150 Years on Pyrmont Peninsula

Text copyright © 2017 remains with the author

All rights reserved. Except for any fair dealing permitted under the Copyright Act, no part of this book may be reproduced by any means without prior permission. Inquiries should be made to the publisher.

National Library of Australia Cataloguing-in-Publication entry
Creator: Fowler, C. F., author.

Title: 150 years on the Pyrmont Peninsula : the Catholic community of Saint Bede 1867 - 2017 / Colin Francis Fowler.

ISBN: 9781925486865 (paperback)
       9781925486872 (hardback)
       9781925486889 (ebook : epub)
       9781925486896 (ebook : Kindle)
       9781925486902 (ebook : pdf)

Notes: Includes bibliographical references and index.

Subjects: St Bede's Catholic Church (Pyrmont, N.S.W.)--History.
 Catholic Church--New South Wales--Pyrmont--History.
 Church committees--Catholic Church.
 Pyrmont (N.S.W.)--Church history.

Cover design and Layout by Astrid Sengkey

Text Minion Pro Size 10 &11

Published by:

An imprint of the ATF Press Publishing Group owned by ATF (Australia) Ltd.
PO Box 504
Hindmarsh, SA 5007
ABN 90 116 359 963
www.atfpress.com
Making a lasting impact

150 Years on Pyrmont Peninsula

The Catholic Community of Saint Bede

1867–2017

C F Fowler

ATF Theology
Adelaide
2017

Table of Contents

Acknowledgements   vii
Chapter 1
    A New Name for an Ancient Peninsula   1
Chapter 2
    The Mother Parish   18
Chapter 3
    Founder of the Pyrmont Mission   28
Chapter 4
    Toole/O'Toole Families of Pyrmont   40
Chapter 5
    1867: Building the Church of St Bede   53
Chapter 6
    Pyrmont's Catholic School   82
Chapter 7
    Pyrmont's First Resident Priest   99
Chapter 8
    Pyrmont's Monks   120
Chapter 9
    'Mighty Dean Lynch' Takes Charge   138
Chapter 10
    Zealous French Missionary   156
Chapter 11
    Good Samaritan Sisters   177
Chapter 12
    Irish See of Sydney   199
Chapter 13
    Church and School for Ultimo   215
Chapter 14
    Towards the End of the Century   234
Chapter 15
    Ecclesiastical Scandal in Sydney   262

Chapter 16		
	Crossing the 'Bridge of Sighs'	296
Chapter 17		
	Impact of War	319
Chapter 18		
	'Pyrmont Native' Ordained Priest	335
Chapter 19		
	Still a Mission District	359
Chapter 20		
	At War Again	377
Chapter 21		
	Parish Decline & Port Chaplaincy	395
Chapter 22		
	Centenary Celebrated	411
Chapter 23		
	Continued Population Decline	425
Chapter 24		
	Revival of Peninsula and Parish	443
Chapter 25		
	Patron Saint	460
Bibliography		477
Appendix 1	Centenary Booklet	483
Appendix 2	Pyrmont Clergy	519
Name Index		523
Place Index		535

Acknowledgements

Interest in the history of the Pyrmont parish began soon after my appointment as parish priest of Pyrmont and Forest Lodge parishes in 2004. Whenever a family history enquiry came to the parish I would, without hesitation, pass it directly to the parish secretary. However, one particular enquiry caught my attention and I undertook my own research. The enquirer stated that the 1882 marriage certificate of her great-grandparents noted that the wedding had taken place, not in the church of Saint Bede, but in the parish presbytery. She requested a copy of the entry in the parish registry and an explanation of why this had happened. I had heard of 'mixed marriages' being celebrated in church sacristies in previous generations, but never of weddings conducted in the priest's house. On consulting the parish marriage registry, I found 'presbytery' entered as 'place of marriage'. I noted with interest the French name of the priest-celebrant—Joseph-Marie Garavel. This set me an initial two pronged investigation—the history of the Canon Law of mixed-marriages and the story of Pyrmont's French priest

The realisation that the parish was approaching its sesquicentenary in 2017 led me to expand the investigation to cover the story of the 150 years of the Catholic community in Pyrmont and Ultimo. This book is the result of the research conducted initially over ten years in the spare time available to a parish priest, and finally in a year of full-time attention to the project, while resident in the Pyrmont presbytery. I am grateful to the current Parish Priest, Anthony Walsh, and to the members of the Parish Council for formally commissioning the work, and for allowing me that year in residence in the house where my predecessors, who have such a prominent role in the story, had lived since 1880.

Early in 2014 my research was transformed with the digitising of the various Australian Catholic newspapers, 1839-1954, by the National Library's 'Trove' project. Easy desktop access to the Trove website and its sophisticated search engine enabled the tracing of newspaper reports about Pyrmont parish and many of its priests and parishioners. I commend this work of the National Library and the many volunteer correctors of the 'Trove community'.

I wish to acknowledge with gratitude the assistance I have received in this project. Access to the Sydney Archdiocesan Archives was granted by the Chancellor, Monsignor John Usher, and facilitated by the welcome and assistance of the archivist, Ms Jo Robertson, and her staff. Sister Lia van Haren of the Good Samaritan Archives at Glebe was generous in her assistance and advice, as was the late Sister Marilyn Kelleher, historian of the Good Samaritan Sisters. I am grateful also for information provided by the archivists of Melbourne Archdiocese and Lismore Diocese, and the secretaries of the many parishes that I have contacted. Various chapters have been read and commented on by colleagues, to whom I express my thanks. I especially acknowledge the assistance of Damian Gleeson, historian of Pyrmont's O'Toole family. I owe a particular debt of gratitude to Hilary Regan for accepting the text for publication by ATF Press. His patience and guidance have been crucial in seeing the work emerge into print.

Throughout the project I have been encouraged by the parishioners of Saint Bede. They are a community to which I was privileged to belong. They are the bearers into the future of a story of highs and lows, of faith and hope. To them I humbly dedicate this work.

Abbreviations

Adjutor Deus: M Xavier Compton et al (eds), *Adjutor Deus. Documents and resource material relating to the episcopacy of Archbishop John Bede Polding OSB*, 2 vols, Sydney 2000

Polding Letters: M Xavier Compton et al (eds), *The Letters of John Bede Polding OSB*, 3 vols, Sydney 1994.

SAA: Sydney Archdiocesan Archives

Chapter 1
A New Name for an Ancient Peninsula

The first reference to the naming of the peninsula between Cockle Bay and Blackwattle Swamp, projecting into Johnston's Bay within Sydney's Port Jackson, was found in an 1806 edition of the first and, until 1824, the only newspaper in the colony of New South Wales, *The Sydney Gazette and New South Wales Advertiser*. The *Gazette* had been established in 1803 by Governor Philip Gidley King as the official organ of the administration of the penal colony. In addition to publishing official decrees this weekly journal also contained items of interest and assistance to the local readership including shipping news, advertising and announcements. One historian has described its contents as ranging from 'fulsome flattery of Government officials' to 'inane twaddle on other matters'.[1]

An item that appeared in the *Gazette* on Sunday 21 December 1806 could be said to be firmly in the category of 'inane twaddle', but it has significance in the history of Pyrmont:

> On Thursday a select party of Ladies and Gentlemen, twenty-one in number exclusive of attendants, made an aquatic excursion from Parramatta to Captain McArthur's estate in Cockle Bay; being highly favoured by the uninterrupted serenity of a salubrious atmosphere and after examining with inexpressible satisfaction the picturesque beauties which that romantic scene afforded, a handsome collation ushered in the evening's festivity beneath the shelter of a spreading fig tree, whose waving foliage whispered to refreshing breezes. To this enviable retirement one of the fair visitors was pleased to give the appellation *le Répos de l'Amitié*, the estate receiving at the same time the name of Pyrmont, from its pure and uncontaminated spring, joined to the native beauties of the place, of which the company took leave at five much gratified with the rational festivities of the day.[2]

---

1. Henry Mayer, *The Press in Australia*, Melbourne 1968, 10.
2. *Sydney Gazette and New South Wales Advertiser*, 21 December 1806.

The membership of the select party can be speculated to have included the Macarthur family, John and Elizabeth and their children, Elizabeth, Mary, James, William and Edward, who had recently returned to the Colony after his schooling in England. Eldest son John had sailed to England with his father in 1801 for his education and never returned to the colony. Other members of the excursion would have included friends, neighbours, business partners and their families. In attendance there would have been some of the many convict workers assigned to the Macarthur household and estates, but not meriting to be numbered in the party. The whole group sailed down the Parramatta River from Elizabeth Farm, the Macarthur Estate, thirteen miles from Sydney. The most obvious point for landing would have been one of the two sandy bays on the northern headland of the peninsula

There was no mention in the story of the local inhabitants, people of the Cadigal clan of the Eora nation, who perhaps advisedly withdrew at the approach of the boats carrying the 'select party'.[3] Pirrama was the name they used for this area, where they camped at a relatively safe distance from the effects of the smallpox outbreaks that had already halved the Port Jackson indigenous population. Unknown to the Cadigal people, their Pirrama with its 'picturesque beauties' had already been several times exchanged among members of the New South Wales Corps. In 1795 fifty-five of the 288 acres of the rocky peninsula stretching north from Parramatta Street had been granted to Private Thomas Jones by Captain William Paterson, continuing the indiscriminate land grants to members of the Corps begun by Captain Francis Grose as acting Governor after the departure of Captain Arthur Phillip. The grant was located at the north-eastern end of the peninsula. In 1794 two grants of 24 and 18 acres on Cockle Bay south of the Macarthur estate had been made. The rest of the peninsula, including these two portions, would end up in the hands of Corps Surgeon John Harris in grants and purchases made between 1803 and 1818.

The name given to the estate in 1806 was suggested to the picnickers by the discovery of a "pure and uncontaminated spring", which would have brought welcome refreshment on a mid-December summer's day in Sydney. The spring seems to have been slightly to the west of the demarcation of the Macarthur land. It became known as Tinkers Well; it disappeared with the excavating of stone quarries in the vicinity later in the century. One of the ladies in the party was reminded of the famous German spa town of Pyrmont, whose waters not only refreshed but reputedly healed an impressive range of diseases: "[Pyrmont water] is better supported than most waters of

---

3. Recent research proposes that there was a distinct sub-group of the Eora nation, tentatively named the Gommerigal clan, living on the peninsula (Keith Vincent Smith, *Eora Clans: A History of Indigenous Social Organisation in Coastal Sydney, 1770–1890*, MA thesis, Macquarie University, Sydney, 2004, 70–72).

this class; and when it can be procured, merits a decided preference over others, especially in cases of general debility remaining after loss of blood, copious discharges, parturition, or severe illness."[4] In 1806 the town and county of Pyrmont was a member state of the Confederation of the Rhine, which had been carved out of the Holy Roman Empire by the conquering Emperor Napoleon as a source of conscripts and supplies for his continuing campaigns, perhaps including supplies of bottled Pyrmont water.

Life in Sydney in 1806 was not all about aquatic excursions, picturesque beauties, handsome collations, fair visitors and rational festivities. The accompanying articles in the Sunday 21 December edition of the *Gazette* gave a truer picture of the penal colony. Immediately after the delightful story of the Macarthur picnic enjoyed on the Thursday, there followed news of hangings on the Monday and Wednesday of the same week and on the Tuesday punishments of 500 and 200 lashes for theft. The Monday executions had a Macarthur connection. Brothers James and Stephen Halfpenny and three accomplices, described at their trial as 'bushrangers'— an early use of the word— had been indicted on four counts, all of 'capital tendency', one of which was the theft of 'a cow, two ewes and two lambs, the property of John McArthur Esq'. All were found guilty and sentenced to death. However, as reported by the *Gazette*, it was 'His Excellency's pleasure to extend the Royal Grace in behalf of William Gorman, James Kelly, and James Sheedy, their accomplices; which act of mercy they accepted with every mark of gratitude'. The Halfpenny Brothers were duly hanged. In the same overwrought prose of the report of the Pyrmont picnic, the *Gazette* described the executions: 'Those whose melancholy fate it was to expiate their offences by a public execution, were visibly imprest with a dread which increased as they approached the fatal spot. The three who were respited attended the sufferers, James and Stephen Halfpenny, reading by them as they walked, and were the near witnesses of a spectacle, which under their circumstances must doubtless have made an impression that time cannot obliterate.'

It is not known whether there were any Roman Catholics among the Pyrmont picnickers. The only likely candidates would have been among the assigned convict servants in the party. The Catholic population of the penal colony in 1806 was variously estimated. A muster conducted in August in the Sydney region had returned a total population of 7148, of whom 10% were free settlers, 45% convicts, 40% emancipated convicts.[5] It is estimated that between 25 and 30 per cent of the convicts were Irish, the majority of these

---

4. Samuel Hanbury Smith, *Medicinal Mineral Waters, Natural and Artificial: their efficacy in the treatment of Chronic Diseases* (Hamilton, Ohio, 1855), 59.
5. Carol J Baxter (ed), *1805–06 Musters of New South Wales and Norfolk Island* (Sydney, 1989), xvii.

being Roman Catholic. Among the approximately two thousand Catholics in 1806 there was one priest, James Dixon, described in the muster as 'EC [emancipated conditionally]; self [employed]; Roman Catholic Priest'.[6] He and two other priests, Peter O'Neil and James Harold, had been transported for involvement in the 1798 rebellion in Ireland, arriving in 1800. O'Neil had been allowed to return home in January 1803 after his conviction was overturned. Harold, within months of his arrival, had been exiled to the harsher penal colony on Norfolk Island. Neither Harold nor Dixon had permission to minister to the Catholic population in their respective locations. However, for a brief period between April 1803 and March 1804 Roman Catholicism became a 'tolerated sect', and Dixon was authorised to celebrate public Mass on alternate Sundays at Sydney, Parramatta and Hawkesbury. Permission was withdrawn following the convict rebellion at Castle Hill. Governor King considered that the gathering of Irish convicts at Sunday Mass had contributed to the planning of the rising. There is evidence that James Dixon, 'self-employed', continued an unofficial ministry of Divine Service, baptism and marriage in Sydney and Parramatta, until full emancipation was granted him in June 1809, after which he sailed from the Colony for England and eventually to Ireland.[7] For the next eight years, apart from the fleeting clandestine ministry of the erratic Father Jeremiah O'Flynn from November 1817 to May 1818, the Catholic community of convicts, emancipists, free settlers and soldiers was again without priestly ministry.[8]

Following O'Flynn's expulsion from Sydney, Governor Macquarie had written to Lord Bathurst, Secretary for the Colonies, with a suggestion for any future appointment of Roman Catholic chaplains: 'If it should at any time be considered advisable to sanction the Ministry of Popish Priests in New South Wales, I would beg to suggest that they should be Englishmen of liberal education and sound constitutional principles, and they should not come hither with any special authority from the Pope, as Rev O'Flynn represented himself to have done.'[9] In 1819 when two priests were formally appointed chaplains by authorities in both London and Rome, these 'Popish priests' were not Englishmen as recommended by Macquarie, but Irishmen, one of whom the Scottish Governor would come to consider to be of decidedly unsound constitutional principles, indeed ungentlemanly. It

---

6. Baxter, *1805–06 Musters of New South Wales and Norfolk Island*, 30
7. Vivienne Keely, *Dixon of Botany Bay: the convict priest from Wexford*, Sydney 2003
8. Paul Collins, *A very contrary Irishman: the life and journeys of Jeremiah O'Flynn*, Northcote, Victoria, 2014.
9. Governor Macquarie to Colonial Office, 18 May 1818 ((Historical Records of Australia, series 1, vol 9, 801).

would be an Irish Governor who would welcome the first English Catholic clergy, a Vicar-General in 1833 and a Bishop in 1835.

Meanwhile on the Pyrmont peninsula, in the years following the 1806 Macarthur picnic, a few business ventures had been undertaken. The first was of brief duration—a salt-boiling works, for producing fine white table salt, transferred by Macarthur from Broken Bay, north of Sydney, to the western shore of Cockle Bay. The next was a windmill erected high on the estate's sandstone ridge, adding another set of sails to the Sydney skyline. It belonged to a Macarthur business partner, Garnham Blaxcell, who intended to use the mill for the production of flour for the growing Sydney population. The wheat would be provided from the the cultivation of the generous land grants held by Macarthur and Blaxcell.

By 1826 the windmill was a ruin, but rising on the same elevated ridge was a 'most splendid mansion after the Grecian style'. This latest Macarthur project was described in the usual effusive style of the *Sydney Gazette* as a 'rising empire': 'There are some 25 or 27 stone-masons and stone-cutters already employed, and the free stone, of which there is a plenitude for ages, is allowed to be the finest in the Country.'[10] The article, as well as providing an accurate assessment of the quality and quantity of Pyrmont sandstone, also noted the rapid increase in shipping within Cockle Bay, an increase which would soon draw attention to the great potential for the development of the west shore and especially the Macarthur Estate:

> Cockle Bay, which should most certainly be designated DARLING HARBOUR, is growing into that kind of notice which we have long been predicting though no great foresight was required for the purpose. Many of the owners and captains of vessels prefer that harbour to Sydney Cove, and we think they are in the right for so doing, since it must become the principal harbour within the heads of Australia. The east side of this capacious bay is becoming lined with stupendous edifices.

The next month the *Gazette* presented its readers with a version of the naming of the estate at odds with its 1806 Pyrmont picnic report: 'The expensive and engaging edifice that is erecting at Pierpoint by Mr John McArthur is advancing as rapidly as circumstances will admit. Mr G Blaxcell, of olden time, we understand, gave the name of Pierpoint, or Pierre-point, to this fascinating spot, and Mr McArthur became the purchaser upon its being put up for sale.'[11] A name reflecting the peninsula's harbourside setting, *Pierpoint*,

---

10. *Sydney Gazette*, 24 May 1826.
11. *Sydney Gazette*, 10 June 1826.

or its sandstone assets, *Pierre-point*, must have seemed more appropriate than the obscure reference to a German spa town.

The mansion did not reach completion, the cut stone being transported upriver to be used on extensions to Elizabeth Farm, as reported in the *Australian*: 'So we are not to have the pleasure of seeing the fine house built in Cockle-bay, on Pierre-point, or some such named place, by Mr John MacArthur. All the stones etc are to be sent up to Parramatta by water. An order has been issued to that effect—old people are as fickle as young ones!'[12] The Pyrmont Estate would remain undeveloped for another ten years, until after John Macarthur's death in 1834.

While the northern end of the peninsula lacked a residence, at the southern end, since 1804, there had stood a fine brick house, near Parramatta Street, on land granted to Surgeon John Harris by Governor King in December 1803. The grant was made in celebration of Harris' acquittal on a technicality from a charge of behaviour unbecoming an officer. There was a mistake in the court document stating the charge, which was dated 23 February 1803 and which referred to the crime as being committed on the '19th ult' (*mense ultimo*: in the previous month), when it should have stated '19th inst' (*instante mense*: in the current month). Though the court found him guilty, the Governor refused to confirm the finding, citing the error. Harris was proud of his classical education and delighted in the outcome, based as it was on a mistake in Latin. The Governor too delighted in the restoration of one of his few supporters among the members of the NSW Corps, and expressed his satisfaction by the modest land grant of 34 acres in a fertile area on the western edge of Sydney town. Harris, already in possession of extensive acreage at Parramatta, named his new estate 'Ultimo' and the new brick residence 'Ultimo House' in cheeky celebration of the little Latin word that had set him free. More grants were to follow, most significantly that of 135 acres, extending to the northwest headland of the peninsula and bordering Macarthur's estate. This was given by Governor King in 1806, his last year in office. On the southern portion of this grant of land Harris built another house which he, still delighting in his acquittal, named Ultimo Cottage.

The unpopularity of Governor William Bligh, whom Harris came to regard as a cross between Caligula and Robespierre, led to Harris' reconciliation with his fellow officers and to his participation in the Rum Rebellion. In the evening of 25 January 1808 a group of officers met and dined at Ultimo House before proceeding into Sydney to call out the troops and arrest the Governor. The day of the coup was the twentieth anniversary

---

12. *Australian*, 7 June 1826; Barrie Dyster, *Servant & Master: building and running the grand houses of Sydney 1788-1850* (Kensington: New South Wales University Press, 1989), 18–19.

of the arrival of the First Fleet in Port Jackson. Harris was required to sail to England to testify at the court-martial of the leaders of the coup, and did not return to Sydney until 1814, with a young wife in tow. They took up residence at Ultimo House and did not work the estate, but turned the area around the house into a country retreat which included deer imported from India. Harris engaged Francis Greenway to design extensions for the house, transforming it into a rural mansion set on the Ultimo ridge with views of the Cockle and Blackwattle bays. In 1821 the couple moved west, to their property at St Mary's; they leased Ultimo House but retained Ultimo Cottage as their Sydney base. Apart from small leases along the northern side of Parramatta Street, the Harris estate remained largely undeveloped during the lifetime of Dr Harris and beyond, due to the complications of his will.

One other residence was erected on the peninsula prior to the subdivision of the Pyrmont Estate. This was on a small parcel of land made available by Harris to a business associate, Captain George Bunn, on the occasion of his marriage in 1828 to Anna Maria Murray, daughter of another Harris connection, Captain Terence Murray of the 48th Regiment. The friendship with Harris was honoured in the naming of their second son—George Harris Bunn. The couple built Newstead House on their four acre acquisition on the western shore of Cockle Bay, just south of the Macarthur estate. They had barely taken up residence with their two infant sons when, soon after the death in child-birth of a baby daughter, Captain Bunn died suddenly in January 1834, as announced in the *Sydney Monitor*: "WE are sorry to announce the rather sudden Death of Captain BUNN, at his new residence across the water, yesterday, at 3 pm, to the great grief of his family, and a numerous circle of friends. Captain BUNN had been many years a Justice of Peace, and one of the principal merchants of Sydney."[13] Anna Maria continued to live at this rather isolated location 'across the water' with her sons and father, who died in 1835. In 1841, just as the peninsula began to be developed, she leased the house, generally known as 'Bunn's Cottage', and moved to live with her brothers on their properties, Woden and Yarralumla, in southern NSW. Ten years later she moved to St Omer, the property near Braidwood granted to her husband in 1827. The widow Anna Maria Bunn with her sons and her father had formed the first Catholic household in the area that would become the Mission District of St Bede in 1867.

Apart from the tiny Bunn enclave, the whole of the peninsula was divided between Macarthur and Harris. However, neither owner sought to farm or develop his portion. The unworked land and its untouched resources were beginning to attract the attention of trespassers. In June 1833 the following

---

13. *Sydney Monitor*, 10 January 1834.

typically aggressive notice was inserted by James Macarthur in the *Sydney Gazette* on behalf of his confined father: 'NOTICE is hereby given, that any person found cutting Timber, quarrying Stone, or otherwise trespassing upon the Estate of JOHN MACARTHUR, Esq, called "PYRMONT" and situated on the westside of Cockle Bay, adjoining the property of Dr Harris, will be proceeded against according to law'.[14] However, in June there was a change in tone which arose from the transfer of ownership, the eldest Macarthur son Edward having purchased the estate from his mother, who had inherited the estate on the death of her husband in 1834. The London-based Edward was determined to turn his property into a source of income. Threatening notices were replaced with invitations to acquire the estate's only readily available assets, stone and timber:

> PERSONS desirous of Quarrying Stone on the Pyrmont Estate are requested to apply to Mr A Murray, Ultimo Cottage.[15]

> SEASONED FIREWOOD. TO BE SOLD BY AUCTION, By Mr Samuel Lyons, Opposite Morton's London Tavern on Friday, the 1st day of July, at 11 o'clock precisely, THE TIMBER felled and standing upon forty-five acres (more or less) of the Estate of 'Pyrmont', situate at the rear of the Ultimo Estate, and within a mile of the Old Toll Bar. It may be seen on the ground, by application to Mr A Murray, Ultimo Cottage. Terms and further particulars made known at the time of sale[16].

This initial clearance of timber was preliminary to a subdivision which had been drawn up in the name of Edward Macarthur. However, the timber failed to sell at first attempt and the subdivision in an altered version did not take place until 1839.

In the meantime the undeveloped peninsula continued to be just a pretty view completing the panorama seen from the grand houses on the heights of the Rocks, as gushingly described in an auction notice:

> The particular beauties connected with these Properties, renders it only imperative upon Mr B[odenham] to point out but a solitary few of their intrinsic advantages: they command some of the finest, most enlivening, and delightful scenery in the whole Colony; the fine majestic view of the Harbour of Port Jackson, the Lighthouse, the noble line of mansions upon the Woolloomooloo Hill, the Surry Hills, and to the rear the marine and delightful Estate of 'Pyrmont', the 'Crow's Nest', and others, with the

---

14. *Sydney Herald*, 6, 13 & 27 June 1833.
15. *Sydney Herald*, 19 May 1836.
16. *Australian*, 28 June 1836

whole expanse of the Parramatta River and its varied sinuosities, with their concomitant advantages in point of health, surpassing the bounds of an advertisement in their description.[17]

An earlier notice of Bodenham had referred to 'the rear view' from the Rocks: 'that beautiful and romantic Estate, called "Pyrmont", admirably calculated for marine villas.'[18] Here was a clear indication to the public about the MacArthur plan to create an upper-class development on the western peninsula, which would further add to 'the lustre and beauty of the Town of Sydney'.

While the western shore of Darling Harbour was languishing, the Catholic community in the Colony was undergoing rapid change. In the same advertisement columns of the *Australian*, 28 June 1836, in which Pyrmont timber was offered for sale, there appeared a public notice calling on all Catholics to gather the next Sunday at the 'Cathedral Church of St Mary', and to linger after Mass for a meeting to be chaired by the bishop, to consider the completion of the cathedral. This was a much changed situation from the first Mass celebrated by the convict priest, James Dixon, in 1803, during the brief period of approved public ministry. Not only was there a formal church building, albeit still unfinished after fifteen years, but there was a formal structure of church governance with a bishop at its head. The Catholic community was considered by papal authority to be sufficiently developed in numbers and in potential to be given the status of a Vicariate Apostolic, with the expectation that it would later become a fully-fledged Diocese. The bishop was John Bede Polding, a forty-year-old English Benedictine, consecrated in London in June 1834, who arrived in the colony in September 1835. With the arrival of Polding and a priest companion, the Catholic clergy on the continent of Australia, numbered six only: two English Benedictine monks (the bishop and his Vicar-General, William Ullathorne), two Irish diocesan priests (John Joseph Therry and John McEncroe) and two Irish Dominican friars (Christopher Dowling and James Vincent Corcoran).

Polding had been appointed Vicar Apostolic of New Holland and Van Diemen's Land. The Papal Curia continued to use the old name for the southern continent, even though the British Government had for some years been using the name Australia, and the name New South Wales for the colony along the east coast. Indeed, the first Anglican bishop, William Broughton, had been styled 'Bishop of Australia' at his London consecration in February 1836. Polding in the meantime, until the formal establishment of the Catholic archdiocese of Sydney in 1842, bore the title 'Bishop of

---

17. *Sydney Gazette*, 29 May 1832.
18. *Sydney Gazette*, 27 October 1831.

Hiero-Caesarea.[19] During the pre-Diocese, Vicariate Apostolic stage of a region, bishops were given the title of an ancient Diocese, now extinct, where Christian communities no longer flourished, 'in partibus infidelium'—in the lands of the unbelievers, or the regions conquered by the Muslims. Hiero-Caesarea was located in Anatolia within the Ottoman Empire. Polding chafed under this foreign title. He complained to Rome: 'It is openly said that these titular bishops are nothing but aliens and foreigners, whose flocks are in other and distant places, and this is the precise reproach brought against me in letters sent to our Governor by Mr Broughton, the Pseudo-Bishop of the Anglican Church in New Holland.'[20]

A second attempt to develop the Macarthur's Pyrmont estate was undertaken in 1839. Throughout September and October all the Sydney newspapers of the day, *The Sydney Gazette*, *The Sydney Herald*, *The Sydney Monitor* and *The Colonist* carried advertisements announcing that Mr Smart had 'been honoured with instructions to offer for public competition ... a considerable portion of the Pyrmont Estate, divided into allotments'. The agent boasted that this was the 'most important and valuable property yet submitted to public competition'. In support of this claim he highlighted the location of the allotments with extended frontage on the western side of Darling Harbour, directly opposite the Market Wharf and the steam boat wharves, giving ready access to the commercially important eastern shore. There appeared a further enticement to investors with the suggestion that, in anticipation of the subdivision of the Pyrmont Estate, a causeway or bridge linking the east and west shores would be undertaken. Such a development would 'lay open the whole of Pyrmont and Ultimo to the heart of the Town', and the lucky owners of allotments there would be able to leave their homes and be at their place of work in five minutes.[21] A wooden bridge was not constructed until 1858.

The 1839 subdivision offered for auction only the part of the estate around Pyrmont Bay, divided into 99 allotments. Three separate sites were reserved for a church, a fortification, and a wharf at Darling Point. Major Edward Macarthur honoured family and friends in the naming of the streets. The family was already honoured in Macarthur Point and Elizabeth Bay, to which he added Edward and John streets, and Bowman Street after his brother-in-law, Dr James Bowman, while Harris and Murray streets paid homage to friends and neighbours. The choice of the name Union Street for the main east-west road could have been for the simple fact that this road united the peninsula with Darling Harbour. A more political motive would have been the commemoration and affirmation of the 1801 Act of Union

---

19. A 20th century bearer of the title was Franz Justus Rarkowski, military bishop of Nazi Germany.
20. Polding to Propaganda Fide, 17 January 1842 (Polding Letters I.192)
21. *Sydney Herald*, 27 November 1839.

between Great Britain and Ireland, the repeal of which, at the time of the subdivision, was being actively sought through a series of 'Monster Meetings' organised in Ireland by Daniel O'Connell, 'the Liberator'. A Sydney branch of O'Connell's 'Loyal Irish Repeal Association' was established in October 1842.[22]

The auction announcements defined the area of the subdivision as 'that most valuable portion of the Pyrmont Estate, situate to the southward of the old Windmill and adjoining the northern boundary of the Ultimo Estate'. Late in November 1839 a description of each of the 41 allotments, which would be offered at auction on 12 December, appeared in many editions of the local newspapers. Twenty-nine of the lots had a water frontage. Six of these were located on Murray Street, nine on Union Street, and fourteen on the eastern side of Pyrmont Street. The remaining lots were situated on the western side of Pyrmont Street, between Union and John streets. On one of these allotments the Catholic church and school would be built in 1867.

The subdivision was described in relation to the only two structures then standing on the northern end of the peninsula. Lot number one was described as 'nearest to the residence of Mrs Bunn'. The full list of allotments was followed by an announcement that 'on the site of the old Windmill the proprietor has made an ample reservation of land for the erection of a Church'. On this the highest point of the peninsula the Anglican parish church, rectory and school would be built in 1850.

In April 1840 the agent T W Smart announced a second offer of Pyrmont allotments, noting by way of encouragement to buyers that already, in just a few months, lots purchased in the first sale had increased significantly in value: '[T]he fortunate purchasers at that sale have, in several instances, already been offered bonuses on their bargains more than equal to the whole of their preliminary outlay.'[23] The new area on offer was described as lying 'to the northward of that already sold, extending to the outer Darling Harbour (reserving only, for particular purposes of intended public benefit, the neck of land or peninsula known as Darling Point) and to Elizabeth Bay, with extensive frontage in deep water, to each'. The properties were promoted as a last-chance opportunity for 'the man of limited means as well as the capitalist'. Again the bridge enticement was prominent in the advertisement.

With the estate now subdivided and largely sold off or leased, and with houses and cottages being constructed and occupied, and wharves projecting from the shoreline, Pyrmont was taking on the appearance of a quaint village. A sure sign of this evolution was the application for a public-house licence as reported in *The Sydney Monitor* of 19 April 1841:

---

22. *Australasian Chronicle*, 4 October 1842; *Sydney Gazette*, 8 October 1842.
23. *Sydney Monitor and Commercial Advertiser*, 27 April 1840.

> Amongst the applications for Public-house licences exhibited at the Police-office, we perceive that two parties have applied for that indulgence, at places which only a year or two ago, was a continual scrub, and we may say unprofitable wilderness, but which has now been converted by the industry of man into thriving villages. We allude to the Estates of Pyrmont and Balmain, situated on the west side of Darling Harbour.[24]

Fast on the trail of the pub came the first of the churches. In April 1842 the Reverend John Dunmore Lang bought one of the lots in Mount Street and had a chapel built for the peninsula's small Presbyterian community. The story was told that Lang had approached Major Macarthur asking him to donate the land for the church, but the Major declined stating that donating land to one church was generosity enough. In 1864 Lang proudly reminisced about his foresight in purchasing land and building a church on the peninsula: 'Foreseeing, so early as the year 1842, the future importance both of Pyrmont and Balmain, as rising suburbs of this great city, I purchased a suitable allotment of ground for the erection of a Presbyterian Church, unconnected with the State, and had a neat, commodious weatherboard building erected for the purpose in each of these localities.'[25]

Going to church was not the only Sunday morning option on the peninsula. In March 1842 *The Australasian Chronicle* carried an article headed 'Prize Fighting':

> Three or four of those disgraceful scenes called prize fights came off on Sunday morning, on the west shore, somewhere near Pyrmont Point, where from thirty to forty of the lowest blackguards in Sydney were assembled to witness these brutal exhibitions. We believe this practice is very common in that neighbourhood on a Sunday morning, and it would perhaps be as well if an extra constable or two were placed there on duty upon Sundays.[26]

Nor was the licensed public-house the only place to slake a thirst. In October 1841 the *Sydney Herald* reported: 'SLY GROG SELLING. Yesterday a stonemason named Munro, residing at Pyrmont, was brought before the Sydney Police Court, to answer a charge of sly grog selling. After a lengthened hearing he was convicted and fined £30 with costs.'[27] Prize-fighting and sly-grog sales regularly featured in the newspaper reports from Pyrmont over

---

24. *Sydney Monitor and Commercial Advertiser*, 19 April 1841.
25. *Empire*, 13 October 1864.
26. *Australasian Chronicle*, 8 March 1842.
27. *Sydney Herald*, Saturday 2 October 1841.

the following decades of the nineteenth century, even after the appointment of a resident constable in the mid-1860s.

Neither its isolated location nor small population prevented Pyrmont from being incorporated into the newly formed City of Sydney in July 1842. The incorporation of Sydney was not everywhere popular, because it brought with it direct taxation in the form of rates. Citizen contributions to government coffers had until 1842 been largely limited to market dues and road tolls, but pressure from the Imperial government for direct taxation of the colonists was growing and finally led to the contested decision of the Legislative Council in July 1842 to pass 'An Act to declare the Town of Sydney to be a city, and to incorporate the Inhabitants thereof'. The city boundaries were generously devised to include all the developed and developing areas of Sydney, and were not based on density of population or any other considerations which interest groups might favour. In fact the boundary of the new city was taken unaltered from the Police Act of 1833. This was an 'Act for regulating the Police in the Town and Port of Sydney and for removing and preventing nuisances and obstructions therein'. Under the Act local justices could fine people for 'nuisances and obstructions', including polluting the water supply, indecent exposure and kite flying. In that year, apart from the Bunn residence and the windmill, the only potential source of nuisances and obstructions on Pyrmont peninsula would be found towards the southern end, along Parramatta Street.

Pyrmont was not to remain a village of commuting residents forever. Some of the allotments at the northern end unsuitable for building because of steep rocky terrain were sold or leased for the quarrying of sandstone. The bays of the peninsula proved attractive to shipbuilding enterprises. However, growth stalled with the onset of the 1840s depression which resulted in many cases of insolvency in the colony. The stifled demand for the peninsula's two resources of sandstone and harbour space led to local entrepreneurs falling into insolvency. The abundant surface stone alone was sufficient to serve the local, small-scale building needs, and serious quarrying would wait until the arrival of a building boom in need of quality sandstone. In this economic climate it was not profitable to undertake the building of the much vaunted linking bridge between Pyrmont and the city across Darling Harbour, essential for further development.

It was the discovery of gold in 1851 in the Bathurst region that brought the long awaited economic revival. One of the first beneficiaries was the shipping industry. The Australian Steam Navigation Company (ASNC) undertook the development of Darling Island which had been deliberately excluded from housing subdivision. A giant patent slip was installed on the island in 1855, providing Sydney with a facility for repairing ships and steamers of up to 2000 tons for the coastal and even the London and Pacific runs. The shipping boom had an impact on quarrying with the need to provide ballast.

The expansion and upgrading of the colonial road network and the laying of railway tracks also called for large quantities of stone. But the biggest impact on local quarrying came from the recognition of the high quality of local sandstone. Pyrmont replaced the other Sydney quarries as the preferred source of sandstone when its superiority was recognised by the Colonial Architect, William Weaver. In 1855 he demanded that the stone for the work on the Australian Museum must come from 'the best bed of the Pyrmont quarries'.[28] The most ambitious Sydney project in the mid-1850s was the building of the University of Sydney on the Grose Farm ridge along Parramatta Road, just west of Doctor Harris' Ultimo Estate. The architect for the project was Edmund Blacket who had resigned as Colonial Architect to undertake the task. He convinced the University Senate to build in stone and not in the brick which they had proposed, and he insisted that the stone be sourced from the Pyrmont quarries which were just two miles away. This was a great boost to the quarry owners who were kept busy supplying stone for the six years of the project. Completed in 1861, the modestly named 'Main Building' of the University is an architectural gem in a mix of Gothic, Renaissance and Tudor styles. An early visitor, the English novelist, Anthony Trollope, wrote home in 1874 describing the Great Hall as 'the finest chamber in the colonies', and stating that he could remember no college of Oxford or Cambridge which possessed a hall 'of which the proportions are so good'.[29]

Pyrmont stone was used extensively in monumental buildings, civic and ecclesiastical, in the city of Sydney and far beyond. In 1852 the *Freeman's Journal* reported that Bishop Pierre-Marie Battaillon, Vicar Apostolic of Central Oceania, was collecting sandstone for his island churches.[30] Reminiscing in 1859 the *Freeman's* was more specific about the origin and destination of the stone: 'At Apia, an island of the Navigator's Group ... there is a Catholic church built of stone from our Pyrmont quarries. Old residents in Sydney will remember how ... Dr. Battaillon and a number of natives whom he had brought up from the islands were for some time employed in quarrying and preparing the stone near Lyndhurst'.[31] The new St Mary's Cathedral, begun in 1865, after the destruction by fire of the 1821 church, was built of Pyrmont sandstone at the direction of the architect William

---

28. Shirley Fitzgerald and Hilary Golder, *Pyrmont and Ultimo Under Siege* (Sydney, 1994), 32.
29. Joan Kerr, *Our Great Victorian Architect, Edmund Thomas Blacket, (1817–1883)* (Sydney: National Trust of Australia, 1983).
30. *Freeman's Journal*, 29 July 1852; cf John Hosie, *Challenge. The Marists in colonial Australia*, Sydney, 1987, 108.
31. *Freeman's Journal*, 28 May 1859.

Wardell. In 1881 with only the northern section reaching completion, and with the congregation still using the temporary brick pro-cathedral, Archbishop Roger Bede Vaughan launched yet another appeal for funds. At the meeting of three thousand he publicly thanked by name several chief benefactors: 'Mr Robert Saunders of Pyrmont "who provides the splendid stone for our building" was thanked for the five guineas sent "in reply to my petition" (Cheers).'[32]

Robert Saunders had taken over the family quarries at Pyrmont and Ultimo from his father Charles, who had founded the business in 1853, while continuing as landlord at the Quarryman's Arms on the corner of John and Mount Streets. The family worked three main quarries which became known to the quarry workers as Hellhole, Purgatory and Paradise. Hellhole was located on the western side of the Ultimo Estate along Blackwattle Cove, and was so-named because of its depth; it would quickly fill with water after heavy rain, making the task of quarrying very difficult and dangerous. Purgatory was further north, producing a very hard stone, but one prone to cracking. The Paradise quarry was located towards the end of the peninsula and produced the best 'Pyrmont Yellow-block'. This highest quality stone from the Paradise quarry not only had excellent hardness, texture and colour, it was also suitable for carving; it could be incorporated into buildings in the form of sculptures and finely carved detailing.

Even though much of the stone for the university and city projects came from quarries which were, strictly speaking, in that part of the Ultimo Estate at the north-west end of the peninsula, by this time the whole of the northern end was being referred to as Pyrmont—an imaginary line had been extended from Union street to the shoreline of Blackwattle Cove, and south of this was Ultimo and north was Pyrmont.

Any nostalgia for the pristine Pyrmont peninsula with its 'salubrious atmosphere', 'picturesque beauties', 'romantic scene' and 'native beauties' celebrated in 1806, had completely faded by 1855. In a *Sydney Morning Herald* article headed 'Improvements in Pyrmont' the author delighted in the transformation of the estate: 'The primeval wilderness which it so lately presented has been completely changed. The monotony of rock and scrub, which everywhere prevailed, has given place to an aspect eminently indicative of the progress of civilisation in its busiest and, pecuniarily speaking, its most prosperous forms.'[33] Nature had yielded to 'civilisation'.

The bridge-building project, linking the east and west shores of Darling Harbour, had been revived in response to the increased activity on the peninsula. In 1855 the Pyrmont Bridge Company, a private enterprise, was

---

32. *Freeman's Journal*, 31 August 1881.
33. *Sydney Morning Herald*, 13 June 1855.

formed with the intention of building a toll bridge across Darling Harbour from Market Street to Union Street. The company directors readily gained the financial support of Pyrmont's landlords, quarry-masters, engineers and ship builders, the major beneficiaries of a direct road link with the city. The only other access was the roundabout route along the Harris Street track to Parramatta Street, then east along George Street West. The company even enlisted the influence of workers' wives to press the need for a bridge, claiming that quarrymen and stonemasons had to commute to the Pyrmont quarries, because they could not persuade their wives to live in such an out-of-the-way place.[34]

The bridge project evolved to include a link in the westward direction with a road extending beyond Union Street and continuing along a viaduct across Blackwattle Cove and linking up with Parramatta Road and the road north to Balmain. All this posed a threat to the development of Ultimo and Darling Harbour to the south of the proposed bridge which would be cut off by the project. The company sought partially to appease concerns by including an iron central 'swing panel' to allow ships access to the wharves on both the eastern and western shores of the inner harbour.

The new wooden bridge was ready for opening early in 1858. The day chosen was Wednesday, 17 March, St Patrick's Day, in conjunction with the Pyrmont Regatta, an event that had been inaugurated in 1848 and originally held on the Queen's Birthday, and which would become Pyrmont's premier annual sporting event. The *Empire* reported on lack of formalities at the opening of the bridge and commented with some reserve on its appearance:

> The Pyrmont Bridge was yesterday for the first time thrown open to the public. It bad been made a question with the proprietary whether there should be a ceremony in commemoration of the event; but it was eventually decided, that as the bridge had been erected mainly as a public convenience, the most fitting way of commemorating the opening would be by throwing the bridge open to the public gratis for one day, which was accordingly done . . . The eastern and western shores of Darling Harbour are now therefore united by means of a strong substantial bridge, combining as it does great strength with a somewhat graceful appearance.[35]

The main attraction for the people crowded onto the bridge seems to have been the regatta. The Company Chairman and board members were not among the throng on their new bridge, but were more comfortably ensconced

---

34. Fitzgerald and Golder, 33.
35. *Empire*, 18 March 1858.

on board the flag ship of the regatta, where they enjoyed an excellent spread and high quality wines. The Chairman proposed the first toast to Pyrmont which 'now that the bridge was completed, would, he prophecied [sic], comprise in less than ten years one-fifth of the population of Sydney'. At the conclusion of the many speeches and toasts, 'it being now nearly six o'clock the visitors to the flagship, who had been pretty numerous in the afternoon, all sought the shore, after having quaffed a few more bumpers of champagne in commemoration of Saint Patrick's day and the Pyrmont Regatta'.[36]

With the new road access across the bridge and with the rapid increase in demand for Pyrmont's resources there was significant growth in population on the peninsula and hence an urgent need for housing. Landowners quickly started subdividing their allotments and erecting small workers' cottages. Many of the workers were newly arrived immigrants, among whom the Irish were a significant element, thus opening a new chapter in the Catholic story of Pyrmont

---

36. *Empire*, 18 March 1858.

Chapter 2
The Mother Parish

In March 1842 Bishop Polding personally presented an official written report on his Vicariate to the Cardinal Prefect and Cardinal Members of the Sacred Congregation of Propaganda Fide, the papal curial department responsible for mission territories.[1] He tried to impress on his superiors the geographical size of his mission, comparing the Colony of New South Wales, part of the eastern portion of New Holland, to the size of Italy, extending about 1400 miles along the east coast of the continent, with its inland reach varying from 100 to 300 miles. After relating the story of the Catholic presence from 1789 he brought Their Eminences up to date with a description of the state of the infant Church which he had left just five months before. Beginning with the most distant mission at Melbourne he briefly described the ten districts into which he had divided the Vicariate, concluding with Sydney, bounded on the south by the Illawarra, on the north by Maitland, and extending east to Concord, where the district of Parramatta commenced. His ten districts were less than the sixteen found in Duncan's *Directory*, because the Bishop wanted to claim that each district was served by two priests 'whenever such an arrangement is possible'. This was an ideal to which he aspired so that no priest would be without 'consolation, mutual counsel and help'. The ideal was rarely achieved; one wit commented that he was so far from his neighbouring priest that to travel for confession was 'too distant for a venial sin, and too dangerous for a mortal'. Most of the priests were alone in extensive districts, and this took a heavy toll, as Polding reported to Rome:

> [T]he health of some of the clergy has been considerably impaired by their labours in faithfully discharging their arduous duties. The Rev Father Gregory has been obliged by order of the physician to desist for a time from the duties of the sacred ministry. The life of the Rev Mr Lynch was despaired of for the same cause; whilst the aged appearance of Rev

---

1. Polding to Propaganda Fide, 17 January 1842 (Polding Letters I.192ff)

> Mr Brady, though he is, comparatively speaking, young, tells at once the fatigue he has endured in his most useful career, and his promptness to consummate the sacrifice of his life at the altar of God.[2]

Polding was justly proud of what had been achieved since his arrival in the Colony in 1835 and he gave a succinct summary of the progress:

> Having thus set forth in detail the condition of the Australian Church, I may summarize, as follows, our relative position in 1835 and 1841:
> In 1835 there was the Vicar-General and two priests. Three churches were in course of erection. There were ten schools. The number of communicants was 200.
> In 1841 there was a Bishop and 24 priests, a Convent of Sisters of Charity, nine churches completed, six others in course of erection; some small chapels have been opened, and others are being completed. Total number of churches and chapels 5. There is a seminary with six ecclesiastics, 20 students and 20 extern scholars. There are 31 schools. The number of those confirmed was 3,150 and of Holy Communicants 23,130.[3]

He was effusive in attributing to Governor Richard Bourke credit for the Church Act of 1836 which removed any notion of 'establishment' privilege for the Anglican Church and gave to Anglicans, Presbyterians and Catholics equal recognition and access to government assistance in financial support of clergy and grants for the building of churches and schools. Bourke, an Irish Protestant, had been appointed governor and arrived at Sydney in 1831. In 1829 the Catholic Relief Bill had been passed by the Westminster Parliament, and the first fruit of that legislation in New South Wales was the arrival of two Irish Catholic lawyers who took up government appointments, which until 1829 had been denied to Catholics. They were Roger Therry and John Hubert Plunkett who arrived in Sydney in 1829 and 1832. Therry had been appointed commissioner of the Courts of Requests (small debts), with the right of private practice, and Plunkett solicitor-general. Bourke drew on the legal skills of Therry and Plunkett, and together they were able to draft the Church Bill which was one of the foundations of the remarkable Catholic progress from 1835 to 1841. The other foundation was the recruitment of Irish clergy, also in part due to Governor Bourke who recommended to the Colonial Office the granting of additional stipends for Catholic priests. The ground-work for this recruitment was in the hands of William Ullathorne who toured Ireland in 1837 and began sending volunteers to Australia in 1838.

---

2. Polding Letters I.192ff.
3. Polding Letters I.192ff.

Most of this growth and expansion of the Catholic community took place beyond Sydney. Most the priests arriving in the Colony were quickly dispersed to the rural districts. According to Polding's report to Propaganda Sydney had a population of 40,000 of whom 14,000 were Catholic. The few town clergy had a busy schedule as outlined in the *Catholic Directory* of 1841. Ministry to the convict population took up much of their time: visits to the Old Gaol in George Street for divine service every Sunday morning and devotions in the evening; visiting the Sydney Hospital daily, or more often if called for; visits to the iron gang at Woolloomooloo every Sunday and to the solitary cells frequently; Carter's Barracks and House of Correction visited weekly; Debtor's Gaol visited occasionally; Iron Gangs on Cockatoo and Goat Islands attended monthly. The prisoners due to be transferred to Pinchgut for building the fortifications were to be added to the list. There were daily visits to the Benevolent Asylum for the aged and infirm. The priests were on call for visiting the sick and dying within an eight mile perimeter of the town.

During the six years of continual church building in the other districts, Sydney, for all its growth in population, had only gained two new Catholic structures, serving as schools and temporary chapels, in addition to the the still unfinished St Mary's. Polding described these as 'situated at the extremities of the city'—in Kent Street in the Rocks, at the northern end of town, and in Abercrombie Place, at the southern end. There was another church under construction, but experiencing slow progress due to high wages for masons and carpenters. This was St Patrick's on the lower slopes of Church Hill, not the more elevated site requested from the Government by Polding, between Prince and Clarence streets, but a much more acceptable location, it having been donated by William Davis. Polding blessed the foundation stone a few months before heading off to Europe in 1840. The still incomplete church was dedicated on St Patricks's Day 1844.

In 1843 with the return of Polding, bearing the new title Archbishop of Sydney and Metropolitan of Australia, the focus of expansion and church building shifted back to Sydney. As well as the new title, Polding was also carrying a series of church designs which he had commissioned from the celebrated leading architect and designer of the English Gothic revival, Augustus Pugin. While in England, Polding visited the Pugin designed church of St Barnabas, which had been commissioned by Father Robert Willson, whom Polding was encouraging to accept nomination as the first bishop of Hobart Town. In October 1842, Polding was finally able to consecrate Willson in Pugin's Cathedral of St Chad in Birmingham. It was the impact of these buildings on Polding that moved him to seek out their architect for designs for churches, sacred vessels and vestments for the Australian mission.

The first move was to transform the temporary chapel-school at Abercrombie Place, on George Street West, into a permanent stone church dedicated to St Benedict, as an expression of the devotion of the Archbishop and his small group of Benedictine monks to their sixth-century founder. The laying and blessing of a church foundation stone was an occasion of great celebration for the local Catholic community and followed a fixed pattern incorporating liturgical, social and financial elements. The event at Abercrombie place was no exception. The day chosen was a Monday, 28 July 1845; the ceremony was set to begin at 9am. The builders had marked out the perimeter of the church and the location of the altar was indicated by a cross. The members of St Patrick's Benefit Society, bearing their splendid banner and accompanied by the excellent band of St Patrick's Total Abstinence Society, had set out from Macquarie Street and begun their march through the city in time to be in place for the event. The Archbishop was accompanied by the 38-year old French bishop Jean-Baptiste Epalle, newly consecrated Vicar Apostolic of Melanesia and Micronesia, who had arrived in Sydney with a group of Marist priests and brothers on their way to the Solomon Islands. In December that year he was hacked to death on Isabel Island.

The crowd at the laying of the foundation stone was estimated to be between two and three thousand, an impressive number for a Monday morning. The choir's singing of the 83rd Psalm, *O quam dilecta Tabernacula*, 'How lovely is thy dwelling place', accompanied the procession of clergy, with the proud Benedictine community forming a distinct contingent. Standing by the corner stone the Archbishop recited the prayers prescribed by the Pontifical and then addressed the congregation. Ever conscious of the Protestant accusations of superstition and idolatry against the Catholics, Polding began by stating that 'though the ignorant or bigoted might look on such ceremony as so much idle pomp, or superstitious exhibition, yet to the sincere Christian nothing was dearer or more venerated than the rite of imploring the blessing of God on that place where a temple was to be dedicated to his most holy name'. He concluded by way of preparing the congregation for the next part of the ceremony, the collection: 'Do not reckon the expense, but count the fruit . . . What a thing it is to go and enter the House of God, and to see that even you built it.' And then to the accompaniment of some 'enlivening airs' by the band, the Archbishop, Bishop Epalle, the Vicar General and the clergy came forward and set the example by laying their offerings on the foundation stone itself. And then 'the people with the most praiseworthy and generous emulation imitated this example'. Newspaper reports always included the important detail of the total amount collected. On this occasion it was three hundred and five pounds. The liturgy then resumed with the bishops and clergy processing around the perimeter of the foundation while the Litany of the Saints and appropriate psalms were intoned. As always an inscribed plaque recording the event was attached to the foundation stone. The inscription on this occasion read: 'John Bede Polding, Archbishop of Sydney, laid the corner stone of this Church, dedicated to Almighty God, in honour of St Benedict, on the 21st day of July, 1845, in the Pontificate of Gregory the 16th, and ninth year of the reign of Victoria, Queen of Great Britain and Ireland, Sir George Gipps, Knight, being Governor of the Colony, John Morris, Builder'. The usual memento of an inscribed trowel used for the cementing of the stone was presented by the builder to the Archbishop. The *Morning Chronicle* concluded its detailed report stating that the church of St Benedict 'promises to be a great ornament to that end of the city'.[4]

The next distinct mission to be established was that of Balmain, which, with Pyrmont, constituted what was commonly known as the West Shore, but which unlike Pyrmont was not included in the municipality of Sydney. The district underwent subdivision and development in the 1840s, paralleling the growth of Pyrmont. The location of the proposed church was described as being on 'a conspicuous eminence', and here the foundation stone of St Augustine's was laid and blessed on Monday, 4 September 1848. Monday seemed to have been the preferred day for blessing foundation stones, but in Balmain's case, given the distance from the city, the later time of 11am was chosen. Archbishop Polding was accompanied by Bishop Alipius Goold of Melbourne and Bishop Francis Murphy of Adelaide, both men well known to the Catholics of Sydney. The Benedictine community had sailed from Woolloomooloo, while the bishops had taken the circuitous land route.[5] There was no mention of the presence of the St Patrick's brass band.

The choice of the patron saint was again influenced by the Benedictine Order of which St Augustine of Canterbury was a member. He was the apostle to the English people, sent by Pope Gregory, also a Benedictine monk, arriving in Kent in 597. Polding suggested to the congregation that they were one with Augustine's English converts in joining in the same prayers and psalms that accompanied the foundation of churches in England eleven hundred years ago. The usual concluding event of placing donations on top of the newly blessed stone was carried out, but the amount realised was not recorded by the *Morning Chronicle* journalist; he simply noted that 'a generous collection was hereupon made, each one depositing his mite or his bounty on the stone itself'.[6] The failure to record an exact amount suggested that mites outnumbered bounty.

---

4. *Morning Chronicle*, 30 July 1845.
5. *Sydney Chronicle*, 9 September 1848.
6. Sydney Chronicle, 9 September 1848.

The dedication of the Balmain church would be transferred to another Saint Augustine in January 1885, when the newly installed Irish Archbishop of Sydney, Patrick Francis Moran, declared that Augustine of Hippo would henceforth be the patron saint of Balmain parish. The Parish Priest, John Joseph Carroll, solemnly recorded the decision in the Baptimal Register: 'In accordance with the unanimmous opinion or belief of the Catholics of Balmain, His Grace Archbishop Moran has declared the great Saint Augustine, Doctor of the Church, Bishop of Hippo and son of St Monica, to be, and ordered that he be henceforth considered, the true and only Patron of that church known as St Augustine's Church in Balmain East.'[7] The dismantling of Sydney's Benedictine connections was underway.

The St Benedict mission area was reduced in its western extension by the establishment of the Petersham district in 1851. It still expanded north to Johnston and Rozelle bays, encompassing the Pyrmont peninsula and The Glebe. To the south it extended to Botany Bay. The Catholics in the northern part of the district had several options for the practice of their faith. They could trudge along rough Harris Street, little more than a country track, to the parish church where Sunday Mass was celebrated at 7.30am without preaching and at 11am with a sermon, and where catechetical instruction was given at 3pm followed by Vespers and a lecture at 4pm. Alternatively they could catch a ferry or sail across Darling Harbour and head either to St Mary's or St Patrick's. At St Mary's Sunday Mass was celebrated at 7am and 8am, with High Mass and sermon at 11am, and at St Patrick's at 7am and 11am with sermon. The completion in 1858 of the bridge from Union Street to Market Street across Darling Harbour made access to St Patrick's and St Mary's the easiest option for the Pyrmont faithful.

Another Sunday worship option for Glebe and Pyrmont Catholics was the chapel of the Monastery and College at Lyndhurst on the western side of Blackwattle Cove. Lyndhurst was the estate and mansion developed from 1833 to 1836 by Dr James Bowman, principal Colonial Surgeon, who had married the Macarthurs' second daughter, Mary Isabella. Edward Macarthur had named Bowman Street on the Pyrmont Estate after his brother-in-law. Bowman fell into insolvency during the depression of the early 1840s, and his properties were conveyed to the Macarthurs and then to the Australasian Bank to cover debts. In 1846 the Anglican bishop leased part of the property and transferred his school at St James in the city to Lyndhurst. The venture succumbed to church divisions with the conversion of two prominent Anglican clergymen to Catholicism in 1848. Both had taught at St James Lyndhurst, which was now identified as a hot-bed of Tractarianism and

---

7. Peter Reynolds, *On Balmain Hill: 150 Years of the Catholic Church in Balmain* (Balmain, 1998), 7.

Roman-leaning theology and practice. The college was closed the following year. Archbishop Polding purchased twenty acres of the estate in 1852 and established a boarding and day school called St Mary's College, to which the two convert Anglican clergymen returned as staff members. The story is told that when one of them, the Rev Mr Makinson, had come alone to see Polding to announce his decision to convert, the Archbishop asked: 'And where, Sir, is your congregation?' Makinson became Polding's faithful and long-serving personal secretary.

In 1857 it was announced that the monastic community at the cathedral was being transferred to Lyndhurst, in this way 'securing the universally acknowledged advantages derived to a house of education from the presence and discipline of a religious community'.[8] With the monks in residence, the chapel of the monastery then became an option for the local Catholics for Sunday Mass. The presence of St Mary's Lyndhurst postponed the need to build a Catholic church in The Glebe for twenty years, until the closure of the monastery-college in 1877. Accessibility to Lyndhurst for Pyrmont Catholics was made possible by the completion in 1859 of two causeways connected by a small bridge across Blackwattle Cove, completing the Pyrmont Bridge Road link between Pyrmont and western Sydney. The monks took this route to the city, as evidenced by an incident in 1860. At a coroner's enquiry into the death of a woman found lying in the mud behind Lyndhurst, Father Anselm Curtis, was called to give evidence. 'He had been crossing the small bridge at the causeway on his way to Pyrmont and into the city, when he happened upon a group of fishermen trying to retrieve the body from the mud and successfully directed their efforts from the bridge'.[9]

The Catholics of the southern parts of the St Benedict district did not enjoy the alternative Mass centres available to Pyrmont residents, so it was in that direction that the priest-in-charge turned his attention late in the 1850s for the building of churches and schools. Michael Andrew Corish was one of the very few Irish secular priests recruited for Australia who chose to join the Benedictine community. He received the monastic habit soon after his arrival in 1847, receiving the name 'Mellitus', by which he was often known. The taking of monastic vows of poverty, chastity and obedience by the clergy had been Polding's ideal, mainly with the intention of removing the temptation for priests to be preoccupied with the accumulation of money and property and distracted by other temptations. However, most of the Irish clergy resisted strongly the monastic call and the few that made profession as monks did not always remain immune to the usual range of temptations.

---

8. *Freeman's Journal*, 19 September 1857.
9. *Sydney Morning Herald*, 6 April 1860.

Father Corish made monastic profession in 1848 and he was given various rural appointments. In 1850 he was called back to St Mary's from where he served St Benedict's temporary chapel and the surrounding district. All Sydney-based priests lived at St Mary's Monastery until 1857, even the diocesan clergy. The Benedictine Journal for these years indicated the various locations to which priests from St Mary's were assigned for Sunday Mass. For example, on 17 August 1851, the Tenth Sunday after Pentecost, three Masses were celebrated at the Cathedral, two at St Patrick's, two at St Benedict's, one at Sacred Heart, Darlinghurst, one at Balmain, one at Petersham, one at the Gaol, one at the House of the Good Shepherd, Pitt Street, and one at Subiaco, the monastery-school of Benedictine nuns, 14 miles up the Parramatta river. Father Corish was regularly assigned to duties at St Benedict's. However, the Archbishop insisted that all baptisms and weddings be celebrated at St Mary's. Corish took up residence closer to St Benedict's when he joined some of his fellow monks at Lyndhurst, as indicated in the *Catholic Directory* of 1854: 'When the Rev Father Corish cannot be found at the Church, he may, in all probability, be seen at the College, Lyndhurst.'

That year Corish was among the dissident monks who petitioned Rome concerning the state of the Benedictine Monastery at St Mary's. In fact he and a junior monk, Anselm Curtis, boarded a steamer for Europe in September 1854, six months after Polding's departure, to present a petition to the Roman authorities. The *Catholic Directory* of 1855 no longer listed Corish as priest at St Benedict's. In Rome, Polding asked that the Cardinal Prefect of Propoaganda discipline these vagrant monks who were spending 'their time now in pleasure in the City': 'I very respectfully request your Eminence to consider the deplorable result which the conduct of these young persons, if unpunished, will produce on the infant church in Australia.'[10]

Corish and Curtis sailed back to Sydney with Polding, arriving in January 1856. At the conclusion of the huge reception at St Mary's to welcome the Archbishop, Corish stepped forward and in front of the hushed congregation read the following statement as reported in the *Sydney Morning Herald*:

> I have now rather a painful duty to perform on the part of Mr Anselm Curtis and myself; however, as I hope we have acted most conscientiously throughout, we hesitate not to do so now that we are aware of our error. We gladly embrace this earliest opportunity of publicly expressing to you our deep regret for the dissedification that may have been caused by our departure from Sydney. We acknowledge that we did wrong in taking that step, and that we thereby incurred the censure of excommunication . . . We have written this of our own accord, and have obtained permission to

---

10. Polding to Fransoni, 16 December 1854 (Polding Letters II.218-219).

make it public lest any erroneous impression might remain on the minds of any of you.[11]

The Archbishop graciously accepted the apology:

> His GRACE, addressing the Rev Mr Corish, expressed his approbation of the noble and manly conduct of the two reverend gentlemen in thus publicly acknowledging the error they committed by leaving the colony subsequently to the departure of his Grace without his permission. He willingly received this proof of' their contrition, and stated his readiness to forget the past.[12]

Polding was true to his word, and all was forgiven—Curtis resumed his ecclesiastical studies and Corish was reinstated as pastor of the St Benedict district, as recorded in the *Catholic Directory* for 1857.

Back in the saddle Corish undertook the building programme that would see the establishment of new missions in the southern section of his district. He began with the laying of foundation stones at Cook's River in June 1858, at Waterloo in August 1859 and at Botany in September 1860. As well as building churches, Corish had also been busy establishing schools. The 1861 *Directory* listed the following Catholic denominational schools in his district: Waterloo Estate, Newtown, Camperdown, Redfern and Pyrmont.

In March 1864 he was assigned to Bathurst as Dean of that vast western district beyond the Blue Mountains, but he died at the age of 46 within a few months of arriving. In the extensive obituary which appeared in the *Freeman's Journal* and which became available as a separate pamphlet, Corish's work in providing churches for the St Benedict district was recalled and celebrated:

> When he first came to St Benedict's district as many our readers are aware, the only church in that large and populous quarter was but a small structure miserably insufficient for the wants of the congregation. This affected Father Corish deeply and he resolved on remedying the want. Long he laboured, earnestly he strove to attain this end. That he has done so the beautiful church of St Benedict's is proud testimony . . . But it is not alone St Benedict's that remains as a proof of his zeal!—on the hill of Mount Carmel, conspicuous from afar stands a goodly edifice dedicated to the worship of Almighty God, the work also of the good priest who has been called away . . . Nor did his labours cease here; he was ever engaged in similar good works, never content while any portion of his

---

11. *Sydney Morning Herald*, 28 January 1856.
12. *Sydney Morning Herald*, 28 January 1856.

district was unprovided with a house wherein the people could hear the consoling truths of religion and assist at the holy sacrifice of the mass, the redeeming sacrifice for the sins of mankind. And always and ever working to attain this end, Father Corish did not cease his efforts until even the outlaying district of Botany was possessed of a church.[13]

Pyrmont had made a significant contribution to this remarkable growth of church building in Sydney, not only through the modest subscriptions of local residents, but especially through the provision of high quality sandstone quarried on the peninsula. The use of the 'best Pyrmont stone' was noted particularly in the construction of St Benedict's and Mount Carmel at Waterloo, where the use of Pyrmont sandstone was extensive: 'The foundations, base course, door and window jambs, sills, arches, label mouldings, buttress caps, string courses, carved and moulded crosses, with their sockets, together with the bases, shafts, and caps of columns, the corbels and blocks, are all of the best Pyrmont stone.'[14] However, Pyrmont itself was still without a local place of Catholic worship.

---

13. *Freeman's Journal*, 6 July 1864.
14. *Freeman's Journal*, 3 April 1861.

Chapter 3
Founder of the Pyrmont Mission

Father Corish was succeeded at St Benedict's by Father Timothy McCarthy. The Catholics of Pyrmont were fortunate in the appointment of Father McCarthy as priest-in-charge of the mother-parish. The new priest continued the work of Father Corish in responding to the needs of the growth areas of the mission district; he turned his attention to the north, to the Pyrmont peninsula. He might well have adopted the argument of John Dunmore Lang in his justification of re-establishing a Presbyterian church in Pyrmont in 1864, substituting 'Catholic' for 'Presbyterian':

> The necessity for a Presbyterian church at Pyrmont, for the comparatively numerous Presbyterian population of the locality, must be evident to any intelligent and candid person. The distance from the different places of worship in Sydney is very considerable, and either a very hot or a very wet day forms an excuse for staying at home on Sabbath. Besides the expense for a mechanic's family, if at all numerous, in crossing the bridge to and fro twice on Sabbath is so considerable—half crown in some cases—that the children are sent to the Sabbath-schools and places of worship of other denominations in the place, and in all probability lost to the Presbyterian Church.[1]

Within a few months of his arrival from Carcoar in 1864, McCarthy had met with the local Catholics and formed a committee to acquire property and undertake the building of a temporary structure which would serve as both church and school. A notice was placed in the *Freeman's Journal* in September calling on the support of Catholics of other districts:

> It is hereby notified that the Catholic residents of Pyrmont having resolved on erecting a public building, temporarily answering Church

---

1. *Empire*, 13 October 1864.

and School purposes, on a suitable site in Pyrmont, beg to solicit the assistance of their Sydney Catholic friends generally, whom they have at all times assisted in the erection of their respective Churches—to enable them to complete the erection of their much needed Church. (Signed) Thos. Quinn, Secretary to the Church and School Building Fund, Pyrmont.[2]

This notice was quickly followed ten days later by a clear indication that Father McCarthy was committed to forming a local congregation by arranging for himself or his assistant to celebrate Sunday Mass at the rented premises used by the local Catholic Denominational School in Pyrmont Street. On Saturday 24 September 1864 the following advertisement appeared in the *Freeman's Journal*: 'TO THE CATHOLICS OF PYRMONT. On to-morrow morning at half-past nine the Holy Sacrifice of the mass will be celebrated in the school-room Pyrmont by one of the Clergymen from St Benedict's Church.'[3] The notice was repeated two weeks later, the location nominated as 'the temporary chapel', rather than 'the school-room', and the pattern of regular Sunday Masses at Pyrmont was in place, with no need for further newspaper announcements.

In the same edition of the *Freeman's Journal* there appeared a 'LIST OF SUBSCRIBERS to the Fund for the ERECTION of a ROMAN CATHOLIC CHURCH and SCHOOL in Pyrmont'. The notice began by recording the collections taken at the first three Masses celebrated in the rented school-room in Pyrmont Street. The results showed a disappointing decline over the three Sundays: one pound, one shilling and 8 pence; 19 shillings; 14 shillings. There followed acknowledgement of individual donors to the fund. Among the subscribers were many Pyrmont residents, including Patrick O'Toole and his son Master Hugh, and the brothers James, Michael and John Toole. These two families would emerge as significant in the life of the parish. Alderman John Hurley gave one pound. The call for donations from Catholics of other districts was not without success—'two friends from Parramatta' gave five shillings. The results of the efforts of the four officially appointed district collectors were given—Father McCarthy gave to each of them, a total contribution of five guineas, by far the most generous subscription. The newly appointed pastor of St Augustine's Balmain, Father George Dillon, gave twice—ten shillings and one guinea. The total collected in the first month of fund-raising was £46/9/2.[4]

---

2. *Freeman's Journal*, 14 September 1864. Thomas Quinn was a tailor at 111 Harris Street, as recorded in the *Sands Directory* for 1863.
3. *Freeman's Journal*, 24 September 1864.
4. *Freeman's Journal*, 8 October 1864.

The 35-year-old McCarthy was well experienced in forming parish communities. Born in Ireland, at Ballinhassig, County Cork, in 1829, the year of Catholic Emancipation, he studied theology at Carlow College, having first opted for law. After completing priestly formation, he was ordained in 1852. It was initially intended that he would head to the diocese of Hyderabad in India, where a Cork priest, Daniel Murphy, was bishop. However, a meeting with Sydney's Vicar-General, Abbot Henry Gregory, who was on a recruiting tour of Ireland, led to a change of plans and McCarthy set sail for Australia with four other Irish clergy, arriving in Sydney in February 1853. As it happened, Bishop Daniel Murphy, who had initially volunteered for New Holland as a newly ordained priest with eight other Maynooth students in 1837, the 'Men of '38', would be transferred to Australia, becoming the second bishop of Hobart in 1866. He was the longest lived of his ordination group, dying in 1907.[5]

After arriving in Sydney, McCarthy remained just long enough to attend the Levee at Government House in honour of the Queen's birthday in May. Soon afterwards Archbishop Polding, true to his pattern, quickly dispersed the new recruits, keeping two in Sydney, and assigning the others to country regions—Newcastle, Carcoar and Armidale. The 24-year-old new arrival was sent alone to begin the new mission in Armidale, which until then had belonged first to the Moreton Bay district, and then to the Maitland mission. Armidale had been visited only intermittently from Ipswich and Maitland. Father Luckie, the first priest at Pyrmont, had been at Ipswich when it included New England region, and Dean Lynch of Maitland, responsible for that region before McCarthy's arrival, would be assigned to Pyrmont in 1875, and in 1878 would welcome an ailing Fr McCarthy into his home, 'Hawthorne', on The Glebe Road.

McCarthy's new district extended indefinitely to the west, east to the Pacific Ocean, and north to Queensland, which would become a separate colony in 1859. He was indefatigable in providing chapels and planning churches for the New England and northern rivers district of New South Wales. Of particular interest is the church he planned for Tenterfield, similar to St Bede's in its architecture. Similar too were his organisational skills used in both locations. A Tenterfield correspondent to the *Freeman's Journal* in 1857 described the approach of their smooth-talking pastor:

> [T]he Catholic clergyman of Armidale, the Rev T McCarthy, who is at present remaining at Tenterfield, [is] engaged in the organisation of

---

5. Anon, 'Murphy, Daniel (1815–1907)', *Australian Dictionary of Biography*, National Centre of Biography, Australian National University, http://adb.anu.edu.au/biography/murphy-daniel-4274/text6911, published in hardcopy 1974, accessed online 22 September 2014.

means and the collection of funds for the erection of the Church that he has in contemplation. On Sunday, the 12th instant, that gentleman convened a meeting of his congregation after Divine Service was over, and, in a lengthened and evidently well matured discourse, entertained his people with a discussion of the means and principles necessary for their observance in the event of their undertaking to accomplish the object proposed for their consideration. The meeting retired into an adjoining room, and after some deliberation, which principally referred to the probable cost of the building etc, they unanimously arrived at the conclusion that the realisation of the funds necessary for the erection of the church was perfectly practicable, and they adopted a resolution accordingly. Immediately after this resolution was recorded, a subscription list was opened in the room, and the sum of £60 was subscribed, which soon after increased to £80. A Committee of Management was formed, and two collectors appointed.[6]

The obituary published in the *Freeman's Journal* after news of his death in Ireland in October 1878 summarised his New England ministry:

For this mission he seemed to be specially cut out by Nature, as he was a splendid horseman, and possessed wonderful powers of endurance. Numberless are the local reminiscences of his escapes from floods and other dangers during the ten years he did missionary duty in the New England district. Equally numerous and well recorded by the squatters and settlers of the vast region he had to traverse—from the Macquarie to the Manning one way, and from the Liverpool Range to McPherson's Range on the other—are his acts of generosity and self-abnegation akin to those referred to by our Armidale correspondent.[7]

One of those fondly remembered northern acts of generosity was perhaps sometimes repeated as he rode from Abercrombie Place through the Ultimo Estate along Harris Street to morning Mass at Pyrmont:

'There are residents in this district now,' says our Armidale correspondent, 'who well remember Father McCarthy meeting a poor tramp upon one occasion, whose boots were completely worn out, and who was suffering much pain from blistered feet. The charitable heart of Father McCarthy was at once touched by the poor fellow's sufferings, and in an instant the

---

6. *Freeman's Journal*, 26 July 1857.
7. *Freeman's Journal*, 25 October 1879.

priest's boots were transferred to the weary traveller's feet, and the rev. gentleman had to ride home, a distance of some miles, in his socks.'[8]

In November 1861 Archbishop Polding undertook an extensive tour of the northern regions of his Archdiocese. Back at St Mary's in December he wrote to his exiled former Vicar-General, Henry Gregory, 'my dearest Child', who had been his regular companion on his missionary tours over the previous twenty-five years. He wrote glowingly of McCarthy's horsemanship which he compared favourably with Gregory's own skills: 'Maccarthy handles the reins much after your fashion. I felt quite safe with him, though we had fearful creeks to cross, and now and again cuts across the bush to avoid deep ruts and stumps, but he steered through the fallen timber admirably ... [W]e rattled over some 800 miles of country within four weeks.'[9]

Late in 1861 there was a major redistribution of clergy in New South Wales resulting in the transfer of Fr McCarthy from Armidale to Carcoar in the Bathurst region. His replacement in Armidale was Dean Lynch, who had spent 24 years in West Maitland. As often happens with sudden changes in clergy, some parishioners of the Carcoar district were not happy with the replacement of their priest, Fr Bernard Murphy, who had been transferred to Singleton. In an exchange in the regional newspaper, *The Bathurst Free Press and Mining Journal,* a Cowra resident had welcomed the change saying what a 'great boon' the new priest had been with his decision to celebrate Mass monthly at Cowra, a place that 'had been neglected'. A reply soon came from 'a Catholic of the Western Plains' who resented the slur on the reputation of Father Murphy. It was pointed out that Murphy, at Carcoar since his arrival in Australia in 1853, had been a builder of churches, including the stone church at Cowra, and an indefatigable missioner, 'administering single-handed a district now attended by three priests from Wellington to Forbes, and many hundred miles further down that now famous river on which that later town is built, and from Burrangong to King's Plains'. The dour Western Plainsman concluded with a caution: 'be not led on by first gushings of the tide of popular opinion, no matter in whose favour they may run.' Whatever the differing clerical preferences of the laity, however, there was no friction between these two priests themselves, for they were friends and, indeed, shipmates, having been together during the six month voyage from Ireland to Australia in 1852-1853.[10]

At the same time as he announced the clerical changes, Polding issued an official warning, a Pastoral Monitum, to all the clergy of the Archdiocese,

---

8. Freeman's Journal, 25 October 1879.
9. Polding to Gregory, 21 December 1861 (Polding Letters III.51).
10. TJ Linane & FA Mecham (eds), *The Men of '38 and other pioneering priests by 'John O'Brien'*, Kilmore, 1975, 183.

against any encouragement of lay petitions opposing the removal of popular priests. He singled out as models of proper priestly behaviour in this regard three nameless priests involved in the current transfers, among whom were surely Timothy McCarthy and Bernard Murphy: 'In proof, I may mention that three priests of great worth, and of long service in this mission, were lately removed from their honourable, and honourably occupied, positions—there was no word of reluctance, or of petition, from them or for them; if any movement of the kind was contemplated, it was wisely, and in a priest-like spirit and discretion, suppressed.'[11]

In the Carcoar district, to which McCarthy was sent, bushranging had become endemic. The first occurrence of the word 'bushranger' was found in *The Sydney Gazette and New South Wales Advertiser,* Sunday 17 February 1805, and it quickly came to be applied to every escaped convict or bolter. In 1837 Polding, in a letter home to Downside Priory, gave a report that must have given pause to any monk who was thinking of volunteering for Botany Bay: 'Mr Corcoran has been the only clergyman who has been attacked, since we came, by Bushrangers. The man pretended to be the Constable of the Road and stood at his horse's head till a severe blow made him retreat. After their wont, another man came out of the bush a few yards further on, and was treated in the like manner.'[12] Polding hastened to add some faintly assuring words: 'Mr Corc was not known to be a priest, otherwise he would not have been attacked'. Polding was always fond of pet-names and used to refer to McCarthy as 'Mac'. John Henry Curtis who was train-bearer and page-boy to Polding and then joined the monastery in 1848, but scandalously abandoned the priesthood in 1864, reminisced in 1902 about the Dominican Corcoran and bushrangers:

> I had the honour, as the Bishop's page, of travelling to Parramatta, for some sacred function, in the same carriage with him [Corcoran] . . . I nearly had my five or six years' growth frightened out of me by Father Corcoran pretending that he saw two bushrangers coming toward us. I gave a little cry of terror, but he instantly comforted me by saying: 'Don't be afraid, my little boy, there's no bushranger that will harm one of God's priests.'[13]

With the end of transportation in 1840 and the onset of the gold rushes in the 1850s the mantle of bushranging fell to loosely organised gangs of

---

11. John Bede Polding, 'Pastoral Monition to the Clergy of the Archdiocese 1861', in P O'Farrell, *Documents in Australian Catholic History* (Melbourne, 1969), volume 1, 96.
12. Polding to Brown (Polding Letters I.83-84).
13. JHB Curtis, 'John Bede Polding', *Austral Light*, Oct. 1902, 701.

disaffected local lads, reckless and hard-riding. The gold mines at Lambing Flat, now Young, attracted the gangs to the district, and by 1861 there was a reign of terror around Carcoar. The most active gang at the time of Father McCarthy's arrival was led by Ben Hall, heir to the notorious Frank Gardiner, and included Johnnie Dunn, Mickey Burke, Patsy Daley, John Gilbert, Jack O'Meally and Johnny Vane. They were known as the 'Weddin Mountain boys', named after the range of scrub covered hills running from Carcoar to Cowra. In October 1863 the Archbishop was passing through the district on his overland journey from Melbourne to Sydney. Always focussed on the most wayward of his flock he took the opportunity of his presence in 'the Bushranger country' to seek out the lost. He deliberately travelled to the Weddin Mountains and spent four days 'in the hope of meeting with the gang of Bushrangers whose resort is there'. In a letter to Father Henry Gregory, his former Vicar-General, now exiled in England, he recounted the outcome of his visit, making a nostalgic comparison with the ministry to the newly arrived convicts which they shared in Sydney in the 1830s:

> I had received notice that they were about to cross the Lachlan to me but unfortunately just at the crossing place 7 troopers came on them, and they scampered off in a different direction. However, my great object was to see and instruct those of their families who might be tempted to join them. These I saw and instructed, and never met with persons so ignorant of the first truths, just as our prisoners used to be. I spent 10 hours in the days I was there in instructing some 7 or 8 young persons.[14]

This was Polding at his most relaxed and happiest—in the bush, remote from Sydney, ministering to those most in need. However, the letter went on to express to Gregory his deep distress and sadness at betrayal by disaffected Irish clergy and laity. He had received a stinging rebuke from the Cardinal Prefect of Propaganda Fide based on inaccurate reports received from Australia about his favouring Englishmen in recommendations for the newly proposed dioceses of Goulburn and Armidale. He applied to the Cardinal the greatest criticism an Englishman could make—'no Gentleman':

> If the Cardinal has no respect for our rank in the Ch[urch] he should not forget that we are entitled to common courtesy—but to be hoisted into the pillory and to be pelted by [some]one's representation and slander, he seems to consider a matter for no account. The conclusion is evident. He is either no Gentleman, or he does not consider me to be one. I would not treat a Schoolboy as he treats Bishops. Cardinal though he be, he

---

14. Polding to Gregory, 20 December 1863 (Polding Letters III.136).

is only a Priest . . . I can have no respect for a man who has no respect for his office, allowing it to be the vehicle of slander and insult—and no respect for the Princes of the Church, Brothers even of the Holy Father himself.[15]

There was worse to come from Rome in 1867, the year of the completion of St Bede's at Pyrmont, as will be discussed in a later chapter.

Meanwhile at Carcoar Father McCarthy was having better success with contacting the Bushrangers. In December 1863 he convinced the convicted bushranger John Foley to reveal the whereabouts of some of the £5,700 in old bank notes he and Fred Lowry had stolen from the manager of the Mudgee branch of the Joint Stock Bank when they held-up the Mudgee Mail Coach in July 1863. McCarthy himself related the incident in a long letter he wrote to the *Sydney Morning Herald* in 1865 during a controversy about 'bushranging and the confessional':

> Foley, who was arrested at the Fish River when I was some 300 miles distant from that place, namely, in the north (New England), must have experienced some of Vane's better thoughts, for, of his own accord, after one or two interviews that I had with him, he informed Dr. Palmer, the Police Magistrate, Mr McIntosh, and myself, where notes to the amount of £2700 were secreted, which money I subsequently had restored to the Australian Joint Stock Bank.[16]

The better thoughts of John Vane were that he would accompany Father McCarthy to Bathurst and surrender himself to the Police Magistrate. The *Bathurst Times* carried the full story in its edition of 21 November 1863. It described Vane as 'a native of the colony, twenty years of age, stands six feet high, and has a ruddy complexion, with black hair, and is said to be a Wesleyan'. He was wanted for a range of robberies under arms from August to October, culminating in 'the shooting with intent, of Mr Keightley, the Commissioner, at Dunn's Plain, Oct. 24th'. McCarthy had come across him by accident in the bush and Vane, after being reassured that the intruder was a priest and not a policeman, offered McCarthy a meal, during which the conversation turned to his life of crime. The priest urged him to abandon bushranging and surrender himself. Vane promised to consider the advice and after three days to let the priest know of his decision. In the meantime Father McCarthy located Vane's mother and urged her to reinforce his advice to her son. This she did and in the words of the journalist, 'the arguments

---

15. Polding Letters III.136–137.
16. *Sydney Morning Herald*, 22 May 1865.

and prayers of the mother and the priest prevailed'. The report concluded with high praise for the 'Bushrangers' Priest':

> Too much praise cannot be given to Father McCarthy for the service he has rendered to the community, in thus, by his moral persuasion, prevailing upon this misguided youth to surrender. He has arrested, in a headlong career of crime, one who might otherwise have steeped himself beyond all hope of recovery, and prevented, perhaps, the commission of offences more heinous than those with which the young bushranger is at present stained. There is another thing which should not be forgotten, though of infinitely less moment, he has saved the country a thousand pounds... His sphere of usefulness has been still more extended, as we are informed that he has had several interviews with the other bushrangers, and, on every occasion, has done his utmost to induce them to throw themselves on the mercy of the law; and we have reason to believe that Gilbert and Ben Hall will yet place themselves in his hands.[17]

Vane was tried at Bathurst in April 1864. Father McCarthy had been transferred to Sydney, but he returned for the trial. Vane pleaded guilty to four charges and was found not-guilty on the fifth. Barrister William Bede Dalley had 'addressed the jury at great length and in a most eloquent manner in behalf of the prisoner'. While the jury was still deliberating, Chief Justice Sir Alfred Stephen, in an unusual move, addressed Vane's family assuring them 'for the relief of their minds, that whatever might be their verdict, it was not his intention to pass sentence of death upon the prisoner'. John Vane was sentenced to fifteen years 'on the roads or other public works of the colony'.[18]

In 1894 there appeared a charming reminiscence about the Vane trial in the *Windsor and Richmond Gazette*:

> I remember meeting Father McCarthy at a road-side inn on the Bathurst-road after the trial. I was in company with the late Mr Samuel Armour of MacGrath's Hill—we having left Mitchell's creek together the previous day. We had just had a nip at Greenhalgh's pub, the other side of Hartley, when the coach drove up, and Father McCarthy and the late Hon W B Dalley alighted, I had seen the good priest before, but the stout little gentleman in a fashionably-cut lavender suit, colored tie, and a choice 'button-hole', was a stranger. At any rate, both insisted upon our drinking with them; and in the bar I learnt who the 'swell' was, and what had been

---

17. 'THE BUSHRANGERS. BREAKING UP OF THE GANG, SURRENDER OF VANE' (From the *Bathurst Times*), *Empire*, 24 November 1863.
18. *Sydney Morning Herald*, 15 April 1864.

their errand to Bathurst. I met Father McCarthy on several occasions since then, and found him one of the most genial of men, while as Priest he was as liberal as he was popular.[19]

Father McCarthy was eligible for monetary rewards for his involvement in Vane's surrender and the retrieval of Foley's stolen cash, but 'he considered that he had done these things in his ministerial capacity; he declined to accept any reward whatever.'[20]

Johnny Vane was released from Darlinghurst gaol in 1870 after six years because of exemplary behaviour. In answer to a question in the Legislative Assembly, the Colonial Secretary stated that the recommendation for release had come from Chief Justice Stephens, who was of the opinion that Vane, if liberated, would never return to a course of crime.[21] An early sign of Vane's exemplary conduct was the extraordinary revelation, found in McCarthy's long letter of 1865, that prisoner Vane was a member of the choir at St John's Anglican church, Darlinghurst. On release one of his first jobs was working on the building of the new St Mary's cathedral as a stonemason, a trade he had learnt while a prisoner. It just so happened that in 1869 Timothy McCarthy had been transferred to the cathedral as Administrator and chief fundraiser for the new cathedral that was being built following the disastrous fire of 1865. His name was regularly found in the *Freeman's Journal* over the next four years, often in relation to the collecting tours for the building of the new cathedral in the country districts where he had ministered from 1853 to 1864. At the meeting of the Cathedral Building Committee for 26 December 1874 it was recorded that 'the Dean entertained the audience by allusions to some sparkling episodes of his travels in the northern districts', and that on the following Tuesday he would leave on the steamship *Agnes Irving* for Grafton, to continue the collections there.[22]

By 1878 he was exhausted and had begun to withdraw from his role as Cathedral Dean, accepting the hospitality of his old friend Monsignor Lynch at his residence, 'Hawthorne', on Glebe Road in The Glebe. However, he made a final official appearance at St Mary's in January 1878 at the ceremony of the placing of the *pallium* on the shoulders of the new Archbishop, an event that usually took place in Rome. It was reported that Dean McCarthy preached for 'fully an hour and a half': 'Notwithstanding the crowded state of the church, and the intense heat of the day, the Very Rev Dean's auditors did not appear to weary, but hung with evident interest on his words throughout.'

---

19. *Windsor and Richmond Gazette*, 10 November 1894.
20. Correspondent of the *Bathurst Free Press* quoted in *Freeman's Journal*, 23 March 1864.
21. *Bell's Life in Sydney and Sporting Chronicle*, 12 March 1870.
22. *Freeman's Journal*, 2 January 1875.

The reporter concluded, with reference to the Dean's recent withdrawal from duties : 'It is not often that Dean McCarthy is heard at St Mary's, and we are not saying too much when we state that many were surprised at his very able, learned, and eloquent address on the Pallium ceremony.'[23]

Later in the year it was decided that he needed to return home to Ireland for full recovery after 25 years in the Colony. A large crowd of well-wishers gathered at St Mary's seminary to make a farewell presentation. The following address was read:

> We, the undersigned colonists, who have learned to know and respect your many sterling qualities, and your great missionary labours, beg leave to present you with an address and testimonial. We earnestly desire, on the eve of your departure for Rome, to record our estimate of the zeal, liberality, and generosity which have marked your long and eventful career. During more than a quarter of a century you uniformly succeeded in fulfilling the duties of your sacred office without wounding the religious feelings or impugning the conscientious convictions of those who do not belong to your communion, and hence men of all shades of opinion and of conflicting political views have joined in paying this tribute to your enlightened and unsectarian philanthropy. We sincerely hope that your visit to Europe may, whilst affording you pleasure, benefit your health. We shall watch with interest your progress through 'the dear old land', and your return to the colony (which we fondly trust may be at no distant period) will be hailed with joy by all classes and creeds.[24]

The Committee Treasurer presented him with a cheque for £850. An emotional Dean McCarthy replied in simple words marked by the 'ecumenism' which characterised his Australian ministry: 'My dear friends, the very complimentary address which has been just presented to me, coming as it does from all classes and creeds in the colony, is most welcome and consoling. In it I distinctly recognize the spirit of liberality, with which, in my efforts to advance religion and collect for the Cathedral, I was always met by members of every denomination.'

The new Archbishop, Roger Bede Vaughan, had asked him to pass through Rome and provide Cardinal Simeoni, Cardinal Prefect of Propaganda, with a report on the current state of church life in New South Wales. The report was very supportive of Polding and Vaughan, cautiously critical of the Irish Suffragan Bishops of Brisbane, Maitland, Bathurst and Goulburn, and realistic about the challenges facing his fellow Irish clergy. Dean McCarthy

---

23. *Freeman's Journal*, 19 January 1878.
24. *Freeman's Journal*, 15 June 1878.

concluded his report: 'We have our clouds, but we are not bereft of Sunshine, and please God, we will always have this, whilst at peace with ourselves and enjoying the full encouragement of the Holy See.'[25]

After 18 months of rest and recuperation in Ireland, plans were in hand for the Dean to return to Australia in the company of the newly appointed bishop of Armidale, the Italian Capuchin friar Eleazar Torregiani, but there was a relapse in health. Father Timothy McCarthy died at his sister's home in County Cork on 25 August 1879, aged fifty. On the headstone of his grave in the churchyard in Ballyheeda, County Cork, is a lengthy inscription which concludes: 'To the casual beholder, it might not be immediately apparent that this is where all that is mortal of one of the most beloved Priests ever to labour on the Australian Mission was interred. Yes, this is indeed the last resting place of the famous "Fr Tim".'[26]

This then was the remarkable priest who ranks as the founder of St Bede's parish. His name is engraved in stone, beneath the cross, high on the facade of the church:

SAINT + BEDE'S
CHURCH
ERECTED ANNO DOMINI 1867
INCUMBENT
REVd. T. McCARTHY

---

25. T McCarthy to Cardinal Simeoni, 5 August 1878, in M A Kelleher, *Compassionate Samaritans. The experiences of active Benedictine women in New South Wales from 1857 to 1877*, PhD thesis submitted to Department of Studies of Religion, University of Sydney, 2000, appendix vi, 565.

26. 'A condensed history of the Catholic Church in Armidale to the Year 2000', http://www.arm.catholic.edu.au/about/history/armidale/diocese.htm (accessed 9 May 2012).

Chapter 4
Toole/O'Toole Families of Pyrmont

The committee established in 1864 to organise the building of a church-school in Pyrmont continued its work into 1865 and in February sent a letter to the *Empire*. The letter, signed by the Honorary Treasurer, Patrick O'Toole, again called for help from fellow Catholics, and indicated progress on the project.

> TO THE EDITOR of the EMPIRE.
> Sir,—Feeling assured that you are always ready through your journal to give publicity to a good cause, I believe you will do me the favour to publish this letter. Pyrmont has been built upon upwards of a quarter of a century, and boasts now of a large population, but I regret to say there is not yet any place of worship for Roman Catholics.
>
> In August last a few labouring men commenced exerting themselves to raise a sufficient sum for building to be used as a place of worship, as well as for a school; a few of the more wealthy joined them, but up to this time £80 only has been collected; most of the Roman Catholic residents at Pyrmont are persons with large families, and but small means. I therefore earnestly call upon co-religionists in other places to come forward and help us. We, of Pyrmont, have often been called upon to assist other places, and other denominations, and I know it cannot be said that we have not responded to the call as far as our means would allow.
>
> Mr Archibald Telfer (who I now thus publicly thank for the residents at Pyrmont), has kindly and gratuitously given us a plan and specification of the building we are anxious to erect, and we find that its cost will be £550; so that we now require £470.
>
> Our friends will perhaps kindly bear in mind that it is a long way to send our young children to divine service or to school, either into Sydney, or to St Benedict's, Parramatta-street

Collectors are furnished with books, in which entries of subscribers to date are inserted, bearing the signature of the Rev. Timothy McCarthy as a guarantee of safety. The reverend gentleman has kindly undertaken to receive any subscriptions forwarded from the country.

I am, Sir, your most obedient servant, PATRICK O'TOOLE, Hon. Treasurer.

Pyrmont, 27th February, 1865.[1]

Patrick O'Toole had called upon Archibald Telfer, a fellow member of the Loyal Victoria Lodge of the Independent Order of Oddfellows of the Manchester Unity, to draw up a plan and specifications. Telfer would be elected Grand Master of the Lodge for the following year.[2] The Oddfellows were the largest of the 'Friendly Societies' registered in New South Wales in 1861, as reported to the Parliament by the Registrar:

> It appears that the number of Societies established in the Colony does not exceed five, viz:
> 1st. The Ancient Order of Foresters, numbering 830 members;
> 2nd. The Grand United Order of Oddfellows, numbering 989 members;
> 3rd. The Australian Mutual Benefits Society, numbering 130 members;
> 4th. The St Patrick's Total Abstinence Society, numbering 64 members;
> 5th. The United Shipwrights Society, numbering 34 members.[3]

Archibald Thompson Telfer was born in Glasgow in 1831 and died at Randwick in 1911. In 1851 he married at the Presbyterian church in Maitland, where he was a prominent citizen, until moving to Sydney in the early 1860s, where he rose to be Grand-Master of the Oddfellows. Like his Lodge-Brother, Patrick O'Toole, Telfer was a stone-mason. His impressive career was outlined in the 1911 obituary:

> For many years he was associated with the Government Architect's Office, and supervised the erection of many important buildings, notably the Darlinghurst Gaol and Callan Park Asylum, while he acted in a similar capacity during the building of nearly all the lighthouses along the seaboard. He was a prominent Oddfellow (Manchester Unity), and was the oldest Grand Master of the order in New South Wales, as well

---

1. *Empire*, 28 February 1865.
2. *Clarence and Richmond Examiner and New England Advertiser*, 20 February 1866.
3. The Australian Centre for Fraternalism, Secret Societies and Mateship (http://www.fraternalsecrets.org/fraternalism/, accessed 14 March 2015)

as the oldest member of the order, his connection dating back nearly 60 years.'[4]

Telfer, in providing plans and specifications to the Pyrmont Building Committee, would have met Father McCarthy in 1865. Perhaps Patrick O'Toole had some involvement in putting Telfer and McCarthy in touch again in 1870, when they combined their efforts in supporting the early release of Johnnie Vane from Darlinghurst gaol and finding him a job as a stonemason on the St Mary's site, as recounted by Vane: 'three days after my release I got employment at St Mary's Cathedral building, through the recommendation of Mr Telfor [sic], the gaol overseer.'[5] Johnnie could also have been a subject of benevolent concern among Patrick's and Archibald's Lodge Brethren at their Sussex Street meetings.

In 1870 there was a remarkable conjunction around the fate of Johnnie Vane, prisoner at Darlinghurst. At the time of his early release in 1870, Father Timothy McCarthy was Administrator of St Mary's Cathedral where new building was underway, and Archibald Telfer was overseer of stone works at the Gaol. Thanks to Telfer, Vane had become skilled in working stone as he explained in his memoirs edited by Charles White in 1908. The Gaol Governor advised Vane to choose his company carefully while in prison, pointing out to him several of the quietest and best behaved prisoners, mentioning particularly John Bow. In February 1863, at the age of twenty, Bow had been sentenced to death for his involvement in the Eugowra escort armed robbery carried out by the Gardiner gang. The sentence was commuted to imprisonment for life, the first three years to be spent in chains. At the time of Vane's arrival at Darlinghurst gaol in 1864 Bow had become one of the stone-cutters, each of whom was allowed an assistant, known as a 'bullock'. Vane applied to Mr Telfer, the overseer of the stone works, for permission to serve as Bow's 'bullock'. It was in this way that Vane 'became handy with the mason's tools'.[6] Both McCarthy and Telfer were impressed with Vane's rehabilitation during six years of imprisonment, as was the Chief Justice who recommended his release. And so when Vane was unexpectedly set fee in 1870, his two patrons combined to provide him with immediate employment.

Catholic membership of secret societies was repeatedly condemned by papal documents throughout the 18th and 19th centuries. However, it was not until the arrival of the Roman educated Irish bishops of the new dioceses of the colony in the 1860s, and their influence at the second Provincial Council

---

4. *Sydney Morning Herald*, 23 January 1911.
5. Charles White, *John Vane, Bushranger: Being a true narrative of his career faithfully depicted*, Sydney, 1908, 206.
6. Op cit, 228-229.

of Australian Bishops in 1869, that the full impact of papal teaching on a range of topics was felt. These matters included rules concerning mixed marriages and membership of Masonic style organisations. Until then there had generally been a more relaxed approach to a range of church rules, including membership of non-catholic mutual assistance societies. This approach had been articulated by bishops of the USA in 1866 at the second Plenary Council of Baltimore in an effort to restrain blanket condemnation of the proliferating benefit societies, including the Odd-Fellows: 'We do not wish that anyone in these Provinces, in any ecclesiastical dignity, whatever, should from now on condemn by name any society, unless it certainly and beyond all doubt is clearly one of those comprehended in the Pontifical Constitutions, insofar as they were interpreted by the Sacred Congregation of the Inquisition.'[7]

There were, however, some Australian clergy who followed a stricter approach. One such was Dean John Lynch of Maitland, later of Pyrmont, who refused to perform the burial service for Catholics at whose funerals the Odd Fellows were in attendance in their regalia, as required by their Society's rules:

> One of the principal topics of conversation during the last two or three days has been the dispute between the Rev Dean Lynch and the Loyal Good Design Lodge of Oddfellows of the Manchester Unity. This dispute occurred some time back, but the circumstance was revived at the funeral of the late Dr Macartney. It may be remembered that at the decease of a young man named Andrew Watt, a Roman Catholic—who distinguished himself at the time of the floods, in rescuing from danger persons whose lives were imperilled—the Rev Dean Lynch positively refused to perform the burial service over his remains, if the members of the Lodge in question attended, according to their usual custom, dressed in their funeral regalia.[8]

This stricter approach was formalised by the Plenary Council of Bishops in 1885 and incorporated into Sydney church regulations at the Diocesan Synod in April 1888, as announced in the *Freeman's Journal*:

> NON-APPROVED SOCIETIES. The following diocesan regulations concerning non-approved societies was adopted: 'That as regards the Oddfellows, Foresters, Druids, Good Templars, Rechabites, and all kindred societies, they have not the approval of the Church, and all

---

7. W Fanning, 'Secret Societies', *Catholic Encyclopedia*, New York 1912, volume 14.
8. *Sydney Morning Herald*, 30 July 1860

Catholics who after this date shall join such societies, disregarding the instructions of their clergy, shall be deprived of the benefit of the presence and services of the priest at their funeral.' We understand that this regulation has been decided on in consequence of services other than those prescribed by the Church taking place at funerals of members of the societies named.[9]

Papal condemnation reached a climax in 1894 when a decree addressed to the bishops of the United States condemned the Odd-Fellow societies by name, instructing the bishops to exclude Catholic members from reception of the sacraments. Two years later there was a mitigation allowing nominal, passive membership on condition that a Catholic promise among other things that 'in the case of death the society will have nothing to do with the funeral'.[10]

Patrick O'Toole combined faithfulness to the Catholic Church and to his Lodge membership. At his funeral in 1879, Oddfellow officers and brethren were invited to gather at his residence, while family and friends were invited to gather at St Bede's for the Requiem Mass. One expects that Archibald Telfer was one of the Oddfellow officers gathered in funeral regalia to farewell their Lodge brother Patrick, as his body was removed from his home. Perhaps some of the Catholic Oddfellows removed their regalia and descended the hill to St Bede's for the Requiem.

Basic information regarding Patrick O'Toole is available from his death certificate:

Date and place of death: August 24th 1879; Way Terrace, Pyrmont
Occupation: Stonemason
Where born: Ireland
How long in Australasian Colonies: 37 years
Place of marriage: Dublin
To whom married: Teresa Boyle
Children of marriage: Hannah (34 yrs), Teresa (30 yrs), Hugh (28 yrs)

A further detail is found in a death notice where it was stated that he came from County Wicklow: 'O'TOOLE. August 24, at his residence, Way-terrace, Pyrmont, Patrick O'Toole, native of the county Wicklow, aged 71 years, after a protracted illness, which he bore with Christian fortitude. *Requiescat in pace*.'[11]

The first clear evidence of the residence of the Toole or O'Toole family in Pyrmont was in the baptism record of Hugh Toole, born on 10 September

---

9. *Freeman's Journal*, 28 April 1888.
10. Fanning, *Secret Societies*.
11. *Sydney Morning Herald*, 25 August 1879.

1849 and baptised on 7 October at St Mary's Cathedral, in the Parish of St James, County of Cumberland. The abode of parents Patrick and Teresa was given as Pyrmont. The celebrant was Rev J E Gourbeillon, a French Benedictine member of St Mary's Monastery, and an accomplished sculptor.

Patrick Toole was noted in the 1855 edition of the *Assessment Book* as renting a two roomed stone and shingled house in John Street. By 1858 there had been a significant change in his socio-economic circumstances, with Patrick being recorded as the owner-occupier of a two-storeyed, four room stone and slated house in Mills Lane, and as the owner of a more modest house in the same street—two rooms, wooden with iron roof. The family's continued residence in Pyrmont, in the Municipal Ward of Denison, can be traced through the *Assessment Books* for 1861, 1863, 1867, 1871, 1877 and 1880. The 1880 *Book* contained information gathered in 1879, the year of Patrick's death. Each of the Books showed Patrick as a property lessee or owner. In 1861, now no longer Toole but O'Toole, he was recorded as in possession of three houses on Way Terrace, a street that was created in 1860, looping around the eastern side of the Anglican Church estate, running off Point Street in the north and joining Mill Street at the southern end. The street name 'Way' came from the shipping-related use of the word, as in 'slip-way', and found in a boyhood reminiscence about Pyrmont in the 1870s: 'At Chowne's there were the remains of the old 'ways' used by the port's premier shipbuilder in launching his vessels, of which we made good use in our harbourside play.'[12]

'Way's Terrace', a spelling that soon became standard, was sometimes described as being 'off Mill Street'. At first houses were built on the west side, and in 1867 on the eastern side. In 1861 Patrick O'Toole's three houses varied in size and material—one was single-storied with two rooms and made of wood with a zinc roof, more a cottage than a house; two were double-storied, made of stone, one with a slate roof and one with shingle roofing. Patrick and his family lived in the house with the highest 'gross annual value in pounds', namely the stone building with five rooms and a slate roof, valued at thirty-two pounds. The other two properties were rented to tenants. In 1863 another house had been added to the O'Toole portfolio, and this was how things remained at Patrick's death in 1879. His wife Theresa died in July 1880. In 1882 their son Hugh O'Toole was listed as the lessee/owner of two houses on Way's Terrace, and residing in number 33, the family home. In 1918 he was still at 33 Way's Terrace, but listed as 'sub-lessee'. All the Way's Terrace properties had reverted to the Macarthur family under the formality of the Camden Park Estate Limited, formed by the heiress Elizabeth Macarthur-Onslow in 1899.

---

12. 'Pyrmont Boy's Recollections', *Sydney Morning Herald*, 4 July 1933.

From 1916 to 1923 Sydney Council resumed the northern section of the Anglican Church property on which the rectory and school was built, as well as the houses on the western side of Way's Terrace, which the Mayor described in 1923 as 'a slum area', the houses having been condemned as unfit for human habitation. After demolition of these houses and the Anglican school and rectory, the Council built the block of workers flats which took the name of the street, with a slight variation in spelling. 'Ways Terrace' was designed by Leslie Wilkinson, professor of architecture at Sydney University, and completed in 1925. The flats still stand, and the design of more recent government housing at the northern end of the peninsula deliberately reflects the style of the Wilkinson building.

Patrick's and Teresa's first born, Hannah, entered the Good Shepherd Convent in 1862, becoming Sister Elizabeth; she was the first religious vocation from the Pyrmont peninsula. Hugh O'Toole, while a pupil at the Model School at St Mary's Cathedral in 1866, won a scholarship to attend Lyndhurst College. Two scholarships had been established by the clergy during their annual retreat, and the results of the examinations were announced at a mid-year assembly of staff, students and parents presided over by the Archbishop. The *Freeman's Journal* gave an effusive and lengthy report of the gathering, proclaiming that 'Catholics may well feel proud to hear that an institution founded by their beloved Archbishop is rapidly entitling itself to be considered the premier school of the colony'. The article concluded with the awarding of the scholarship:

> The result of the examinations for the two scholarships founded by the clergy was next announced. These had been conducted in the college by written examinations and were open to any boys attending any Catholic Denominational school. The candidates were examined in Latin, English, Arithmetic, Dictation, History, Grammar, Geography, Catechism, and Composition. To give assurance of perfect fair play fictitious names were assumed by the boys, the real one not being known till a decision had been arrived at. Eleven candidates offered themselves, and the two successful ones were from St Mary's Model School, the first having assumed the name of Plautus, the other that of Terence. 1150 was the full number of marks and Plautus gained 597 and Terence 545. On Plautus being called for, Walter Edmonds [sic], a boy of extremely youthful appearance, stepped forward amidst the enthusiastic cheers of all present. Hugh O'Toole, or Terence was not present.[13]

---

13. *Freeman's Journal*, 30 June 1866.

In the Christmas examination reports published in the *Sydney Morning Herald* from 1866 to 1869 Edmunds and O'Toole jostled for pre-eminence in Catechism, Latin, Greek, Geography, History, Geometry and Arithmetic. In the ranking of 'Order of the School' in 1869, Edmunds was placed first and O'Toole fourth.[14] Walter Edmunds was appointed senior judge of the NSW Industrial Court in 1920. In the same year Hugh O'Toole died, his death certificate recording 'occupation: labourer'. Interestingly the certificate noted the place of death as Mill Street, while the newspaper death notice stated 'late of Way's Terrace', reflecting the persistence of the original name of Mills Lane.[15]

Throughout the *Assessment Books* from 1861 into the twentieth century there were many occurrences of the names Tool, Toole and O'Toole, residents of Denison Ward, at Pyrmont addresses. The variation in the spelling of the surname, with a preference for the omission of the Gaelic prefix 'O', had become common after the failure of the 1798 Irish rebellion and the Act of Union of 1801, which had produced a sense of inferiority among large sections of the Irish population, and a move to eliminate specifically Irish identifiers. Though never declared illegal, the Gaelic form of surnames was often dropped in favour of a more Anglo-Saxon version. The retention, adoption or restoration of the Gaelic version was taken as a forthright declaration of Irish nationalism. The determination of Daniel O'Connell, the Liberator, to retain the prefix, against family custom, was an example of such a forthright statement.[16] In 1847, the year of O'Connell's death, Bishop William Higgins of Ardagh, an ardent supporter of the campaign to repeal the 1801 Act of Union between England and Ireland, restored the prefix to his family name in honour of the Liberator.[17] A contemporary and local example of this pattern was Hobart-born Daniel Connell, monk of St Mary's in Sydney, who changed his surname to O'Connell at his ordination in 1843 as the first Australian born priest. At the time of receiving the Benedictine habit he had been given the name Maurus in honour of one of the first followers of St Benedict. Bishop James Quinn of Brisbane changed his surname to O'Quinn in 1875, the centenary of the Liberator's birth.[18] The name of Patrick O'Toole of Way's Terrace was the first occurrence of the Gaelic form recorded in Pyrmont. Rarely between 1861 and 1880 was the

---

14. *Sydney Morning Herald*, 20 December 1869.
15. *Sydney Morning Herald*, 11 May 1920.
16. Patrick Woulfe, *Irish Names and Surnames* (Dublin, 1922).
17. D Bowen, *Paul Cardinal Cullen and the Shaping of Modern Irish Catholicism* (Dublin, 1983), 65.
18. See John Molony, *The Roman Mould of the Australian Catholic Church* (Melbourne ,1969), 32.

prefix omitted in his entries in the *Assessment Books*, and probably never at his instigation.

Another Toole family in Pyrmont, first noted in the *Assessment Book* of 1858 and the *Sands Directory* of 1861, did not restore the prefix until 1878 with the appearance of the funeral notices for the matriarch Hannah O'Toole placed in the *Sydney Morning Herald* of 23 September by her sons, sons-in-law and grandsons. This adjustment of the family name to the Gaelic form could very well have been made in response to the celebration of the centenary of Daniel O'Connell's birth in 1875.

This County Wexford family was of no known relationship to Patrick O'Toole, the Pyrmont stone-mason from neighbouring County Wicklow. Two sisters were the first members of the family to arrive in Sydney as sponsored immigrants in 1853 and 1854, paving the way for an influx of Toole relations, among whom was their brother Tobias, arriving in 1856. Tobias in turn sponsored his parents, Thomas and Hannah, three siblings, a nephew, and a cousin in the following year. They arrived on 31 January 1857. The next day Tobias married his second cousin, Eliza Neal, at St Augustine's Church, Balmain, where the priest-in-charge was Fr John Joseph Therry, veteran pioneer priest of the Colony. Neither bride nor groom could sign the marriage register, nor could the witnesses, Tobias' parents Thomas and Hannah.[19] By 1861 many of the clan were established in Pyrmont. In the *Sands Directory* for that year there were four Tooles mentioned, only one of whom was listed with a trade—Patrick Toole, the stonemason of Way's Terrace. The lack of trade against the names of John, Tobias and their father Thomas indicated that they were unskilled labourers, from a farming background in Ireland.

The names of both Toole families occur on a list of 800 parishioners of St Benedict's, signatories to an address expressing support of their priest, Father Mellitus Corish, following the criticism he had received in the *Freeman's Journal* in May 1858.[20] The names of Mr and Mrs Toole (Thomas and Hannah) and their children John, Bridget, Michael, James and Ellen were listed, as were those of Patrick Toole and two of his children, Hannah and Hugh, among others from the northern extreme of the St Benedict's mission district.[21] A dissenter from the supportive resolutions moved at the parishioners' meeting dismissively described the gathering as 'a medley of small boys and girls, adventurous mammas, and not very bright papas' summoned 'from the extreme boundaries of the parish . . . to do something

---

19. DJ Gleeson, *Irish dusk, colonial dawn: the Dooly, Hickey, O'Brien, O'Neill (Neale), O'Toole (Toole) & Ryan Septs*, Concord 1999.
20. *Freeman's Journal*, 15 May 1858.
21. *Sydney Morning Herald*, 26 May 1858.

very desperate'.[22] Another dissenter expressed scepticism about the names appearing on the list:

> I see by the Sydney Morning Herald just received, that Father Corish has had a demonstration in his favour. I never supposed that it was reserved for a Catholic clergyman to be the first to carry into practice the principle of universal suffrage in Australia. For, in addition to all the fictitious names I think I can discover attached to that precious document, it is besides signed by ladies and their 'suckling babes'. I do not wish to impugn the respectability of a single individual who signed that address; but, if they are the signatures of those who assembled in the school room of St Benedict's on the evening of the eighteenth of May Father Corish has little cause to pride himself upon the respectability of his foolish demonstration. I have carefully gone over the large array of names to that document—and I must say they bear a strange, if not a suspicious similarity, throughout its whole length. For instance, we find 10 Clunes, and, strange coincidence, 4 of these are distinguished by the Christian name of Thomas. I hereby offer a reward of £1 (one pound) to any person who will find 4 Tom Clunes in the Parish of St Benedict. Then again, there are 19 O'Brien's, 17 O'Neil's, 16 Walshes, 13 McMahon's, 20 Murphy's, and 15 Grath's, besides a whole legion of Ryans, Byrnes, Hogans, and Tools (the latter specially predominating) all bearing a similar affinity in the Christian name to each other as the 4 Tom Clunes.[23]

Though not exactly a 'suckling babe', the signatory Hugh Toole was only eight years old.

In the 1858 edition of the municipal *Assessment Book*, Toby Toole was listed as resident at 55 Pyrmont Street in a single storey, two room house. This was the year of the birth of the first of the twelve children of Tobias and Elizabeth. In the 1865 *Sands Directory*, Tobias was listed as resident at the northern end of Harris Street. His mother Hannah was listed as conducting a dairy in Harvey Street. Her husband Thomas died in October 1865 aged 69. Three years later in the *Sands Directory* for 1868 Tobias was listed as a 'quarryman', and still resident in Harris Street. James, Tobias' youngest brother, took over the Harvey Street dairy from his mother after her death in 1878.

Tobias and Elizabeth's family increased during their early years in Pyrmont, from 1858 with the arrival of first-born Bridget to1874 with

---

22. *Freeman's Journal*, 22 May 1858.
23. *Freeman's Journal*, 2 June 1858.

the birth of the youngest, Andrew. There were twelve children altogether, including twins who were born in 1867, the year of the building and opening of St Bede's Church. Twins Elizabeth and Tobias were according to family tradition, in the absence of the original baptismal register, the first infants baptised in the new church, built by members of the local Catholic community, among whom were mason Patrick O'Toole and quarryman Tobias Toole.[24] A first Elizabeth had been born in 1864 and died in April 1867 during her mother's pregnancy with the twins. As often happened, the name of the deceased child was given to the next born.

In 1875 Tobias moved from quarrying to conducting a public house, the Green Tree Hotel, on the corner of Harvey and Bowman streets, and moved into the premises with his family. He died there in October 1879: 'O'TOOLE. October 2, at his residence, Green Tree Hotel, Harvey-street, Pyrmont, Tobias O'Toole, aged 46 years, leaving an affectionate wife and eleven children to mourn their loss.'[25] His wife Elizabeth took over the licence. Several of the following generation would follow in their parents' footsteps as publicans. A grandson, John, followed a less-trodden path and he studied for the priesthood, being ordained at St Mary's Cathedral in 1930. Three grand-daughters joined the Good Samaritan Sisters.

The funeral service for Tobias was celebrated in the parish church of St Bede by Father Joseph-Marie Garavel, newly appointed priest-in-charge. There was something rather confusing about the funeral announcement—the five notices placed in the *Sydney Morning Herald* indicated four different times for the departure of the cortege from the church: 1.45pm, 2pm, 2.15pm and 3.15pm. The notices had been placed by the undertaker, by Tobias' adult sons Thomas, Patrick, Michael and James, by his brothers Michael and John, by his nephew John, and by the Secretary of the Australasian *Holy Catholic Guild* of St Mary and St Joseph. The Guild secretary called on members to 'attend the Funeral of Brother TOBIAS O'TOOLE, to move from St Bede's Church, Pyrmont, TO-MORROW (Sunday), at 2 o'clock, for Petersham.'[26] The Guild had been founded by Archbishop Polding in 1845 as a Catholic alternative to the benevolent Protestant lodges flourishing in Sydney, as he explained to Cardinal Barnabo in his 1866 Report: 'In opposition to secret societies known by the name of Oddfellows and also Freemasons, the Society of the Most Holy Virgin and St Joseph has been established.'[27] Unlike the funeral of Patrick O'Toole in August 1879, which had occasioned a gathering of brother Oddfellows at his Pyrmont residence, Tobias' October funeral

---

24. Victor J Doyle, *St. Bede's Church Pyrmont. Centenary 1867–1967* (Sydney 1967).
25. *Sydney Morning Herald*, 3 October 1879.
26. *Sydney Morning Herald*, 3 October 1879.
27. 'Report of the State of Religion in the Diocese of Sydney given by the Archbishop, Monsignor Polding', 19 August 1866 (Polding Letters III.245).

brought his Catholic Guild brethren into St Bede's church, resplendent in their regalia which consisted of 'a black cloak made very full, with wings of half capes falling from the shoulder to each wrist, and a white collar, to which is suspended a sort of medal termed a shield, embossed with various devices'. The officials of the Guild wore cloaks trimmed with various colours according to rank, and matching collars. At funerals the brethren walked behind a large processional cross.[28]

Six of the patriarch's children named their first-born sons Tobias in honour of their father.[29] When his wife Elizabeth died in July 1902 there were twelve funeral notices printed in the *Sydney Morning Herald*, submitted by sons and daughters, grandchildren, sisters-in-law, nephews and nieces. Father Philip McIntyre was the priest-in-charge, recently returned from Ireland, and the curate was Father Michael MacNamara, recently demoted for his suspected involvement in the Monsignor O'Haran case, and soon to be removed to Cobargo.[30]

In 2005 Tobias' only living grandchild, the 92-year-old Phillip Bede O'Toole, son of Joseph and Mary Therese, gave a videoed presentation for an exhibition at the Powerhouse Museum entitled: 'Paradise, Purgatory and Hellhole, a history of Pyrmont and Ultimo'. He reminisced about family life and death in Pyrmont. He spoke of the tragic death of his sister Molly. Although Phillip was not born until two years after Molly's death, his parents and older siblings had shared with him their attachment to the little girl as 'the delight of the family'. She was tragically killed outside the family home in Cross Street in 1911, as reported in the newspaper:

> RUN OVER BY A CART. At the City Coroner's' Court yesterday an inquiry was held into the death of Mary Theresa O'Toole, 18 months, who was run over by a cart in Cross-street, Pyrmont, on August 15, and died in Sydney Hospital the same day. It was proved that the little one had followed her brother across the street, and that the driver did not see her until it was too late. A verdict of accidental death was returned, no blame being attached to the driver.[31]

Phillip remembered fondly that his older brother Joseph each Saturday would drive one of his father's trucks from the Austral Sawdust Company

---

28. The details of the regalia were described in an article entitled 'Religious doings in Sydney' in the *South Australian Register*, 31 January 1846.
29. DJ Gleeson, 'Tobias (O')Toole in History', MSS, Sydney, 2011.
30. Michael McNamara had, as early as 1902, begun to spell his surname 'Macnamara': M Macnamara, 'The Catholic Church in NSW and the Census', *Australasion Catholic Record*, 8 (1902): 292–315.
31. *Sydney Morning Herald*, 24 August 1911.

fleet, with his brothers and sisters crowded on board, to Curl Curl on the northern beaches, where the family had a holiday house. The children spent the months from Christmas to Easter at the beach, commuting to Sydney each day when school resumed. Back in Pyrmont Phillip and his school-age brothers followed a week-day routine beginning with serving the 7am Mass at St Bede's, then running back up the hill for breakfast, then running to catch a small ferry from the wharf adjacent to the Goods Railway tracks for an 8.30am departure across Darling Harbour to Erskine Street Wharf, then catching a rickety tram up King Street, heading across Hyde Park, walking through the Cathedral and finally arriving at St Mary's College for the 9am start to the school day.[32] During the recorded interview he recalled the visits of his Good Samaritan cousins who were granted the honour of being entertained in the 'front room' of the Point Street home. The family Rosary was prayed each evening, with the leading of the five decades being shared among the youngest children and their father. Fingering his beads, Phillip qualified his account by noting that on some Saturdays the evening Rosary was omitted, allowing the younger family members to socialise. He devotedly showed the interviewer his father's prayer book which he had inherited; the pages were interspersed with the many mortuary cards which recorded the deaths of O'Toole family members over three generations.[33]

---

32. Phillip O'Toole, 'Some Memories' (manuscript 2003).
33. 'Paradise, Purgatory and Hellhole, a history of Pyrmont and Ultimo', Powerhouse Museum Exhibition, 19 March 2005 to 16 October 2006 (http://www.powerhousemuseum.com/exhibitions/paradise.php; accessed 11 March, 2014).

Chapter 5
1867: Building the Church of St Bede

Fund raising for the Pyrmont church-school was slow from the beginning. The first six months of the appeal from September 1864 to February 1865 netted a mere eighty pounds. Five months later, collecting for the project met a major setback. During the night of Thursday 29 June the uninsured St Mary's Cathedral was devastated by fire, as headlined in the *Herald* of the next morning:

> By far the largest and most disastrous conflagration which has ever occurred in Sydney happened last night, and resulted in the total destruction of St Mary's Cathedral. This noble edifice, which was one of, if not the finest example of Church architecture to be found in the colony, is now an unsightly ruin . . . The fire was still burning when we went to press and is likely to smoulder for several days. The large engine of the Insurance Brigade has been playing on the ruins all night.[1]

The date was a very significant one for Sydney Catholics; as well as being a major feast in the Church's calendar, that of St Peter and St Paul, it was the anniversary of their Archbishop's episcopal consecration in 1834. At St Mary's Cathedral and at the attached monastery the feast was always celebrated with grand liturgy and festivities. Polding happened to be absent on one of his pastoral tours in the Western Districts that month, but the pattern of celebration was maintained. The weekly edition of the *Freeman's Journal* of Saturday 1 July, in which the destruction of the cathedral was lamented, also carried a report of the festive events of the day:

> Long before daylight on Thursday morning the bells of St Mary's Cathedral sent forth their merry peals in honor of the feast of St Peter and St Paul. It was also the feast of his Grace the Archbishop of Sydney,

---
1. *Sydney Morning Herald*, 30 June 1865.

who on that day celebrated the 30th anniversary of his consecration as a prince of the Church. High Mass was celebrated in the Cathedral and other churches, and many a prayer was offered up that his Grace might long be spared to preside over the flock committed to his care.[2]

The festivities had concluded with evening Benediction of the Blessed Sacrament attended by a large congregation. The cathedral was locked at the end of the service soon after 8pm. The gas lighting was turned off and the many burning candles that were traditionally part of this service were extinguished, except for the sanctuary lamp, 'which as our readers are aware is far removed from the possibility of any danger'. An hour later a fire was observed by a passer-by who alerted the only priest who was present at the monastery, Father Joseph Marie Garavel, a French missionary recently arrived from New Zealand. The rest of the clergy were at St Benedict's with Father Timothy McCarthy for a vigil service on the first anniversary of Father Corish's death.

The first person into the burning Cathedral was Garavel. He found the sanctuary ablaze, but courageously rushed to the tabernacle and successfully removed the vessels containing the consecrated hosts. A large crowd quickly gathered in Hyde Park across from the cathedral, and many joined in trying to rescue vestments, liturgical vessels and books, altar furniture and paintings from the sacristy. Steel safes containing documents and registers were retrieved from the Archbishop's private apartments adjoining the Cathedral. All the rescued items were safely deposited in the bell-tower that stood a safe distance to the north of the burning cathedral. The police had arrived to direct the operation and they were soon followed by the fire brigade, which had great difficulty in accessing water, the nearest available source being at the corner of Macquarie and King Streets. Sailors from the French war-schooner *Gazelle*, which had been anchored in Farm Cover since 12 June, took part in unsuccessful attempts to limit the damage to the Cathedral. However, their efforts contributed to saving the surrounding buildings and contents.[3] On the previous Sunday the *Gazelle* had joined all harbour shipping in flying its flags at half-mast in memory of President Abraham Lincoln, the news of whose assassination had just reached Sydney.[4] On the Wednesday, mourning was replaced on board the *Gazelle*, now 'gaily decked with flags' in celebration of the 27th anniversary of the Queen's coronation.[5]

The ferocity of the Friday night cathedral blaze was such that according to the *Herald* report, 'Captain Heselton, of the steamer *You Yangs*, which

---

2. *Freeman's Journal*, 1 July 1865.
3. *Freeman's Journal*, 1 July 1865.
4. *Empire*, 26 June 1865.
5. *Sydney Mail*, 1 July 1865.

arrived from Melbourne, in port last night, saw the reflection of the fire when off Port Hacking, and states his opinion that it would be visible for a distance of twenty miles at sea.[6] The *Freeman's Journal* concluded the story of the devastating night: 'Through the long and weary night these exertions were sustained with unextinguished ardour, and the day dawned upon the roofless blackened mass, upon the bare walls of our dear Cathedral upon which thousands of the faithful were looking with hearts filled with sorrow.'[7]

Devestated though they were, Sydney Catholics soon rallied to make arrangements for the building of a new and grander cathedral. That Friday evening, with the ruined Cathedral still smouldering, there was a meeting in the St Mary's school-room or seminary, as it was called. Father McEnroe chaired the meeting in the absence of the Archbishop who had received the shocking news at Bathurst and was preparing to hurry back to Sydney. The hall was crowded and among those present were 'most of our clergy, the leading Catholics and many of our Protestant friends' and it was not long before a subscription was underway, and 'before the meeting closed the sum of £6000 had been subscribed by those present'.[8]

On the Sunday following the fire, the city congregations held special collections with the following results: St Mary's parishioners, gathered in the school building for Mass, contributed £1200; at St Benedict's £1445 was subscribed, at St Patrick's £250, and at the Sacred Heart, Darlinghurst, £630. The extraordinary result from St Benedict's was achieved at an evening meeting convened by the incumbent, Fr Timothy McCarthy, and attended by a large gathering of parishioners, including those from Pyrmont. He spoke powerfully of the need for funds for rebuilding the Cathedral and he movingly expressed the other constant theme in this period of loss, namely, deep concern about the impact of the disaster on the seventy-year-old Archbishop. The official booklet published in the week following the fire expressed the anxieties about the well-being of the Archbishop: 'The long and arduous labours of the venerated Prelate have told upon his health, and great dread was felt by the Faithful lest the shock should be too much for him.'[9] The grieving Archbishop arrived back in Sydney the following Tuesday.

That same evening a scheduled meeting of subscribers and members of the Church of England was held in the school room in Castlereagh Street to receive the report of the St Andrew's Cathedral building committee, and to devise measures for the immediate completion of the long-delayed project,

---

6. *Sydney Morning Herald*, 30 June 1865.
7. *Freeman's Journal*, 1 July 1865.
8. *Freeman's Journal*, 1 July 1865.
9. Henry Norbert Birt, *Benedictine pioneers in Australia*, 2 vols, London 1911, II.295

which was taking even longer to complete than had the destroyed St Mary's—the first foundation stone was laid in 1819 and the finished cathedral was consecrated in 1868. The Governor, Sir John Young, chaired the meeting and in his opening address referred to the fire at St Mary's: 'I am sure that there is no one in this assembly who does not heartily deplore the calamitous fire which has burnt the Roman Catholic Cathedral to the ground [Applause].'[10] He proceeded to call on the Anglican communion to have the same spirit in advancing their building project as shown by the Catholics over the last few days—'amidst all their sorrow their energy has not failed'. In his concluding address Bishop Frederick Barker joined the Governor 'in expression of deep regret that many of our fellow colonists should have been subject to such a great calamity as the destruction of their place of worship'. However, he went on to assert that 'he could not regard it as consistent with the principles of our Reformed Church that any member of the Church of England should contribute towards the erection or the re-edification of a place of worship belonging to the Church of Rome'. This statement was received with 'long and prolonged cheering from all parts of the room', according the report in the *Empire*. The bishop continued, venturing into a criticism of the architecture of the destroyed cathedral: '[F]or the deliverance of my own conscience I felt bound to make such a statement (Renewed cheers). Then let us hope that they (the Roman Catholics) would bring their work speedily and happily to its completion. And they might even have cause to rejoice that a building more adapted to ecclesiastical uses than the former had been erected.'[11] 'Frederick Sydney' had not gone quite as far as his predecessor, 'William Australia', who had described Protestant donations to old St Mary's as a sin.

An overwhelming rejection of Barker's sectarianism was displayed at public meetings in the following days. On the Wednesday afternoon Sydney's mayor, John Woods, called a meeting of citizens, mostly of Protestant allegiance, to express solidarity with the suffering Catholic community, and especially to express sympathy for 'that grand old gentleman', Archbishop Polding, affirming the high estimation in which he was held throughout the colony. City Aldermen lined up to propose and second resolutions of financial commitment to the project of building a new cathedral, with the repeated expectation that it would be completed within two or three years, and be consecrated by the present Archbishop. Each speaker committed himself to adding his 'mite' to the appeal. Alderman Joseph Raphael, speaking for the Jewish community, recalled that 'when an appeal was made for the starving Jews of Palestine, that good old man, Archdeacon McEncroe, came forward

---

10. *Sydney Morning Herald*, 5 July 1865.
11. *Empire*, 5 July 1865.

and pleaded their cause'. He expressed his concern for the sorrow of that other 'good old man', Archbishop Polding, 'returning to see that magnificent pile of building in ruins'. He was confident that the 'sensible, enlightened, and those of free toleration would give a helping hand'.[12] The repeated call at the meeting for a generous, non-sectarian response to the needs of the Catholic community in rebuilding their cathedral met with sustained cheers, applause, and 'hear hear', effectively drowning out the 'loud and prolonged cheering' at Bishop Baker's meeting the previous evening.

The largest indoor meeting ever held in the colony took place on the Thursday afternoon at the Prince of Wales Opera House, with Archbishop Polding in the chair. With him on the podium were the Governor and Sir Terence Aubrey Murray, President of the Legislative Council. The Archbishop spoke of the shared grief of all, expressing particularly his gratitude for the support of those of other religious faiths:

> I was at Bathurst when this dreadful calamity befell us. The intelligence was communicated to me by the electric wire. I need not say that I was prostrate—stunned—at first, by the blow. But in a very short time after the first intelligence was received, a second communication informed me of the promptitude with which all classes came forward to make good that which had been so destroyed; and thus, my friends, you raised me up at once . . . I could readily suppose that those united to me by the relationship of Sacred ties would come to my assistance and enable me to bear up against so grievous a blow; but that they should also have so many around them of every denomination to enable them to bear their loss and to assist me was much more than I could possibly anticipate (Cheers). While the reports which reached me prepared me to meet a very large number of those who are involved in the same calamity with myself, I could scarcely have thought—nay, what right had I to expect—that on this occasion I should not only have you, my friends, before me, but that I should be environed by the representatives of all that is honourable in the country—by so many who are distinguished for their positions in life—that they should one and all leave their ordinary duties to come and mingle their sympathies with our own (Continued applause). Yet, why should I not have expected it? (Cheers). Have I not known New South Wales for thirty years?[13]

When it was the Governor's turn to speak, the gathering showed its deep appreciation of his presence at the meeting—'His Excellency Sir John Young

---

12. *Empire*, 6 July 1865.
13. *Freeman's Journal*, 8 July 1865.

on rising to speak was greeted with enthusiastic applause (the audience standing while the cheering continued)'. The Governor was emphatic in distancing himself from sectarian sentiments, citing criticism of his attendance at this Roman Catholic meeting:

> My Lord Archbishop, ladies and gentlemen, in the position which I hold as presiding over all classes of her Majesty's subjects in this colony I have thought it a duty—but a duty which I most willingly accept—to attend on this occasion to offer sympathy and to lend a helping hand towards the re-erection of the cathedral so calamitously destroyed (Cheers). Doubts have been expressed as to the propriety of this course, and the opinion has been given that greater stress should be laid on differences of religion. I do not entertain those doubts—(applause)—nor should I give way to them even if the occasion were one of less special emergency than the present (Cheers).

He deliberately used the theme of conscience, on which Bishop Barker had based his advice to his congregation, to contradict His Lordship: 'I am happy to think that the testimony of my conscience in this particular is borne out by the long array of names of Protestant gentlemen—the foremost in position and intelligence in New South Wales—who signified their intention to being present at this meeting, and of furthering its objects by their influence and assistance (Applause). I think their decision was right (Applause).' This former Chief Secretary for Ireland drew an 'hurrah' and continuous cheering when he expressed his sympathy towards 'the Catholics of this colony, who I believe to be as faithful, as intelligent, and as industrious a class of the community as any that exists', and who 'besides being mostly Irishmen or of Irish descent, and although being scattered over distant lands' have a common country.

He rejected the advice of Bishop Barker in announcing his own intention of contributing to the appeal: 'I hope that my sympathy, and that of Lady Young (continued cheering), will go beyond a mere phrase, as I have shown it does, by the act of attending at this meeting, and as I hope to show still further by a contribution which I shall offer, and which I hope your Grace will do me the honour of accepting, more as a token of good will than on account of pecuniary value (Applause).' His concluding remarks brought the cheering assembly to their feet:

> There is no need then to import that which wisdom and patriotism deprecate—no need to import the passions of bygone ages, or the hatreds of another hemisphere. I trust that the union displayed at this meeting will raise up one other effectual barrier against their admission—

(cheers)—and that as your Cathedral arises—as arise it will—in renovated grandeur,—(cheers)—the sense of the calamity which has overtaken you will be lost in the joy of the successful restoration, or only be recalled in association with pleasant memories of the good will, and the active sympathies which have been elicited by the occasion from all classes of your fellow citizens.[14]

At that Thursday afternoon meeting in Sydney Governor Sir John Young became a hero to the Catholic community, second only to one of his predecessors, Sir Richard Bourke. At the conclusion of the gathering another 1200 pounds had been added to the rebuilding fund.

In his first letter after the fire, Archbishop Polding wrote to his brother bishop in Melbourne, James Goold, summarising the catastrophe: 'Alas! Our calamity is great'; but adding: 'Happily no lives lost'. He enclosed the *Herald* report on the meeting and praised the Governor for his address: 'The Governor's speech and that of several others were in marked condemnation of Barker, the Ch[urch] of England Super[ior], who the day before held a meeting in wh[ich] he distinctly expressed his disapproval of all countenance and assistance being given to the Catholic body. It has greatly injured him and his cause very much.'[15] He went on to express his anxiety to resume his mission in the country districts.

The extraordinary initial successes of the fund-raising drive led the Archbishop and the committee to think in very grand terms of a replacement cathedral. On 25 July Polding wrote to his Vicar-General, Father Austin Sheehy, also chairman of the committee formed to oversee the construction of a new cathedral, approving arrangements made for continuing the fund-raising and rules governing the work of the committee. He was able to inform the committee of his intention to 'procure from a Catholic architect, whom you all know, and whose genius is stamped on one of the confessedly grandest buildings the Colony contains, a plan for a Cathedral as noble as the devotion of our people shall enable us to accomplish within a reasonable time.'[16] That architect was William Wardell, a friend of John Henry Newman, who had led him into the Catholic church in 1843 aged twenty, and of Augustus Pugin, the leading Gothic Revival architect and designer. Wardell's 'confessedly grandest building', referred to by Polding, was St John's College at the University of Sydney.

In October, Polding wrote to Wardell giving him wide freedom in designing the cathedral and acknowledging that the building might need to

---

14. *Freeman's Journal*, 8 July 1865.
15. Polding to Goold, 8 July 1865 (Polding Letters III.186).
16. Polding to Sheehy, 25 July 1865 (Polding Letters III.189).

be reoriented from the traditional east-west alignment of the old St Mary's to a north-south orientation:

> And now for the design itself of our new Cathedral: I have but little to say beyond this, that I go to the Architect of St John's College to ask him for something that shall again be an honour to himself and to the Catholics of the diocese ... I place everything at your disposal ... I imagine that you will decide to make the new Cathedral range from North to South along College St. It is the site most nearly level and soundest for foundations ... I say again I leave all to you and your inspiration in the matter.[17]

The Archbishop was more realistic than the over-optimistic speakers at the various meetings who had expressed the expectation that the new cathedral would be completed within two or three years. Polding required of his architect that 'it shall be possible to complete within two or three years so much of the body and of the shell of the building as will enable from 3 to 4 thousand Christians to hear Mass, and attend the other offices of their Church'.[18] It was not until 1882 that the northern end was able to be roofed and made available for liturgical use. The whole cathedral was not completed and consecrated until 1928, even then lacking the spires of Wardell's plans which were not added until 1988, as a bicentennial project of the New South Wales Government.

Within days of writing to Wardell, Polding was again heading west along Parramatta Road, leaving the burdens of Sydney behind and resuming the itinerant mission work he loved most. On 19 October he wrote to a Benedictine nun in England: 'I suppose you are wondering, my dear Child, into what strange isolated parts of this vast Island Continent I have strayed. Well then if you have a map of N.S.Wales, as you ought to have, you will find not far from Yass—which is not far from Gunning—which is not far from Goulburn—a hamlet town, or collection of huts, houses, etc. called Burrowa; and there I am at this present time.'[19] His delight in his travels and the work among his rural congregations and his distance from Sydney was evident.

Back in Sydney all responsibilities were in the hands of Austin Sheehy and the committee. A few months after the fire a temporary, wooden building had been erected at the northern end of the site. No sooner was it in use than Wardell confirmed that the new cathedral would be aligned from north to south, and that work would commence at the northern or sanctuary end, necessitating the removal and relocation of the temporary building to the south-eastern end of the site. This repositioned building would itself be

---

17. Polding to Wardell, 10 October 1865 (Polding Letters III.195).
18. Polding Letters III.195.
19. Polding to Sister Justina Merewether, 19 October 1865 (Polding Letters III.196).

completely destroyed by fire in January 1869. A brick building, known as the Pro-Cathedral, was then erected on the foundations of the destroyed wooden structure and remained in use until 1882, when the northern end of the new cathedral was available for congregational use. The erecting, relocating, replacing and demolishing of temporary buildings added to the growing expense of the project. Fund-raising continued well into the twentieth century.

With all attention focused on fund-raising for a new cathedral, it was not until May 1866 that Father McCarthy felt able to turn his attention to the postponed project of building a modest church-school for the Pyrmont section of his mission district. With the initial Cathedral appeal a success beyond all expectations and an architect appointed, the local Catholic community felt free to attend to its own needs and return to the task of fund-raising for the building of their church. Land for a church-school had been purchased in December 1865. The site was Lot 32 of the original Macarthur subdivision, with a frontage of 66 feet. The original subdivision along Pyrmont Street had provided for allotments with generous frontages of 66 feet in order to attract middle-class purchasers and house builders. However, another pattern later set in with most buyer-investors dividing their allotments into three lots of 22 foot frontages and building humble workers' cottages for rent. Lot 32, with the original generous frontage, was an undeveloped property owned by Thomas Ware Smart, the auctioneer who had presided over the sale of the Pyrmont estate and who had purchased several allotments for himself at the 1840 auction. Smart was a long serving member of the Legislative Assembly; from 1860 to 1869 he was member for The Glebe. The church paid £330 for the land, which was flanked on the north by a vacant lot and five small cottages leading to John Street, all with frontages of 22 feet; on the south side was a house on an allotment with a frontage of 33 feet, which would be initially rented and later purchased as the presbytery. The trustees listed on the sworn document of 23 February 1866 were Archbishop Polding, Rev Timothy McCarthy, John Henry Wiles and Patrick O'Toole. Wiles was a prominent parishioner of St Benedict's, a teacher at the parish school, the founder of the Catholic Teachers Association in 1857, the secretary to the Catholic Denominational School Board since 1856 and a staunch defender of the Benedictines during the lay revolt in 1858.[20] After the dissolution of the Denominational Board in 1867 his fellow teachers honoured him with the presentation of 'a handsome carriage'.[21]

---

20. Kelvin Cavanagh, *St Benedict's School, Broadway: a history of a Catholic school*, Sydney 2014, 11.
21. *Freeman's Journal*, 8 June 1867.

In August 1866 there was an oblique reference to the plans for a Pyrmont church in Archbishop Polding's report personally presented to Cardinal Barnabo, Prefect of the Propaganda Congregation in Rome. In a section entitled, 'The city of Sydney—Churches and Schools', the Archbishop, after listing the four churches in the city and the three in the suburbs, reported that 'we are employed in building as well two dependent Churches'.[22] One of these was the Pyrmont church, which was intended to be dependent on the clergy of the mother church of St Benedict's and without its own resident priest.

The first fund-raising venture of 1866 drew on Father McCarthy's organisational skills and resulted in a most successful 'Party and Musical Soiree', held on the evening of Tuesday 28 May at the rented school premises in Pyrmont Street. Interestingly the newspaper reports stated that the function was held 'in aid of the funds for the erection of a church in that locality'[23] or 'in that increasing neighbourhood' as the *Sydney Morning Herald* described Pyrmont.[24] There was no mention of a school. The papers agreed in estimating the gathering at one thousand, a number far exceeding the capacity of the wooden school building, necessitating the borrowing of two large tents from the Pyrmont Volunteer Force. Even then not everyone could get in. Not all the participants at the soiree had been locals. Fr McCarthy had invited clergy colleagues—Very Rev Dean O'Connell, Fathers Dwyer and O'Reilly—and there was even a sprinkling of politicians and Sydney identities. McCarthy enjoyed a wide circle of friends on whom he called to support his projects. It was part of the 'Father Tim' legend that 'public men, especially politicians, cultivated his genial company'. Among his intimate friends were said to be the NSW premiers of different political and religious persuasions, Sir Charles Cowper, Sir James Martin and Sir John Robertson.[25] These political contacts had brought him close to suspension during the 1864-1865 election campaign, as indicated in a letter received from the Vicar General, Austin Sheehy:

> Complaints have again been made to His Grace the Archbishop that you are again taking an active part in electioneering matters. I did hope that after the last admonition you would not meddle with politics. I can assure you that your conduct has given occasion to remarks very afflicting to His Grace and many of your confreres ... I have now to warn you that if

---

22. *Report of the State of Religion in the Diocese of Sydney given by the Archbishop. Monsignor Polding*, 19 August 1866 (Polding Letters III.241).
23. *Freeman's Journal*, 2 June 1867.
24. *Sydney Morning Herald*, 31 May, 1867
25. *Freeman's Journal*, 29 October 1925. .

you take any part, directly or indirectly, in favour of any candidate at the forthcoming elections, you will *ipso facto* incur suspension.[26]

A week later Sheehy wrote again, following the receipt of a reply, not extant, from McCarthy:

Your letter in reply to my monition was laid before His Grace and his Council. I have now to inform you that there will be no investigation held. You have been already admonished by His Grace's letter of 28th September [non-extant]. You were afterwards admonished by the Archdeacon and myself, and whatever you may think of the matter, allow me to tell you that Your Archbishop was grieved and felt himself degraded when Mr Robertson in Mr Cowper's presence styled you their best electioneering agent.[27]

Almost two years after Patrick O'Toole's letter to the *Empire* calling on fellow Catholics to support the project of building a church-school at Pyrmont, a notice appeared in the *Sydney Morning Herald* in November 1866 inviting tenders for the building of a school at Pyrmont: 'PYRMONT CATHOLIC SCHOOL—Mr P O'TOOLE, Way terrace, has been authorised by the Rev T McCarthy and the Pyrmont School Committee, to receive tenders for the immediate erection of the above school. Plans and specification can be seen at his residence. No tenders will be acknowledged after the 12th instant, JOHN FINLAY, Secretary.'[28] John Finlay, like Patrick O'Toole, was a member of one of Sydney's Friendly Societies, the Ancient Order of Royal Foresters.[29]

The success of the fund-raising event of May would have contributed to the advancement of the project, but that alone could not account for the imminent commencement of the building indicated in the notice. Perhaps there was a clue from the change in description of the project found in the call for tenders. The project was no longer described in terms of erecting 'a building to be used as a place of worship as well as for a school'. It was now a school alone that was on the drawing board. There is evidence that a Government grant had been given for the building of a Roman Catholic denominational school at Pyrmont. In 1866 Government grants were still available for denominational schools, but no longer for places of worship. In February 1868, five months after the opening of the new church, a letter from the Secretary of the Council of Education, William Wilkins, was sent to the Vicar-General reminding him that a grant of £100 had been committed

---

26. Sheehy to McCarthy, 17 November 1864 (*Adjutor Deus* II.120).
27. Sheehy to McCarthy, 24 November 1864 (*Adjutor Deus* II.120).
28. *Sydney Morning Herald*, 7 November 1866.
29. *Sydney Morning Herald*, 9 April 1866.

in 1866 and given in May 1867 towards the building of a Catholic school at Pyrmont.[30] The expectation of receiving this grant can help explain why Father McCarthy and the committee felt they were in a position to call for tenders in November 1866. It also explains why public notices now referred to the project as the building of a school and not a church-school.[31]

The next such public notice to appear was a month later, in December: 'TO BUILDERS—SEPARATE TENDERS are required for building a Roman Catholic School at Pyrmont. Plans and specification may be seen at the office of Mr MUNRO, 61, Pitt-street, where tenders will be received until the 8th instant.'[32] The month between the notices calling for tenders had brought another change of direction. The 'plans and specification' on view at Patrick O'Toole's residence in the November notice would have been those given by Archibald Telfer as indicated in O'Toole's letter to the *Empire* in February 1865. These plans were set aside and in December builders were directed to view 'plans and specification' at the office of William Munro in Pitt Street. Munro was the preferred local architect of Archbishop Polding.

William Munro was a carpenter by trade and had arrived in the Colony from Scotland with his two brothers in 1839, initially finding abundant work in the Liverpool area. Polding first came across his work as the contractor on the building of the Holy Trinity Anglican church at Berrima, designed by Edmund Blacket. Munro had received high praise from Bishop Broughton both at the laying of the foundation stone in 1847 and at the consecration in June 1849, when he was thanked for his part in creating 'one of the best and handsomest churches in the Diocese'.[33] At this stage he had already been contracted by Polding to build the Berrima Catholic church. The foundation stone of this church, originally dedicated to St Scholastica, the sister of St Benedict, yet another Benedictine connection, was blessed and laid by Polding in February 1849. The Archbishop had provided Munro with one of the drawings and sketches that he had been given in England by Augustus Pugin. The Berrima church, later dedicated to St Francis Xavier, was completed in 1851. The Australian Pugin Foundation credits William Munro as a skilled builder:

> Munro was a very competent builder, and this is reflected in the quality of workmanship in the church. St Francis Xavier's was built of ashlar sandstone laid in 12 in. (30 cm) courses. The nave and north porch interiors were likewise finished in ashlar, the only instance of a Pugin

---

30. Wilkins to Sheehy, 19 February 1868 (Polding Period Papers, volume P38, n 4 [SAA]).
31. This matter will be addressed in detail in the following chapter.
32. *Sydney Morning Herald* & *Empire*, 4 & 5 December 1866.
33. *Sydney Morning Herald*, 12 June 1849.

church, apart from his own Church of St Augustine, Ramsgate, being so treated. His interiors were normally plastered, as indeed are the sacristy and chancel walls at Berrima. Pugin would have designed the latter as such, intending them to carry a program of painted and stencilled decoration...[34]

Following the Berrima contract Munro, although a Presbyterian, became fully engaged in work for the Catholic Archdiocese, being set up with an office in the grounds of St Mary's and initially engaged as clerk of works, overseeing the implementation of the Pugin designed additions to the cathedral. Polding's confidence in and increasing dependence on Munro provided him with the opportunity to make the transition from builder-supervisor to architect. The first reference to Munro as an architect was in a public notice of April 1858 calling for tenders for the completion of alterations and additions to the priory of the Benedictine nuns at Subiaco on the Parramatta River.[35] 'Subiaco', formerly known as 'The Vineyard', had been the estate and stately home of Hannibal Macarthur, nephew of the 'Great Perturbator'. Purchased in 1849, this was the first of the Macarthur family estates and mansions acquired by Archbishop Polding; the second was 'Lyndhurst' at The Glebe, acquired in 1852. Both mansions had been called 'Polding's Palaces' in the anti-Benedictine attacks of 1854. Judge Roger Therry had roundly refuted this 'calumny without a parallel' at a huge meeting at St Mary's following the Archbishop's sudden departure from the Colony for Rome, where he intended to submit his resignation:

> [At] Lyndhurst ... he had not reserved to himself a single room at all. He gave up the whole occupation to the pupils and their instructors, and only visited it when his general duty of superintendence occasioned him to do so ... As to Sub-Iacho [sic], which was distant about twenty miles from Sydney, the Archbishop had a small room or nook in the building, when he occasionally visited it in the performance of a similar duty of superintendence, and if the slanderous inventor of these 'tales of the palaces' had before his eyes, when he uttered these calumnies, the rude iron bedstead, and the hard pallet laid upon it, his voice must have stuck in his throat before he could have uttered calumnies so gross and groundless (Cheers).[36]

---

34. Brian Andrews, 'St Francis Xavier's Church, Berrima, New South Wales', Pugin Foundation (http://www.puginfoundation.org/assets/Berrima_Essay.pdf; accessed 22 March 2014)
35. *Sydney Morning Herald & Empire*, 8 April 1858.
36. *Sydney Morning Herald*, 28 March 1854.

Later in 1858 Polding asked William Munro for a set of plans for St John's College to be built at the western end of the campus of the University of Sydney. These plans were handed to the building committee of the College Council in December. However, the Committee had already received a letter from William Wardell, recently arrived in Melbourne from England, making himself available for a commission as architect for 'the proposed Catholic University of Sydney'. He had been urged to write by College Fellow, Archdeacon John McEncroe, who he had met Wardell in Melbourne, while in transit to Europe on commission from the College Council to recruit an inaugural Rector for St John's. Polding was aware of Wardell's excellent reputation in England and, putting aside Munro's proposal, encouraged the Committee to take up the new offer.[37] In 1862 Munro submitted to the College Council a claim for £125 for provision of the 1858 plans, being ½% of the £25,000 quoted as the cost of the building designed by him. He added that those drawings had been commented on favourably at the time by the Governor, Sir William Denison. However, his claim was not entertained, since it was the Archbishop and not the Council who had authorised him to produce the plans.[38]

Difficulties with the Council led Wardell to resign in 1860 from the role of supervising architect. Edmund Blacket, the architect of the Main Building of the University and St Paul's Anglican College on campus, was appointed to 'undertake the ordinary duties of an architect and, if necessary alter and remodel the plans and specifications already made by Mr Wardell and prepare working plans for the building'.[39] William Munro would eventually make his mark on the university campus as architect of the Presbyterian College, St Andrew's, begun in 1874 and completed in 1877.

Although disappointed at having been replaced by Wardell on the St John's project, Munro was fully occupied by his episcopal patron in designing and building Catholic churches, church-schools, chapels, presbyteries and schools in Sydney and country districts until 1868. These included churches at Ryde and Mudgee, based on Pugin drawings, and at Singleton, Waterloo, Raymond Terrace, Morpeth, Numba on the Shoalhaven, St Leonard's and Waverley, using simpler designs, either his own or from Polding's collection.[40]

Munro had relocated his office from St Mary's to Pitt Street in 1862 and began to mix his ecclesiastical work with secular commissions. Although missing out again to Wardell in the major commission for the new cathedral

---

37. RA Daly, *One Hundred Years on Grose's Farm: the Story of the College of St John the Evangelist, within the University of Sydney*, typed manuscript 1977, 188.
38. Daly, *One Hundred Years on Grose's Farm*, 544 n 54.
39. Daly, *One Hundred Years on Grose's Farm*, 219.
40. Mark Edward Twynam Horn, *William Munro: a report*, B.Arch Thesis, Department of Architecture, University of NSW, 1973.

after the 1865 fire, he was involved in building the temporary wooden cathedral and then in supervising its relocation to make way for Wardell's creation. His ecclesiastical commissions were focused on small Catholic church and school contracts. One of these was the 'school' at Pyrmont, as indicated by the call for tenders in December 1866. This contract turned into the 'church' of St Bede, built between February and September 1867. The question of this transition from the church-school of 1865 to the school of 1866, and then to the church of 1867 will be addressed below.

Munro's connection with the Catholic Archdiocese of Sydney ended abruptly in 1868. His determined move towards only accepting Presbyterian Church and civil contracts seemed to indicate that this termination was influenced by the sectarian fever resulting from the attempted assassination of Prince Alfred, Duke of Edinburgh, at Clontarf in March 1868 by the 'Fenian' Henry O'Farrell. Members of the Munro household were prominent among the Glebe contributors to the 'Prince Alfred Hospital Fund'.[41] It could also be speculated that his involvement in the school/church ambiguity of 1867/1868 could have contributed to the separation of the Presbyterian architect from his Catholic patron. Munro's practice continued to flourish. In August 1868, under the name 'Bunyip', he submitted a design for the Sydney Town Hall. He gained the third prize of £50 in the competition. The winning entry was submitted by John Henry Wilson under the name ''Treu und Fest', the motto of the late Prince Consort, a choice carrying a strong declaration of Empire loyalty in that troubled year of 1868.[42] Munro's work as architect of St Andrew's College, from 1872 to 1874, was considered to be his 'magnum opus'. He was an Alderman of the Glebe Council 1865 to 1872, responsible for having Forest Lodge proclaimed as a ward within the Glebe municipality. He died at his home, 'Forest House', on Pyrmont Bridge Road, in 1881.[43]

At Pyrmont a foundation stone was laid and blessed at 11am on Wednesday morning, 6 February 1867. Prior to this event the ground would have to have been levelled; this involved the quarrying of the cliff at the rear of the property, a task which provided some of the sandstone for the building. The ceremony of setting the corner stone required that the foundations had been dug and that the stone was 'suspended from shears' above the point at which it would be set, ready to be lowered, and a wooden cross was erected at the point where the altar was to be located, as described

---

41. *Sydney Morning Herald*, 7 May 1868.
42. *Sydney Morning Herald*, 18 August 1868.
43. Max Solling, *Sydney's Aldermen* (http://www.sydneyaldermen.com.au/alderman/william-munro/ [accessed 1 January 2014]).

in detail at a similar ceremony for another church dedicated to St Bede, at Morpeth in 1861.[44]

The *Empire* and the *Freeman's Journal* carried the following unambiguous headlines for their articles describing the ceremony: 'NEW CATHOLIC CHURCH OF ST. BEDE, PYRMONT'[45] and 'DIOCESE OF SYDNEY: NEW CATHOLIC CHURCH, PYRMONT'.[46] Other city newspapers referred to the foundation stone as that of a church. The newspapers of the other colonies carried extracts of these articles in their 'Telegraphic News' sections. Nowhere was there mention of a school. The plans and specification on display at William Munro's office in December 1866 must have been of the church which would be built on the foundations blessed on that February morning.

The report in the *Freeman's Journal* outlined the emergence of this new Catholic Church:

> The district of Pyrmont belongs to the parish of St Benedict, and within the last few years the Catholics have increased so rapidly that Father McCarthy felt himself justified in undertaking the task of erecting a handsome structure to replace the wooden building, which up to the present time has been used both as a church and school. In this he has received the hearty co-operation of the local Catholics as well as those other warm hearted and generous friends, who are ever ready with their subscription when the object tends to the greater glory of God and the furtherance of the church.[47]

The article located the church for its readers and provided the dimensions of the building, misleadingly comparing it in style to St Patrick's, and exaggerating its capacity:

> The church is to be built on the western side of Pyrmont-street, half way between Union-street and the Church of England, the front commanding a fine view of the harbour. The plan of the church will be somewhat after the style of St Patrick's though of course much smaller: the body will be 50 feet long, by 23 feet wide; the porch 10 by nine, the sacristy 16 feet by ten, and the height from floor to spring of roof, 15.5 feet. Until the gallery is built there will be accommodation for 400 seats, but after that fully 600 will find room in the church.[48]

---

44. *Maitland Mercury*, 9 November 1861.
45. *Empire*, 7 February 1867.
46. *Freeman's Journal*, 9 February 1867.
47. *Freeman's Journal*, 9 February 1867.
48. *Freeman's Journal*, 9 February 1867.

At the time of the building of a second church in the parish at Ultimo it was stated more accurately that the Pyrmont church with gallery had a capacity of 200.[49]

It was announced that the new church would be dedicated to Saint Bede in honour of 'the learned English saint', and that Mr W Munro was the architect and Henderson and Hill the builders. The *Sydney Morning Herald* complimented the architect's design: 'It will be, when erected, a very neat and elegant structure; and the designs, which have been prepared by Mr W Munro, display a considerable amount of architectural merit.'[50]

In the absence of the Archbishop, who had sailed to Europe in November 1865 in order to fulfil his obligatory 'ad limina' visit to Rome, the foundation stone was blessed by the Vicar General, the Very Reverend Samuel Austin Sheehy, whom the Freeman's Journal designated as 'Bishop elect'. One of the few successes of Polding's negotiations in Rome was finally to have an auxiliary bishop appointed for the archdiocese of Sydney. Since the death of Bishop Charles Henry Davis in 1854, Polding had been without an assistant, leaving the question of succession uncertain. By February 1867 it was known in Sydney that Rome had appointed Samuel Austin Sheehy 'Bishop-elect of Bethsaida among the Infidels' and assistant bishop to Archbishop Polding. On 19 January, the *Freeman's Journal* had announced excitedly: 'We feel great pleasure in announcing that in a Consistory held on the 29th October last, the Holy Father elected the Very Rev SJA Sheehy, OSB, Vicar-General of the City and Archdiocese of Sydney, to be Bishop of Bethsaida, in partibus, and assistant to his Grace the Archbishop of Sydney.'[51]

Less enthusiastic was the reaction of Sir Roger Therry, former judge of the NSW Supreme Court and prominent Catholic layman, now retired in Europe. From Paris he wrote to a disaffected Irish priest, Patrick Bermingham, expressing his deep misgivings about the choice of Sheehy as bishop:

> Sheehy's appointment to the co-adjutor-bishopric has been a step little expected. When I left Sydney [1859] he was very young—had given no proofs of talents—and his theological education must have been very slight. He was, I believe never out of the Colony, and I am not aware that there was what could be regarded as a regular course of divinity taught in Sydney while I was there. Is then (one naturally asks) the prospect of

---

49. *Freeman's Journal*, 21 February 1891.
50. *Sydney Morning Herald*, 7 February 1867.
51. *Freeman's Journal*, 19 January 1867.

his being at the Head of the Catholic Church in Australia for probably the next 25 years a cheering prospect for the success of the Missions.'[52]

Rome's suspension of this appointment six months later would be the source of much distress for the Archbishop and his Vicar-General and much rejoicing among disaffected Irish bishops, clergy and laity.

Accompanying the Bishop-elect at the foundation stone were fifteen members of the Sydney clergy. The list was headed by the Venerable Archdeacon McEncroe, Pyrmont's neighbour in charge of the St Patrick's district across Darling Harbour, and Father Timothy McCarthy 'under whose special care the district of Pyrmont is placed'.[53] Also present was the neighbour to the north across Johnston Bay, Father George Dillon of St Augustine's at Balmain. In attendance too was Father Edmund Walsh, passing through Sydney in transition from the Hunter Valley to the Illawarra; he would return to Pyrmont seventeen years later as priest-in-charge.

Foundation-stones at this period did not bear carved inscriptions on the surface. A cavity was formed in the stone and into this was placed a bottle containing coins of the realm, copies of the local newspapers, the weekly *Freeman's Journal* and the dailies, *Empire* and *Herald*, and a Latin inscription written on vellum. The cavity was closed with a copper plate also bearing the inscription, which in the case of St Bede's, Pyrmont, read:

> In the faith of Jesus Christ,
> and to the honour of the most High God,
> this foundation stone
> of the Church of St Bede
> was laid by the Very Rev S F A Sheehy, VG,
> on the 6th day of February, in the year of salvation, 1867,
> the Rev T McCarthy missionary presbyter of the district
> and many other priests assisting,
> a very large concourse of the faithful being also in attendance,
> Pope Pius IX, happily reigning,
> the most illustrious and most Rev John Bede being Archbishop of Sydney,
> Victoria Queen of Britain and its dependencies,
> the Honorable Sir John Young, Baronet, Governor of the colony.[54]

The ceremony began with the blessing of the cross erected where the altar would stand, followed by a circuit of the foundations accompanied by prayers and the singing of psalms. The celebrant then approached the

---

52. Therry to Bermingham, 20 January 1867 (*Adjutor Deus* II.157).
53. *Freeman's Journal*, 9 February 1867.
54. *Freeman's Journal*, 9 February 1867.

suspended corner-stone which had mortar spread on its base and applied the trowel to each corner, invoking the name of the Trinity. The stone was then lowered into position. Included in the prayers was an invocation of blessing on all who would offer thanksgiving in the church to be raised on the foundations, including the parishioners who would gather to celebrate the sesquicentenary: 'In the faith of Jesus Christ we lay this first stone in this foundation, in the name of the Father, and of the Son, and of the Holy Ghost, that true faith may flourish here, and the fear of God, and brotherly love, and that this place may be devoted to prayer, and to the invocation and praise of the name of the same our Lord Jesus Christ, who with the Father and the Holy Ghost lives and reigns forever and ever. Amen.'[55] The ceremony concluded with another circuit of the perimeter, and the sprinkling of the trench with holy water.

After the placing of the stone into position Father Thomas Keating, member of the Lyndhurst College teaching staff, stepped forward and delivered a sermon on the text of St Matthew's Gospel, 'And the mustard seed became a mighty tree, so that the birds of the air came and dwelt in its branches.'[56] The preacher did not miss an opportunity to slight the Protestant sects and exalt the Roman Catholic Church:

> There is no sect of Protestants that can boast of 200,000,000 of members; there is no sect that is the exclusive religion in any one locality on earth. But the Catholic Church . . . that mighty tree which was planted by Christ will flourish till the end of time. After various illustrations of the greatness and power of the Church, the preacher referred to the proofs given in this their adopted country of the vitality of the Catholic Church. Forty years ago they had no schools, no bishop, and scarcely any priests to break the bread of life on this vast continent. Now they had twelve bishops, presided over by the venerable Archbishop, who would be called in future ages the father and apostle of Australia. They had churches, schools, convents, and colleges through the length and breadth of the land.[57]

Next, Archdeacon McEncroe stepped forward and gave the traditional appeal for contributions to the project and, as was his custom, he accompanied his own donation with some personal reminiscences: 'He had applied to the Government fifteen or sixteen years ago for a site for a church in Pyrmont. But various difficulties had prevented the fulfilment of their desire until

---

55. Benedictine Monks of Buckfast Abbey, 'The Laying of the Foundation-Stone of a Church', *Homiletic & Pastoral Review*, January 1927.
56. Matt 13:31–32.
57. *Empire*, 7 February 1867.

now. They must endeavour to erect a church and school there worthy of Catholicity (Cheers). He commenced their collection with £5 (Cheers).[58] That application, from the then Vicar-General McEncroe, for a grant of land would have followed soon after the laying of the foundation stone of St Bartholomew's Anglican Church at Pyrmont in August 1849.[59] Archbishop Polding was always keen to match Anglican expansion in the Colony with Catholic growth; indeed, he preferred to get in first. However, in the case of Pyrmont the Catholics were last on the block, a quarter century after the Presbyterians and eighteen years after the Anglicans and Wesleyans.

The traditional contributions placed on the foundation-stone realised a respectable total of £174, with a further promise of £200. When the ceremony was concluded, the Vicar-General and many of the priests and their friends partook of a luncheon in a tent near the site of the church.[60] That evening a 'Grand Tea Party and Musical Soiree', by now a specialty of Father McCarthy, was held at the Masonic Hall in York Street. The *Freeman's Journal* reported on the soiree, particularly complimenting the host: 'There could not have been less than 1500 persons present and Father McCarthy can congratulate himself on having got up the largest tea-party ever held in Sydney'.[61]

In the same edition of the *Freeman's Journal* which carried the story of the commencement of the Pyrmont church, there appeared several references to the Irish Fenian movement's 'physical force' activities in Ireland, England and Canada. One item was headed 'An Alarming State of Affairs in Ireland':

> London, December 8, 1866—The Fenian troubles in Ireland are evidently assuming still more alarming proportions, as it is reported here to-day that in addition to the troops already despatched to that island two cavalry regiments have been ordered to leave immediately for the scene of disturbance.
>
> London, Dec. 10—The Times, in an editorial this morning, says that the Fenians have been fairly checkmated, and that it would be madness on their part to attempt rebellion. Cardinal Cullen has issued a pastoral, urging the Irish people to obedience to the law and the avoidance of all secret societies. Arrests still continue to be made, and more artillery will leave for Ireland soon.[62]

---

58. *Freeman's Journal*, 9 February 1867.
59. *Sydney Morning Herald*, 25 August 1849.
60. *Empire*, 7 February 1867.
61. *Freeman's Journal*, 9 February 1867.
62. *Freeman's Journal*, 9 February 1867.

There was also a report of a lecture given in Melbourne two days previously at which the audience was alerted to the expected news of an imminent rising —'by the December mail they might expect to hear of a *Fenian* insurrection in Ireland.'[63] In May 1867 the colonial newspapers carried headlines about 'another Fenian rising' in Ireland which had begun in February and petered out in March. Arrests, imprisonment, transportation and executions followed, resulting in intense newspaper reporting on the movement throughout 1867. In September the last convict ship bound for Australia carried 62 Fenian prisoners to Fremantle. The year ended with news of the execution of three Fenians for the murder of an English policeman; among Irish republicans the three became known as the 'Manchester Martyrs'.[64] In the following year New South Wales would experience its own Fenian frenzy.

The next fund-raising event for the Pyrmont church was organised for Easter Monday, 22 April 1867. It was a 'Grand Steam Excursion to Balmoral Gardens at Middle Harbour'. Father McCarthy's events were always 'grand'. The report of the day was, as usual, glowing and highly complimentary of the charm and organisational skills of the popular Father McCarthy:

> Throughout the day Father McCarthy did his utmost to make his friends enjoy themselves, and it is only fair to state that he succeeded admirably. Good humour and pleasure were supreme during the whole time . . . Not the least accident or mishap marred the pleasures of the day, and we feel quite sure that everyone who attended this excursion will only be too happy to attend the next, whenever that shall be got up by the same Rev. gentleman for any purpose he thinks deserving of his help.[65]

All stops were pulled out in June to produce the grandest event of the season in aid of the Pyrmont Church, now rising from its foundations. The Pyrmont Catholic school was added as a beneficiary of the fund-raising, as indicated in the advertisement in the *Sydney Morning Herald* on the morning of the concert: 'THE GRAND CONCERT in aid of the CATHOLIC CHURCH and SCHOOL, Pyrmont, will take place THIS (Wednesday) EVENING, in the Masonic Hall.'[66] Father McCarthy called on all his friends and admirers to be patrons of the concert—the published list included 8 members of the

---

63. *Freeman's Journal*, 9 February 1867.
64. Already in January 1868 the *Freeman's Journal* was referring to the executed Fenians as 'martyrs' (*Freeman's Journal*, 24 January 1868). In Melbourne *The Age* published an article about a Fenian demonstration in New Zealand in which the phrase 'Manchester Martyrs' was used (*The Age*, 18 March 1868 [extracted from *New Zealand Celt*, 21 February 1868]).
65. *Freeman's Journal*, 20 April 1867.
66. *Sydney Morning Herald*, 5 June 1867.

Legislative Assembly, the Mayor and 8 Aldermen, and 43 other prominent gentlemen.

The *Freeman's Journal* reported the event, noting the number of encores called for and given, which resulted in the concert running overtime. The coachmen booked for 10.45 were kept waiting in the chill of a winter's night:

> It was half past eleven before all was over, and when the large audience separated, each individual must have gone impressed with the conviction that he or she had listened to one of the best concerts ever given in Sydney. We trust the monetary part of the business was something nearly as satisfactory to Father McCarthy, as the musical part was to the listeners. If that be so, the 'Pyrmontese' may expect to see their Church all right very soon.[67]

That night, between 11.30pm and midnight, the time when the fashionable members of the audience were climbing into their carriages and the 'Pyrmontese' were heading home across the Pyrmont bridge, or catching a late ferry ride across Darling Harbour, there was a fire discovered burning in the rented Catholic school premises in Pyrmont Street. The *Freeman's Journal* summarised the incident from the evidence heard at the first day of the enquiry held in the Royal Oak Hotel, on the corner of Pyrmont and Union Streets, not far from the burnt out rented premises:

> On Wednesday week [5 June] a fire was discovered on the premises used as a Catholic school at Pyrmont, and, but for the prompt assistance of the neighbours, the whole structure would have been destroyed. There were very suspicious circumstances connected with this fire, and, in order to sift the whole matter, the City Coroner commenced an inquest on Tuesday morning [11 June], at the Royal Oak Hotel Pyrmont. The following is the summary of evidence taken. The building where the fire took place is a wooden one and was leased by the Catholics as a schoolroom and chapel, and the lease expired last September; it has however been used for the same purpose ever since, but owing to the new catholic school being nearly completed, possession would be given up at the end of the present month. The premises were the joint property of Alexander Downie, and Edward and Shepherd Buchan, and were insured for £100. The fire was first discovered by Teresa O'Toole who was returning home with her parents late on Wednesday night, the alarm, was at once given when Mr Creed a neighbour burst open the door, and succeeded in extinguishing the fire.

---

67. *Freeman's Journal*, 8 June 1867.

Teresa O'Toole, her mother Teresa and father Patrick were returning from the Grand Concert late that night, walking up Union Street from the bridge, and turning into Pyrmont Street, on their way home to Way Terrace, up the hill from the 'nearly completed new catholic school'. William Creed was the publican of the Royal Oak Hotel. The fuller report of the inquiry in the *Empire* stated that Teresa had deposed that after noticing the fire she encountered a young man called Toole and that together they sounded the alarm.[68] A leading candidate for this young man was John Toole, the eldest nephew of Tobias Toole, the publican of the Green Tree Hotel. Perhaps this 'young man called Toole' was in Pyrmont Street so late at night because he too had been at the Grand Concert, or perhaps at the Royal Oak.

At the end of the first day of the inquiry, evidence seemed to point to Edward Buchan as the guilty party, and he was arrested. At the commencement of the resumed hearing on 17 June the landlord, Alexander Downie, stood and made a confession:

> It's no use doing anything to that boy (pointing to his step-son) it was me who set fire to the place. I was the one who put the fire to it ... I wanted the people to go out of the place as I wanted to use it as a paint shop, but I could not get them to go out, the people who had the place wanted me to give it to them; and a person named McElhinney told me if I did not give it to them it would be set fire to. I don't want the family to be ruined through me; I want to get out of Pyrmont and I hope I shall get a good long sentence to the blacksmithing; I did not take out that (pointing to the policy) to burn it, but it was for fear it would be burnt for me.[69]

The coroner ordered that Downie be immediately taken into custody. However, His Honour remarked that the statement was very improbable in that the landlord could have recovered his premises when the lease had expired in September 1866. The inquiry continued with the calling of several witnesses, among whom was the Catholic schoolmistress, the widow Groberty.

Insights into the nature of the building and its use as a school-church emerged from the hearings. It was a wooden structure with a single partitioned room and a shingle roof, situated at the rear of the landlord's house, which fronted Harris Street. Though the lease had expired, the church was continuing in occupation, paying a weekly rent of eight shillings. The owner had an insurance policy of 100 pounds on the building. It was used for Divine Service on Sunday mornings. An interesting Sabbath practice

---

68. *Empire*, 12 June 1867.
69. *Freeman's Journal*, 22 June 1867. Thomas McElhinney was a local Catholic and a coal and wood merchant located in Union Street.

had allegedly been observed by Downie: 'persons getting over the fence during service in church, to avoid payment on going into the church front way.'[70] Based on his observation of local Catholic resentment to the 'entrance fee', Downie ventured that the fire could have been started by disgruntled parishioners. However, Mrs Groberty informed the Coroner that a new chapel and school were being built in the locality and that it was well known 'all over Pyrmont' that the school would soon be moving from the rented premises to the new location.[71] Downie was facing the imminent loss of rental income.

The jury retired to consider their verdict at 1pm and, not having reached agreement within a reasonable time, 'they were locked up in charge of the police', returning at 8pm with the following verdict: 'We find that the premises were feloniously and maliciously set fire to on the night of the 5th of June, 1867, by Alexander Downie, and that Edward John Buchan was an accessory thereto.'[72] Downie and Buchan were then committed for trial at the Central Criminal Court. The newspaper reports concluded by noting that the case had created great excitement in Pyrmont, with large crowds milling around the public house in the evening, waiting to hear the result of the jury's deliberations.[73]

At the trial on 14 August before Mr Justice Cheeke, Downie was charged with arson with intent to defraud the Commercial Union Insurance Company. The prisoner pleaded not guilty and was defended by William Bede Dalley. Dalley argued that Downie was intoxicated on the morning he made his confession. He called witnesses to that effect, several of whom 'swore positively that the prisoner was on that occasion as drunk as he could possibly be, while others said that he was in a wild and excited state'. The Coroner, however, stated that he considered him to have been sober. The jury returned a verdict of guilty. The following day Downie was sentenced to twelve months hard labour.[74] It is not known whether he was able to fulfil his wish of joining the Darlinghurst Gaol blacksmithing department, but he certainly achieved his other desire of leaving Pyrmont. There was no reference to the young co-accused in the trial reports.[75]

In the meantime work on the Pyrmont church or church-school was progressing well. Indeed, the seven months from the laying of the foundation stone to the dedication of the building was a remarkably brief time in comparison to other church projects. On 31 August the Sydney

---

70. *Empire*, 18 June 1867.
71. *Sydney Morning Herald*, 18 June 1867.
72. *Empire*, 18 June 1867.
73. *Empire,* 18 June 1867.
74. *Sydney Morning Herald*, 15 & 23 August 1867
75. *Sydney Morning Herald*, 15 & 16 August 1867.

newspapers carried the announcement that St Bede's Church would be blessed on the following day: 'ST. BEDE'S ROMAN CATHOLIC CHURCH, PYRMONT. The Solemn DEDICATION and BLESSING of the above Church, by His Grace the ARCHBISHOP OF SYDNEY, will take place TO-MORROW SUNDAY, at 11 am SOLEMN HIGH MASS will commence after the ceremony of Blessing the Church is concluded. Omnibuses will leave St Benedict's for Pyrmont at 10.45 am.'[76] The allocation of fifteen minutes to get from St Benedict's along Harris Street to Pyrmont Street by horse-drawn omnibus was somewhat optimistic.

The *Freeman's Journal* prefaced its report on the church opening by announcing that a resident priest had been appointed to the newly formed district: 'Hitherto the district of Pyrmont has been an appendage to the parish of St Benedict, and its spiritual wants have been discharged by Father McCarthy, but now that the Catholics are numerous, and they have shown their zeal in the cause of religion by erecting a very neat and commodious church, they are about to be blessed with the presence of a resident priest.'[77] This was somewhat unexpected. It had been presumed that Pyrmont would remain part of the St Benedict district, with its new church as a local 'chapel of ease', served from the mother-church on Parramatta Street. Indeed, for some years after 1867 the St Benedict reports defined the area of the district as still extending north to Johnston's Bay. The fact that there was never any mention of the provision of a presbytery in the planning from 1865 to 1867 was a clear indication that Pyrmont would continue to be 'an appendage to the parish of St Benedict'. It seems that the sudden return to Sydney of the experienced missionary, Father Eugene Luckie, led the Archbishop to avail of his services by assigning him as resident priest to Pyrmont. Fr Luckie had opted to return after the creation of the new diocese of Goulburn and the arrival and consecration of the new bishop, William Lanigan, in June 1867. Four of the ten priests ministering in the area of the new diocese took the option available in Canon Law of returning to their diocese of origin, leaving Lanigan with six priests for seven mission districts.[78]

The borders of the separate 'district of Pyrmont' were not defined in any contemporary documentation. Parish maps that emerged many years later marked the boundaries as Johnston Bay to the north, Darling Harbour to the east, Blackwattle Creek and Bay to the west, and William Henry Street to the south. The southern border meant that most of the Ultimo Estate, virtually undeveloped and without population in 1867, remained part of St Benedict's parish.

---

76. *Empire*, 31 August 1867.
77. *Freeman's Journal*, 7 September 1867.
78. B Maher, *Planting the Celtic Cross. Foundations of the Catholic Archdiocese of Canberra-Goulburn* (Canberra, 1997), 44.

The Archbishop was present for the solemn blessing and dedication of the church named in honour of his personal patron saint, the Venerable Bede. Polding had arrived back in Sydney from eighteen months absence in Europe on Wednesday, 7 August, to a rapturous reception. When it was known that his ship was off Kiama, a steamer with five hundred well-wishers and a German band on-board, set out from Port Jackson for a rendezvous off Botany Bay. The *Morpeth* accompanied the *Alexandra* up the coast, through the heads into the harbour, while the band played 'Home Sweet Home' and 'See the conquering hero comes'. The ships docked at Darling Harbour where an estimated ten thousand people had gathered, and the procession proceeded to the Cathedral for the liturgical welcome. On arrival at St Mary's the organist, Mr Cordner, heightened the excitement with his pipe-organ version of 'See the conquering hero comes' and then, reverting to a more liturgical tone, he accompanied the choir in the traditional hymn of rejoicing, the *Te Deum*.[79]

The Archbishop had expected that his 'first pleasant duty' would be to consecrate his newly appointed auxiliary. However, awaiting him on his arrival was a letter from the Cardinal Prefect of Propaganda Fide containing what Polding described as 'charges of a shocking nature against my V G, F Sheehy ... and implicating also another'. The other was Mother Scholastica Gibbons, co-founder with Polding in 1857 of the Sisters of the Good Shepherd, later renamed Sisters of the Good Samaritan.[80] In a letter to his agent in Rome, the distressed Archbishop wrote of 'vile infamous calumnies' involving 'immorality and insobriety'. He expressed his suspicion that 'the slander came from Brisbane', thus identifying Cardinal Barnabo's unnamed informer as Bishop James Quinn. He concluded his letter in deep distress at Rome's acceptance of gossip and accusations communicated from the Colonies: 'Where will this dreadful system lead to? I am sick at heart.'[81] In another letter written on the same day he wrote to his dear friend and confidant, the exiled Abbot Gregory, spelling out the accusation made against Father Austin and Mother Scholastica: 'Worse—it is incredible—but a nasty insinuation is made resting on the testimony of one *fide dignus* [worthy of belief]—that M[other] Scholastica (Mrs G[ibbons] of the Good Shepherd) was seen coming out of his room *valde ebria*!! [heavily intoxicated]. And this miserable calumniator's story is preferred to my testimony.'[82]

---

79. *Freeman's Journal*, 10 August 1867.
80. Marilyn Kelleher, "Sister Scholastica Gibbons Co-Founder of the Sisters of the Good Samaritan", *Journal of the Australian Catholic Historical Society*, 20 (1999): 25–26.
81. Polding to Smith, 24 August 1867 (Polding Letters III.274).
82. Polding to Gregory, 24 August 1867 (Polding Letters III.275).

On the eve of presiding at the blessing of St Bede's, the Archbishop penned his reply to Cardinal Barnabo. He did not hide his distress or his sense of abandonment by Rome:

> I had been under the impression that I had somewhat merited the confidence of the Holy See and I learnt, however that my thirty years of Missionary Episcopate, so many calumnies already refuted, have had no avail in sheltering me from an accusation such as your Eminence's letters disclose to me on the subject of my Vicar General ... My administration is paralysed and will of necessity remain paralysed until I know the name of the accuser, his details and his proofs, and until I vindicate first myself and then my Vicar General from every blemish.[83]

On the same day Austin Sheehy wrote to the Cardinal in forthright and gallant defence of the 'holy nun', his co-accused. He also enclosed the Papal Bull confirming his 'election' as bishop, the document that Polding had brought from Rome:

> If the matter had a bearing only upon me in my nothingness, I, on my part, would never have dared to put before your Eminence any defence or protest, but an obligation of charity and justice towards the good reputation of a holy nun compels me to ask and to beseech that anyone connected with the accusation and the character of the accusers should be unmasked.
> May it be acceptable to your Eminence for me to lay at the feet of His Holiness gratefully, humbly and reverently, the Bull by which the Holy See had honoured me, though I am unworthy, and which is enclosed in this letter.[84]

On 1 September 1867, Sheehy, who had been hailed as bishop-elect when he laid the church foundation stone at Pyrmont in February, and who had now returned his document of appointment to Pope Pius IX, chose to absent himself from the consecration of the completed church of Saint Bede. It was with a heavy heart that Archbishop Polding arrived at Pyrmont on that Sunday morning. However, he had always drawn greatest comfort from being among his people, and the Catholics of Pyrmont had gathered in strength to welcome him and participate in the blessing of their new church. The dedication of the church to St Bede was as much a way of honouring their English monk-Archbishop John Bede, present among them, as honouring the seventh-century English monk-saint.

---

83. Polding to Barnabo, 31 Augusr 1867 (Polding Letters III.275-76).
84. Sheehy to Barnabo, 31 August 1867 (*Adjutor Deus* II.176).

The Archbishop spoke to the people gathered outside the church and explained the ceremony that was about to unfold. Accompanied by the clergy, he began by walking the perimeter blessing the walls and then, entering the church, he did the same on the inside, accompanied by the choir of St Benedict's singing the appointed psalms. The people then entered their new church for the celebration of the first Mass. The Solemn High Mass was sung by Father Michael Dwyer. The preacher was Father Octavio Barsanti, an Italian Franciscan who had come to Sydney from New Zealand in 1865. Later in September he would be formally commissioned by the Archbishop to proceed to Rome to act as his representative in the affair of the bishop-elect and other matters: 'Agreeing with the wishes of the Missionary Priests of our Archdiocese who constitute our Clergy and who have observed your wisdom, experience and tactfulness, by this letter of ours we appoint and constitute you our Extraordinary Minister for the discussion with the Sacred Congregation of Propaganda Fide and we wish you thus constituted and appointed to present yourself to our Superiors in Rome.'[85] Barsanti's 'wisdom, experience and tactfulness' failed him in 1875 when he was suspended by Coadjutor Archbishop Roger Bede Vaughan. Other clergy present at the church blessing were Fathers McCarthy, Luckie, Keating, Crone, Athy and Colletti. Prominent laymen in the congregation were named: 'Amongst the laity we noticed Mr W B Dalley, W Cummins, MLA, Alderman Caraher, Messrs Mullins, Hurley, Moore, Rubie, Curran, O'Neill, Clune, McCarthy, etc, etc. Several members of the Guild were also in attendance, wearing their costumes.'[86]

Before the final blessing and dismissal Father McCarthy stood on the steps of the sanctuary and gave a finance report:

> From this it appeared that the land and the building had cost a little above eleven hundred pounds, and every shilling had been paid on the building. The altar furniture and the sittings were yet unpaid, but what with the balance in hands and the collection on that day he would be able to liquidate any claim. There remained rather more than half the purchase money on the land to be paid, but this he hoped would also be soon liquidated.[87]

To have been able to liquidate the debt on a church by the time of its opening was quite an achievement, only made possible by the fund-raising skills of the incumbent, with a little help from the government. A final collection resulted in 80 pounds. At the conclusion of the liturgies Father McCarthy

---

85. Polding to Barsanti 24 September 1867 (Polding Letters III.277).
86. *Freeman's Journal*, 7 September 1867.
87. *Freeman's Journal*, 7 September 1867.

hosted a dinner at St Benedict's for 'his Grace the Archbishop, several of the clergy and a large number of the principal laity of Sydney, numbering altogether between 70 and 80 persons'.[88]

The entry in the *Benedictine Journal* for 1 September 1867 gave further interesting details about the church dedication. It noted the presence and participation of two of the Benedictine students from Lyndhurst monastery at The Glebe, Brother Bonaventure Curr, who acted as sub-deacon, and Brother Bernard Callachor, who assisted the Master of Ceremonies, Father Colletti, and who would become parish priest of St James at neighbouring Forest Lodge in 1882. The monastic journal expressed pride in having yet another Sydney church dedicated to a saint of the Benedictine tradition, 'the great Saint Bede'. The entry mentioned a 'temporary sacristy', suggesting that the workers were a little behind schedule in completing every detail of the church in time for the opening. A well fed monk-chronicler, either Bonaventure or Bernard, concluded the entry: 'Fr McCarthy gave a splendid dinner in the school room at St Benedict's.'[89] The need for the guests to climb aboard the omnibuses and head along bumpy Harris Street to Abercrombie Place for the dinner raises the question of whether there was at this stage a new schoolroom squeezed onto the narrow piece of land next to the new church at Pyrmont. This is a question for the following chapter

---

88. *Freeman's Journal*, 7 September 1867.
89. *Benedictine Journal*, 1 September 1867 (Sydney Archdiocesan Archives).

Chapter 6
Pyrmont's Catholic School

The first indication of the presence of a Catholic school in the Pyrmont district was found in a reference in the *Freeman's Journal* to a schedule of examinations planned for the end of the school year in 1857: 'Due notice will be given when the schools of Balmain, Pyrmont, North Shore, and Waverley shall be examined'[1] In the list of Denominational Schools in the *Catholic Directory* for 1858 a Mrs Mortimer was named as the school-mistress at Pyrmont. The *Directory* for 1861 and 1862 named Mrs R Searson as the teacher. In the same years a Mr John Searson was school-master at the Public School in Mount Street, perhaps indicating a husband-wife professional bond. This was not uncommon.

The earliest indication of the school's location was found in the *Sands Directory* of 1863: at Pyrmont Street, with Theresa Vaughan as schoolmistress. The first reference to an exact address occurred in *Sands* for 1867, giving number 59 on the west side of Pyrmont Street, at the southern end towards Union Street. This pre-fire listing located the school between Alexander Downie, wheelwright and landlord of the leased school building, and Joseph Wardrop, blacksmith, who was a witness at the inquest into the fire. The inquest heard that the three-year lease had expired in September 1866. This indicated that the school was at that address from 1863, if not earlier. A few houses along in the direction of John Street, at number 47, was the residence of Mrs Catherine Groberty, the school-mistress who had given evidence at the fire inquest. Further along still was the plot of vacant land on which the new church or church-school was being built, between numbers 9 and 17. At number 17 was the house which would be rented and later purchased as the priest's residence, and in which this book was written.

The question of the ambiguity about the building erected by the Catholic community at Pyrmont Street between March and September 1867 was

---

1. *Freeman's Journal*, 5 December 1857.

raised in the last chapter. In 1860s there seems to have been a practice developed by the church administration of applying to the Denominational School Board for grants to build schools and then diverting the funds to the building of churches. That a church was intended for Pyrmont was evident in February 1867 at the laying of the foundation stone in Pyrmont Street. The Empire and the *Freeman's Journal* carried the following unambiguous headlines for their articles describing the ceremony: 'NEW CATHOLIC CHURCH OF ST. BEDE, PYRMONT',[2] and 'DIOCESE OF SYDNEY. NEW CATHOLIC CHURCH, PYRMONT'.[3] Other city newspapers referred to the foundation stone as that of a church. The newspapers of the other colonies carried extracts of these articles in their 'Telegraphic News' sections. Nowhere was there mention of a school. The plans and specifications on display at William Munro's office in December 1866 must have been for the church which would be built on the foundations laid on 6 February 1867.

A similar case occurred on the other side of Darling Harbour from Pyrmont, where there was a move by Catholics in June 1867 to build a church in Kent Street South, between Market and Druitt Streets, as reported at length and with shimmering prose in a *Freeman's Journal* article, in which the good example of Pyrmont, with its church under construction, was cited:

> We have been requested to call the attention of the Catholics of Sydney to the necessity of providing church accommodation for the congregation which assembles every Sunday at the school room Kent-street south. With the view of making this provision, there will be held a public meeting in the schoolroom next Tuesday evening at seven o'clock, the Archdeacon presiding, and we hope that Catholics who have the best interest of their holy religion at heart will come forward and aid in the good work. There is no part of our large and increasing city in which a Catholic church is so much needed. The present building is altogether inadequate for the purpose of a church, and for the number of Catholics who come there every Sunday. We can scarcely imagine that it is necessary to urge upon Catholics the necessity of having a suitable building in which to offer up the ever Adorable Sacrifice of the altar ... We congratulate the people of Pyrmont on the success which they have achieved in the erection of a very handsome Church which is now almost completed, and we hope ere long to be able to chronicle the same good news with regard to the people of Kent-street south and its neighbourhood.[4]

---

2. *Empire*, 7 February 1867.
3. *Freeman's Journal*, 9 February 1867
4. *Freeman's Journal*, 15 June 1867.

Despite all these clear references to a church, in February 1868 William Munro called tenders for the building of 'a Catholic School in Kent Street'.[5] However, as at Pyrmont, it was a church that was erected, the church of St John the Evangelist, now the Genesian Theatre.

A letter received at the Vicar-General's office from the Council of Education in February 1868 provides an explanation of what was happening in the case of Pyrmont, and probably also in the case of the Kent street building. The letter deserves to be quoted in full:

Council of Education Office
Sydney, 19th February 1868
Very Reverend Sir

Referring to my letter, under the date the 7th of November last, No. 67/5033, relative to the refusal to permit the use of the building recently erected for the purpose of a Schoolhouse in connection with the Certified Roman Catholic Denominational School at Pyrmont, I have now the honor, by direction of the Council of Education, to make application, through you, to His Grace the Archbishop, as one of the Trustees of the land for Roman Catholic Church and School purposes at Pyrmont, for the return of the sum of one hundred pounds, paid by the Council of Education on the 17th of May, 1867, under the circumstances thereafter detailed.

2. The late Denominational School Board on the application of the Venerable Archdeacon McEncroe as representative of the Head of the Denomination, promised the sum of one hundred pounds towards the cost of erecting the Schoolhouse at Pyrmont. In March 1867, a Schedule of Work performed at that school was forwarded to the Council with a view to obtain payment of the sum promised, and on the 8th of the following May the necessary vouchers were submitted. In all the correspondence up to that date the building is spoken of as a School, and upon the facts of this correspondence and of the Vouchers before mentioned the money was paid on the 17th of May. On the 16th of October the Council was informed that the building was a church and not a school, and that the Teacher had been prevented from removing the School furniture into it and commencing the duties of the school. On the 7th of November His Grace the Archbishop was requested, through you, to give the necessary directions for removing the prohibition to occupy the building for School purposes. No reply has been received to that communication, but

---

5. *Sydney Morning Herald*, 1 February 1868. See Mark Edward Twynam Horn, *William Munro: a report*, B.Arch Thesis, Department of Architecture, University of NSW, 1973.

on the 6th of December following a letter was received from the Reverend E. Luckie, from which the following passage is extracted:

'Judging from the tenor of this communication that the Council of Education still persists in demanding entrance to the Church, I beg to say in reply that, since the Council will not accept the use of the commodious and, in every respect, suitable Schoolhouse lately erected, it has permission to open the School in the Church adjoining'.

In a further communication the Reverend Mr Luckie again describes the building as St Bede's Church.

3. As it thus appears that the building in question is not a school, but a Church, the Council is of opinion that the money granted for the erection of a School, but appropriated towards the erection of a Church, should be refunded.

4. Copies of correspondence with late Denominational School Board and other papers are forwarded herein.

I have the honour to be, Very Reverend Sir, Your most obedient Servant,

W. Wilkins, Secretary
(The Reverend SJA Sheehy, Vicar General) [6]

This letter, found in the Sydney Archdiocesan Archives, has not been able to be located in the State Archives, nor has the cited correspondence from McEncroe and Luckie been located. There is no record of any reply from the Vicar-General, or of the repayment demanded by the Council of Education.

The body that had approved the grant was no longer in existence. The Denominational Schools Board had been abolished with the passing of the Public Schools Act in October 1866, and replaced with the Council of Education which had responsibility for both public and 'certified denominational' schools. The DSB had been made up of representatives of the four main denominations, Anglican Roman Catholic, Presbyterian and Wesleyan. Government funds for the establishing of schools were allocated to the Board and applied in proportion to the numbers in each denomination at the previous census. It was this system that was being used by the Catholic authorities, and perhaps not only they, to gain grants for schools and then divert them to church building, possibly with the connivance of the Catholic member of the Board.

During 1867 there was no direct reference to the building of a school on the site where the church was being erected. However, from the scanty evidence available the likely scenario can be constructed. Wilkins' letter

---

6. Wilkins to Sheehy, 19 February 1868 (Polding Period Papers, volume P38, n 4 [SAA]).

implies that there was a Catholic school operating in the vicinity of the completed church, because his informer the local teacher, Mrs Groberty, had been 'prevented from removing the School furniture' into the new stone building at some time after its completion in August or September. The suggestion is that after the June fire at the leased premises, a temporary wooden structure was quickly erected on land next to the church building, under construction since February. The school-mistress must have been of the opinion that the building in progress was a new church-school, as it had been styled in the call for tenders in the previous December. The 'new chapel and school' referred to by Mrs Groberty in her evidence at the fire inquest in June could have been a single building, which was often the way of providing for the dual needs of worship and education in new mission districts in the Archdiocese.

The letter of 6 December sent to the Council of Education by Father Eugene Luckie, the new priest-in-charge, as quoted in Wilkin's letter, confirms these surmises. Luckie referred to two separate new buildings: 'the commodious and, in every respect, suitable Schoolhouse lately erected' and 'St Bede's Church'. The Council's refusal to accept the 'Schoolhouse' as the building for which it had provided one hundred pounds was probably based on it not matching the 'Schedule of Work' submitted in March. That document was the basis for the release of the funds in May. That the newly erected school building was not as 'commodious' as Father Luckie claimed was suggested by the fact that the dinner for VIP's after the church blessing had not been held there but back at the St Benedict's school. The school-mistress and her pupils did not gain access to the sandstone building, despite Father Luckie's grudging concession to the Council of Education granting 'permission to open the School in the Church adjoining'. Mrs Groberty had to struggle on in the makeshift wooden building next to the sandstone church.

At this point it is worth diverting and focusing on the story of Catherine Groberty for an interesting glimpse of colonial life in New South Wales. She was identified as a widow at the 1867 fire inquest. Her husband, Edwin Groberty, had died in May 1849: 'At his residence, Campbelltown, on the 22nd instant, Mr Edwin Grobity, aged 33 years, formerly of Berne, Switzerland, and for many years organist at St John's Church, in this town, after a short and painful illness of three days, much regretted by all who knew him; leaving a wife and two young children to deplore their loss.'[7]

The name Groberty received a variety of misspellings in official documents and newspaper articles: Grobity, as above, as well as Grobety, Grobetty, Grobelty and Grobeti. Edwin Groberty was born in Switzerland in

---

7. *Sydney Morning Herald*, 25 May 1849.

1816. He was charged with embezzlement at the Central criminal Court in London on 23 October 1837. The court records state that Edwin was 22 years old and was clerk to a coachmaker. Edwin was to pay a bill of his master that was due, and was given £126.6.0 to do so—'two £50 Bank notes, one £5 and the rest in sovereigns and silver'. He absconded with the money, but four months later he gave himself up to the police and threw himself on the mercy of the court. He was sentenced to transportation to New South Wales for 14 years.[8] On 21 July 1838 he arrived in Port Jackson on board the *Bengal Merchant*, one of 266 fellow convicts; three had died on the voyage. The Convict Indent gave the following details of the prisoner:

Education: Reading and Writing
Religion: Protestant
Native Place: London
Trade/Calling: Music Teacher (piano-forte)
Sentence: 14 years
Former Conviction: 3 months
Height: 5' 3"
Complexion: fair; ruddy
Colour of Hair: sandy
Eyes: grey
Particular Marks / Scars / Remarks: small scare outside left eye; raised mole on left jaw; finger nails short.[9]

In 1841 he was located at Campbelltown, where he had been assigned to a local resident, and where he found time to exercise his talent at the keyboard. Edwin Grobety [sic] was identified as the organist at St Peter's Anglican Church, Campbelltown, in a newspaper notice advertising a Grand Oratorio to be held at St Mary's in June 1841. Edwin's participation in the Oratorio was not as the organist but as a 'vocal performer'. The Grand Oratorio of Sacred Music had been organised by the recently arrived Isaac Nathan, composer and musician and newly appointed choirmaster of St Mary's Cathedral. A much anticipated item was a new national anthem, 'Long Live Victoria', written by W A Duncan and set to music by Nathan. The concert was the largest yet held in the colony and received detailed and glowing reviews.[10]

Edwin made himself available for playing at Catholic services, as well as Anglican, at Campbelltown. In 1842 he played the 'seraphine' to accompany

---

8. Proceedings of the Central Criminal Court, 23 October 1837, 66. (http://www.oldbaileyonline.org/images.jsp?doc=183710230066, accessed 15 April 2015).
9. *Convict arrivals, 1788-1842: Convict indents*, Archives Authority of New South Wales.
10. *Sydney Monitor and Commercial Advertiser*, 2 July 1841.

the choir and soloists at St John's during the High Mass celebrated on the feast of St Augustine in 1842, as described in the *Australasian Chronicle*:

> THE FESTIVAL OF ST AUGUSTINE AT CAMPBELLTOWN. At an early hour this morning (Wednesday) our little town presented a most animating sight. From all parts of the neighbourhood might be seen hundreds of happy faces, every person dressed in his Sunday suit, wending his steps towards the church of St John, which was soon filled to excess; indeed so great was the press for room that numbers were compelled to remain outside the doors, through the disappointment of not being able to procure sittings. At half-past eleven o'clock the service of the mass commenced by a most beautiful chorus in the key of G major, which was given with fine effect; immediately afterwards the Rev N Coffey officiated as high priest, assisted by the Very Rev the Vicar General, and the Rev Messrs McEvoy and Grant as deacon and sub-deacon. The mass of Count Mazzinghi, in B flat, was sung with great precision and taste by the Rev Messrs Sumner and Macginnis, and the choir, accompanied on the seraphine by Mr Grobety, the organist, of Campbelltown. This splendid composition we believe was never before sung in this colony, and we can only say that it was performed with a judgment and ability that did ample justice to the composer.[11]

Convict Groberty was granted his ticket of leave in April 1844. Two years later he applied for permission to marry. The application named 22-year-old Catherine Brady as his intended bride. Catherine was described as a free colonist who had arrived on the immigrant ship *China*. Prior to the marriage Edwin had been instructed in the Catholic faith by Father James Alipius Goold and was baptised at St John's in December 1845. Edwin and Catherine were married at St John's by Father Goold on 27 April 1846.[12] Goold was appointed first bishop of Melbourne in 1847 and consecrated at St Mary's Cathedral in August 1848.

In February 1849 the *Government Gazette* published the following proclamation:

> His Excellency the Governor directs it to be notified, that her Majesty has been graciously pleased to authorise the issue, in conformity with the provisions of the Act of Parliament, 6 Vic, cap 7, of pardons to the

---

11. *Australasian Chronicle*, 23 August 1842. The 'seraphine' was a musical instrument devised in the 1830s; it was a portable and inexpensive substitute for a pipe organ, ideal for colonial churches.
12. Information from parish registers of St John's, Campbelltown, supplied by Marilyn Baert, parish secretary.

undermentioned persons, on condition that, during the remainder of their respective sentences, they do not return to the countries or colonies below particularly specified. Pardons available everywhere save in the United Kingdom of Great Britain and Ireland. Dated 1st February 1849.[13]

Edwin Groberty was listed as a recipient of a conditional pardon. As indicated above Edwin died that year on 22 May at the age of 33, leaving a wife and two infant children, without having received notification of his pardon. In June of the year following his death, the *Sydney Morning Herald* published a notice from the Principal Superintendent of the Convicts' Office:

> The 'Absolute,' 'Exceptive Absolute,' or 'Conditional Pardons,' granted to the undermentioned individuals, being still in my office unapplied for, it is hereby notified that the parties in whose favour these Pardons have been prepared, are required by the Government within three months from this date to make application for the same, either at my Office, or to the Clerk of Petty Sessions of their respective Districts, and failing in so doing, they will become liable to all the consequences that may arise from their not possessing those Instruments. J McLEAN.[14]

On the accompanying list of names, under conditional pardons, was found 'Groberty, Edwin; Bengal Merchant 1838'.

The 25-year-old widow later relocated to Sydney with her daughter, taking up teaching, first at Camperdown, then at Parramatta in 1851.[15] In 1852 she transferred to the Catholic School attached to St Benedict's, where Mr J Dwyer was master of the boys and Miss Garnham in charge of the infants.[16] In 1854 she was placed in charge of the girls. As a parishioner of St Benedict's she was listed as a regular contributor of five shillings, from May 1853 to April 1854, to the fund for the completion of the church. In 1857 she moved to the Macquarie Street Denominational School, again in charge of the girls. At the conclusion of the mid-year examinations in June she and her colleague were commended by the examiners: 'The annual examination took place on Wednesday June 10. The Rev Mr McClennan, Rev E Corish, and Mr TH Wiles, assisted at the examination and expressed their approval at the progress of the children, and the manner in which Mrs Grobity and Mr Moloney conduct the school.'[17] Catherine continued

---

13. *Maitland Mercury*, 31 March 1849.
14. *Sydney Morning Herald*, 22 June 1850
15. Peter Reynolds, *On Balmain Hill: 150 Years of the Catholic Church in Balmain*, Balmain Historical Monograph No 3, 1998, 15
16. *Catholic Directory*, 1855.
17. *Freeman's Journal*, 20 June 1857.

at Macquarie Street School until its closure at the end of 1862, when she was transferred to Balmain, where she was assisted by her fourteen year-old daughter in an unpaid capacity. Catherine's annual salary was £70. The 1864 inspection noted that 'Mrs Groberty was given the end of the church under the gallery to teach each subject in two semicircular classes of 26 boys (12 present) and 25 girls (10 present)'.[18] Replaced at St Augustine's parish school by the Good Samaritan Sisters at the end of 1864, she spent the first half of 1865 teaching at the Cook's River district school. Her next move was to the Pyrmont School. The *Sands Directory* of 1867 listed Catherine Groberty, 'RC teacher', as renting a house at 43 Pyrmont Street, about halfway between the temporary school and the vacant land on which St Bede's would be built. It was in this house that her daughter Annie Mary died in March 1866 as reported in the death and funeral notices of the *Sydney Morning Herald*:

> On Wednesday, the 14th instant, at Pyrmont, ANNIE MARY, only daughter of the late Mr ERWIN GROBETY, of Campbell Town, NSW, and grand-daughter of the late Mr T Brady, of Limerick, Ireland, aged 17 years.[19]
>
> FUNERAL—The Friends of Mrs GROBETY are invited to attend the funeral of her deceased daughter ANNIE MARY; to move from her residence, Pyrmont-street, Pyrmont, TO-MORROW (Saturday) MORNING, at a quarter to 9 o'clock, and proceed to the cemetery, Petersham. JAMES CURTIS, Undertaker, 59 Hunter-street.[20]

The reference to Annie Mary as the 'only daughter' raises a question about the 'two young children' mentioned in Edwin's death notice. No other Groberty/Grobety/Grobity born between 1846 and 1849 is traceable in NSW civil records. However, the baptismal register of St John's, Campbelltown, records the birth and baptism of Eliza Catherine Grobety, born 7 September 1848 and baptised 26 October 1848. Church records also show that the infant Elizabeth was buried at Campbelltown on 1 December 1849, the same year as her father's death; prayers were offered by Father P S Farrelly.

Catherine was next found teaching at Catholic schools in the country regions of the colony. In 1871 she was reported as having resigned from the Gunnedah school.[21] In the following year she was at Kincumber where again she received high praise for her impact on examination results as reported by the Brisbane Water correspondent of the *Freeman's Journal*'s:

---

18. Reynolds, *On Balmain Hill*, 15.
19. *Freeman's Journal*, 24 March 1866.
20. *Sydney Morning Herald*, 16 March 1866.
21. *Freeman's Journal*, 18 November 1871.

Having (in a former communication) glanced at the Kincumber school, I will only say about it now that on last Tuesday there was a general examination of the children (33 in number) that the examination was conducted in the presence of many of the parents, and gave great satisfaction to all. Mrs Groberty, the teacher, was complimented on her success—for at the time of the last examination there were only (12) twelve children in attendance, and the Inspector's report was anything but flattering, since then Mrs Groberty has taken charge of the school. And Tuesday's examination testifies as to the results.[22]

The final traces of Catherine's long teaching career find her having transferred to the Public School system and in 1880 assigned to a Provisional School at Baerami Creek a small settlement near Muswellbrook in the Upper Hunter region.[23] Such elementary schools were established where there were fewer than 25 children, but more than 15, on the condition that the local community provided the building and furniture, with the Department of Education appointing and paying the teacher and supplying books and equipment. In 1888 her retirement from the Civil Service was announced: 'The following officers have retired from the Civil Service: . . . Mrs Catherine Grobety, teacher, public school, Clairvaulx.'[24] Clairvaulx was described as being 'beyond Glen Innes' in the New England district.

At the time of her death in 1891 Catherine had returned to Sydney, living again within the district of St Benedict. The *City Assessment Book* for that year located her in Rose Street, Chippendale, in a rented two-storied brick and stone house with five rooms. In September her death notice appeared in the *Sydney Morning Herald*: 'Of your charity, pray for the soul of C Groberty, daughter of the late T Brady, Limerick, Ireland, who died at her residence, 32 Rose-street, South Sydney, on the 4th instant, aged 71. Buried on Sunday at Campbelltown.'[25] After forty-two years of widowhood she was finally laid to rest with Edwin and their daughters in the Campbelltown Roman Catholic Cemetery.

In January1868 it was announced that the proceeds a lecture, 'On the Labours of Catholic Priests in the Field of Scientific Discovery', to be given by a visiting Irish Jesuit from Melbourne would be applied to 'liquidating the debt on the new school lately erected in connection with St Bede's Church'.[26] The wording of this announcement confirmed that a separate building had been erected next to the new church. The 'new school' was obviously

---

22. *Freeman's Journal*, 9 November 1872.
23. *Sydney Morning Herald*, 22 September 1880.
24. *Sydney Morning Herald*, 10 March 1888.
25. *Sydney Morning Herald*, 5 November 1891.
26. *Freeman's Journal*, 11 January 1868.

too humble a building to host the lecture, which was held in the 'large hall of St Mary's Seminary'.[27] The event, attended by the Archbishop and the senior clergy of Sydney, including Fathers McCarthy and Luckie, Pyrmont's priest-in-charge, was reported in the *Freeman's Journal*: 'Notwithstanding the extremely unfavourable state of the weather, and the very natural preoccupation of many in regard to the expected arrival of the Duke of Edinburgh, the attendance was a very numerous one, the lecture, in all respects, proving to be a remarkable success.'[28]

The day following the lecture, 21 January, Prince Alfred Ernest Albert, Duke of Edinburgh, Earl of Kent, Earl of Ulster, Prince of Saxe-Coburg and Gotha and second son of Queen Victoria, sailed into Port Jackson in command of the steam frigate HMS *Galatea*. On the day of the lecture another ship had reached Australian shores; the *Hougoumont*, carrying the last cargo of convicts, including the 'much dreaded Fenian importation', docked in Fremantle, adding to the growing anxiety about Irish conspiracy.[29] On the Duke's return visit to Sydney in March there took place an incident that would have huge repercussions for the Catholic community in Australia. The attempted assassination of His Royal Highness during a picnic at Clontarf beach on Middle-Harbour by a self-confessed Fenian, Irish Catholic Henry James O'Farrell, will be treated in the following chapter.

The *Sands Directory* of 1869 gave the following description of the Pyrmont Street properties from the corner of John Street in the direction of Union Street:

> 5 houses, numbered 1 to 9
> Vacant land,
> ST BEDE'S ROMAN CATHOLIC SCHOOL,
> ST BEDE'S ROMAN CATHOLIC CHURCH,
> n 17 Luckie, Rev Eugene J
> (here lane)
> n 19 Paterson, Rev R S

This description indicated that the 1867 wooden school building was squeezed into the narrow space between the church and the vacant allotment. The house at number 17 was rented by Father Luckie and would be purchased as the presbytery in 1880. In 1869 Father Luckie's neighbours at number 19, separated by a lane, were the family of the Reverend Robert Smith Paterson, the local Presbyterian minister.

---

27. *Freeman's Journal*, 21 January 1868.
28. *Freeman's Journal*, 21 January 1868.
29. *The Herald* (Fremantle), 29 February 1868.

The cramped dimensions of the school building were indicated in a *Freeman's Journal* article of September 1870 reporting the establishment of the Pyrmont branch of the St Francis Total Abstinence Society: 'By the time they arrived there the school room of St Bede's Church was well filled, and there was not room enough to accommodate one quarter of those assembled ... The platform was crowded by the band, vocalists and speakers quite as much as the body of the room.'[30] In May 1871 an inspector from the Council of Education visited St Bede's School. His findings were published in the Annual report of the Council on Certified Denominational Schools:

Numbers present: Boys, 45; girls, 31
1. The schoolhouse is in a satisfactory condition; its appointments, internal and external, are sufficient and good.
2. The general organisation may be rated tolerable; the discipline induces cleanliness and order, but it might with advantage be made to influence the mental tone of the classes more than it does.
3. The instruction, which deals with the prescribed subjects, is methodical and tolerably spirited.
4. The proficiency ranges from fair to very fair.[31]

As boys and girls were always separated, it can be presumed that the school room was divided by a partition as had been the case in the earlier leased premises. St Bede's compared well with the schools of the 'mother parish' of St Benedict's, where the boys' schoolroom was found to be in need of a ceiling, 'as the dust falls through in large quantities', and the infants' facilities were rated 'very unsatisfactory'.

In 1880 Father Luckie's 'commodious and, in every respect, suitable Schoolhouse' was described in less glowing terms by a correspondent to the *Sydney Morning Herald* in which he detailed the shortcomings of the denominational system in the heated debate concerning the proposed withdrawal of all government funding from church schools: 'Then, with reference to the character of the Denominational school buildings, many of them are very inferior, and many of them very deficient in accommodation ... Take the Roman Catholic School at Pyrmont; it is a mere weatherboard shed, without any proper playground.'[32] In that very year the weatherboard shed was marked for demolition and replacement. A foundation stone was laid and blessed in August and the new wooden building on brick

---

30. *Freeman's Journal*, 10 September 1870.
31. NSW Council of Education, *Report of the Council of Education upon the condition of the public schools and of the certified denominational schools for 1871*, Sydney 1872.
32. *Sydney Morning Herald*, 20 January, 1880.

foundations was formally opened in December ready for the 1881 school year.

The schoolmaster at St Bede's in 1880 was Stephen Pegum assisted by Pupil Teacher Catherine Lang. Stephen's first teaching appointment had been in the Burragorang region of NSW where he had settled and begun a farm after arrival in the Colony. In 1870 he became the teacher at the properties of the Blackman and Pippin families, some of the earliest settlers in the valley. In the following year he married Ellen Gorman of another local Irish clan. In 1870 they moved to Sydney where Stephen had been appointed by the Education Council to the Catholic school at Petersham. Since the abolition of the Denominational Schools Board in 1867 the Council was responsible for appointments to Certified Denominational Schools, an arrangement which was yet another point of contention in the struggle over education between the Catholic hierarchy and the Colonial Government. At a public meeting in January 1870 the Vicar-General cited the example of a successful teacher, perhaps Catherine Groberty, being removed without notice from St Bede's and sent elsewhere. Sheehy complained that 'the school at Pyrmont, in consequence of this sudden change, had to be closed for a week, and thus lost thirty scholars'.[33] As invariably happened the controversy spilled over into the correspondence columns of the *Sydney Morning Herald*.

From 1874 to 1877 Pegum was schoolmaster at the Newcastle Catholic School from where he was transferred to Pyrmont in 1877. He was the schoolmaster at St Bede's at the time of the building of the new school in 1880. The family resided in a rented house in Edward Street, as recorded in the *Sands Directory* of 1879. The question of the housing of Denominational teachers became the subject of much controversy. Public school teachers were provided with a residence or given a housing subsidy. This did not apply to their Denominational colleagues. This issue brought Stephen Pegum into the public domain from where he was rarely absent for the rest of his life.

In December 1878 the principal teachers in the Certified Denominational Schools in Sydney District began a series of meetings to prepare a petition calling for equal treatment and justice on the housing issue. The *Freeman's Journal* was loud in its support of the teachers, even calling on the church authorities to see justice done should the government fail to do so:

> Great dissatisfaction exists among teachers of Denominational schools, at what is justly considered the unfair way in which they are treated in not being allowed house rent in common with their more fortunate confreres in the Public schools, and this dissatisfaction is not confined to those who are immediately affected by this invidious distinction, but extends to all impartial minds throughout the country . . . Advocates

---

33. *Freeman's Journal*, 25 January 1870.

of Denominational schools, should effect either of these two things—obtain a motion of the House to do away with the injustice referred to, or provide their teachers with residences.[34]

Pegum emerged among the chief spokesmen for the aggrieved teachers, being one of the two signatories, 'joint honorary secretaries', of the petition sent to Parliament in December 1878. The Council of Education claimed that the responsibility for housing teachers lay with the local school boards of the denominational schools. With the question in limbo a delegation of three teachers was formed in May 1880 to take the case to the Minister of Public Instruction, former premier Sir John Robertson. Pegum was one of the delegates. The Minister was sympathetic, but nothing changed. It would not be long before all funding for denominational schools was withdrawn and the question of housing catholic schools teachers became the question of providing convents and monasteries for religious sisters and brothers.

Pyrmont was Stephen's last Catholic School appointment. In 1881 he was moved from the city and sent to be schoolmaster at the Public School at Lochinvar in the Hunter Valley where he remained for two years before being appointed to Morpeth in 1883. Besides campaigning forthrightly for essential improvements to his schools he found time to become involved in establishing a local volunteer army corps. Soon after his arrival in the Colony Stephen had joined the NSW Volunteer Regiment and for many years held officer rank, making him a key participant in the project. The *Maitland Mercury* strongly argued the case by encouraging interest among the young men of the district:

> The colony has grown in material wealth, in social and commercial prosperity, and has exhaustless resources at its command. It is therefore a gem worthy a foreign potentate's grasping, and to prevent aggression the Government is anxious to afford every aid and encouragement to young men of patriotic sentiments. Volunteers are now provided with arms, with two regimental suits, have £12 per annum, and the volunteer movement, in point of discipline, efficient training, and general military deportment, is said to compare favourably with the Imperial army. Mr Pegum, of the Public School, is a retired officer of the volunteer force—this by effluxion of time.[35]

Stephen emerged from military retirement and in May 1884 the East Maitland and Morpeth Volunteer Corps was formed. Later that year,

---

34. *Freeman's Journal*, 7 December 1878.
35. *Maitland Mercury*, 22 September 1883.

following a reorganisation of the colony's military forces, the units then situated at Newcastle, West Maitland, Singleton and East Maitland were united to form the 4th Regiment of New South Wales Volunteer Infantry. In 1885 Stephen was appointed as first lieutenant of the Morpeth Corps of the 4th Regiment, and later promoted to captain.[36]

His final teaching appointment was at Islington, a suburb of Newcastle, from 1887 until 1890 when he retired from the Education Department and returned to farming, firstly back at Burragorang and then at Camden. During these last years of the nineteenth century he became involved in the campaign for the formation of the federation of the Australian colonies. In 1898 the *Sydney Morning Herald* made encouraging reference to an anthem that he had composed some years before, recommending its adoption: 'The New South Wales Federal Association has received a copy of Captain S Pegum's spirited song, "The Federal Banner". Though written and composed 10 years ago, it appears exceedingly appropriate at the present moment The music is melodious and inspiring, and arranged as a march has for years been a favourite marching tune of the 4th Regiment, of which corps Captain Pegum was first lieutenant.'[37] The full title of the anthem was 'Federal banner of United Australia', and the first verse and chorus were as follows:

> Australians all, come sing a noble song,
> Come raise the chorus loud and long,
> And let the echo of the joyous strain
> Be heard o'er Australia's wide domain,
> Until on high the Fed'ral Banner o'er
> Australia floats from shore to shore,
> A mighty nation, great and proudly free,
> United, one from sea to sea!
>
>
> Then, steady and ready, hearts of the brave,
> Let your unity nothing dissever;
> The Federal Banner proudly shall wave
> O'er Australia United forever.

In retirement Stephen was an inveterate writer of letters to and articles for newspapers. He wrote long letters on political themes to the *Catholic News*, expressing fears that the recently formed Labor Party was veering towards socialism. His local *Camden News* also published his letters and articles. The *News* always referred to him as 'Captain Pegum'. In the year before his death,

---

36. *Evening News*, 9 December 1885.
37. *Sydney Morning Herald*, 26 May 1896.

from October to December 1913, he submitted a series of nine articles, entitled 'Pro Aboriginibus. CEREMONIAL CHANTS AND SONGS', to *Camden News*. Earlier that year he provided four articles on bird song, the first of which began with his return to verse: 'Where the Bell-birds sing (a picnic song)'. He concluded these articles: 'I have already occupied more space than I intended, and yet have said nothing of the aboriginal race and their language, but with the editor's kind permission, will do so on some future occasion'. He did not disappoint. Captain Pegum died on 27 July 1914.

Meanwhile back at Pyrmont in 1881 a new schoolmaster had arrived to take Stephen Pegun's place. He was Matthew Patrick Ryan. Ryan's stay at St Bede's school was not without incident. In May 1882 he was charged with assaulting a ten-year-old boy named Edward Kenny, one of the scholars at that school. The details were provided by Kenny himself and a class-mate: '[O]n the 18th instant the defendant called Kenny out of the class and beat him with a cane; and they both averred that the beating continued for three-quarters of an hour, and that during that time Kenny was shrieking out as loud as he could. The neighbours heard his cries, and spoke about it. The beating was down the boy's back and legs, a cane being used. He was black and blue afterwards.'[38] In the cross-examination Ryan declared that Kenny was a disobedient and unruly child who that morning had knocked down another pupil, and that he was generally a 'great deal of trouble in the school'. In the schoolmaster's opinion the punishment meted out was 'no more severe than was necessary in the circumstances'. At this point in the proceedings, for some unstated reason, the Evening News reporter left the court. The story was taken up by the *Town & Country* which reported the evidence of the boy's mother: 'She deposed that one of the neighbours had informed her that her son was being cruelly beaten at school. She at once found that the doors were locked so that she could not get in. She, however, heard her boy shrieking from the inside, and also heard the sound of the blows. She deposed to the condition of her son's body that night when she examined him. It was a mass of weals from top to bottom.'[39]

Catherine Lang, the pupil teacher at Pyrmont for the last four years, was called by the defence. She deposed that she had witnessed the 'flagellation', but she was of the opinion that the punishment of one of the 'most unruly boys in the school' had not exceeded the crime. She stated that 'she could not conceive it possible that the 'correction' could have made the bruises which she had seen that day on the boy's body'. Magistrate Dillon in giving his decision began by defending the use of corporal punishment in schools but concluded that in the case before him the beating inflicted had gone far

---

38. *Evening News*, 25 May 1882.
39. *Town & Country*, 27 May 1882.

beyond what was acceptable. He imposed a fine of three pounds and costs, or in default seven days' imprisonment. The proceedings concluded with a question from the floor of the court: 'The wife of the defendant (who is quite a young man), asked if the bench would give any time for payment. Mr Dillon: "Yes; you can have 24 hours." The parties then left the court.' Matthew Ryan was the last lay teacher at St Bede's. In December 1882 it was announced that the Sisters of the Good Samaritan would be taking charge of the school in the New Year.

Chapter 7
Pyrmont's First Resident Priest

Eugene John Luckie, the man who was unexpectedly appointed as resident priest at Pyrmont, had been most recently at work in the Goulburn district. In June 1863 he had been transferred from Raymond Terrace in the Hunter River area south to Bungonia. As noted above he returned to the Archdiocese of Sydney in June 1867 soon after the creation the new diocese of Goulburn. The new bishop, William Lanigan, immediately after his consecration, called a meeting of his priests. In his diary he noted the names and mission districts of his clergy. Against the name of Eugene Luckie was the district of Young. In a later annotation he noted the 'exodus' to Sydney of four of his ten priests. Referring to Luckie, Lanigan wrote that after the conference he had been transferred to Burrowa but 'at once returned to Goulburn, and without any letters is received in Sydney'.[1] The new bishop complained to Archbishop Polding about the desertion of the four priests, which had left him with only six missioners for his seven districts. Polding replied justifying the situation in terms of law and compassion:

> I have not yet told Your Lordship that on this very subject of the removal of old Missionaries from a newly-erected diocese to that of their old Bishop, I had obtained a direction from the Holy See. The Cardinal Prefect's answer to my enquiry is distinct: in any new arrangement of dioceses and clergy the Archbishop may take or leave priests according to his own wish and judgment. Irrespective of that authority there is something reasonable in yielding to the claim of an old Missionary to abide by the side of him who first received the devotion of his services—a human feeling, perhaps, but excusable. At any rate it will be seen that I have not been acting wantonly or thoughtlessly. My own bitter experience of the scarcity of Priests for the vast work we have before us would surely

---

1. Brian Maher, *Planting the Celtic Cross: Foundations of the Catholic Archdiocese of Canberra and Goulburn* (Canberra, 1997).

make me very cautious of aggravating the scarcity in a Brother's diocese. And I do trust I have not done it unawares.

The Archbishop concluded with a barbed comment on Lanigan's rejection of offers of help: 'It is commonly and persistently reported that new priests (I do not know how many) are expected, and on the way for the Diocese of Goulburn. This on the one hand; on the other I know that my own necessities have made me gladly accept the services of an excellent Franciscan and of others whom your Lordship had been able to refuse.'[2]

Being forty-four, Luckie could not be rightly described as an 'old missionary' in terms of years, but experienced he certainly was. With Polding on the high seas returning to the Colony in June 1867, perhaps it was the Vicar-General, Bishop-elect Sheehy, who took the initiative in encouraging Luckie to return to the mother diocese, to the Archbishop 'who first received the devotion of his services', with the idea of appointing him to St Bede's. The limited demands of the small mission of Pyrmont would leave him time to employ his talents in the fight against the new education bill. In fact soon after the appointment in September 1867 he was elected as one of the two secretaries of the newly established Catholic Association for the Promotion of Religion and Education, at the inaugural meeting of 5 December.[3] He had been prominent at a meeting of clergy and laymen a month before when six resolutions were moved and passed regarding Catholic concerns about the functioning and purpose of the Education Act of 1866. The sixth resolution concerning the rules for the proposed association was read and moved by Father Luckie. The purpose of the Association was to collect, manage and apply funds:

> To aid the establishment of new Catholic primary schools as they may be required.
> To assist existing schools where provision made by Government is inadequate.
> To establish and maintain a Catholic training school for teachers.
> To invite from Europe, and to aid in establishing here, competent teachers of religious congregations to take charge of the said training school, and also to conduct primary schools where provision can be made for them.[4]

The duties of the secretaries required their presence at the Association's committee rooms at St Mary's each Tuesday and Friday from 10am to 4pm, as well as attendance at the monthly meetings. In his capacity as secretary

---

2. Polding to Lanigan, 4 January 1868 (Polding Letters III.287)
3. *Freeman's Journal*, 7 December 1867.
4. *Sydney Morning Herald*, 6 November 1867.

Father Luckie emerged as the chief spokesman for Catholic education in the colony. Letters to editors from 'Eugene J Luckie, St Bede's, Pyrmont' appeared regularly in the Sydney newspapers; he did not use ecclesiastical titles when signing these letters. Pyrmont's first priest-in-charge was a busy man.

Born in County Armagh, Ireland, in 1822, he entered the newly established missionary seminary of All Hallows, located at the village of Drumcondra on the northern edge of Dublin. Following the British Government's threat to withdraw funding from the Royal College of St Patrick's Maynooth, if priest graduates continued to be allowed to go to the missions, the special missionary seminary was established in 1842.[5] Its task was to provide priests for 'the white missions', the Irish diaspora—England, Wales, Scotland, South America, South Africa, Canada, Australia, the West Indies, New Zealand, and the United States—also known at All Hallows as the 'Greater Ireland beyond the seas'. During Archbishop Polding's recruiting visit to Ireland in 1847 he invited Luckie, a cleric in deacon's orders, to accompany him to Australia. Eugene did not need much persuading, as recounted many years later:

> Father Luckie's adoption of the Australian mission as his future sphere of labour took place in that mysterious way in which it occurred to many a missionary before, and which undoubtedly indicated a call of grace. About the time he was making up his mind to go on some foreign mission, to which he always gave the preference, two pamphlets fell into his hands—the one was the *Catholic Mission in Australia* [London 1837], by Dr Ullathorne, then VG of the Archbishop of Sydney, but now bishop of Birmingham, England; the other was called the *Horrors of Transportation*, by an anonymous author. But both these pamphlets gave him such a harrowing account of the state of religion and society in New South Wales, that he at once resolved to go upon the Australian Mission conceiving it to be then the most arduous on the face of the earth.[6]

He sailed for Australia with Polding in 1847 together with a fellow All Hallows deacon, Michael Harrington Ryan, and a motley group of Polding recruits, priests and students, and two Benedictine nuns. He was ordained priest at St Mary's on 7 May 1848, three months after his arrival. His first assignment as a newly ordained 25-year-old priest was to Ipswich in the district of Moreton Bay, 650 miles from Sydney. His colleague, Michael Ryan, found himself sailing the 1,000 miles to the much more difficult mission on

---

5. *Catholic Press*, 14 May 1903.
6. *Freeman's Journal*, 19 April 1873. *Horrors of Transportation* was also by Ullathorne and published in Dublin in 1838.

Norfolk Island, a penal settlement which Ryan later described: 'This dark degraded little speck of creation . . . synonymous with everything that is horrible and degraded in human nature . . . an Ultra penal station or, in the convict dialect, the next door to the gallows, where the worst of the worst, where all the most abandoned and helpless characters even of NSW and Van Diemen's Land are congregated'.[7]

At Ipswich, Luckie was responsible for a huge district spreading north and west indefinitely and south to the Clarence River on the coast and to Armidale on the Great Dividing Range. Within a month of his arrival, he and the Catholic community were being compared favourably with the Church of England minister and his congregation for the 'energy' that had resulted in a government grant towards the construction of a 'good-sized building, to be used as a school-room on week days and for Divine Service on the Sabbath': 'How is it that the members of the Church of Rome have procured so handsome a subscription, and the Church of England been refused any assistance? Is it on the part of the latter a want of that energy which so eminently characterizes the former?'[8]

It was significant that the building of a school was his first undertaking. Education would remain his chief pastoral focus throughout his long priestly ministry. An early involvement in the perennial colonial debate on the provision of education occurred in Ipswich when at a meeting on the government proposal to institute the Irish system of public education Luckie 'spoke strongly in favour of establishing a National School'.[9] The meeting had been called by George Rusden who was appointed in 1849 as one of two agents for the National schools, first at Port Phillip and later at Moreton Bay, and then for the whole of the Colony of New South Wales. The task of the agents was to promote the National system throughout the Colony and to assist in the establishment of such schools. Rusden 'threw himself into his work and in his several tours rode 10,000 miles as far south-west as Portland and as far north as Brisbane, taking in the Hunter Valley and Armidale'.[10]

The first attempt to introduce the so-called 'Lord Stanley system of education', a system of bringing Protestant and Catholic school children together, initiated in Ireland to address Catholic disadvantage, was made

---

7. Letter of M H Ryan to All Hallows, quoted in Roger Wynne, 'From Portland Bay to Moreton Bay', *Australasian Catholic Record*, 53 (1976): 278.
8. *Moreton Bay Courier*, 14 October 1848.
9. *Moreton Bay Courier*, 29 June 1850.
10. Ann Blainey and Mary Lazarus, 'Rusden, George William (1819–1903)', *Australian Dictionary of Biography*, National Centre of Biography, Australian National University, http://adb.anu.edu.au/biography/rusden-george-william-4523/text7405, published first in hardcopy 1976, accessed online 1 April 2013.

by Governor Richard Bourke in 1836. Bishop Polding had supported the proposal, but this only intensified the Protestant opposition which interpreted Catholic support as a Romish plot to dominate education, and the plan failed. In 1848 Governor George Augustus Fitzroy tried again. This time there were to be two systems existing side by side—approved church or denominational schools governed by their own board with membership from the four main churches and the national schools under a board of commissioners. Both systems were publicly funded and members of the two boards were appointed by the government. The change has been described as a move from an independent to an organized denominational system.[11] Luckie's support for the dual system was an expression of the official Catholic response expressed in a letter from Father John McEncroe to Campbell Drummond Riddell, chairman of the newly established Denominational Board: 'His Grace is happy to learn that the Board of which you are the Chairman is anxious and disposed to render the Denominational schools more efficient than heretofore. The Archbishop and the clergy under his jurisdiction will most cheerfully co-operate in every measure to improve and extend Public Education, thereby making it commensurate with the wants and wishes of the great body of our colonial population.'[12] A third phase in the nineteenth century history of Catholic education began in 1867 with the move from an 'organized' to a 'controlled' denominational system. This would evoke a dramatically different response, neither cheerful nor cooperative, from the Archbishop and his clergy. Eugene John Luckie of St Bede's, Pyrmont, was the public voice of this response from 1867 to 1873.

By the end of 1850 Luckie had taken up work in the Illawarra district, which extended from Botany Bay to Pambula on the far south coast. Here one of his first acts was to revive the Total Abstinence Society which had been the first established in the Colony ten years previously, but which had fallen into abeyance. As reported in the *Freeman's Journal* he paid tribute to the reformed alcoholic, Father John McEncroe, at the Wollongong meeting: 'He said, that in commencing here his humble efforts to promote the good and holy cause of Temperance, he was complying with the request of the Venerable Archdeacon McEncroe, of Sydney, whose able and successful services in the cause of Total Abstinence required no eulogium from him.'[13] The newspaper report gave an insight into the Luckie style when it stated that 'the Rev speaker went on at great length and with effect'. The description, 'at great length', would continue to characterise his communications, whether in spoken or written form.

---

11. Ronald Fogarty, *Catholic Education in Australia 1806°1950* (Melbourne: Melbourne University Press, 1959), volume 1, xiii.
12. McEncroe to Riddell, 23 February 1848 (*Adjutor Deus* I.170); Fogarty, I.52
13. *Freeman's Journal*, 14 November 1850.

In November 1852 he was sent from Wollongong to Sofala, a tent township on the Turon River, beyond the Blue Mountains. Because of the discovery of gold in 1850 the Sofala district at times had a population exceeding that of the whole Ipswich and Illawarra districts combined, and sometimes even rivalling that of Sydney. In January 1853 the *Sydney Morning Herald* published the second of ten articles in its series, 'Notes from the Turon', in which the 'Special Reporter' commented on Sunday in Sofala:

> The Sunday which I have now passed here was as well spent by the bulk of the population as it could have been in any of the settled towns. There is an Episcopalian Church and a Wesleyan Chapel, both well attended. The minister of the latter I have not the pleasure of knowing, but the Church of England clergyman—the Rev. Mr Palmer—is a most amiable and gentlemanly man, universally and deservedly respected. There is also a priest of the Roman Catholic Church—the Rev Mr Luckie—who has the good word of everybody. But, although the members of this communion are very numerous, they have no place of worship. Between £200 and £300 were collected a long time ago for the purpose of erecting one, but for some reason no commencement has been made.[14]

The report of the Reverend Mr Palmer to his Diocesan Committee was not as rosy as that of the 'Turon Special Reporter':

> The Church of England Minister of Sofala, the Rev JH Palmer, has addressed a statement to the Secretary of the Diocesan Committee requesting assistance to enable him to prosecute his ministerial duties at that place. He states the population of Sofala to be about 2000, the number of public-houses coming beneath his personal notice forty, or at the rate of one for every fifty souls. His calculation, based upon the soundest evidence, discloses a fearful contingency of crime and consequent misery.[15]

Palmer's co-worker in the goldfield's mission was the Reverend William Allworth who was rector of St Bartholomew's at Pyrmont in 1867 when Luckie began his ministry at St Bede's. Their shared experiences at the diggings would have made for convivial encounters.

By March 1854 the Rev Mr Luckie was back in Sydney, assigned as priest-in-charge to the Petersham mission, which had been separated from the St Benedict district in 1851. In 1857 he was back in rural New South Wales, appointed to Raymond Terrace with the added responsibility of assisting

---

14. *Sydney Morning Herald*, 31 January 1853.
15. *Freeman's Journal*, 17 March 1853.

the ailing old missioner at Newcastle, the Dominican Christopher Vincent Dowling. Luckie was diligent in the task of building. In the six years he spent at Raymond Terrace, the longest appointment in his missionary career, he built 'the beautiful stone Church of St Bridget, Raymond Terrace, the neat brick Church of St Malachy, Port Stephens, and the large, commodious new school-house at Miller's Forest', as detailed in a farewell address.[16] Both churches were given Irish patron saints from his home diocese of Armagh, a custom of naming not uncommon among Irish clergy. However, he did not improve the worship facilities of the Novocastrians, who had to make do with 'a miserable little shed, shaking under every wind'.[17] This situation led to a controversy between Luckie and the Newcastle congregation which was played out in the local newspapers.

In March 1863 Eugene Luckie took his leave of Raymond Terrace, clutching the traditional purse of sovereigns. He took the steamer to Sydney, from where he rode south-west to Bungonia, his new mission field in the vicinity of Goulburn. Soon after settling in, he received a letter from the Council of St John's College reminding him of a promise he had made to give one hundred pounds to the subscription fund for the building of the College. It was in August 1857 that the commitment was made, as recorded in the list of subscribers covering four columns of the *Freeman's Journal*, and in more enduring form in the 57 pages of subscribers in William Dolman's 1858 *Catholic Almanac and Directory of Divine Service*, and reprinted in the 1860 edition.[18] The letter from the College Council was part of an effort to persuade, if not compel, defaulters to make good their promises. Luckie's response was not encouraging:

> I made this liberal offer solely through my ardent love for the advancement of education in this land. Indeed such a liberal offer may be considered a great sacrifice of my humble means and everyone was astonished at it, knowing that since I came to this mission, His Grace has been pleased to appoint me to a succession of the most wretched missions in the Archdiocese, when I could only spare a little for local wants, but nothing for the general purposes of benevolence. To be brief the amount I expected from Dr. Gregory I never received and His Grace has, some time ago, decided that I should lose it.

---

16. *Freeman's Journal*, 27 May 1863.
17. *Sydney Morning Herald*, 9 May 1860; *Freeman's Journal*, 12 May 1860.
18. *Freeman's Journal* 15 August 1857; *Catholic Almanac and Directory of Divine Service*, 1858 & 1860.

He proceeded to comment on his current situation: 'I have a most miserable mission where I can only live; I have not even the necessaries, much less the comforts of life; but whenever I am able I shall subscribe to St John's.'[19]

The St John's Council, on receiving Luckie's response, approached the Archdiocese with the letter in which he requested that one hundred pounds of his claim on Gregory be made over to the College. Sheehy, a member the College Council, strongly rebuked Luckie and exposed his duplicity: 'With reference to your remarks about the missions entrusted to your care I will say nothing. In reply to your claim I read for the Council of St John's portions of your letters to me and to the Archbishop—that to His Grace of the 20th May 1862—in which you express your sincere regret for any expressions that would seem to discharge Dr. Gregory with injustice, and apologise to His Grace, in the absence of Father Abbot.'[20] The smitten Luckie agreed to subscribe twenty pounds, which was duly received by the College. The historian of St John's concluded his footnote on this matter with the wry observation: 'Apparently the reverend gentleman who complained of being committed to a succession of most miserable missions in his earlier days was somewhat more fortunate thereafter, for at his death in 1883 his estate amounted to no less than seventeen thousand pounds.'[21] It was more likely that it was precisely the 'miserable' mission of Sofala that was the source of Luckie's wealth. The Irish diggers were apparently in the habit of placing nuggets on the collection plate for their 'Soggath Aroon', their 'dear priest'. In fairness it must be noted that the seventeen thousand pounds were left to Luckie's old seminary, All Hallows College, for the creation of bursaries for students preparing for the Australian mission. Also to be noted is that 'the reverend gentleman' managed to spend his final years in comfortable retirement in a Waverley mansion.

On his arrival at Pyrmont, Luckie took rental accommodation in the house next to the new church. This residence would be bought by the parish as the presbytery thirteen years later in 1880. His next door neighbours were Reverend and Mrs Paterson of the Harris Street Presbyterian Church. It is not recorded whether Father Luckie joined the Patersons in celebrating the birth of a daughter at their house in May 1868. Robert Smith Paterson, who had arrived in Australia from the Orkney Islands in 1864, was called by local Scots Presbyterians to restore the ministry that had been established in Mount Street by John Dunmore Lang in 1843. Unable to gain access to the original church building, Paterson arranged to share the use of the Wesleyan Church in Harris Street while his community set about erecting a

---

19. RA Daly, *One Hundred Years on Grose's Farm: the story of the College of St John the Evangelist, within the University of Sydney*, typed manuscript 1977, 562 n 57.
20. Sheehy to Luckie, 24 December 1863 (*Adjutor Deus* II.110).
21. Daly, *One Hundred Years on Grose's Farm*, 562 n 57.

weatherboard church further down the street, just beyond Union Street. He ministered there until 1883, when a fine new Presbyterian church was built on land given by the Harris family in Quarry Street, Ultimo.

With his dual responsibilities of pastoral care of St Bede's and secretary of the Catholic Association, Eugene Luckie set about acting on one of the aims of the Association, namely establishing branches in every parish. He called together a Sunday evening meeting at St Bede's church and delivered a typically long discourse during which he made unflattering references to Julian the Apostate, Thomas Carlyle and John Stuart Mills, naming them as prime influences on the Public Education system, which the Association was formed to oppose. He appealed to the pride of his Irish listeners:

> It is the most touching and beautiful incident in the History of your race, how when it was made a felony to teach the alphabet in Ireland, our race, to satisfy their proverbial thirst for knowledge, set up the school behind the hedge, in the cave, in the caverns, and by various devices, eluded the pursuit the miscreant informers hired to scatter the children and shed the teachers' blood. I feel confident that the descendants of that manly race, that by passive and active resistance conquered the execrable policy of a government even more savage than the apostate Julian, will guard the interests of religion and education here.[22]

He stirred the gathering by raising the sensitive issue of government inspectors entering the schools conducted by nuns:

> How absurd is it not for the Council to send the Jews and the Gentiles to examine the nuns schools or I should have rather said, what an insult does it not appear in the eyes of Catholics. No doubt it is congenial to the taste of a Protestant Inspector to be empowered by law to leer a nun, but it outrages the feelings of every Catholic to see or hear of them being in the school at all. Whilst the religious Sister must loathe his very presence when she reflects that he is a member of a church that professes detestation for her order.[23]

A branch of the Association was established that evening and a committee formed to gather subscriptions in Pyrmont. The ever faithful Patrick O'Toole volunteered for committee duty, happily dividing his spare time between the Catholic Association and the Brotherhood of Oddfellows.

Having led by example in forming a local branch of the Association in his own district, Luckie enthusiastically launched into his Archdiocesan role

---

22. *Freeman's Journal*, 30 November 1867.
23. *Freeman's Journal*, 30 November 1867.

as secretary. His frequent letters to the editors of the Sydney newspapers were forthright in defence of Catholic schools and often aggressive in denunciation of the public system of education, and in particular of its chief architect, the Colonial Secretary, Henry Parkes. Always given to historical allusions, he compared Sydney's Archbishop, in his stand on education, to the martyred Archbishop of Canterbury, Thomas Becket: 'One is once more reminded thereby of the sainted and noble A'Becket of old when he was compelled to rise in resistance to the unlawful encroachments of the civil powers. This noble example of episcopal firmness will shine as one of the brightest incidents in the beautiful biography of his Grace.'[24]

Concerning Parkes he wrote that 'he is at war with everything we were taught to reverence and respect, and does not desire to conceal his contempt for all we hold most sacred.'[25] His announcement the next day that the Marist Brothers would be coming to the Colony to establish a training school for teachers for Catholic schools, carried sentences that would have raised Protestant cries of papal aggression: 'I need scarcely observe that the members of this Order will be thoroughly imbued with the same zeal and Catholic spirit that pre-eminently characterise the French Church at the present day, and which spoke out so energetically of late, from one end of France to the other, as to compel the Emperor of the French to hasten to the rescue of his Holiness the Pope, and place Pius the Ninth immovably on the ancient throne of the Caesars.'[26]

With tensions rising over education, in March an event took place in Sydney which increased the mistrust between the Catholic community and the civil Government far beyond their differences over the education issue. On the evening of Thursday 12 March 1868 as the members of the Central Council of the Catholic Association for the Promotion of Religion and Education gathered at the offices attached to the temporary cathedral of St Mary's for their monthly meeting, the news was spreading through the city that there had been an attempt on the life of the Duke of Edinburgh that afternoon at Clontarf on the shores of Middle Harbour. The Council was unanimous in expressing 'indignation and horror of the dastardly act' which had been committed, the shooting of the Duke in the back. They called on their eloquent reverend secretary to formulate a resolution expressive of their feelings.

> The Rev EJ Luckie said that he felt at some loss to find words which would justly express what he felt on the occasion. Still the language of

---

24. *Freeman's Journal*, 14 December 1867.
25. *Sydney Morning Herald*, 13 February 1868.
26. *Sydney Morning Herald*, 14 February 1868.

spontaneity was the language of the heart. He therefore begged to move the following resolution: That, owing to the sad intelligence which has just reached us of the outrage committed upon his Royal Highness the Duke of Edinburgh, we desire to express our abhorrence of that abominable outrage, and our sincere sympathy with his Royal Highness on this occasion.[27]

The Council members were apparently aware that the assassin was an Irishman who claimed to be acting as a member of the Fenian Brotherhood, because Luckie proceeded to protest most vigorously the loyalty of the clergy to the British crown and government:

They had assembled there for the peaceful agitation of a very important matter affecting their civil and religious rights; but always as citizens— men who earnestly desired to live on the best possible terms with members of all other denominations. They desired to guard those rights by all constitutional means, but they were good and loyal subjects of her Majesty's Government. They were heartily and sincerely loyal—loyal from their hearts, whatever some might choose to say to the contrary. Whoever said they were not loyal said what was not true. When he heard of this shameful outrage he felt as if a dagger had been plunged into him. They were, in his opinion, called upon to denounce the outrage in the strongest possible language, and it was because he felt this to be the case that he moved the resolution he had read.[28]

With the late arrival at the meeting of the Vicar-General, Father Austin Sheehy, there arose an animated conversation 'in which Fenianism was very emphatically condemned by several gentlemen (and especially by the Vicar-General and the Rev Mr McCarthy)'.[29] There was obviously a spectrum of views expressed about the Fenians during the heated exchange. The meeting was adjourned for a week and secretary Luckie was directed to record the resolution in the minute book and communicate it to the press. The clergymen would have been well aware of how weighted with Irish significance were the time and location of the attempted assassination: it took place in the week before St Patrick's Day, the celebrations of which were quickly cancelled; Clontarf in Ireland was the site of the great victory of Brian Boru over the Danes in 1014, and was the planned location of Daniel O'Connell's Monster Repeal Meeting of 1843, a rally that was banned and led to the Liberator's arrest and conviction for conspiracy.

---

27. *Sydney Morning Herald*, 13 March 1868.
28. *Sydney Morning Herald*, 13 March 1868.
29. *Sydney Morning Herald*, 13 March 1868.

On 13 March an estimated 17000 people attended an 'indignation meeting', held in a pavilion erected in Hyde Park and chaired by Sydney's Lord Mayor, to protest 'yesterday's outrage' and to offer prayers for the recovery of Australia's first royal visitor. The meeting moved the following resolution:

> That this meeting, impressed with a sense of the thorough and abiding loyalty of the colony of New South Wales, desires to convey to her Majesty the Queen the undeviating devotion of the people of that colony to her Majesty's person and throne, and their profound regret that their hospitality to her beloved son should have been disgraced by the crime of a wretch whose citizenship they repudiate.[30]

The next week, with the Prince recovering, another public meeting was held at which it was resolved 'to raise a permanent and substantial monument in testimony of the heartfelt gratitude of the community at the recovery of HRH'.[31] It was decided to erect a public hospital in his honour. An early subscriber to the public fund was the Rev EJ Luckie with a donation of one pound.[32] The resolution eventually found expression in Sydney's Royal Prince Alfred Hospital, opened in 1882. The Latin inscription on the commemorative plaque at the entrance to the hospital refers to Queen Victoria as 'Regina Mater' and to the unnamed O'Farrell as 'homo fanaticus'.[33]

O'Farrell stood trial at the end of March. He had first claimed to have acted on instructions from a group of Melbourne Fenians, but later retracted, stating that he had acted alone, motivated by his preoccupation with the troubles of Ireland. At his trial the defence team, which included William Bede Dalley, sought to have him acquitted on the grounds of insanity, drawing parallels with the 1840 case of 'Regina v Oxford', in which Edward Oxford, accused of attempting to assassinate Queen Victoria, was acquitted on the grounds of insanity.[34] However, the jury found Henry O'Farrell guilty of attempted murder of Victoria's son, and he was sentenced to death. Despite Prince Alfred's intercession to spare his life, O'Farrell was hanged at Darlinghurst Gaol on 21 April. Archbishop Polding visited the prisoner in his cell the night before the execution. O'Farrell was attended at the gallows by the Benedictine Father John Dwyer, grandson of emancipist Michael Dwyer, the 'Wicklow Chief'.

---

30. *Sydney Mail*, 14 March 1868.
31. *Sydney Morning Herald*, 21 March 1868.
32. *Sydney Morning Herald*, 25 April 1868.
33. *Sydney Morning Herald*, 25 September 1882.
34. *Sydney Morning Herald*, 31 March & 1 April 1868.

The NSW Government's initial reaction to the Clontarf shooting was, on 18 March, to bring in the draconian Treason Felony Act, which made it illegal to voice or publish statements 'disrespectful to the Queen', or to be one 'avowing a determination not to join in any loyal toast or demonstration in honour of Her Majesty, or who expressed sympathy with or approval of any offence under the Act'. It also gave police 'extraordinary powers . . . for entering any suspected house and searching for persons, papers, or arms'.[35] After the execution, Henry Parkes, the Colonial Secretary, continued to pursue the alleged Fenian connection, vigorously asserting the existence of further plots and raising anti-Irish and anti-Catholic feeling throughout the Colony to fever pitch. There had even been a call for the proposed memorial hospital to be restricted to Protestant patients.[36] Eventually a parliamentary select committee in February 1869 found that there was no foundation to Parkes' allegations. The *Freeman's Journal* welcomed the finding on behalf of the Irish Catholic community: 'To sum up there never was, and could not be any Fenian organization here . . . Only ignorance and credulity of the grossest nature, or else the basest hypocrisy, could for a moment express belief in the existence of organized Fenianisrn in this country.'[37]

The increased tensions arising from the attempted assassination did not, however, cause the Catholic Association's reverend spokesman to soften his hostile tone on the education issue. Letters from Eugene Luckie continued to flow to the newspapers throughout 1868. Reaching once more into his store of historical allusions, he likened Henry Parke's determination to enforce the regulations of the Public Schools Act, especially the role of school inspectors, to the 'irritating and offensive spirit that has characterised despotism in every age, whether encountered in Nero's councils, or amongst the demagogues of Jerusalem, some 1,836 years ago'.[38] The 'unlawful encroachments of the civil powers' of New South Wales were described in lurid terms in June. He accused the government of introducing a 'godless system of education' and of crushing the denominational system. He accused the Colonial Secretary of setting about this evil task under 'specious forms, aided by various devices, and supported by popular appeals to all that is selfish and seductive in human nature'.[39]

In 1869 there was a sudden end to letters from Eugene J Luckie. Wiser and calmer counsels prevailed as part of the effort to lower the temperature of sectarianism. This was indicated in an article that appeared in the *Freeman's Journal* in April 1873 headed 'Departures for Europe. Rev Father

---

35. *Freeman's Journal*, 21 March 1868.
36. *Freeman's Journal*, 28 March 1868.
37. *Freeman's Journal*, 27 February 1869.
38. *Sydney Morning Herald*, 30 May 1868.
39. *Freeman's Journal*, 6 June 1868.

Luckie'.[40] The combined apologetic and self-justificatory tone of the article would suggest that it was written either by or for Luckie, on the eve of his extended leave-of-absence. It suggested that it was with reluctance that he had accepted the role of spokesman for the Association, and that he was compelled by the circumstances of the education crisis to adopt a 'hostile attitude'. The need for such an approach had now passed, with the arrival of the teaching Brotherhood and some unspecified concessions in the Public school administration 'made to the Catholics'. His yearning 'to return to congenial privacy and retirement' could now be fulfilled. The article proceeded to describe in some detail his twenty-five years of ministry in the Colony, and concluded with the recounting of an incident calculated to remove any lingering suggestions of clerical avarice:

> There is a feature in connection with the temporary severance of Father Luckie and his late flock which deserves both commendation and adoption. His parishioners who are ardently attached to him, not satisfied with presenting him with a handsome Easter offering, resolved to present him with a testimonial and purse, but he respectfully and thankfully declined both, stating that he could not accept another generous offering from a devoted people who had a few days before handed him such a substantial token of their duty and regard, and as to the expression of their esteem and regard for him of that he was certain, and no public manifestation of it was needed to confirm the conviction.[41]

The 'late flock' was not that of St Bede's, for in September 1869 Eugene Luckie had been transferred from Pyrmont to the Paddington Mission, ministering at the church in Albert Street, Edgecliff. On leaving St Bede's he took with him the civil register of marriages, with the result that the first nine marriages celebrated in the Pyrmont parish, from January 1868 to May 1869, are to be found in the opening pages of the first volume of the marriage registers of St Joseph's, Edgecliff.[42] There are no records of weddings conducted at St Bede's after Luckie's departure until August 1874, the date of the first entry in the oldest extant marriage register.

Marriage, specifically 'mixed marriage', was a major item on the agenda of the bishops gathered in Melbourne for the second Provincial Council in April and May 1869. In Australia the approach to marriages between Catholics and Protestants had followed the more relaxed practices of the Catholic Church in England, where the bishops enjoined a prudent attitude

---

40. *Freeman's Journal*, 19 April 1873.
41. *Freeman's Journal*, 19 April 1873.
42. Damian Gleeson, 'Marriages performed at St Bede's Catholic Church, Pyrmont, 1868-69', typed manuscript, 2000.

on the part of priests. The only legislated requirement was that the Protestant party promise not to interfere with the faith of the Catholic and the children of the marriage. Such marriages were solemnised in churches in the same way as marriages between catholic spouses. In Australia, the marriage was often celebrated in both a Catholic and Protestant church. In Ireland the attitude of the bishops was very different; strict observance of Papal Decrees, not prudence, was enforced by the bishops gathered at the National Council of Thurles in 1850. Mixed marriages were forbidden; they could only be permitted by formal dispensations, which were severely discouraged; if permitted they could not be celebrated in a church; no sacred rites or blessings were allowed; the priest, dressed in his black cassock, was to act as witness only. Archbishop Paul Cullen of Armagh, as Primate and Apostolic Delegate, had presided at the Thurles Council, and was instrumental in bringing the Irish church into strict conformity with Rome. Cullen was also instrumental in the appointments of at least five bishops in Australia; he was cousin to three of them. These Cullenite bishops formed the majority among the bishops at the 1869 Provincial Council in Melbourne, and succeeded in imposing the same conformity. Discussions were preceded by a request from the majority of the thirty priests present that the legislation on mixed marriages be benign. Polding held out for the wearing of the stole at such marriages.

After the formulation of the strictest decrees by vote of the bishops, the priests presented a formal petition (*supplex libellus*) asking that it be left to the prudent discretion of the local priest to decide on where, and under what form of ceremony, a mixed marriage would be celebrated. These interventions did not succeed. There were eight priests of Polding's Archdiocese present at the Council—five Irish, two Italians, one Frenchman.[43] Back in Sydney two of them, John Lynch and Joseph Garavel, each during his incumbency at St Bede's Pyrmont, would have to consider whether to implement, moderate or ignore the new legislation. Concerning the Cullenites at the Council, Polding commented laconically to his confidant in England, Henry Gregory: 'The young Bps [Bishops] go in much for rigour or something like it.'[44]

In the Pastoral Letter addressed to the clergy and laity of Australia and signed by the eight bishops assembled in Council mixed marriages were characterised as 'irreligious connections' and 'mischievous alliances', as 'dangerous and disgraceful'. Clergy were exhorted to preach frequently against such unions, 'but if unhappily, they fail to dissuade mixed marriages, then they are to take care that the holy, unswerving discipline of the Catholic Church is observed': 'The dispensation is not to be expected except for just

---

43. *Freeman's Journal*, 10 & 17 April 1869.
44. Polding to Gregory, 24 April 1869 (Polding Letters III.326).

and grave reasons; there must be risk of grave consequences . . . not to be otherwise avoided; and even when under these conditions the mixed marriage is permitted, there is to be no solemn benediction. The minister of the Church is to stand by, almost a passive witness of an act which the Church has always deprecated and deplored.'[45] An Australian canonist-historian has concluded that 'the Australian legislation was more rigorous than the Roman instructions, which at least tolerated the rite in the ritual (without Mass) in order to avoid greater evils'.[46]

Protestants considered that the papist bishops were severe in the matter of mixed marriages in order to increase the pressure on the Catholic party to lure the non-Catholic to conversion, especially since the majority of such marriages involved a Catholic woman and a Protestant man. John Dunmore Lang had in 1848 warned the British public against Caroline Chisholm's programme of female immigration:

> These young women, who are almost exclusively Roman Catholics . . . have been selected as free emigrants for Australia, expressly with a view to their becoming the wives of the English and Scottish Protestant shepherds and stockmen of NSW, and thereby silently subverting the Protestantism and extending the Romanism of the colony through the vile, Jesuitical, diabolical, system of 'mixed marriages', a system which the Romish priesthood systematically employ as an instrument for the advancement of the Papacy in all countries.[47]

A similar but less acerbic interpretation was taken by an 'ex-journalist' in the *Newcastle Chronicle* following the publication of the 1869 Pastoral Letter:

> These marriages usually take place between the Roman Catholic women, and men who are, perhaps, professedly Protestant, but who, in reality, are nothing at all. The consequence is that the wives, if they are at all zealous themselves, get their husbands to go along with them in the course of a short time. The Catholic Church, therefore, almost invariably gains by

---

45. *Freeman's Journal*, 22 May 1869.
46. Ian Waters, *Australian Conciliar Legislation prior to the 1917 Code of Canon Law: a comparative study with similar conciliar legislation in Great Britain, Ireland, and North America*, dissertation submitted to the Faculty of canon Law, Saint Paul University, Ottawa, in partial fulfilment of the requirement for the degree of Doctor of canon Law, 1990, 176.
47. Lang to editor of *British Banner*, 15 November 1848 in *Letters of Dr.John Dunmore Lang in the 'British Banner'*, edited by Margaret Kiddle (Melbourne, 1953), n 36.

such marriages, and I am somewhat surprised that the bishops express themselves so strongly against them as they do in their pastoral.[48]

The *Protestant Standard* was dismissive of the bishops' attempts to curtail marriages between Catholic and Protestants: 'as to mixed marriages, until they make a proselyte of Cupid and engage him to be always on their side, we fear their fulminations against his free archery will be equally vain.'[49]

Practice in Sydney did not immediately conform to the severe requirements of the 1869 decrees. In January 1871 Polding was informed by Cardinal Barnabo of allegations of continuing abuses, 'forbidden practices', in the Sydney Archdiocese—mixed marriages being celebrated with full solemnity; couples having a second ceremony performed by a Protestant minister. Having alerted Polding to these matters 'most pressing for our pastoral solicitude', His Eminence disingenuously concluded: 'I myself believe these things have happened either in Your Grace's absence or at least without your knowledge through the inexperience or laxity of some priest.'[50]

The priests of Pyrmont were slow to implement the new rules. The first instance of a marriage 'witnessed' in the priest's house did not occur until July 1879. The clerical witness was Father Norbert Quirk, who would have welcomed the couple, if such courtesy was permitted, into his rented premises on Pyrmont Street. Monsignor John Lynch, Quirk's predecessor, who had been present at the 1869 Provincial Council, did not celebrate any weddings in his residence, perhaps because he lived some distance away, in salubrious Glebe. Between August 1879 and March 1883 Father Joseph Garavel conducted all mixed marriages, 15 out of a total of 49 weddings, in one or other of his various rented houses, and finally at 43 Pyrmont Street, which he purchased as the permanent presbytery in July 1880. However, in April 1883 he witnessed a wedding in the 'vestry', and from then until January 1884 all 21 marriages, whether 'Catholic' or 'mixed', took place in the church. None of the 54 weddings conducted by his successor, Father Edmund Walsh, between 1884 and 1889 took place in the presbytery or sacristy. Even though the civil registers did not indicate the religion of the spouses, it may be presumed that among the weddings celebrated by Walsh, there would have been a proportion of mixed marriages similar to those celebrated by his predecessor, namely 33%. Neither Joseph Garavel nor Edmund Walsh were 'inexperienced' priests, so their indulging in 'forbidden practices' must have been due, in Cardinal Barnabo's terms, to 'laxity'; or perhaps Garavel and Walsh simply chose to be benign in their approach to

---

48. *Newcastle Chronicle*, 6 May 1869.
49. *Protestant Standard*, 15 May 1869.
50. Barnabo to Polding, 19 January 1871 (*Adjutor Deus* II.244).

couples of mixed faith. In 1889 Father Furlong, neither inexperienced nor lax, resumed the implementation of the strict prohibition on mixed couples entering the church for their wedding.

The decree on mixed marriages emerging from the 1885 Plenary Council, presided over by Cardinal Moran in Sydney, allowed the local bishop to dispense, for serious reasons, from the prohibition on conducting mixed marriages in a church. Locations of such weddings could, in rare instances, now be shifted from the presbytery to the sacristy, but not in front of the altar. This concession allowed the bride to process down the church aisle, before disappearing into the sacristy, and the couple to exit together. Apart from Garavel's maverick 'vestry' wedding of 1883, the first transfer of a marriage ceremony from presbytery to sacristy at St Bede's did not take place until June 1892. Pyrmont clergy were slow to implement both the severest and the more benign rules. After 1892 the only wedding in the Pyrmont presbytery was conducted by Father Cletus Heffernan in June 1939, not in compliance with Canon Law, but because the marriage was, as noted in the register, a 'revalidatio', a private renewal of vows in the presence of the Catholic priest and two witnesses. A solemn blessing would have been bestowed by Father Heffernan wearing the stole. Following the reforms of the Second Vatican Council in the 1960s all marriages could be celebrated 'in front of the altar'.

The parish marriage registers, as well as giving an insight into the application of Church Law, also provide a glimpse of the socio-economic status of Pyrmont. Against the name of groom and bride it was required to enter information under the heading 'Rank and Profession'. An analysis of the nine weddings witnessed by Father Luckie in 1868 and 1869, and the 197 weddings recorded in the first extant parish register, from August 1874 to November 1893, covering the incumbencies of O'Connell, Lynch, Quirk, Garavel, Walsh and Furlong, yields interesting information. Of the grooms, 113 or 57% were labourers in unspecified areas; another 18 were quarrymen. Among those connected with shipping there was one sea-captain, one chief office, one mariner, one ships-engineer, 7 seamen, two shipwrights, one boat-builder. One of the shipwrights was Patrick Gorman who, at St Bede's on 22 July 1876, married Teresa O'Toole; she was the daughter of Patrick the stonemason. Teresa, who had discovered the fire in the Catholic schoolhouse in June 1867, had no entry in the register under 'profession'. Among 40 tradesmen were represented the following: cabinet-maker, boiler-maker, painter, French polisher, wheel-wright, carpenter, compositor, harness-maker, coach builder, brick-maker, printer, iron moulder, saddler, mason, compositor, baker, butcher, iron founder, boilermaker, smelter, electrician, plumber, glazier. There were four bridegrooms associated with the hotel trade, variously described as publican, hotel manager, hotel keeper and barman. Sundry 'professions' were waiter, jeweller, policeman, fireman, storekeeper, carter, grocer, railway porter, barber, post office clerk, gardener. There was an actor and a jockey. All of these could have gone about their work while maintaining residence in Pyrmont. There were some whose 'profession' indicated that they would have left the city after marrying their Pyrmont bride—farmer, drover, gold miner, and an American 'gold-digger'.

The majority of brides, 105, were classed either as 'housekeeper', or as 'living at home', an expression favoured by Father Furlong. Under the range of headings, 'servant', 'domestic servant', 'house servant', 'service', 'housemaid', there were 33 brides. The next largest category was 'dressmaker' with 14. Other 'professions' were dairywoman, storekeeper, upholsterer, tailoress, seamstress, teacher, milliner, cook, machinist, waitress. Curiously, there were three 'labourers' among the ladies. Perhaps these were mistaken entries made by a weary clergyman. Six brides wrote 'lady' as their rank, while only one bridegroom chose to indicate 'rank' rather than 'profession', and wrote 'gentleman'. Herein was a significant insight into the socio-economic ranking of the Pyrmont population. The district had become almost exclusively working-class, a far cry from the elegant, middle-class harbour-side suburb envisaged by Edward Macarthur in his 1840 subdivision.

In 1873 Eugene Luckie, after 25 years in the Australian mission, prepared for his first return voyage to Ireland to visit his aged mother. Sadly, shortly before his departure from Sydney he received news of his mother's death at the age of ninety. The Archbishop commissioned Eugene to 'collect as much statistics and information on school management and improvement as he will be able to obtain of a reliable nature and from the best sources.'[51] He fulfilled this commission on his way to and from Ireland. He travelled extensively visiting Ceylon, India, Arabia, Egypt, the Holy Land, Italy, Germany, and France. In Rome he was granted a private audience with Pius IX, no longer seated 'immovably on the ancient throne of the Caesars', but a 'prisoner of the Vatican', despoiled of all his territories by the armies of a newly united Kingdom of Italy. Luckie visited the Irish communities in Rome, including the Dominicans at San Clemente, where the prior, Father Joseph Mullooly, took him on a guided tour of his recent archaeological discoveries under the ancient basilica. He returned to Australia via the United States, renewed in his forebodings of the evils of public education.

He arrived back in the Archdiocese in October 1874, 'in the enjoyment of excellent health and spirits'.[52] He was soon assigned to St Bridget's church and parish, north Kent Street, which had recently and controversially been separated from St Patrick's, Church Hill.[53] In a charming gesture, at the

---

51. *Freeman's Journal*, 19 April 1873.
52. *Sydney Morning Herald*, 16 October 1874
53. Peter McMurrich, *The Harmonising Influence of Religion: St Patrick's, Church Hill, 1840 to the Present* (Sydney, 2011), 21.

celebration of the profession of Sisters of Charity in St Vincent's Convent, Father Luckie presented Sister Clare with 'a flower which he plucked in the garden of Gethsemene, whilst visiting that holy site . . . a rare and valued souvenir of his travels in the holiest spots on earth'. Sister Clare was the daughter of 'an old and much esteemed friend', William Augustine Duncan.[54]

In 1876 Father Luckie was moved out of Sydney to All Saints Church in the extensive Liverpool district. In 1882 he took retirement in a residence described as a 'Victorian Mansion' in Leichhardt Street, Waverley. The following year, planning to return to Ireland he arranged for the sale of his 'substantial household furniture and effects' and his extensive library of over 500 books. However, his health underwent a rapid decline and he died on 12 May 1883 at the age of 61. The obituary in the *Freeman's Journal* gave a detailed account of his final illness:

> [A]bout twelve months ago, when, completely broken down in health, and utterly incapable of continued service, it was seen that he should be totally exempt from active life. He placed himself under the care of some of the most eminent members of the medical faculty, and was advised to make another trip to the old country. Acting on this advice the rev. gentleman procured his cabin on board the *Orient*, and it was after he had made all necessary preparations for his departure that he was seized with the attack of illness which, unfortunately, proved fatal. At his own request he was removed from his residence at Waverley to St Vincent's Hospital, where he received the consoling attentions of the good Sisters. It was on Saturday morning last, 12th instant, at half past ten, that the angel of death came with the summons, and Eugene Luckie, the priest, scholar, and gentleman, calmly breathed his last, and gave his soul into the hands of his Divine Master.[55]

An interesting detail emerged from the obituary—Father Luckie's interest in writing a history of the Australian church was noted: 'every spare moment was devoted to the acquisition of knowledge, and the compilation of matter for an ecclesiastical history of Australia.' Unfortunately, Eugene's research did not result in a published text; he missed the opportunity of becoming a latter-day Bede. The obituary was generous in its assessment of his achievements, not least of which was the considerable estate that he had accumulated and generously bequeathed:

> The deceased was a man of general learning and considerable literary attainments, and his writings, especially his contributions some years

---

54. *Freeman's Journal*, 21 November 1874.
55. *Freeman's Journal*, 19 May 1883.

ago to this journal, were always marked by soundness of judgment. With, matured ideas on the question of education he devoted himself heart and soul to the establishment and maintenance of thoroughly Catholic schools, and he also showed himself deeply interested in the founding of a fund for the education at home of priests for the Archdiocese. By his last will and testament he bequeathes £17,000 for his Eminence Cardinal McCabe, Archbishop of Dublin, and the Right Rev Dr Woodlock, Bishop of Ardagh, the sum to be devoted by them to the maintenance in the College of All Hallows, Drumcondra, near Dublin, of ecclesiastical students who may adopt the archdiocese of Sydney, or become affiliated thereto, provision being made for the outfit and passage of such students to this colony when ordained.

It was noted that 'the only other bequests are £300 to St Vincent's Hospital, and £100 each to the niece and nephew of the deceased clergyman'.[56] St John's College did not receive a mention in the will.

In the absence of Archbishop Roger Bede Vaughan, who had left for Europe via America in April 1883, Dean Felix Sheridan, who had sailed to Australia with Eugene Luckie in 1848, presided at the Requiem Mass on 14 May in the unfinished St Mary's Cathedral. On 20 August news was received in Sydney that Archbishop Vaughan had died suddenly in England at the age of 49. Thus ended 64 years of English Benedictine rule in the Australian Church. It had begun with the appointment in 1819 of the Downside monk, Edward Bede Slater, as Vicar Apostolic of the Cape of Good Hope, Madagascar, Mauritius and New Holland with adjacent islands.

---

56. *Freeman's Journal*, 19 May 1883.

Chapter 8
Pyrmont's Monks

Pyrmont had its own period of Benedictine rule, albeit brief. A few months after Eugene Luckie's transfer to Woollahra in September 1869, James Austin Byrne OSB, barely four years ordained, was appointed to the St Bede mission. Just two years previously, Polding, in a letter to his exiled confidant, Henry Gregory, had expressed his despair as to where and with whom to place Byrne, given certain problems: 'Austin Byrne, whom you may recollect I brought as a Boy from the Turon, has betrayed a propensity to drink which has taken me by surprise. What to do with him I know not—he cannot remain at Lyndhurst and with whom to place him on the Mission?'[1] In 1851 Polding had brought James Byrne, possibly as young as eight years-old, to St Mary's Monastery after the first episcopal visit to the goldfields along the Turon River, west of the Blue Mountains. The recruiting of young boys was a common practice at the Sydney monastery.[2]

After schooling at St Mary's, James Byrne had been clothed with the Benedictine habit in 1857, taking the name Austin, in honour of the Benedictine monk, Saint Augustine, first Archbishop of Canterbury. That year the monastic community relocated to Lyndhurst where the young monks continued their ecclesiastical studies. As well as preparing for the priesthood, Brother Austin, after being ordained a sub-deacon in 1862, became a member of the staff of the boarding school at Lyndhurst, teaching Latin and Greek.[3] After an unusually lengthy four-year delay, he was ordained a priest on 7 September 1866 and continued as a teacher in the College. As Polding's letter indicated, it was soon necessary to remove him from Lyndhurst. His name appeared as celebrant of marriages at St Mary's temporary cathedral from October 1868 to August 1869. In this pastoral role

---

1. Polding to Gregory, October 9 1868 (Polding Letters III.306).
2. T Kavenagh, 'Romanticism and Recrimination: the Boy Postulants at St Mary's, Sydney', *Tjurunga* 46 (1994): 21–42.
3. *Catholic Directory* 1862.

he was under the watchful eye of the cathedral administrator, Father Timothy McCarthy. In September 1869 his appointment as chaplain at Darlinghurst Gaol was announced. However, in January 1870 he was replaced: 'The Rev John Kelly has been appointed Roman Catholic chaplain of Darlinghurst Gaol, *vice* the Rev J A Byrnes [sic]'.[4]

It was then that he began his ministry at Pyrmont in place of Father Luckie. Soon after his appointment, Austin announced that a Lenten mission would be held in the parish during March 1870. Thanks to the *Protestant Standard*'s careful scrutiny of Catholic matters, the wording of the 'small printed card' issued by 'the Romish priest of Pyrmont' announcing the event has been preserved:

>
> ST BEDE'S CHURCH, PYRMONT
> Regulations for the Jubilee
> DEVOTIONS
>
> 5am MASS
> 5½am MEDITATION
> 7am MASS
> 7½pm NIGHT PRAYERS. SERMON. BENEDICTION of BLESSED SACRAMENT.
> The Confessionals will be attended from 6 to 10am and from 4 to 10pm
> *Conditions for gaining the Indulgence*
> 1. To visit the Church twice and there pray for the intention of the Holy Father.
> 2. To Fast three days.
> 3. To approach the Sacraments of Penance and the Holy Eucharist.
> 4. To give some Alms.
>
> The solemn public exercise of the Jubilee will commence at 7 o'clock pm on Sunday, 13th inst, and conclude by Mass at 7 o'clock am Thursday morning, 17th instant.
>
> The Rev Father MONNIER will conduct the Retreat.[5]

Joseph Monnier was the Marist parish priest of St Patrick's at Church Hill.[6] In typical fashion the *Protestant Standard* was scathing of the Jubilee held

---

4. *Sydney Morning Herald*, 29 January 1870.
5. *Protestant Standard*, 2 April 1870.
6. John Hosie, 'Monnier, Joseph (1825–1874)', *Australian Dictionary of Biography*, National Centre of Biography, Australian National University, http://adb.anu.edu.au/biography/monnier-joseph-4222/text6807, published first in hardcopy 1974, accessed online 11 November 2015.

in 'the miserable little church at Pyrmont': 'What a fortunate name—Father Monnier will take the money! Jubilee, indulgences, fasts and penances—confessionals and masses—holy popes and holy wafers—and Father Monnier will take the money! All for money!'[7] The *Standard* would later contrast 'miserable little' St Bede's with neighbouring St Bartholomew's: 'Founded upon a rock, both literally and spiritually . . . a prettier little building we have not yet visited.'[8]

Archbishop Polding would have been pleased that Austin Byrne's 'propensity to drink', which had led to his removal from Lyndhurst, seemed to have been conquered, as strongly indicated in the headline in the *Freeman's Journal* of 10 September 1870: 'Temperance in Pyrmont'. The article recounted the rather extraordinary event of the inauguration of the St Bede's Branch of the St Francis Total Abstinence Society. At 7.30 on the evening of Monday 5 September the parent society met at St Francis de Sales church on the corner of Campbell and Elizabeth Streets, Haymarket, and led by the Temperance Band and carrying their banners and wearing their regalia, they marched with their pastor, the Benedictine John Felix Sheridan, to Market Street, then down to Darling Harbour, across the Pyrmont Bridge, up Union Street and into Pyrmont Street towards St Bede's. The article continued:

> By the time they arrived there the school room of St Bede's Church was well filled, and there was not room enough to accommodate one quarter of those assembled. Father Sheridan was loudly cheered by the crowd on his arrival. So soon as a passage to the platform could be attained, the Rev Austin Byrne of St Bede's took the chair. The platform was crowded by the band, vocalists and speakers quite as much as the body of the room. After a selection by the band, the Rev Chairman introduced Father Sheridan, who in a pithy speech stated the object of the meeting.

Father Sheridan, who had been Principal at Lyndhurst College during Austin's time as a professor there, told the crowd about a 'gigantic crusade', which was being undertaken on behalf of sobriety in Sydney, and stirred them to enrol as 'soldiers of temperance'. After a collection on behalf of the band and a bracket of solo items, including 'Believe me if all those endearing young charms', 'I'll Meet Thee in the Lane' and the crowd-pleasing comic song 'The Irish Schoolmaster', Father Sheridan adjourned to the Church, where he administered the pledge to a hundred parishioners. The following was the text of the pledge: 'I promise, with the Divine assistance and through

---

7. *Protestant Standard*, 2 April 1870.
8. *Protestant Standard*, 1 June 1872.

the intercession of the Blessed Virgin Mary, to abstain from all intoxicating drinks and to discountenance the cause and practice of intemperance in others.'[9] It was not stated whether Father Byrne participated in making this promise.

Father Sheridan was back in Pyrmont with his band two weeks later to recruit more soldiers for the crusade and to announce a 'grand monster social temperance picnic shortly to come off in connexion with St Francis' Total Abstinence Society, to which all the boys and girls of the Pyrmont Cadets of Brothers and Sisters of Temperance would be invited to attend free'.[10] Felix Sheridan continued attentively to nurture his Pyrmont recruits and their pastor, appearing again early in October, but without the band. Father Austin began to take a more active role; this meeting was concluded with an 'earnest practical speech from the Rev Father Byrne' and several names were added to the roll.[11]

There is no record, either in the *Assessment Books* or the *Sands Directory*, of Austin Byrne living in the Pyrmont district during his ministry there. Father Luckie had rented the house next to the church during his incumbency. However, there is a hint that Byrne may have resided at St Benedict's, reverting to the pattern, begun in 1864 by Father McCarthy, of ministering to Pyrmont from Abercrombie Street. The suggestion is found in the report that in November 1870 Father Byrne, in the absence of Father John Dwyer, had welcomed Father Sheridan and his band to St Benedict's for the inauguration of the Abstinence Society in that district.[12] This was confirmed by an earlier reference to the St Benedict's clergy present at the funeral of Father John Kelly who had succeeded Byrne as Gaol chaplain, but died suddenly just five months later: 'Among the clergymen present we noticed ... the Rev Messrs Dwyer, Athy, Byrne and Mahony, St Benedict's'.[13] The clergy were housed at Eveleigh House which had been purchased by the Archbishop in 1869 for the Sydney Benedictine community as an alternative to Lyndhurst. The house was in the vicinity of St Benedict's church.[14] Perhaps

---

9. *Freeman's Journal*, 10 September 1870.
10. *Freeman's Journal*, 24 September 1870.
11. *Freeman's Journal*, 8 October 1870.
12. *Freeman's Journal*, 12 November 1870.
13. *Freeman's Journal*, 18 June 1870.
14. F Mecham & A Brown, 'Eveleigh House'. *Footprints* 9 (1973): 9–10. 'Eveleigh House is believed to have been built in the late 1840s it is shown in various maps from 1850 onwards. It was named after Holden's mother's maiden name, Everleigh (later known as Eveleigh). Eveleigh House (demolished) was located in the vicinity of Louis Street just south of Vine Street, east of Abercrombie, west of Eveleigh Street and north of Caroline Street, in the area now referred to as 'The Block'.' (Australian Heritage Database, Australian Government, Department of

this communal domestic arrangement was an aid to Byrne's new-found commitment to temperance.

Other activities of the Pyrmont pastor were recorded in the *Freeman's Journal* in 1870. In November Father Byrne led his congregation across Darling Harbour back to the Masonic Hall in York Street, the preferred site of fund-raising events, for a Grand Tea-Party and Musical Soiree under the auspices of the United Temperance Societies of New South Wales.[15] It was an event to raise money towards liquidating the Pyrmont church debt. Though over 700 people were present, the ladies had catered for many more. Fathers Byrne and Sheridan seem to have formed a team by now and 'they were everywhere in their desire to ensure success'. Also present was the choir of St Mary's girls' school and, of course, Father Sheridan's Temperance Band, which concluded the evening at 10pm with 'God Save the Queen', during which all would have stood, it being a criminal offence since the Treason-Felony Act of 1868 to remain seated during the anthem.

In January 1871, with the parish debt still not liquidated, the committee organised a lecture by the visiting Melbourne Jesuit academic, William Kelly, on 'Sarsfield and the Irish in France' to be held at the Masonic Hall. Tickets were on sale at two shillings for reserved seating, and one shilling for unreserved.[16] A cautious estimate of the attendance was given—'a very numerous audience assembled', many of whom were Sydney clergy. The theme of the lecture was the heroic exploits of Irish patriots in the service of the French monarchy against the English. 'The lecturer interspersed his lecture with several patriotic and pathetic verses, and was continuously greeted by loud and enthusiastic applause.'[17] The *Protestant Standard* added its usual sour note: 'A real live Jesuit has made his appearance in Sydney . . . [He] lectured on Monday last, in aid of St Bede's school, Pyrmont, on Saarsfield and his Irish Brigade. It was a chance for the Jesuit to declaim against William, Prince of Orange, and he availed himself of it. Of course, a Jesuit is to be forgiven for hating the man who set England free from the priestly policy of the imbecile James.'[18]

In May a local academic, Rev Dr John Forrest, Rector of St John's College, was at the podium delivering a very topical lecture on the Franco-Prussian War, which had recently concluded with the resounding defeat of France and the abdication of Emperor Napoleon III. An estimated seven hundred attended the lecture given on behalf of St Bede's church and school. The

---

the Environment website, http://www.environment.gov.au/cgi-bin/ahdb/search.pl?mode=place_detail;place_id=101630 [accessed 6/7/2014]).
15. *Sydney Morning Herald*, 15 November 1870.
16. *Evening News*, 13 January 1871.
17. *Empire*, 17 January 1871.
18. *Protestant Standard*, 21 January 1871.

regional newspaper, the *Quaenbeyan Age*, gave a very thorough summary of the lecture. The Irishman Forrest was clearly on the side of the defeated 'French Celts', blaming their generals for the army's failures, rhetorically asking his audience: 'Did they lack courage? No; they lacked Generals. They were "heroes led by asses." (Cheers). There was Leboeuf, whose name aptly expressed his fitness for his functions (Laughter).' Referring to the Prussian annexation of Alsace and Lorraine the lecturer concluded: 'She may annex and partition, but she never can annex the affections nor partition the loyalty of a French parish, much less of a French province.' These remarks were loudly cheered, and the applause was renewed when the Doctor proceeded to speak of the fidelity of Alsace to its French traditions and its long sustained hostility to the Teutons, who now laid claim to its allegiance.[19]

The following month there was a 'Grand Jubilee Tea Party and Concert', organised by the parishioners, not to raise money, but to congratulate their committee on the liquidation of the church debt. This event was held in the local school-room and attended by two hundred parishioners. The pastor of St Benedict's sat in the place of honour flanked by members of the Church Building Committee. Father Byrne was 'in attendance during the evening, and was assiduous in his desire to bring the matter to a successful issue'. At the end of the evening 'three cheers were given for the Rev MJ Dwyer, the Rev A Byrne, and the Church Building Committee'.[20]

With the church debt liquidated and fund-raising events no longer necessary, St Bede's ceased to attract regular press attention. Without newspaper reports it is difficult to ascertain how long Father Byrne continued as pastor of Pyrmont. Except for a passing reference in September 1871 to the presence of 'Rev A Byrne (Pyrmont)' at a city meeting of the Catholic Association, Austin Byrne faded from public attention.[21] There are references to his conducting weddings at St Benedict's during 1872 and at Sacred Heart, Darlinghurst, in 1873. The final citing of Byrne in an ecclesiastical context occurred in the *Freeman's Journal* in 1874, when he was noted assisting in the elaborate celebration of the Forty Hours Devotion at Windsor: 'On Tuesday the Mass was sung by the Rev Père Garavel. After Mass the Blessed Sacrament was again borne in procession as on Sunday, *mutatis mutandis*. The litanies were sung on each occasion by the Rev SJA Sheehy and the Rev Austin Byrne. The latter gentleman discharged very efficiently the onerous duties of master of ceremonies.'[22] He had been appointed in April to assist Austin Sheehy in the Richmond district as reported in the local newspaper:

---

19. *Quaenbeyan Age*, 11 May 1871.
20. *Freeman's Journal*, 6 June 1871.
21. *Freeman's Journal*, 9 September 1871.
22. *Freeman's Journal*, 26 September 1874.

> A MEETING of the Parishioners of the Catholic Church at Richmond took place after Divine Service on Sunday morning last, for the purpose of inaugurating a Committee to carry out in the most suitable manner a system of collecting, and maintaining a fund for the support of the clergyman, the Rev Austin Byrne, who has recently been appointed to assist the Rev Dr Sheehy in the charge of his district, which includes a very large area, extending as it does from Castlereagh in one direction to the lower McDonald in the other. It is a pleasing fact to observe that since the Rev Doctor's arrival amongst us, the congregation in each of the churches has largely increased.

With the passing of the 1862 'Grants for Public Worship Prohibition Act', government support for clergy appointed after the Act was not available. While Sheehy continued to receive his stipend, voluntary contributions were needed for the support of Byrne: 'An opinion was expressed that it would require £150 to be raised as an annual salary for the Rev Austin Byrne. Several gentlemen put their names down for subscriptions, amounting to between five and twenty and thirty pounds.'[23] The good people of Richmond would not have needed to support Father Austin for much longer, because by 1875 he had left the priesthood and would soon marry a former Good Samaritan sister. However, he would make a re-appearance in Catholic affairs a few years later when he became a source of information concerning the alleged misdemeanors of his fellow Benedictines.

After the death of John Bede Polding in March 1877, his successor, Roger Bede Vaughan, moved with haste to fulfil his Roman commission to report on the state of the Benedictine community in Sydney:

> Your Eminence,
> Having received the Decree of the Congregation of Propaganda Fide dated Nov. 5 1874, by which I was ordered to conduct an Apostolic Visitation of the Benedictines of this Diocese after the death of my predecessor, and to transmit to the Holy See an accurate account on their condition, I have the honour to submit to the Holy See the following Report and my own opinion on the matter.[24]

---

23. *The Australian, Windsor, Richmond, and Hawkesbury Advertiser*, 25 April 1874.
24. Roger Bede Vaughan, 'Report on the Australian Benedictines' (27 October 1877) in T Kavenagh, 'Vaughan and the monks of Sydney', *Tjurunga* 25 (1983), 183-206. Addressed to the Cardinal Prefect of Propanda Fide, Alessandro Franchi, the report bore the title: 'I Benedittini di Sydney. Il risultato della Visitazione Apostolica'.

To assist him in this task Vaughan had called upon William Augustine Duncan to provide details of the behaviour of the monks prior to his own arrival in 1873, and this sad saga was attached to his report. He introduced Duncan to the Cardinal disingenuously as 'a great friend of the late Archbishop'. Duncan, in fact, had become a vocal opponent of the Benedictine establishment during the lay revolt of the late 1850s. He had referred obliquely to this opposition at a meeting in December 1873 to organise a welcome to Sydney for Vaughan as the new Coadjutor Archbishop. He reminisced about his youthful, energetic involvement in ecclesiastical affairs in Sydney, especially his early support of the Benedictines; indeed, in 1844 he had referred to Polding as 'the ornament of the Benedictine body, and successful vindicator of English talent ... a gentleman and a scholar'.[25] Duncan acknowledged his subsequent 'disappointment at the results I fondly expected', and deferred to 'younger men to keep the affairs of Church and State from stagnation'.[26] However, in 1877 he enthusiastically re-entered the lists and gave ample expression to his opposition to the Benedictines in his narration of the 'irregularities' which allegedly occurred at Lyndhurst College: 'Monsignor, I gladly comply with the request of Your Grace to put down some notes on the irregularities which occurred at Lyndhurst (where the Benedictines were staying), with the intention of assisting Your Grace in putting a remedy to the evils about which the Catholics of this Colony have complained.'[27] In 1876 the *Protestant Standard*, ever alert to Catholic gossip, had described Duncan as 'the pet layman of Dr Vaughan'.[28]

Duncan relied for his report on the recollections of three witnesses, two of whom had died before the report's submission on 29 August 1877. James McGirr, was an Irish priest who after his arrival in Sydney in 1855 was appointed to teach at Lyndhurst. In *Catholic Almanac* for 1857 he was listed as Principal of the College. He was dismissed from the Archdiocese and eventually found his way to the new diocese of Bathurst where he became the first priest in the Parkes mission district. He died in June 1874.[29] The second deceased witness was Father Patrick Francis O'Farrell who was a clerical student at Lyndhurst under McGirr. In the same letter in which Polding had expressed alarm at Byrne's problem with drink, he wrote kindly of O'Farrell: 'Young Father O'Farrell, brought up in Lyndhurst, an excellent Priest, good Preacher, has had a most severe attack of Lung disease—the right is much affected and I fear for his recovery—so as to be useful—is very

---

25. *Weekly Register*, 30 March 1844.
26. *Freeman's Journal*, 13 December 1873.
27. 'Report on the Australian Benedictines', 184.
28. *Protestant Standard*, 5 February 1876.
29. L Grant, *Salt of the Earth: a Bathurst Necrology*, Bathurst 2005, 185.

uncertain.'[30] O'Farrell died at Newtown in January 1877, just two months before Archbishop Polding.

Duncan's living witness was James Byrne of whom he wrote: 'notwithstanding that he wrote and spoke the truth, [he] followed the bad example of his superiors'. The bad example was that of Anselm Curtis OSB, Prefect of Studies at Lyndhurst, who had eloped to Melbourne with the college housekeeper in 1864. To Curtis' scandalous defection Duncan linked Austin Sheehy, the Vicar-General and Bishop-elect, who had blessed the foundation stone of the Pyrmont church in February 1867. Duncan, though scathing about the monks' drunkenness in his report, made no direct mention of Byrne's 'propensity to drink' as a monk, although he could be considered to be included among the Benedictine students, all of whom, according to Duncan, were drunk on an boating outing in January 1863—'it was a miracle that they were not drowned into the sea.'[31] Perhaps it was Byrne who reported the incident to Duncan. Be that as it may, 'the boy from the Turon', the witness who 'wrote and spoke the truth', the founder of the Pyrmont branch of the St Francis Total Abstinence Society, was finally exposed by Duncan in his 1877 report as a drunk: 'The last time I saw him, he was staggering into a pub of ill-fame, and later I heard that he got married to one of the ex-nuns who left or had been expelled from the Good Shepherd Convent.'[32]

In the meantime, back at Pyrmont, it is to be presumed that St Bede's continued to be attended by one of the priests from St Benedict's, between the fading away of Austin Byrne in 1871 and the first entry in the earliest extant Baptism Register, the baptism of William Follers on 30 August 1874 by Daniel Maurus O'Connell. In the centenary booklet of 1967 the author, Pyrmont Parish Priest Victor Doyle, noted concerning the parish baptismal registers: 'No baptismal records from 1867 to 1874. Maurice O'Dwyer [parishioner since 1899] states that these were burned.'[33] A tradition among the descendants of Tobias and Elizabeth Toole is that the first baptisms at the newly dedicated St Bede's were of their twins Elizabeth Anne and Tobias, born in August 1867.[34] The florid signature of Daniel O'Connell was misread by Fr Doyle as 'W McCormack'.[35]

Dean O'Connell had been at St Benedict's since 1872 and was likely to have begun ministry at Pyrmont in that year. A letter of March 1873 from the Vicar General, Austin Sheehy, to the Secretary of Education, suggests

---

30. Polding to Gregory, 9 October 1868 (Polding Letters III.306).
31. 'Report on the Australian Benedictines', 188.
32. 'Report on the Australian Benedictines', 199.
33. Victor Doyle, *St Bede's Church Pyrmont. Centenary 1867–1967* (Sydney, 1967), 13.
34. Gleeson, *Irish Dusk Colonial Dawn*, 23.
35. Gleeson, *Irish Dusk Colonial Dawn*, 29.

that the priest-in-charge of St Benedict's, John Dwyer, was formally in charge of St Bede's during the interim between Byrne and O'Connell: 'In answer to your letter of the 12th instant I have the honour to report, that the Rev J M Dwyer has retired from his connexion with the Certified Roman Catholic Denominational School of St Benedict's in Abercrombie St, but that His Grace the Archbishop wishes him to continue his connexion with the similar School at Pyrmont.'[36]

Daniel Vincent Connell was born in Van Diemen's Land in 1825, son of John and Maria Connell, who later became prosperous land owners in the north of Tasmania, as the island was officially named after the grant of responsible self-government in 1856. They called their property 'Glen Connell'. At the age of thirteen Daniel was sent to Sydney for schooling at the newly established St Mary's Seminary, a boarding school for boys. The name 'seminary' did not imply preparation for priesthood. However, Daniel did choose to enter the monastery in February 1843 at the end of his schooling, receiving the Benedictine habit and taking the name Maurus, in honour of one of the first followers of St Benedict. He also changed his surname to O'Connell, in honour of the Great Liberator, Daniel O'Connell. Perhaps he was inspired to make the change by reading in the *Morning Chronicle* in September 1840 the account of O'Connell's speech at 'a very numerous meeting of the St Patrick's Catholic Total Abstinence Society' in Dublin. One of the priests present 'pointed to Mr O'Connell as a glorious proof of its [teetotalism's] compatibility with the discharge of onerous duties'—an inspiration for a young monk embarking on an onerous mission under a religious superior, Bishop Polding, who was an enemy of 'cordials, gin and strong whisky'.[37]

After ordination in 1848 Father Maurus was appointed to various mission stations in Sydney. Within the monastery he held the position of sub-prior from ordination until 1858. He was a popular member of the community as evidenced by the many fond references to him in the *Benedictine Journal*.[38] In 1851 he accompanied his Archbishop on the arduous journey to the Turon gold-fields, where they recruited young James Byrne for the Sydney monastery. In 1857 he was named Dean of St Mary's Cathedral. He would continue to be known as Dean O'Connell even after concluding his appointment. William Dolman's *Catholic Almanac* for 1858 carried a 'highly finished steel engraving ... of the Very Rev Dean O'Connell', together with a brief notice which emphasised his significance as 'the first native priest, the first native monk of the Australian Colonies', presenting him as 'the *primitiae* [first fruit] of the great harvest, which, we trust, the native population of

---

36. Sheehy to Wilkins, 17 March 1873 (*Adjutor Deus*, II.270).
37. *Morning Chronicle*, 20 September 1842.
38. See Kavenagh, 'Vaughan and the monks of Sydney', 173–174.

our land will yield to the service of the Church': 'If only our youth would employ thought and imagination on splendours which no imagination can exaggerate, then surely would many follow those examples of whole devotion to God's immediate service, which we have already witnessed among us.'[39] From 1858 to 1860 he also held the position of interim Rector of St John's College, to which he had been nominated by Archbishop Polding. It was a temporary appointment pending the outcome of Archdeacon McEncroe's journey to Ireland in search of a worthy academic clergyman for the position. Dr John Forrest arrived in September 1860. O'Connell's first appointment outside Sydney was to East Maitland from 1860 to 1863, and then in the Illawarra district from 1863 to 1872, when he returned to the city and took up residence at Eveleigh House, from where he commuted to his mission to the Catholics of Pyrmont.

In 1873 a significant gathering of quarrymen took place in the St Bede schoolroom which resulted in the formation of the 'QUARRYMEN'S PROTECTIVE SOCIETY'. The organisation continued to meet at St Bede's into 1874.[40] In 1881 the Society held its eighth annual picnic at Chowder Bay and after the toasts the chairman, Mr Cuke, used biblical imagery to express the importance of the eight-hour day:

> He said that the eight-hour movement was to the quarrymen what the deliverance of the Children of Israel from the house of bondage was to them . . . The very fact of him presiding over that important gathering was an evidence of the progress which had been made by the quarrymen (hear, hear), and he had no doubt that they would go on progressing until, perhaps, in ten or fifteen years hence, they would have a quarryman in Parliament as their representative (Cheers.)[41]

With their own premises in Union Street and under a new name, 'Quarrymen's Eight Hour Protective Society', the workers at Saunders Pyrmont quarries called a strike in 1888 over pay and conditions. One of the conditions demanded was that the custom known as 'smoke-ho' should be granted. Mr Saunders conceded this privilege of 10 minutes intermission at 11am to allow the men time to smoke a pipe.[42]

Dean O'Connell's period in Pyrmont can be traced through entries in the baptismal register—the last baptismal entry with his name is dated 3 September 1875—and through two items in the *Freeman's Journal*. In December 1874 he presided at a very parochial event, the annual prize-

---

39. *The Catholic Almanac and Directory of Divine Service in the Archdiocese of Sydney, and the Diocese of Maitland, for the Year of Our Lord, 1858* (Sydney, 1857), v-vi.
40. *Sydney Morning Herald*, 3 July 1873 & 25 February 1874.
41. *Sydney Morning Herald*, 1 November 1881.
42. *Sydney Morning Herald*, 2 October 1888.

giving at the parish school: 'The children were dressed in holiday attire and presented a neat, respectable, and orderly appearance. Many of the parents attended as well as several members of the local board. Several classes were examined on the ordinary subjects and answered in a creditable manner. The Very Rev. Dean O'Connell, chairman of the Local Board, awarded handsome prizes to the most deserving children.'[43]

In July 1875 there was an event with a much wider resonance. It was a local Pyrmont meeting organised by the O'Connell Centenary Committee. The committee had been formed in June to arrange the celebration of the centenary of the Liberator's birth on 6 August 1775. Delegates were despatched to the Sydney parishes to stir up interest in the events, which involved a formal oration by Coadjutor-Archbishop Vaughan, a celebration of Irish music and sports and a concluding banquet. Dean O'Connell welcomed the visitors to St Bede's and opened the meeting with an 'eloquent speech' in praise of his namesake, the 'greatest man of his age'

> [He] explained the reasons why all admirers of truly liberal principles should do honour to the man who, by his powerful advocacy and wise counsels, had broken down the barriers of religious and political intolerance in the British dominions, and placed Catholics, Dissenters, and Hebrews on a platform of equality, and also gained substantial advantages for the oppressed Negro . . . [T]he great Liberator had so large a claim upon the gratitude of all right-thinking men that he had no doubt the 6th of August would be celebrated in Sydney as it would be elsewhere in a way in which the memory of no other man has ever yet been celebrated.[44]

The delegates encouraged the parishioners to attend the events as a group, and Dean O'Connell 'intimated his intension of being present at the head of his flock'. None of the newspaper reports of the centennial celebrations mention the presence of the Dean and his Pyrmont parishioners.

His subsequent appointments saw him regularly 'removed', a word that did not necessarily imply any ecclesiastical censure. It was the frequency of 'removal' that could carry such an implication. From Sydney he was sent north to the Brisbane Water district in 1875, from there back to Sydney in 1877, stationed at Newtown, from there in 1879 west to Windsor and then in 1881 south to the remote town of Araluen. He was back in Windsor the next year and finally in neighbouring Richmond from 1884 to 1888.[45]

---

43. *Freeman's Journal*, 19 December 1874.
44. *Freeman's Journal*, 24 July 1875.
45. Cf P J Wilkinson, 'Daniel Vincent Maurus O'Connell OSB: first Australian-born priest', *The Swag*, 21 February 2013.

The Duncan report of 1877 on the misdemeanors of the Sydney Benedictines did not spare the Dean.[46] A whole paragraph was dedicated to his drunkenness. It began by stating that the 'terrible drunkard' had been 'an excellent young man before becoming a monk'; this was faint praise indeed given that Daniel was eighteen when he took the monastic habit. Duncan referred to his succession of placements 'around the country side', claiming that wherever he went 'he brought dishonour to the priesthood'. In addition to a general condemnation of his being drunk at Lyndhurst 'for entire weeks', Duncan cited three specific incidents: a dinner at Campbelltown where Fathers O'Connell and Dwyer were 'publicly drunk'; an accident involving his carriage and an omnibus in George Street for which he was placed in gaol, from where he managed to escape; an incident in Pitt Street where he was seen by a 'crowd of two hundred persons' in the company of a 'public woman'. The fact that neither of the witnessed, spectacular events received coverage in the press casts doubt on the telling.[47]

Be that as it may, O'Connell did have a propensity for drink, as noted by his Archbishop. In 1861 Polding wrote to Henry Gregory about another monk with a drink problem, Bede Sumner, not named by Duncan, and mentioned Maurus O'Connell: '[I] renewed the condition on which he [Sumner] held his faculties, in writing, and so trust he will go on blamelessly. F[ather] Maurus at E[ast] Maitland holds his faculties on the same condition.'[48] In October 1868 in the letter to Gregory in which Byrne's 'propensity to drink' was sadly noted, Polding reviewed each of the members of 'our little community [which] is in a poor way'. When he came to O'Connell he commented: 'If F[ather] Maurus had always been as he has been these last few months—what a comfort he would be to me—but I fear I am disturbing you with my miseries.'[49]

In 1890 Dean O'Connell retired to Glen Connell, his family home in Tasmania. He died at Launceston on 12 September 1901 aged 77. The *Freeman's Journal* concluded its obituary noting that 'the late Dean O'Connell was scrupulously exact in everything connected with the vestments and adornment of the altar' and that he was 'a ripe scholar, a well-equipped theologian and a man of practical ideas in the management of a mission.'[50] O'Connell was succeeded at Pyrmont by Monsignor John Thomas Lynch. Consideration of the Monsignor will be delayed until the next chapter, so

---

46. 'Report on the Australian Benedictines', 190.
47. See comments on Duncan's credibility in Kavenagh, 'Vaughan and the monks of Sydney', 190–192.
48. Polding to Gregory,17 February 1861 (Polding Letters III.11)
49. Polding to Gregory, 9 October 1868 (Polding Letters III,307)
50. *Freeman's Journal*, 28 September 1901.

that the third of the Pyrmont monks can be treated in company with his Benedictine confreres.

John Aloysius Quirk was born in Ireland in 1831 and arrived in Sydney with his family in 1841. Educated at St Benedict's school by the Christian Brothers during their brief initial stay in Sydney, he joined St Mary's monastery in 1849, receiving the name Norbert. He taught at the school while undertaking his studies in divinity. He was a signatory to the young monks' petition to Rome questioning the validity of their vows. The petition was taken to Rome by the absconding monks Mellitus Corish and Anselm Curtis in September 1854. Even after the formal resolution of the crisis, Brother Norbert remained unreconciled and quit the monastery in August 1856. After a year's absence he sought readmission and was welcomed back by Polding. He was ordained in September 1862 and taught at Lyndhurst, being appointed President of the College in 1865. At the same time he pursued legal studies at the University of Sydney, graduating LLB in 1864 and being awarded the Doctorate of Laws in 1866. In 1867 he combined the role of Prior of the Benedictine community with the College Presidency.[51] Fitness for the role of superior among the local Benedicitnes was a constant problem and it seemed to apply to Dr Norbert Quirk, as evidenced in a letter from Austin Sheehy in Armidale to Archbishop Polding: 'I promised your Grace to write respecting Lyndhurst and the Community . . . I have all before my mind now and I could not say I would wish any of them to be superior. When Fr Norbert was made such, it was through dire necessity. He is well fitted for carrying on the school, but, I fear, he has no care for the community.'[52]

Norbert took leave from his work at Lyndhurst at the end of 1873, though not of his title of President, and sailed to Europe in February 1874. He was not forgotten at Lyndhurst, where Father John Dwyer had taken over as prior. At the regular College reunions the mention of his name was always greeted with cheers, as happened in May 1875:

> The vice-chairman (Mr P Callachor) then proposed the health of The Very Rev Prior Dwyer, which was well received and responded to. The vice-chairman then in a complimentary speech gave 'The President of Lyndhurst, Dr Norbert Quirk', which was received with rapturous cheers. Father Quirk [Placid] replied on behalf of his brother, and was glad to see that the memory of his brother was still green in their heart. He was sure though he was separated from them by 18,000 miles of sea that he

---

51. Kavenagh, *'Vaughan and the monks of Sydney'*, 176–177.
52. Sheehy to Polding, 15 September 1869 (*Adjutor Deus* II.228)

was present among them in spirit, and nothing, he was sure, would have given him greater pleasure than to be present there that night.[53]

He arrived back in Sydney in September 1875. The Lyndhurst Old Boys quickly organised a 'welcome home' banquet. The event was reported in the *Evening News*:

> Last evening, the Rev Dr Quirk, principal of Lyndhurst College, who has lately returned from a visit to Europe was entertained at a banquet in the hall of the college by the students of the institution. About sixty gentlemen sat down to the tables... The toast was received with loud and prolonged cheering, and Dr Quirk made a feeling and suitable reply... Speaking of the education imparted to the youth at Lyndhurst College, he said as far as he could see, comparing the results with those of kindred institutions elsewhere, the education imparted here was equal to that of any other institution, and the youth of the colony had equal natural talents with those of any in the world. The only thing was, to use well the gifts God had given them, and they would be certain to succeed in whatever paths they walked.[54]

Norbert Quirk resumed his work at Lyndhurst until the visitation of the monks conducted by Archbishop Vaughan after the death of Archbishop Polding. While Quirk was spared in Duncan's appended report, he did not escape censure in Vaughan's formal document forwarded to Rome. Vaughan summarised his findings crudely:

> It is certain that:
> 1. If these Australian monks were put together in one house to live the regular life, after a week that house would be turned into a devil's house.
> 2. Such an attempt would only provoke laughter among the people, for the character of the monks is well-known and they have a poor reputation. They have lost irrevocably the respect and good opinion of the general public.
> 3. There is not a single one among them to take the place of Abbot or Superior.[55]

---

53. *Freeman's Journal*, 1 May 1875.
54. *Evening News*, 15 October 1875.
55. 'Report on the Australian Benedictines', p 204.

He supported his findings with dismissive comments about the four monks resident at Lyndhurst, two of whom were Norbert and his younger brother Placid, of whom he wrote:

> D[om] Norbert Quirk who of late has left the College on account of *delirium tremens* caused by immoderate drinking of strong spirits.
> D[om] Placid Quirk (brother of the above Quirk) who many times has been put to bed by his own pupils—being too drunk to walk.[56]

Perhaps it is not surprising that Dom Norbert took to the bottle after Vaughan's aggressive visitation and the subsequent hasty mid-year closure of the college, to which he had dedicated his fifteen years of priesthood. Just three years before the closure of the monastery and school, the *Herald* had published a feature article entitled 'THE UNIVERITY AND COLLEGES OF NEW SOUTH WALES', in which Lydhurst College received high praise: 'About thirty graduates, and four under-graduates, have from time to time, proceeded to the Sydney University from Lyndhurst; and those have for the most part been successful in winning a high academic standing, with scholarships and prizes, etc, to the glory of their Alma Mater.'[57]

Vaughan arranged for the subdivision of the substantial Lyndhurst Estate in preparation for a quick sale, and relocated the monastic library to his own apartments at St John's College. In January 1878, just six months after the closure, Vaughan gave an address at the opening of the St John's College Library, in which he lauded the great monastic tradition of creating and maintaining libraries: 'They preserved the relics of the past for the enlightenment of the future, and handed down the torch which but for their hands would have fallen to the earth.'[58] He placed himself in this great tradition, but not his fellow Sydney monks.

In November 1877 it was announced that the Quirk brothers had been assigned to pastoral duties: 'The other clerical changes involve Father Placid Quirk's acceptance of the Mission of Cook's River, with a residence in the presbytery at Newtown. His esteemed and learned brother, Dr Quirk is at present at Campbelltown officiating in the absence of the Rev P Roche, who has retired on leave of absence from the mission, caused by severe illness that will require some time of rest and medical skill on the part of his advisers.'[59] Norbert was back in Sydney in 1878 and assigned to the Pyrmont mission.

---

56. 'Report on the Australian Benedictines', 204.
57. *Sydney Morning Herald*, 10 July 1874.
58. Roger Bede Vaughan, 'Address on the occasion of opening the library, January 16 1878', *Occasional Addresses*, (Sydney, 1881), 36.
59. *Freeman's Journal*, 10 November 1877.

His first baptism at St Bede's was conducted on 23 June 1878. In August he was reported as having forwarded a donation from Pyrmont to the St Mary's Building Fund.[60] The new Archbishop's renewed drive for funds for the completion of the cathedral was reflected in the regular reporting, sometimes weekly, of parish contributions in the *Freeman's Journal*. Dr. Quirk's last entry in the baptismal register was dated 13 July 1879. *Sands's Sydney and Suburban Directory* for 1879 located the Reverend Doctor Quirk at number 14 Pyrmont Street, flanked by a tollkeeper on one side and a watchman on the other.[61]

In September 1879 Norbert was removed to Newtown. The following June it was announced that he had been appointed to St Benedict's: 'The many friends of the Very Rev Dr in Newtown will be glad to hear that his health, which had improved much during his residence there, will be equal to the more arduous duties of that extensive parish.'[62] In August 1881, in the 'Acta Populi' column by 'The Flaneur' of the *Freeman's Journal*[63], there appeared a charming reminiscence of the Rev President of Lyndhurst, 'the good and gifted Dr Quirk, a gentleman whose kindly heart has always run level with his clever head, and who thoroughly appreciates the ancient maxim that "it is better to rule by love than fear".'[64] Perhaps 'Flaneur' was drawing a less than subtle contrast with Archbishop Vaughan.

John Aloysius Norbert Quirk died in April 1883 at the age of 52, four months before Roger Bede Vaughan's sudden death in England. One of his funeral notices was placed by his mother Mary. His obituary in the *Freeman's Journal* described him as 'a scholar, and a ripe and good one, a good priest, and a worthy gentleman of culture and geniality'.[65] His collection of 700 books was added to the old Lyndhurst monastic library relocated to St John's College. Soon after his death it was announced that the ex-students of Lyndhurst intended to establish a 'memorial of the late Very Rev John Aloysius Norbert Quirk, OSB, LLD.' In September the plan took shape with the decision to create an annual prize in the University of Sydney, to be called 'Norbert Quirk Mathematical Prize'.[66] The prize is current, as described in 'List of All Prizes with Conditions' of the University:

---

60. *Freeman's Journal*, 24 August 1878.
61. *Sands Directory* 1879, 117.
62. *Freeman's Journal*, 5 June 1877.
63. 'The Flaneur' was the pseudonym of John Ignatius Hunt (1846-1912). cf John Arnold & John Hay (eds), *The Bibliography of Australian literature to 2000*, St Lucia, Qld. University of Queensland Press, 2000, 522.
64. *Freeman's Journal*, 27 August 1881.
65. *Freeman's Journal*, 5 May 1883.
66. *Freeman's Journal*, 29 September 1883.

Norbert Quirk Prize Best Essay in a Mathematical Subject: Founded in 1886 by a gift of 144 pounds from the subscribers to a memorial of the Rev John Norbert Quirk, LLD, Principal of Lyndhurst College. Four prizes may be awarded annually, one each for the best essay on a given mathematical subject by a student enrolled in Junior, Intermediate, Senior and Honours units of study in mathematics (Pure Mathematics, Applied Mathematics or Mathematical Statistics), provided that the essay is of sufficient merit in each case.[67]

Clearly there was much more to Norbert Quirk and his Benedictine confreres than was indicated in the exclusively negative assessments found in Vaughan's report to the Congregation of Propaganda Fide in 1873.

---

67. http://sydney.edu.au/scholarships/docsprizes/science_prizes.pdf, accessed 9 July 2014.

Chapter 9
'Mighty Dean Lynch' Takes Charge

Between the Pyrmont appointments of Dean Maurus O'Connell and Doctor Norbert Quirk, Monsignor John Thomas Lynch was priest-in-charge at St Bede's from November 1875 to August 1878. Unlike the Pyrmont Benedictines, Lynch did not ever manifest a propensity to strong drink. Clerical ambition, or 'mitre-mania', was the Monsignor's besetting weakness, as will be seen in the relating of his remarkable career.[1]

Born in Dublin in 1816, Lynch was one of the young Maynooth seminarians who responded enthusiastically and generously to Bernard Ullathorne's request for missionaries for New Holland during his recruiting tour of Ireland in 1837. With seven clergy, he a deacon and they priests, Lynch arrived in Sydney on the barque *Cecilia* in July 1838. They became known as the 'Men of '38', celebrated by Monsignor Patrick Hartigan in his series of articles entitled 'In diebus illis' [*In those days*] published between 1943 and 1945 in the *Australasian Catholic Record*. The articles were collected and published in 1975 in book form, *Men of '38 and other pioneering priests by 'John O'Brien'*.[2] The chapter on Lynch is entitled 'The mighty Dean Lynch'.[3]

Soon after arriving in Sydney, he was sent north with shipmate Edmund Mahoney to Maitland. He was back in Sydney for ordination to the priesthood in October:

---

1. 'Mitre-mania' was an expression in use in Irish clerical circles in that era, as evidenced in Bishop O'Mahony's letter to Propaganda, 14 June 1875 (cited in JJ Farrell, *A Great Storm Arose: the saga of the resignation of Bishop Timothy O'Mahony*, unpublished manuscript based on a thesis 'The O'Mahony Case' submitted for Degree of Master of Letters at the University of New England, 1991, 55), and in Father Michael Foley's 'Notes for the History of the Diocese', in the Archives of the Diocese of Armidale.
2. TJ Linane & F A Mecham [eds], *The Men of '38 and other pioneering priests by 'John O'Brien'*, Kilmore [Victoria], 1975. 'John O'Brien' was the 'nom de plume' of Monsignor Hartigan.
3. Linane & Mecham, *The Men of '38*, 80–96.

Mr Lynch is to be here on next Sunday from Maitland to be ordained about the 22nd *inst*. He has been preaching and baptising almost all nations in the extensive territory consigned to his Diaconal care—the circumstance of his not being in the Priesthood has been kept by him a profound secret, so much so that I fear that the parents whose children he has baptized will be calling out for a re-baptizing when they discover he was only a deacon.[4]

Back on the mission it was not long before it was considered necessary to create a separate ministry for Lynch, and Maitland found itself in the unique situation of having two missioners for a single settlement—East and West Maitland, one mile apart. This was an early manifestation of Hartigan's description of Lynch as the type who worked best by himself, suffering no rival, 'be it bishop or curate'.[5] He would spend twenty-four years at West Maitland, having responsibility initially for a district which extended indefinitely north and west.

In the *Catholic Directory* of 1841 ten mission stations were listed as in the care of John Lynch, including West Maitland itself. Three wooden chapels were in existence and two under construction. He used to make periodical visitations, passing along the Hunter River valley from settlement to settlement by way of Lochinvar, Branxton, Singleton, Muswellbrook up to the tablelands and Armidale, then struggling down the escarpment to the coast, and sailing south, calling in at Kempsey, Port Macquarie and other places on his way back to headquarters in Maitland. The 1841 *Directory* entry concluded rather forlornly with the comment: 'There is a clergyman wanted for the upper Hunter, and another at the Paterson'.[6] Help would not come until the appointment of John Rigney to Singleton in 1848 and Timothy McCarthy to Armidale in 1853.

After the death of Dean Mahoney in 1845 the title and responsibility of Rural Dean passed to John Lynch. As early as 1841 he had founded St John's Total Abstinence Society in West Maitland. Promotion of total abstinence, modelled on the Irish movement founded by Capuchin Father Theobald Mathew in 1838, would be the constant concern of John Lynch throughout his long priestly career in New South Wales. News of the phenomenal early success and impact of Father Mathew's movement began to appear in William Duncan's *Australasian Chronicle* early in 1840, which printed extracts from

---

4. Francis Murphy to John Fitzpatrick, 10 October 1838, in Brian Condon, *Letters and Documents in 19th Century Australian Catholic History* (http://www.library.unisa.edu.au/condon/CatholicLetters/18410412.htm, accessed 9 July 2015).
5. Condon, *Letters and Documents*, 81.
6. *The Australasian Catholic Directory for the Year 1841* (Sydney, 1841), 29.

the *Dublin Herald*.[7] Early praise for the Irish Society came from the Colony's Irish Catholic Attorney General, John Herbert Plunkett, who stated that Father Mathew had done 'more for Ireland in the cause of temperance than ninety-nine bishops'.[8] In Sydney in May 1841 Vicar-General Francis Murphy rose to the challenge and established the first 'St Patrick's Total Abstinence Society' in Sydney, followed by those of John Lynch in Maitland in August and of John Rigney in the Illawarra district in September.[9] Lynch became known 'the *Father Mathew* of the Hunter'; his earnest prayer was often heard: 'May the salutary waters of sobriety and brotherly affection, as they pursue their rapid and onward course, hurry along the foul demon of intemperance, and cast him into the ocean of eternal oblivion.'[10]

In addition to the usual Catholic cluster of buildings—Church, school and presbytery —Dean Lynch added to his mission stations the Temperance Hall. In Maitland it was called the 'Temple of Concord', in Singleton the 'Ark of Peace' and in Muswellbrook the 'Conciliation Hall'.[11] Weekly meetings were held with Dean Lynch in the chair and concluded with the taking of the pledge to abstain from alcohol: '[M]any a cold and wintry night has he left his warm fireside to come to the "Temple of Concord". Many a long and weary hour has he sat in the President's Chair to advocate the objects of the society, and receive the lost sheep within its peaceful fold.'[12] Happily, however, the meetings were not all gloom and doom. An early report in the *Maitland Mercury* painted a more attractive picture of events at the Ark of Peace:

> The teetotallers give a grand tea party this evening, in their large hall, which has been named 'the ark of peace.' There is no doubt, from the admirable arrangements which have been made, the meeting will go off with great eclat. Mr Fanning, 'of noted fame', has been engaged for the occasion to 'perform his extraordinary feats on the fiddle', and to sing some of his favorite songs. This young man is certainly an amusing person, and is justly entitled to all the commendation which has been bestowed

---

7. *Australasian Chronicle*, 5 & 25 May 1840. See M Allen, 'Sectarianism, respectability and cultural history: the St Patrick's Total Abstinence Society and Irish Catholic temperance in mid-nineteenth century Sydney', *Journal of Religious History*, 35 (2011): 374–392.
8. *Sydney Herald*, 21 September 1840.
9. *Australasian Chronicle*, 6 May & 8 December 1841.
10. *Maitland Mercury and Hunter River General Advertiser*, 1 March 1845.
11. H Campbell, 'Dean Lynch: laying the foundations for Maitland Diocese', *Journal of the Australian Catholic Historical Society*, 3 (1971): 53.
12. *The Catholic Almanac and Directory*, 1855.

upon him. The Rev Father Lynch presides; and many gentlemen who 'speak trippingly on the tongue' are expected to address the meeting.[13]

Forty years later in its obituary the *Mercury* returned to the 'Temple of Concord' and summed up the Dean's approach to temperance meetings:

> [H]e knew human nature too well to make good advice nauseous, and the Temple of Concord was a sort of ordered free-and-easy, and every Monday night was looked forward to by hundreds as a season of delight. Admission was threepence, and subsidiary to the main business of the meetings were musical selections by an excellent brass band, led by the late Edward Fanning, and better than all, truly popular songs sung by Fanning, songs which are now forgotten, such as 'Billy Barlow', 'Paddy Malone'—ditties full of local allusion and possessing a strong local colouring. A tone of wholesome fun pervaded these meetings, which attracted all classes, and yet the real reformatory work done at them was as great as any that the Dean performed.[14]

The first mention of John Lynch in connection with the possibility of elevation to the episcopacy came in 1858 when Archbishop Polding included his name on a list of potential candidates for a diocese at Ipswich or Brisbane in the Moreton Bay district, which was under consideration in Rome. Patrick Moran, in his history of the Australian Church, quoted Polding as recommending Lynch, citing his qualities and achievements: 'He is strictly moral, has done a great deal of good as the head of the total abstinence movement, and has acquired immense influence with all parties, Catholic and Protestant, in the Maitland district ... he possesses considerable means which could be laudably applied to develop the work of religion in Brisbane.'[15] However, Polding's recommendations were put aside by the cardinals of Propaganda Fide and, as would become a pattern in episcopal appointments in Australia, the influence of Archbishop Paul Cullen of Dublin prevailed, with the papal nomination going to James Quinn, a priest of Cullen's archdiocese and His Grace's cousin.

The need for more bishops in the Colony would soon emerge. The diocese of Brisbane was established at the time of the proclamation of the new Colony of Queensland in 1859. When the southern border of the new colony was decided, Armidale, chief town of the New England area, which under one proposal would have been part of Queensland, then emerged as a candidate for a bishop in northern New South Wales. Another

---

13. *Maitland Mercury*, 7 September 1844.
14. *Maitland Mercury*, 19 February 1884.
15. PF Moran, *History of the Australian Church in Australasia* (Sydney, 1896), 59.

motive was also operating, because in 1863 the Anglicans had founded the dioceses of Grafton-Armidale and Goulburn. Whenever Polding heard that an Anglican diocese was to be established he would rush to urge Rome to create a Catholic diocese in the same town or region, hoping to have the Catholic bishop in place before the arrival of the Anglican. Rome responded to Polding's urging and in the same year created the dioceses of Armidale and Goulburn, even though he had favoured Yass as the seat of a Catholic bishop in the south. Maitland, a titular See since 1847, would be given a resident bishop in 1865. In the same year, Bathurst would be raised to the episcopal rank by both the Catholics and Anglicans. Following this growth in dioceses the scramble began to find suitable candidates to occupy the new episcopal thrones. This was a period during which the hopes of priests with a 'mitre in the saddle-bag' rose to new heights. Dean Lynch had missed out on Brisbane, but new opportunities were emerging, and as Dean of Maitland he had extensive experience in both new dioceses in the north.

During his long ministry at Maitland the Dean prided himself on his reputation as a good citizen, avoiding sectarianism and forming his congregation into a sober, law-abiding and respected community. However, there were occasions when he found himself in open, public conflict with the local Protestant clergy. John Lynch had cause to call upon the support of his faithful parishioners in 1860, during a conflict that the newspapers headlined the 'Maitland Riot'. In the heat of the saga the *Freeman's Journal* emphasised the Dean's high reputation for good citizenship: 'Of all Catholics in the country, he has been looked upon as the most liberal by such of our Protestant fellow citizens as know him. He has practically cooperated with Protestants in educational and philanthropic movements much more unreservedly than any other Catholic clergyman in the Archdiocese.'[16]

It all began on 24 February 1860 at a public meeting held in the Baptist Chapel at nearby Hilton on the topic of state aid to religion, with the aim of producing a petition to the parliament advocating the abolition of government stipends for clergy. One of the vocal advocates for this change was a local minister, the Rev William McIntyre of the Free Church of Scotland. As recounted by the *Freeman's Journal* the reverend 'availed himself of that public opportunity to assail our holy Church, in the manner usual to gentlemen of his class and temperature'.[17] The insult was colourfully described in a letter to the *Freeman's Journal* signed 'A Blarney Man, Maitland':

---

16. *Freeman's Journal*, 7 April 1860.
17. *Freeman's Journal*, 4 April 1860.

> [I]t is reported that amongst the speakers was a certain individual named McIntyre, who, in his course to have a dig at Popery, and in a most rabid and frenzied strain (such as might be expected from one originally imported from the back slums of Edinburgh) was pleased to launch forth in bitterest invective against the Roman Catholics (Papists, as he termed them) and their Church, by designating them 'baptized heathens', and saying of their Church that in his opinion 'their Church was no church at all'.[18]

On the following Sundays Dean Lynch in his sermons referred to the insulting comments, refuting and ridiculing McIntyre's arguments, as recounted by the 'Blarney Man':

> The Very Rev. Dean Lynch brought the matter before his congregation on Sunday evening last, in St John's Church, which was crowded almost to suffocation, and in a lecture of one hour and forty minutes (which for brilliancy of thought and elegance of style has seldom, if ever, been surpassed in the colony) laid bare the whole matter, and at the conclusion promised to deliver a series of lectures in St John's, in refutation of Mr McIntyre's unchristian tirade... And now, Mr Editor, as Parson McIntyre has fallen into the safe keeping of Dean Lynch, I shall not say more at present, but simply offer him a friendly advice, which, if he take it, will do him some service—which is to mind his own affairs in future, and let the Papists alone.[19]

McIntyre declined to accept the 'friendly advice' and retaliated in the following weeks by advertising a public lecture entitled, 'The Heathenism of Papacy Proved and Illustrated', to be given on 24 March at the Presbyterian Church in Maitland.

In the face of this provocation Dean Lynch issued an instruction to his congregation to observe the laws and to prove themselves worthy of his teaching by 'acting up to the precepts of Christian charity, peace, and good will'.[20] However, on the evening of the advertised lecture, a large crowd had gathered at the Presbyterian Church, not all with the intention of entering and listening to Rev McIntyre—most of them were the Dean's parishioners, determined to prevent further insults to the faith of their fathers. The 'riot' began with the arrival of the Reverend and his family in their carriage. They were 'assailed by the rash-headed members of the mob', William's reverend brother Alan 'receiving a number of blows with sticks and other implements'.

---

18. *Freeman's Journal*, 17 March 1860.
19. *Freeman's Journal*, 17 March 1860.
20. From the *Northern Times* as quoted in *Freeman's Journal*, 4 April 1860.

Mrs McIntyre and Master McIntyre, sister-in-law and nephew, were 'much terrified at the alarming fracas', she getting her bonnet crushed, and the boy being 'somewhat disagreeably pummelled by a brawny female hand, and knocked into insensibility'. The reverend brothers escaped unharmed, having been advised to flee the scene; 'the advice was not disregarded'.[21] With the meeting cancelled, the triumphant crowd then set about demolishing the church.

Throughout April the 'Maitland Riot' occupied the columns of the Sydney and country newspapers, taking opposing sides in the assigning of responsibility. The *Freeman's Journal* accused the *Sydney Morning Herald* of 'besmattering Dean Lynch's character in an attempt to indemnify the Rev. McIntyre', concluding that 'the *Herald*'s Catholic news is always one-sided—a dull, sickly orange hue suffuses every column of it'.[22] Of Henry Parke's *Empire* the *Freeman* wrote, assiduously refusing to use the word 'riot': '[T]he friends of Dr. Lang and the fanatics of the Presbyterian body, are indispensable to its vitality. We do not care what the writers in the *Empire* think about the Maitland business, because we know they will not give their candid opinion on the provocation which the Catholics of the district received.'[23] The local newspapers, the *Maitland Mercury* and *Northern Times*, were more even-handed in their assessments of the event, finding fault with both the reverend gentlemen and their congregations.

In April 1862 the Dean received his first curate at West Maitland, Andrew Phelan, recently arrived in the Colony. By June, Lynch was manifesting some restlessness. In a letter to Polding he wrote emphasising his long service and loyalty, even in the face of ill health. He stated that when he had left Dublin his exeat was for three years only, but that he had already spent twenty-three years of uninterrupted faithful service in the diocese, even when, on two separate occasions, he had received medical advice to leave Australia and sail back to Ireland.[24] The following month the curate put pen to paper and wrote to the Vicar General, Austin Sheehy, complaining that since his appointment he had been treated as the Dean's mere servant boy, doing minor tasks as he commanded. He proceeded to question the Dean's pastoral style and made a slighting comment on his 'mitre-mania'.

He emphasised that he in no way wished to express any doubts about the Dean's ecclesiastical training or about his personal sanctity, nor about his missionary practice. He added a sting in describing Lynch as a dignitary of the church, but one aspiring to even higher dignities. He concluded by apologising to Sheehy for his strongly worded letter, excusing himself as a

---

21. *Freeman's Journal*, 4 April 1860.
22. *Freeman's Journal*, 7 April 1860.
23. Freeman's Journal, 7 April 1860.
24. Lynch to Polding, 29 June 1862 (SAA archives, Lynch File).

recent arrival having to work in difficult circumstances under the Dean's authority.[25]

In August, Sheehy, in typically blunt fashion, wrote a letter of correction to the Dean, stating that the general direction of the mission belonged to him, but that the second priest was not to be rendered so dependent upon the head of the mission as to render him a mere servant, instead of being a co-operator.[26] For the curate Sheehy had a word of encouragement, emphasising that it was not the Archbishop's wish that he or any other priest should be so dependent upon Dean Lynch as to hinder his usefulness on the mission.[27]

Things moved quickly after this and in September Sheehy wrote to Lynch welcoming his agreement to be appointed Vicar Forane in the New England district, in place of Timothy McCarthy.[28] The new title was considered to be the equivalent of Archpriest, a slight elevation above that of Dean. The *Maitland Mercury* announced the appointment with a mixture of pride in the promotion and regret at the parting:

> His Grace Archbishop Polding has been pleased to promote Dean Lynch in the church, by appointing him Vicar Foran [sic], with spiritual jurisdiction over the members of his church in the districts of New England, Grafton etc. The change in itself will confer additional honour and dignity upon the Dean, but his removal from a district in which he had resided nearly twenty five years will be much regretted by the many friends he has made during his long public career.[29]

Lynch had not been among Polding's recommendations for bishop of Armidale, and when it was revealed that Dean James Bernard Hayes of Geelong had been appointed, rumour quickly followed that Dean Lynch would be on the move:

> It is announced by the papers that we may expect shortly among us the Catholic Bishop of Armidale, and consequent thereon it is currently rumoured that the Very Rev Dean Lynch, who has been some time among us, will he removed at an early date. The departure from among us will be generally regretted, not only as a minister of God, but also as a

---

25. Phelan to Sheehy, July 1862 (SAA archives, Lynch File).
26. Sheehy to Lynch, 1 August 1862 (*Adjutor Deus* II.87).
27. Sheehy to Phelan, 1 August 1862 (*Adjutor Deus* II.87).
28. Sheehy to Lynch, 23 September 1862 (SAA, Lynch file).
29. *Maitland Mercury*, 28 October 1862.

friend to all in the dissemination of improvements, and his willing aid in every project for the advancement of the district.[30]

However, this first attempt at an appointment failed. News of the appointment had brought written complaints from clergy in Australia about the suitability of the nominee. Rome quickly withdrew the nomination after receiving denunciations of Hayes as being too worldly and given to banqueting and attending dances. Also withdrawn was the nomination to Goulburn of James Hanly of Yass, who had been denounced as being poorly educated and addicted to shooting kangaroos.[31] With Armidale continuing without a bishop, the Vicar Forane, unchallenged in authority, remained active in ministering to the district. The year 1866 witnessed the blessing of foundations stones for new permanent churches in Grafton, Tenterfield and Glen Innes. The year ended with high praise from the *Freeman's Journal*: 'It must be a source of gratification to the Dean's friends to see that he still retains the energy which marked his early efforts in Maitland.'[32]

1866 saw another failed attempt to appoint a bishop for Armidale. The latest nominee was a Polding suggestion, John Crookall, a secular priest of the English diocese of Southampton. At the September meeting the cardinals of Propaganda had nominated William Lanigan, the Irish secular missioner at Berrima, as bishop of Goulburn, and Austin Sheehy as auxiliary bishop to Polding. On hearing the news of his nomination, Crookall wrote immediately to Cardinal Barnabo, Prefect of Propaganda, to decline the appointment, offering a litany of excuses, including the clinching argument that he had never ridden a horse. This was backed up with a medical certificate emphasising that his health was not up to long horseback journeys.[33] His excuses were accepted and Armidale remained without a bishop, but retained its Vicar Forane.

In April 1869 the Dean was present at the Provincial Council of the Australian Catholic Church in Melbourne. The *Freeman's Journal* explained for its readers that this was only the second such gathering in Australia, the first having been held 23 years previously in Sydney when there were only three bishops in the Colonies, those of Sydney, Hobart and Adelaide. The work of the Council was summarised: 'There are many questions for the council to consider, especially the operation of the laws relating to marriage, education, and the establishment of churches, besides affairs of discipline.'[34] No sooner was Lynch back in Armidale than it was announced that he

---

30. *Maitland Mercury*, 7 October 1865.
31. Farrell, *A Great Storm Arose*, 28.
32. *Freeman's Journal*, 29 December 1866.
33. Farrell, *A Great Storm Arose,*, 32.
34. *Freeman's Journal*, 24 April 1869.

intended sailing to Europe by the September mail steamer. Having travelled south through the various parishes of the district, and being honoured with the traditional addresses and purses of sovereigns, Lynch arrived in Sydney and sailed on the same steamer which was carrying Archbishop Polding and Bishop Quinn of Brisbane together with their theologians to the Vatican Council in Rome. The aged and ailing Archbishop would turn back after reaching Galle, in Ceylon.

It has been speculated that Lynch's decision to head to Rome was taken in a last attempt to gain appointment as bishop of the still vacant See of Armidale.[35] However, if that were so, then the scheme was thwarted by the realisation that awaiting him in Rome was the freshly consecrated Bishop of Armidale, Timothy O'Mahony, yet another Cullen cousin. The Dean received the consolation prize of being nominated Vicar General of the diocese by O'Mahony until his arrival in Australia, which did not occur until March 1871. No sooner was the Dean back in Armidale than he chaired a huge temperance meeting in August 1870 at which a petition was addressed to the Legislature asking for a reduction in the number of liquor licences in the town.[36] Temperance fever had arrived in New England, and this would turn out to be an unfortunate atmosphere into which the bishop would step the next year.[37]

When Bishop O'Mahony finally arrived in his diocese, Lynch's old characteristic of 'suffering no rival, be it bishop or curate' re-emerged, and within a few months he moved from Armidale to Tenterfield. An item in the *Newcastle Chronicle* in October 1872 referred in glowing terms to the Tenterfield church, so similar in design to the one in which John Lynch would preside in Pyrmont three years later: 'The most imposing structure in Tenterfield appears to be the Roman Catholic Church, which is a stone building, where the Rev Dean Lynch officiates.'[38]

Already rumours were circulating concerning the new bishop's propensity to drink, and these were communicated to Archbishop Polding at the consecration of the Armidale cathedral in February 1872. O'Mahony would later blame the teetotaller Lynch for having advised him to take a little brandy for his stomach's sake soon after his arrival in the stomach-challenging environment of a new climate and a bush diet.[39] Soon after his arrival the bishop had referred to Armidale as 'this miserable place'.[40] A more serious

---

35. Farrell, op cit, 54.
36. *Armidale Express*, 13 August 1870, cited in Farrell, op cit, 65 n22.
37. Farrell, op cit, 65.
38. *Newcastle Chronicle*, 29 October 1872.
39. 'O'Mahony's Replies to the Formal Allegations', March 1876, cited in Farrell op cit, 62 n 4.
40. O'Mahony to Lanigan, 9 November 1871, cited in Dowd, op cit, volume II, 432.

allegation involved that of having fathered a child in Armidale. Although ultimately vindicated on both counts by an investigation commissioned by Propaganda involving the new Coadjutor of Sydney, Archbishop Vaughan, and many other clerics, in 1878 Rome required that the bishop resign and accept appointment as Auxiliary in Toronto, Canada. In his first pastoral letter to the people of his diocese, written from Rome in 1870, O'Mahony had declared that by the placing of the Episcopal ring on his finger at his consecration he was 'wedded forever, through weal and woe, to the church of Armidale'.[41] He could not have anticipated that the woes that would afflict him in Armidale would lead to a permanent separation from his diocese.

In the meantime Dean Lynch had been sent back to Europe by the bishop on a recruiting mission in March 1873. The journey was a success from the point of view of recruitment, and also from the point of view of an increase in the Dean's ecclesiastical dignity, for while in Rome he had been appointed a Papal Chamberlain with the title 'Monsignore'. The *Freeman's Journal* was effusive in its praise and exaggerated in its assessment of the significance of the title:

> On the 29th of June this eminent priest, so widely and so well-known in this colony, was honoured as men worthy of honour deserve to be. For nearly forty years Dean Lynch has been a conspicuous and honoured priest. His name is a household word in the districts where he administered the words and sacraments of truth and grace. His was no partial, no stunted charity. The oldest and most trusted public men of the colony are witnesses of the facts we state. In every special movement he was prominent; in the esteem and affection of those not of his denomination he was honoured and happy. The priest, and emphatically the gentleman, he was the welcome guest of all. The first Australian priest to be made 'Monsignore', next in dignity to a bishop, with the badges and appertenances of his dignity as Pope's chamberlain, Monsignore Lynch, after two visits to Europe in the interests of religion and his diocese, will be welcomed with large and hearty welcome by the Catholic and Protestant people who have known him so well and so long.[42]

Henceforth he would be known as the Very Reverend Monsignor Lynch.

The Monsignor arrived back in Sydney in November 1874 and, still Vicar General of Armidale, headed home. However, on learning of a transfer to Inverell he returned to Sydney for Christmas, only returning north at the end

---

41. 'THE PASTORAL LETTER Of Timothy, by the Grace of God and Favour Of the Apostolic See, Bishop of Armidale, to the Clergy and Faithful of the Diocese of Armidale', *Freeman's Journal*, 17 September 1870.
42. *Freeman's Journal*, 12 September 1874.

of January. When Bishop O'Mahony was preparing to answer a summons to Rome in May 1875, he sought a Sydney priest to act as Administrator of Armidale in his absence. Having rejected the Archbishop's first offer of Timothy McCarthy, too close a friend of John Lynch, he accepted John Kenny. Monsignor Lynch and his many admirers and supporters in the diocese were indignant that as Vicar General he had not been appointed Administrator. Lynch resigned in May and returned to Sydney, to the service of the Archbishop who had welcomed him in 1838. He was quickly assigned to St Mary's temporary cathedral.

The Monsignor was a guest-of-honour at the O'Connell Centenary Banquet held at the Masonic Hall in York Street in August. The Chairman, praising 'the sympathetic and heart-felt utterances of such a practised elocutionist as our reverend friend, Monsignor Lynch', called on him to respond to the toast, 'Ireland and her patriots'. He concluded his speech by calling on the largely Irish Catholic gathering to turn from sectarianism: 'Let them, as Irishmen do honour and credit in this country to the memory of these noble men [Cheers]. To-night he asked them as an Irishman, and as a priest to throw aside all bitter feelings, all of these bitter animosities that had disfigured the fair face of this country [Cheers]. In this free and happy land let them live as brothers [Cheers].'[43]

The Monsignor was appointed to the Pyrmont mission in November 1875 in place of Dean O'Connell. His appointment to the small mission district enabled him to be available for a wider ministry, as had been the case with Eugene Luckie. The Monsignor's renown as a preacher meant that he was in high demand for special occasions. He continued residing at 'Hawthorne', a grand 1844 house in The Glebe, and commuted on horseback to his mission district.

In February 1876 the Monsignor welcomed to St Bede's the Coadjutor Archbishop, Roger Bede Vaughan, to inaugurate in the district the renewed appeal for the completion of St Mary's Cathedral. At the end of March 'the Jubilee was commenced at this City Mission ... and was ably and successfully conducted throughout by the Very Rev Monsignor Lynch, the venerated pastor of the place.'[44] The newspaper report, in its praise of the 'venerated pastor', carried a barely concealed criticism of his mission district:

> The Very Rev Monsignor in his introductory sermons, strenuously directed his efforts towards inducing his people en masse to avail themselves of the benefits of the Jubilee, and having succeeded, it may fairly be said, beyond expectation, he then, in several forcible addresses,

---

43. *Freeman's Journal*, 14 August 1875.
44. *Freeman's Journal*, 1 April 1875.

dwelt on the necessity of perseverance. His second last discourse, delivered on Wednesday evening, was a magnificent appeal on behalf of devotion to the Mother God. The congregation were visibly affected. As a result of his discourses, the numbers who approached the sacraments were such as to astonish those acquainted with the place.[45]

The Mosignor's light pastoral duties at Pyrmont allowed him to be in attendance at most church events in Sydney and beyond—liturgies, lectures, anniversaries. On 21 March 1877, at the funeral of Archbishop John Bede Polding, who had died on 16 March at the Darlinghurst Presbytery, strict precedence was observed and Australia's only *Monsignore* claimed his privileged processional position immediately in front of the bishops. Later in the month he was one of 'a large and brilliant assemblage' in the Great Hall of the University for the Annual Commemoration. The Chancellor announced the vacancy in the Senate membership caused by Polding's death: 'It is with very great regret that I have to announce the loss which the University has sustained by the lamented death of his Grace Archbishop Polding, who, for a period of upwards of twenty-one years was a member of the Senate, and took an active part in the proceedings.'[46] Polding had filled the vacancy resulting from the death of Bishop Charles Davis, who was a foundation fellow of the University Senate. The Benedictine coat of arms, featuring a deer, symbol of the immortal soul, is among those of the original Senators adorning the northern external wall of the Great Hall.

Following Polding's death, Lyndhurst College was closed and the Benedictine community dispersed. The loss of the college chapel which had served the local Glebe Catholic community necessitated the establishment of a mission church in the area. The foundation stone of the church of St James was laid and blessed by the new Archbishop on 7 July 1877. This was the last of the parishes carved out of the district of St Benedict's, and it became the western neighbour to St Bede's. The first parish priest was John Pollard, the assistant priest at St Benedict's, originally an Armidale priest and well known to Monsignor Lynch—they had both found refuge in Sydney.

In September Archbishop Vaughan visited New England as the newly nominated Administrator of the vacant diocese of Armidale. Wisely he had chosen to be accompanied by the ever popular Timothy McCarthy, 'so well and favourably known in this district as one of the earliest pioneers of Catholicity in New England'. Vaughan attempted finally to bring closure to the controversial O'Mahony saga: 'The Archbishop, after High Mass on Sunday, preached to one of the largest congregations ever assembled

---

45. *Freeman's Journal*, 1 April 1875.
46. *Sydney Morning Herald*, 18 June 1877.

within the walls of the Cathedral. Previous to entering on the subject of his discourse, his Grace made some explanation respecting the resignation of the Right Rev. Dr. O'Mahony, the late Bishop of Armidale, and stated that the Pope had accepted the resignation, voluntarily made.'[47]

In November the annual St Bede's school picnic was held at Chowder Bay. During the clergy luncheon the Monsignor's close friend, Père Garavel of Waverley, delivered a 'handsome eulogium' which was applauded by the assembled guests:

> Whilst Father Garavel was responding to the toast of the clergy, he gracefully and happily alluded to a remarkable speech made at the Monsignor's dinner table by the late Archbishop Polding. His Grace, in proposing the Monsignor's health, said that his dear friend the Monsignor had passed so many years with a blameless character, and that his long friendship with him was not marked with a single break. Once his child and subject and now almost a brother, his career was in all respects priestly.[48]

Garavel would have had a twinkle in his eye as he quoted Polding's reference to the Monsignor as 'now almost a brother'—almost a fellow bishop.

By this time Dean McCarthy was in the constant company of John Lynch; he had moved into 'Hawthorne' for convalescence following a break down. Concerning this situation, Patrick Hartigan wrote: '[B]y 1878 it became evident that he was breaking up. The gruelling and the hard years had brought the athlete down, and sadder still, the collapse threatened to be mental as well as physical. He had to leave St Mary's and went to live at 'Hawthorne', Glebe Road, as the guest of Mgr Lynch, his kindly mentor in the happy old New England days. Everybody was deeply touched at the news of his retirement.'[49] A delightful reminiscence was handed down among the clergy of Armidale recalling the fond relationship between the two pioneers of the district. In his 'Notes for the History of the Diocese' Father Michael Foley recorded the story that Timothy McCarthy, 'who was always full of fun and fond of playing tricks', would tease Lynch about his episcopal ambitions by producing a mitre, placing it on Lynch's head, and inviting all the priests present to admire the mitred Dean.[50]

In April Monsignor Lynch organised a meeting to raise funds so that Dean McCarthy could undertake his first journey home to Ireland since his arrival in the Archdiocese 25 years before. One of the many speakers at

---

47. *Maitland Mercury*, 29 September 1877.
48. *Freeman's Journal*, 17 November 1877.
49. Linnane, op cit, 199.
50. Cited in Farrell op cit, 108 n 21.

the meeting 'eulogised the Dean as a man who was respected by all classes and creeds. His allusions to the Dean's declining health were most affecting, and his wishes for his speedy restoration to his wonted strength were re-echoed with applause by the meeting'.[51] The fund-raising was extraordinarily successful and Timothy McCarthy was able to sail from Sydney on Saturday 8 June. Two ferries were needed to accommodate all who wanted to escort the Dean's steamer to the heads. On their return to the Circular Quay, Monsignor Lynch warmly thanked his Pyrmont parishioner, Captain Matthew Byrnes, 'on behalf of the Committee, for the kindness and courtesy which they and their friends had that day received at his hands, and, he added, that it was not the first time that the Catholics of the city had been under obligations of a like kind to Captain Byrnes'.[52]

The following day Monsignor Lynch was farewelled by his Pyrmont parishioners with an address and testimonial. In his last year at St Bede's he had submitted a report on the state of the mission, by completing a questionnaire formulated by the new Archbishop. He described his district as 'rather confined' and 'peculiarly situated'. He estimated that there were 400 Catholics in the district, but that only twenty of these were weekly communicants at the one Sunday Mass. He noted that many of the parishioners still attended Mass and confession at St Benedict's, the mother-church of the area. During the previous year, confirmation of the Pyrmont children, though they had been prepared at St Bede's, had taken place at St Benedict's.[53] Perhaps the development and consolidation of the local Catholic community had been hindered by not having a resident, full-time priest. His next appointment was to Campbelltown where he continued his widespread ministry for the next six years.

In January 1879 he was welcomed to Campbelltown by a gathering of clergy, 'nearly all of them old missionaries, and some of whom travelled a long way to be present'. Their formal address teasingly concluded with the hope that the Monsignor would finally be granted the longed-for mitre: 'We fervently hope that if in the arrangements of Providence you should again remove from amongst us, it may be to a position of eminence, suited to your earliest and persuasive eloquence, and worthy of your distinguished and successful efforts for the glory of the church, the good of your fellow-colonists, and the benefit of mankind in general'.[54]

When news reached Sydney in October 1879 of the death of Timothy McCarthy at his home town in Ireland, a Requiem High Mass was celebrated

---

51. *Freeman's Journal*, 13 April 1878.
52. *Freeman's Journal*, 15 June 1878.
53. 'State of the Mission', Form A, District of Pyrmont, 1878 (SAA, Pyrmont file).
54. *Maitland Mercury and Hunter River General* Advertiser, 28 January 1879 (reprinted from *Catholic Times*, 23 January 1879).

at the pro-Cathedral with the Archbishop presiding. Monsignor Lynch preached the panegyric:

> At the conclusion of the Requiem the Very Rev. Monsignor Lynch proceeded to the pulpit and there delivered a brief but truly eloquent and most impressive panegyric upon the late lamented Dean of St Mary's, in which the Monsignor spoke with such pathos and tenderness that many of the congregation were moved to tears. The rev. gentleman himself, although he spoke with power and fervour, evidently felt the loss of his dear friend and companion very keenly.[55]

From January to March 1880 a series of letters on the 'education question' from 'J T Lynch' was published in the *Sydney Morning Herald*.[56] In June the letters were collected in a brochure under the title, 'Denominational versus Secular Education: letters written by the Right Rev Monsignor Lynch in favour of Denominational Education'. Archbishop Vaughan's newly launched newspaper, *The Express*, welcomed and recommended the publication: 'We cordially congratulate the Right Rev. Monsignor on the ability and zeal which he has displayed, and heartily recommend his work to the perusal of our readers.'[57]

In September 1882 the northern end of the new cathedral was advanced enough in construction to be dedicated by Archbishop Vaughan for public worship. Present was a young visiting priest from Bathurst, Michael Macnamara, who would minister at Pyrmont in 1901. At his golden jubilee of ordination in 1931, he recalled with delight being in the presence of some of the pioneer priests of the Archdiocese, among whom was 'the Right Rev Monsignor Lynch . . . in all the glory of the purple which he made the young priests respect'.[58]

On 10 July 1883, the 67 year-old Monsignor preached at a remarkable gathering in St Patrick's Church, Parramatta. He joined Archdeacon Rigney as the last survivors in New South Wales of the eight pioneer priests who arrived at Sydney aboard the barque *Cecilia* on 15 July 1838—their colleague, Dean John Fitzpatrick of Melbourne, was not able to attend. The Monsignor recalled the names of their deceased companions and reminisced about the progress of the Catholic Church in Australia over 55 years:

---

55. *Freeman's Journal*, 25 October 1879.
56. *Sydney Morning Herald*, 10, 22 & 28 January, 10 & 18 February, 10 & 23 March, 1880.
57. Quoted in *Freeman's Journal*, 3 July 1880.
58. *Freeman's Journal*, March 1931.

These faithful priests maintained the prestige of the Island of Saints, and left a glorious example to their successors. To-day I am carried back in thought to the state of religion in 1838. A vicar-apostolic having jurisdiction over the Australian Continent with only six priests received us; dear old St Mary's was just roofed; the Catholic body had very little influence in the social scale; morality languished through the want of pastors and through the low standard of public opinion; vice stalked unblushingly in high places and permeated all classes. The prospect before the youthful band was gloomy and uninviting. They courageously faced their work. Animated by the example of their apostolic and zealous bishop—the ever to be remembered and revered John Bede Polding—and of those grand Irish priests, Fathers Therry and McEncroe, who in the darkest days of the colony kept the lamp of faith brightly burning—the young missioners helped to lay deep and wide the foundations of the Australian Church, and to-day, thanks be to God, the Church stands in a grand position before the world. When in 1874 I had the privilege of addressing Pius IX of blessed memory, I said, 'Holy Father, religion has progressed wonderfully in Australia. There are now more bishops there than there were priests when I first saw it'. He raised his eyes to heaven, and thanked God.

The Monsignor concluded his sermon: 'Join with me in the wish, that we three, who remain, may walk to the end in the footsteps of our departed colleagues and companions, and that their souls may, through the mercy of God, rest in peace.'[59]

John Thomas Lynch died at Campbelltown on 17 February 1884:

At the Obsequies held at St Mary's the following Tuesday, Dr Murray, of Maitland, presided—the See of Sydney being vacant. Archbishop Vaughan had died in 1883 and Archbishop Moran was not appointed till March 1884. The Mass was sung by Archdeacon Rigney, the only survivor, this side of the Murray, of the band who came in 1838; and priests from every diocese in New South Wales—all of whom have long since been gathered in—stood round the open grave in the old Petersham Cemetery.[60]

His body was laid to rest between the graves of two fellow Pyrmont missioners, Eugene Luckie and John Norbert Quirk. Obituaries appeared in the principal newspapers of city and country, and of the other colonies.

---

59. *Freeman's Journal*, 14 July 1883.
60. Linane & Mecham, *The Men of '38*, 95.

The deceased estate was assessed as in excess of £11,000, not including Irish assets. The will specified that the library of 1600 books was to be relocated at St John's College, which also received a bequest of £1000. The College's Lynch Scholarship was created from this income. Other beneficiaries were the St Mary's Building Fund, St Vincent's Hospital of the Sisters of Charity, the Dioceses of Maitland and Armidale, St Ignatius Jesuit College at Riverview, the Sisters of the Good Samaritan, the Marist Fathers, the Sisters of Mercy, the Poor Sisters (Josephites).[61] The only clergyman to be named in the will, with a bequest of £200, was Père Joseph-Marie Garavel, the incumbent since 1879 at St Bede's, Pyrmont.[62]

---

61. *Freeman's Journal*, 1 March 1884.
62. Mistakenly named as 'Mr N. J. Garavel' in the *Freeman's Journal*, 22 March 1884.

Chapter 10
Zealous French Missionary

Joseph-Marie Garavel succeeded Father Norbert Quirk as priest-in-charge of Pyrmont in August 1879. He was born in Savoy in 1823, when this duchy, though francophone, was part of the Kingdom of Sardinia. The Duchy was ceded to France in 1860 in exchange for a French alliance against the Austrians in the campaign for the unification of the Italian States under the Sardinian-Piedmontese dynasty. Garavel attended the minor seminary in Pont-de-Beauvoisin and the diocesan seminary at Belley, and then transferred to the Missionary Congregation of the Holy Spirit in Paris. He entered a troubled seminary in a troubled France. During his presence at the seminary there were two bloody revolutions in Paris, in February and June 1848. There were barricades around the building and gunfire in the streets—not exactly conducive to the recollected life expected in a seminary. Internally there were troubles as well. There were the standard student complaints about the quality of food, the meanness of the bursar and the severity of superiors, but there were also at this time deep divisions arising from the merger of two different congregations. The seminary superior, described as mentally and emotionally unbalanced under a pious exterior, was in conflict with the Superior General.[1] It is not surprising that deacon Garavel seized an opportunity to escape from this environment when the aristocratic bishop Jean-Baptiste Pompallier, newly appointed Apostolic Administrator of Auckland, visited the Seminary in 1849 looking for volunteers for his mission.

Garavel joined an impressive party of two priests, two deacons, two subdeacons, four clerics in minor orders, four seminarians and eight Irish Sisters of Mercy, which set out from Antwerp in August 1849 on a seven month voyage to New Zealand via Sydney. Pompallier presided over this ship-board seminary, turning the voyage into the equivalent of an academic

---

1. Henry J Koren, *The Spiritans. A History of the Congregation of the Holy Ghost*, (Pittsburgh, 1958), 112–113.

year.[2] In addition to the range of ecclesiastical studies, English and Maori languages were also on the curriculum, though judging from Garavel's later reminiscences not much Maori was learnt.

Eager to set his team to work, the bishop had ordained all candidates to the priesthood within two months of their arrival in Auckland in April 1850. In August Garavel, competent in English but with nothing of the Maori language, was sent south with a native servant to the Waikato region. In Sydney in 1864 he recalled the first encounter with the locals:

> He well remembered the difficulties he was placed in when upon his first arrival in New Zealand and totally ignorant of the language he was sent into the interior. He was met by a multitude of natives all of whom were much concerned at the loss of their old Father his predecessor. He trusted in God but made sure by their manner they were going to kill and eat him ... [T]he chief addressed the assembly in his favour deciding that he was Kapai, that is good-looking, a decision which at once gained the good graces of the people and he soon gained sufficient knowledge of the language to be able to preach and catechise.[3]

A large wooden church was completed in the following year, as well as a presbytery and school. His energy and success attracted a Crown grant of 197 acres in 1857 which he turned into a lucrative farm, producing food for the Auckland market. In five years he had become the outstanding Catholic missionary, a priest of great influence among the Maori. The number of Catholics in his mission area was estimated in 1860 to be 5000.

Open war broke out between the Maori and the British in March 1860 and lasted until March 1861. Government documents revealed Garavel's high status among the Maori and the increasing suspicion regarding his Imperial loyalty among some of the British. As a Frenchman he was not associated by the Maori with the army or Government. However his ability to pass between the Maori and British camps made him the object of suspicion to many settlers and especially the Anglican missionaries. The Anglicans continued to be convinced throughout the conflict that bishop Pompallier and his priests were fomenting rebellion among the Maori. Open conflict again broke out in July 1863 with the British pre-emptive invasion of the Waikato region.

---

2. In a Sydney Archdiocesan questionnaire in 1877 Garavel concluded his answer to the question 'Where did you go through your theological course?' with the response: '8 months at sea' ('State of Mission', Waverley 1877, SAA).
3. *Freeman's Journal*, 14 September 1864.

By the end of 1863 Garavel had been moved to the Bay of Islands, where he resumed his roving ministry among the Maori, while all other Catholic priests were recalled to Auckland because of the ongoing warfare. Complaints to Governor Grey from Protestant clergy about Garavel's activities led Pompallier to recall him too, and then to exile him from New Zealand. 'Persona non grata' with both his bishop and the Governor, he sailed from Auckland to Sydney in August 1864 with the intention of proceeding from there to Europe. In the 1877 Archdiocesan questionnaire he responded to the question 'Date of arrival?': '12 August 1864 after 14 years of hard mission in New Zealand (on vacation!)'.[4]

The *New Zealand Herald* reported on the farewell given by Auckland Catholics: 'We have much pleasure in laying before our readers the following address presented to the Rev. Father Garavel, by the friends of that gentleman, on the occasion of his approaching departure for the mother country, by the *Prince Alfred*.[5] The suddenness of his departure and regret at his leaving were expressed in the address: 'The short notice of your intended departure allowed but a few hours in which to collect the present amount (£70). We are only sorry that there has not been sufficient time to enable us to show, in a far more substantial manner, the high esteem which you are held, and the sincere regret with which your departure is witnessed, not only by your co-religionists, but by the whole community'. In his reply he flattered the largely Irish gathering, an approach that would endear him to the Irish at his next mission in Sydney: 'I esteem the gift the more, knowing that it does not proceed from any national feeling (being myself a foreigner), but from a pure and laudable Catholic spirit, by which the Irish Catholic, when led and rightly instructed, is distinguished through the whole world.'[6]

When Garavel crossed the Tasman to Sydney in August 1864 he was welcomed by Archbishop Polding, who encouraged him to cancel plans to continue to Europe and remain in Sydney. He was appointed to St Mary's Cathedral, where his ministry was less dangerous than in New Zealand. Within a month of arriving he was invited by Archdeacon McEncroe to give a lecture at St Patrick's Hall. The *Freeman's Journal* reported the event as a lecture by 'Father Garavelle, a missionary priest from Savoy, on "Manners and Character of the New Zealanders among whom he lived for a space of fifteen years".[7] He was accompanied by two Maori chiefs who 'appeared in the costumes worn on occasions of state, and imparted additional interest to the lecture by the performance of the war-dance'. Garavel left no doubt as to his sympathies with the Maori land claims:

---

4. 'State of Mission', Waverley 1877, SAA.
5. *New Zealand Herald*, 6 August 1864.
6. *New Zealand Herald*, 1 August 1864.
7. *Freeman's Journal*, 14 September 1864.

The King movement was commenced against the treaty of Waitangi, executed at the Bay of Islands in 1840, between Governor Hobson and some of the chiefs. That treaty transfers the sovereignty over the whole of New Zealand to the British Crown. Now, the Maoris admit the existence of the treaty, but they deny that its provisions are valid; 1st Because they were ignorant of its purpose; 2nd Because the five Northern chiefs had no right to sell what did not belong to them. It was that treaty which led to the war now raging in New Zealand . . . It was impossible not to recognise and admire their courage and patriotism in fighting for their own homes and country against a powerful nation which possesses all kinds of material of war perfected by modern science, and a regular well provided commissariat, while the Maoris are few in numbers, half-naked, half-starving and half-armed with a few old worn out flint guns.

He concluded with the hope that 'justice would be done both to Maori and colonist'.[8]

At the Cathedral, Garavel was regularly assigned to weddings and was especially in demand for sung parts in the grand liturgies. He was the celebrant at High Masses on New Year's Day 1865 at the Cathedral and at St Patrick's for the patronal feast in March. On both occasions the Mass was 'coram episcopo', in the presence of the bishop. On Palm Sunday he took one of the parts in the singing of the Passion. In February the *Freeman's Journal* had announced: 'The new church of St Francis Xavier at the Haymarket has lately been opened for divine service by Father Garavelle, and mass will be celebrated on stated Sundays.'[9] The church was in fact dedicated to St Francis de Sales, a Savoyard like Garavel.

He was on duty the night in June 1865 when Old St Mary's burnt to the ground. He became a hero among the clergy and Catholics of Sydney for his courage in retrieving the contents of the tabernacle from the burning cathedral, as reported in the *Freeman's Journal*:

Father Garavel, who had officiated at Benediction in the Cathedral, was . . . in his room at St Mary's. The Rev Gentleman immediately hastened to the sanctuary of the Cathedral and removed the Blessed Sacrament . . . There was but just time for the Rev Gentleman to accomplish his mission and speed back from the high altar through the Cathedral fast filling with fire and blinding smoke, and seek refuge in the cloisters; and from this moment no attempt could be made to enter the Cathedral, for the purpose of saving anything.[10]

---

8. Freeman's Journal, 14 September 1864
9. *Freeman's Journal*, 18 February 1865.
10. *Freeman's Journal*, 22 July 1865.

Some of his fellow countrymen, sailors from a French man-of-war in Sydney harbour at the time, also played a heroic role in preventing the fire spreading to the adjoining monastery. At the City Coroner's inquest into the fire, Garavel gave his personal testimony:

> The Rev J M Garavel deposed: I am a French priest, and for the last ten months have been attached to St Mary's; I was the officiating clergyman on the 29th of June; after the service Father Woolfrey, the sacristy boys and myself went into the sacristy in procession; when I left the church at twenty-five minutes past 8 o'clock, I saw that everything was right; people were leaving the church; the sacristan was in the church; I was in my room about three-quarters of an hour reading my office, when the housekeeper ran to me saying the church was on fire; it was about a quarter past 9 o'clock; I rushed to the church; I was about five yards from the altar, and could see behind and in front of the altar, I looked up, and saw the fire spreading from the organ gallery towards the sanctuary like waves of fire; the fire was falling in great quantities; I believe that the fire did not originate from charcoal; I believe that the fire was caused by the gas or was the work of a malicious person; the fire fell in flakes from above, and it struck me that some person had put liquid fire in the roof. When I entered the fire was above and the back of the altar was not on fire; the two pillars near the altar at the top were on fire; I believe the fire originated in the organ gallery; a number of persons were in that gallery during the service.[11]

The jury returned an open verdict, but attached some blame to the altar boys who had shown carelessness in the use of the thurible.

In November 1865 Garavel was assigned as priest-in-charge at Newtown, a district to which the southern areas of St Benedict's had been added— Mount Carmel, Cooks River, and Botany—and which extended north across the Parramatta Road to Leichhardt. He temporarily lodged with the Rev Dr John Forrest at St John's College in neighbouring Camperdown. With Forrest he would attend the local 'indignation meeting' in March 1868 following the attempted assassination of Prince Alfred, and each priest would move motions of disgust and abhorrence at the 'late diabolical outrage'.[12] During Garavel's incumbency at Newtown he was responsible for the building of St Joseph's Church, and for churches and schools in other parts of his extensive mission. In recent years his work in the district has been honoured by the naming of the 'Garavel Playground' in Chelmsford St, Newtown.[13]

---

11. *Freeman's Journal*, 5 August 1865.
12. *Sydney Mail*, 28 March 1868.
13. http://www.australiahistoryblog.com/great-reserves-and-public-parks-of-

With the church finally completed and blessed in May 1869, Father Garavel was able to resume his journey to Europe, which had been interrupted by his five years of ministry in Sydney. In his 1877 report to the Archdiocese, under the heading 'Dates of Removal' he included: '12 August 1869 my departure for the Vatican Council.'[14] His visit to Rome coincided with the meeting of the Council, though he was in no way officially involved. At the time of his departure the *Protestant Standard* had commented drily concerning his supposed participation in the Council:

> What humble part Père Garavel, of Newtown, is to perform at Rome during the great gathering, which is expected as the Ecumenical Council of Pio Nono, we do not know, for no less personages than *Bishops* form part of the infallible Council of the Church; but it seems that the said Père is off to meet the Church at Rome, and his parishioners have given him a purse to assist in his expenses of travel.[15]

In Savoy, by then annexed to France, he was reunited with his parents after more than twenty years. While there he was called upon to bless the new chapel at his old college at Pont-de-Beauvoisin.[16]

In the 20 November 1870 edition of the Melbourne *Argus*, his name was mentioned as a passenger on the *Geelong*, which had arrived from Southampton on its way to Sydney. The same edition carried reports of Prussia's crushing victory over the French: 'SURRENDER OF METZ WITH ONE HUNDRED AND FIFTY THOUSAND PRISONERS . . . Bismarck, anticipating the attempt of France eventually at revenge, deems the security of Metz and Strasbourg as German possessions necessary.' There would have been little consolation for Garavel in the news of continuing French naval action against Prussia in the Indian and Pacific Oceans: 'The French ironclad frigate *Belliqueuse* left the Sound on the 13th on a cruise for German vessels, and towards New Caledonia.'[17]

While he was still at sea, papal Rome had fallen to the troops of his former monarch, Vittorio Emmanuele II of the House of Savoy, now King of a unified Italy. In August 1870, after the outbreak of the Franco-Prussian War, Garavel's emperor, Napoleon III, had withdrawn French troops from Rome where they had been protecting the city on behalf of Pope Pius IX. This allowed the Italian army to enter on 20 September, thus ending the

---

sydney-11/, accessed 21 August 2014.
14. 'State of Mission', Waverley 1877, SAA.
15. *Protestant Standard*, 21 August 1869.
16. Information supplied by Professor Christian Sorrel, Universite de Lyon, 4 August 2011.
17. *The Argus*, 21 November 1870.

millennial history of the Papal States, and the formal suspension of the Vatican Council. News of what seemed a disaster to Catholics reached Sydney in November and was acclaimed by the secular press, with the *Sydney Morning Herald* publishing a detailed account, including the text of the proclamation by the conquering General Raffaele Cardorna, which had been placarded throughout the conquered papal city:

> Romans! The excellence of our right and the valour of our arms have in a few hours brought me among you to restore you to liberty. Now your destinies, those of the nation itself, lie in your own hands. Strong by your sufferings, Italy will at last have the glory of solving that great problem which has been so terrible a burden to modern society. Thanks, Romans, also in the name of the army, for the heartfelt reception you have given us! Continue to preserve as you did to this day public order, because without it there is no liberty possible. Romans! The morning of the 20th September, 1870, makes a memorable epoch in history. Rome is again restored, to be now and forever the great capital of a great nation. Long live the King! Long live Italy![18]

A few months after his return to Sydney, Garavel attended a lecture in aid of St Bede's by his friend Dr John Forrest, Rector of St John's College, on the Franco-Prussian War, in which the lecturer's sympathies were decidedly with the defeated French.[19] In July he was celebrant in the presence of Archbishop Polding at the Solemn Dirge and Requiem for the Archbishop of Paris, Georges Darboy, who had been executed by a Communard firing-squad in May 1871.[20]

He had, in the meantime, been appointed to the Waverley mission, which extended towards Botany Bay, where the French explorer La Perouse had established his last encampment before disappearing into the Pacific in 1788. The land route followed by the French sailors, when visiting the British settlement at Port Jackson, was named Frenchman's Road, a path that followed the high ridges, avoiding the coast on one side and the swamps on the other.

In addition to the usual building and maintenance responsibilities—St Charles church, presbytery and school—Garavel inherited the chaplaincy to the Randwick Asylum for Destitute Children. The Asylum had been opened by the Society for the Relief of Destitute Children in 1858 with an initial intake of 89 children, a number which swelled to over 800 in the 1880s. He was soon appointed to membership of the Governing Board which involved

---

18. *Sydney Morning Herald*, 22 November 1870.
19. *Freeman's Journal*, 6 May 1871
20. *Freeman's Journal*, 15 July 1871.

him not only in monthly meetings but in regular sectarian conflicts over the treatment of the Catholic children, especially given that the bigoted John Dunmore Lang was a fellow board member. Some of the conflict concerned the assignment of Catholic children as apprentices to Protestant tradesmen. At least one Catholic apprentice from the Asylum had been assigned to a Catholic employee. That employee was Father Garavel himself. In January 1875 a police document, under the heading 'Deserting Wives and Families, Service, &c', reported: 'A warrant has been issued by the Water Police Bench, for the arrest of James Darby, charged with absconding from his apprenticeship with the Rev Joseph Maria Garavel of Waverley. Darby is about 15 years of age, medium size, red hair, has a habit of winking when speaking; dressed in gray tweed suit, and a small round hat. He was apprenticed from Randwick Asylum.'[21] In March James was arrested, and then discharged. It was not recorded whether he was returned to his indented apprenticeship.[22] In a scoffing pen-picture in the *Protestant Standard*, there was a suggestion that, while at Waverley, Garavel continued the practice of engaging young apprentices: 'We remember also to have seen Father Garavel sitting in his buggy, with his juvenile footman, pushing out to Waverley, looking as rosy and fat as if he fed on good dinners.'[23]

Another Catholic grievance with the practices of the Randwick Asylum was the prohibition on celebrating Mass on the premises, which meant that the children had to trudge along Frenchman's Road to Waverley on Sunday mornings. Relief for the foot-sore Catholic children came with the establishment of the separate mission district of Randwick in 1881: 'Instead of eighty only of the Randwick Institution children who were able to hear Mass at Waverley, a hundred and seventy-five are now in attendance every Sunday at the Holy Sacrifice; all receive religious instructions. In the afternoon all the young people are thoroughly indoctrinated in Butler's Catechism.'[24] Garavel had been recommending the establishment of a separate Randwick mission for some years during his Waverley incumbency, and he especially argued that the land allocated by the Government in 1856 for the Roman Catholics on Chapel Street, off Frenchman's Road, was not central enough, being at the northern end of the district. The eventual site of church, presbytery and school on Avoca Street, was within easy walking distance for the 'Destitute Children'.[25]

In August 1872 there occurred an incident at a house near the Randwick Asylum which led to a court hearing at the Water Police Court, Circular

---

21. *Police Gazette*, 13 January 1875.
22. *Police Gazette*, 3 March 1875.
23. *Protestant Standard*, 20 April 1878.
24. *Freeman's Journal*, 2 April 1881.
25. John F McMahon, *Randwick Catholic Church Centenary* (Kensington, 1985).

Quay. On Wednesday 14 August an ailing Mrs Sarah Richardson of 'Brighton Cottage', Whale Street, later Coogee Bay Road, had asked to be visited by the Catholic priest, whom she had first met at a fund-raising event at Waverley some months before. The following day Father Garavel arrived, and the lady, who was a member of the fashionable St Jude's Anglican parish at Randwick, expressed her wish to become a Catholic. In the dining room Mrs Richardson was reclining on a sofa and after prayers with two servants present, the priest gave some instructions and administered conditional baptism, fearing that Mrs Richardson was close to death. He continued to visit her every day walking or riding from Waverley, twice accompanied by the Archbishop who gave instructions in the Catholic faith and prayed with the lady, until what would be the eventful day of 21 August. When he arrived that morning, though being warned by the servants not to go up to the lady's room, he climbed the stairs and found a Doctor Reginald Reid 'standing like a soldier at the door'. Reid was attending the patient who was suffering from severe attacks of '*delirium tremens* ensuing from what may be called chronic intemperance'.[26] On being told that Mrs Richardson had been very ill all night and was now sleeping, Father Garavel said that he would like to administer the sacrament of extreme unction. The doctor stood his ground and the priest withdrew, only to return that afternoon when he was due to attend the monthly meeting at the nearby Asylum. This time the priest entered the room and found Mrs Richardson in bed attended by the doctor and his wife. There then occurred the incident that would lead to a charge of assault being brought by Doctor Reid against Father Garavel, and a counter charge by Garavel against Reid.

The unfolding of the saga in the evidence given at the ensuing hearings, before a bench of five magistrates, kept journalists busy and entertained readers in Sydney and beyond for several days. Newspaper headlines ranged from 'Extraordinary Case of Assault' to 'THE COOGEE ASSAULT CASE', culminating in the New Zealand *Evening Post*'s 'Clerical Soul-Snatching'.

The incident that led to the charge and counter-charge was the scuffle that took place between doctor and priest around and on the bed of the dying woman on Wednesday 21 August. The hearing began on Thursday of the following week. The two cases, charge and counter-charge, revolved around the question of who struck the first blow. That there was a scuffle was not contested. It began when the doctor objected to the priest waking Mrs Richardson and inviting her to join him in prayer, and when he told him to leave the room, to which the priest had responded: 'Now, I will put you out.' Dr Reid, whose charge was heard first, after announcing that Mrs Richardson had died that morning, deposed: 'He grasped me by the

---

26. *Freeman's Journal*, 7 September 1872.

whisker—the right one—and threw me upon the bed, he falling on top of me. He pulled some of my whisker out. (Witness here produced a quantity of whisker which he stated had been pulled out by defendant.) The bed he threw me on was the patient's, and the patient was in the bed. Since the quantity of whisker has been torn from my face I have had the whisker on the other side shaved to make both sides even.'[27] The fate of the doctor's mutton-chop whiskers would become the focus of the hearings to the great entertainment of journalists and the crowded court room, and indeed the whole of the newspaper-reading public.

Before delivering a verdict on Reid versus Garavel, the Magistrates, on the next day, heard the case of the priest against the doctor. Garavel's version of events was significantly different. His grasp of English idiom let him down in his description of the doctor's location in the bedroom: 'Dr. Reid was standing on my back.' The defendent's counsel, who would make much play with Garavel's malapropisms, interjected: 'Standing on your back?' To which the witness replied: 'I am a foreigner; but you understand.' Whiskers re-entered the saga as Garavel described his reaction to the alleged assault by Reid:

> When I saw that, I turned round and grasped him also by the shoulders and his whiskers, and pinned him against one of the bedposts, at the foot of the bed, still holding him by the long whiskers on the right side. At the moment that I pinned him against the bedpost, the whiskers gave way (Great laughter in court). I then let them (the whiskers) go, still holding him by the shoulders. Both of us then went spinning or waltzing out of the room. We were both pushing one another out.

With the bedroom door closed against them, and with Mrs Reid attending the still insensible Mrs Richardson, a theological discussion ensued between priest and doctor, as recounted by Garavel:

> I began to give him a friendly admonition, by speaking to him quietly. I said, 'You know how guilty you are before God and man for interfering with my ministry, and assaulting me in such a manner.' He said to me, 'You should have asked me.' I said, 'Are you not a doctor?' He said, 'Yes. I am.' 'I am also a doctor,' I said, naming of souls, of course; 'Do I interfere with you, while you administer your medicine? Why should you interfere with me when I administer mine?'

---

27. *Empire*, 30 August 1872.

At the conclusion of the evidence given at the Friday hearing, the day of Mrs Richardson's funeral, the five magistrates withdrew to consider their verdict. They found the 'reverend gentleman' guilty of assault and ordered that he 'pay a fine of 20 shillings, together with 5s 0d, or, in default, to stand committed to gaol for three days'. Reid's attorney interjected: 'I am instructed, Your Worships, to make no application for costs whatever.' The report in the *Empire* concluded on a positive note: 'Father Garavel and Dr Reid shook hands with each other as they left the court.'[28]

In July 1879 Garavel concluded his ministry in the Waverley district, being succeeded by a community of Irish Franciscans. He was warmly farewelled by his congregation with a formal address and a purse of sovereigns:

> Reverend and Dear Father,
> After having been our Priest for upwards of nine years, we, the parishioners of Waverley and Randwick, feel that we would be wanting in gratitude, were we to allow you to leave us without some acknowledgement of our obligations to you. We have ever found you a good shepherd, a fearless priest, the friend of the poor and afflicted, one whose character commanded our respect, and whose kind heart enlisted our affection. Your good work in this parish will, we trust, be evidenced—not by the poor accompanying offering—but by its influence on our daily lives. May He, in whose path you have tried to lead us, bless you in your future mission; and grant you that reward hereafter which He promised to His good and faithful servant.[29]

The future mission was towards the west, in the much smaller district of Pyrmont, even though the *Protestant Standard* had speculated that 'the famous Father Garavel' would be promoted to 'the yet vacant diocese of Armidale'.[30]

One sign of a new approach to ministry at Pyrmont was the new pastor's determination to reside in the district. Of his five predecessors only two had lived in rented premises in Pyrmont. Eugene Luckie had leased the house next to the new church, and Norbert Quirk, during his twelve months, had lived on the other side of Pyrmont Street from the church. Austin Byrne and Daniel O'Connor had resided at Everleigh House near StBenedict's, and John Lynch had commuted from his private residence at The Glebe.

The exercise book serving as sacrament register also served as the church accounts ledger, committee minute book and journal. The impact of the

---

28. *Empire*, 30 August 1872.
29. *Freeman's Journal*, 26 July 1879.
30. *Protestant Standard*, 7 June 1879.

newly resident priest-in-charge was expressed in Garavel's own early brief entries in which his French accent can be detected:

Principal events in Pyrmont since the 25 of August 1879.

Arrival of the Rev J M Garavel on the 25 of August 1879. Jubilee is given to the people by the Rev Muraire, Marist father. The presbytery is at Bowman street. House rented at £5 per month.
(1880)
On the 27th of January Father Garavel removes from Bowman street to Bunn street at the rate of £6.0.0 per month calendar.
On the 29 of July the house next to the church is bought for presbytery and mortgaged for the sum of £625 at the rate of eight per cent payable every quarter at the rate of £12.10.0.
On the 29 August 1880 first communion at ½7 and confirmation at 11 o'clock.
Names of those confirmed: [56 names] ... NB—some adults not on the list.
On the same day the 29th of August 1880 the foundation stone of the addition to the school was laid by His Grace the Archbishop at ½3 o'clock pm before a crowded assembly.[31]

One of the adults on the confirmation list was Captain Matthew Byrnes, who lined up with the boys and girls of the parish to be anointed by the Archbishop.

The first item on Garavel's agenda was to organise the preaching of the jubilee at St Bede's. In February Pope Leo XIII had declared 1879 to be a Jubilee Year in commemoration of the first anniversary of his election.[32] Garavel engaged for the task a very experienced French colleague, the Marist Zépherin Felicien Muraire. Père Muraire had arrived in Sydney without any English in 1864, and had been assigned as assistant priest to Père Claude Marie Joly in the Ryde mission district.[33] He must have had a talent for languages, because he was soon in demand as a preacher. In his obituary it was stated that 'he preached with a zeal and a fire and a depth of feeling that a Lacordaire never surpassed'.[34] Muraire was known

---

31. *Pyrmont Parish: various accounts and historical notes 1870's & 1880's* (SAA, Pyrmont Box).
32. *The Tablet*, 22 February 1879.
33. J Hosie, *Challenge. The Marists in Colonial Australia*, Sydney, 1987, 118-119.
34. *Freeman's Journal*, 7 February 1903. Henri-Dominique Lacordaire (1802-1861) was a French ecclesiastic, preacher, journalist and political activist, who re-established the Dominican Order in post-Revolutionary France.

to have incorporated sermons on the vexed education question into the Jubilee programme. At Father Luckie's Liverpool district in September, 'the eloquent preacher devoted one of his discourses to explaining and enforcing the duties prescribed to Catholics in the now celebrated Pastoral'. It may be presumed that, like all preachers, he was given to repeating his sermons, and that the same theme was trotted out at St Bede's. Perhaps, he was able to say of Pyrmont what he said of Liverpool, that 'it is a gratifying characteristic of this ecclesiastical district that the Public School system has never obtained acceptance amongst the Catholics, notwithstanding all the cajolery and other devices which the influential promoters of that system ... have used to win them over to it'.[35]

The Australian bishops had sought to link the observance of the Jubilee in every parish with the public education controversy. The bishops had met in May 1879 and agreed on issuing a Joint Pastoral Letter on education. Archbishop Vaughan was commissioned to draft the letter and it was issued in June, addressed to 'our dearly beloved brethren and children in Christ, the clergy, secular and regular, and the faithful under our jurisdiction'. It was also intended that it would be read by politicians and by citizens not under the bishops' jurisdiction. The Joint Pastoral attacked Henry Parkes' plans for a free and secular school system. It provocatively asserted that education without religion was 'a system of practical paganism, which leads to corruption of morals and loss of faith, to national effeminacy and to national dishonour'. And in words calculated to cause particular offence, the existing public schools were called 'seedplots of future immorality, infidelity and lawlessness, being calculated to debase the standard of human excellence, and to corrupt the political, social and individual life of future citizens'.[36]

On Sunday 27 July, Archbishop Vaughan announced to the children gathered to receive the sacrament of confirmation in St James church in neighbouring Forest Lodge that he would not be confirming those who were attending Public Schools. With the rejected children in tears, there was a whispered consultation with the pastor, Father John Pollard, and His Grace relented, on the understanding that the offending parents would withdraw their children from those godless schools in the coming week and enrol them at the local Catholic school.[37] It is to be presumed that the 56 children confirmed at Pyrmont in the following year were all dutifully attending St Bede's school.

---

35. *Freeman's Journal*, 6 September 1879.
36. Archbishop and Bishops of N.S.W. Pastoral, *Catholic Education* Sydney, 1879, in P O'Farrell (ed), *Documents in Australian Catholic History*, volume 1, London, 1969, 386-99
37. *Sydney Morning Herald*, 28 July 1879.

The house at number 17 Pyrmont Street, next to the church, was purchased in 1880. The first record of an occupied house on the site is found in the 1858 *Assessment Book*, making it at least ten years older than the church. It was described as being of stone with a slate roof and containing five rooms. The negotiated price was £600, and the house was mortgaged for £625. The names of the trustees were recorded on the title deed: Roger Bede Vaughan, Archbishop, Joseph Marie Garavel, priest, Mat Byrnes, shipowner. Renovations and additions to the front of the house were undertaken to make it suitable as a presbytery. The new presbytery was ready for blessing in March 1881 as announced in the *Freeman's Journal*: 'ST. BEDE'S NEW PRESBYTERY, PYRMONT. On SUNDAY, March 27, at 11 a.m., His GRACE the ARCHBISHOP of Sydney will lay the Foundation stone of St Bede's Presbytery, Pyrmont. The parish is a very poor one, and the Catholics of Sydney are invited to attend and assist in the good work. The Archbishop will deliver an address on the occasion.'[38] An insight into the description of Pyrmont parish as a 'very poor' was found in the January 1880 list of contributions to the St Mary's Building Fund. The St Bede contribution of £7.10.0 was the eighth on the list of the nine parishes listed; £62.10.0 given by Sacred Heart Darlinghurst was the most, and Manly's £5.19.0 the least.[39] The advertised blessing did not take place 'in consequence of the inclement state of the weather' and had to be postponed until after Easter. However, in the meantime, the 'worthy pastor received a number of donations to the building fund from kind friends', including £2 from the Right Rev Monsignor Lynch, £1 from an anonymous clerical friend and three guineas from Captain Byrnes. The *Freeman's Journal* noted that the debt on the purchase and improvements stood at £1000.[40]

After the conclusion of the Easter celebrations, during which, as usual, Père Garavel's fine voice was in great demand at the cathedral liturgies, the blessing of the Pyrmont presbytery was rescheduled and took place on 22 May. Archbishop Vaughan presided in the presence of an estimated 300 parishioners: 'His Grace congratulated the worthy pastor and his parishioners upon having completed the much-needed Presbytery, and referred in highly complimentary terms to Père Garavel's zeal and energy'. The traditional collection harvested more than seventy pounds, with His Grace setting a fine example with a gift of five guineas. Monsignor Lynch donated £2 and the ever-generous Captain Byrnes gave another three guineas. The Archbishop took the opportunity to promote his favourite cause, the building of St Mary's Cathedral, referring 'at considerable length'

---

38. *Freeman's Journal*, 26 March 1881.
39. *Freeman's Journal*, 10 January 1880.
40. *Freeman's Journal*, 2 April 1881.

to the work which he felt was 'as dear to them as to the Catholics in every other part of the archdiocese'. He expressed his confidence that the project would be completed by the beginning of 1882, which would leave him free to devote his energies to a 'still greater work—the cause of Catholic education.'[41]

That 'greater work' had not exactly been neglected by Vaughan. During his earlier visit to Pyrmont in August 1880 he had given a widely reported, rousing and lengthy address at the laying of the foundation stone of the new St Bede's school. The editor of Sydney's short-lived *Echo*, an afternoon newspaper from the stable of the *Sydney Morning Herald*, took up the cudgels against the Archbishop's speech and threw down a challenge. Opinions of the Archbishop which brought cheers from the Catholics of Pyrmont, were treated with alarm in the *Echo* editorial, which was reprinted in the *Goulburn Herald and Chronicle*:

> If anything could ensure that the education question shall be the turning-point of the next general election in the colony, it is such speeches as the one uttered on Sunday by Archbishop Vaughan. He still denounces the common schools of this land, with which his predecessor, Archbishop Polding, was satisfied, as 'death-bringing public schools' ... The whole issue to which the world is coming he describes as follows: 'The catholic church in this colony will be flourishing when some other churches have melted into dissent, and when dissent has well-nigh melted into infidelity. There are but two logical positions: Rome or rationalism, the catholic church or no church at all.' These are the positions assumed by Dr Vaughan on Sunday, and enumerated with his usual vigour of language ... If the catholic hierarchy forbid parents to make use of the common schools because sectarian creeds are not an inseparable part of the state curriculum, that is their fault, not the state's, and by their refusal they give clear evidence that what they want is religious ascendancy, not religious equality. Let Dr Vaughan carry this cry to the hustings, and he will get his answer.[42]

The *Freeman's Journal* which, like the *Sydney Morning Herald*, had published Vaughan's Pyrmont speech in full, was swift to the defence, drawing on a cartoon and satirical poem published the previous week in *Sydney Punch*, headed 'PARKES AMONG THE BISHOPS': 'The cartoon in Saturday's Sydney Punch is capital. Parkes, seated on the Papal throne, robed in Primatial vestments, with tiara on head and crozier in hand, two idiots with censers burning, Bishop Barker [Anglican bishop of Sydney] on his knees

---

41. *Freeman's Journal*, 28 May 1881.
42. *Goulburn Herald and Chronicle*, 1 September 1880.

proceeding to kiss the toe of Parkes, which rests upon the cushion of 'Secular Education', Dr Vaughan looking from behind the scene with amazement.' The last three of the fifteen verses in the accompanying poem contrasted Vaughan's position in the education debate with that of the Anglican bishops:

> Yet, stay! there is one who at least is sincere,
> Who stoops not for favour, who quails not for fear,
> One who follows his path, as the sun follows dawn,
> With unfaltering footsteps—'tis Roger Bede Vaughan,
>
> Small care hath this man for the world or its carks,
> No yearnings towards Mammon, no leanings toward Parkes,
> No will but his Master's, no purpose save one,
> No thought but its final fruition alone.
>
> Be his views what they may, be they narrow or wide,
> No self-seeking motive can turn him aside!
> And those who care little for parson or priest
> Must honour consistent adherence at least.[43]

The outcome of the conflict would be the withdrawal of all government funding for denominational schools in 1882 and the determination of the Catholic bishops to create an independent system of education. The inability of local Catholic communities to fund the salaries of lay teachers led to the recruitment of religious congregations of nuns and brothers to staff parish schools. This happened at St Bede's at the beginning of the school year in 1883 with the coming of the Good Samaritan Sisters, who walked to Pyrmont each day from their convent at the southern end of Pitt Street.

The impact of a resident priest without extra-parochial commitments, apart from command performances at cathedral liturgies, was found in the full programme of parish activities as recorded in the *Catholic Almanac* of 1882:

> PYRMONT. ST BEDE'S.—Mass, Sundays and Holidays of Obligation, at 7.30 and 11am. The hour for Mass on ordinary weekdays is 7am. The Confessional every Saturday at 4pm and whenever application is made. Benediction, etc, every Sunday at 7pm. The children assemble for catechism every Sunday, at 3pm. There is 1 school, under the Minister for Education, with 3 Teachers. Number of pupils, 250. There are about

---

43. *Freeman's Journal*, 4 September 1880.

1000 Catholics in the District. The Rev J M Garavel has charge of the District.

Père Garavel did not neglect the social life of his parishioners. Soon after his arrival he restored the McCarthy tradition of annual picnics and fund-raising concerts. In December 1879 with the assistance of Captain Mat Byrnes and his steamers *Prince* and *Princess*, running regularly across the harbour from Pyrmont and Circular Quay to Chowder Bay, 'taking there a large number of visitors', a most successful day was enjoyed. The usual clerical mates were in attendance—Dwyer, Forrest, Quirk, Fleming, Slattery, McGrath, Fitzpatrick and Pollard—and they were entertained at a sit-down luncheon, 'prepared in splendid style at Thompson's Hotel'. The Imperial brass band had been engaged to provide the music. In June 1883 a concert to raise money for the Presbytery Fund was held in the local public hall and included, in addition to solo vocalists, some quite exotic items: 'Mr G. Bell in his female impersonations showed much talent . . . while in the Terpsichorean art Messrs Delohry, Ratcliffe and Ferguson, Fagan, Fowler and Charles, gave creditable exhibitions.'[44]

Music remained a constant theme in Père Garavel's life; he continued to be regularly in demand for special liturgical celebrations such as Easter at the Cathedral, Solemn High Masses at city churches and Parramatta, All Souls Mass at St Mary's, to name just a few. An insight into Père Garavel's singing prowess was given in the amusing 'Acta Populi' column of 'The Flaneur' in the *Freeman's Journal* in May 1884. In reviewing priestly voices he started on a negative note: 'In Sydney, our good clerical singers can be reckoned on the fingers of a one-armed man.' But he proceeded to identify a few priests of outstanding talent, beginning with the recently deceased Italian Franciscan Ottavio Barsanti, of whom he commented: 'Dr. Barsanti's singing, however, drew me to church much oftener I'm afraid than ever learned sermons did.' Also singled out was Dean Michael Flanagan: 'The sweet Wollongong Warbler declared his vocal efforts were so charming that he could coax sparrows down off the telegraph wires by standing underneath and chanting the *De Profundis*. What he did with the sparrows when he got them down is not recorded, but as his fighting weight is about 18 stone, I presume he stuffed them in a pie and eat them.' But highest praise was reserved for Père Garavel, whose extraordinary talent even Dean Flanagan, now promoted to the city parish of St Peter's Surry Hills, acknowledged: 'Père Garavel is the only singer St Peter's Soggarth Aroon is jealous of, and it is said that the first time the Dean heard the really splendid voice of the gifted Frenchman he

---

44. *Freeman's Journal*, 23 June 1883. Terpsichore was one of the nine Greek muses of dance and chorus.

turned away, and observed, "Never mind—if I can't take the top F as easy as he can, I can sit a buck-jumper with any man that ever came from his blessed country."[45]

In January 1882 Garavel returned to New Zealand after 18 years absence for a well-earned holiday. By a wonderful coincidence, on the Sunday before his arrival in Auckland, the Maori King Tawhiao had recalled Père Garavel with affection in a conversation with one of the priests after Cathedral Vespers. He expressed his regret that missionary activity had almost ceased among the Maori: 'The King referred to an old friend of his, Father Garavel, one of the French priests who were in the Waikato just before the war, and enquired after him, and expressed great regret that he was not again in the colony.'[46] Garavel's return to New Zealand was announced with enthusiasm in the Auckland newspapers: 'Many of our readers will be glad to know that, after an absence of 18 years from Auckland, the Rev. Father Garavel, so well-known both to the European and native population, is at present in this city. The rev. gentleman ... intends visiting Tauranga and Hot Springs for the purpose of recruiting his health. He will officiate at the 11 o'clock Service to-morrow in St Patrick's Cathedral.'[47] The Service was, of course, a *Missa Cantata*.

He was back in Sydney in September 1882, and joined eighty priests of the Archdiocese gathered for the solemn dedication of the northern end of the unfinished St Mary's Cathedral for public worship.[48]

The New Year began for Garavel with attendance at events associated with the Good Samaritan Sisters. As well as welcoming the sisters to begin their teaching at the Pyrmont school, he joined his former parishioners at the opening of the Convent of St Bede in the Newtown parish.[49] A week later he was at the Sisters' Motherhouse in Pitt Street for the clothing of six new novices.[50] A few days later he led parishioners and clerical mates across the harbour for the annual St Bede's picnic at Athol Gardens.[51]

On 23 August Père Garavel was among the clergy called upon to participate in chanting the *Dirge* at the Requiem Mass for Archbishop Vaughan, the news of whose death had arrived in Sydney by cable on the previous Sunday: 'Telegram from Liverpool Station. Archbishop Vaughan died suddenly today. Signed Salford. Dated Saturday, 18th instant. Time,

---

45. *Freeman's Journal*, 31 May 1884; Roger Wynne, 'Dean Flanagan's last years', *Australasian Catholic Record*, 48 (1971): 171–172.
46. *New Zealand Herald*, 2 February 1882.
47. *Auckland Star*, 11 February 1882.
48. *Freeman's Journal*, 15 September 1900.
49. *Freeman's Journal*, 13 January 1883.
50. *Freeman's Journal*, 20 January 1883.
51. *Freeman's Journal*, 20 January 1883.

9.20 p.m.'[52] That Sunday evening, while the bells tolled the death-knoll, the Cathedral Dean solemnly announced to an immense congregation: 'The hand of the Lord is heavy upon us tonight. We are orphans. Our Archbishop, our father, is dead.'[53] 'Salford', the signatory of the telegram from England, was the deceased's brother, Herbert Vaughan, Bishop of Salford, who would later become Cardinal Archbishop of Westminster and clash with the Cardinal Archbishop of Sydney over the financial responsibility for the final resting place of Roger Bede Vaughan.

The black mourning drapes, 'trappings of woe, solemn in the extreme', prepared for the Requiem of Archbishop Vaughan were brought out again in February 1884 to adorn the Cathedral sanctuary for the funeral of John Thomas Lynch: 'Rarely had the Cathedral held so large and distinguished a gathering of priests and dignitaries, and no service within its walls ever exceeded in solemn grandeur the Office and Requiem of last Tuesday.'[54] As already recorded, the Monsignor's will included a bequest of £200 to 'Mr N J Garavel[sic]'.[55]

During his last few years at St Bede's, Garavel's neighbour at the top of the hill at St Bartholomew's Anglican church was Francis Bertie Boyce, rector from 1882 to 1884. In his memoirs published in 1934 Archdeacon Boyce recalled the contrast between his new parish of Pyrmont and those of the far west of New South Wales where he had spent his early years as a minister: 'My work in the parish of Pyrmont brought me into touch with an entirely new set of conditions . . . My new charge was in a closely populated industrial area. It was anything but a wealthy parish, and the financial problems were considerable. The church itself was a handsome stone building, standing in a commanding position.'[56] His reminiscences brought to light the presence of entrenched sectarianism in Pyrmont in those years:

> I remember that, on one occasion, I was surprised to find the church crowded to the doors. The subject of my sermon has been announced as 'A Sunday in Paris,' and the rumour had gone abroad that I intended to deliver a philippic against the Church of Rome. That was not my intention at all, but the mistake had secured me an overflowing audience

---

52. *Freeman's Journal*, 25 August 1883.
53. *Sydney Morning Herald*, 20 August 1883.
54. *Freeman's Journal*, 17 October 1885.
55. *Freeman's Journal*, 22 March 1884.
56. Francis Bertie Boyce, *Fourscore Years and Seven. The memoirs of Archdeacon Boyce, for over sixty years a clergyman of the Church of England in New South Wales* (Sydney, 1934), 71.

which had to listen to a sermon on Sabbath observance, which, I hope, did it good.[57]

There is no record of encounters between the reverend gentlemen of Pyrmont, but Boyce's biographer describes him as an 'advocate of inter-church cooperation', and 'a convinced Evangelical but no narrow "party" man'.[58] From Pyrmont he went to St Paul's, Redfern, where he ministered for 46 years, paralleling the 42 years of incumbency of his Catholic neighbour at St Vincent's, Archdeacon Richard O'Regan, curate at St Bede's from 1889-1890. Both had received their first introduction to the social problems of poverty, inadequate housing and intemperance at Pyrmont, and applied the lessons learnt to their ministry in Redfern.

The improvement in Père Garavel's health brought about by his holiday in New Zealand did not endure, and in March 1884 it was announced that he had been transferred to the district of Petersham with the assistance of an energetic young curate, Father Philip McIntyre, who would become priest-in-charge at Pyrmont in 1899. Before leaving St Bede's it was reported that Père Garavel had 'performed a generous and graceful act' in giving £50 to his successor, Father Edmund Walsh, to be used in further reducing the presbytery debt of £800.[59] His health improved at Petersham and he responded in typical fashion to the challenge of providing churches and schools for Ashfield, Canterbury and Leichhardt. And he was well enough to join the Pyrmont community at the annual Chowder Bay excursion in October 1884.

A minor theme that can be traced in the advertisement columns of the *Sydney Morning Herald* was a certain carelessness in losing his horses. In September 1881 a reward of one pound was offered for the return of 'one bay carriage horse, branded 2 on cheek and MP near shoulder'.[60] Again in February 1885 the same reward was offered for a 'bay horse marked OK on left shoulder and 41 on right'.[61] To lose one horse may be regarded as a misfortune; to lose two looks like carelessness!

On 10 October 1885 the *Freeman's Journal* carried distressing news of Garavel's sudden decline in health, announcing that 'the Very Rev. Dr. Sheridan on Tuesday returned to the city in order to attend to Père Garavel,

---

57. Boyce, *Fourscore Years and Seven*, 71-72.
58. KJ Cable, 'Boyce, Francis Bertie (1844-1931)', *Australian Dictionary of Biography*, National Centre of Biography, Australian National University, http://adb.anu.edu.au/biography/boyce-francis-bertie-5319/text8983, published in hardcopy 1979, accessed online 25 August 2014
59. *Freeman's Journal*, 29 March 1884
60. *Sydney Morning Herald*, 23 September 1885.
61. *Sydney Morning Herald*, 5 February 1885.

whose serious illness caused his friends grave alarm'.[62] On the same day the *Sydney Morning Herald* announced his death: 'October 10, at St Thomas' Presbytery, Petersham, Rev. Joseph M. Garavel, aged 61 years. R. I. P.'[63] The *Freeman's Journal* headlined its obituary: 'Death of Père Garavel. Close of an Heroic Missionary Career'. It lavished high praise on him:

> One who for over twenty years occupied a singular place in the affections of the priests and people of the archdiocese, and of whom—so great was the reverence for his goodness, his gentleness, his charity, and his simplicity—no living soul was ever heard to say a hard word, ended his days in the peace of a holy death, at the close of last week ... In the whole archdiocese no priest ever so completely surrendered himself to duty, or ever manifested a keener pleasure in the performance of kindly acts, however arduous and fatiguing, for his brother priests than poor Père Garavel.[64]

His will specified the following bequests: '£100 to the church at Leichhardt [in the process of erection], £100 to the presbytery at Pyrmont, and £50 each to the Convent of the Good Samaritan, Pitt-street, and St Joseph's Providence.'[65] A newspaper notice in January 1886 announced the final winding up of the estate with the auctioning, at the Petersham presbytery, of 'the whole of the Furniture, a Milch Cow, Poultry &c'.[66] It would seem that the missing nag branded 'OK' had never been recovered.

---

62. *Freeman's Journal*, 10 October 1885.
63. *Sydney Morning Herald*, 10 October 1885
64. *Freeman's Journal*, 17 October 1885.
65. *Freeman's Journal*, 17 October 1885. The St Joseph's Providence Home, Cumberland-street, The Rocks, was described in *the Catholic Almanac* of 1887: 'Home for old and infirm women. There are also a number of destitute children. It is conducted by the Sisters of St Joseph, and supported entirely by public charity.' (*Catholic Almanac 1887*, 88)
66. *Sydney Morning Herald*, 28 January 1886.

Chapter 11
Good Samaritan Sisters

After the withdrawal of all government funding from denominational schools at the end of 1882, the Good Samaritan Sisters consented to Father Garavel's request that they staff the St Bede School, commencing at the beginning of the 1883 school year. Two sisters walked from their Pitt Street convent, where Central Railway Station now stands, to Pyrmont each day. The most direct route would have been along Pitt Street to Market Street, then down Market Street and across the Pyrmont Bridge, up Union Street and then along Pyrmont Street. This routine of Sisters setting out on foot each day to teach in city schools had begun as early as 1861, when the Pitt Street nuns undertook to teach in the nearby Sussex Street Denominational School. In the following year this school was relocated to the site of the Pitt Street Mother House. The walking pattern quickly resumed with commitments accepted at St Mary's Cathedral in 1864 and in 1867 at St John's, Kent Street South. Distant Balmain was too far to walk and required a different solution. In 1864 the first branch teaching community was established there to serve the parish school of St Augustine.

Unlike the Sisters of St Joseph, founded by Mary McKillop in 1866 specifically for the education of poor children, the Sisters of the Good Shepherd, as the Good Samaritans were first called, were founded in 1857 to staff the 'House of the Good Shepherd', a home of refuge for 'penitent women', established by the Sisters of Charity in 1848 at the Carters Barracks in Pitt Street South, opposite Christ Church School.[1] The original group of three Charity Sisters was reduced to one, Scholastica Gibbons, in 1853. Three lay women came forward to assist in this work with the 'frail daughters of Eve'.[2] Sydney's need of the refuge, and the refuge's need for more support, became

---

1. *Catholic Almanac* 1862, 79.
2. Sister de Sales Smith, *The Annals of the Institute of the Sisters of the Good Samaritan from 1857 to 1938* (Sydney, 1939), 2.

clear in an 1856 report submitted to the Government, which had provided the former prison building for accommodation:

> Number of inmates:
> No. admitted in 1855: 84
> Number in the House on 31st December 1855: 40
> How supported: by the work etc, of the Penitents, and by Voluntary subscriptions.
> Remarks: In 1855, 84 were admitted to the House, of whom 17 were sent to situations,
> 17 taken by their friends, 3 sent to the infirmary and seven left before their Probation.
> 45 voluntary applicants were refused admission for want of rooms and means.[3]

To place the refuge on a more secure footing Archbishop Polding decided to establish a Sydney version of the Order of Our Lady of Charity of the Good Shepherd, founded at Angers in France in 1835. The French Order had been established 'to labor for the conversion of fallen women and girls needing refuge from the temptation of the world', as expressed in a fourth vow.[4] In July 1857 the first five sisters of the Sydney foundation were clothed with the habit and began their novitiate formation in the rules and spirit of the new Institute under the guidance of John Bede Polding, an experienced former novice Master at his home monastery, the Benedictine Priory of Downside. Bernard Ullathorne had been one of Polding's novices in 1825 and in his autobiography he wrote affectionately of the Master and his qualities: 'Father Polding was our prefect and our director, and in him I found all that my soul needed . . . [He] was a man of warm and tender heart, with true religious instincts, who formed our souls to detachment and the spirit of the Benedictine Rule with unction and genuine solicitude. We were devoutly attached to him.'[5] In 1875 Ullathorne, by then bishop of Birmingham, gathered with three of his fellow former novices to celebrate the golden anniversary of their novitiate, sent an affectionate memorial of thanksgiving to their old Novice Master in Sydney: 'Besides the vivid image of our old master that is imprinted on our mind, and the affectionate remembrance of his spirit as it dwells in our consciousness, we could have

---

3. McEncroe to Colonial Secretary, 5 January 1856, (*Adjutor Deus* I.310).
4. AM Clarke, *Life of Reverend Mother Mary of St Euphrasia Pelletier, First Superior General of the Congregation of Our Lady of Charity of the Good Shepherd of Angers* (London, 1895), 48.
5. William Bernard Ullathorne, *From cabin-boy to Archbishop: the autobiography of Archbishop Ullathorne* (London, 1941), 35–36.

wished that in person he might have presided over our spiritual festival, and that we might have heard the accent of that voice, which first awakened in us the knowledge and love of the religious life.[6] The same gentle formation in the Benedictine way of life was available to the Good Shepherd novices in Sydney thirty years later. Mother Scholastica, known in civil documents as 'Mrs Gibbons', was the superior of the community, though she remained officially a member of the Sisters of Charity.

The first expansion beyond Pitt Street came soon after the formal profession of vows in July 1858, when the Sisters were asked to take over the work at the Parramatta Catholic Orphanage. Three of the new sisters moved west, and the Congregation conducted the Orphanage, funded by the Government, until 1886. The *Catholic Almanac* of 1862 published an appeal for the support of the Sisters, giving a thorough description of their apostolate and their needs at Pitt Street:

> HOUSE OF THE GOOD SHEPHERD, PITT STREET SOUTH.
> Under the patronage of His Grace the Archbishop. Superioress: Mrs Gibbons.
> The attention of the benevolent public is earnestly solicited to the claims of this Institution. Nowhere is a more blessed work of charity to be found, and nowhere has Christianity been more successful in its contest with sin and misery. It is now twelve years since, in this House of the Good Shepherd, religious Ladies who, for the love of the Saviour of the lost, devote themselves, strength, and health, and life, to reclaim and console the most unhappy of their sex, began their task, and God has richly rewarded them. Out of more than nine hundred penitents who, during these twelve years, have been received into the House, upwards of eight hundred have left it rescued and reformed. So much reparation has God's blessing wrought in this dreary waste of ruin, wrought by human vice. There are in the House at present sixty-four, and the present appeal is made in order to secure, and, if possible, to increase the means of support. It is perhaps, not generally known, that the Institution is self-supporting. There is no Government aid, no private endowment. Everything is provided by the labour of the penitents themselves, assisted in a very uncertain and scanty degree by some rare private contributions. The labour consists of washing, mangling and sewing. The public are solicited to supply additional labour, in the shape of plain sewing, tailoring and mangling especially. Fine sewing is also done, but the majority have not

---

6. Moran, *History*, 177.

the necessary skill. An effort must now be made to establish some little reliable assistance in the way of charitable contributions.[7]

The move into education, begun in 1861, was motivated by the need for teachers in the schools of the Catholic Denominational System, and by the need of the Congregation for a secure flow of income in addition to benefactions and money from the work of the penitents. Teachers in denominational schools were in receipt of Government stipends until 1882.

A change of name for the Congregation was explained in a letter from Archbishop Polding to Mother Scholastica, sent from Rome in April 1866, where Polding was seeking approval for the Constitutions of the new Institute. He said that he had received advice from the Cardinal Prefect that 'to prevent unseemly jealousy, and apparent encroachment upon the Congregation now extensively spread throughout Europe, it would be well, it would be advisable, to take another name'. Indeed four nuns from the Angers mother-house of 'Les Soeurs du Bon Pasteur' had already arrived in Australia in 1863, in Melbourne, where the generous grant given by the Victorian Colonial Government for their work—'24 acres of excellent ground, two large houses, space and means for every purpose'—occasioned a sigh from Polding: 'I only wish our Government was as equally liberal.'[8] Without revealing the new name he had in mind for his Sydney group, he assured Mother Scholastica and her community that 'you will all be delighted, and find in the very name the nature and extent of your duties'.[9] He himself used the new name in his report to Cardinal Barnabo in August 1866, and proudly provided some statistics about the flourishing congregation:

> There is also the Society of Religious Women or Sisters of the Good Samaritan. They are 30 in number with two Novices and five Postulants. These have care of the institution for the reform of the fallen of their own sex and also of the schools for Orphans containing some 230 to 300 children and in the schools they have from 750 to 800 pupils or students ... The blessing of God descended on this little Institute ... From their foundation up to this present time they have been, under the gentle Providence of God, instruments that have returned to Society more than 800 of those fallen women.[10]

---

7. *Catholic Almanac* 1862, 79.
8. Polding to M. Scholastica, 2 December 1865 (Polding Letters III.198).
9. Polding to M. Scholastica, 21 April 1866 (Polding Letters III.211).
10. 'Report of the State of Religion in the Diocese of Sydney given by the Archbishop, Monsignor Polding', 19 August 1866 (Polding Letters III.243-245).

When Polding arrived back in Sydney in August 1867 he was carrying the papally approved 'Rules of the Sisters of the Good Samaritan of the Order of St Benedict'. It took many years for the new name to replace the old. The *Catholic Directory* of 1876 was still listing 'Sisters of the Good Shepherd'.[11] As late as May 1879 the *Freeman's Journal* was still referring to the Good Samaritans at Balmain as 'Sisters of the Good Shepherd'.[12] Even within the Institute there seemed to have been some initial resistance to the change—in 1869 Sister Catherine Egan, one of Pyrmont's early teachers, made profession as a Sister of the Good Shepherd.[13] The *Annals* commented that 'gradually, the old order changed yielding place to the new, the old generation passed away, and to the new one, the title of the *Good Samaritan* is as familiar as was that of the *Good Shepherd* to their parents'.[14]

In 1883, as well as the two sisters setting out for Pyrmont from Pitt Street each morning, there were groups of nuns heading to St Peter's at Surry Hills, to St Benedict's and to St James at Forest Lodge. The *Catholic Directory* for 1884 detailed the work of education carried out at and from the Pitt Street convent:

> Sisters of the Good Samaritan, St Scholastica's, Pitt-street, South, Sydney:
> Mother Foundress, Rev. Mother Mary Scholastica (Gibbons);
> Superior-General: Rev. Mother Mary Magdalene (Adamson).
> Number of Community, 30; average number of Penitents, 74.
> There are six schools under the care of the Sisters:
> one a High School, number of pupils, 70;
> another attached to the Convent, average number of pupils, 400;
> a third at Forest Lodge, average number of pupils, 350;
> a fourth at St Peter's, Surry Hills, number of pupils, 350;
> a fifth at St Benedict's, average number of pupils, 500;
> and a sixth, St Bede's, Pyrmont, average number of pupils, 200.[15]

Additional branch convents had been established at the Sydney suburbs of Balmain, Five Dock, Manly, Rozelle, Newtown and in the country towns of Braidwood, Wollongong, Windsor, Campbelltown, Queanbeyan and Moruya. In all these localities the Sisters had established High Schools as well as staffing parish primary schools.

---

11. *Catholic Almanac* 1876, p 69.
12. *Freeman's Journal*, 10 May 1879.
13. Obituary, GS Archives.
14. Sister de Sales Smith, *The Annals of the Institute of the Sisters of the Good Samaritan from 1857 to1938*, Sydney 1939, 29.
15. *Catholic Almanac 1884*.

The *Sands Directory*, which listed the occupiers of properties against addresses, in its editions from 1884 to 1889 listed the names of teaching Sisters against 'St Bede's school (R.C.), Pyrmont Street'. Presuming the names listed were for the previous year, the sequence of Pyrmont appointments was as follows:

1883: Sister Clement O'Donovan
1884: Sister Laurentia Maher
1885: Sister Bede Kelleher
1886-87: Sister Catherine Egan and Sister Alexius
1888: Sister Catherine Egan and Sister Ligouri Howard, (misspelt 'Legory' in *Sands*)

It may be presumed that at least two sisters were always assigned to Pyrmont. When only one name appeared in *Sands* the Sister was designated 'head teacher'.

The six women listed provide interesting insights into the teaching apostolate of the Good Samaritans. The pattern of formation was that, after receiving the habit and a period of novitiate, a sister would be invited to make profession of vows and a life commitment. During the novitiate, ranging from eighteen months to two and a half years, the novices, wearing white veils and not yet the black, would also participate in the work of the Institute, either assisting in the Refuge or teaching in one of the schools. The Pyrmont nuns reflected this pattern. Cork born Sister Clement O'Donovan, the first 'head teacher' at Pyrmont had entered the convent in February 1882 at the age of 27, and made profession in October 1884. During her time at St Bede's school Sister Clement was a Novice, but perhaps not a novice at teaching. It is possible, indeed likely, that she had been a lay teacher at a denominational school before joining the Good Samaritans. This was certainly the case with Sister Catherine Egan, at Pyrmont from 1886, as stated in the *Annals*: 'When in 1867 Sister Catherine became a member of the Institute, the Kent Street School, over which she presided as a secular teacher, passed into the hands of the Community.' As a Novice she remained in charge of St John's School, Kent Street South, walking to school each day from the Pitt Street Convent with her Good Samaritan assistant teacher.[16]

Sister Laurentia Maher was only eighteen when she commenced at St Bede's School in 1884, having entered the convent in 1882. Born at Menangle she had a sister and four cousins in the Institute. Her talents as a teacher were soon recognised, as recalled in her obituary: 'Sr Laurentia made her first vows of perseverance, conversion of life and obedience according to

---

16. *Annals*, 21.

the Rule of St Benedict in the presence of Archbishop Moran and Mother M Magdalen Adamson on 8 April 1885. Although Sister was very young, it says something of her competence and the regard that her superiors had for her that in the same year as she was professed Sr Laurentia was appointed principal of St Mary's School at Manly.[17] She was a pioneer sister at Marrickville in 1887 and at Charters Towers in 1900 with Sister Matthew Byrnes, a Pyrmont vocation.

In 1885 St Bede's gained a senior nun in Sister Bede Kelleher, who had been born in Hyderabad, India, and sailed to Australia as a child with her family in 1854. With Sister Elizabeth O'Toole, the first Pyrmont vocation, she was one of the pioneer sisters at the Manly Industrial School in 1881. Most of her fifty years as a Good Samaritan sister were spent in caring for the penitent women at the Pitt Street Refuge and at Tempe.[18] She died at Rosebank in July 1915.

In 1886 St Bede's gained the experienced Sister Catherine Egan, who had established the schools at Balmain West (Rozelle) in 1880 and Newtown in 1883. She was assisted at Pyrmont in 1886 and 1887 by Tipperary born Novice, Sister Alexius O'Flaherty.[19] During 1888 Sister Ligouri Howard accompanied Sister Catherine on the daily walk to and from St Bede's. She was born at Merrygoen in the Dubbo region. She was a niece of Father Paul Fitzgerald who as a boy postulant had joined the Benedictines at St Mary's in 1852, and as a priest had established the Kent Street South Mission, near Market Street, where the Good Samaritans were teaching from 1867, and where in 1868 he built the church of St John, which is now the Genesian Theatre. Father Fitzgerald's last appointment was at St Joseph's, Newtown, where he ministered for twenty-one years, dying in 1893. At Sister Ligouri's Diamond Jubilee celebration in 1947 past pupils gathered at Rosebank Convent, where she was in retirement; they flocked from far and near— Pyrmont, Balmain, Haymarket, Chippendale, Moruya, Forest Lodge, Five Dock, Wollongong, Queanbeyan, Manly, Rozelle and Richmond. She died in 1960 at the age of 91 and in the 73rd year of her life in vows.[20]

Twenty years before the commencement of the daily journey of the Good Samaritans from Pitt Street to Pyrmont in 1883, one young Pyrmont woman made a one-way journey from her home to the Mother Convent. In 1862 the 19-year-old Hannah O'Toole, eldest child of Patrick and Teresa of Way Terrace, entered the novitiate, receiving the name Elizabeth, and made profession of vows on 31 March 1864. Sister Elizabeth O'Toole had a remarkable life of service as a Good Samaritan. She was among the

---

17. Obituary, Good Samaritan Archives.
18. Obituary, Good Samaritan Archives.
19. Obituary, Good Samaritan Archives.
20. Obituary, Good Samaritan Archives.

first nuns who taught at St Mary's Cathedral School during 1864. The school was set up under the Cathedral in rooms which had been part of the Benedictine monastery before its transfer to Lyndhurst in The Glebe. All school equipment was lost in the devastating fire of 1865, after which the school was relocated to premises in Macquarie Street.[21] After the fire Sister Elizabeth was assigned to the short-lived Good Samaritan convent at Maitland. The new bishop, James Murray, before leaving Ireland for his new diocese, had arranged that Dominican Sisters would undertake teaching in the Maitland school, and before their arrival in 1867, the Good Samaritans had been required to vacate their convent and school. Some ill-feeling regarding their eviction after just two years in Maitland was recorded in the journal of the Dominicans' journey from Ireland and arrival in Australia. Their guided tour around Sydney brought them up the Parramatta River where they visited the Benedictine nuns at Subiaco and the Good Samaritans at the Orphanage. The diarist recorded their welcome at the Parramatta convent: 'Arrived at the convent of the Good Shepherd, Parramatta, a branch from Sydney. We were introduced to Reverend Mother, an Englishwoman, who very humouredly, asked were we coming to see the nuns we had turned out, for 3 or 4 of the Maitland Sisters are here in charge of the orphanage.'[22] Sister Elizabeth O'Toole was one of those 'turned out' Maitland nuns. The Dominicans referred to the Good Shepherd Sisters as 'active Benedictines'.[23] Concerning Sydney's monks they adopted the irony of their Irish patron, Bishop Murray of Maitland: 'It seems the Benedictines are not favourites of the Australians, although apparently favoured in every way by heaven.'[24]

Sister Elizabeth O'Toole remained at the Orphanage until 1881. Her father had died at Pyrmont in 1879 and her mother the following year. From Parramatta she was transferred to Manly to establish a new foundation to meet a newly perceived need. In 1881 the Good Samaritan Sisters purchased from William Bede Dalley a fifty-acre property and family residence near the lagoon at Manly with the intention of providing a home for older girls without parents or relatives to care for them. Experience had shown that it was not suitable to accommodate young girls brought in from the streets at the Pitt Street facility; a separate home was needed for them. The Good Samaritans established accommodation and an Industrial School for the girls' vocational training on the Manly property. The *Annals* recorded the impact of the work of Sister Elizabeth and two of her community, both of whom would spend time teaching at Pyrmont:

---

21. Smith, *Annals of the Institute of the Sisters of the Good Samaritan*, 22.
22. Elizabeth Hellwig (ed), *An Account of a Journey from Kingstown, Ireland, to Maitland, Australia in 1867 during the Age of Sail* (Strathfield, 2001), 106–107.
23. Hellwig, *An Account of a Journey from Kingstown*, 103..
24. Hellwig, *An Account of a Journey from Kingstown*, 105.

To Mother Mary Elizabeth O'Toole was entrusted the charge of the great undertaking. Her first assistants were Sister Mary Bede Kelleher and Sister Mary Barbara Furber, under whose management, based on divine charity, the hitherto neglected girls became, by degrees, susceptible to the best impressions and silently led to good. Formed to tidy habits, gentleness, order and strict cleanliness, instructed in domestic affairs—laundry work, cooking and needlework—many, who would have otherwise gone to swell the pauper population, became thoroughly efficient and capable of earning an honest livelihood.[25]

After the forced closure of the Parramatta orphanage in 1886, boys and girls for whom homes could not be found were transferred to Manly, and additions were built to accommodate them. In 1884 some of the community began conducting the parish school; one of those nuns was Sister Laurentia Maher, who would later teach at St Bede's. Sister Elizabeth O'Toole's leadership was remembered by her community: 'The main source of income was the laundry and Sr. M. Elizabeth rose at 4 a.m. each morning to light the fires. She worked in the laundry until she joined the other Sisters at prayer at 5.30am. She superintended the High School (also conducted on the premises for a time), the children's dormitories, the kitchen and the whole household. She saw to the sorting of the linen as it arrived at the laundry and checked it before it was sent off again.' Her sisters marvelled 'at her wonderful powers of endurance, her business capacity, her love of fine things for the chapel, her interest in good reading.'[26] The orphanage was relocated to Narellan in 1910.

In 1893 Elizabeth O'Toole was again called on to pioneer a new foundation, this time at Nowra, south of Sydney, where the sisters took over the parish school. The following year she was heading further south to Braidwood where, for the next ten years, she was superior of the community teaching at St Bede's parish school. She retired to the Rosebank convent at Five Dock and died there in1917 at the age of 75, and in her 55th year of religious life.

Another young Pyrmont parishioner joined the Good Samaritans in 1894. Catherine (Kate) Byrnes, born in 1875, was the daughter of Captain and Mrs Matthew Byrnes. The family name was variously given as Byrnes or Byrne, even in official civic and ecclesiastical documents as well as in newspaper articles.

Kate's father was born at the coastal town of Kingstown (now Dun Laoghaire) near Dublin in 1839. From boyhood he undertook a seafaring life, beginning with the coastal trade on the Irish Sea. There followed more

---

25. *Annals*, 90.
26. 'Hannah O'Toole', Good Samaritan Archives.

adventurous journeys across the Atlantic and around Cape Horn into the Pacific Ocean. He finally arrived in Sydney in 1862. He was initially engaged along the Pacific Islands trading routes before switching his attention to Port Jackson steam ferries.

In 1865 Matthew married Mary Cosgrove and they lived at Balmain and had two children, Mary born in 1866 and Matthew in 1868. He was widowed in 1868 as announced in the *Sydney Morning Herald*: 'The Friends of Mr MATTHEW BYRNES are respectfully invited to attend the Funeral of his deceased and beloved Wife, MARY, to move from his residence, Smith-street, Balmain, and proceed to the new Catholic Cemetery, Balmain.'[27] An accompanying funeral notice identified Matthew as a member of the Oddfellows, like his West-Shore neighbour at Pyrmont, Patrick O'Toole: 'OOFMU—LOYAL BALMAIN LODGE, No 4329—The Officers and Brothers of the above lodge, together with the officers and brethren of the various lodges in the Sydney District, are hereby respectfully invited to attend the funeral of the wife of Brother MATTHEW BYRNES, THIS DAY, Saturday the 12th instant. Brethren to meet at the Oddfellows' Hall at 2 o'clock sharp.'[28]

In 1870 Captain Byrnes was the initiator of a meeting of sixty mariners at Greville's Commercial Rooms to form an association of shipowners. The aim was achieved with the passing of the following resolution: 'That an association be now formed, to be called the New South Wales Shipowners' Association, having for its objects the protection of mutual interests, and the adoption of measures to obtain the redress of grievances in connection with the colonial mercantile marine.'[29]

In the same year he married Catherine McCarthy, with whom he had two daughters, Annie and Catherine, born in 1872 and 1875 respectively. In 1878 the family relocated to Church Street in Pyrmont when Matthew purchased the Pyrmont steam ferries, which operated across Darling Harbour between the John Street and the Lime Street wharves. He expanded his business by initiating ferry connections to Glebe and Balmain in 1881, for which he was congratulated for supplying 'communication to the centre of the city by water.'[30] He also began hiring out the steamers of his growing fleet for harbour excursions, as advertised in the *Freeman's Journal*: 'To Picnic Parties, &c. MR M BYRNES of the Pyrmont Ferry, wishes to intimate to persons getting up Picnics and Excursions that he has added a new steamer (the Princess), and the steam launch Fawn, to his fleet of steamers, and is now prepared to supply large or small picnic parties with boats at Reasonable Rates. Address:

---

27. *Sydney Morning Herald*, 12 December 1868.
28. Sydney Morning Herald, 12 December 1868.
29. *Newcastle Chronicle*, 1 September 1870.
30. *Freeman's Journal*, 30 April 1881.

M BYRNES, Lime-street Wharf, Sydney.'[31] He also entered into competition with the Pyrmont Bridge Company, undercutting the weekly pedestrian toll of two shillings and sixpence by eighteen pence, achieving great success.

Captain Mat received regular praise in the *Freeman's Journal* for his generous free service in ferrying picnickers to and from Catholic events at the various coves on the northern shore of the harbour. The newspaper summarised this commitment in its obituary notice in 1895: 'It was in connection with the school and confraternity picnics that Captain Mat was best known to the Catholic community. For more than 18 years he enjoyed a monopoly in this respect. Thousands of children have been under his care, and many more thousands of grown-up people, yet there is scarcely a record of any accident. He was always careful and courteous, a little boisterous, perhaps, but ever overflowing with fun and Cap'n-Cuttle-like good nature.'[32] His steamers were always available for the annual St Bede's school picnic, ferrying children, parents and clergy to and from the much favoured Chowder Bay.

He was particularly in demand for the grand occasions involving the arrival and departure of church dignitaries. In June 1878 he provided the steamers *Fawn* and *Breadalbane* free of charge so that the friends of the much-loved Timothy McCarthy could escort him down the harbour and through the Heads on his return to Ireland. When Archbishop Vaughan was farewelled in April 1883 the clergy clambered on board the captain's steamer to accompany His Grace to the Heads, on a voyage to Europe from which he would not return. It was later commented: 'On this occasion the captain had 94, out of 104 Roman Catholic priests then in New South Wales, on board his steamer, and, to use his own words, they formed "the most valuable cargo he ever had on board". Captain Byrnes was the last man in Sydney to shake hands with the Archbishop.'[33]

As well as directing the fleet at Archbishop Moran's arrival in September 1884, he was also 'master of Port Jackson' for his departure, summoned to Rome in May 1885, and for his return as Cardinal. Whenever a prelate from one of the other colonies visited Sydney, it was the Captain who was entrusted with showing him over the harbour. In 1888 the Cardinal chartered one of the captain's steamers to ferry the clerical participants at the Diocesan Synod across the harbour to Manly for an informal celebration of the completion of the St Patrick's Ecclesiastical Seminary: 'In a trifle over half an hour Capt Mat Byrnes, who seems to exercise a sort of Lord-high-admiralship over all the ecclesiastical marine movements in or about our harbour, had his party

---

31. *Freeman's Journal*, 12 October 1878.
32. *Freeman's Journal*, 16 March 1895. Captain Edward Cuttle is the endearingly eccentric mariner in Charles Dickens *Dombey and Son* (1846).
33. Digby, *Australian Men of Mark*.

safely landed near the estate at Manly on which the Cardinal's palace and the seminary have been erected.'[34]

In July 1880 Captain Byrnes, 'shipowner', stepped forward to join the Archbishop and priest-in-charge as Archdiocesan trustees for the house next to the church purchased as the presbytery by Father Garavel. At this stage Matthew and Catherine Byrnes and their four children were neighbours to Father Garavel; they were living at 31 Pyrmont Street, on the other side of the church and school from the presbytery. In August his penny ferries were on Sunday duty 'every five minutes' to carry visitors across the harbour for the laying of the foundation stone of the new school at which the Archbishop would give a keynote speech on the education question. In February 1881 Matthew had received news of his mother's death in Ireland, and he and his sister placed a simple notice in the newspaper: 'BYRNES. October 10, 1880 at her residence Balthenglass, County of Wicklow, Ireland, Julia Byrnes, aged 84, beloved mother of Matthew Byrnes, proprietor of Pyrmont steamers, and Mrs Durning, Balmain. RIP'[35]

The Captain's name was often to be found on subscription lists for church projects and in December 1880, in a lengthy recital of the names of donors and their gifts to the St Mary's Cathedral fund, Archbishop Vaughan came to that of Matthew Byrnes: 'I will now read out the few shillings that I have collected during the past month (Cheers and laughter) . . . Captain Byrnes, of Pyrmont, known to all here I suppose, and an energetic man in his profession, promised me something some time ago, and he sent me, so as to be in time for the meeting, these three one-pound notes, which I hand over to Mr Hollingdale (Cheers).'[36]

The Captain's steamers were always available for the St Patrick's Day celebrations, as in March 1880 when the Hibernian Australian Catholic Benefit Society organised an excursion to Chowder Bay. The proceeds were to go to the Irish Famine Relief Fund. Captain Byrne's favourite steamers *Prince*, *Princess*, and *Prince of Wales*, and the huge and powerful steamer *Breadalbane* were engaged for the day, and the Imperial Brass Band of 20 performers, and an Irish Piper and Violinist were to be on hand for Irish National Jig Dancing.[37] The theme of the day was: 'Faithful to the Old Land, True unto the New.'[38] In November 1889 the Captain's Irish national credentials were on display when he volunteered the *Princess*, with a green flag flying at the mast-head, to ferry across the harbour John Dillon MP and other delegates of the Irish Parliamentary Party who were visiting from

---

34. *Freeman's Journal*, 28 April 1888.
35. *Evening News*, 16 February 1881.
36. *Freeman's Journal*, 11 December 1880.
37. *Sydney Morning Herald*, 10 March 1880.
38. *Sydney Morning Herald*, 18 February 1880.

Dublin in promotion of Home Rule. The Chowder Bay pavilion resounded to rousing speeches, with Dillon concluding that 'if Home Rule were granted to-morrow religious dissension would disappear within five years, and that all classes of Irishmen, Orange or Catholic, would work together for the good of the country'.[39]

Captain Byrnes somehow found time to engage in and promote his favourite aquatic sports, sailing and rowing. He was a member of the Pyrmont Regatta committee, and in February 1886 at a meeting at the Caledonian Hotel, still standing on the corner of Point and Herbert Streets, he was appointed to a delegation to wait on the Governor and request his presence on the flagship during the races. Added to the programme at that year's regatta was 'a race for quarrymen belonging to their protective society for a trophy of the value of £6'.[40]

In 1888 he was honoured by a biographical entry in *Australian Men of Mark*, two volumes published in commemoration of the centenary of the arrival of the First Fleet. The article was fulsome in its appreciation of the 'old salt': 'Among the old salts, who have made Sydney their home, none is better known nor more widely popular than the subject of this sketch. His skill is unquestioned, and his liberality and largeness of heart are proverbial.' The article concluded with unusual praise for an Irishman: 'He does not interfere in politics.'[41]

Tragedy struck the Byrnes family in November 1888 with the death of the 22-year-old Mary, his first-born. The *Freeman's Journal* wrote movingly of the family's grief and loss, giving an insight into the fragility of life in nineteenth century Sydney:

> The troop of friends of Captain Mat Byrne, we are sure, will be deeply sorry to learn that his bright, amiable and accomplished daughter Mary, after whom the gallant and genial skipper named his well-known boat, has been taken from him by the hand of Death. The comely and gentle maiden whose decease we record with an unfeigned feeling of sadness had grown up to be the pride and happiness of Captain Mat's life; she was the light of his house and the object of all his tender and all his fond thoughts and fatherly hopes. Miss Byrne was in her 22nd year, and the illness which carried her off first set in about six months ago, Miss Byrne was by nature of a singularly sweet disposition, and to this fairy gift was added a gaiety of heart and winning grace of manner that made her character attractive and admirable to a rare degree. In her

---

39. *Maitland Mercury and Hunter River General Advertiser*, 2 November 1889.
40. *Evening News*, 23 February1886.
41. Everard Digby (ed), *Australian men of mark* (2 volumes), Sydney, 1888.

early schooldays in the Good Samaritan Convent, Balmain, she was the well-beloved of her school companions, and her cleverness was shown by the easy way in which she passed the Civil Service and Junior Public Examinations at the University. When she had finished her studies at the Balmain Convent Miss Byrne's services were retained for the teaching staff, and she was afterwards appointed one of the assistants at St Mary's Cathedral Girls' School, with the approbation, we believe, of his Eminence Cardinal Moran. During her illness at her father's residence, Pyrmont, the Rev Father E Walsh was constantly in attendance, and the good nuns, with whom she was so great a favourite, paid many a visit. She died fully fortified by the rites of the Church, and on Thursday afternoon all that remained of Mary Maria Byrne was deposited in the Catholic portion of the cemetery at Waverley. The affliction that has befallen Captain Byrne in the death of his daughter evoked many expressions of sympathy from the clergy and laity of the city and suburbs, and of this sympathy the large attendance at the funeral afforded a consoling testimony.[42]

The article, with nineteenth-century decorum, did not mention the grief of Mary's step-mother Catherine.

A happy event took place on 11 February 1895 when Kate, the Byrnes' youngest daughter, joined six other young women in being clothed in the habit of the Good Samaritan Sisters at their convent in Pitt Street, becoming Sister Matthew. Present at the ceremony with Captain Byrnes was Father Patrick Ryan, curate at St Bede's. His Lordship Dr Joseph Higgins, Sydney's auxiliary bishop, addressed the postulants 'in words of fatherly counsel and strong encouragement':

> He made clear the extent of their surrender from a worldly point of view, explained the duties they were undertaking, the new responsibilities they were putting on, emphasized the necessity for cultivating by prayer, self-sacrifice and holiness of thought and deed the grace of God which could alone sustain them in their noble resolve, dwelt on the immense treasure of spiritual gifts open to them, and concluded by picturing with eloquent felicity the perfect peace on earth and the eternal joy in heaven which would be theirs if, meek of heart, pure in purpose, strong of soul, they followed loyally and lovingly in the footsteps of the Good Shepherd.

---

42. *Freeman's Journal*, 24 November 1888.

The *Freeman's Journal* concluded its report by stating that 'it need scarcely be added to the record of a happy event that the visitors as usual had experience of the hospitality of the Sisters'.[43]

On the afternoon of Thursday 7 March 1895 the *Evening News* carried the following heading on page three: 'Found Drowned. CAPTAIN MATTHEW BYRNES DEAD. A MYSTERIOUS ACCIDENT.' The article described the situation in detail:

> Shortly after 6 o'clock this morning the dead body of Captain Matthew Byrnes, the well-known ferry boat proprietor, was found floating in the water between his own steamer Princess and the stone wharf at Pyrmont. The discovery was made by a man named Thomas Piper. Captain Byrnes, who resided at 57 Point-street, Pyrmont, was last seen alive about 8 o'clock by John Hunter, engineer of the ferry boat, Leipoa, at which hour he crossed over in the vessel from the city. How deceased got into the water is not known. It must, however, have been very shortly after he reached the Pyrmont side, as his watch when examined this morning was found to have stopped at seventeen minutes past 8. A man named William Thomas Price, in the employ of deceased, lives at the ferry landing, and he states that he was at home about the hour of the occurrence, and frequently about the wharf, but heard no noise such as would be made by a man falling into the water. What is more extraordinary about the affair is that the night was unusually bright. The body now lies at deceased's late residence awaiting the inquest, which will probably be held to-day.[44]

During the day the body was brought to the nearby Caledonian Hotel where the inquest was held. The Coroner's report, having noted that the 54-year-old deceased was born in Dublin, and that no autopsy had been conducted, read as follows:

> I found that the said Matthew Byrnes in the waters of Darling Harbour at Pyrmont Ferry landing place at foot of John Street Pyrmont in the District of Sydney in the said Colony on the 7th day of March 1895 was found dead without any marks of violence appearing on his body. I further found that this death took place on the 6th day of March 1895 and was caused by asphysia by drowning, but how or by what means he became drowned the evidence adduced does not enable me to say.[45]

---

43. *Freeman's Journal*, 16 February 1895.
44. *Evening News*, 7 March 1895.
45. NSW Register of Inquests held during 1895 (7/3/1895), 368.

The burial took place the next day at Waverley cemetery with the two Pyrmont priests, Fathers O'Reilly and Ryan, conducting the service in the presence of Father Furlong, the previous priest-in-charge, and Franciscan Father Kennedy, who was conducting a mission at St Bede's, which the captain had been faithfully attending. Also present were 'many representative citizens, the shipping trade being strongly in evidence'.[46] The Requiem Office and Mass were held at St Bede's four weeks later on Thursday 4 April.

The *Freeman's Journal* devoted three columns of its 16 March edition to an obituary which summarised the Captain's qualities:

> He could count his friends in hosts—an enemy he could not have discovered with the largest telescope or the finest microscope. Apart from what might be called the romantic side of his character Mat Byrne was a big-hearted and sterling man. Frank, open and generous, he made his way in the world by robust energy, but whenever a kindly hand was needed by 'a forlorn and ship-wrecked brother,' whenever succour was asked by a victim of misfortune 'fainting by the way,' it was not in his nature to turn a deaf ear. He was a practical patriot, taking a warm interest in every Irish movement, taking little, but always dipping his hand into his pocket when money was needed for the old land.[47]

Matthew's daughter Kate, being a white-veiled novice at the Pitt Street Convent at the time of his death, was not permitted to attend his funeral. As Sister Mary Matthew she lovingly bore her father's name and memory, and in her teaching vocation she manifested many of his endearing characteristics.

Kate's high-school days were spent at the Convent of the Immaculate Conception, Balmain, 'where she learnt to know and venerate the early members of the Institute of the Good Samaritan, and from them to inherit a strong love for the poor, the sick and the suffering'.[48] At the end of 1893, her final year at school, in the Great Hall of Sydney University she sat the Theory of Music examination of Trinity College. The papers were carefully numbered and sealed and forwarded to London to be assessed by the Trinity College examiners. When the results were received in Sydney in September 1894 the *Freeman's Journal* was triumphant in reporting the success of the Irish Catholic candidates: 'The readers of the morning papers at first glance must have thought a Dublin list had been sent to Sydney by mistake, fully two-thirds of the names being unmistakably Irish. But there had been no mistake. It was a triumph, under favourable conditions, of the old Irish knowledge and love of music—a proof as striking as gratifying

---

46. *Evening News*, 9 March 1895.
47. *Freeman's Journal*, 16 March 1895.
48. Obituary, *Catholic Weekly*, 16 April 1942.

that the spirit of "the land of song" lives afresh in the bright and emotional Irish-Australian.' The detailed results for each Catholic school were given, including the 'Convent of the Immaculate Conception, Balmain (Sisters of the Good Samaritan)': 'Honours: May Samliss, Kate Byrnes, Minnie Shine, Lily Sullivan, Gertie Aiken, Agnes Gooud. Total 6. These were all the pupils that went up for the examination. Miss Samliss and Miss Byrnes (daughter of Captain Byrnes, Pyrmont) have since entered the Convent of the Good Samaritan in Pitt street, Sydney.'[49] Kate became a postulant on 15 August 1894, aged 19, and she received the habit and began her two-year novitiate in March 1895. On 13 February 1897 Sister Mary Matthew made her first vows of perseverance, conversion of life and obedience.

Kate's mother died in 1898. The obituary spoke of her daughter as having chosen 'the better part':

> Although for many years an invalid, and for the past six months confined to her house, Mrs Byrnes' death came as a surprise to many of her friends. The good lady had been suffering from partial paralysis, but acute symptoms presented themselves for which her medical advisers thought an operation necessary. The operation was skilfully performed, but revealed a serious malady, and Mrs Byrnes survived the ordeal but a couple of days. Born at Cork 58 years ago, the deceased lady had spent 40 years in N.S.W., and like her husband was held in general respect. Her daughter—Sister M. Matthew—years ago 'chose the better part,' and is now engaged in the holy mission of religious education as a Good Samaritan nun at St Benedict's School. During her protracted illness Mrs Byrnes was assiduously attended by her spiritual adviser, the Rev D O'Reilly, of Pyrmont.[50]

Daniel O'Reilly was St Bede's disabled, long-serving curate, acquainted with suffering. The Byrnes' residence was a rented house at 31 Pyrmont Street, just a few doors up from the school and church. It was described as containing ten rooms and made of stone with a slate roof.[51] After Mrs Byrnes' death the house was leased by the parish, and in 1900 it became the Good Samaritan convent, accommodating six nuns, bringing a welcome end to the long daily walk from Pitt Street.

Sister Matthew Byrne's life as a teaching sister provides an overview of the spread of the Good Samaritan Order beyond the Archdiocese of Sydney. After her apprenticeship at St Benedict's she was appointed as a member

---

49. *Freeman's Journal*, 29 September 1894. A week later the FJ corrected its mistake in printing 'Samliss' instead of 'Lawliss' (6 October 1894).
50. *Freeman's Journal*, 5 November 1898.
51. *Sydney Assessment Book* 1907.

of the pioneering community established at the Institute's first Queensland foundation in Charters Towers, a booming gold-mining town. The twelve sisters sailed from Sydney in January 1900 on the steamer 'Aramac' to Keppel Bay, Rockhampton, where they were met by Bishop Joseph Higgins, former auxiliary bishop of Sydney, who had presided at Sister Matthew's reception of the habit five years before. The Good Samaritans were replacing the Sisters of Mercy, who were not able to staff the expansion of schools planned by the bishop. He had withdrawn them and sought help from Sydney. In this delicate situation, reminiscent of the change of guard at the Maitland schools in 1867, the bishop addressed the misgivings of parishioners, who had become attached to the Mercy Sisters over many years. At the Sunday Mass in the parish church he acknowledged that 'the Sisters of Mercy have been among the first pioneers of the faith to you', and went on to explain the changes that led to the presence in Charters Towers of a new Congregation of nuns, whom he urged them to welcome and support: 'It was my privilege to conduct a community of 12 Sisters here last evening, who have come all the way from Sydney, to take up the work of your schools, to maintain the high standard of literary merit they have already attained, and, at the same time, to bring to the bed-side of the sick and dying the support and sweet consolation, which the visit of such ministering angels of charity never fail to impart.'[52] Bishop Higgins spoke eloquently of the double mission of the Good Samaritans, school teaching and the care of the needy. Young Sister Matthew and a companion were assigned to teach in the nearby township of Millchester, to which they walked each day.

In 1905 Sister Matthew was sent south to Melbourne, where the Congregation had established a convent at Northcote the previous year. She was again to be a pioneer as a member of a new teaching community at South Yarra. Here she became principal of the parish school of St Joseph and continued in that role until 1922. In 1923 she headed west to South Australia, where in 1890 the Good Samaritan's had established their first foundation outside of New South Wales, at Port Pirie in the new diocese of Port Augusta. As the convent superior Sister Matthew became Mother Matthew, and she served as school principal successively at St Anthony's, Solomontown, St Mark's, Port Pirie and St Catherine's, Crystal Creek until 1932. After another year in Melbourne she was sent back north in 1933 as superior at Lawson, in the Blue Mountains, west of Sydney. She was back in familiar territory at South Yarra from 1936 to 1939, and returned to Sydney as superior and primary school teacher at Stella Maris College, Manly, a girls' primary and high school that had been established on the original Good Samaritan property in 1931. Manly was to be Sister Matthew's last posting.

---

52. *Annals*, 156–157.

She died in March 1942 at the Wollongong Convent, where she was staying for a brief holiday.

The Catholic newspapers had always provided obituaries of priests, but rarely of nuns. Mother Matthew Byrne was an exception, reflecting her family connections with the Church in Sydney and her exceptional career:

> Mother Matthew belonged to a staunch Catholic family . . . In 1894 she entered St Scholastica's Convent, the Mother-House at Pitt-street. Since then, in four States of Australia, she spent herself in nearly 50 years of constant and untiring labour for the generations of children entrusted to her care . . . [M]any of her former pupils are now priests and religious of different Congregations . . . As Superior, she entered into all the intimate details of her community, and her sympathy and insight into difficulties found a remedy for all perplexities. She made all under her care, religious and children, very happy and enthusiastic. As Superior, she supervised the details of study and conduct of the pupils, with very happy results.[53]

Back at Pyrmont during the 1880s the daily slog from the Pitt Street convent continued. In 1892 with the opening of St Francis Xavier School at Ultimo, the St Bede nuns were joined on their daily walk by their colleagues heading for Ultimo. Perhaps this led to a changed route, heading down George Street South and then along Harris Street. This routine continued until 1900 when the first convent was established at Pyrmont. That was the year in which notice to vacate the Pitt Street convent was received from the Government, in order to commence the development of Sydney's Central Railway Station. This led to the relocation of the mother-house in 1901 to the Toxteth Mansion in The Glebe, the former home of the Allen family, leading members of Sydney's Methodist community.

Information about the changing locations of the Pyrmont-Ultimo convent is found in an undated letter of Sister Elizabeth O'Toole written from the Coffs Harbour convent, where she was stationed from 1965 to 1967. She was the second Good Samaritan of that name, not directly related to the first 'Sister Elizabeth O'Toole' (1844-1917). The three eldest daughters of Andrew O'Toole, youngest son of Tobias and Elizabeth Toole of Pyrmont, joined the Good Samaritans: Elizabeth, born in 1898, became Sister Brigid Mary and made profession in 1916; Christina Ann, born in 1899, became Sister Mary Elizabeth and made profession in 1919; Catherine Mary, born in 1901, became Sister Mary Lidwina and made profession in 1924. In 1901 the growing family was living in Harvey Street, at the *Green Tree Hotel*, which

---

53. Obituary, *Catholic Weekly*, 16 April 1942

Andrew had taken back into O'Toole hands.[54] The three sisters and their ten siblings and their many cousins were pupils at St Bede's parish school. One of those cousins was John O'Toole ordained priest in 1930. At their father's funeral the former pastor of St Bede's, Monsignor John O'Gorman, recalled asking Andrew, known as Dick, whether he begrudged giving three daughters to the Church: 'My good Monsignor', he replied, 'I would willingly give away every one of my children to assist in God's work.'[55] The next generation of the O'Toole clan is represented among the Good Samaritans by Sister Elizabeth Carr, a great grand-daughter of Tobias and Elizabeth, and the niece of her three Good Samaritan aunts.

The Mother-General in the 1960s, Mother Mary De Sales Rowe, asked Sister Lidwina O'Toole for some recollections about the early days at Pyrmont to fill out the history of the Sisters' involvement at the St Bede School. The official *Annals of the Congregation 1857- 1938*, compiled by Sister de Sales Smith, the first Good Samaritan university graduate in 1920, had been unusually brief in its recounting of the Pyrmont story.[56] Sister Lidwina handed on the request to her older sister Christina, Sister Elizabeth O'Toole. Sister Elizabeth began her response: 'My dear Mother—Sister M. Lidwina wrote a couple of days ago and asked me to send a few lines about the early days of Pyrmont. I do not know much, and perhaps you have been told that little before. I shall write just as it comes to me.'[57] She then recounted her memories of the two locations of the convent in Pyrmont Street:

> The first Convent was in Pyrmont Street, close to John Street . . . There was a fair space of land at the back for a garden. Sr Brigid Mary and I used to help Sr M[ary] Barbara now and again, doing a bit of gardening. The chapel in that convent was smaller than the one in the hollow of Pyrmont Street, where wool stores are now. The Sisters moved there about 1908 or 1909. It was high up—fifteen steps up to the front door—the rooms were larger. Srs [Sisters] had a prie-dieu instead of stalls. Sr [Sister] would allow you to make a visit when you went for a music lesson.

The *Catholic Directory* of 1901 listed the first convent: 'Pyrmont Convent— founded 1900 (Mother M. Gabriel Robinson), 6 in community.'[58] The same edition of the *Directory* gave the current statistics of the Good Samaritan

---

54. 'CENTRAL LICENSING COURT', *Sydney Morning Herald*, 27 May 1901.
55. *Catholic Press*, 23 December 1926.
56. 'School at Pyrmont', *Annals*, 110; 'Attendance of Sisters at Universities', *Annals*, 333.
57. Sister Elizabeth O'Toole to Mother de Sales, n.d. (Good Samaritan Archives, Pyrmont File)
58. *Australasian Catholic Directory* 1901, 15.

Congregation in the Archdiocese of Sydney: 'number of communities, 20; number of religious, 191.'[59] Pyrmont was the latest and smallest of the 20 convents. The *Sands Directory* for 1909 located the convent at 55 Pyrmont Street: 'Convent of the Good Samaritan—Mother Superior Xavier'. The relocation of the convent from 31 to 55 Pyrmont Street happened in 1908.

From 1900 the Ultimo teachers walked south each day from the Pyrmont convent to their school, a welcomed shortening of the walk from Pitt Street. A reversal would begin in 1910 when the parish purchased two semi-detached houses next to the Ultimo church-school to be used as the convent, from where the St Bede's staff would walk north each day to school. Sister Elizabeth recollected that 'the move to Ultimo must have been about 1910 or 1911. Sr M [Sister Mary] Elizabeth Highfield was there at the time. I think Monsignor O'Gorman bought the two houses from the Misses McCaffery'.[60] The new convent was blessed by Cardinal Moran in July 1910. In his address he congratulated the parishioners 'on their having the devoted nuns residing in their midst. A convent was like a *pharos*, a light house, and spread around it far and wide the radiance of heavenly blessings.'[61]

Sister Elizabeth, in her letter, went on to express her fond attachment to the parish church of St Bede:

> It was a beautiful building as we all thought. The altar is a cedar one (some person painted it white). It was its natural colour when we were young. A heavy red curtain cut the sanctuary off from the body of the church. Sometimes a class had lessons in it; so that must have been the reason of its being there. The sanctuary was a blue that looked heavenly when lights were on for Benediction. Gold fleur-de-lis and crosses were painted on the blue. Our Lady's statue is one that made you look at it again and again. At any moment you thought the eyes might open.[62]

William Wilkins of the Council of Education, who had protested in 1868 that the 'church' was funded to be a school, would have been mollified somewhat to know that lessons were sometimes conducted in the church, behind the 'heavy red curtain'. Classes were also later held in the church gallery in 1924, during the building of a new brick school replacing the 1880 weatherboard building, as recounted by Phillip O'Toole.[63] A new church-school at Ultimo was also ready for use at the beginning of 1925.

---

59. *Australasian Catholic Directory*, 1901, 14.
60. Sister Elizabeth O'Toole to Mother de Sales, n.d. (Good Samaritan Archives, Pyrmont File)
61. *Catholic Press*, 4 August 1910.
62. *Catholic Press*, 4 August 1910.
63. Phillip O'Toole, 'Some Memories' (manuscript 2003).

The St Bede's school closed at the end of 1954, ending almost 100 years of Catholic education in Pyrmont. After the closure the Pyrmont children were offered places at St Francis Xavier's at Ultimo. The Good Samaritan Sisters were again walking to school in 1971 after the Ultimo convent was closed and the community amalgamated with that at St Benedict's, Broadway. The nuns' choir stalls were relocated from the chapel in the Ultimo convent to St Bede's church. The Ultimo school was closed in 1973, ending ninety years of Good Samaritan ministry on the Pyrmont peninsula. The St Francis Xavier pupils were distributed between the parish schools at Forest Lodge and Broadway.

Chapter 12
Irish See of Sydney

In January 1884, on successive days, Sydney newspapers announced the appointment of a new Archbishop for Sydney—the secular press named Patrick Moran, Bishop of Ossory; the *Freeman's Journal* named Thomas Croke, Archbishop of Cashel and formerly Bishop of Auckland.[1] These contradictory announcements added confusion to the speculation that had circulated since the death of Archbishop Vaughan in August 1883. The weekly *Freeman's Journal* finally caught up with the latest news in its next edition, and excused its mistake:

> There were ever so many speculations, all sorts of rumours were circulated, and at least half a dozen names were mentioned in connection with the filling of the vacant See. The Venerable Archpriest Sheehy's name was the first to appear in print; and then the newspapers had it that Prior Jerome Vaughan would succeed his brother. Only within the past weeks the news flashed over the world that the appointment had been offered to the illustrious Archbishop of Cashel, and now last of all we have Dr Moran named as the prelate actually selected by the Holy See for the Archdiocese of Sydney.[2]

Jerome Vaughan was prior of the Benedictine Abbey and College at Fort Augustus in Scotland. Speculation also swirled around another of Vaughan's six clerical brothers, Herbert, bishop of Salford. In 1892 he would become archbishop of Westminster and cardinal in 1893. Apart from Sheehy, another local candidate spoken of was Bishop James Murray of Maitland. Earlier in January 1884 it had been announced in all the newspapers that the bishops of the Sydney Province, meeting after the Vaughan Requiem in September 1883, had submitted to *Propaganda Fide* the required list of their three

---

1. *Sydney Morning Herald*, 18 January 1884; Freeman's Journal, 19 January 1884.
2. *Freeman's Journal*, 26 January 1884.

suggestions for the Sydney vacancy. They were ranked, as required by Rome, as 'most worthy', 'more worthy' and 'worthy'. First on the all-Irish shortlist, *dignissimus*, was Father William Walsh, President of St Patrick's College, Maynooth, in second place, *dignior*, came Patrick Moran, and in third place, *dignus*, was Murray of Maitland.[3] Walsh would be appointed Archbishop of Dublin in the following year. The publication of this list did not put an end to wild speculation which spread to include the name of the convert English auxiliary bishop of Westminster, James Laird Patterson. The most unlikely, perhaps most mischievous rumour emerged in the *Launceston Examiner* which on Christmas Eve announced 'advices from America which state that Monsignor Capel is spoken of as the successor of the late Archbishop Vaughan'.[4] Thomas John Capel was a high-profile English Monsignor, an 'apostle of the drawing room', who, following a spate of accusations and scandals, was sent in mid-1883 to the United States where, despite an enthusiastic welcome, repeated scandalous behaviour led to his suspension from the priesthood in 1886.[5]

The *Potestant Standard,* which in reporting Vaughan's sudden death had hailed him as 'always our chief opponent' with no one 'worthy to take up his mantle'[6], in January 1884 added its own version of the process of choosing his successor:

> Who dictates the ecclesiastical messages sent or supposed to be sent from the Vatican respecting episcopal appointments? Every few days we have had a new name positively announced as that of the successor to Dr Vaughan as Archbishop over the Pope's children in New South Wales. When Prior Vaughan was mentioned, the Sydney Popish papers at once took up the matter as settled and wrote of Vaughan as the coming man. Sheehy the rusticated was equally adopted and praised by the *Freeman* to the skies as the real rising sun. Archbishop Croke was so certainly the man, that the *Freeman* again filled its sails with wind in his honour, and broke out in laudatory biologies, and eulogistic poeans. Lo! before the advertised eulogies appeared, the telegrams laugh them to scorn, announcing that Moran not Croke is the friend . . . It will certainly be a matter of congratulation to the respectable part of the Romish people here that they have escaped the calamity of Dr Croke's rule; and it will be a further satisfaction to them should Dr Moran of Ossory be their chief.

---

3. *Tablet*, 2 February 1884.
4. *Launceston Examiner*, 24 December 1883.
5. *Freeman's Journal*, 2 November 1911.
6. *Protestant Standard*, 25 August 1883.

> He is quiet, scholarly and a gentleman—three very rare attributes in the Hibernian Popish Church.[7]

The *Standard* maintained its interest in the succession, mocking Austin Sheehy's 1867 encounter with episcopacy as 'delightfully all but', and finally offering a dismissive interpretation of his current candidacy: 'The story of the selection of Dr Sheehy originated in the waggery of Dr Colletti and priest Dillon who were in Rome. Whoever gathered it, it was a joke.'[8]

The vacant see of Sydney had become the focus of Irish nationalism in Australia and in Ireland itself. The Dublin newspapers carried editorials vigorously arguing the need for an Irish bishop for an Irish people. The most forthright expression of this campaign was an article in Dublin's *Nation* reprinted in the *Freeman's Journal* in December 1883. It referred to Vaughan's appointment in 1873 as 'hazardous', given that he was 'a Benedictine monk, with little experience of the world, and none whatever of the sympathies or aspirations of the people whose spiritual interests were entrusted to his keeping'. It referred to Polding as 'a man of strong English if not anti-Irish proclivities'. The hope was expressed that the 'experiment' of appointing 'spiritual rulers of the hated English race' would not be repeated in 1884, and the article concluded: 'In short, there is no longer any reason whatever for repeating the anomaly of importing an Englishman into the Irish See of Sydney, and accordingly it is only reasonable to hope that the Holy See will not make so risky an experiment.'[9]

In the midst of this speculation, at Pyrmont in March 1884, the Irishman Edmund Walsh succeeded the Frenchman Joseph-Marie Garavel as priest-in-charge of the St Bede mission district. Born in 1823 in County Tipperary, Walsh had studied for the priesthood at St John's College, Waterford. He was a fellow recruit for the Australian mission with Father Timothy McCarthy, arriving in Sydney in 1853. Unlike his colleague, who remained in charge at the Armidale posting for nine years, Walsh was regularly transferred as a curate from city to country. Edmund was joined in the Colony by his brother Martin, also a priest, in 1859. Martin was assigned to the Sacred Heart Mission at Darlinghurst, under the tutelage of Dean Felix Sheridan. Edmund joined them there from 1861 to 1862. After this brief city posting the brothers were again on the move, Edmund heading to the northern rivers of New South Wales, the coastal district of the Armidale mission centred at Grafton on the Clarence River. Martin went south to the Bungonia mission near Goulburn. Both brothers were among the clergy gathered at Pyrmont

---

7. *Protestant Standard*, 26 January 1884.
8. *Protestant Standard*, 12 January & 15 March 1884.
9. *Freeman's Journal*, 1 December 1883.

for the laying of the foundation stone of St Bede's in February 1867.[10] Edmund was passing through Sydney on his way south to a new posting; Martin, like Eugene Luckie, a refugee from Lanigan's Goulburn Diocese, would soon be heading north to Newcastle.

Both brothers were soon undertaking longer journeys back to Europe. Martin left in August 1869 and was absent for two years. Early in 1871 Edmund departed and on arrival in England took charge of an 'important mission'. On his return to the Colony he spent a further fifteen months as curate at Queanbeyan, after which he finally received appointment as priest-in-charge of St Bede's, Appin

Two years later he was on the move again, heading further south to the remote gold-mining town of Araluen which had been part of the Braidwood mission district until 1878. Walsh was the second resident priest. The *Catholic Almanac* recorded that there were four churches in the district and two schools, with a population of about 700 Catholics.[11] Araluen's improvised church, St Patrick's, had originally 'served as a hotel, later to become a hay and corn store, and then (after having several partitions removed), to be dignified by the title of a church'.[12] The district received a mention at the monthly meeting of the St Mary's Cathedral Building Fund in March 1880, when Archbishop Vaughan announced that he had received 'a handsome donation that evening of £20 from Father E Walsh of Araluen'. His Grace went on to comment that this was Fr Walsh's 'own private subscription, and he was all the more to be thanked, when they considered the fact that the district in which that rev gentleman resided was not in a very flourishing or prosperous state, but was on the contrary going down, for the gold, which at one time was so plentiful, was not now to be found'. Father Walsh's generosity was held up as a fine example which the Archbishop hoped 'many other country priests would imitate'.[13]

In March 1884, Edmund moved to Pyrmont. His five years at St Bede's would prove to be the longest appointment that he held during his almost forty years of ministry in the Archdiocese of Sydney.

His first and only entry in the surviving parish ledger recorded the financial situation at the end of his first year. The income included the proceeds of two concerts and an 'entertainment' held in the favoured venue of the Masonic Hall in York Street, bringing in a total of £57. A minor amount of £4.16 was a loan from Father Walsh 'to settle some unpaid bills'. The total income for the year was £108.16.3, which comfortably exceeded

---

10. *Freeman's Journal*, 9 February 1867.
11. *Catholic Almanac*, 1882, 62.
12. *Catholic Press*, 25 September 1941.
13. *Freeman's Journal*, 13 March 1880.

the expenditure of £79.5.7. The major item of expense was the quarterly interest repayment totalling £62; Father Walsh's timely loan was duly repaid.

In September Edmund was among the clergy who clambered on-board harbour ferries to welcome the new archbishop to Sydney. The Irish clergy finally had an Irish 'chief'. Patrick Francis Moran took possession of the 'Irish See of Sydney' on 8 September 1884. He was welcomed through the Heads by a flotilla of 40 vessels, a scene unsurpassed in the history of the city—'a royal reception of unprecedented magnitude and unrivalled grandeur'. This was in stark contrast to the entry into the harbour of the manacled convict priests in 1800, and in contrast also with the arrival of the first bishop in 1835—Polding was 'pulled ashore in a waterman's boat and there was but one priest to meet him'.[14]

With the Irish Archbishop triumphantly among his Irish subjects the *Freeman's Journal* could be less aggressive in its nationalism. It discreetly noted that on that Monday the reception had 'a decidedly national tone' in celebrating the fulfilment of 'the universally expressed wish for an Irish Archbishop'. The crowds were more exuberant in their Irish patriotism: 'A large and most remarkable looking steam barge, freshly painted a flaring green in honour of the occasion, and flying an enormous Irish flag, made a circuit of the *Liguria*, while a strong-chested cornet performer, conspicuously pedestalled in the centre of the deck, played "Killarney" and "The Harp that once" with most commendable patriotic fervour combined with the concentrated power of a full brass band.' Meanwhile on the *Annie*, named after the second of Captain Mat's daughters, the band, gathered on the bow, 'made the air ring . . . with the stirring strains of "Garryowen" and "St Patrick's Day".'[15]

In November 1885 Edmund Walsh received the sad news of the death of his youngest brother in South Africa. Andrew, the third of the Walsh brothers to become a priest, died at the age of 46. The Freeman's Journal printed an obituary from the Kimberley local paper, the *Diamond Field Advertiser*, confident that it would be 'read with interest in Sydney, the good Father referred to being the brother of the Rev Edmund Walsh and the Rev Martin Walsh, both well known in Sydney and the Archdiocese'. High praise was heaped on the deceased who had functioned as a military chaplain:

> In the Zulu war and the Transvaal war he attached himself to the British troops as chaplain, and invariably contrived to gain the love and respect of the soldiers, no matter what creed they professed. He was fearless in administering rebuke, and unflinching in giving caution and advice; the

---

14. Anon, 'The Church and the Centenary', *Freeman's Journal*, 21 January 1888.
15. *Freeman's Journal*, 21 January 1888.

tenderest of all nurses, the most unselfish of comrades . . . He was one of the numerous subjects of her Majesty who in many an engagement has won the right to the Victoria Cross, if ever true valour won it; but the innate modesty of this truly brave and thoroughly unselfish man made him shrink from anything like a trumpeting of his deeds. 'My duty' was his motto, and never did priest militant or loving pastor do that duty more loyally.[16]

In the same edition of the *Freeman's Journal* three full broadsheet pages were dedicated to the 'Landing of the First Australian Cardinal': 'Returning amongst us with a twofold title to our veneration and affection—coming back to our shores not alone as Archbishop but as a prince of the Church—bringing with him, for our honour, the highest glories of ecclesiastical rank and dignity—what marvel that his Eminence the Cardinal should have received a magnificent and fitting welcome!'[17] Also published was a circular from Cardinal Moran setting out the preparations for the first Plenary Council of the Australasian Church to be held later in the month. All the bishops of the Australian Colonies, as well as the bishops of New Zealand and Fiji, were to gather in Sydney for the Council, under the presidency of Cardinal Moran as Delegate Apostolic 'representing the Sovereign Pontiff'. They would be assisted in their deliberations by theologians and representative clergy of the various dioceses, together with the heads of religious orders. The Cardinal involved the visiting dignitaries in public events—the blessing of the foundation stone of the seminary at Manly and the blessing of the cathedral memorial window in honour of Archbishop Vaughan.

On the agenda of the Council was the question whether 'irremovable parish priests' should be instituted in Australasia. Irremovability would bring stability to priests appointed to certain nominated parishes. Stability of locality was not considered to be desirable by Polding and the early bishops, Australia being a vast missionary territory requiring the mobility of the small numbers of clergy.[18] As late as 1865, Polding complained to his Melbourne colleague, James Goold, that James Quinn in Brisbane was 'instituting parish priests', and thus changing 'the missionary character of the colonies'.[19] Already there had been calls for clerical irremovability from the Irish laity in the disputes of the late 1850s. The situation was summed up by 'Vindicator' writing to the *Freeman's Journal* in 1876: 'We have no parishes

---

16. *Freeman's Journal*, 7 November 1885.
17. *Freeman's Journal*, 7 November 1885.
18. See Ian Waters, 'Stability of Parish Priests: The Australian History', *Australasian Catholic Record*, 74 (1997): 307–314.
19. Polding to Goold, 26 August 1865 (Polding Letters III.192).

or parish priests. The veteran priest of thirty years standing, however good he may be, is liable to be removed at the will of his bishop, which he could not do without a great fault on the part of the priest, had he been canonically appointed to a parish.'[20]

In 1885 the bishops were still divided on the issue, those against arguing the necessity for bishops to be free to relocate their priests according to the changing needs of the Catholic population. Conformity to the status available to senior priests in Ireland carried weight with some bishops. The passing of the resolution required the casting vote of the presiding Delegate Apostolic, Cardinal Moran. The legislation proposed that each diocese would turn some of its mission districts into canonical parishes, appointees to which would enjoy life appointments. Districts would be eligible for upgrading by reason of developed and separate facilities for worship and education and minimal debts. Qualifications for appointment as a parish priest would include faithful ministry of at least seven years in the diocese and proven capacity for spiritual and temporal administration. Listed causes, which would lead to an 'irremovable rector' being removed by his bishop, included inebriation and causing scandal.[21] The Council Fathers explained the decision in a pastoral letter addressed to their priests and faithful:

> As regards our clergy, those who left home and kin, and who deny themselves so much that they may work with us in the Master's vineyard, we have decided to submit to the Holy Father our opinion that they have a title to share, to some extent, that permanency of position which hitherto has been possessed by bishops only in Australia. For years back the necessities of these missions require that every priest should be ready, at the beck of authority, to start in any direction . . . Half a century does not record a word of refusal . . . The extent of country now settled makes an opening to give a comparatively greater permanence to some of the priests.[22]

The Cardinals of Propaganda Fide insisted on an adjustment in terminology, from 'parish priest' to 'irremovable rector', as more accurately reflecting the Australian Church's status as mission territory and the hierarchy's subjection

---

20. *Freeman's Journal*, 30 December 1976.
21. See Ian Waters, *Australian Conciliar Legislation prior to the 1917 Code of Canon Law: A Comparative Study with Similar Conciliar Legislation in Great Britain, Ireland, and North America*, dissertation submitted to the Faculty of Canon Law, Saint Paul University, Ottawa, in partial fulfilment of the requirement for the degree of Doctor of canon Law, 1990, 113-127.
22. Patrick Moran, *History of the Catholic Church in Australasia*, Sydney, 1895-96, 685.

to the Roman Congregation. Cardinal Moran, during his remaining 25 years as Archbishop of Sydney, moved slowly to implement the decrees, creating only 17 parishes with irremovable rectors. These priests enjoyed a vote in the choice of a coadjutor bishop. By 1928 Moran's successor, Michael Kelly, had created an additional 41 formal parishes, making a total of 58 out of 108 separate districts in the Archdiocese. Pyrmont was never formally elevated from missionary district to parish.[23] The terminology eventually fell into disuse, all districts being called parishes and resident pastors being called parish priests, whether removable or irremovable. In 1965 the Vatican Council constitution on the pastoral office of bishops, *Christus Dominus*, formally abolished the distinction between removable and irremovable parish priests. The revised Code of Canon Law in 1983 opened up the possibility of fixed-term appointments, at the expiry of which the priest could be moved by the bishop without any process. In 1986 the Australian Episcopal Conference chose to eliminate permanent tenure for parish priests.[24]

In October 1886 St Bede's hosted an important meeting of the Irish National League. 1886 was a year of great expectation for the granting of Home Rule in Ireland. Following the British general election in November 1885 the Irish Parliamentary Party held the balance of power in the Westminster Parliament. After a brief flirtation in support of a Tory government, Charles Stewart Parnell swung the party's support in February 1886 to the Liberals led by William Gladstone, who had committed himself to legislating for a separate parliament in Dublin.

The Irish National League had been formed by Parnell in 1882 and managed to bring together contending groups, including the Catholic hierarchy, in a united drive for the overturning of the 1801 Act of Union and the restoration of an Irish Parliament. Branches of the League were quickly formed among the diaspora Irish, including the Irish population in Australia. Delegates from Ireland became regular visitors to maintain interest and financial support of the Home Rule cause. In 1883 the Redmond brothers, John and William, toured Australia. Their visit was not without controversy. During their presence in Australia allegations emerged implicating the Irish Land League, the banned predecessor of the INL, with the assassination of the Irish Chief Secretary, Lord Frederick Cavendish, and his Under Secretary, Thomas Burke, in Phoenix Park, Dublin in May 1882. This led to their often being denied access to suitable venues for their meetings. The Redmonds' arrival in Sydney coincided with the cricket match between the visiting

---

23. *Freeman's Journal*, 22 November 1928.
24. Brian Byron, 'The Stability Necessary for a Parish Priest', *Australasian Catholic Record*, 73 (1996): 310.

English and Australian teams, which they gladly attended. The short-lived evening paper, *The Echo*, commented on their presence at the cricket ground and on their deceptive appearance—'inoffensive looking gentlemen, with no suspicion about them of Lowie knives or dynamite, or anything of "dark treason's deadly garb".'[25] The Orange Lodges' *Protestant Standard* took grave offence at the flags flown during the match:

> Can anyone explain why, when the Messrs. Redmond were at the Cricket Match, the Irish flag and two American flags were flying on the Pavilion, and nowhere the English flag? On no other occasion that we remember was that green flag with the harp and the inscription Cead Millia Failthe [sic] on it flying on the Pavilion. Who were the hundred thousand welcomes for? If they were for the cricketers, and not for the sedition mongers, why was the flag not hoisted before? It has an ugly look.[26]

John Redmond's Sydney lecture had to be held in the small and inadequate Academy of Music, which only half the assembly was able to enter. The *Freeman's Journal* was effusive in its praise of the address and concluded with the hope that 'the next time Mr Redmond speaks . . . the accommodation will be better', and with confidence after hearing him that all 'will know more of the truth about Ireland than they can find in the daily Press of Sydney'.[27] Prominent among the few clergy attending the Sydney lectures was the Irish Franciscan Patrick Kavanagh, patriot-priest and author of a famous history of the 1798 rebellion.[28] He proposed the vote of thanks at the February meeting and was warmly acknowledged by John Redmond at the farewell lecture in December, even though Redmond's interpretation of 1798 did not follow Kavanagh's emphasis on clerical heroes and his downplaying of the role of Protestant United Irishmen.[29] Among the few clergy present at the lecture was Edmund Walsh, who would be appointed to Pyrmont in March of the following year. The Redmonds' visit had a great impact on the Irish population of Sydney and led to an increase of membership of the INL and the opening of suburban and country branches.

---

25. *The Echo*, 20 February 1883.
26. *Protestant Standard*, 21 February 1883. see Jeff Kildea, 'Tours Downunder: John Redmond MP and the English Cricket Team of 1883', posted on 19 February 2013: http://jeffkildea.com/category/trivia/ (accessed 26 August 2014).
27. *Freeman's Journal*, 3 March 1883.
28. Patrick Kavanagh, *A Popular History of the Insurrection of 1798*, Dublin 1870.
29. *Freeman's Journal*, 24 February & 8 December 1883; see Malcolm Campbell, 'John Redmond and the Irish National League in Australia and New Zealand, 1883', *History* 86 (2002): 360.

In January 1886 Sydney played host to Dr Kevin Izod O'Doherty a member of the Queensland Legislative Council who had been elected to the Imperial Parliament as member for the Irish seat of North Meath in the 1885 elections. He was on his way back to England to participate in the Home Rule debate and vote. O'Doherty was one of the Young Irelanders or Fenians in the 1848 rising who were convicted of treason and transported to Tasmania in 1849. He was given a conditional pardon after five years, one of the conditions being that he not return to the British Isles. He sailed back to Europe, resumed medical studies in Paris, and made a clandestine visit to Ireland where he married his beloved, the poetess known as 'Eva of the Nation', the *Nation* being the Fenian daily newspaper suppressed in 1848. She had been hailed as 'one of the singers of the new patriotic movement'.[30] On receipt of an unconditional pardon in 1856 O'Doherty returned to Dublin, completed his studies, graduating as a fellow of the Royal College of surgeons and setting up a medical practice. In 1860 he returned to Australia with his young family and found his way to Queensland in 1865.[31]

O'Doherty was welcomed to the INL meeting with encouragement for his mission at the Imperial Parliament and flattering words about his dear wife: 'We cannot conclude this address without wishing Godspeed and eternal happiness to that loving partner of your life, 'Eva', whose writings have contributed so largely to keep the spirit of patriotism alive in the breasts of all Irishmen (Prolonged cheering).'[32] O'Doherty shared his great confidence that Ireland, under Parnell's leadership, was on the verge of self-government: '[W]e have, never before so nearly reached the goal of victory (Applause). Never in the past history of this struggle has the hope of victory presented itself so prominently to our view as it does to-day (Cheers) ... You have a commander in Mr Parnell the like of whom has never before been seen in Ireland (Enthusiastic cheering).'[33]

The optimism generated by news from Ireland and the visit of O'Doherty culminated in the preparations for the 1886 St Patrick's Day celebration. The expectation of imminent self-government for Ireland led to an unprecedented gathering of the various Irish groups in preparation for the 17 March event:

---

30. *Brisbane Courier*, 24 May 1910
31. Mella Cusack, 'Kevin Izod O'Doherty and the Roman Catholic Bishops of Hobart and Brisbane', *Journal of the Australian Catholic Historical Society*, 22(2001), 59-70; G. Rudé, 'O'Doherty, Kevin Izod (1823–1905)', *Australian Dictionary of Biography*, National Centre of Biography, Australian National University, http://adb.anu.edu.au/biography/odoherty-kevin-izod-4319/text7007, published in hardcopy 1974, accessed online 26 August 2014.
32. *Freeman's Journal*, 30 January 1886.
33. *Freeman's Journal*, 30 January 1886.

Irishmen will be pleased to note that there is to be a unity of action in celebrating the National Festival this year. It is important for many reasons that this spirit of unity should be manifested by the sons of Erin, for the unity and devotion of the Irish abroad will give courage to our countrymen struggling for Home Rule in the old country. In response to an invitation from the Hibernian Society, the Irish National League, Shamrock Club, and Hurling Club sent representatives to a general meeting of delegates of the Hibernian Society which was held at the Bible Hall, on Sunday, the 14th inst.[34]

The 1886 St Patrick's Day events were an outstanding success, the speeches on the day were full of the anticipated triumph of Gladstone's Government of Ireland Bill which was to be tabled in April. The journalist of the *Freeman's Journal* was so excited that he inadvertently canonised Sir Joseph Banks, reporting that 10,000 people had gathered at the 'St Joseph Banks Grounds' at Botany. The key-note address was given by the President of the Sydney Irish National League, Francis Bede Freehill. He reminded the crowd that they were there to make 'a large contribution to the Irish cause by sending home, not bayonets or bullets, but golden sovereigns, to enable Mr Parnell and his party to carry on the movement which they had laboured over for so long a time'.[35] James Toohey, brewer and member of Parliament for South Sydney, captured the feeling of the day in declaring that 'it would be their unspeakably great joy, consolation and privilege next year to celebrate a twofold anniversary festival in honour of their National Saint and their National Parliament (Great cheering)'.[36] The repeated mention in the speeches of the name of their hero of the moment, Prime Minister Gladstone, was met with sustained applause and cheering.

The optimism was misplaced, for the Government of Ireland Bill, which became known as the First Home Rule Bill, was defeated in the House of Commons in June 1886. In the election that followed, with Home Rule now the central issue, the Tories, with the support of the Unionists, were victorious and formed the new Government. Gladstone devoted the next six years trying to convince the British electorate to favour Irish Home Rule. Campaigning on the issue, the Liberals won the 1892 election, and he returned for a fourth administration. He once more introduced the Irish Home Rule Bill in 1893, but it was rejected by the House of Lords. Further frustrated attempts by subsequent British Governments led to the armed rebellion in Dublin at Easter in 1916.

---

34. *Freeman's Journal*, 20 February 1886.
35. 'Our National Festival', *Freeman's Journal*, 20 March 1886.
36. *Freeman's Journal*, 20 March 1886.

The speakers at the Botany rally, Freehill and Toohey, led the delegation to Pyrmont in October 1886 in order to form a local branch of the INL. The double aim of the meeting, held in the St Bede's schoolroom, was to express continued support and encouragement for Parnell and Gladstone in the cause of Home Rule, and to collect funds for the Irish Parliamentary Party. John Douglas Young MP, one of the local West Sydney members of the Legislative Assembly, was in the chair, and 'in opening the proceedings said that the object for which they had met had his warmest sympathy', and that 'as a Scotchman he was pleased to see the stand his countrymen at home had taken on this question'.[37] Then followed the first resolution put by Edward O'Sullivan MP for Queanbeyan and seconded by a familiar local, Captain Mat Byrnes: 'That this meeting of citizens of Pyrmont and surrounding districts, in public meeting assembled, heartily approves of the Right Honourable W E Gladstone's policy of Self-Government for Ireland.' Francis Bede Freehill stepped forward to propose the second resolution: 'That a subscription list be now opened, for the benefit of the Payment of Irish Members Fund, such a fund being essentially necessary to enable the Irish members to successfully aid Mr Gladstone in his endeavours to perpetuate friendly relations between Great Britain and Ireland.' Members of Parliament at the time were not remunerated and the Irish members were at a grave financial disadvantage regarding travel to and from London for the parliamentary debates and votes. The final motion proposed 'that a branch of the Irish National League be now formed, in order to augment the constitutional organization that is endeavouring to place the peasants of Ireland on an equal footing with the peasants of other countries'. All resolutions were carried unanimously.[38]

A few weeks after the Pyrmont meeting the task of keeping Irish spirits buoyant was greatly assisted by the return visit to Sydney of Kevin O'Doherty, back in Australia after the defeat of the Home Rule Bill. At the INL meeting in Sydney, O'Doherty was able to rouse the crowd by his personal account of 'the glorious Session in which the measure for granting Home Rule to Ireland was introduced and practically carried by the foremost English statesman of our times', and proclaiming that he had been 'a witness of the greatest political event of the century'.[39] He expressed his confidence that 'the granting of a national Parliament to Ireland . . . was as much a matter of certainty as the rising of the sun to-morrow morning (Cheers).' The question of fund-raising was not neglected and there was great cheering when he triumphantly announced that 'he had received the permission of the Cardinal Archbishop to place his Eminence's name for 100 guineas on

---

37. *Freeman's Journal*, 16 October 1886. Young was a convert from Presbyterianism to Catholicism.
38. *Freeman's Journal*, 16 October 1886.
39. *Freeman's Journal*, 30 October 1886.

the list for Irish Tenants' Relief Fund opened at the meeting'. O'Doherty acknowledged the importance of the support offered by the Irish Catholic hierarchy, and ventured to address the misgivings often expressed about Cardinal Moran's perceived reserve towards Irish independence:

> Speaking for himself, he (Dr. O'Doherty) thought it only right to say that he for one never had the slightest doubt in the matter, and indeed he could scarcely imagine anyone who really knew anything of his Eminence seriously doubting his patriotism for a moment. It should be remembered that the Cardinal was above all things a Churchman, and that it was his habit to act with the greatest prudence and discretion in matters of a political nature. His Eminence in the opinion of some may have been reserved, but they had now a convincing proof if one were needed that his heart was thoroughly Irish. It was something for them to have as their spiritual head in Sydney one who was recognized as the great modem historian of the Irish Church, and acknowledged to be perhaps the first scholar among all the Irish prelates of the world. There can, therefore (said the speaker in conclusion) be little doubt that the example of his patriotism and his generosity will do more than anything else—winning the support of clergy and laity—to bring about the success of the Irish National movement—a magnificent success –throughout the length and breadth of Australia.[40]

The hierarchy had a chance to reciprocate O'Doherty's praise in June 1887 when they wrote in support of a testimonial organised for the Irish patriot: 'His Eminence the Cardinal, in the course of a letter to the treasurers, said: "Dr O'Doherty has been foremost in giving a helping hand to every good cause in the Australian colonies during the past 30 years, and I know of no one amongst us who is more deserving of a grateful and generous testimonial"'. His Lordship the Bishop of Maitland went further, accompanying his letter with a donation: 'Dr O'Doherty, in good report and, evil report, has never been ashamed of his Church or of his country, and supported by his patriotic and gifted wife, he has ever rendered his influential aid in advancing the interests of our holy religion in Australia; and for his native land, I need scarcely say, in his youthful days he passed through fire and water. I have great pleasure in enclosing a cheque for £10, and wishing the movement every success.'[41]

In January 1888 the Australian Colonies celebrated the centenary of the arrival of the First Fleet. The population in the first hundred years had

---

40. *Freeman's Journal*, 30 October 1886.
41. *Freeman's Journal*, 18 June 1887.

increased from a thousand in 1788 to almost three million; the number of aborigines had decreased from an estimated 251,000 in 1788 to approximately 67,000 in 1888; expected to disappear entirely, they formed no part of the centennial celebrations.[42] The *Sydney Morning Herald* published a list of churches where special services were held to give thanks for the event on the Sunday preceding the 28 January celebration.[43] The only Pyrmont church listed was the local Congregational Church in Harris Street where the Rev James Buchan MA held services in the morning and evening. The focus of the local Catholics would have been on the Cathedral events, not on their little local church.

Cardinal Moran made sure that Catholic loyalty to the Empire was on display. The focus of Catholic celebration was at the Cathedral where all the bishops of Australia had gathered for the opening of the Provincial Synod, especially scheduled to coincide with the centenary. St Mary's was the setting for 'the greatest and grandest gathering in connection with the Church that has ever taken place in Australia.'[44] The assembly included the Cardinal, three Archbishops, seven Bishops, the Governors of the seven Australian colonies, the leading public men of New South Wales and a congregation of 5000. The gathering was held to initiate a centennial memorial project for the completion of the Cathedral. The *Freeman's Journal* described the scene with exuberance:

> What a gathering it is, and what a splendid spectacle the platform presents! There is his Excellency Lord Carrington, the Governor of our own colony, in the centre, his richly gemmed star glittering on his breast; by his side the Cardinal, radiant in his robes of red, while in a semi-circle stretching at either side to the tall pillars of the great sanctuary arch are the collected colonial representatives of Royalty in this province of the British Empire, all wearing their knightly decorations and their insignia of office ... Then the prelates seated in the next row to the Governors in their rich purple.[45]

The ailing William Bede Dalley had been invited to give an address of welcome to the Governors. He reminded Lord Carrington that 'nearly seventy years ago, one who then occupied the high and responsible office which your Excellency now fills and adorns laid himself with his own hands the foundation-stone of' this building, declaring that he felt himself very much honoured in having been selected as the representative of his King

---

42. CMH Clark, *A History of Australia*, Melbourne 1987, volume 5, 1.
43. *Sydney Morning Herald*, 23 January 1888.
44. *Freeman's Journal*, 28 January 1888.
45. *Freeman's Journal*, 28 January 1888.

in laying the first stone of the first Roman Catholic church attempted to be erected in Australia'.

Governor Charles Carrington, in the concluding speech, placed himself firmly in the tradition of his predecessors, Lachlan Macquarie and John Young, both of whom had publicly become involved in the building and re-building of the Catholic Cathedral:

> [I]t is in the hope that I may by my presence here assist in the good work in some manner, that I have availed myself of the courteous invitation of his Eminence and that I am here to-night (Applause). While, of course, I hold personally to the doctrine and system of that branch of the Christian Church to which I myself belong, I conceive that in these great colonies it is the duty of the Queen's representative, when acting in his public capacity, to know no distinction of creed or denomination— (great cheering)—and I am very glad to be able to show my sympathy with any work which is intended to serve our common Christianity, and which commands the religious adhesion of so large a section of her Majesty's subjects in this colony (Cheers).[46]

An important change came to the Pyrmont mission district in February 1889 with the arrival of the first curate. Three years previously the growth of the local population had been noted in a *Freeman's Journal* article reporting an intense mission conducted at St Bede's by the Vincentian Fathers. One of the outcomes of the week was the reestablishment of a local abstinence society. Another sobering result was the realisation that after just twenty years the church was proving too small for the growing population in Pyrmont and Ultimo. As noted by the *Journal*: 'The little church on all occasions was crowded to excess, showing the need for a larger or an additional church in the rapidly-increasing suburb of Pyrmont.'[47] Cardinal Moran eventually took note of the needs of the district, and a curate was appointed to assist Father Walsh towards the end of his incumbency in 1889. Richard O'Regan, newly arrived from Ireland, was the first of a succession of young Irish assistants, a pattern that would continue over the next forty years. The arrival of the new curate enabled a smooth transition to a dynamic successor with a proven record for church building. Pyrmont was no longer seen simply as a convenient location for an elderly, semi-retired priest.

Edmund Walsh received the traditional 'address and purse' farewell from his Pyrmont parishioners in April 1889: 'The occasion of the removal of Father E Walsh from St Bede's, Pyrmont, was taken advantage of by the

---

46. *Freeman's Journal*, 28 January 1888.
47. *Freeman's Journal*, 6 November 1886.

committee and parishioners to present him with an address and purse of sovereigns on Thursday evening. Father Walsh replied in feeling terms, expressing his sense of the obligation he owed to the people for their generous support; though removed to another place he would always take great interest in their welfare.'[48] He moved west to Holy Trinity, Granville, where he ministered until his death in 1894 at the age of 71.

---

48. *Freeman's Journal*, 6 April 1889.

Chapter 13
Church and School for Ultimo

Edmund Walsh's dynamic successor, with a proven record for church building, was James Furlong. Born in 1852 in the County of Wexford, he was educated at St Peter's College, Wexford, affiliated to the Catholic University of Ireland. He undertook post-graduate studies at the University of Louvain in Belgium. Ordained in 1875 he served in his home diocese of Ferns until being hand-picked by Patrick Moran, newly appointed Archbishop of Sydney, to accompany him to Australia. Three other Irish priests were in the group sailing to Sydney in 1884—Moran's newly appointed private secretary Dr Denis O'Haran from the Irish College in Rome, and two other young recruits, William Coffey of Dublin and David Fahey of Tuam. The ship-board clerical entourage picked up another Moran protégé on arrival at Adelaide—Patrick Coonan, a graduate of the Kilkenny seminary and ordained by Moran in 1879 for the Adelaide diocese, but now poached for Sydney, where Coonan would become a Monsignor, Vicar-General and parish priest of Forest Lodge for 44 years. The flow of Irish priests to the Sydney Archdiocese increased significantly after the arrival of Archbishop Moran.

James Furlong's first appointment was to St Mary's Cathedral. In 1886 he was sent west to Rookwood as the first resident priest. He immediately began his church building career, inviting Cardinal Moran to bless the foundation stone of the district's first church-school, St Joachim's. The patron saint was chosen because the Rookwood district was a neighbour to St Anne's at Concord—Joachim and Anne were the names traditionally given to the parents of Mary of Nazareth. In 1889 he was transferred south to Camden, a mission with five churches. From there he came back to the city in April 1889, to St Bede's Pyrmont.

The nature of the mission district to which Furlong was appointed was summarised in a report prepared for the incoming pastor by the transitory Pyrmont curate, Richard O'Regan, early in 1889. Entitled, 'Summary of a house to house visitation in the Roman Catholic parish of St Bede's Pyrmont', the report was signed by O'Regan who styled himself 'coadjutor'. The local population was described as 'working class with the exception of about half a dozen Hotel Keepers, as many store-keepers, and about half a dozen private families'. The average Sunday Mass attendance was placed at 500, with Masses at 7am, 9am and 11am. Catechism was taught from 10am to 11am, and on Sunday evenings there was the Office of Vespers at 7pm followed by a sermon and concluding with Benediction. The visitation had identified ten heads of families who never attended Mass, and 'only two cases of concubinage in the parish, otherwise we know of no public scandal'. The school attendance totalled 260 children, taught by two Good Samaritan sisters, assisted by three 'seculars'.[1]

In June Furlong drew on the results of O'Regan's visitation to submit, as required, detailed statistics on the mixed-marriage cases in the district.[2] There was a total of 114. Reporting on the 'Catholic parties', the report divided them into the following categories:

Good	36
Perverts	10
Perpetual absentees from Mass and Sacraments	22
Go occasionally to Mass; very rarely to Sacraments	37

The report did not specify whether the Catholic party was male or female. 'Pervert' was the crude term for a Catholic who had converted to Protestantism and had been married by a parson. Nine 'parties' seemed to have escaped categorisation. Turning to the children of the marriages, Furlong reported:

Marriages without issue	16
Protestant children	13
Infidels	5
Good Catholics	41
Indifferent Catholics	39

These statistics suggest that the canonical requirement that children of mixed-marriages be baptised catholic was being observed in the majority of cases. 'Infidels' were unbaptised children. In the same year, from the neighbouring parish of Forest Lodge, the Benedictine Hugh Bernard Callachor submitted a more nuanced report, avoiding the words 'pervert' and 'infidel':

---

1. *Summary of a house to house visitation in the Roman Catholic Parish of St Bede's Pyrmont*, 1889 (Pyrmont Box, SAA).
2. 'Mixed Marriages in Pyrmont', 12 June 1889 (Furlong File, SAA).

- Out of the 16 Mixed Marriages, one of the non-Catholics parties became a Catholic after the marriage.
- There are 15 non-Catholic husbands.
- There are 75 children, the issue of the above marriages, and out of this number 9 boys and one girl are lost to the Catholic Church, and one wife, I fear, has utterly lost the Faith.[3]

At the age of 37 James Furlong had the energy of the 1867 founder of the mission, Timothy McCarthy. He immediately addressed the problem of church space. The *Freeman's Journal* had succinctly summarised the situation: 'The present church holds only 200 people and the Catholic population is about 1200'.[4] The cramped site of St Bede's, hemmed in on one side by the school and on the other by the presbytery, and restricted at the rear by a high sandstone cliff, allowed no scope for expanding the size of the church. The solution pursued by Furlong was to build a church-school in the southern area of the district. William Henry Street marked the border with St Benedict's parish, so it was in this northern section of the suburb of Ultimo that Father Furlong went looking for an appropriate location for his building project. He purchased a block of land, measuring 122 by 60 feet, with frontages to Crown Road (now Bulwara Road) and Bannister Street (now Henry Avenue) in Ultimo, near the junction of Harris and Quarry Streets. The price was £1904. The land was close to the *Lord Wolseley* Hotel, built in 1878 as the *Glasgow Arms*, and the Presbyterian Church, erected in 1883.

The basic and functional building, which would serve as a church on weekends and a school on weekdays, was designed by Herbert Wardell, son of William Wilkinson Wardell, the architect of the new St Mary's Cathedral and St John's College. The foundation-stone was laid and blessed on Sunday 22 February 1891, twenty-four years after the laying of the St Bede foundation-stone. The newspaper report carried comments about the 'out of the way district' and its inhabitants: 'Pyrmont does not force itself much into public notice, but all the same, it is a populous and fairly enterprising district, and the enthusiasm which marked the ceremony on Sunday proved that when the Catholic residents, though not the happy possessors of much wealth, put their shoulders to the wheel for any good object, they do so in no half-hearted way.'[5] James Furlong seemed to have the drawing power of Timothy McCarthy, and a distinguished group of visitors joined the crowd of locals for the ceremony. The Cardinal presided, accompanied by Bishop

---

3. 'List of Mixed Marriages in Forest Lodge', 30 May 1889 (Callachor File, SAA).
4. *Freeman's Journal*, 21 February 1891.
5. *Freeman's Journal*, 28 February 1891.

Doyle of Grafton who gave the occasional address. Senior clergy of Sydney were present together with the local member of the Legislative Assembly and Postmaster-General, the Honourable Daniel O'Connor, and, of course, the ubiquitous and generous Captain Mat Byrnes. O'Connor, member for West Sydney since 1877, spoke with pride in his constituency; he 'felt justified in saying that in no part of Australia had greater zeal been manifested in proportion to circumstances than in this district'. He won the approval of clergy and laity in identifying closely as a fellow Catholic:

> For his own part he could assure them that he was delighted as one of the household of the faithful, if he might so speak (laughter and applause), and one proud of his membership (applause), to be present that day to assist in his own poor way in this work ... He had only to say by way of conclusion that it was to him a matter of special gratification, interested as he was in West Sydney (laughter and applause), to see this portion of the city so successfully competing in the cause of religion and education with all the other portions of the colony (applause).[6]

Applause at the blessing did not seem to translate into votes for O'Connor at the next election, for he lost his seat in the Assembly in the June elections. He was appointed to the Legislative Council, but was compelled to resign when he was declared bankrupt in the following year.

Cardinal Moran congratulated the priest and people on choosing Francis Xavier as patron saint of the church and school, the first such dedication in Sydney. He highlighted the connection between the great sixteenth-century Jesuit missionary to Asia and the missionary nature of the church in Australia. His comment gave an interesting insight into the selection of parish patrons, a choice that was traditionally thought to be the prerogative of the bishop.

The custom of placing money on the foundation stone resulted in a collection of £180 towards the cost of land and building, the estimated total of which was £700. The major donors were the Cardinal and Father Furlong, £10 each, the Postmaster-General, five guineas, and Captain Byrnes, £5. At the conclusion of the ceremony Cardinal Moran expressed the confident expectation that he would be back at Ultimo in three months-time to bless the new building. The project took a little longer, longer than the building of St Bede's, and it was in October 1891 that the blessing took place, with the auxiliary bishop, Joseph Higgins, presiding.[7] However, the Cardinal had been back at Ultimo in June to open a week-long fund-raising bazaar.[8]

---

6. *Freeman's Journal*, 28 February 1891.
7. *Freeman's Journal*, 10 October 1891.
8. *Freeman's Journal*, 27 June 1891.

Furlong's plan had been that the ample grounds would be big enough to accommodate a future 'substantial and commodious church'.[9] That development never happened. The original church school was replaced with another such practical building in 1924, with the church on the ground floor and the school above. The school was closed in 1973. After the closure of the school two Sisters of St Joseph took up improvised residence in the upstairs portion of the building, and worked among the people of Ultimo. The convent was made available to the St Vincent de Paul Society for the housing of Vietnamese refugees. The church was closed in 1991. The property and buildings were then sold to the City Council and a child-care centre established. The Josephite sisters moved to a parish house in Bulwara Road and continued their mission until 2011.

During 1889, his first year at Pyrmont, James Furlong established a conference of the St Vincent de Paul Society. The founding president of the Society in New South Wales, Scotsman Charles Gordon O'Neill, was present to explain the objects and operations of the Society to the local parishioners. This was not Charles' first visit to Pyrmont. By profession he was an engineer, also styling himself as an architect in newspaper advertisements.[10] In 1888 he had established a business in Elizabeth Street called 'Harbour Tunnels Office'. He and his partners had submitted plans to the government for the construction of railway tunnels under the harbour in 1885 and 1887. Preliminary underwater soundings and borings of the harbor bottom were even undertaken. Also included in his proposals was a railway extension that would run from Union Street, Pyrmont, at an angle across Darling Harbour to King Street, and from there via a tunnel to the Circular Quay.[11]

Born in 1828 Charles studied at Glasgow University and after graduating as a civil engineer he joined the St Vincent de Paul Society in Dumbarton in 1851, within the lifetime of the founder, Frederick Ozanam, who died at Marseille in 1853 at the age of forty. The Society had been founded in Paris in 1833 by Ozanam and fellow university students. Charles had risen in 1863 to become president of the Superior Council of Glasgow and a member of the Council General in Paris. After migrating to New Zealand in 1864 he eventually became provincial engineer at Wellington, overseeing railway and tramway works, and was a member of the House of Representatives from 1866 to 1875. He established the first New Zealand conference of the St Vincent de Paul Society in Wellington in 1876. Moving to Sydney with the express commission of establishing the Society, he founded the

---

9. *Freeman's Journal*, 28 February 1891.
10. *Freeman's Journal*, 7 May 1887.
11. S Utick, *Captain Charles, Engineer of Charity: The Remarkable life of Charles Gordon O'Neill* (Sydney, 2008), 200.

first conference in Sydney in 1881 at St Patrick's, Church Hill, with the encouragement of the French Marists.[12]

In 1885 there was a proposal that the Society establish a Catholic Mission to Seamen to match the long established Protestant Bethel Union and its 1859 Mariners' Church at the Rocks, and the more recent Church of England Mission to Seamen established in 1881 with a temperance meeting held on board HMS *Nelson*: 'Mr Shearston, the new-appointed missionary amongst seamen, inaugurated his work by a temperance meeting on board HMS Nelson. The meeting was held on the main deck, a portion of which had been screened off for the purpose. The attendance was very good, and Mr Shearston gave an excellent address on the temperance question.'[13]

HMS *Nelson* and its sister naval vessels were the focus of the Catholic trial-run in August 1885. The Catholic sailors of the three British warships moored in the harbour were invited to attend Sunday morning Mass at St Patrick's and presented with prayer books by the Society:

> At the last council meeting of St Vincent de Paul Society, it was decided to present a prayer book, as a souvenir, to each Catholic man on board HMS Nelson and the other war vessels of the fleet. Captain Lake, of HMS Nelson, Captain Paul, of HMS Miranda, and Captain Pike, of HMS Harrier, were communicated with and informed of the society's intention. These gentlemen not only approved of the project, but most cheerfully gave permission for the men to wait at St Patrick's Church on Sunday last, after the 9.30 o'clock Mass (at which the sailors attend), for the purpose of receiving the books. Accordingly, shortly after 10 o'clock on Sunday last the sailors assembled in St Patrick's Hall. There were present the Very Rev Father Le Rennetel, SM, the president and officers of the council of the society, and a large number of members. The president (Mr Charles O'Neill) said he hoped the little gift would be accepted in the same spirit of friendship, kindness, and fraternal love which prompted the members of the society.[14]

It was another twenty years before the Catholic Seafarers Mission was established by Cardinal Moran in 1906. Located initially in George Street North, near the Circular Quay, the Mission, later called the Stella Maris Club, was relocated to Kent Street in 1924. The new building, three storeys high,

---

12. CJ Foley, 'O'Neill, Charles Gordon (1828–1900)', *Australian Dictionary of Biography*, National Centre of Biography, Australian National University, http://adb.anu.edu.au/biography/oneill-charles-gordon-4333/text7033, published in hardcopy 1974, accessed online 27 August 2014.
13. *Evening News*, 29 June 1881.
14. *Freeman's Journal*, 22 August 1885.

was blessed and opened by Archbishop Michael Kelly, Moran's successor, who claimed a special 'soft spot for sailors', being the son of a sailor himself.[15] An additional floor was added to the building in 1929 to accommodate a chapel and other facilities. The first chaplain of the Mission was Father William Barry, who later became bishop of Hobart. From 1911 to 1958 one of the members of the Marist community at nearby St Patrick's filled the role. From 1959 to 1992 the Parish Priests of St Bede's combined the chaplaincy with their pastoral ministry among the declining number of parishioners in Pyrmont and Ultimo.

By 1890, within ten years of the establishment of the St Vincent de Paul Society in Sydney there were ten parish conferences, including Pyrmont. On the evening of Sunday 12 August 1889 Charles O'Neill and two of his fellow Councillors accompanied by members of the city conferences crossed Darling Harbour to St Bede's to address a gathering of parishioners, with the intention of inaugurating a local conference of the Society. The President spoke of 'the great good done by the Society in the places where it had been established, not only to the poor whom it visited, but also to its members'.[16] One of the accompanying councillors was the young William Coogan, who would be back at St Bede's fifty years later to participate in the celebration of the golden jubilee of the Pyrmont Conference. James Furlong explained his urgent desire to establish the Society at St Bede's in terms of the social needs of Pyrmont and Ultimo: 'Father Furlong expressed the pleasure it gave him to know that they had a branch of the excellent Society of St Vincent de Paul established in their midst. During the short time he had been in Pyrmont he had been made painfully aware that there was a large amount of poverty and distress in the district, and he believed that no better means existed to meet that poverty than by the establishment of the conference of the society.'[17] The new conference of St Bede's was formed that evening with 12 members, Father Furlong being appointed spiritual director, Mr William Howell, president, Mr J Sullivan secretary, and Mr John Corliss, treasurer.

The 'poverty and distress in the district' would increase dramatically over the next twelve months with the onset of a deep financial depression extending into the 1890s, increasing unemployment and labour unrest, culminating in the great maritime strike of August 1890. The *Sydney Morning Herald* carried an alarming banner headline on 21 August 1890:

THE STRIKE.
BOTH SIDES CONSOLIDATING THEIR POSITION.

---

15. *Catholic Press*, 31 October 1935.
16. *Freeman's Journal*, 24 August 1889.
17. *Freeman's Journal*, 24 August 1889.

NEARLY FIVE THOUSAND MEN ON STRIKE.
ALLEGED INCENDIARISM.
RUMOURS OF STRIKES BY AFFILIATED BODIES.

It may now truly be said of the long-expected conflict between the representatives of capital, and labour that the dogs of war have been slipped, and that the struggle has fairly begun.[18]

Pickets were set up at the harbour wharves, including Pyrmont:

> The wharf labourers at a mass meeting appointed 150 pickets. Their duties have been apportioned as follows: East district—Woolloomooloo and city, first watch, 6pm to 2am; second watch, 2am to 10am; North district—Circular Quay, Miller's Point and Dawes Point; West district Railway, Darling Harbour, Pyrmont, and Sussex Street. Two watches have in each instance been appointed, and each watch consists of about 25 men.[19]

Cardinal Moran's bond with his specially chosen recruit was evidenced by his willing attendance at the fund-raising events organised by Father Furlong. The presence of His Eminence at the opening of the annual week-long parish bazaar, announced in all the metropolitan newspapers, was a drawcard for Catholics from other parts of Sydney and for curious Protestants. Moran could always be counted on to address some topical subject and find his way into the press during the coming week. At the 1889 bazaar the Cardinal spoke in enthusiastic support of the move towards a Federation of the Australian Colonies.[20] His comments were reported as far afield as the northern rivers:

> Cardinal Moran, in declaring a bazaar open to the public at St Bede's, Pyrmont, recently, made brief reference to the federation movement now so prominently before the public. He described the growth of Australasia during the past half-century as phenomenal in the history of the world. They saw a great effort being made to unite the Australian colonies, and the very fact of such a political scheme attracting the serious consideration of all leading statesmen was proof of this wonderful growth. No one could say that Australasia did not possess the possibilities of a great nation, and it augured well for the future that rival statesmen of the hour laid aside

---

18. *Sydney Morning Herald*, 21 August 1890.
19. *Sydney Morning Herald*, 21 August 1890.
20. *Freeman's Journal*, 16 November 1889.

party prejudices and individual interests to devote their united energies to the building up of that great future.[21]

Just before Christmas 1893, Father James Furlong made an unannounced appearance in the pulpit of St Peter's church, Surry Hills, and told the congregation that he would immediately be assuming duties in their district:

> On Sunday morning the Rev Father Furlong, of St Bede's Catholic Church, Pyrmont, announced from the pulpit of St Peter's Church, Surry Hills that he had been offered by the authorities the position of their pastor in succession to the Rev Father Glasheen. It had, he said, been a pleasure to him to accept the position on account of the character given the Surry Hills congregation by the clergy, and it would be his effort to labor assiduously amongst them for a period. The notice thus given came as a surprise to the congregation, who had no notice of the contemplated removal.[22]

The former pastor of St Peter's would re-emerge in New Zealand in the following year as the administrator of St Patrick's Cathedral, Auckland.

The sudden vacancy left at Pyrmont was temporarily filled by the disabled assistant priest, Daniel O'Reilly, who would become St Bede's longest serving curate, assisting four pastors from 1893 to 1900. An All Hallows graduate, he was one of the junior members of a large number of priests arriving in Sydney in October 1885. His first appointment was to St Peter's, Surry Hills, and then in 1887 to Pambula on the far south coast, where he incurred a permanent injury as the result of a riding accident. The accident was described in the 1921 obituary in the *Catholic Press*: 'He had to travel over distances of 15 and 20 miles to reach his outlying churches; and for such long journeys a spirited steed was necessary. On one of these occasions . . . his horse became frightened, and leapt over an embankment. Father O'Reilly was pinned to the ground by his horse, and in trying to extricate himself his spine was injured, which affected him for the rest of his life.' An endearing detail was added: 'after the accident, his parishioners presented him with a carriage', and 'when he was transferred to Sydney, he ordered that the gift be sold, and the proceeds distributed amongst the poor.'[23] That transfer to Sydney found him located at St Bede's, where a carriage would have been more a hindrance than a help. Perhaps some of the poor of Pyrmont were the beneficiaries of his generosity.

---

21. *The Richmond River Herald and Northern Districts Advertiser*, 22 November 1889.
22. *Freeman's Journal*, 18 December 1893.
23. *Catholic Press*, 23 June 1921.

The parish-priest/curate relationship was one fraught with challenges. The arrival of a freshly ordained priest in a parish shifted the focus from the priest-in-charge towards the new young arrival. There was potential for petty jealousies arising from the alienation of affections of parishioners, especially the young ones. Theoretically the curate was the apprentice with much to learn from the experienced pastor, but he was often treated as the servant, as in the Maitland clash between John Lynch and Andrew Phelan, recorded above. An example with a Pyrmont connection was the case of Thomas Ryan, curate at St Bede's from April 1890 to October 1891, who as parish priest at Penrith in 1923 was called before the Archdiocesan Assessors, among whom was his former superior from Pyrmont days, James Furlong. They had been gathered to consider whether the spiritual and financial conditions of the parish of Penrith were greatly prejudiced by the methods of the Reverend Thomas Ryan PP in:
1. the administration of the parish, collections
2. treatment of assistant priest, Father John O'Flaherty
3. his unpopularity on account of various causes.[24]

The report of the assessors noted the curate's complaint that he had not received payment from Ryan for the month of August, and that Ryan was always insulting him. Ryan said he had no intention of paying a curate who was disrespectful and often absent, and who was 'the most surly person' he had ever met. He further threatened that if the curate were not removed, other measures would be taken. The finding of the Assessors was that, everything considered, Father Ryan's spiritual and financial administration was satisfactory, and that, while the relationship of parish priest and curate was not harmonious, Father Ryan had undertaken to work amicably with an agreeable assistant.[25] The next month John O'Flaherty was transferred to Newtown and Austin Bradstreet, a future parish priest of Pyrmont, was sent to assist Thomas Ryan at Penrith.[26]

There were exceptions to such troubled relationships, one notable example being instanced in the neighbouring parish to the west of Pyrmont, St James, Forest Lodge, where the priest-in-charge dedicated a stained glass window to his curate in 1890—the curate happened to be the senior of the two priests: 'Erected to the memory of the Rev Myles Edmund Athy OSB by his brother in religion Rev Hugh Bernard Callachor OSB BA.'[27] The ideal

---

24. Thomas Ryan File, S.A.A.
25. Thomas Ryan File, SAA.
26. *Freeman's Journal*, 15 November 1923.
27. Anne Wark, *Armour of light: the stained glass windows of St James' Church, Forest Lodge, those to whom they are dedicated and their families*, (Forest Lodge, 2010).

episcopal report following parish visitations was: 'There is harmony in the presbytery, all the priests quite happy.'[28] This was rarely achieved.

With the annual increased influx of young priests from Ireland following the appointment of Sydney's first Irish Archbishop, there arose the custom of shifting the new arrivals through a range of different parishes under the supervision of a variety of parish priests. This was a far cry from the Polding style of sending new arrivals to establish new missions alone in remote regions, as instanced by the newly ordained Eugene Luckie sent to Ipswich in 1848, Michael Harrington Ryan to Norfolk Island in 1848 and Timothy McCarthy, aged twenty-four, dispatched to Armidale in 1853.

During the 1890s the staffing of St Bede's presented an example of the Moran approach to clerical appointments. Except for the case of the lame Daniel O'Reilly's seven years at Pyrmont from 1893 to 1899, the other four curates under James Furlong from 1890 to 1893 served terms of eighteen, nine, six and two months. The same pattern was resumed from 1900 to 1920 with a succession of twelve curates assisting three priests-in-charge.

The subsequent careers of the Furlong curates provide an insight into the development of the Archdiocese of Sydney and its clergy. Richard O'Regan remained just a few weeks at Pyrmont, his first appointment, after James Furlong's arrival. His subsequent moves were recorded in the obituary printed in the *Catholic Press* in October 1936 headed, 'Redfern's Great Bereavement':

> Born in Bathcannon, Killmallock, County Limerick, Ireland, on All Saints' Day, 1802, Archdeacon O'Regan was educated at the national schools, and received his training for the priesthood from the Cistercian monks at Mount Melleray and at St Patrick's College, Carlow. He was ordained in 1888 at St Patrick's College, and came to Australia the same year. His first labours were at Pyrmont and Newtown—in the latter suburb he was with the Benedictine priest, Father Paul Fitzpatrick; then followed successive appointments at Gosford, Parramatta, and St Mary's Cathedral before he began his long ministry in Redfern, succeeding the late Father Tuckwell. He celebrated his first Mass there on the first Sunday of August 42 years ago.[29]

O'Regan succeeded to the unique title of Venerable Archdeacon after the death of James Furlong, his neighbour at Enmore, in 1927.

---

28. J Fletcher & M Hogan, *St James' Parish, Forest Lodge. 125 years: 1877-2002* (Forest Lodge, 2002), 24.
29. *Catholic Press*, 8 October 1836.

Pyrmont's next curate, Thomas Ryan, arrived a year after O'Regan's departure, in April 1890. His priestly ministry in the Archdiocese was summarised in the obituary printed in the *Catholic Press* in November 1931:

> The death occurred in Lewisham Hospital on Saturday, 7th. inst., of Rev. Father Thomas Ryan P.P., who was pastor of Penrith for the last 16 years . . . Father Ryan was born at Newport, Tipperary, Ireland, 66 years ago. He studied for the priesthood at All Hallows College, Dublin, and came to Australia in 1889, taking up priestly duties on the mission. He was assistant priest in turn at Mt. Carmel, Waterloo, Pyrmont, and Redfern. From the early part of this century, Father Ryan was priest-in-charge at Milton, Araluen, Michelago, Burragorang (twice), South Grafton, Smithtown, Gosford, and Redfern (twice), and Parramatta (for a few months). He was relieving P.P. at Windsor, and 16 years ago went to Penrith, where he continued till his death. It is a large parish, and includes important outlying places, such as St Marys, Rooty Hill, Mulgoa, Castlereagh, &c.[30]

The pattern of frequent appointments as curate and 'priest-in-charge' reflected the policy of the Archbishops in 'removing' priests at will, 'for the good of the ministry', until a final appointment as 'irremovable parish priest'. Canon Law, however, did allow for the removal of an irremovable priest in the case of misdemeanours, as inferred from the Archdiocesan Assessors' investigation of Father Ryan in 1923, cited above.

Edmund Riordan Creagh succeeded Thomas Ryan as curate at Pyrmont and remained for nine months from November 1891 to July 1892. He had arrived in Sydney from Ireland in November 1889. His first recorded appointment was as chaplain to the Benedictine nuns at Subiaco, on the Parramatta River. From March 1890 this work was combined with ministry at the new Holy Name of Mary church-school at Rydalmere, part of the Parramatta parish. The building had been designed by Charles O'Neill, President of the Vincent de Paul Society.[31] The young engineer had an established reputation for gothic-revival architecture in Scotland. In 1858 the *Glasgow Free Press* wrote of him that his 'architectural talents have won him the same place among the Catholics of Scotland as that of J J McCarthy in Ireland and Edward Pugin in England'.[32] The simple structure at Rydalmere displayed little sign of 'gothic-revival'.

In 1891 Creagh was briefly at Cooma, from where he was assigned to Pyrmont. There were no references to him after his last entry in the St Bede's

---

30. *Catholic Press*, 12 November 1931.
31. Utick, *Captain Charles*, 203.
32. Quoted in Utick, *Captain Charles*, 33.

Baptismal Register in July 1892 until his appearance on the passenger list of the steamer *Pilbarra* which arrived in Adelaide from Sydney in June 1901.[33] He was next found at the isolated goldfields town of Cue in Western Australia in the diocese of Geraldton, which had been established in 1898. In 1903 the local newspaper reported the destruction by fire of the church and residence at Cue, and the loss of the personal property of Father Creagh and the visiting Bishop of Geraldton, William Kelly.[34] The details of the tragedy were recorded by the diarist of the local Dominican convent:

> It seems that flames had quickly spread after a sudden gust of wind unexpectedly blew a curtain on top of a lamp that Father Creagh had been carrying between rooms. The combination of flaming material and the exploding lamp soon set fire to the presbytery and, fanned by strong winds, the fire soon carried the flames along to the church and into the eaves and the roof. The Anglican rector, who was one of the first on the scene, thoughtfully ran into the church and rescued the Blessed Sacrament. He then passed the ciborium to the sacristan, Sister Hyacinth Carroll, who carefully wrapped it in her scapular.[35]

Father Creagh spent the rest of his life in the Geraldton diocese. In 1906 he was located at coastal Greenough where he built the new church of St Peter in 1908: 'The Catholic people of Greenough may feel a pardonable pride in the possession of such a magnificent church. To their zealous and indefatigable pastor, Father Creagh, they must realise that they owe a deep debt of gratitude, for were it not for his untiring energy and unflagging determination, great results could never have been so quickly achieved.'[36] He continued as parish priest until his death in June 1917 at the age of 52 after a long incapacitating illness. In August 1913 he had addressed a pitiful begging letter to all his fellow priests on the Australian mission:

> If you refer to the *Ordo* you will find my name on the Sick List. For more than 20 years I have suffered from a very painful spinal disease, now resulting in my being almost a complete cripple. I am confined to my room and mostly to my bed. By the aid of a stick I am able only to move a few steps. In the progress of the disease my sight has been so impaired that reading and writing are a great difficulty. I have not been able to attend to any of my active duties for a year. During the last six years I

---

33. *Adelaide Advertiser*, 17 June 1901.
34. *Western Mail*, 5 December 1903.
35. Ruth Marchant James, *Fields of Gold: a history of the Dominican Sisters in Western Australia*, Doubleview WA, 1999, 79.
36. *Geralton Express*, 1 February 1909.

have had strenuous work to cope with in my District, and had to grip on to the Altar to say my Mass. I have been in hospitals often and long, and have left no remedies untried that are known to medical science. All to no purpose, except to leave me penniless. I have determined now, when I have found the needful [sic], to visit Lourdes and see if it may please Our Lady to do there something for me. This is my last plank. There is so far no Infirm Fund in this Diocese. The Diocese is poor and has few priests. I would like to have 30 more years of active work. Father, please help with a trifle so that I can make Lourdes.

Yours in much pain and misery, Edmund Creagh.[37]

There is no evidence of any response from fellow clergy; the invalid did not reach Lourdes. The death notice in the local newspaper named the disease from which Father Creagh suffered: 'The death occurred on Saturday night, at the Presbytery, Greenough, of the Rev Father E R Creagh who had been an invalid for some years, the cause of death being *locomotor ataxy*. Deceased, who was 52 years of age, came to the district about fifteen years ago, and had charge of several parishes in the diocese, and was held in high esteem.'[38]

Following Edmund Creagh at Pyrmont was Patrick O'Shea, who briefly served as curate from October 1892 to April 1893. He was a graduate of All Hallows College, which supplied most of the young Irish priests destined for Sydney. After just a few years in the Archdiocese, with appointments in quick succession at Pyrmont, Braidwood, Camden and Gosford, he transferred to the Goulburn diocese in 1898 where he gained his first appointment as parish priest of Wyalong in 1904, followed by Murrumburrah in 1907. His decision to leave Sydney for Goulburn was related by historian Roger Wynne as the first of many flights from Cardinal Moran's rule in Sydney:

> [Moran's] appointment as Archbishop was regarded with a degree of apprehension by many who had vivid memories of the Fenian and Tenant Right League days. One such person was Father Patrick O'Shea, who was particularly proud of the fact that he was a nephew of the patriotic Father Thomas O'Shea, the 'people's priest', who in 1852 had incurred the grave displeasure of Cardinal Cullen by boldly espousing the stand taken by Frederick Lucas against the betrayers of the Tenant League . . . A few years spent in Gosford and other such places in the backblocks were sufficient to convince him that this distinction was really no asset in the

---

37. TJ Linane, *From Abel to Zundolovich. Biographies of priests on the Australian scene up to 1900* (volume 2, 'Byrne' to 'Dixon'), Armadale 1979, 103-104.
38. *Geraldton Guardian*, 19 June 1917.

diocese of Cardinal Cullen's nephew, so he promptly betook himself to the more congenial atmosphere of Goulburn.[39]

While a curate at Wagga, Patrick O'Shea had occasion to write to the Catholic newspapers in Sydney and to the local *Wagga Wagga Express* questioning the findings of a Coroner's jury concerning the death in May 1903 of Joseph Bunbury, with whom he had sailed to Australia in 1892. The Sydney *Evening News* reporting the inquest had carried the eye-catching headline:

> A PRIEST'S SUICIDE.
> RELIEVED OF HIS POSITION
> ON THE GROUND OF HIS ECCENTRICITY.[40]

Father O'Shea wrote with the intention of removing 'a stigma which I consider has been unjustly attached to the memory of an old and esteemed friend of mine, the late Rev. Joseph Bunbury, whom a coroner's jury pronounced to have committed suicide by poisoning himself with strychnine'.[41] He offered an alternative explanation of his friend's death:

> For years past it was well known to his friends that Father Bunbury suffered from a weak heart, and as a corrective of this malady he was in the habit of taking strychnine. It was done with the full knowledge of a medical practitioner, but it would appear that with the growth of the disease Father Bunbury had increased the dose of his medicine to an extent disapproved of by his medical adviser. This, it will be allowed is by no means an uncommon practice with patients, who are apt to become careless through the constant use of a drug and naturally imagine that having become habituated to its effects a little more than the usual quantity is not likely to injure them. What happened in Father Bunbury's case was, I presume, that it being his intention to leave Sydney by the *Medic* on the following day for Europe he being in a weak state of health, with the object of strengthening himself to make the necessary preparations for his departure, took a larger dose of his medicine than he should have done, thus bringing about the fatal result his friends so deeply deplore.[42]

---

39. Roger Wynne, 'The coming of Cardinal Moran', *Australasian Catholic Record*, 47(1970): 205.
40. *Evening News*, 22 May 1903.
41. *Freeman's Journal*, 13 June 1903.
42. *Freeman's Journal*, 13 June 1903.

He also wrote in praise of Joseph Bunbury's impressive talents: 'Father Bunbury was a ripe scholar having completed his theological studies for the priesthood at the College of the Propaganda, Rome, where he was ordained priest in 1892. The deceased priest, if I may be permitted to say so, was a journalist by instinct, his power as a leader writer and caustic paragraphist being acknowledged by experienced pressmen to be up to a very high standard.'[43] The young Bunbury had been appointed inaugural editor of the new Catholic newspaper, the *Catholic Press* in 1895, and was a regular contributing journalist, while acting as curate in a range of Sydney parishes, including Surry Hills, as James Furlong's curate, and Forest Lodge.

The report in the *Evening News* reminded readers that in 1902 Bunbury had made controversial 'remarks at a Hibernian gathering on the question of Imperialism', a dinner at which Cardinal Moran presided.[44] In fact, he had advocated a republican form of government for both Ireland and Australia, and had been publicly rebuked at the dinner by the Catholic Minister of Public Works and former editor of the *Freeman's Journal*, Edward O'Sullivan.[45] Over several years Bunbury had also been an outspoken opponent of the Boer War, seeing parallels between the Empire's aggression towards the Irish and the Boers. As a result of his controversial public interventions he had been re-assigned away from Sydney. Both Cardinal Moran and his coadjutor Michael Kelly were strongly opposed to any voices advocating a form of Irish self-government separate from the British Empire. Indeed, following the departure of Moran for Europe soon after the Hibernian banquet, it was Kelly who assigned Bunbury from Forest Lodge in Sydney to Appin and then to Camden.

At the coroner's inquest Dean O'Haran, Cardinal Moran's private secretary, gave evidence that Bunbury had been 'relieved of his position as a priest on the ground of his eccentricity', and had been living for three weeks at the Lloyd Hotel, George Street North, where he was found dead.[46] The inference was that he had been distressed at the re-assignments and was abandoning the mission, and that he had finally lost all hope. The tragedy received widespread reporting throughout Australia. A Northern Rivers newspaper added further details, both disedifying and edifying: 'The medical evidence was to the effect that . . . the appearance of the liver, stomach, and kidneys were those usually found in persons addicted to the use of alcohol . . . Deceased left a will in favour of the poor.'[47] The *Freeman's*

---

43. Freeman's Journal, 13 June 1903.
44. *Evening News*, 22 May 1903.
45. *Sydney Morning Herald*, 26 February 1902.
46. *Evening News*, 22 May 1903.
47. *Clarence River Advocate*, 26 May 1903.

Journal published a summary of the tragedy which very respectfully reflected on the pressures placed on a talented but vulnerable young Irish priest:

> The tragic close of the Rev Joseph Bunbury's life on Thursday in last week caused a painful shock to the Catholic community, to whom both in city and country he was well known. He came to the Archdiocese of Sydney a young priest of brilliant parts, bringing to his work unbounded enthusiasm and the Celtic temperament—two qualities which in a priest promised a future of much service in the cause of religion. He saw great possibilities for Catholicity in this country, and perhaps he allowed his zeal for the quickening of Catholic progress in some respects to outpace his discretion. A nature such as his—and the remark is made in no censorious way—was probably impatient of that safe policy of 'Festina lente' [*hasten slowly*] which has done so much for the Church in Australia; for at the back of his mind there were forces which brooked no delay. But these forces were lodged in a body never very robust, and mainly nerves, and the mental balance once lost, the evolution from eccentricity to the mania which produced last week's tragedy may easily be accounted for. But in remembrance of the brilliant early promise of Father Bunbury's life the manner of its close may be allowed to drop into oblivion; and very general, very sincere, will be the charitable aspiration—'May he rest in peace!'[48]

Patrick O'Shea was visiting Sydney in 1918 when he suddenly fell ill and was hospitalised at St Vincent's. He was diagnosed with pneumonia and died on 16 May at the age of 51. The news was a great shock to his parishioners at Murrumburah. The *Freeman's Journal* reported the eulogy given by the Bishop of Goulburn, John Gallagher:

> Model of a devoted priest and Christian gentleman, how amiable and accessible he was to all, rich and poor; how sincerely humble, how retiring he was, yet with that genuine sympathy and warmth of heart which enabled him to enter, just as one of themselves, into all the little cares and worries, sports and pastimes of his children and his people. Although no duty connected with his sacred office was ever neglected, yet he found time for study; and through continuous reading in those leisure hours when the labors of the day were over, he was conversant with affairs, and had a more than average acquaintance with science and literature, ancient and modern, sacred and profane. Always dominated by a high sense of duty, courteous and affable to all, 'a priest according to

---

48. *Freeman's Journal*, 30 May 1903.

God's own heart,' he has been taken from us too soon for the wants of the diocese and the affectionate longings of his flock.[49]

The long serving curate, Daniel O'Reilly, was transferred in 1900 to St Peter's, Surry Hills, where he rejoined James Furlong. He served there as curate until 1909 when he became seriously ill. The parishioners made a special presentation to him:

> Mr Hoyle read an address expressive of' deep regret and sympathy with the Rev. Father O'Reilly in his affliction, and in a few well-chosen words conveyed to the rev. gentleman the high esteem in which he was held by the parishioners of St Peter's for the self-sacrificing way in which he had always carried out his duties as a priest and a citizen ... Notwithstanding his suffering, Father O'Reilly was in one of his humorous strains. He had hopes of a recovery, but whatever happened he would always joyfully remember his happy days among the people of St Peter's, Surry Hills.[50]

The issues of the *Catholic Directory* from 1910 to 1916 listed Daniel O'Reilly as 'on leave of absence'. He returned to Ireland and died in 1921 at the family farm. The *Catholic Press* obituary concluded: 'He was one of the most popular priests in Sydney.'[51]

James Furlong himself had an impressive career as a Sydney priest, outliving three of his five Pyrmont curates. On leaving St Bede's at the end of 1893 he was priest-in-charge at Surry Hills until 1904 when he became administrator of St Benedict's, where the Coadjutor Bishop, Michael Kelly, was the resident titular rector. In 1910 he was appointed the first parish priest of Enmore when it was separated from the Newtown district. In the tradition of priest-builders he provided his new parish with church, convent, school and presbytery. In 1926 he was elevated to the position of Archdeacon with the accompanying title of 'Venerable'. Sydney had several deans, and many monsignors, but a diocese could have but one archdeacon and one archpriest, titles that would disappear in years to come. He died in November 1926 at the age of 73. Archbishop Michael Kelly reminisced about his friend in the panegyric at the Requiem Mass, slipping in and out of the 'royal plural':

> He was companionable, sincere, and possessed fidelity and to us he stood in more than one relation since we became Australians. Providence kept him by my side at St Benedict's, and other places, and we had the benefit

---

49. *Freeman's Journal*, 23 May 1918.
50. *Freeman's Journal*, 2 December 1909.
51. *Catholic Press*, 23 June 1921.

of his counsel. We met first over 60 years ago. He was educated at St Peter's Seminary, and when I went there it was to join one of the higher classes. In the priesthood I was in advance of Father Furlong, and well I remember him for he had little changed in demeanour or of general appreciation from those days. During my mission in Ireland I found him as a curate, and when I arrived in Sydney Father Furlong was before me.[52]

In his will the established a 'scholarship of £120 a year for the purpose of giving a post-graduate course to a cleric of the Archdiocese of Sydney in Sacred Orders at his old Alma Mater, the great University of Louvain in Belgium'.[53] In 1919 he had already funded a bursary for students preparing for the Sydney Archdiocese at St Peter's College, Wexford.[54] The first beneficiary of the Louvain scholarship was Justin Simonds, who would become the first Australian-born Archbishop in 1937, initially of Hobart and then of Melbourne in 1963.[55] Subsequent scholarship holders were historian Eris O'Brien, future Archbishop of Canberra-Goulburn, and Monsignor Thomas Veech, Vice-President of St Patrick's College at Manly and Rector of St Columba's College, Springwood.

---

52. *Freeman's Journal*, 4 November 1926.
53. *Freeman's Journal*, 26 July 1928.
54. KJ Walsh, *Yesterday's Seminary. A history of St Patrick's Manly* (Sydney, 1998), 360, n 10.
55. *Freeman's Journal*, 26 July 1928.

Chapter 14
Towards the End of the Century

The successor of James Furlong at Pyrmont was Patrick Matthias Ryan. This Irish priest had had an unusual preparation for ordination. Born in Westmeath in 1851, he began his priestly studies at St Edmund's at Ware in Hampshire, the seminary of the Westminster Archdiocese centred in London. He completed his studies and was ordained in 1879 at the famous seminary of Saint-Sulpice in Paris. His bypassing of the Irish seminaries came about through the influence of his uncle, Michael Harrington Ryan who was for a time a priest of the Westminster Archdiocese.

Michael had been recruited with Eugene Luckie for New South Wales while students at All Hallows Dublin; they were ordained together in Sydney in 1848. Ryan then spent twelve years ministering to the most hardened convicts at Norfolk Island and Van Diemen's Land. He left Tasmania in 1861 following a dispute with Bishop Robert Willson over his defiance of the bishop's prohibition on clergy support for a newspaper edited by Irish nationalist John Donnellan Balfe.[1] He was received into Westminster by Cardinal Wiseman and assigned to the mission of Turnham Green where he built a church, presbytery and school.[2] In 1869 he returned to Australia ministering at Grafton and then at Newcastle, where he was Vicar General to Bishop Murray of Maitland diocese. He also cared for the veteran Newcastle missioner, the Dominican Christopher Dowling who died in 1873. In 1878 he was invited to Sydney by Archbishop Vaughan to succeed Timothy McCarthy as Dean at St Mary's, with the chief task of continuing to collect for the building of the new cathedral. Michael Ryan had displayed an impressive flair for fund-raising when he persuaded his Newcastle congregation to provide a carriage and pair for the Coadjutor Archbishop

---

1. WT Southerwood, *The Convict's Friend: Bishop R. W. Willson* (Hobart, 1989), 142.
2. *The Tablet*, 9 April 1864.

soon after his arrival in 1873.[3] As Dean he laboured for five years on the task of completing the northern section of the cathedral, which was dedicated and opened for public worship in September 1882.

In that year Michael was again influential in his nephew's life, urging Patrick to seek a canonical '*exeat*', leave of absence, from Cardinal Manning of Westminster, so that he could transfer to the Sydney Archdiocese. Several members of the Ryan family had migrated to Australia, beginning with Michael's sister Mary in 1842, then followed by the two other sisters and his brother Peter, Patrick's father. This was a pattern for many Irish immigrant families, as was the influence of a priest brother and uncle in encouraging family members to migrate to Australia. With Patrick's arrival in Sydney in 1883 the Ryan family's relocation to Australia was almost complete, his parents, Peter and Margaret, having arrived in 1879. Patrick's first appointment from Archbishop Vaughan was as assistant to his uncle Michael at St Mary's Cathedral, where he became fondly known as 'little Father Ryan'.[4]

After seven years as Cathedral Dean, Michael's health had completely broken down.[5] Vaughan's successor Patrick Moran relocated the Ryans, uncle and nephew, away from the cathedral in 1885, sending Michael to the small mission of St Bede at Appin, and Patrick across town to St Francis de Sales at the Haymarket as senior curate. Later in the year the still ailing Michael Ryan was assigned to Camden where his siblings resided and where he was joined by his nephew as his assistant. The following year Patrick was assigned as priest-in-charge of the new district of Leichhardt, and his uncle Michael joined him as assistant, where he would be in easy reach of medical attention at the Royal Prince Alfred Hospital. But the 'years of hardship and neglect had taken their toll' and he died in November 1887.[6] His obituary in the *Freeman's Journal* concluded: 'His last appointment to Leichhardt was intended as a rest for him, but he persisted in doing work, and died literally "in harness" at the fine old age of 66.'[7] Patrick celebrated the Requiem Mass for his uncle at their church of St Fiacre in the presence of Cardinal Moran and Bishop Murray of Maitland.

A succession of appointments followed for Patrick, taking him from Leichhardt to Hurstville, Camperdown, Kogarah and, in 1893, to the chaplaincy to the Benedictine nuns at Subiaco Monastery, which encompassed ministry in the Rydalmere district. In February of the following year he was appointed as priest-in-charge at St Bede. The Pyrmont

---

3. *Freeman's Journal*, 16 May 1874.
4. *Sunday Times*, 15 July 1917.
5. Wynne, 'The Coming of Cardinal Moran', 284.
6. Wynne, 'The Coming of Cardinal Moran', 284.
7. *Freeman's Journal*, 19 November 1887.

peninsula with its docks and wharves and working-class population must have seemed very much like the setting of his first parish appointment as curate at St Edmund's, Millwall, in the East End docks area of London. Awaiting him at Pyrmont was the curate Daniel O'Reilly, who had held the fort over the Christmas period after the sudden transfer of Father Furlong. For the brief two and a half years of his incumbency, Patrick and Daniel, residing together in the Pyrmont Street presbytery, shared the ministry at the two churches and schools of the mission district, St Bede's at Pyrmont and St Francis Xavier's at Ultimo.

The New Year at Pyrmont had been inaugurated with a bonfire in one of the quarries which drew crowds of the local youth 'who apparently enjoyed themselves'.[8] There was not much source of entertainment for the young people of Pyrmont. Their fathers had an abundance of pubs at which to relax after a hard day's work, if they were lucky enough to be employed; their mothers had the traditional range of interests as expressed in the Italian phrase: 'casa, chiesa, spesa'—'home, church and shopping'. The Pyrmont baths, built in 1875 at the bottom of steep stairs leading down from Point Street, constituted the only recreational area for the local children and youth. The pool was tidal, and the floor was sand. One resident remembered: 'You could see the bottom, clear as you like. We used to catch yabbies in that pool'.[9] The future of the baths was threatened in 1888 by an attempt by timber merchants to lease them. The Municipal Council opposed the grab, but failed to maintain them. They fell into a deplorable state and the water became so polluted as to be dangerous to health. The situation was lamented at a meeting of the Municipal Council in January 1893:

> Discussion took place as to the necessity for repairing the Pyrmont baths. Several letters were received, complaining of the state of the baths. It was pointed out that some time since the council had decided, on the recommendation of the city surveyor, to spend £153 in repairs, but that the matter had been afterwards referred back, as there was very little income from the baths. Alderman M Harris said that filth surrounded the baths, and alterations were absolutely necessary. It was resolved to recommend the council to carry out the alterations.[10]

However, no action was taken until 1902. The adventurous youth of the district resorted to the even more dangerous diversion of swimming in flooded quarries, which led to several drownings. Sporting teams provided a more organised and safer outlet for youthful energies. The Pyrmont Rangers

---

8. *Sydney Morning Herald*, 1 January 1894.
9. *Port Pyrmont: historical walking tour*, Sydney, circa 1995, 5.
10. *Sydney Morning Herald*, 20 January 1893.

soccer club and its junior teams, the Swifts and Rovers, were regularly triumphant in the annual inter-suburban competitions. The local churches organised junior versions of their adult groups: the Methodists had the Rose of Pyrmont Juvenile Temple[11], and the Catholics had their junior section of the Temperance League of the Cross, which each year gathered the children from local branches to the Cathedral for the annual procession and pledge renewal.[12]

The major local concern during 1894 was the state of the Pyrmont Bridge. An accident in January, when a steamer rammed and severely damaged the bridge, had led to a two week closure, bringing great inconvenience to both commercial and pedestrian users. The Council provided free ferry service across Darling Harbour for the foot traffic, but vehicular traffic was required to take the long route from the city to Pyrmont via Parramatta Road and Harris Street. During the repair of the bridge it was discovered that the forty-year-old timbers were riddled with termites and in danger of collapse. Vehicles were restricted to a walking pace. The *Sydney Morning Herald* sent a special reporter to investigate. He began his inspection by observing the 'transit commissioner' stationed at the centre of the bridge vainly attempting to restrict the speed of horse-drawn wagons and carts:

> It is his duty to see that the walking regulation is carried out, and as far as the heavy wagons are concerned he has no difficulty. But it is otherwise with the lighter fry, the hansoms and dogcarts. Time is money to the drivers, and as soon as the commissioner is passed one can see them furtively urging the horse into a trot, which increases in speed as the distance from the officer becomes greater.[13]

He reported that every plank of 'this crazy structure' vibrated under his feet, and the piles trembled, and a collapse seemed imminent. He rehearsed the history of the bridge from its construction by a private company in 1857 to its acquisition by the Government in 1884, when it was already in a dilapidated state, and the subsequent abolition of the toll. He concluded that the only way forward was to demolish the bridge and provide a westward crossing from the city by reclaiming the southern end of Darling Harbour up to Bathurst Street:

> It is not probable that we will ever see another Pyrmont Bridge. The changed conditions of city traffic, and especially the heavy shipments made from the railway wharfs, have rendered the bridge rather an

---

11. *Sydney Morning Herald*, 9 May 1894.
12. *Freeman's Journal*, 3 November 1894.
13. *Sydney Morning Herald*, 24 March 1894.

obstruction than an aid to traffic, and in all probability we will be able, by reclaiming a small portion of Darling Harbour, to do away with the bridge altogether.[14]

The Public Works Committee of the Council was set the task of coming up with a firm, costed recommendation, and it met regularly throughout the year, receiving a large range of proposals. One of them came from Charles O'Neill, engineer, but better known as the founder of the St Vincent de Paul Society in Sydney. His proposal was an expansion of the favoured reclamation proposal—from the head of the Harbour as far as Market Street. He suggested 'reserving five acres for salt water baths', and 'erecting jetties along the line of reclamation'. His advocacy of filling in such a large area of Darling Harbour was based on health reasons: 'Mr O'Neill considers the reclamation a sanitary improvement of the greatest consequence to the health of the citizens, as this portion of the harbour in its present state is a huge cesspool.' From his visits to poor households Charles was well aware of the health hazards in the slum areas of Sydney. His proposal for the associated extension of the rail system also carried social advantages by addressing the aggravated unemployment situation:

> The scheme also includes the extension of the Redfern railway from Pyrmont over the reclaimed land, thence by two double-line tunnels direct to Circular Quay . . . This would connect Circular Quay with the Redfern Railway, and thus afford wonderful facilities for great traffic to and from Circular Quay and the interior of the country. If this scheme was carried out employment would be given to a large body of men, and thereby ease the great distress now existing, while it would create a splendid profit for the Government.[15]

The locals were alarmed at the prospect of losing their convenient bridge access to and from the city, and meetings were held and letters sent to the newspapers in support of building a new bridge. 'E Thompson' wrote on behalf of the 'Ultimoites and Pyrmontese' strongly urging the acceptance of a proposal that not only provided a replacement bridge, but also incorporated a tramway, 'long needed locomotion to save our time and our legs'.[16] Local businessmen called a meeting at Elder's Hall in Harris Street and passed resolutions calling for a larger bridge: 'If it was deemed necessary to construct the bridge 37 years ago when the population did not exceed 50,000, how much more necessary was it now when it had increased to 250,000?

---

14. *Sydney Morning Herald*, 24 March 1894.
15. *Freeman's Journal*, 19 May 1894.
16. *Sydney Morning Herald*, 24 May 1894.

(Cheers)[17] A recommendation against reclamation and in favour of bridge replacement was finally made by the Works Committee in December, but not implemented by Council until 1899 when the construction of a new bridge parallel to the old was begun. It was completed and opened and the old bridge was demolished in 1902.

1894 was an election year in New South Wales. From January to July hopeful candidates addressed electors on street corners and from hotel balconies, the most favoured being the Caledonian on the corner of Herbert and Point streets and the Quarrymen's Arms on the corner of John and Mount streets, both still standing, though as private, not public houses. On Saturday 14 July at a meeting of electors in Pyrmont Street the local district returning officer formally announced the four candidates for the next Parliament.[18] That night a huge torchlight procession of 'several thousand members' of the Labour Leagues moved through the city electorates:

> On passing the branch office of the *Herald* [King-street] groans were given and a similar compliment was paid to the other newspaper offices as they were passed on the line of march. The chorus of the familiar marching song 'John Brown's Body', was parodied to 'We'll hang George Dibbs on a sour apple-tree,' which was lustily sung, both here and at some other points. When passing the headquarters of any obnoxious candidate a demonstration of groans was made, this occurring at several points in the three hours' journey of Saturday evening . . . The route of the procession was from Chancery-square along King-street, Pitt street, Market street, across Pyrmont Bridge to Harris-street and along that street through Ultimo-road, Engine-street, back to George street, along Park-street, William-street, Riley-street North, Woolloomooloo street, Brougham-street to Willliam-street, Bourke-street, Oxford-street, Crown-street, Albion-street, Randle-street, Elizabeth-street and Cleveland-street to Prince Alfred Park where the assemblage arrived just at ten minutes before half-past 11 o'clock.[19]

Pyrmont's status as a division of the City of Sydney was still a source of bewilderment to the *Herald*'s reporter who commented with amazement that 'the working men who took part in the procession . . . cheerfully allowed themselves to be led all over the city and suburbs, right away into far Pyrmont'.

Life at St Bede's and St Francis Xavier's followed a well-established pattern, with special events punctuating the weekly church and school activities. The

---

17. *Evening News*, 29 May 1894.
18. *Sydney Morning Herald*, 16 July 1894.
19. *Sydney Morning Herald*, 16 July 1894.

annual picnic at Chowder Bay continued to be the major social event of the year for both adults and children and for local and invited clergy. An annual visit from the Cardinal to Pyrmont or Ultimo for confirmation or bazaar openings could be counted on. An annual week-long mission conducted by members of one of the increasing number of Sydney-based religious orders was on the agenda. The Franciscans and the Passionists were the most regular missioners at Pyrmont and Ultimo.

Father Ryan brought a new element to parish administration when in January 1895 he printed and distributed a financial report: *St Bede's and St Francis' Parochial Account 1894*. It showed a total debt of £1131 serviced by an annual interest payment of £82, more than a third of the annual income of £220, of which £137 came from church collections and £68 from the 'proceeds of Socials and Harbour Excursions'. It was this unhealthy situation that gave rise to the report and a tear-off section: 'I wish to pay . . . weekly towards the Church Debt'. A hint as to the poor state of the finances of the local Catholic community was given in a report of the St Mary and St Joseph Friendly Society in January 1894, which showed that Pyrmont's annual subscription of £41 ranked well below that of the highest—St Benedict's at £251.[20] This was a period of severe unemployment, but financial difficulties would continue to be a challenge for the parish for the next generations, until the socio-economic transformation of the district a hundred years later. Despite the financial constraints in 1895, much needed repairs and enhancement to the interior of St Bede's were undertaken during November. The reopening of the church in the presence of visiting clerical dignitaries was announced in the 'Amusements' column of the *Catholic Press*: 'This little church, one of the oldest in the city, has been undergoing a series of long-delayed and very necessary repairs during the last two weeks. The work of repairing and decorating the sanctuary has been carried out by Mr John Shaw, a worthy member of the congregation, for whom it has evidently been a labour of love.'[21]

Both the pastor and his curate combined their parish duties with active participation in the Irish Home Rule cause. They were the only clergy present at a meeting held at the Australia Hotel in May 1895 to organise a reception for Michael Davitt, former Fenian, several times imprisoned and now an Irish Federation member of the Westminster Parliament.[22] Davitt was on an Australian fund-raising tour. The paucity of clergy participation would seem to indicate Cardinal Moran's disapproval of the visitor. Moran was no stranger to Davitt; in the early 1880s, as bishop of Ossory, he had deplored

---

20. *Sydney Morning Herald*, 23 January 1894.
21. *Catholic Press*, 7 December 1895.
22. *Freeman's Journal*, 25 May 1895.

what he perceived as the 'communistic and irreligious elements' of the Irish Land League which had been founded by Davitt and led by Charles Stewart Parnell. Moran later moderated his attitude to the League in conformity with his brother bishops, following Davitt's and Parnell's renunciation of violence on their release from prison in 1882.[23]

Fear of offending the Cardinal would have been sufficient to keep most of the Sydney clergy from the Davitt welcoming committee. Even the fearless French Marist and ardent advocate of Home Rule, Father Pierre Francois Le Rennetel of St Patrick's, whom the Sydney Irish affectionately called 'Father O'Rennetel'[24], stayed away, discretely indicating his support with a written apology. An apology was also received from Sir Henry Parkes who wrote that he 'would go to hear Mr Davitt at whatever inconvenience', perhaps to cheer his ideas on secular education. The meeting, chaired by Francis Bede Freehill, brought together 'a large number of citizens, including Irishmen, Scotchmen, Englishmen, and Australians'. There was much talk of Davitt's significance, not just as an Irish patriot, but as a 'great mover in labour reform' in all nations. The executive committee decided on a public reception, procession, presentation of addresses and banquet, to be followed by a series of lectures for Davitt's Sydney visit. It was later announced that the Hibernian Society had cancelled the banquet without any explanation, perhaps in response to archiepiscopal pressure.[25]

When the lectures took place between July and September 1895 the clergy were present in large numbers in the Theatre Royal and the Guild Hall, led by the Vicar General, Dr. Carroll. Whatever disincentives prevailed in May, there was no stopping the Irish priests' enthusiasm for the lecturer and his theme, 'The Progress of the Home Rule Cause'.[26] The platform was packed with clergy for the farewell lecture held at St Benedict's Hall. At their head and chairing the gathering was Cardinal Patrick Francis Moran. Michael Davitt, while acknowledging that Moran was present principally in support of the beneficiary of the evening's takings, St Martha's Industrial Training Home at Leichhardt, stated that it was 'one of the highest compliments that had been paid him in Australia to have the Cardinal occupying the chair at one of his lectures'.[27]

1895 saw the emergence of a new Catholic newspaper. The first challenge to the *Freeman's Journal*'s monopoly of Catholic and Irish journalism in Sydney had come in 1877. It was called the *Catholic Times*. The *Illawarra*

---

23. P Ayres, *Prince of the Church. Patrick Francis Moran, 1830-1911*, Sydney 2007, 101-125.
24. J Hosie, *Challenge: the Marists in Colonial Australia*, Sydney 1987, 265.
25. *Freeman's Journal*, 25 May 1895.
26. *Freeman's Journal*, 13 July 1895.
27. *Freeman's Journal*, 21 September 1895.

Mercury wryly noted the simultaneous emergence of two 'New Religious Journals':

> The first number of 'The Catholic Times' and also of 'The Orangeman and Protestant Catholic' have been issued almost simultaneously in Sydney. It would thus appear that the 'Freeman's Journal' and the 'Protestant Standard' have been proving themselves altogether too meek, and mild in their treatment of each other and the respective subjects advocated or denounced by them.[28]

In 1880 Archbishop Vaughan purchased the *Times* from the Irish nationalist Joseph (J G) O'Connor, changed the name to *The Express* and sought to place more emphasis on Catholic, rather than on Irish matters. 'Clericus', a correspondent to the *Freeman's Journal*, referred to the new weekly scathingly as 'your Anglo-ecclesiastical contemporary, the *Express*'.[29] The *Freeman's* editor, Thomas Butler, himself considered that 'the establishment of the *Express* was intended as a protest against our existence, and that its daringly speculative proprietary contemplated among other noble but happily hitherto unattained achievements nothing short of our suppression.'[30] The *Protestant Standard* delighted in describing a public dispute between the two Catholic journals: 'The Freeman's Journal, Irishlike, seized upon the opportunity for sitting upon its English co-religionist rival and has very effectually done so . . . How these two Roman Catholic journals love each other.'[31] The Melbourne Catholic paper, the *Advocate*, commented on Vaughan's newspaper: 'No one can say that the Sydney *Express* is not a thoroughly loyal paper. It is, in fact, loyal amongst the loyal, and its views on Irish affairs are sure to be dispassionate and in no way influenced by Irish feeling.'[32] After Vaughan's death in 1883, O'Connor resumed control of the *Express*, and it reverted to strong Irish advocacy; it ceased publication in 1887.

The next challenge to the dominance of the *Freeman's Journal* came early in 1895 with the appearance of the *Irish-Australian*, a weekly broadsheet published and edited by Father Joseph Bunbury and Major Frederick Shawelhood. This was a challenge to the *Journal* on the issues both of Irishness and catholicity. Lack of capital prevented it from succeeding. However, its enthusiastic reception indicated that there was an opening for a second Catholic paper. It was decided at a meeting of the clergy in June to

---

28. *Illawarra Mercury*, 27 March 1877.
29. *Freeman's Journal*, 26 March 1881.
30. *Freeman's Journal*, 4 February 1882.
31. *Protestant Standard*, 28 January 1882.
32. *Advocate*, 10 June 1882.

purchase the *Irish-Australian* and to change its title to *The Catholic Press*.[33] The first number appeared in November 1895. The editor turned to poetry to introduce the new journal:

> With joyous hearts we launch this argosy,
> Our journal, on the literary sea.
> 'Too many journalistic barques,' some say,
> 'Tack here and there upon the breezy bay.'
> We care not; there is sea-room for us all;
> We'll do and dare what hap soe'er befall.
> . . .
> God's Holy Church will be our first concern—
> The hinge on which our labours all will turn
> . . .
> Ireland, home of patriot, saint, and sage,
> Shall be the theme to fill our brightest page;
> But our own sunny land, Australia fair,
> Will ever be our dearest, tenderest care.[34]

The editorial differences between the two Sydney Catholic newspapers would become stark during the First World War, when the *Journal* supported and the *Press* opposed the first conscription referendum, and when the *Press* cheered and the *Journal* jeered the 1916 Easter Rising in Dublin. The papers were amalgamated in 1942, becoming the *Catholic Weekly*.

Father Joseph Bunbury was the interim inaugural editor. He was much praised by Patrick Ryan, who became a regular contributor to the paper. In December 1895 Ryan wrote to the new editor, Mr John Perrin, formerly of the *New Zealand Tablet*:

> I desire to place on record the deep sense of gratitude and appreciation which I feel sure every friend of Catholic journalism in New South Wales entertains for the efforts of Father Bunbury in the past. In its initial stages the Catholic Press, under another name, had very grave difficulties to overcome, and it is mainly if not altogether owing to the courage, energy, and patience of Father Bunbury that the Catholic Press of to-day is an accomplished fact ... Our late editor pegged away with his little paper, and forced an entrance for it into thousands of our humblest Catholic homes where no Catholic paper had ever been, before ... In conclusion, I must express the hope that the bright and cheery paragraphs from

---

33. *Catholic Press*, 13 September 1928.
34. *Catholic Press*, 9 November 1895.

his pen which have been a feature of the Catholic Press in the past may continue to be the same in the future. Wishing you the fullest measure of success in the great work you have come to take up amongst us.[35]

Bunbury's 'bright and cheerful paragraphs' continued, especially in his regular literary contribution, 'Father Bunbury's Sketches'.

Patrick Ryan's ministry at Pyrmont came to an end in July 1896 with his transfer across town to St Mary of the Suburbs at Erskineville, formerly called McDonald Town. This move involved a swap with Father Edward O'Callaghan who moved from Erskineville to Pyrmont. In March 1898, after less than two years at Erskineville, Ryan asked to be transferred from the Sydney Archdiocese to the new Diocese of Grafton, which would later become the Diocese of Lismore. His letters to Cardinal Moran carry hints of dissatisfaction with his placements in Sydney. Referring to the appointments he had received during the latter years of his time in the Archdiocese, he expressed his wish to offer his humble services where they were more wanted and would be of more value.[36] Moran gave permission for the transfer but suggested that he may wish to remain a priest of the Archdiocese while on loan to Grafton. Ryan was emphatic in declining the offer, in no way wishing to avail himself of it.[37]

Ryan's popularity among his fellow Sydney priests was shown in the farewell banquet held in April 1898 at the Prince of Wales Hotel, at Sandringham Point at the mouth of the Georges River. Monsignor James O'Brien, Rector of St John's College, chaired the gathering, at which neither the Cardinal nor any of his cathedral clergy were present. The chairman followed his effusive praise of Ryan's 'many estimable qualities' with the comment that he was leaving the Archdiocese 'at his own request, simply and solely through a desire to discharge a more useful and necessary duty in the Diocese of Grafton', a remark perhaps calculated to suppress other opinions as to motives. Patrick's Pyrmont curate, Daniel O'Reilly, 'delivered a most eloquent address', emphasising Ryan's 'culture, literary abilities and eloquent powers', and 'endorsed what had been said by the Right Rev. Chairman in reference to the noble part Father Ryan had taken in the intellectual, social and truly priestly sphere of duties assigned to him during, his long connection with the Archdiocese of Sydney'.[38]

A year after his arrival in the Grafton Diocese he wrote to Cardinal Moran asking about the validity of the exeat from the Westminster Archdiocese given him by the late Cardinal Manning. He stated that he was anxious to

---

35. *Catholic Press*, 14 December 1895.
36. PM Ryan to Cardinal Moran, 22 March 1898 (P M Ryan file, SAA)
37. PM Ryan to Cardinal Moran, 28 March 1898 (P M Ryan file, SAA)
38. *Catholic Press*, 9 April 1898.

know what diocese he could regard himself as belonging to.[39] Perhaps he was making canonical enquiries with the idea of resuming ministry in London. In fact when in 1901 he left on a trip to England for the benefit of his health, he lingered and took charge of a Westminster parish for a year.[40]

It was while sailing south to Sydney on the steamer *Bundah* that he died on 10 July 1917 at the age of 65. A surprising and charming glimpse of Patrick Ryan was given in a report of his death in the *Port Macquarie News and Hastings River Advocate*: 'The deceased was a cultured and affable gentleman, wielded a facile pen, and, better still, was a great lover of nature. It was during his incumbency that the ornamental trees that now adorn St Agnes' church grounds were planted, and they form a fitting and pleasing tribute to his memory. Might we be permitted to say that through arboral culture: "He, being dead, yet speaketh".'[41] Perhaps it was this love of nature and his yearning for 'arboral culture', so little available in the crowded inner Sydney suburbs of Pyrmont and Erskineville, that were the principal motivations in his relocating to the far north coast. A letter from the Diocesan Treasurer of Westminster to the Vicar General of Lismore in June 1918 acknowledged the receipt of £275 from the estate of Patrick Matthias Ryan: 'The Cardinal will see that the money is well spent amongst the destitute poor of Millwall'.[42] His poor former parishioners of Pyrmont do not seem to have been beneficiaries of the will.

In July 1896 at the Pyrmont Street presbytery to welcome Edward O'Callaghan was the long-serving curate Daniel O'Reilly. Amid the regular changes of priest-in-charge, O'Reilly provided welcome continuity for the parishioners of St Bede's, especially when it came to initiating their babies into the Christian way of life. A perusal of the Baptismal Register for the years of his curacy, 1893 to 1900, reveals that O'Reilly performed two out of every three baptisms.

Edward O'Callaghan was born in the Irish capital, and studied in Rome before being ordained for the Dublin archdiocese. Shortly after his ordination in 1884 he suffered from ill-health, and at the invitation of Cardinal Moran he came to Australia in the hope of the change of climate proving beneficial. He arrived in Sydney in October 1887 and after a brief appointment at the cathedral he was assigned as curate at Petersham. An unusually quick promotion in 1890 found him as priest-in-charge at McDonald Town, later called Erskineville, at the church of Our Lady of the Suburbs, variously named Our Lady of the Rosary, of the Assumption, of Perpetual Succour,

---

39. Patrick Ryan to Cardinal Moran, 7 August 1899 (P M Ryan file, SAA).
40. *Catholic Press*, 15 June 1901.
41. *Port Macquarie News and Hastings River Advocate*, 14 July 1917.
42. Diocesan Treasurer of Westminster to the Vicar General of Lismore, June 27 1918 (P M Ryan file, Lismore Diocese Archives).

and simply St Mary's. At the time of his appointment this mission district extended south to Tempe and included the church of Saints Peter and Paul. However, towards the end of his appointment in 1896 Tempe was placed under the Passionist priests of Marrickville.

In August 1894 'the Rev E O'Callaghan appeared before Mr Delchery SM in the Newtown Police Court . . . on a summons laid by George Huggard, charging him with having assaulted William Huggard, son of the plaintiff, residing in Erskineville'.[43] The nine year old William had some time previously been removed from the nuns' school because of the beatings he had received there, and placed in the Public school. The boy stated in court that he was walking past the priest's house one morning on his way to stay at a neighbour's place. He had not cried out or done anything to the clergyman's house. However, O'Callaghan followed him and struck him with a stick on the back and across the legs. A neighbour corroborated the boy's story. O'Callaghan stated that he had struck the boy because he had thrown a stone at his house, but that 'it was a most trivial stroke'. He considered it his duty to do so to 'suppress larrikinism'; 'he beat the boy as a corrective'. The defendant was found guilty and fined £2 with costs, or, in default of payment, one month's imprisonment. This case reflected the continuing tensions over the vexed education question.

Beginning in May 1896 the *Catholic Press* ran regular playful reports on the Catholic schools of the Archdiocese, beginning with the Josephite school on 'the giddy heights of Mosman's Bay', and concluding with remote Araluen in April 1897. At the end of each article the percentage mark recorded at the last formal school inspection was given. The turn of Pyrmont and Ultimo came in November 1896. The articles would have made entertaining and instructive reading for the new priest-in-charge:

> The word Ultimo, of course, suggests the last place in Sydney, and yet the Technical College, built in the centre of the district, is the first institution in the colony . . . The school-church of St Francis Xavier attracts hundreds of pupils. Under the able direction of the accomplished Sisters of the Good Samaritan, it is not surprising to find a prosperous school. But within easy reach of St Benedict's immense lyceums it is something unexpected. And to my mind, although these children live in Ultimo, they are not the last in the way of education or manners. Pious, good, and amiable, these children do credit to the district. They do not sneer, jeer, or jostle on their way to or from school. They behave well because they are taught that to hurt the feelings of others betrays a

---

43. *Sydney Morning Herald*, 21 August 1894.

want of education, and an ignorance of the most elementary Christian principles. Percentage, 64.

St Bede's Church and school at Pyrmont are very old institutions, and consequently they have dwindled in size. Crippled by age, they seem to have been erected by Lilliputians, who may have had possession of this country in the time of Gulliver. For all that, there is life and activity among the Catholics of Pyrmont. Their schools are crammed to the door with good, intelligent children; and if these children are not the very best in the colony, you will find that the fault is not theirs. Percentage, 69.[44]

The inadequate size of St Bede's church weighed on Father O'Callaghan, and in 1898 the *Freeman's Journal* reported: 'The church may have been considered big enough for Pyrmont in 1867, but Father O'Callaghan is fully convinced that it is by no means large enough for 1898. Before very long we shall hear of a new church, which will be built in all probability on a new site.'[45] A reminiscence about this proposal for a new church emerged in 1967 in a response to Father Victor Doyle's attempt to gather information for the centennial booklet. Mrs Mary Thom of Waverley replied and provided some stories which she had heard from her father, Michael Joseph Maher, who was born on 27th October 1862 near where the Ultimo Powerhouse then stood. He was the second eldest of the 9 children of Thomas and Brigid Maher, who had emigrated from County Clare in 1857. She recalled that it had been the custom in those days for small private schools to be conducted by a couple of genteel ladies. Her father at first went to one of these and then, like most local Catholic boys, to the Marist Brothers at St Benedict's. Her father used to tell the family that, as the years went on, there was a move on foot to combine Pyrmont and Ultimo churches and build a new one on the corner of Harris and Allen Streets, where the Imperial Meat Company later stood. However, someone let the cat out of the bag, and before the deal could be clinched, the land in question was snapped up by another denomination and a church built there. From memory she thought it was a Presbyterian Church, which was used for some years and then demolished.[46] It was the Congregationalists who had snapped up the property and built a fine church with a capacity of 400 worshippers.

Though thwarted in his desire to leave a legacy in bricks and mortar, Fr O'Callaghan did, however, succeed in leaving a magnificent legacy of

---

44. *Catholic Press*, 7 November 1896.
45. *Freeman's Journal*, 5 September 1898.
46. Mary Thom to Victor Doyle, 13 August 1967 (Centenary File in Pyrmont Box, SAA)

church music for his parishioners. There followed him from Erskineville to Pyrmont the very talented musical director, Captain Frederick Augustine Shawelhood, who became active in creating a local church choir, which was soon 'able to sing at sight in four parts'.[47]

Frederick Shawelhood began his teaching career in 1875 at the age of 19 as a pupil-teacher at Marrickville Public School.[48] He soon transferred to Catholic schools; the next ten years found him teaching successively at West Maitland, Wollongong and Balmain. He was among the last lay teachers employed by the church in its schools. After the withdrawal of the government funding of teachers' wages in the denominational system at the end 1882, Catholic primary schools were largely staffed by a plentiful supply of nuns from the several Irish Congregations already well established in New South Wales—Sisters of Charity, Sisters of Mercy, Dominicans, Presentation Sisters—and the two home-grown Congregations—the Sisters of the Good Samaritan and the Sisters of St Joseph. When called upon by the bishops, these groups, which had been recruiting successfully among local women, responded generously. In short supply in New South Wales were members of the male teaching Orders available for staffing boys' schools. In 1882 only the Marist Brothers were established in Sydney. They had arrived in Sydney in 1872 and over the next ten years opened schools at St Patrick's, Church Hill, St Patrick's, Parramatta, St Benedict's, George Street West, and St Mary's Cathedral. The Brothers of Saint Patrick had come to St John's Maitland, Shawelhood's old school, in 1883 and spread to Goulburn and Bathurst in 1884, three dioceses governed by Irish bishops. The Irish Christian Brothers first came to Sydney as early as 1843 and taught at St Mary's and St Benedict's, but because of perceived Benedictine interference in their independence as a separate religious Congregation, they sailed back to Ireland in 1847. When they returned to Australia in 1868 it was to Melbourne they headed, and not to Sydney. Despite invitations from particular parishes, they did not come to Sydney until 1887, to staff the boys' school at Balmain.

1885 brought a change of direction for Sergeant Shawelhood when he volunteered for the New South Wales expedition to the Sudan. In January news of General Charles George Gordon's death had stirred the call for vengeance against the rebel Muslim forces in the Sudan, and the acting premier of New South Wales, William Bede Dalley, rushed to cable London with an offer of local troops, with the further inducement of undertaking to cover the contingent's expenses. The home government accepted, but stipulated that the contingent would be under British command. The

---

47. *Catholic Press*, 19 February 1898.
48. *NSW Teachers Roll*, 1871–1908, volume 2.

contingent, 767-strong, consisting of four infantry companies, artillery and a field ambulance, was ready to sail on 3 March 1885. It left Sydney amid much public fanfare, generated in part by the public holiday declared to farewell the troops. Archbishop Moran presided at a special service on the Sunday before the departure. The *Freeman's Journal* reporter noted the presence of the newly appointed chaplain, Father Charles Collingridge, and observed Frederick Shawelhood in the front pew. The *Journal* proudly estimated that there were 180 Catholics among the volunteers. It appointed Frederick as its special correspondent and published his letters until the return of the contingent in June. Frederick also acted as Fr Collingridge's sacristan at sea and on land. His first report from the *Iberia* three days after departure lauded the chaplain: 'There is no doubt the Government has conferred a boon on the Catholic members of the contingent by appointing a chaplain, especially one so earnest and energetic as Father Colleridge [sic].'[49] The expedition was short-lived. By May 1885 the British government had decided to abandon the campaign. The colonial contingent did not participate in any battles and casualties were few; those who died were victims of disease rather than of enemy action. The Australians sailed for home in May 1885.

There is a permanent reference to the Sudan war within the parish of Pyrmont. A local Ultimo hotel, opened in 1878 as the *Glasgow Arms*, a few doors along from the site of the St Francis Xavier church and school in Crown Street, now Bulwara Road, underwent a name change in 1882. The Irish parishioner Thomas Leahy renamed his pub in honour of the British General, Garnet Joseph Wolseley (1833-1913), who, after his successful suppression of an Egyptian rebellion, was raised to the peerage in 1882 as Lord Wolseley of Cairo and Wolseley. In 1884 he was placed in command of the Nile Expedition sent to the Sudan to relieve the garrison of General Gordon besieged at Khartoum. The expedition arrived too late—Khartoum had been taken and Gordon and his troops had been slaughtered. Wolseley withdrew from the Sudan. The 1885 expedition, in which New South Wales troops participated, was the British Government's next failed response to the Sudan situation. It has been suggested that Catholic publican Thomas Leahy, an ex-convict, took the unlikely step of naming his hotel after a British General and Freemason, because he admired the fact that Wolseley, Dublin-born and one of seven children raised by their army-widow mother, had risen to military eminence without the advantage of wealth or patronage.[50] Wolseley became the darling of the British public and was lightly parodied as the 'very model of a modern Major-General' in Gilbert and Sullivan's

---

49. *Freeman's Journal*, 14 March 1885.
50. Shirley Fitzgerald, *Lord Wolseley Hotel: A Social History of a Very Small Pub* (Sydney, 2016), 36.

'The Pirates of Penzance' (1880).[51] The comic opera had its first Sydney performance on 19 March 1881.[52] Within a year of his appointment as Commander-in-Chief of Her Majesty's Forces in Ireland in 1890, Wolseley was reported as supporting Home Rule: 'The Commander of the Forces now openly declares that he sees no danger, from the military point of view, in the granting of Home Rule to Ireland.'[53] This would have further endeared the General to the Ultimo publican.

Back in Australia from the Sudan in mid-1885, Frederick Shawelhood was engaged by the Public School administration to teach at Cooba Creek, in the south of the Colony between Junee and Gundagai. From there he was moved to Bookham. He resigned in 1888 for health reasons and tried his hand at journalism as proprietor and editor of the *Dinalong Argus*. The editor of *The Gundagai Times and Tumut, Adelong and Murrumbidgee District Advertiser* wished this 'youngest member of the fourth estate' every success.[54] Success did not follow; the next year Frederick was back in Sydney, making a return to schools, not as a classroom teacher, but as an instructor of cadet corps. By 1891 he was a very popular instructor to all Sydney's Catholic schools and colleges. In 1892 he was a member of a committee of devoted young men, including William Coogan, looking after some six or seven homeless boys. They had a small cottage in Riley-street, Surry Hills, to begin with, and later they moved to a much larger house at Five Dock with 42 boys. The St Vincent de Paul Society soon took over the work, which was relocated to Westmead, where the Marist Brothers took charge.[55]

In 1895 he returned to journalism when he combined with Father Joseph Bunbury to establish the short-lived *Irish-Australian*, a weekly broadsheet. It was in the following years that Shawelhood turned to music and became a choir-master in several Sydney parishes, including Pyrmont in 1898. The first opportunity for him to display his skills at Pyrmont was at a concert in the schoolroom to welcome Father O'Callaghan back from holidays in New Zealand in April 1898. The ambitious programme included works by Beethoven, Mozart, Mendelssohn, Rossini and Wallace. The newspaper report commented that 'considering that this singing class has only been a few months in existence, and that the concert was the outcome of a few days'

---

51. OA Cooke, "WOLSELEY, GARNET JOSEPH, 1st Viscount WOLSELEY," in *Dictionary of Canadian Biography*, vol 14, University of Toronto/Université Laval, 2003, accessed April 30, 2016, http://www.biographi.ca/en/bio/wolseley_garnet_joseph_14E.html.
52. *Sydney Morning Herald*, 21 March 1881.
53. *Freeman's Journal*, 27 June 1891.
54. *Gundagai Times and Tumut, Adelong and Murrumbidgee District Advertiser*, 11 May 1888.
55. *Freeman's Journal*, 22 March 1917.

preparation, the programme was remarkably well carried out'. Singled out for special mention was 'Nellie Maunsell, a child of about 11 years, who gave an exquisite rendering of the ever-popular *Last Rose of Summer*'. Nellie was the daughter of Constable Daniel Maunsell, who had been widowed in July 1895 and who remarried at St Bede's in October 1896. The 'Star of the Sea' window in St Bede's church was restored in 2013 by the Maunsell family in memory of their forebears. The report on the April concert concluded: 'As to Captain Shawelhood, he was the life and soul of the entertainment, and as vigorous with his baton as we hope he will be with his sword should ever an enemy invade our shores.'[56]

The following month the new choir had the sad duty of singing at the Requiem Mass for one of its young members:

> On Sunday, the 22nd instant, at Waverley, the remains of Miss Mary Ann Coleman were laid to rest ... Only fifteen years and ten months old, she had endeared herself to all with whom she had come in contact, and although one of the youngest members of St Bede's choir and singing class, the respect in which she was held was amply testified by the attention given to her mother in her dire distress. Prominent among the wreaths sent were those from her friends and companions of the choir and singing-class. At Mass and Vespers special prayers were offered up, and both occasions concluded with the Dead March in Saul on the organ. A special service was held by Father O'Reilly at St Bede's on Sunday afternoon prior to the funeral leaving for Waverley. At the cemetery the coffin was carried by Captain F A Shawelhood and Messrs Weslan, O'Haiher, and Cameron, most of the other members of the choir and singing-class following. Out of respect to the deceased, the usual meeting of the singing-class will not be held this week.[57]

The choirmaster's appetite for liturgical music was on display in a very ambitious programme of music to accompany an eleven o'clock Mass in September 1898 celebrated by Father O'Callaghan and attended by a visiting preacher: 'The parishioners of St Bede's had quite a great day on Sunday last. The announcement had been made that the Rev Father Buckley MSH, would preach a charity sermon in aid of the local conference of the Society of St Vincent de Paul, and that there would be music on quite an unprecedented scale of grandeur at the 11 o'clock Mass.' The music was indeed ambitious for the 'Lilliputian church':

---

56. *Freeman's Journal*, 9 April 1898.
57. *Freeman's Journal*, 28 May 1898.

The Kyrie and Gloria were from Mozart's Twelfth, the Credo from Farmer's Mass, and Sanctus, Benedictus, and Agnus Dei from Gounod's St Cecilia Mass. At the Offertory Miss Campion (who studied with Signora Coy in Melbourne) sang with beauty of voice and fine expressiveness Carmusci's Salve Regina. Messrs Behan and Briggs sang the familiar and brilliant Beata Nobis Gaudia. At the end of the Mass the full choir, with organ and orchestra, gave the Hallelujah Chorus from Beethoven's 'Mount of Olives' most impressively.[58]

There does not seem to have been any congregational singing. The use of such classical and 'operatic' settings for the parts of the Mass would be prohibited by Pope Pius X in 1903, in favour of Gregorian chant and Renaissance polyphony. The pope's 'motu proprio' was issued on the feast day of St Cecilia, the patroness of church music.[59] The *Freeman's Journal* headlined its translation of the document: 'Meretricious compositions condemned'.[60] Also condemned was the participation of women in church choirs.

In 1901, after a final musical contribution at the St Bede's parish mission in June, Shawelhood became a late volunteer for South Africa, where the Second Boer War was coming to an end.[61] He lingered in Cape Town and eventually settled there, becoming very involved with the Marist Brothers schools. The *Freeman's Journal* in December 1905 reported on its former journalist:

> A South African contemporary has a very complimentary notice of the production on November 30 of Cardinal Wiseman's drama, 'The Hidden Gem', by the pupils of the Marist Brothers schools Capetown, under the direction of Captain FA Shawelhood—a well-known Sydney gentleman—who is engaged on the school staff. We quote: 'To Capt Shawelhood, whose energy and resourcefulness are something quite out of the ordinary, the main part of the credit for the success of the whole evening must be given, for he planned and supervised the whole of it; is responsible for the physical training of the lads; wrote the prologue to the play; composed some of the music, and conducted throughout the evening while not engaged in superintending behind the scenes.'[62]

---

58. *Freeman's Journal*, 3 September 1898.
59. Pius X, *Tra le sollecitudini*, 22 November 1903. See John de Luca, 'Disharmony among bishops: on the binding nature of a papal *motu proprio* on music', *Journal of the Australian Catholic Historical Society*, 35(2014), 28-37.
60. *Freeman's Journal*, 13 February 1904.
61. *Freeman's Journal*, 22 June 1901.
62. *Freeman's Journal*, 7 January 1905.

In 1907 Frederick was welcomed back on a visit to Sydney, 'where his long connection with pedagogic, military, musical, and Catholic affairs is held in pleasant memory'.[63] The last reference to the Captain in the *Freeman's Journal* was in January 1913, when the receipt of his New Year greetings from South Africa was acknowledged.[64]

Father O'Callaghan, like his predecessor, Patrick Ryan, was an ardent supporter of freedom for Ireland. He was among the clergy who responded to an invitation in October 1897 to attend a meeting at the Oddfellow's Temple in Elizabeth Street to consider how to commemorate the imminent centenary of the Irish Rebellion of 1789, which had been the cause of the transportation of hundreds of Irish patriots and three Irish priests to New South Wales. The meeting was chaired by Dr Charles MacCarthy, the Cardinal's personal physician, and attended by Rev Dr Denis O'Haran, his personal secretary. They represented two different approaches to the commemoration. The chairman put forward a proposal which involved exhuming the remains of Michael Dwyer, the Wicklow Chief, buried at the Devonshire Street cemetery, and reinterring them in a grave surmounted by a monument at some unspecified location. O'Haran spoke in cautious support of the plan, but emphasised that there should be no 'recalling seditious sentiments or of recognising that sentiment either in the past or in the present movement'. This was a clear statement of the Cardinal's attitude to Irish independence—home rule within the British Empire—and his abhorrence of a republic. O'Haran made a move to take control of the proposed event, suggesting that 'he believed it possible, for instance, that the memorial might form an ornament in the grounds of St Mary's Cathedral'.[65]

Some weeks later a public meeting was held in the Guild Hall in Castlereagh Street. Dr MacCarthy was again in the chair and among the few clergy present was Edward O'Callaghan; no priests from the Cathedral attended. There was much emphasis on the commemoration not being an exclusively Catholic affair, but rather 'their movement symbolized the union between the Protestant North and the Catholic South during the Insurrection of 1798'. Father TA Fitzgerald, true to the Irish Franciscan tradition of support for Irish freedom, posed a rhetorical question:

> Why in this case speak of their insurgents of '98 as assassins, and not patriots? (Cheers). They had good reason to celebrate the incidents of 100 years ago. This meeting was gathered in Castlereagh street, next to Pitt street, and it was something to be proud of that, notwithstanding

---

63. *Freeman's Journal*, 14 November 1907.
64. *Freeman's Journal*, 16 January 1913.
65. *Freeman's Journal*, 16 October 1897.

the efforts of the ruffians who bore those names, the Irish spirit still lived (Applause). If you took the average citizen of Sydney and asked him where the '98 movement started, he would probably say in Tipperary (Laughter). No; it was in Belfast (Cheers). In conclusion he might remark that not a sentiment was expressed in the resolution of the United Irishmen, but might be expressed anywhere. What turned their programme into rebellion was the goading-on unprincipled by government (Cheers).[66]

Father O'Callaghan was voted onto the executive committee, and to the concluding collection he contributed three guineas, matching that of the Franciscan and Passionist communities.

Three weeks later Cardinal Moran's attitude to 'the '98' was revealed in a wide-ranging interview he had given to a visiting English journalist of the London *Daily News*. It was reprinted in full by the *Catholic Press* under the heading 'A Sensational Interview':

[Halifax]: Might I ask your Eminence for an expression of opinion upon the present phase of the Irish question?

[Moran]: I really do not know much about it, said the Cardinal. There is only one phase upon which I might remark, and that is the proposed celebration of the centenary of 1798. I would do everything in my power to oppose such a centenary celebration. I look upon the '98 movement as a terrible crime and a terrible blunder—a crime on the part of the Government that forced on the Revolution, and a blunder on the part of every friend of Ireland who took part in it. To celebrate the centenary of what is a great crime and blunder would be I think a crime and blunder in itself. When we celebrate the centenary of anything, it is to set before us something that is noble, something that has been a source of benefit and honor to the people; and I think that to celebrate a national movement that was a blunder and a crime is to lead people in very wrong lines.[67]

In this forthright condemnation of the revolution Moran was echoing the response of the majority of the Irish bishops of 1789. The Dominican Archbishop of Dublin, John Thomas Troy, had threatened excommunication of the rebels within days of the rising; in a pastoral read in all the churches, he described clerical organisers of the rebellion as 'vile prevaricators and apostates from religion, loyalty, honour, and decorum, degrading their

---

66. *Freeman's Journal*, 6 November 1897.
67. *Catholic Press*, 27 November 1897.

sacred character, and the most criminal and detestable of rebellious and seditious culprits.'[68]

The *Sydney Morning Herald* published its own interview with the Cardinal specifically on the planned centennial commemoration. In the *Herald* interview, although repeating the 'sensational' phrase 'terrible blunder', Moran modified somewhat his attitude to the commemoration, making a distinction between celebrating the centenary of the revolution as such and commemorating the heroism of the patriots who lost their lives. He went on the express his misgivings that the planning of the event was in the hands of 'a few who really have no claim to be considered as leaders, either from a religious or national point of view'.[69] Among these few were the four clerical members of the Executive Committee.

Charlie MacCarthy made a vigorous response on behalf of his committee: 'Will it be said that the clerical representatives of our committee are not competent leaders in national as in religious affairs? Speaking of all the members, lay and clerical, I can say that it has never been my privilege to be associated with a more intellectual and a more competent body of men.' He expressed the Committee's suspicion that an attempt was being made to highjack the event for denominational advantage, and insisted that the 'national aspect of the movement' must be strictly adhered to. He concluded:

> Our movement has been called a tentative one. It is not tentative. It is well and safely launched, and progresses rapidly, and I deprecate with all the power that is in me any attempt to narrow its broad significance or any counter blow which would bring disunion amongst our people here. The men who are at the helm now and have been from the commencement, and who have borne the heat and burden of the day, are not going to relinquish their position through any pressure or any consideration whatever . . . I predict for the movement a great success.[70]

It was now the turn of the *Freeman's Journal* to seek an interview with Moran. Its journalist took courage and against all advice sought out His Eminence at his palace in Manly, a venue strictly reserved for episcopal visitors. However, encouraged by reading the word PRESS on the palace's electric doorbell button, the press-man announced his presence and gained admittance. His interview filled two broadsheet pages of the *Journal*. The Cardinal, while reiterating his view of 1798 as a blunder and his lack of confidence in the

---

68. Patrick M Geoghegan, 'The Catholics and the Union', *Transactions of the Royal Historical Society*, 30(2000), 243–258; https://en.wikisource.org/wiki/Troy,_John_Thomas_(DNB00) (accessed 4 September 2016).
69. *Sydney Morning Herald*, 27 November 1897.
70. *Sydney Morning Herald*, 29 November 1897.

committee, further moderated his attitude to the evolving commemoration. He gave great offence to the Protestant members and supporters of the committee, especially 'Tim Fogarty', by describing Wolfe Tone, a Protestant leader of the '98 Rebellion, as no hero, and 'nothing better than an atheistical coxcomb': 'It is my personal opinion that with all his protestations he really did not care a button for Ireland, when it became a matter of personal sacrifice.'[71] 'Fogarty' (William Ellard) was the Sydney agent for the collection of funds to erect a statue of Theobald Wolfe Tone in Dublin.[72]

Moran was flippant in commenting on a proposal for the reburial of Michael Dwyer coming from a committee with three doctors as members: 'When the deputation waited on me, something was said about having a public funeral procession. It was proposed to carry the remains of Michael Dwyer and other patriots to a new place of interment. I thought then that it would hardly do to have a funeral procession headed by three doctors.' When asked by the journalist whether his attitude to the committee may give the impression that he was not in sympathy with commemorating the men of '98, he responded indignantly:

> I sincerely trust not. I fancy if any man in our community has the right to consider himself a rebel, I mean a rebel in blood and by tradition, I am that man ... My grandfather, Mr Cullen, just escaped hanging. He owed his life to the indignation aroused by the ferocity of those model judges Norbury and Toler. Three of my grand-uncles, Mr William Cullen, Mr Brennan, and Mr Walshe, were shot as rebels. My father, who when a young man displayed too much patriotic ardour to suit the authorities, was within an inch of losing his life.[73]

---

71. *Freeman's Journal*, 4 December 1897.
72. *Freeman's Journal*, 30 October 1897. Due to a combination of incompetence and embezzlement an empty plinth was all that was erected on the designated site. 'Eventually the lassitude of the Dublin commemorationists led to the galling usurpation of the site, which was requisitioned by the Corporation for the Dublin Fusilier Boer War memorial', known to Republicans as Traitors' Arch. It was not until 1967 that Wolfe Tone would finally have a statue in Dublin. In 1971 it was targeted by loyalist extremists. The statue was wrecked, leaving only the base; huge slabs of the bronze sculpture were hurled 20 feet in the air. 'The irony in the statue of a Dublin Protestant, who had been instrumental in establishing his political movement in Belfast, falling victim to a Northern Irish bomb was lost on few.' ('Plaques of Dublin: The birthplace of Theobald Wolfe Tone', https://comeheretome.com/2013/01/09/plaques-of-dublin-the-birthplace-of-theobald-wolfe-tone-wolfe-tone-street/ [accessed 23 August 201)].
73. *Freeman's Journal*, 4 December 1897.

Dr MacCarthy was given the right of reply by the *Freeman's* and he seized the opportunity. He stood his ground on the competence of his committee and on resistance to any denominational exploitation of the commemoration. On the question of the Cardinal's Irish nationalist credentials his doctor was not impressed with Moran's blood-line claim. He demurred:

> You do not want to know what I think of his Eminence's attitude towards the Home movement, at a time when the idea of a '98 commemoration had not been as yet broached in the colony. It is too delicate a subject for me to touch. I as a Nationalist can hold very strong convictions, as opposed to the expressed views of his Eminence, while at the same time venerating and admiring him as a great Churchman, a profound scholar, a learned historian and archaeologist, and a powerful defender of that old Faith which is the brightest gem in the diadem of my country.[74]

The centennial year got underway with a production of James Pilgrim's play, 'Robert Emmet, the Martyr of Irish Liberty—a Historical Drama in Three Acts' at the Imperial Opera House, directed by Dr Charles MacCarthy. The performance was remembered by St Bede's director of music, Norbert Chinchen, in 1923: 'I recollect well witnessing a performance of "Robert Emmet" at the old Opera House on the corner of York and King Streets in '98. The production was directed by Dr MacCarthy, and Bernard Purcell cut a manly and effective figure in the name part. My father was cast as the judge, Lord Norbury.'[75]

On Sunday 22 May 1898 the committee's work came to a magnificent conclusion with a Requiem Mass celebrated by Cardinal Moran at St Mary's Cathedral, followed by a procession accompanying the remains of Michael and Mary O'Dwyer along the four and a half miles to Waverley Cemetery, with the participation of an estimated 200,000, the largest gathering in Sydney's history. The Cardinal did not participate in the Waverley commemorations. At the grave-side Dr MacCarthy gave a stirring speech in which he vindicated the questioned patriotism of Wolfe Tone:

> What shall I say of that hero of heroes, the unselfish, the untiring, the unconquerable Theobald Wolfe Tone, the great organiser of the Society of United Irishmen, the men of iron energy, the terror of the myrmidons of Dublin Castle, the friend and lieutenant and military confidant of Hoche the admired of the great Napoleon and the darling of the Irish people; the man of whom Lucian Bonaparte said in his celebrated eulogy

---

74. *Freeman's Journal*, 11 December 1897.
75. *Freeman's Journal*, 12 July 1923.

on Tone's heroism and military capacity before the assembled council of five hundred in Paris in 1799, 'had he lived he would have been the Washington of Ireland'?[76]

Father O'Callaghan of Pyrmont was present throughout the celebrations on that historical day. On the Monday evening a banquet was held at the Guild Hall. O'Callaghan was again present among the clergy, as was the whole community of the Waverley Franciscans. Dr MacCarthy had the last word, perhaps with Cardinal Moran in mind: 'If any other answer were required for those unsympathetic pessimists and Job's comforters who predicted failure and all manner of ill-success for our '98 movement, that answer was given yesterday in the magnificent demonstration at the funeral procession and at the laying of the foundation-stone of the monument to the patriots.'[77]

In 1900 a rectangular platform, 9 metres wide and 7 metres deep, made of white Carrara marble, was raised over the vault containing the bodies of Michael and Mary Dwyer. A white marble cross, with intricate Celtic intertwining, was placed in the rear wall, rising nine metres high. Carved on the base of the cross were the words: 'In loving memory of all who dared and suffered in Ireland in 1798', and the following inscription:

>Pray for the Souls of
>Michael Dwyer the 'Wicklow Chief'
>and Mary his wife whose remains are interred
>in this vault. Requiescant in Pace.

A wall, almost two metres high, runs along the back of the platform. The wall is stepped down at the sides of the platform so as to be only about one metre high at the front. Two bronze wolfhounds crouch on the front terminals at each side. Bronze plaques, bearing images of Wolfe Tone, Lord Edward Fitzgerald, Michael Dwyer and Robert Emmet, and designed by Dr MacCarthy, are placed on the rear wall at each side of the marble cross. Of these four honoured patriots of 1798, three were Protestants. Sydney had its monument to Theobald Wolfe Tone long before Dublin. The inscription at the base of the towering monument is a permanent rebuke to all critics of the 'Men of '98':

>Who fears to speak of 'Ninety-eight'?
>Who blushes at the name?

---

76. *Catholic Press*, 28 May 1898.
77. *Freeman's Journal*, 28 May 1898.

When cowards mock the patriot's fate
Who hangs his head for shame?[78]

Charles MacCarthy, a supporter of the Irish Parliamentary Party and the constitutional path to Home Rule, perhaps would not have been pleased with the addition to the monument in 1947 of the names of the rebels of 1916, or in 1994 of the ten Irish Republican hunger-strikers who in 1981 died in the Maze prison, Belfast. In April 1916 MacCarthy had cabled John Redmond, leader of the IPP, concerning the Easter rebellion in Dublin: 'Sectional pro-German rioting disgusts Home Rulers here. Take heart. Our race with you and gallant countrymen at front.'[79]

One of Edward O'Callaghan's last achievements was the renovation of St Francis Xavier's church at Ultimo: 'The Catholics of Ultimo, a portion of the city of Sydney, are not a wealthy class, but they are strong in faith and devotion. Some time ago a plain building was erected for a church, with the title of St Francis Xavier, but the Rev Father O'Callaghan, of St Bede's, Pyrmont, being about to visit the old country, determined to have certain additions made to the structure, and to have the whole church renovated.'[80] On Sunday 29 January 1899, Auxiliary Bishop Higgins, who was soon to be appointed bishop of Rockhampton, presided at the dedication. He praised the retiring pastor: 'Rev Father O'Callaghan had done great work in the past, but in addition to all his other work, when he saw that they had not a house worthy of Almighty God, he got to work to accomplish that object. He might have left that to his successor, but he chose to work on to the end—and he worked with untiring energy.'[81] Soon after the dedication, it was announced that Father O'Callaghan had been granted sick-leave by the Cardinal, and that he was returning to Ireland after just eleven years in Australia. Like his predecessor Patrick Ryan, O'Callaghan seemed to have been among the not insignificant number of clerical casualties of the administration of Cardinal Moran and his personal secretary, Rev Dr Denis O'Haran, mockingly called 'fidus Achates' by the clergy, and proudly described on his tombstone as 'for 27 years the devoted secretary and faithful companion of Cardinal Moran'.[82]

The parish farewell was held in the Metropolitan Hall in Harris Street, the school-room not being big enough for the 'more than a thousand people' gathered to wish him well. Captain Shawelhood was present to provide the

---

78. Roger Wynne, 'The unfortunate business of '98', *Australasian Catholic Record*, 42 (1965): 203.
79. *Sydney Morning Herald*, 28 April 1916.
80. *Freeman's Journal*, 4 February 1899.
81. *Catholic Press*, 4 February 1899.
82. The bishop's mitre that O'Haran craved to have placed on his head is found on his tombstone—one of the privileges of a Prothonotary Apostolic.

music, together with his now famous parish choir. Father Daniel O'Reilly rose to farewell his third superior from Pyrmont:

> As one who had lived with him and worked with him, he could, if it were allowable, speak of Father O'Callaghan's splendid qualities and virtues. A few days ago he (the speaker) met an old lady of wide experience and matured judgment who volunteered the opinion, in fact pronounced the judgment, that 'Father O'Callaghan is a saint' (Applause and laughter). They could not improve on that (Laughter). In the name of the meeting, he hoped Father O'Callaghan on his arrival in the old land would find his relatives and friends with open arms of welcome. To this he would add the hope of seeing their esteemed friend return to Sydney with renewed energy and strength (Applause).[83]

Other farewells took place at the parish schools of St Bede and St Francis Xavier, where the children presented him with a 'very handsome and beautifully-fitted travelling-bag' and a box of silk handkerchiefs. These gifts were in addition to the traditional 'purse of sovereigns' and £100 from the ladies of the Altar Society. A final fond farewell was given by Captain Shawelhood and his choir. In making the presentation of a framed group photograph of the choir members with Father O'Callaghan as the central figure, the captain recalled that 'Father O›Callaghan had taken a more than usual interest in the choir', and noted that 'the enormous strides they had made during the few years of Father O›Callaghan's charge of affairs at Pyrmont, were due to that gentleman's untiring efforts in the cause of good music'. In his speech of thanks Fr O'Callaghan 'complimented Captain Shawelhood, to whom was due, he said, the great success of St Bede's choir and singing class. Captain Shawelhood had made enormous sacrifices to further the interests of the choir at St Bede's, and had done this without fee or reward.'[84] A final gift of £60 came from fellow priests who gathered at Redfern station to farewell him on the Western Mail.

After a holiday in Bathurst, Edward O'Callaghan joined the German mail steamer *Barbarossa* in Melbourne and sailed for Europe on 28 February. In July the *Catholic Press* published a letter from Father O'Callaghan in Rome describing a papal mass at St Peter's Basilica. His musical ear had not failed him: 'The music of the Mass, as you can well believe, was beyond criticism.'[85] He finally arrived in Ireland and resumed priestly ministry in Dublin. He became the point of contact for Sydney visitors to Dublin. In 1913 he was in the Sydney news for his hospitality to a former Erskineville altar-boy,

---

83. *Freeman's Journal*, 18 February 1899.
84. *Freeman's Journal*, 25 February 1899.
85. *Catholic Press*, 8 July 1899.

Jimmy Russell, the trainer of Australia's welter-weight boxing champion, Pat Bradley. Through Fr O'Callaghan's Roman connections the boxers were able to secure an audience with Pope Pius X.[86] In July 1918 the news of his death was received in Sydney: 'A cable from Dublin announces the death of the Rev Father Edward O'Callaghan, who was well known in Australia, having spent many years of his missionary life in this country.'[87]

---

86. *Catholic Press*, 7 August 1913.
87. *Freeman's Journal*, 18 July 1918.

Chapter 15
Ecclesiastical Scandal in Sydney

Edward O'Callaghan's successor at Pyrmont in February 1899 was Philip McIntyre, an All Hallows graduate who had arrived at Sydney in November 1882. After a brief initial appointment at Mount Carmel, Waterloo, he was called to the Cathedral by Archbishop Vaughan. In August 1883 an insight into his preaching skills, already known to the cathedral congregation, was given to the broader Sydney public in an article published in the *Evening News*. The article was the last in a series of twelve entitled 'Sundays in Sydney', begun in April and written by an anonymous journalist. 'Reflector' began his article on St Mary's: 'A sense of deep regret, akin to melancholy, oppresses me in commencing this sketch'. News of the death in England of Archbishop Roger Bede Vaughan on 18 August had been received in Australia the next day, Sunday afternoon. Reflector's article, based on his attendance at High Mass that morning, was composed after the arrival of the devastating news. In the Saturday 25 August edition of the *Evening News*, the item following *Reflector*'s article was a report of the Requiem Mass for Vaughan celebrated at St Mary's on the Thursday.[1] These dates explain why McIntyre's Sunday morning sermon made no mention of the Archbishop's death.

After describing the 'vast but incompleted' Cathedral and the quality of the music, he turned to the preacher: 'A youngish priest entered the pulpit . . . He then began his sermon, a short outline of which I propose to give. At the close of the service I ascertained that he was the Rev Father McIntyre. His manner was somewhat rapid, I thought a little too rapid. A pause now and then is useful. It seems to be a stepping-stone to something else. It enables the listener to take a glance backward and get ready for another step in advance.' The topic was drunkenness, an interesting theme for a priest who tragically for the last fourteen years of his long life would be suspended from parish ministry by his Archbishop for addiction to intoxicating drink.

---

1. *Evening News*, 25 August 1883.

The journalist was so taken with the sermon, 'its simplicity, its sterling truth, its picturesqueness', that he quoted the preacher's vivid description of the drunkard:

> Take, as an example, the vice of drunkenness; it is a vice found in every section of society. He (Father McIntyre) read a book once, the statistics of drunkenness, which showed Australia to be worse than any other country. His own short experience confirmed that. Go into the streets, or where men are bent on pleasure. Look at the drunkard, the confirmed drunkard, with eyes rolling; he leans against a post; he staggers against you; you look back to see whether he is in the gutter. You know he has given his life to drink. Morning and evening his thoughts are of drink. The sun has hardly shone in the morning, when you find he seeks for more drink. What sights you see in hotels and beer-shops. Listen to the profane songs. Look at the sights at all hours of the day. The drink to which the drunkard gives his mind, wastes his health and strength, and he becomes a disgrace to society. The more he drinks the more it increases his appetite for it . . . The drunkard makes himself wretched and others too. At night his wife sits watching for his coming, and he comes home to her with curses, and the curses become blows, and that wife he promised to support and be a consolation to is made wretched.

Before concluding his article, *Reflector* returned to the tragic death of the Archbishop and especially the implications for the completion of the cathedral: 'But who will be Archbishop Vaughan's successor? Who will with his zeal, eloquence, persistent energy and tact, put as it were the coping stone to a work which Archbishop Polding began, and he, who has so lately died, advanced in so marvellous a manner? These questions the future must answer.'[2] The answer would come within three months with the appointment of Patrick Francis Moran.

In May 1884, before Archbishop Moran's arrival, Philip McIntyre was moved from the Cathedral to Petersham to assist the ailing Joseph Garavel. A year later, Moran relocated him to Parramatta. In March 1886 he was sent south to take charge of the Appin district. This was a relatively swift promotion for a priest during the Moran regime. In going to Appin, McIntyre was on the way to achieving what could be styled the 'St Bede Trifecta'— priest-in-charge at the three churches of New South Wales dedicated to Saint Bede: Appin, Pyrmont and Braidwood.

By February 1889 he was in charge of a much more extensive district on the Illawarra coast, based at Albion Park, south of Wollongong. Six years

---

2. *Evening News*, 25 August 1883.

later McIntyre returned to Sydney in charge of Leichhardt. Early in 1899 he moved the short distance east to Pyrmont. The new pastor was settled into the district in time for Holy Week and the traditional *Missa Cantata* of Easter Sunday which was ably accompanied by the Shawelhood-trained choir, singing portions of Mozart's 12th Mass and Gounod's 'Messe solennelle de Ste. Cécile'.[3] Charles Gounod's Mass, composed in 1854, became the preferred setting for solemn liturgies at Pyrmont and Ultimo into the twentieth century, even well beyond the 1903 Vatican prohibition on 'operatic church music'.[4]

The end of the nineteenth century was commemorated at St Bede's with a 'Grand Century Fair' held at Coffill's Metropolitan Hall in Harris Street. The event was organised by the ladies of the parish to raise funds to address the long-standing debt on the two churches of the district, a debt which had been increased by recent repairs to St Bede's and St Francis Xavier's. The Cardinal was invited to open the Fair on Monday 6 November 1899. The good-humoured pastor received plenty of laughs in his address of welcome: 'The Rev Father McIntyre said that they had been ambitious in their title by calling their fair the "Century Fair", but as they were some centuries in debt (laughter) the title was appropriate enough, especially as they desired to raise some "centuries" by the effort (Laughter). He could assure them that the parish debt amounted to no less a sum than £1319.'[5]

The Cardinal in his remarks took up the theme of the naming of the event, stating that 'he feared he must begin by dissenting from the pastor of this district', and suggesting that 'taking into view the present state of feeling in the colony, they should have called it the "Fighting Fair" (Laughter)'. The 'state of feeling' was the jingoistic patriotism which had accompanied the departure of the Colony's contingent for South Africa at the end of October. The Cardinal flippantly linked his opinion of the Boer War with the aims of the Century Fair: 'One of the special purposes for which their volunteers had gone to South Africa was to annex certain goldfields that had become very dear to their British friends, so, he supposed the purpose of this bazaar or fair was to annex as much gold as possible ... (Laughter).' He went on to state, concerning the Australian contingent, that 'if any of the brave men had asked his opinion he would have advised them to stay at home (Applause)'.[6] Moran's misgivings about Australia's involvement in the war against the Boers expressed at Pyrmont were reported critically by newspapers throughout the Colonies.

---

3. *Freeman's Journal*, 8 April 1899.
4. De Luca, 'Disharmony Among Bishops'.
5. *Catholic Press*, 11 November 1899.
6. *Catholic Press*, 11 November 1899.

Present at the Fair with the Cardinal, as always, was his private secretary Denis O'Haran, who referred to Moran as 'the Chief', and whom Moran called 'dilectus filius' or 'carissimo'. O'Haran was popular with the laity, especially among the ladies, to whom he distributed postcards bearing a photograph of himself. Like all favourites, O'Haran was looked upon with resentment by fellow clergy. Priests unhappy with their appointments focused their disgruntlement on O'Haran's influence with Moran. Stories relating to his arrogance towards fellow priests began on the day of his arrival, and became part of Sydney clerical folklore. In 1970 Sydney priest Roger Wynne recounted a story told to him on his arrival in the Archdiocese in 1936 by a 'very old priest', who had been 'very young' on the day Moran and O'Haran arrived in September 1884:

> The Cathedral, temporarily roofed and unfinished, as Dr. Vaughan had left it, was packed to the doors . . . In the sacristy, where the best set of vestments had been carefully set out, a number of senior priests . . . were vesting in surplices and copes preparatory to proceeding to the main door for the solemn liturgical reception. Suddenly the door swung open and there, framed in the doorway, his tall figure slightly stooped by the weight of the portmanteau he carried, was the new Archbishop's secretary. Stern and unsmiling, without a word of greeting to anyone, he strode straight to the bench where, with what almost seemed a gesture of disdain, he swept the carefully arranged vestments to the floor before proceeding to set out in their place the magnificent cope and dalmatic specially brought from Rome for the occasion.

The whispered words of a senior Sydney priest witnessing this scene were taken as a prophecy: 'This is the man we will need to watch'.[7] Indeed, O'Haran was closely watched from that moment.

Likely candidates for Wynne's 'very old' informant were two priests who served at Pyrmont, Philip McIntyre, who died in 1938 aged 83, and Michael Macnamara, who died in 1939 aged 80, both living long enough to have related the story to Roger Wynne who arrived in Sydney in 1936. Both were present at Moran's welcome—McIntyre as a young priest of the Archdiocese and Macnamara as a newly ordained visitor, the junior member of a delegation of Bathurst clergy. Macnamara was appointed to Pyrmont in March 1901 as administrator during the absence of Father McIntyre who returned to Ireland 'on sick leave' for nine months. The appointment was

---

7. Roger Wynne, 'The coming of Cardinal Moran', *Australasian Catholic Record*, 47 (1970): 202.

the result of a scandal surrounding the much watched and much resented Doctor O'Haran.

During 1899 the Cardinal sought to have his private secretary promoted to episcopal rank. In mid-year Joseph Higgins, his assistant bishop since 1889, was appointed bishop of Rockhampton. Moran, as Metropolitan Archbishop of the ecclesiastical Province of New South Wales, summoned the bishops of the Colony, his suffragans. The eight were invited to propose names for the position of auxiliary bishop. It was well known that Moran wanted the appointment of Denis O'Haran. Only two of the bishops submitted O'Haran's name. In a move reminiscent of the blocking of Austin Sheehy's appointment in 1867, James Murray of Maitland, the senior among the suffragans and suspected of involvement in the Sheehy case, wrote a letter to Michael Kelly, Rector of the Irish College in Rome and Roman agent of the Australian hierarchy, arguing O'Haran's unsuitability because of his lack of respect among the clergy and 'his familiarity with females'. Murray was later joined by the long-serving William Lanigan of Goulburn in a more direct intervention, writing to the Cardinal Prefect of Propaganda Fide, whose congregation would be responsible for proposing a nominee to the Pope. Lanigan cited O'Haran's indiscretions over several years as making him unworthy of elevation to the episcopacy. The Cardinal Prefect informed Moran in April 1900 that, given the information he had received, an appointment of O'Haran would be inopportune. In January, Murray had expanded on vague references to indiscretions and reported to Kelly that Sydney clergy suspected O'Haran of 'fornication or something very near or like it'.[8]

What was written in confidential letters to Rome and gossiped about by Sydney priests at presbytery card-tables entered the public arena in December 1900 with the opening of a divorce case in which O'Haran was named as co-respondent. Test-cricketer Arthur Coningham was suing for divorce from his wife Alice whom he accused of adultery with O'Haran beginning in 1898 at St Mary's Cathedral and 'buildings adjacent thereto', resulting in the birth of a boy in November 1899. Included in the case was a claim of £5,000 damages for petitioner's loss of honour.[9]

During the trial suspicions emerged that Coningham was being supplied with inside information about ecclesiastical matters, especially regarding the finer details of the theory of 'mental reservation' in confessional practice, a topic which always excited anti-Catholic sentiment. After the jury failed to reach a decision at the conclusion of the trial on 14 December, a

---

8. P Ayres, *Prince of the Church. Francis Patrick Moran 1830-1911* (Sydney, 2007), 207–210.
9. *Sydney Morning Herald*, 4 December 1900.

second hearing was scheduled for March 1901. During the interim period the defence team was busy trying to unmask the whistle-blower. Their investigations included having the Catholic Postmaster General, Paddy Crick, intercept and open mail.

Crick, by no means a devout Catholic, was nevertheless keenly alert to slights against the church, which he saw as manifestations of establishment pretensions.[10] Just such an affront was perceived to have been received by Cardinal Moran in conjunction with celebration of the declaration of the formation of the Australian colonies into a Commonwealth on 1 January 1901. The Cardinal, a great advocate of federation, expected that he, being senior to the Anglican Archbishop of Sydney, William Saumarez Smith, who had only been on his throne since 1897, would have the place of honour at the ceremony to be held in the specially erected pavilion in the Centennial Park. Indeed, instructions from the Imperial Government had established the order the precedence with Moran in top position. However, at the last minute the order was reversed and Smith was named as the one to lead the opening prayers. Crick, 'not caring for social matters', did not attend the celebration, and was unaware of the reversal until, watching the procession heading for Centennial Park from his office high in the General Post Office in Martin Place, 'was much surprised at not seeing the Cardinal', as he indignantly explained to the editor of the *Catholic Press*.[11] The Cardinal had deliberately absented himself from direct involvement in the official celebrations, refusing to play second fiddle to 'William Sydney'. Instead he chose to observe the procession from a raised platform at the northern end of his cathedral, attended by Dr O'Haran and flanked by visiting bishops and Sydney clergy. As the procession emerged from the Domain on its long progress to Centennial Park, the cathedral bells were rung, the new national flag unfurled from the central tower and the gathered clergy were heard loyally singing 'God Save the Queen'. The *Catholic Press* made the rather exaggerated claim that 'on all hands it is admitted that St Mary's was the showplace of the day'.[12]

Perhaps it was Crick's outrage at the insult offered to the cardinal that made him susceptible to the suggestion that he provide 'splendid services' to His Eminence and his secretary by undertaking the interception and

---

10. Bede Nairn and Martha Rutledge, 'Crick, William Patrick (Paddy) (1862–1908)', *Australian Dictionary of Biography*, National Centre of Biography, Australian National University, http://adb.anu.edu.au/biography/crick-william-patrick-paddy-5821/text9883, published first in hardcopy 1981, accessed online 20 October 2014.
11. 'The Cardinal and the Procession. A Letter from the Postmaster General', *Catholic Press*, 12 January 1901.
12. *Catholic Press*, 5 January 1901.

opening of mail in the cause of rescuing O'Haran from the church's enemies.[13] Letters from a certain 'Zero' to Arthur Coningham came to light; 'Zero' was uncovered as Father John Kenny, curate at Darlinghurst. Moran summoned Kenny late in February and confronted him with the evidence and demanded to know of any other clergy involved. The name of Michael Macnamara emerged. At the second trial, through the entrapment of Coningham achieved by letters sent by a substitute 'Zero', the case against O'Haran collapsed, and on 2 April the jury found him not guilty. O'Haran was escorted by a jubilant Catholic crowd from the King Street courthouse to St Mary's Cathedral where, from an upper window of the presbytery, 'the Chief' raised his red biretta in welcome to 'carissimo':

> The Cardinal, like the statue of a pontifical saint in a niche, stood at an open window above, and gazed with calm benevolence upon his people below . . . There was something separate and supramundane in his attitude and expression, the look of a Prince of the Church against which the Gates of Hell shall not prevail, as he acknowledged the cheers of the crowd by quietly raising his biretta and inclining his head.[14]

Father Kenny was suspended, or 'crushed out of existence' in his own words, and obliged to leave Australia. However, while at sea he was granted an 'exeat', a document which would allow him to seek admittance to another diocese. He finally settled in the United States. At the beginning of March, Michael Macnamara had been suddenly removed from being priest-in-charge of the extensive district centred on the suburb of Kogarah and sent to Pyrmont in place of Father McIntyre, who had left for Ireland on a year's leave. Now located away from the parish where he was well known and very popular, and placed in one of the smallest and poorest districts of the Archdiocese, Macnamara was confronted within days of his arrival with the accusation of cooperation with 'Zero'/Kenny. In a letter from Moran he was accused of being mixed up in the diabolical conspiracy against Dr O'Haran.[15] In his

---

13. A book on the trial, published soon after the event, carried the following dedication: 'TO THE HON. W. P. CRICK, IN RECOGNITION OF THE SPLENDID SERVICES RENDERED BY HIM IN THE WORK OF VINDICATING THE HONOUR OF DR. O'HARAN, THIS BOOK IS DEDICATED BY THE AUTHOR' ('Zero', *The Secret History of the Coningham Case*, Sydney 1901).
14. Zero, *The Secret History of the Coningham Case*, 349-350. On the Coningham case, see also: Edmund Campion, *Rockchoppers. Growing up Catholic in Australia*, Ringwood 1982, 79-82; P Ayres, *Prince of the Church. Patrick Francis Moran, 1830-1911*, Sydney 2007; A E Cunningham, *The Price of a Wife? The priest and the divorce trial*, Sydney 2013.
15. Moran to Macnamara, 3 March 1901 (Macnamara file, SAA).

reply the next day Macnamara described himself as feeling highly indignant that, after his twenty years record as a priest, such an outrageous charge should be made against him.[16] He further claimed that he had been warned by a cathedral priest, John O'Gorman, that O'Haran suspected him of being 'Zero', and that he had said that when the case was settled he would pay off that little man in Kogarah.[17] Despite further exchanges with the Cardinal, who was continuing an unsuccessful trawl for more clerical traitors, no material evidence of Macnamara's involvement emerged.

The intimate bond between the Cardinal and his personal secretary would continue until Moran's death in 1911. O'Haran's influence over 'the Chief' was dramatically illustrated by the excommunication that Moran imposed on the very popular French Marist, Peter Piquet, in 1907. As Dean of St Mary's Cathedral O'Haran jealously guarded his canonical privileges and complained to the Cardinal about intrusions by the Marist priests of the neighbouring St Patrick's parish into the cathedral district. In a seven page memo he specifically accused Piquet of administering the sacrament of extreme unction to dying Catholics on three occasions without his permission. He went further, accusing Piquet of a scandalous grab for cash under the pretext of piety, describing him as a marauding priest attempting to exploit all the parishes in the city and suburbs, and constantly hanging on to the coat-tails of the rich, while neglecting the poor people of his own parish of St Patrick's at the Rocks . He drew Moran's attention to a clause of Canon Law which stated that such actions attracted ipso facto excommunication. The memo was signed: 'I am Your Eminence's dutiful child, Denis F O'Haran.'[18] The day after receiving the memo the Cardinal wrote to Piquet informing him that he had automatically incurred excommunication reserved to the Holy See. However, the Venerable Archpriest Austin Sheehy, well versed in Canon Law following his own unfortunate experience of 1867, intervened and pointed out that O'Haran's interpretation of the law was faulty. As recounted by Piquet, he was restored to sacred ministry 'on the third day'.[19] The saintly Peter Piquet is commemorated in a window that was created for the Seafarer's Chapel in Kent Street in 1931 and relocated to St Bede's at Pyrmont in 1983.

Michael Macnamara had been appointed to Pyrmont without the assistance of a curate. The long serving assistant at St Bede's, Daniel O'Reilly, had been transferred to Surry Hills in August 1900 and replaced briefly by Peter Paul Power, an All Hallows priest who had arrived from Ireland in

---

16. Macnamara to Moran, 4 March 1901 (Macnamara file, SAA).
17. Macnamara to Moran, 19 April 1901 (Macnamara file, SAA).
18. O'Haran to Moran, 24 September 1907 (Marist Fathers box, SAA).
19. See P McMurrich, *The Harmonious Influence of Religion: St Patrick's Church Hill, 1840 to the present*, Sydney 2011, 48-49.

1890 and had served as assistant in a range of Sydney parishes. When Philip McIntyre sailed for Ireland in February 1901, Power was sent to take charge of the Windsor district in the absence of its pastor who was also heading back to Ireland on leave. Power's subsequent career saw him as pastor at Gosford, Albion Park and Bungendore. He became a priest of the Goulburn diocese when the southern section of the Sydney Archdiocese, including the Bungendore district, was transferred in compensation for Goulburn's loss of territory following the creation of the new diocese of Wagga Wagga in 1918. In 1921 a 'BAILIFF'S NOTICE OF INTENDED SALE' appeared in the *Queanbeyan Age and Queanbeyan Observer* announcing that unless an account were paid by Rev P P Power, a sale of 'a Chestnut Trotting Mare, 5 years, by Lord Elmo out of Memo, Memo by Huen Prince, 1 Hooded Sulky and set of Sulky Harness' would be sold at the residence of the defendant.[20] It is not recorded whether the reverend gentleman was deprived of his elegant means of transport. There is a sad entry against his name in a hand-written list of pioneer Australian clergy: 'mental case'.[21] Father Power died at St Joseph's Hospital at Auburn in April 1927 at the age of 63.[22]

Michael Macnamara was a native of Limerick. Born in 1858 he was recruited in Ireland with nine others by Bishop Matthew Quinn as students for the new seminary the bishop was planning for his diocese of Bathurst. They arrived in Australia in 1875, and began studies at St Stanislaus College, while awaiting the building of St Charles Seminary. The president of the college assessed the new arrivals as 'very pious', but 'generally backward in acquired learning'.[23] Christopher Coveny, Australian born and a lay teacher at the college, mischievously described them all as 'raw youth' with red hair, having one Greek grammar between them, and all sharing the same large pocket handkerchief

Ordained in 1881, Michael Macnamara was sent in the following year as priest-in-charge of the vast district of Bourke in western New South Wales. In 1885 he was appointed Prefect of Studies at St Stanislaus College in Bathurst and, after a period of teaching at the St Charles diocesan seminary from 1887 to 1889, he sought a transfer to the Archdiocese of Sydney. His first brief appointment was as curate at Petersham. In October 1889 he was present at St Mary's Cathedral for the obsequies of Julian Tenison Woods, the famous priest-scientist who had taught him at the Bathurst seminary. Also present were Father James Furlong, newly appointed to Pyrmont, Father Edward O'Callaghan, future pastor of Pyrmont, and Father John

---

20. *Queanbeyan Age and Queanbeyan Observer*, 16 September 1921.
21. TJ Linane, 'Index to priests A - Z to 1900', manuscript (SAA).
22. *Sydney Morning Herald*, 11 April 1927.
23. Kevin Livingston, *The Emergence of the Australian Catholic Priesthood* (Sydney, 1977), 90.

Milne Curran, another Bathurst Seminary graduate and disciple of Tenison Wood and briefly a Pyrmont curate.[24]

From Petersham Macnamara was sent across the harbour to a vast district based at Gordon and extending north-west to the confluence of the Hawkesbury and McDonald Rivers and north-east to Pittwater. He was entrepreneurial in buying land and building churches, convents and schools, as detailed in a letter to Archbishop Kelly in 1922.[25] He brought the same energy and panache to his next appointment at Kogarah in 1896. The extensive St George district was situated 'between the two rivers', the Cooks and the Georges. With a touch of bitterness and regret in reviewing this placement and his subsequent removal, he concluded his letter to Kelly, claiming that he had arranged to purchase a block of land in the district as a site for a church when he was suddenly removed; that block of land, which could have been purchased for two pounds per foot, was now worth ten times as much.[26]

That sudden removal was his relocation to Pyrmont in March 1901, where he was too preoccupied with defending himself from Moran's accusations and conducting parish duties single-handedly to exercise his real-estate skills. However, his public removal did not cause him to withdraw from clergy gatherings. On St Patrick's Day he joined the huge assembly of priests and people which accompanied the remains of Archbishop Polding and the pioneer priests, Therry, Power and McEncroe, through the streets of Sydney from St Benedict's, where the disinterred bodies had been placed overnight, to St Mary's Cathedral for reinterment in the floor of the Irish Saints Chapel.[27] Nor was he absent in April from the Town Hall 'Monster Meeting', a gathering of Catholics 'brought together by the common object at once of demonstrating their undying fidelity to the priesthood from which they derive spiritual sustenance and their scorn for the dastards who sought to wound that body in the person of the Very Rev Dr O'Haran'.[28] Also high on the agenda was a subscription to defray the legal costs of the Monsignor. The meeting opened with the reading of a letter of solidarity from the newly commissioned Prime Minister of the Commonwealth, Edmund Barton, read by the chairman, his colleague, the newly elected Senator Richard O'Connor:

> I am unable to be present, but I hope you will be the bearer of my congratulations to Dr O'Haran on his vindication. He has no doubt

---
24. *Freeman's Journal*, 12 October 1889.
25. Macnamara to Kelly, 21 March 1922 (Macnamara file, SAA).
26. Macnamara to Kelly, 21 March 1922 (Macnamara file, SAA).
27. *Freeman's Journal*, 23 March 1901.
28. *Freeman's Journal*, 13 April 1901.

the sympathy of a large majority of the unprejudiced citizens who throughout have kept themselves informed of the proceedings in the case. As one of these I have already expressed to Dr O'Haran, through the medium of a friend, my agreement with the verdict of the jury. But as the meeting is one of active sympathy I do not wish to have it supposed that I stop at cold concurrence with the verdict. That concurrence was a mere conclusion of reason; but I have a warmer feeling of welcome for the exoneration of a man whose duties are of the gravest, and whose responsibilities are of the heaviest, from charges which I am bound in honesty to say that I never saw reason to believe. Always yours sincerely, Edmund Barton. (Prolonged cheers)[29]

Even Paddy Crick, well known for his avoidance of public gatherings, attended in the name of 'fair play': 'It is seldom that I obtrude my presence to a Sydney audience, but on this occasion, having regard for fair play, I have no hesitation in coming forward and expressing, regardless of any religious feeling, my opinions with regard to certain aspects of the trial, not hitherto touched upon.' He obliquely referred to clerical undermining of the Monsignor in suggesting that there were two motives at play in accusations against O'Haran—blackmail and 'squaring'. At the conclusion of the meeting, at which an estimated 6,000 were in attendance, the Chairman announced: 'You will be glad to hear that the total sum received tonight amounts to £1411, that is, exclusive of £500 already subscribed by the Very Rev Dr O'Haran's fellow-priests (Cheers)'. The evening was brought to a close when 'cheers were called for his Eminence the Cardinal, the Very Rev Dr O'Haran, and the King, and were lustily responded to in the most hearty fashion'.[30]

During April local parish meetings were held throughout the Archdiocese and beyond to express 'sympathy with Dr O'Haran' and to gather more subscriptions to defray his legal expenses which exceeded £5000, much of which had been spent on the inter-trial sleuthing. The *Freeman's Journal* gave regular reports on these meetings and late in April trumpeted that 'the feeling is just as warm in the other States as in New South Wales'. A long list of the inter-state and inter-diocesan meetings was then given, with a report from Pyrmont tacked on at the end:

At a largely-attended meeting of the parishioners of Pyrmont and Ultimo, held in St Bede's Schoolroom on Sunday evening, the Rev Father MacNamara presiding, a resolution congratulating the Very Rev Dr

---

29. *Freeman's Journal*, 13 April 1901.
30. *Freeman's Journal*, 13 April 1901.

O'Haran on the satisfactory termination of the terrible ordeal to which he had of late been subjected was carried unanimously. It was also decided ... to open a subscription list for the purpose of receiving contributions towards defraying the heavy expenses incurred by Dr OHaran's defence, to which those present responded in a very liberal manner.[31]

A meeting of the Pyrmont parish committee had been held on the evening of 2 April, the day on which the jury returned its 'not guilty' verdict. With Father Macnamara in the chair the Committee unanimously resolved by acclamation that 'the Secretary be instructed to write a letter to Dr O'Haran on behalf of the parishioners of Pyrmont and Ultimo congratulating him on the glorious victory gained by him that day as the result of the unanimous verdict of the jury in the Coningham divorce case'.[32] Michael Macnamara was doing everything he could to shake off the suspicions connecting him with the clerical 'squaring' against O'Haran.

A delightful child's view of life at St Bede's in 1901 was given in a letter to the 'Children's Column by Playmate' in the *Catholic Press*. Ten year old Tom McGuirk of John Street wrote:

> Dear Playmate, As this is my first letter to the Catholic Press, I hope it will please your playmates. I am getting on very well at school. I am taught by the Sisters of the Good Samaritan, Saint Bede's School, Pyrmont. The boys of our school formed a Sodality of the Holy Childhood Guild last December. They hold their meetings in the schoolroom on the second Sunday of the month. I am not a member yet, but I hope I will be when I am a few years older. Six more boys were enrolled on the first Sunday in May by the Rev. Father McNamara. He is our parish priest since the Rev. Father McIntyre went to Ireland. I am preparing for my first Holy Communion with a lot of other children at our school. With kindest wishes to the playground, Your fond playmate, Tom McGuirk.[33]

In June Macnamara wrote to the Cardinal on behalf of his former parishioners at Kogarah asking permission for them to organise a belated farewell for him. The event finally took place in August, and was chaired by the mayor of Kogarah and attended by parliamentarians and councillors from Hurstville, Rockdale, Sutherland, Bexley and Kogarah, and a large gathering of parishioners. 'Father Mac' was eulogised by speaker after speaker, praised and thanked for his church and civic activities, and for his financial astuteness. He was wished 'Godspeed and good luck' in his move

---

31. *Freeman's Journal*, 27 April 1901.
32. Pyrmont Committee Minute Book, 2 April 1901 (Pyrmont Box, SAA)
33. *Catholic Press*, 1 June 1901.

to 'the parish by the waterside'. In an unprecedented move Macnamara had indicated his wish to decline the traditional purse of sovereigns; Polding, who had issued an official warning against the practice in 1861, would have been proud of him.[34] In his reply he said that he felt that it had been his duty to join in every movement for the welfare of the district—that was his recreation: 'He felt that he was too old for cricket and had taken up bowls, but after a little experience of that game he found he wasn't old enough.' The *Freeman's Journal*'s full page report of the farewell was accompanied by a large flattering photograph of the 42 year old pastor.[35]

Philip McIntyre returned to Sydney in November 1901, two weeks after the arrival of the new Coadjutor Archbishop, Michael Kelly. Kelly came with a reputation for his strong 'advocacy of the holy cause of temperance'.[36] Perhaps this should have been an early warning for some of the local clergy, including McIntyre, who in later life would be the recipient of suspensions from Kelly because of inebriation. On the eve of McIntyre's return Moran had instructed Macnamara to prepare to accommodate him as the priest-in-charge; Macnamara would be the curate. The reply was immediate: 'I received last night a letter from Your Eminence in which you order me to hand over the administration of the parish of Pyrmont to Fr McIntyre, and myself to remain as his curate.' He complained bitterly of being publicly degraded to the position of curate after 20 years hard work in the archdiocese, of which he was justly proud.[37]

There was general delight on the part of parishioners in welcoming Fr McIntyre home: 'Father McIntyre was warmly welcomed by his parishioners. A big crowd, including a large number of children, by whom he has always been beloved, assembled on the wharf to greet him, and the people of Pyrmont and Ultimo received him with demonstrations of joy. On his visit to the schools he was entertained at a concert.'[38] One of the children, a high school student, shared the joy in a letter to 'Playmate':

> As it is a long time since I wrote to you I suppose you thought I forgot all about you. I am always wishing for Thursday to come around and bring me the 'Children's Columns'. I still go to St Mary's Cathedral school... His Grace Archbishop Kelly visited our school on Tuesday. We are preparing for our Christmas concert. The Rev Father McIntyre, our parish priest,

---

34. John Bede Polding, 'Pastoral Monition to the Clergy of the Archdiocese 1861', in P O'Farrell, *Documents in Australian Catholic History* (Melbourne, 1969), volume 1, 94–97.
35. *Freeman's Journal*, 31 August 1901.
36. *Freeman's Journal*, 16 November 1901.
37. Macnamara to Moran, 24 November 1901 (Macnamara file, SAA).
38. *Catholic Press*, 30 November 1901.

arrived on Friday evening after a tour to Europe. We were so glad to have him back to Sydney once more. Wishing the Catholic Press every success, and wishing to all a Happy New Year, I remain, as ever your fond playmate, Bridget Hynes (Aged 13 years.)[39]

Michael Macnamara's last entry in the Pyrmont Baptismal Register was dated 2 March 1902, the day before Cardinal Moran with Doctor O'Haran departed on the night express to Melbourne in order the board the luxury liner *Ophir* the next day as it set sail for Europe. After four months awkward cohabitation with McIntyre, Macnamara had been assigned to the far south coast, to the small, remote settlement of Cobargo. Lack of firm evidence implicating him in the O'Haran affair precluded suspension and dismissal from the Archdiocese, leaving internal exile as the alternative punishment. In his 1922 letter to Archbishop Kelly he outlined his achievements during his seven years in the rural parish: he had paid the debt off the Church, made improvements, erected a costly bell imported from England, and left one hundred and fifty pounds for the building of a convent.[40] In a questionnaire required to be completed by all priests of the Archdiocese in 1938, the year before his death, maintaining his rage, he wrote of Cobargo: 'seven years, salary £180 out of which a horse had to be fed.'[41] In 1908 he was sent by Cardinal Moran to an even more remote location, the former gold-mining township of Araluen in the Southern Tablelands of New South Wales. Here he built the only presbytery that ever was built in Araluen, as he reminded Archbishop Kelly.[42] From 1909 to 1913 his closest neighbour was Philip McIntyre transferred from Pyrmont to Braidwood, 27 kilometres north of Araluen, a more comfortable relationship than the sharing of the small presbytery at Pyrmont.

Cardinal Moran died in 1911 and was succeeded by Michael Kelly. Kelly appointed Macnamara to Kiama in the Illawarra district in 1913. He was pleased with this arrangement, but was relocated to North Parramatta in 1917. In 1922 in a letter to Kelly seeking appointment to the vacant parish of Strathfield, where he would be a 'rector inamovibilis' and a 'very reverend', he reflected on the perceived injustice of his removal from Kiama, recalling an appeal to the Papal Delegate. He asked His Grace that, in making his claim for Strathfield, he be permitted to remind him that in coming to North Parramatta five years ago, he had been assured in writing that in due time preferment should and would follow. He then recalled that the Apostolic Delegate, as the result of an inquiry into the removal from Kiama, wrote

---

39. *Catholic Press*, 11 January 1902.
40. Macnamara to Kelly, 21 March 1922 (Macnamara file, SAA).
41. Archdiocesan Questionnaire 1938 (Macnamara file, SAA).
42. Macnamara to Kelly, 21 March 1922 (Macnamara file, SAA).

assuring him that His Grace had declared that the present arrangement was a temporary one. The Delegate had exhorted him to devote himself earnestly to his work so that the Archbishop might be able to see his way to entrust to him a parish or position that would be regarded as satisfactory.[43]

Nine years later when he celebrated his Golden Jubilee of ordination in 1932 he was still at North Parramatta, still a simple 'reverend'. Tributes were paid to Macnamara in March 1924 at a gathering to farewell him on a trip to Ireland. Monsignor John O'Gorman concluded his speech with high praise, saying that 'a straighter character he had never met among the priesthood'.[44]

Macnamara and O'Haran played out their mutual dislike in an exchange of correspondence in the *Freeman's Journal* during July and August 1930. O'Haran had written an article on Mother Mary MacKillop as foundress of the Sisters of St Joseph, and made slighting remarks about the role of Father Julian Tenison Woods.[45] Macnamara leapt to the defence of his old professor at St Charles Seminary, Bathurst, crediting him as founder of the Josephites. He took the opportunity to include Cardinal Moran in his critique:

> But the claim that Father Woods was the founder of the Order of St Joseph, which he established at Penola with the help of Mother Mary, who at the time was a teacher in a small country school, receives no support from him [O'Haran] who has a theory of his own. It is a remarkable fact, in conjunction with this, that the name of the great missioner, the noted scientist, and the founder of a religious Order, is not mentioned once in the two volume history of the Church compiled by Cardinal Moran. Penola is there, but Father Woods is not in the picture.[46]

Monsignor O'Haran prefaced his reply: 'I have always carefully eschewed controversy because I realised early in life that a war of words only irritates tempers and leads nowhere.' However, he proceeded to set out 'a plain statement of facts', declining 'to be drawn into devious paths by any scribe, merely for the sake of seeing my name in print'.[47] Denying ever having 'said a word or written a line detrimental to the name of Father Julian Woods', he slyly raised doubts about Woods' reputation:

---

43. Macnamara to Kelly, 21 March 1922 (Macnamara file, SAA).
44. *Freeman's Journal*, 13 March 1924.
45. *Freeman's Journal*, 10 July 1930.
46. *Freeman's Journal*, 24 July 1930.
47. *Freeman's Journal*, 31 July 1930.

I have never had the leisure or the time to follow his works, review his life or study his character. I must, therefore, accept the general version that he must have been a man of more than ordinary genius to have succeeded in accomplishing much, considering that he is not known to have had any classical course or any regular training in Philosophy, Theology or Canon Law. I have never learned under what definite jurisdiction he exercised his priestly faculties, whence he received his obedience or whether he was not a law unto himself, nor why he abandoned his priestly calling for secular or lay pursuits. I did hear that in his preaching he exercised a great influence over women, presumably for their good.

Alluding to Tenison Woods' susceptibility to female visionaries, he concluded that he himself 'had never had any desire of receiving any premature messages from the other world', and therefore he had been robbed of the 'privilege of seeking to meet or form acquaintance with Father Woods. I cannot, therefore, conscientiously take away anything, or add much to the good name and exploits which others credit him with.'[48]

Macnamara replied, characterising O'Haran's letter as 'a final kick at Father Julian Woods'. He referred to the recently published biography of Tenison Woods by the Jesuit George O'Neill, 'where it is clearly shown that Father Woods founded the Sisters of St Joseph with the help of Miss McKillop, a teacher in a country school, and who in the book is called the co-founder'. He concluded by joining with O'Haran 'in the only thing we seem to agree on', namely, 'offering a fervent prayer that God and St Joseph may bless' the work of the Sisters.[49]

O'Haran had the last word, denying any criticism of Woods: 'Regarding Father Tennison [sic] Woods I have carefully abstained from saying anything really detrimental to his life and character lest in doing so I might have hurt the feelings of his relatives or given offence to his friends and admirers ... Fault finding is no part of my domain.'[50] However, he again proceeded to raise the delicate question of Woods' relationship with women:

When shortly before his death Father Woods came here he had no ecclesiastical claims on Cardinal Moran or on the Archdiocese of Sydney. In all charity, however, His Eminence asked me to reserve for Father Woods a private room at St Vincent's Hospital with full attendance and treatment by the Sisters of Charity and the best medical skill, which I did

---

48. *Freeman's Journal*, 31 July 1930.
49. *Freeman's Journal*, 7 August 1930.
50. *Freeman's Journal*, 14 August 1930.

> ... We all felt the extreme delicacy of a priest taking up his quarters with a small community of women where no male had ever slept.[51]

O'Haran concluded the exchange of letters with Macnamara by expressing his confident expectation that 'the character of Father Woods will probably be much clarified', especially the negative aspects, in the biography of Mary McKillop, which Father O'Neill then had in hand, and which would be published in 1931.

Michael Macnamara submitted the completed archdiocesan questionnaire of 1938 from North Parramatta/Waitematta, specifying that he had been there for 21 years. The form also recorded his lingering anger at the way he had been treated during the O'Haran affair and since. Having answered the question 'Papal Dignities and Diocesan Offices, if any, and dates of reception of, or appointment to same?' with 'Never held any, not even a Very Reverend', he addressed the question 'Chronological list of appointments?' To the list he added the observation: 'Father Kenny who made the charge is now a Monsignor in the States. No recompense was ever made to me by the Cardinal or his successor'. The following year he retired from parish duties in May and died in July. At the Requiem Mass Coadjutor Archbishop Norman Gilroy spoke of him as 'always a most courteous and gentlemanly priest', who 'amongst his fellow priests . . . had been esteemed and popular . . . a most companionable man'.[52] The celebrant of the Mass was a nephew of the deceased, John Carroll, on loan from the Irish Vincentian Province, who would volunteer as an army chaplain at the outbreak of war in 1939.

Father 'Mac' was fondly remembered back in Araluen, as reported in an obituary published in the *Braidwood Dispatch*:

> A wonderful type was the late Father 'Mac', as his friends (and they were legion) knew him. Broad-minded, fearless, a grand sport and a true friend, his passing will be deplored by all sections. He was well known in the Braidwood district, having been in charge of Araluen parish many years ago. Members of the old Araluen and Braidwood Rifle Clubs will treasure pleasant memories of their association with the genial priest, who was one of the best shots in the former club . . . He lived frugally, and although strong in character, was most gentle in his dealings with his fellow men.[53]

---

51. *Freeman's Journal*, 14 August 1930.
52. *Catholic Press*, 3 August 1939.
53. *Braidwood Dispatch and Mining Journal*, 18 August 1939.

Back at Pyrmont, after Macnamara's removal to Cobargo in March 1902, Philip McIntyre laboured alone until he was joined by a new curate, Peter Donnelly, in December. Donnelly was born in 1865 at Armagh and was something of a 'late vocation'. He was sent to undertake his priestly studies in Rome, while residing at the Irish College, and was ordained at the Lateran Basilica in 1894 and sailed to Australia soon afterwards. Following a brief placement at the Cathedral he was sent south to Bega, 41 kilometres beyond Cobargo. In quick succession from 1896 he was curate at Surry Hills, Concord, Parramatta and Moruya, before arriving at Pyrmont. When he was farewelled from Parramatta to rural Moruya, instead of presenting him with the traditional purse of sovereigns, the parishioners gave him a present 'useful to a country priest—a neat bridle, whip, leggings, and spurs'.[54]

One of his last pastoral acts before leaving Parramatta involved him in an unprecedented liturgical initiative—the employment of 'altar girls'—as reported by the secular but not the Catholic press:

> The Rev Father Peter Donnelly, from Parramatta, returned home a few days ago, after spending almost a fortnight in the vicinity of Wiseman's Ferry and St Albans. During his stay he visited all the people of his flock. Despite the flood and wet weather Father Donnelly was extremely pleased with his visit. He celebrated Mass to fairly large congregations at St Albans, Webb's Creek and Wiseman's Ferry. As altar boys are not available in this district, the Misses O'Brien and Miss Nagle acted as such at Wiseman's Ferry, and deserve to be congratulated for their knowledge of Latin. The people of his parish were looking forward to another visit from him in the near future, but within the last few days he has been removed from Parramatta to Moruya.[55]

It is not known whether he ever repeated the experiment.

In Pyrmont he would not have needed the equine equipment so necessary at Moruya, for the small parish could be covered comfortably on foot, and for more distant excursions there were the ferries and the new tramway. Donnelly was back in Sydney in time to add to the 'splendid enthusiasm' displayed by the throng of clergy and laity gathered at the Cathedral on December to welcome Cardinal Moran back from his trip to Rome.[56] By his side was the 'faithful companion', Denis O'Haran, who had been honoured in Rome with an appointment as 'Domestic Prelate' by the Pope, in compensation for his failing to be appointed auxiliary bishop. The appointment allowed the bearer to style himself 'Monsignor' and to

---

54. *Cumberland Argus and Fruitgrowers Advocate*, 4 August 1900.
55. *Windsor and Richmond Gazette*, 4 August 1900.
56. *Freeman's Journal*, 13 December 1902.

wear quasi-episcopal garb, but not the mitre. In 1905 he would receive a promotion to 'Prothonotary Apostolic' which allowed the bearer to place the mitre on his coat of arms and on his tombstone, but not on his head. This was the limit of what Cardinal Moran could achieve for his ambitious 'carissimo'. He made up for it with adulation, paying him the following tribute at the conclusion of the Catholic Congress in 1909:

> I owe a special debt of gratitude to Divine Providence in giving me a worthy priest for my constant companion and assistant, one who throughout those 25 years has been unwearying in his devotedness to religion, and incomparable in the ardor with which he promoted the interests of piety and of every good cause—I mean, my excellent, most gifted, most self-sacrificing, and most devoted Secretary.[57]

The Cardinal made a visit to St Bede's in May 1904, not to celebrate a liturgy or open a bazaar, but to preside at a fund-raising meeting on behalf of the completion of St Mary's Cathedral. He was seated in the sanctuary holding a list of local subscribers to the fund. The district of Pyrmont and Ultimo was held up as an outstanding example of selfless generosity. Though very poor, as attested by the pastor and his curate, the people were very generous and had given what they could. Father McIntyre paid special tribute to Mrs Coffill, 'a Protestant lady who was an ornament to the parish'. The Cardinal referred to the list in his hand and commented that 'looking at the list it stuck him that so many had contributed, and though the sums were not large yet everyone appeared to have contributed'. In an article headed, 'The Cardinal at Pyrmont; A Self-Sacrificing People', the *Freeman's Journal* heaped praise on the parish:

> Of the many meetings held in parochial districts around Sydney in aid of the Cathedral Fair none has been marked with more zeal and thorough earnestness than that addressed by his Eminence the Cardinal-Archbishop at St Bede's, Pyrmont, on Sunday afternoon. The parishioners, who included those of St Bede's, Pyrmont, and St. Francis', Ultimo crowded the church and transmuted their sympathy into a very practical form, so much so, indeed, that the donations poured in, until the total went over £100, a sum made up in the main by numerous small donations, which reflected the greatest honour on the givers. This was subsequently increased to £107 5s. Other parishes blessed with wealthy donors of large sums have not approached Pyrmont in results, and taking the number and smallness of the donations into account, St Bede's and

---

57. *Freeman's Journal*, 26 March 1931.

St. Francis' combined have just reason reason to be proud of the Fair meeting.[58]

The subscription list was printed in the *Catholic Press* the following week. The donations ranged from the seven guineas given by Father McIntyre and the two pounds of Father Donnelly to the one-shilling contributions of six of the local ladies—widows' mites.[59]

From Pyrmont Peter Donnelly was sent to Bungendore in 1905, and after a leave of absence granted in 1908 his name did not appear in the *Catholic Directory* again until 1918. During some of that time he was in the United States working in the Diocese of Omaha. In September 1917, on is return to Sydney, he was briefly at Darlinghurst, where he chafed under the authoritarian regime of Monsignor O'Haran, especially regarding the non-payment of the curate's salary. He was at Milton when that parish was transferred to the Goulburn Diocese, and then he received a series of brief appointments until becoming parish priest of Pambula south of Bega in 1934. He retired from the parish in 1940 and took up residence in Goulburn where he celebrated his Golden Anniversary of Ordination in 1944. He died at Lewisham Hospital in Sydney in November 1945 at the age of 80.

Succeeding Peter Donnelly as curate at Pyrmont was Edward Gell. He was born at Bathurst in 1867. His father, Edward, had come to Bathurst from England in 1858 to build the church of St Michael and St John which would become the cathedral with the arrival of Bishop Matthew Quinn in 1866. He also designed St Stanislaus College and St Charles Seminary in Bathurst and many rural churches in the diocese. Mrs Elizabeth Gell was a teacher at the Bathurst Catholic Denominational School. Edward Junior began his studies at St Stanislaus and completed them at Oscott College in England. On returning to Australia he became an apprentice engineer before deciding to enter St Charles Seminary at Bathurst. He was sent by Bishop Quinn to complete his theological studies at Propaganda Fide College in Rome. He was ordained at the Lateran Basilica in 1894, the first Bathurst-born priest. His first years were based at Bathurst, then Orange, Wellington and Dubbo. The popularity of the young priest at Wellington was highlighted in the *Freeman's Journal*: 'The Rev. Father Gell, in addition to being an efficient and popular priest, is an amateur photographer and an accomplished musician and vocalist. He sings occasionally in the church choir, and often presides at the wedding feasts, after he has "tied that knot with the tongue that cannot be undone with the teeth".'[60]

---

58. *Freeman's Journal*, 21 May 1904.
59. *Catholic Press*, 26 May 1904.
60. *Freeman's Journal*, 15 July 1899

In November 1903 he sailed to Europe on sick leave accompanied by his brother-in-law, Louis Francis Heydon, member of the New South Wales Legislative Council and President of the State Conference of the St Vincent de Paul Society. Back in Australia he applied for a transfer from Bathurst to Sydney Archdiocese. All his family, parents and three sisters, had settled in Sydney in the 1890s, his parents in a grand house in Bayswater Road, Darling Point. His father had died in 1899. Given release by the bishop of Bathurst and accepted by Cardinal Moran, he was appointed as assistant to Philip McIntyre at Pyrmont in August 1905. In September 1906 he was initiated into that essential element in parish life, fund-raising. The annual bazaar again drew the presence of the Cardinal, who in turn drew a large crowd. Father McIntyre in welcoming His Eminence commented that 'there were warm hearts in Pyrmont, even if it was the poorest parish in Sydney'. On this occasion Moran chose to address the evil of gambling. He did not advocate legislation against gambling, regarding such a move as useless:

> If he were to take examples of the inutility of endeavouring to abolish such matters by legislation it would be from what were called the 'two-up schools' (Laughter). He was not quite versed in it (Renewed laughter). In his younger days it used to be called 'pitch and toss'. However, it was contrary to the law in New South Wales, and he supposed there was not a citizen amongst them but knew very well that night after night, and especially on Saturday nights, it was carried on without the smallest interference from those who administered the law . . . He merely mentioned this as a proof that legislation was not the means for suppressing gambling.

The context for this intervention was the threat by government to extend the ban to the sorts of gambling which were such a large part of parish bazaars and fund-raising. The politician present on the day, John McNeill MLA, made explicit his objections to the proposal: 'So far as his action was concerned, and whilst gambling on a racecourse was legal, they would never make a child of his or of any of the people he represented a criminal for putting a shilling in a bazaar in aid of the church (Applause).'[61]

A scandalised Protestant gentleman of Lithgow presented, from detailed observation, a 'general synopsis' of gaming practices used by Roman Catholics:

> Race track, 7 horses running, 6d. per race, paying on the winner only, a prize of 2s., which makes 1s. 6d. clear for the Church every race; a

---

61. *Freeman's Journal*, 27 September 1906.

Yankee-sweat wheel, with the following numbers, 1, 2, 3, 4, 5, 6, which gives the Church 5 chances to 1; a Duck-Malloy handicap, which is really a roulette wheel, which wins 2s. for the Church every spin; a race wheel, which is a little too hard for a non-racer to understand, but brings in anything from 5s. to 10s. per spin, and very rarely pays out; raffles or draws in great quantity, some with and some without tickets.[62]

He contrasted these healthy takings in aid of a new church with the Lithgow community's struggle to raise funds for the town monument 'raised to our fallen heroes in Gallipoli, Egypt, and France'. Signing himself 'Interested' he explained his writing to the editor: 'I am forwarding you this, believing that under the power of your pen there is good material for a stinging article in our very valuable little champion *The Watchman*.'

Edward Gell did not have long to wait for a parish of his own, being appointed to St Charles at Ryde in June 1906. He succeeded the most senior priest of the Archdiocese, the Venerable Archpriest Samuel Austin Sheehy OSB, who as bishop-elect of Bethsaida in 1867 had blessed the foundation stone of St Bede's. It did not take Gell long to apply the bazaar lessons of Pyrmont to his Ryde parish. In November he invited the Cardinal to open an unprecedentedly long fund-raising event of ten days. Present to admire his apprentice's achievement was Philip McIntyre.[63]

After his mother's death in August 1907, he was joined at the Ryde presbytery by his spinster sister Frances as his housekeeper. The *Catholic Press* published an obituary of Mrs Elizabeth Gell, which concluded its description of the Requiem High Mass at St Mary's Cathedral: 'A sad incident in connection with the obsequies was the inability of the deceased's son, Father Gell, to attend. He was very indisposed, and was confined to his bed.'[64] Edward and Frances were both personally very wealthy beneficiaries of their father's estate, but together they also shared a deep commitment to the poor. They became supporters of the unique work of a group of nurses at Randwick dedicated to assisting the sick poor in their homes. The group was founded by Eileen O'Connor, a severely disabled young woman and a spiritual visionary, and a local priest, Edward McGrath. In 1913 the Gells each wrote a cheque for the purchase of a large house at Coogee, where Our Lady's Nurses for the Poor, locally known as the Brown Nurses, became established. They also sponsored a pacific cruise and overseas travel for Eileen and Father McGrath, and there were regular motor outings with Father Gell at the wheel. All of this unpriestly behaviour led to censures

---

62. *Watchman*, 21 November 1918.
63. *Catholic Press*, 22 November 1906.
64. *Catholic Press*, 22 August 1907.

from Archbishop Kelly. However, Father Gell weathered every storm and ministered for 42 years at Ryde, witnessing the division of his original extensive district into several separate parishes.[65]

An insight into his sensitivity was revealed in 1917 in his writing to military authorities seeking to be released from the duty of the parish priest to deliver news of a soldier's death to the family home. The military authorities wrote to the Archbishop asking him to nominate someone else in Gell's place for the task. Kelly wrote to Gell asking for an explanation of his attitude. Edward replied that he would not shirk the duty of breaking the news of a soldier's death if he thought any practical benefit could come of it. However, he failed to see how any good could come, because the blow would be felt just as keenly no matter who announced it; it was futile to try to soften it. Moreover, the announcement by a priest had the ill effect of putting the people in a panic whenever they saw a priest approaching. He recalled four cases of people being frightened at a mere visit from him. He offered to Kelly these and the reasons given in the letter to Colonel Lucsombe as sufficient reason to decline so painful an ordeal.[66] The Archbishop replied that he could see no way to decline this wartime service required of priests.[67]

In 1948 Father Gell retired to the Coogee home of the Brown Nurses, and died there in July 1951 at the age of 84. A priest colleague wrote: 'He died in a place and amongst those who had been his dearest work, the one nearest to his heart, a work he had nursed from its infancy . . . He loved that work, he loved those noble nurses. Fitting it was it should be they who would close his eyes in death, and prepare his body for burial—fully clothed in priestly garments as if prepared once again to go to the Altar of God.'[68] Cardinal Gilroy presided at the funeral at St Charles Church. The *Catholic Weekly* published the terms of the will: 'Father Gell's estate of £39,404 was left to various beneficiaries, including the Sisters of Mercy, Ryde; the Patrician Brothers, Ryde; Our Lady's Nurses of the Poor, Coogee; the Clerical Fund for Sick Priests; and Mrs Mary Collingridge (niece). A bequest of £1000 was made to His Eminence the Cardinal.'[69]

In 1953 a Ryde parishioner wrote to Cardinal Gilroy asking why the Arcdiocese had not erected a headstone over Father Gell's grave at the Field of Mars cemetery. Gilroy wrote to the executors of the Gell's will and

---

65. J Hosie, *Eileen: the life of Eileen O'Connor, foundress of Our Lady's Nurses for the Poor* (Sydney, 2004).
66. Gell to Kelly, 31 May 1917 (Gell File, SAA).
67. Kelly to Gell, 7 June 1917 (Gell File, SAA).
68. *Catholic Weekly*, 2 August 1951.
69. *Catholic Weekly*, 20 September 1951.

received the reply from one the executors stating that the will had not made provision for such, and proposing that it was the Archbishop's responsibility. His Eminence replied in measured tones, directing the executors to seek elsewhere for funds to erect a headstone. He wrote that he felt confident that the Brown Nurses, whom, he believed, had received the bulk of the estate, would consider themselves privileged to undertake the obligation of paying for the work. He asked that Dr Baker make the necessary approach to the Nurses, expressing his gratitude in anticipation.[70] A certain resentment can be detected concerning the imbalance between the Cardinal's share of the estate and that of the Brown Nurses at Coogee. The Cardinal's advice was followed and a copy of the Nurses' swift and gracious response was forwarded to His Eminence: they considered it a privilege to pay for the erection of a headstone in memory of one whom they loved and who was a very dear friend, a generous Benefactor and noble priest. They expressed their regret that the matter had been overlooked in their busy life, Father Gell's grave being so far away. They assured Dr Baker that it was not through indifference that they had not acted earlier, and that they would immediately proceed with the work.[71]

Replacing Edward Gell as Philip McIntyre's curate in November 1906 was Joseph Bowers freshly arrived from ordination in Ireland. He displayed his literary and lecturing talent when he gave an address during a fund-raising concert at St Joseph's, Balmain West, later named Rozelle, on the Irish poet and songwriter, Thomas Moore (1779-1852), whose songs were the favourites of parish concerts throughout Australia, especially 'The Last Rose of Summer' and 'Believe Me If All Those Endearing Young Charms'.[72]

Soon after his arrival in Pyrmont the young assistant headed a committee to prepare for the celebration of the pastor's silver jubilee of ordination. The event was held in the school hall and attended by many clergy mates, parishioners and visitors from the jubilarian's former parishes at Albion Park and Leichhardt. Joseph Bowers spoke succinctly in appreciation of his boss: 'The Rev. Father Bowers, as president of the committee, warmly eulogised the good qualities of Father McIntyre. If he were asked to put in one word, the essence of Father McIntyre's good qualities it was his sincerity. He was proud of the co-operation of the parishioners and admirers outside the parish in their efforts to show their appreciation of Father McIntyre's untiring zeal in his labours at Pyrmont (Applause).'[73] There was a passing reference to 'the Soggarth's well-known aversion to personal prominence'.[74] Perhaps it was

---

70. Gilroy to Baker, 8 June 1953 (Gell File, SAA).
71. Theresa McLaughlin to Baker, 16 June 1953 (Gell File, SAA).
72. *Catholic Press*, 14 March 1907.
73. *Freeman's Journal*, 27 June 1907.
74. 'Soggarth aroon' is an affectionate Gaelic expression for a priest.

this aversion that caused McIntyre to let the fortieth anniversary of St Bede's Church in September of the same year pass without celebration.

Bowers was sent across the harbour at the beginning of the academic year in 1908 to join the staff at St Patrick's College at Manly Seminary. On the date of his last baptism at St Bede's, a letter to 'Playmate' appeared in the *Catholic Press* giving a positive assessment of the parish from a young and enterprising parishioner:

> 234 Harris-street. Dear Playmate, I am writing to you for the first time. I work all day, and I go to night-school. There are two churches in Pyrmont—St Bede's and St Francis'. They are crowded, every Sunday morning and evening. A large number of the parishioners are in the Sacred Heart Society, which enables us to keep good resolutions—that is if all are careful to attend the monthly Communion and the meetings regularly. I shall write again, I remain, your now playmate, MARTIN RYAN.[75]

The editor wrote an encouraging reply: 'If I were to give a list of the great men who have graduated from night schools this page would not hold it. You are familiar with some of them. Emulate their example, and perhaps you too will make your mark in the days to come.'[76]

St Patrick's National Seminary to which Joseph Bowers was assigned had been established at Manly by Cardinal Moran in 1888, using the funds from Archbishop Vaughan's sale of the Lyndhurst estate. Although there had been four Australia-born priests, three of them Manly graduates, teaching at the College at various times from 1897 to 1907, the professorial staff in 1908 was all Irish.[77] They were in charge of teaching and forming 80 young Australians who were developing a strong spirit of nationalism. In 1906 the College's Literary and Debating Society had invited a young Manly graduate of 1903, Patrick Joseph Hartigan, then curate at Albury, to address them. He was soon to become well known and much loved as the priest-poet 'John O'Brien'. He spoke to the seminarians on 'a subject that should be dear to us—our native poets—Kendall in particular'. Some of the Irish professors did not share this love for Australia and its literature. In 1908 the students reacted strongly when 'the Reverend J Bowers made disparaging remarks about Australia'.[78] Some of the more rebellious students retaliated in their

---

75. *Catholic Press*, 16 January 1908.
76. Catholic Press, 16 January 1908.
77. KT Livingstone, *The Emergence of an Australian Catholic Priesthood 1835–1915* (Sydney, 1977), 194.
78. P Crittenden, *Changing Orders. Scenes of Clerical and Academic Life* (Blackheath (2008, 156).

essays on the topic, 'On the historical character you admire most', set for them by their young Irish professor, by writing about Australian heroes such as John Batman and Peter Lalor. Bowers tried to explain himself later when he gave an address to the Literary and Debating Society, summarised in the student diary in the following year: 'On the whole he found fault with Australia . . . The love of sport was too general, and too exclusive of the higher branches of culture. Politics was left altogether to the few . . . Australian prose and poetic composition was yet in its infancy. Writers got no encouragement in Australia, and to make a profitable living had to leave Australia.'[79] Perhaps his observation on the local obsession with sport and the neglect of 'higher branches of culture' was based on the fact that his only experience of Australia before beginning his teaching at Manly was his thirteen months on the Pyrmont peninsula.

Perhaps too his time in working-class Pyrmont was valuable in preparing a paper for the Catholic Congress of 1909, entitled 'The Catholic Workman in New South Wales', as announced in the *Catholic Press*.[80] Unfortunately Bower's essay was not among the papers published in the proceedings of the Congress. However, the contribution of one of his successors as curate at St Bede's did find its way into print—'Science Teaching in Catholic Schools' by the priest-geologist, John Milne Curran.[81]

After three years at Manly Bowers was transferred to the new ecclesiastical college of St Columba at Springwood in the Blue Mountains west of Sydney. Cardinal Moran had built the college with the intention that it would become a seminary for training Australian missionaries for China and Japan. He insisted that the entrance to the main building should face north, in the direction of these 'pagan nations'. In the meantime it would serve as a feeder seminary for Manly. After only one year at Springwood, Bowers found himself returning to the role of curate firstly at Surry Hills and then successively at the Cathedral, Lewisham and Rose Bay. In 1915, while at Lewisham parish, he gave a series of three lectures on 'The Church and the War'. He concluded his first lecture by recalling the role of the Vatican in the negotiations following the fall of Napoleon, and commented on the current conflict that 'the Pope and the Church would have to be reckoned with, too, when "scraps of paper" were thrown into the hat at the end of this war of the nations.'[82] However, the Holy See was excluded from the Versailles peace conference at the conclusion of the First World War.

---

79. Livingstone, *The Emergence of an Australian Catholic Priesthood*, 231.
80. *Catholic Press*, 26 August 1909.
81. *Proceedings of the Third Australasian Catholic Congress held at St Mary's Cathedral, Sydney, 26th September–3rd October 1909* (Sydney, 1910).
82. *Freeman's Journal*, 7 October 1915.

He was back at St Columba's College in 1919 and stayed there lecturing for the next thirteen years. In 1928 he made a presentation on behalf of the staff to the Vice-Rector, Justin Simonds, who was proceeding to Louvain University as the first recipient of the James Furlong Scholarship.[83] Joseph Bowers received his first appointment as a 'rector inamovibilis' at Waterloo parish in 1932 and later successfully applied for a transfer to the more salubrious suburb of Chatswood in 1941. On entering into parochial ministry he did not leave his lecture notes behind; he became actively involved with the Catholic Evidence Guild which had been established in Sydney in 1924. However, he does not seem to have been one of the few brave priests who took to the outdoor speakers' platforms in the Sydney Domain and at the Haymarket. His lectures, ranging from philosophical logic to Sacred Scripture, took place in St Mary's Cathedral Chapter Hall, and were part of the formation programme for the budding lay public speakers. His literary interests did not fade, though he does not seem to have extended his range to include Australian poets. In August 1935 he gave a lecture at the inaugural meeting of the Verse-Speaking Association on the English poet Henry Newbolt (1862-1938).[84] It is more likely that Bowers concentrated on Newbolt's lament, 'Ireland, Ireland', than on his imperialistic poem, 'Vitae Lampada', a jingoistic linking of cricket and the Sudan Expedition—'Play up! Play up! And play the game!' He also became involved in the establishment in Sydney of the Campion Society in 1937:

> Last month his Grace the Archbishop of Sydney (Most Rev. Michael Kelly DD) duly approved of the formal establishment of the Campion Society in Sydney . . . The society was formed for the first time in Australia in Melbourne some nine years ago by seven university undergraduates. Its function is to give young Catholic men a true picture of the function assigned to them by the Pope as lay apostles; to increase their knowledge of Catholic principles so that they may be able to answer for the faith that is in them; to train them to speak and write effectively, and to put their ideas clearly in ordinary conversation, and most particularly, to train them to combat the social evils of the age. The method of preparation is by study in groups of about ten members, which study and discuss a course prescribed and set to cover about three years . . . The spiritual direction, of the society has been put in the hands of the Rev Father Bowers PP of Mount Carmel.[85]

---

83. *Catholic Freeman's Journal*, 26 July 1928.
84. *Sunday Mail*, 17 July 1935; *Sydney Morning Herald*, 3 August 1935.
85. *Catholic Press*, 1 July 1937.

Joseph Bowers died in November 1945 at the age of 63. At the funeral Archbishop Gilroy praised his scholarship and referred to his withdrawn, perhaps poetic, nature: 'His was a character not easily known. Because of that shyness and sensitiveness of his, he came little in contact with people, except in the fulfilment of his duties.'[86]

When Joseph Bowers caught the ferry from Pyrmont to his new appointment at Manly in 1908 he was succeeded as curate by Richard Woulfe. Born in Ireland in 1879 he was ordained in 1902, and on arriving in Australia was appointed as assistant at Burwood. Pyrmont was his next move where he became Philip McIntyre's sixth curate. During his stay the parish was in the news regarding various church and school events. In October 1908 the school took pride in its successful candidates in the piano examinations of the Associated Board of the Royal Academy and Royal College of Music; the presence of a music teacher among the sisters in the local convent was paying dividends.[87] Also in October the Forty Hours devotion was conducted at St Bede's with a guest preacher, and beginning and ending with High Mass.[88] Parish pupils won first prize in the Dumbbell Competition at the New South Wales Manufacturers' Exhibition in November.[89]

The sacrament of confirmation was conferred on 14 March 1909, as reported by one of the candidates, ten year old Louis Walsh of Allen Street, in his letter to the *Catholic Press*: 'Dear Playmate, This is my first letter to the "Catholic Press", and I hope to see it in print. I was confirmed on March 14, in St Bede's Church. Ninety-five girls and 49 boys were confirmed, I joined the juvenile branch of the Sacred Heart Society. I have two brothers and two sisters. I go to St Bede's School, and am in upper second class. I remain your fond playmate, LOUIS WALSH (Aged 10 years).'[90] The girls of St Bede's School had success at the St Patrick Day Sports held at the Showground in 1909, gaining first place in the 'Sash Drill' competition, but they had to settle for second behind St Benedict's in the 'Wand Drill' event. Local sales of the *Freeman's Journal* would have soared with the publication of a large photograph of the triumphant Sash Team.[91] The sister-school of Francis Xavier at Ultimo did not get a mention in the *Evening News* report.[92]

In June 1909 the Cardinal must have considered that Richard Woulfe had successfully completed his apprenticeship in parochial ministry, because in May 1909 he placed him in charge of the Picton district. He continued there

---

86. *Catholic Weekly*, 15 November 1945.
87. *Catholic Press*, 1 October 1908.
88. *Catholic Press*, 8 October 1908.
89. *Freeman's Journal*, 8 April 1909.
90. *Catholic Press*, 24 April 1909.
91. *Freeman's Journal*, 8 April 1909.
92. *Evening News*, 20 March 1909.

until 1913 when he was given a year's leave to visit Ireland. On his return he was appointed priest-in-charge in the new mission district of Auburn, and from there he transferred to Hurstville in 1917. In failing health he was granted leave again and sailed home to Ireland in 1921. On his return journey to Australia through the United States in 1922 he became gravely ill in San Francisco and died in April at the age of 43.

Two months after Woulfe's departure from Pyrmont, Philip McIntyre was transferred away from Sydney to his third 'Bede' posting, to St Bede's at Braidwood in the Southern Tablelands of New South Wales. The promotion also involved his appointment as Vicar Forane or Rural Dean of the Southern Region of the Archdiocese. One of his last duties at Pyrmont was to muster and accompany parishioners and local school children across the harbour to the annual Corpus Christi procession at St Patrick's College, Manly. The *Catholic Press* headlined its report on the event that year:

> The Great Corpus Christi Procession at Manly
> A Brilliant Pageant
> Fifteen Thousand March in a Hurricane [93]

The atrocious weather conditions were confirmed a few weeks later by a regular Pyrmont correspondent, young Louis Walsh, in his letter to 'Playmate': 'It gave me much pleasure to see my last letter in print. I walked in the great Corpus Christ procession at Manly. It was very nice, but the wind blew awfully hard.'[94] Crossing the harbour would have been hazardous in those conditions.

A grand farewell for Father McIntyre took place late in June in the school hall. Two of his six former curates were present, Joseph Bowers and Richard Woulfe, as was his nominated successor, John O'Gorman, All Hallows men all, as well as several other clergy mates. Priests lined up to speak in his praise, including Richard Woulfe who spoke movingly of the relationship between parish priest and curate: 'Father Woulfe was very pleased to be present to witness the grand send-off to Father McIntyre, who had laboured amongst them for about nine years. He felt sorry at his departure, for in Father McIntyre he had a true friend. In order to know a man properly one must live with him. He had been under Father McIntyre for about 12 or 14 months, and spent a very happy time.'[95] In his reply Father McIntyre reminisced about his arrival in the district:

---

93. *Catholic Press*, 17 June 1909.
94. *Catholic Press*, 1 July 1909.
95. *Catholic Press*, 1 July 1909.

He thanked the parishioners for their splendid send-off, also the organisers of the function, he thanked not only his own people, but the whole of the people of Pyrmont. During his 10 years amongst them, he had learned to love them all... When he came to Pyrmont ten years ago, and he first saw their church, it was not an impressive building. Thank God, though it was not very fine yet, it was better than it was at that time. A considerable amount of improvements had been carried out.[96]

In concluding he paid a tribute to the 'qualities of his past curates' and introduced his successor.[97] Three cheers were given for Father McIntyre and three more for Father O'Gorman.

Philip McIntyre's ten years at Pyrmont stood as the longest stay of any priest until Victor Doyle's eleven years concluded in 1973. This was in contrast to the experiences of other parishes and can be accounted for by the smallness of Pyrmont-Ultimo parish and the poverty of the area during most of its history. As a mission district with a 'removable' priest-in-charge, the Archbishops tended to assign clergy to St Bede's for relatively short periods. When the bishops did not take the initiative to promote or move the priests, they themselves were busy applying for more rewarding assignments in more salubrious parishes in the Archdiocese.

The motor car made its entry into Archdiocesan history in 1909 when Cardinal Moran and Monsignor O'Haran visited the Southern Tablelands. After a tour of the site of the proposed national capital at Canberra, they were 'conveyed from Goulburn in Mr R J C Maddrell's motor car, thus obviating the necessity of having to undergo a fatiguing coach journey'.[98] Their driver was Braidwood's new parish priest, Philip McIntyre. At the blessing of the new convent Moran hinted that, when Braidwood obtained a rail connection, it could well become the centre of a new diocese, 'and under these conditions with a new cathedral and a new see it would spread far and wide all the blessings of religion, morality, and enlightenment'.[99] Perhaps it was with this vision in mind that the new parish priest undertook to embellish his church of St Bede to prepare it for promotion to a cathedral. Stained-glass windows were created in the nave, and a new high altar was installed. Changes were also made to the flooring: 'A fine velvet pile carpet has been procured for the sanctuary, while linoleum has been laid down in the aisle. The whole of the work has been carried out under the personal supervision of the Very Rev Father McIntyre.'[100] This last 'improvement' was much regretted by later

---

96. *Catholic Press*, 1 July 1909.
97. *Freeman's Journal*, 1 July 1909.
98. *Braidwood Dispatch and Mining Journal*, 24 November 1909.
99. *Braidwood Dispatch and Mining Journal*, 24 November 1909.
100. *Goulburn Evening Penny Post*, 24 February 1912.

generations of Braidwood parishioners, and restoration of the original floor boards was undertaken.[101]

A first indication of Philip McIntyre's drinking problem was found in a report in a southern districts newspaper: 'There was no service at St Bede's Church on Sunday last, owing to the absence of the Very Rev Father McIntyre, and his inability to secure another priest to act for him. The rev. gentleman, we understand, after attending the annual Retreat, became an inmate of a Sydney hospital.'[102] Within two weeks he was being farewelled from Braidwood. The local paper gave a full page report of the event, including the rambling speech of McIntyre. Catholic newspapers did not report the farewell. The departing pastor allowed his resentment to find expression in his speech, seeming to imply that some locals had undermined him:

> He was pleased and grateful for their company, and thankful for the kind spirit that prompted them to be there. There was a good deal of kindness and a good deal of proper spirit in the people. He thanked the people for a great deal of kindness. There was a great deal that was lovable in them; there was a great deal of simplicity in most of them; but there was lot of bad in others. They were like a mob of horses; some were good, and some were kickers, and kicked badly.[103]

He carried the same theme into his comments about his new assignment to Sydney: 'He was going to Rookwood. There were lots of people in that parish who could not talk, and he might say at once that they never would until the Archangel Gabriel sounded his trumpet. He hoped the others would talk and be nice, and he hoped that some would talk better and be nicer than some in Braidwood'. He seemed to protest too much in emphasising that he was leaving of his own free will: 'He had asked to be relieved of the parish, and his wish was a young man would come here with a motor bike or an aeroplane to get around the parish. In the parish where he was going he would have two curates to help him in the work. He was going away at his own request, and he was pleased that Archbishop Kelly had granted his request. He was not going away because someone wanted him to go away.'[104]

Perhaps it was the 'abundant supply of liquid refreshments' at the farewell, and the many toasts honoured in 'bumpers' that led to McIntyre's embarrassingly frank address. He made no mention of sickness as his reason

---

101. Robert Parkinson, *The House of Prayer: St Bede's Catholic Church, Braidwood, NSW* (Braidwood, 2003).
102. *Goulburn Evening Penny Post*, 1 February 1913.
103. *The Braidwood Dispatch and Mining Journal*, 22 February 1913.
104. *Braidwood Dispatch and Mining Journal*, 22 February 1913.

for leaving, even though every other speaker referred to this as the cause of the transfer. Present at the meeting, seated on the platform, was his former curate from Pyrmont, Michael Macnamara, and now his neighbour at Araluen. He spoke generously of his colleague: 'Father McNamara, in a neat and witty speech, referred to the fact that he and Fr McIntyre had been friends for over 20 years. He had always received the greatest encouragement, kindness, and courtesy at his hands. He trusted that Fr McIntyre would soon be restored to good health.' There was a presentation of a purse of sovereigns, and the chairman wisely cancelled any further toasts and bumpers, and the evening was concluded with everyone joining hands and singing 'Auld Lang Syne'.[105]

No longer a 'Very Reverend' he was brought back to Sydney and assigned to the Rookwood district. A newspaper item in 1914 indicated the continuation of a problem: 'The Very Rev. Father McIntyre, it is pleasing to know, has entirely recovered from his recent serious indisposition, thanks to the care of the good Sisters at St Joseph's Hospital. He has resumed duty as priest in charge of the combined parish of Auburn and Lidcombe.'[106] His name was absent from the *Catholic Directory* from 1918 to 1925; from 1926 to 1932 he was listed as 'on leave'. For a year from May 1920 he replaced his former curate Edward Gell while he was on an extended holiday in Europe. In the gathering to welcome Gell back to Ryde and thank McIntyre, the chairman of the event said: 'Wherever he went he claimed the affections of his people; and as for Pyrmont, Father McIntyre's name in that parish was one at which all hats were raised.'[107]

In July 1922 he wrote from St Joseph's Orphanage at Kincumber to Archbishop Kelly asking for an appointment as a curate. The next month the Archbishop, the great advocate of temperance, replied in harsh terms. He stated that without any proof and reassurances of McIntyre's restoration to abstinence from intoxicating drink, and also because no fellow priests would offer such reassurances on his behalf, he did not have sufficient confidence to appoint him to public ministry, despite the need of the Archdiocese for curates. Kelly went further, stating that parish priests preferred double duty to accepting McIntyre as an assistant. He then enumerated the reasons for his refusal – disedification to young and old parishioners; scandal to non-catholics; heart-breaking trouble and annoyance in place of comfort and agreeable cooperation. Kelly concluded the letter by commending McIntyre to Our Lady Help of the Weak and Queen of Clergy.[108]

---

105. Braidwood Dispatch and Mining Journal, 22 February 1913.
106. *The Cumberland Argus and Fruitgrowers Advocate*, **11 July 1914**.
107. *Catholic Press*, 19 May 1921.
108. Kelly to McIntyre, 11 August 1922 (McIntyre file, SAA).

This was not a letter to inspire sobriety. In September McIntyre again wrote to Kelly in reply to yet another refusal to reinstate him. In it he expressed his sad disappointment that he had not been reinstated to active ministry, and his surprise that the Archbishop had not shown his usual kindness and charity. He proceeded to ask humbly for forgiveness for his many shortcomings, and to express his confidence that he could undertake parish work under the guidance of a brother priest. He emphasised that work would be his best safeguard against future lapses.[109]

No offer of parish work was forthcoming from the Archbishop. On the back of the letter Kelly recorded notes for another negative reply, again enumerating McIntyre's failings: unreliability in regard to peaceful and edifying discharge of the office of assistant priest; abandoning treatment; persistent unreliability; his unacceptability among his fellow priests.

Ten years later, in 1932, Philip McIntyre celebrated his Sacerdotal Golden Jubilee at the Mater Misericordiae Hospital, North Sydney, where he was officially listed as acting as chaplain. His deacon and sub-deacon at the High Mass celebrated in the hospital chapel were priests baptised by him. The sub-deacon was John Francis O'Toole baptised at St Bede's in May 1908, ordained in 1930 and died in 1938. Also present were two of McIntyre's former curates at Pyrmont, Edward Gell and Michael Macnamara. Both Catholic newspapers reported that 'Father McIntyre gave many interesting personal reminiscences of his early life in the Archdiocese since he landed here in 1882.'[110] Unfortunately neither paper shared the contents of the speech with the reading public.

In November 1934 he was in receipt of another letter from the Archbishop and his Diocesan Council in reply to a request for retirement into a presbytery household. The answer was negative, but expressed in a slightly more kindly way. While the possibility of Philip's living openly in a parish presbytery was excluded, the Archbishop recommended that he take up accommodation at St Joseph's Sanatorium at Lake Macquarie, where he hoped disedification would cease and a holy death be safely secured. St Joseph's was a new facility established earlier in the year by the Little Company of Mary as a convalescent home for alcoholic and disturbed priests. Kelly directed McIntyre to proceed to the sanatorium, assuring him of remembrance in archiepiscopal prayers.[111]

In May 1938 Philip McIntyre died aged 83 at the Mater Hospital. At the Requiem Mass in St Mary's, North Sydney, 53 priests were present, but no bishops. However, a future Cardinal Archbishop of Sydney, James Freeman,

---

109. McIntyre to Kelly, 16 September 1922 (McIntyre file, SAA).
110. *Freeman's Journal*, 30 June 1932; *Catholic Press*, 30 June 1932.
111. Kelly to McIntyre, 10 November 1934 (McIntyre file, SAA).

acted as deacon. There was a small group of parishioners from well-known Pyrmont families honouring their pastor of thirty years before—William Weslan, former President of St Bede's Vincent de Paul Society, Maurice O'Dwyer and his wife, and Mesdames W Armstrong and C O'Toole. The newspaper report noted that 'Father McIntyre was the last of the priests who came to Australia under the Benedictine regime'. It went on to regret that the deceased had not committed to writing his stories about ecclesiastical life in the Archdiocese during 56 years:

> Despite his years, Father McIntyre was still mentally alert, as was evidenced during the course of a reminiscent speech on the occasion of a dinner in connection with the golden jubilee of Sister Mary Regis, when the aged priest kept his fellow clergy highly entertained with tales of his experiences in years gone by. He had a remarkable memory, stored with reminiscences of persons and events in the ecclesiastical history of Sydney, but he could not be persuaded to commit them to writing.[112]

The regret would not have been shared by Sydney's hierarchy; it is, however, shared by researchers of ecclesiastical history.

---

112. *Catholic Press*, 12 May 1938.

Chapter 16
Crossing the 'Bridge of Sighs'

In 1889 a new church was built to the east of the city, on the Darlinghurst ridge, previously referred to as Woolloomooloo Hill, or sometimes Eastern Hill. The development of the area, beginning in the 1830s, was highly controlled. Grants of land were restricted to the wealthy—merchants, public servants and private citizens. All plans had to be approved by Governor Darling; all houses had to be of a value of £1000 or more, and allotments could contain only a single residence with no other buildings, set within a landscaped garden and, where possible, facing the town. The result was a collection of elegant villas, clearly visible on this ridge east of the town. This up-market residential development was similar to that envisaged at the same time by the Macarthur family for their Pyrmont Estate, but unrealised. The new church was dedicated to St Canice, the patron saint of the Diocese of Ossory in County Kilkenny, where Moran was bishop from 1872 to 1884. Interestingly Saint Canice was already represented in the area as the name of a Darling Point mansion, built by the Catholic barrister and parliamentarian, Edward Butler, a Kilkenny man, former Maynooth seminarian and dedicated Young Irelander.[1]

The land on which the new church was built was the gift of John Hughes, merchant and pastoralist, and local resident at Elizabeth Bay, where he had built an elegant residence, named Kincoppal (Gaelic word for sea-horse) after a nearby rock formation in the harbour.[2] St Canice's was not assigned

---

1. Bede Nairn, 'Butler, Edward (1823–1879)', *Australian Dictionary of Biography*, National Centre of Biography, Australian National University, http://adb.anu.edu.au/biography/butler-edward-3127/text4655, published first in hardcopy 1969, accessed online 12 December 2014.
2. C Cunneen, 'Hughes, John (1825–1885)', *Australian Dictionary of Biography*, National Centre of Biography, Australian National University, http://adb.anu.edu.au/biography/hughes-john-12995/text23489, published first in hardcopy 2005, accessed online 13 December 2014.

a resident priest and remained part of the cathedral district. The serving priest for twelve years from 1898 to 1909 was Father John O'Gorman, a relative of the Hughes family. He resided at the Cathedral presbytery over that period. In June 1909 he was transferred westward to Pyrmont. The contrast between tranquil and salubrious Darlinghurst/Elizabeth Bay and decidedly poor, working class Pyrmont/Ultimo was stark. At a farewell event Monsignor O'Haran, Administrator of the Cathedral and head of the presbytery household, reflected the sadness of the St Canice community in losing their priest by playfully renaming the Pyrmont Bridge, 'the Bridge of Sighs'.[3] Given that the Venetian bridge so named was the crossing from the Doge's palace to the Doge's prison, O'Haran's comment may also have reflected on a transition from opulence to poverty for the departing priest.

John O'Gorman was a County Clare man and a graduate of All Hallows. An older brother, Father James Hugh O'Gorman, was already present in the Colony at faraway Michelago when John arrived, newly ordained, in 1896. John's first year was spent on loan to the Melbourne Archdiocese, but he was back in Sydney at St Mary's with responsibility for St Canice's in 1898. O'Gorman had been resident in the cathedral presbytery during the O'Haran trial. Alice Coningham in her evidence related that in March 1900 she had asked O'Haran to baptise the child she claimed he had fathered, but that he had refused, claiming that he could not baptise his own child, and referred her to O'Gorman. A witness at the trial confirmed that O'Gorman had baptised baby Vincent Francis, adding that O'Haran rarely performed baptisms because of his seniority.[4] Here was an insight into the division of labour between parish priest and curate.

At the farewell event in 1909 Monsignor O'Haran spoke glowingly of his assistant's personal qualities and popularity in the presbytery community: 'There has never been at St Mary's a priest under my charge for whom all the clergy entertained a more sensitive degree of appreciation than for Father O'Gorman.' And he then 'painted a happy word-picture of the esprit de corps which had existed at the Cathedral during the term Father O'Gorman had been a member of the staff.'[5] This was praise indeed coming from someone who had a growing reputation for severity towards his subordinates. For John O'Gorman, leaving the cathedral presbytery and crossing the Pyrmont Bridge, the 'Bridge of Sighs', may well have seemed like a release from prison.

His appointment had been greeted by his new parishioners at St Bede's with enthusiasm. However, there was no curate at the presbytery to welcome him. Richard Woulfe had already left for Picton. But with two churches in

---

3. *Freeman's Journal*, 29 July 1909.
4. AE Cunningham, *The Price of a Wife? The Priest and the Divorce Trial* (Sydney 2013), 33 & 51.
5. *Freeman's Journal*, 29 July 1909.

the district assistance was needed. From 1908 to 1912 the *Catholic Press* each week published an item headed 'LEADING CHURCHES IN SYDNEY. Hours of Devotion. USEFUL INFORMATION FOR VISITORS'. In October 1909 Father O'Gorman had his new parish of Pyrmont and Ultimo added to the list with the following details:

> St Bede's, Pyrmont—Masses: Sundays, 7 and 10; week-days, 7. Evening devotions on the first and third Sundays of the month, at 7. Rosary and Benediction on Thursday evenings at 7.30. Baptisms on Sundays, at 3.30 p.m.
> St Francis Xavier's, Ultimo—Masses: Sundays, 7.30 and 10. Evening devotions on the second and fourth Sundays of the month, at 7. Devotions and Benediction on Friday evenings, at 7.30.[6]

This programme indicated a busy schedule requiring the weekend assistance of a visiting priest when there was no curate in residence. O'Gorman immediately enlisted the help of the Missionaries of the Sacred Heart from their Kensington monastery, and occasionally called on the Passionists from Marrickville for weekend supplies. Their names appeared regularly in the baptismal register in 1909 and 1910.

A few months after John O'Gorman's arrival in Pyrmont in June 1909, the *Catholic Press* published a photo gallery of 143 priests spread over eleven pages, each page headlined: 'Prominent Australian Priests'.[7] Included on the first page was 'Rev Father J O'Gorman, Pyrmont', an entry that was surely a source of pride and boasting for the local parishioners. Also included were three former pastors of St Bede's, Fathers Furlong, Ryan and McIntyre, a former curate Peter Paul Power, and John Hyland, who would later assist and then succeed O'Gorman. Perhaps cut-outs were framed and placed on mantle-pieces of Catholic households in Pyrmont and Ultimo. The much photographed Monsignor O'Haran was not among the 'Prominent Australian Priests', but the much loved and briefly excommunicated Père Piquet was there.

In November 1909 a prominent Pyrmont parishioner was honoured with 'a complimentary concert and social' at St Bede's School Hall. Maurice O'Dwyer was treasurer of the local St Vincent de Paul Conference, and he and his wife Nellie, a member of the O'Toole clan, had just completed ten active years in the district.[8] Maurice would be present at the parish centennial celebrations in 1967, and was described in the commemorative booklet as

---

6. *Catholic Press*, 14 October 1909.
7. *Catholic Press*, 30 September 1909.
8. *Catholic Press*, 11 November 1909.

the last Vincentian to have known the Society's founder in New South Wales, Charles O'Neill.[9]

In 1910 the new pastor set himself the task of arranging better accommodation for the Good Samaritan Sisters teaching at the two schools, and then living in a rented house at 55 Pyrmont Street. The lease was about to expire—the house was one of several marked for demolition to make way for a huge new wool store, as announced in the *Evening News* in April: 'A contract has been let for a wool store for Messrs Schute, Bell, and Company, and which will have frontages to Pyrmont and Harris streets. The stores will be equipped in an up-to-date manner, and will be fitted with elevators.'[10]

Father O'Gorman feared that the sisters 'whose work in the parish was beyond all praise, would be forced to leave the district, owing to the difficulty of securing a home'. He acquired a double terrace next to the church at Ultimo, and a short time afterwards bought the three small cottages, 33 to 37 Pyrmont Street, adjoining St Bede's school, which would be leased to tenants. He explained the advantageous financial arrangement to the parishioners: 'Of course, they would have to pay off the £2000 expended on the property, and then the property would not only be their own, but they would be £117 per year better off than they were now. For the convent previously occupied by the nuns the rent was £65 a year, and they received as rental for the new building £52 a year, which met the interest.'[11]

When it came to fund-raising it must have seemed that Father Timothy McCarthy was back in town. In July O'Gorman inaugurated an annual 'St Bede's and St Francis' Reunion'. The *Catholic Press* article described the event under the headline 'A SPLENDID GATHERING': 'The combined efforts of the parishioners of Pyrmont and Ultimo to raise funds for the church debt have been successful far beyond anything anticipated. The reunion held in the Odd fellows' Temple, Elizabeth-street, on Tuesday evening was crowded, and dancing was difficult at times, but it was a most enjoyable affair, everyone being so pleased with the very representative gathering.'[12]

The following week the Cardinal was at Ultimo to bless the new convent and dedicate it to Our Lady of Good Counsel. In welcoming His Eminence the pastor emphasised the 'honour and privilege they enjoyed in having a great Prince of the Church in their midst'. Concluding his summary of the funding of the project he expressed his confidence that with anticipated annual income from rents, supplemented by two or three bazaars, the debt would be liquidated in the course of eight or nine years. The Cardinal, in his address, said that he disagreed with Father O'Gorman regarding the length

---

9. VJ Doyle, *St Bede's Church Pyrmont. Centenary 1867—1967* (Sydney 1967), 31.
10. 'New Buildings in Sydney', *Evening News*, 13 April 1910.
11. *Catholic Press*, 16 February 1911.
12. *Catholic Press*, 28 July 1910.

of time they would be paying off the debt; 'he would not give him more than five years (Laughter and applause).'[13]

In September a resident assistant was sent to Pyrmont. He was Albert George Clarke BA. The son of a Church of Ireland minister, he had studied for the ministry at Trinity College Dublin, and was ordained an Anglican priest at St Paul's Cathedral in London in 1882. After three years at Colombo in Ceylon he returned to England and ministered at York and Leeds for the next four years. In 1889 he was received into the Catholic Church and sent to the English College in Rome by the Bishop of Portsmouth to prepare for Catholic ordination, which took place on the isle of Jersey in 1892. Because of ill health he sailed to the South Seas in 1905, visiting the New Hebrides, New Caledonia and North Queensland. He returned to England early in 1910, but because of the severity of the winter he sailed south again. Arriving in Sydney in October he was appointed to Pyrmont. After four months assisting Father O'Gorman, he sailed to New Zealand in February 1911 and for four years was chaplain to the Little Sisters of the Poor at Ponsonby. In an article 'REMINISCENCES OF A CONVERT' written in 1930 he summarised his ministry after returning from Auckland:

> The Archbishop of Brisbane asked me to accept work in his diocese, and I took charge of the mission at Helidon. There I remained till November, 1918, when failing health caused my return to Sydney. In 1919 the Archbishop of Sydney appointed me chaplain at the Boys' Home, Westmead, but in six months' time I became very seriously ill, and had to go into hospital at Auburn. When partly recovered I was able to do a little Sunday work, and to assist in the confessional. The latter is now the only clerical work (besides saying Mass when able) that I (in my 72nd year) can discharge.

He also took the opportunity to reconfirm his Catholic faith: 'For my own part, I become daily more convinced that the church whose centre is Peter's See, and whose circumference is the whole earth, is the only Church which can validly claim to be the depository of the Christian revelation. To withdraw from her is spiritual death.'[14] Albert George Clarke died in September 1931 aged 73. In its obituary notice *the Catholic Press* commented on his letters to newspaper editors: 'Until very close to the termination of his life Father Clarke cherished his favourite topic of pointing out to those in the Anglican communion the false position they were occupying.'[15]

---

13. *Catholic Press*, 4 August 1910.
14. *Catholic Press*, 6 November 1930.
15. *Catholic Press*, 8 October 1931.

In February 1911, Father O'Gorman sailed to Europe, on a year's leave of absence, to visit his family in Ireland. Under Cardinal Moran's regime, Irish priests were granted leave to return home after about ten years of service in the Archdiocese. John O'Gorman had been ministering in Sydney for fifteen years when he set sail, but for only twenty months at Pyrmont. He received a grand send-off from his parishioners, with glowing tributes from members of the parish committee and from the journalist of the *Catholic Press*, of which O'Gorman was a board member. The unanimous opinion was that he was cheerful, buoyant and confident, genial and good-humoured, with a 'love-compelling personality', a true friend and consoler to the poor and afflicted. During his brief time in Pyrmont and Ultimo he had shown that 'the district was no Sleepy Hollow'. In his speech in reply the pastor outlined a project to be undertaken on his return: 'If they had 300 or 400 young men paying threepence a week, and the same number of young ladies, there was no rational amusement, they could not have, and there was no way in which they could not promote their material interests. People in working-class districts, such as Pyrmont, could then have their clubs as well as the rich. They had the means of forming such a club if they wished to set about it.'[16] At the farewell, one of the soloists entertaining the gathering was Nellie Maunsell, by now an accomplished contralto and a regular singer at Sydney's Tivoli Theatre, and soon to be a member of Williamson's Opera Company.

During Father O'Gorman's twelve month absence Father John Francis Hyland was brought from Queanbeyan to administer Pyrmont, but without a curate. During his year as administrator he prepared a report in connection with the episcopal visitation of the district. He gave a summary of income from the collections in both churches:

Sunday collection average:	£9
Christmas dues:	£90
Easter dues:	£85
Baptism and marriage stipends:	£50

With John O'Gorman back in harness in 1912, it was John Hyland's turn to take a holiday back home.

On his return Father O'Gorman was interviewed at the Pyrmont presbytery by a *Catholic Press* journalist. He identified the audience with Pope Pius X as the highlight of the trip: 'When we mentioned we were from Australia he took a great interest in us, looked surprised to see five priests from the Antipodes, and spoke in loving terms of our country.' In the interview O'Gorman drew a lesson for Australia from his experience of state

---

16. *Catholic Press*, 16 February 1911.

subsidised Catholic schools in Switzerland, Holland, Germany and England: 'Countries that want to go ahead do not try to crush any portion of their population, but find it a more progressive and fruitful policy to encourage the work of education everywhere. They recognise that the greatness of a nation depends upon the education of its people as a whole ... Hence, we are lagging behind the nations in education, a sad state for a country whose motto, strange to say, is "Advance Australia".'[17]

In October 1912 the pastor made one final push to reduce the debt on the Ultimo convent by organising a two week bazaar at the Pyrmont school hall. The Rector of St John's College at the university, Monsignor James O'Brien, was invited to do the honours at the opening. The Monsignor had been one of John O'Gorman's seminary professors at All Hallows College in Dublin, and in his address he insisted that 'he was no longer the master, but was proud to be the pupil of Father O'Gorman, who commanded the respect of his fellow-priests in the diocese (Applause)'. He commented on the patron saints of the parish churches, describing St Bede as the light and glory of the Church in England and St Francis Xavier as the apostle of India, China, and other countries of the East, and concluded that 'the people of the parish were singularly blessed in having their two temples erected under the invocation of these saints'.[18]

From August to November 1912 John O'Gorman was joined in the presbytery by John Milne Curran. Curran is the only Pyrmont priest to have merited an entry in the *Australian Dictionary of Biography*, not for his achievements as an ecclesiastic, but as a scientist.[19] Born in Tipperary in 1859 he was recruited with Michael Macnamara and others in 1875 by Bishop Matthew Quinn for the Bathurst seminary. It was while he was a student at St Charles Seminary in Bathurst that he came under the influence of Father Julian Tenison Woods whom the bishop had invited in 1871 to come from Adelaide to teach in his seminary and conduct parish missions. The influence was scientific rather than theological, and it set Curran on a lifetime's adventure in geological studies. Ordained in 1881, his first appointment as curate was in Dubbo from 1881 to 1885 where he combined pastoral ministry with geological studies and field work. Between 1884 and 1891 Curran authored 12 papers published in the journals of the Linnean and Royal Societies. During 1889, whenever he was in Sydney, he would visit his ailing mentor, Julian Tenison Woods, who was housebound and

---

17. *Catholic Press*, 29 February 1912.
18. *Freeman's Journal*, 24 October 1912.
19. CJ Duffy, 'Curran, John Milne (Michael) (1859–1928)', *Australian Dictionary of Biography*, National Centre of Biography, Australian National University, http://adb.anu.edu.au/biography/curran-john-milne-michael-3302/text5027, published first in hardcopy 1969, accessed online 20 December 2012.

dependent on the pious women whom he had formed into a community in a house in Strawberry Hills. Soon after Woods' death in October, Curran published a delightful tribute to him in the second volume of the *Centennial Magazine* of 1889-1890. He described his master's room: 'Let me introduce my readers into his study. A small room plainly furnished, every table and chair laden with books and specimens, all in that healthy disorder that betokens genuine work. A Madonna and Child, of considerable merit as a painting, and a few sketches of his own hang round the walls; a crucifix with some texts in Greek from the old Testament stand above his desk.'[20] He recalled that 'shortly before his death he was given to understand that he should comply with an exceptionally exacting Church regulation.'[21] This was a reference to Cardinal Moran's instruction that Tenison Woods must leave the household in Elizabeth Street to avoid scandal. The invalid priest disregarded the Canon Law and died surrounded by his community of women.[22]

The *Catholic Directory* of 1892 contained a section called '1891 An Eventful Year', in which the following item appeared: 'Father T. Milne-Curran, F.G.S., of the Diocese of Bathurst, was in April appointed by the New South Wales Government travelling lecturer in connection with the Technical Education Department. In July Fr Curran received the medal and £25 offered by the Royal Society for the best paper on the microscopic structure of Australian rocks.'[23] His bishop had given permission for him to spend weekdays in Sydney at his new task while returning on weekends for pastoral work in the diocese. The *Catholic Directory* from 1893 to 1907 listed him under the heading 'Diocese of Bathurst: Secular Clergy absent on leave'. In June 1897 the *Government Gazette* announced his appointment by the Governor to the position of 'teacher of Geology and Assaying, in the connection with the establishment of a School for Miners, at the Sydney Technical College'.[24] The Sydney Technical College had been established at Ultimo in 1882 in succession to the Working Men's College formed in 1878 from the Sydney Mechanics' School of Arts founded in 1833.

In August, 1912, Father Milne Curran joined Father O'Gorman in the Pyrmont district mission, an area familiar to him from his years at the Ultimo Technical College. His stay was brief, but according to the *Catholic Directory* of 1916 he was back at St Bede's with Father Hyland. His presence was noted in a *Freeman's Journal* item in September reporting on a recruitment

---

20. JM Curran, 'Julian Tenyson Woods', *Centennial Magazine*, 2 (1889-1890): 408.
21. Curran, *Julian Tenyson Woods*, 411.
22. Margaret Press, *Julian Tenison Woods: 'Father Founder'*, second edition (North Blackburn 1994), 226.
23. *Catholic Directory*, 1892. He would be awarded the medal again in 1896.
24. *NSW Government Gazette*, 10 June 1897.

campaign for the Catholic Club: 'The visits to Pyrmont and Ultimo by the committee resulted in increased membership, and the club is indeed greatly indebted to Rev Father Hyland and Rev Father Milne Curran for their practical help in the matter.'[25] Later that year, when he was living privately at an address within the Franciscan parish of Paddington, he received a letter from Archbishop Kelly stating that he had received information 'affecting you in point of disedification'. The information came from a Franciscan conducting door-to-door parish visitation, who had observed that Curran had been receiving various women into his home. This was an echo of the gossip surrounding his mentor Tenison Woods in 1889. The Archbishop warned him that his faculties would be withdrawn unless, within ten days, he had obtained a 'commendation' from the Parish Priest.[26]

During his career Milne Curran became involved in several mining ventures that failed, leading to court appearances and declarations of bankruptcy. His final years found him maintaining his interest in mineral and artesian deposits and travelling throughout New South Wales advising the mining industry. In June 1928 he died at a private residence at Centennial Park in Sydney, aged 69. Regional and city newspapers published obituaries of the 'noted geologist'. His Requiem Mass at St Peter's, Surry Hills, was celebrated by his old classmate of Bathurst Seminary days, Michael Macnamara.[27]

Towards the end of his Pyrmont appointment Father O'Gorman had published an article, 'A Personal Experience in the United States', in the *Australasian Catholic Record*, a learned journal which had been founded at St Patrick's College, Manly. In it he recommended the 'peculiar style' of the sermon as preached in the USA, particularly for its brevity: 'The style of sermons is quite distinct from any previous experience. Long sermons have gone out of fashion. Their motto is that a short bad sermon is better than a long bad one. And they hold exactly the same in regard to discourses that are good.' Also urged on his fellow priests was the frequency of preaching, which in Australia was traditionally restricted to the High Mass on Sundays: 'But the chief characteristic is that they speak so often. It is a rule that at every Mass on Sundays a five minutes' sermon, in addition to notices, is delivered, generally on a dogmatic subject.'[28] It may be presumed that he practised what he preached, and adopted the peculiar American style in his final year at Pyrmont and Ultimo.

In November 1912 the new Archbishop Michael Kelly transferred John O'Gorman from Pyrmont and appointed him administrator of St

---

25. *Freeman's Journal*, 16 September 1916.
26. Kelly to Milne Curran, 27 November 1916 (Milne Curran File, SAA).
27. *Freeman's Journal*, 5 July 1928.
28. *Catholic Press*, 5 December 1912.

Mary's Cathedral in place of Monsignor O'Haran, who was removed to the Darlinghurst parish. Father Hyland was back from his leave of absence in time to replace his colleague at Pyrmont and preside at his farewell.[29] One of the main tasks of the Cathedral administrator was the raising of funds for the completion of St Mary's. O'Gorman brought all his personal qualities and talents to bear with great success. His achievements were summarised in his obituary notice:

> Then began his herculean work—raising funds for the completion of the mother church. In a vigorous drive throughout his term of office, from the beginning of 1912 to 1919, he triumphed in this special work beyond the expectations of all; and fully £100,000 for the fund is attributed to his zealous prosecution of the cause. His big part therein culminated in 1919 with a final rally, a great Cathedral bazaar, which was a huge success from all angles.[30]

In August 1920 Father O'Gorman was appointed parish priest of Parramatta, and in the following year was appointed 'Antistes Urbanus', or domestic prelate of the papal household, with the right to style himself 'Right Reverend Monsignor', to wear quasi-episcopal regalia and to use a special candle-stick (*palmatoria*) in Solemn High Masses, but not to carry the crozier or wear the mitre.

In 1927 O'Gorman was appointed official secretary of the organising committee for the 1928 International Eucharistic Congress. In May 1928 he was back at Pyrmont opening that year's bazaar in the new brick school, erected in 1924 on the site of the three cottages that he had bought in 1910. He had very complimentary words for the locals, declaring that his three years at Pyrmont were the happiest of his life, and that it was with great reluctance that he had left to take up the task of administrator at the Cathedral. Also present with the new pastor and curate, William McDonald and John Lynch, was O'Gorman's Pyrmont predecessor, Philip McIntyre. McDonald in his speech of welcome had commented that 'people in other districts were in ignorance of the wonderful spirit of Catholicity existent in Pyrmont'.[31]

In March 1930, following repeated bouts of sickness, Monsignor O'Gorman sailed with Archbishop Kelly to Europe. The Archbishop was fulfilling his obligatory *ad limina* visit to Rome and attending the Eucharistic Congress in Carthage. In January 1931 news was received in Sydney that the Monsignor had died in Dublin at the age of 60. The *Catholic Press* concluded

---

29. *Catholic Press*, 19 December 1912.
30. *Catholic Press*, 29 January 1931.
31. *Catholic Press*, 24 May 1928.

its obituary by quoting one of his colleagues: "'He was a wonderful scholar,' said Father O'Kelly, "and whenever in conversation we were always proud of him, for he was most ready and clear with all his explanations of Church and national affairs. He was, besides, a most lovable companion, and very quick in winning himself into the hearts of others. We all recognise we have lost one of the grandest representatives of the Church in Australia'."[32]

John O'Gorman's successor at Pyrmont in December 1912 was John Hyland, familiar to the parish community from his 'locum tenens' during O'Gorman's leave of absence in 1911. A native of Kilkenny, Hyland was a student at the Irish College in Rome and was ordained in 1895. He had a range of appointments during his first five years in the Archdiocese, beginning at Surry Hills, moving south to Bega, and back in Sydney at Waterloo in 1898. In 1900 he was given compassionate leave to visit his ailing father in Ireland. Back in Australia in 1901 he resumed his peregrinations through parishes—Pymble, Balmain West (Rozelle), Camden, and then Queanbeyan in 1905, his first appointment as priest-in-charge. It was from there that he came back to Sydney 1911 as administrator at Pyrmont. From November 1912 to March 1916, during war years, he was pastor at St Bede and St Francis Xavier.

One of his first acts was to write to the Archbishop and request the appointment of a curate. Hyland argued in support of his formal appeal for assistance by pointing out that for over two years he, as the only resident priest, had been striving to do the work formerly conducted by two. The fact of having two churches, both of equal importance, made it difficult, if not impossible, for one resident priest to keep parish societies together, catechise the children, visit regularly the homes and perform the various other duties inseparable from the proper administration of a district.[33]

Archbishop Kelly responded immediately, sending the newly ordained William Paul McNally, the first of the Manly seminary graduates to serve at Pyrmont. He was a Balmain boy, son of a wharf labourer. He was educated by the Christian Brothers at Balmain and then went to St Ignatius College Riverview on a scholarship. His school achievements, academic and sporting, were summarised in his obituary in 1936: 'In his scholastic progress he was first in the Cardinal's examination in four successive grades (3rd to 6th), and also received the Cardinal's special prize for Irish History. In State

---

32. *Catholic Press*, 29 January 1931.
33. Hyland to Kelly, 1 December 1912 (Pyrmont File 1912, SAA).

examinations he was placed first in NSW in several subjects. At athletics he also excelled. He was the leading footballer and cricketer of his college.[34]

Like most young curates he was very popular with parishioners, and especially so because he was 'native born', and a West Shore local boy. When he was assigned to Nowra after only ten months at Pyrmont, he was given a grand and fond farewell. The *Freeman's Journal* headlined its report: 'Tribute to Young Australian Priest: Rev W McNally Honoured'. Father Hyland spoke 'in very warm terms of the splendid priestly and manly qualities of Father McNally, and of the zeal with which he had worked during his term at Pyrmont'. He spoke movingly of the bond between Catholic people and their priests, venturing that 'as far as he could see, that union was nowhere more strong than in Australia'. A parish committee member, Sydney Dalton, an old school mate of William at Christian Brothers Balmain, 'paid tribute to the self-sacrificing labours of their guest and said that he carried away with him the greatest respect of all the parishioners'.[35] When it was William's turn to respond he emphasised his bond with Father Hyland and the district: 'His association with the parish had been of the happiest, and he regarded his connection with his pastor, Father Hyland, as one of the greatest privileges which their revered Archbishop could have bestowed upon him. The parting was difficult, and though he was told that Nowra was a very beautiful place, no place could ever be to him what his first parish had been.'[36]

A quick succession of appointments followed at Nowra, Wollongong, Waterloo and St Mary's Cathedral. His first placement as pastor was at Mittagong in 1922, followed by Burragorang, Windsor and Richmond. In 1932 he was appointed to St Michael's at Baulkam Hills in succession to Daniel Hannan who was moving to Pyrmont. On Christmas Day 1935 he collapsed; he died the next day, aged 47. He had at times been a 'guest' of the nuns at St Joseph's Convalescent Home for priests at Morrisset, a facility for troubled clergy. Coadjutor Archbishop Michael Sheehan presided at the Solemn Requiem Mass, and William's Manly classmate, Justin Simonds, was the celebrant. Especially noted in the newspaper report was the presence at the obsequies of the eminent professor of physics at the University of Sydney, Oscar Ulrich Vonwiller, 'who had a high regard for Father McNally'. Also present was the parish priest of Pyrmont, Austin Bradstreet, and other priests with Pyrmont connections, Michael Macnamara and Edward Gell. The obituary concluded: 'A priest of dignified and courteous manner—one with a great sense of honour—Father McNally will be much missed by the many who benefited by his ministrations and company.'[37]

---

34. *Catholic Press*, 2 January 1936.
35. *Freeman's Journal*, 20 November 1913.
36. *Catholic Press*, 20 November 1913.
37. Catholic Press, 20 November 1913.

Succeeding McNally as curate at Pyrmont in November 1913 was Thomas O'Farrell, fresh from ordination in Ireland. His stay was brief, being sent across the harbour to Mosman in March 1914. John Hyland was without a curate for two years after O'Farrell's departure. He was not absent from the parish for a single weekend during that time, as evidenced by his signature in the register against all, except one, of the 160 baptisms performed from March 1914 to March 1916. He would have been assisted with Sunday Masses by priests of various religious congregations.

In April 1914 Archbishop Kelly urged Sydney priests to follow the example of the Cathedral parish in establishing 'poor schools'—St John's in Kent Street under the care of the Sisters of St. Joseph, and St Joseph's in William Street conducted by the Sisters of Mercy—where the children were fed and clothed as well as being educated:

> His Grace said that the greatest glory of the Cathedral parish was these schools. These were the children dearest to God. They were not shunted out of line with the others, but were the pet schools. He would be glad if his words reached the ears of every priest in Sydney when he said that they had still to add to the greater glory of their administration by the inauguration of a school like St Joseph's and St John's. If one parish could not do it alone, let two or three combine—for example, say St Benedict's and Golden Grove, Pyrmont and Glebe Point.[38]

Pyrmont and Glebe already had two schools each, and while not formally called 'poor schools' they served poor families, and the Good Samaritan Sisters often found themselves providing food and clothing for the children. A stong bond between St Bede's and St James would be created eighty years later when the two parishes found themselves sharing one school and one parish priest.

In June 1914 the St Bede cricket team celebrated its success in the Catholic Young Men's competition. Father Hyland, who possibly had never known the game at home in Ireland, and certainly not at the Irish College in Rome, took the opportunity to give some words of spiritual advice to the team members:

> The Rev Father Hyland, before presenting the prizes, said he was in favour of all field games, because they helped the player to control his natural tendencies and to subject his will to authority. This had a very good effect in many ways, and he maintained that, not only in sport should they 'play the game', but in all things in the game of life. He took the opportunity of

---

38. *Catholic Press*, 23 April 1914.

reminding all the young people present that their religious practices did not cease on their leaving school, and the narrow, thorny pathway led to a more lasting glory and fame than did the enticing and satisfying field of sport. Both should be combined and then complete happiness would result. He congratulated the team on its successful season and wished them greater results during the coming summer. He then handed the winners their trophies amidst applause.[39]

The gold medal for bowling was awarded to a young parishioner who during the season achieved 'a somewhat phenomenal average as a bowler, taking 89 wickets at 5 runs apiece'. Father Hyland donated the prize for the best fielder, and his former curate William McNally, a champion cricketer himself, had funded the trophy for the best batsman.

A lay initiative in Sydney had been the commencement of a Catholic Club in July 1909. The founder was Patrick Scott Cleary of Woollahra who drew his inspiration from the Catholic Workmen's Clubs of nineteenth century Germany and France, which not only provided recreational facilities but led to increased Catholic political influence. Already in Adelaide in 1899 a Club had been established with the encouragement of the Dominican Prior, Robert Spence, who would later become Archbishop. In Sydney, Cardinal Moran lent his support to the venture and even forwarded a subscription of ten guineas, becoming the first life member of the Club.[40] It was not until 1915 that Pyrmont and Ultimo appeared on the Club's recruiting programme, as reported to a meeting of the Club committee: 'The propaganda work is proving a decided success. Rev Father J Hyland has very kindly placed at the disposal of the committee, on Sunday (September 5) after 10 o'clock Mass, a meeting of the parishioners of Pyrmont and Ultimo, and it is expected that a large number will be enrolled.'[41]

An offshoot of the Catholic Club was an organisation with would develop an explicitly political agenda, the Catholic Federation. Again it was Patrick Cleary who took the lead, urging Archbishop Kelly to follow the example of his Melbourne colleague, Archbishop Carr, and approve the establishment of the Federation. Sydney's Irish archbishops had been reluctant to authorise lay pressure groups for advancing Catholic interests. There was always the fear that too aggressive a push would result in backlash from the majority Protestant community. Moran and Kelly preferred to use their personal influence with politicians, especially when the Labor Party, with its significant Catholic membership, was in government. However,

---

39. *Freeman's Journal*, 25 June 1914.
40. *Catholic Press*, 23 September 1909.
41. *Catholic Press*, 2 September 1915.

there had been no progress in gaining funding for Catholic schools. Kelly and the bishops of New South Wales finally agreed to the establishment of the Catholic Federation, and the inaugural meeting was held at St Mary's Cathedral on 13 April 1913, with Father John O'Gorman in the chair. The *Freeman's Journal* welcomed the development and headlined its article:

> Catholic Federation of NSW
> Inauguration of First City Branch.
> Remarkable Demonstration of Catholics.
> Politics Barred. [42]

Branches were quickly formed in suburban and country parishes, with parish priests acting as local 'presidents'. In November a branch was formed at Pyrmont and Ultimo.[43] By this time the Federation had been drawn from a rather cautious agenda to a militancy advocated by the fire-brand president of St Stanislaus College at Bathurst, Father Maurice O'Reilly, who boldly proclaimed on behalf of Catholic voters: 'We are going to sell ourselves to the highest bidder'.[44]

One of the many criticisms of O'Reilly's 'fighting policy' came in a letter to the *Sydney Morning Herald* from 'M Macnamara, Araluen'. Michael Macnamara may have been removed from Sydney, but exile had not silenced him. His biting sarcasm was on display as he cast scorn on Father O'Reilly's attempt at Bathurst to prod the new Federation into militancy:

> The Catholics, or some of them, in that beautiful sanatorium have now started a movement, which, if it succeeds, will prove that Bathurst is a place which must always be reckoned with. They are not in favour of the milk-and-water variety of federation that is proposed. The founders of the society, Mr Cleary and his friends certainly deserve the sympathy, if not the support, of their fellow-Catholics. They have been at considerable expense travelling round the country, forming branches of a federation for laymen only, which is not to be a political organisation, and they have been practically told that they do not know what they are talking about.

Also on display in the letter was Macnamara's insight into the mind of the Catholic voter, especially the labouring class that he had got to know at Pyrmont and Ultimo in 1900. He accurately predicted the outcome of any attempt to coerce Catholics into voting in a particular way: 'The great majority of Catholics belong to the labouring class. No advice—I will use no

---

42. *Freeman's Journal*, 17 April 1913.
43. *Freeman's Journal*, 13 November 1913.
44. *Catholic Press*, 31 July 1913.

stronger term—will induce them to vote against the party that has provided them with a living wage.'[45]

O'Reilly responded to the widespread reaction, both Catholic and Protestant, against his proposed aggressive politics, by publishing an article in the *Catholic Press* entitled 'A Plea for a Fighting Policy in the Catholic Federation'. In it he listed 'classes of Catholics [who] have always and everywhere turned down the fighting policy'. Perhaps he had Sydney bishops and priests in mind in one of his categories: 'The naturally weak-kneed and timid, who have a most amiable and optimistic belief in the efficacy of gentle and polite representation of their grievances. Those are the peace-at-any-price men, who are always, like Micawber, hoping for something to turn up. They alone, of all the people in the State, still cling to the superstition that politicians are guided by considerations of justice or equity, and not determined by political pressure.'[46] The other categories listed by O'Reilly were Catholic politicians, high-society Catholics and Catholic businessmen protecting their profits.

The President-Warden of the Federation, Patrick Cleary, urged on by the lay editor and clerical directors of *Catholic Press*, succumbed to O'Reilly's influence and adopted the 'highest bidder' approach to the parties—Labor, Liberal and Independents—preparing to contest the state elections in December 1913. The *Freeman's Journal* clung to the Federation's original brief of educating rather than confronting the politicians and society generally. The result was that the Catholic community was deeply divided and the Protestant majority increasingly united in hostility. As the elections approached, sectarianism reached alarming levels. The Federation produced a questionnaire on Catholic grievances and sent it to all candidates for responses. The Labor Premier, William Holman, instructed his candidates not to respond. O'Reilly added fuel to the fire when he visited Holman's electorate at Cootamundra for the laying of a foundation stone and urged parishioners to oust the Premier from his seat. It was a rash move by O'Reilly to target Holman directly, for the Premier had been popular among Catholics for his consistent support of Irish Home Rule.[47] In the midst of the controversy Archbishop Kelly remained fair minded and condemned both the Labor and Liberal parties for their neglect of Catholic claims for funding of schools and hospitals; the Liberal party had even proposed withdrawing bursaries for Catholic students made available by Holman's government.

---

45. *Sydney Morning Herald*, 8 August 1913.
46. *Catholic Press*, 28 July 1913.
47. J Kildea, 'Troubled Times: An Overview of the History of the Catholic Federation of New South Wales', *Journal of the Australian Catholic Historical Society*, 23 (2002): 15.

The outcome of the election was a dismal failure for the Federation's 'fighting policy'. Neither party made a bid for Catholic votes. In Cootamundra Holman increased his majority. Macnamara of Araluen was vindicated; in October, when the Federation's aggressive approach was set in place, he had predicted that 'defeat and discouragement are certain'. In February 1914 he wrote to the *Freeman's Journal* with his analysis of the election and advice for the Federation: 'Ninety per cent of the Catholic vote at Cootamundra went to Labor, and possibly more than ninety at Rozelle and the neighbouring constituencies. Let the Rozelle Federation try and convert that ninety instead of calling them names.' He concluded: 'The Catholic community, with that good sense which remains with the majority, and which seems to be wanting in those who would assume the position of guides, will not give up the substance for the shadow. They will continue to be Labourites and followers of Holman till they see something better.'[48]

One of the constituencies neighbouring Rozelle was Phillip, to which Pyrmont and Ultimo belonged, districts very familiar to Father Michael Macnamara from his time there in 1900-1901. Dick Meagher, the sitting Labor member and old-boy of St Stanislaus College Bathurst, had a resounding victory, as noted in the *Sunday Mail*: 'Mr Eden George attacked a formidable antagonist in Phillip. It was judged that with his old Parliamentary experience he would not have confronted Mr Meagher, only that he had some David sling to use against his Goliath. But it turned out that he had neither sling nor stone, and was simply slaughtered.'[49] Perhaps it was thought that the Catholic vote would be his sling and stone. It is not recorded what the local priests and the members of the local branch of the Catholic Federation made of the result, but they certainly refrained from joining their neighbouring Rozelle branch in the sycophantic sentiments communicated to the Very Reverend O'Reilly:

> Dear Father—On behalf of the members of the committee of the above branch I am instructed to forward on to you a copy of resolution which was carried at meeting lately held: 'That the thanks of this branch of the Catholic Federation be tendered to the Very Rev. Father M O'Reilly CM, for his patriotic and disinterested labours in the cause of good citizenship, and for his stately and dignified protest against the actions of unscrupulous politicians, and the great services rendered to his co-religionists in pursuance of his duty as a citizen and a priest. We also beg to offer Father O'Reilly our sincere sympathy in the annoyance he has lately been subjected to when, like a lion of the fold, he stepped

---

48. *Freeman's Journal*, 19 February 1914.
49. *Sunday Mail*, 17 December 1913.

into the breach in defence of honour, justice and uprightness, there was found a few miserable Catholics base enough to dispute his position and challenge his authority.[50]

No such resolution of support for Father O'Reilly was passed at the March meeting of the Pyrmont branch, chaired by the curate in the absence of the pastor:

> The schoolroom at St Bede's Pyrmont, was well filled on Tuesday evening last, when the monthly meeting of the Ultimo and Pyrmont branches of the Federation was held. The Rev Father O'Farrell was in the chair. Mr Cleary (president of the Federation) addressed the members on the social principles of the Federation, and traced the effect of these principles on the industrial conditions of to-day. Dr C J Fallon dealt with the treatment given to Catholic institutions in this State. A programme of music and singing helped to make a very enjoyable and interesting evening.[51]

The Church's relationship with the Labor Party, especially with Premier Holman and its Catholic Members of Parliament, was severely damaged. Damaged too was Father O'Reilly's reputation, despite the efforts of the *Catholic Press* to vindicate him for 'his fearless championship of Catholic rights, his uncompromising policy, and his assistance rendered to the Catholic Federation.'[52] At the end of 1914 he was called back to Ireland to head the Vincentian College in County Dublin, never expecting to return to Australia.[53]

War in Europe was declared on Tuesday 4 August 1914, and the following Sunday clergymen throughout Australia addressed the situation in their sermons. At St Mary's Cathedral, at the evening service, Archbishop Kelly expressed sentiments similar to those heard from Anglican and Protestant pulpits.[54] The *Catholic Press* reported Kelly's sermon under the headline:

THE ARCHBISHOP AND THE WAR
'Shoulder to Shoulder'
THOSE WHO ARE ABLE MUST TAKE A PART

---

50. *Catholic Press*, 12 February 1914.
51. *Freeman's Journal*, 12 March 1914.
52. *Catholic Press*, 12 February 1914.
53. J Wilkinson, 'Father Maurice O'Reilly, a Controversial Priest', *Journal of the Australian Catholic Historical Society*, 7(1983): 11.
54. M McKernan, *Australian Churches at War. Attitudes and activities of the major Churches 1914-1918*, Sydney 1980, ch 3 'August 1914', 14-39.

He called for unity across all sections of society in supporting the cause, and for an end to sectarianism: 'Soldiers did not ask their companions in arms whether their faiths agreed.' He expressed the hope that the war would be quickly concluded: 'Let not the war be carried on a single day after it has been decided which side is likely to conquer, or when it is clear that to continue will only mean absolute destruction.' He emphasised that 'war, dreadful as it was, could, in God's providence, be made to do good', and that 'from chastisement sometimes desirable results ensued'. Where his sermon was specifically Catholic was in his analysis of when a war is justifiable. He outlined the classic 'just war' theology, naming the three conditions necessary:

> The first was that it should be proclaimed by public authority; the second, that there should be a just cause for it; and the third, that those who went out to fight should be actuated by an upright intention. A war of aggression, or extermination, was not justifiable, except by the express will of God in punishment for wickedness. War must not be actuated by spite or from a pleasure taken in killing these who were hateful to us. With these three conditions, as a basis of war, the war would be blessed by God.[55]

Also specifically Catholic was the good he hoped would come from the evil of this war—justice for Catholic schools and Catholic workers: 'If this war pleased God, the people of the various religions would have such esteem for one another that there would be no more disabilities put upon their schools, and the question would not be asked in connection with their public work whether a person was a Catholic or not.' He also included Home Rule for Ireland as a hoped for fruit of the conflict. He concluded with an unambiguous declaration of Catholic loyalty to the Empire: 'And whether our schools are treated fairly or not, we will do our duty.'[56] The Catholic Federation added its weakened voice to support for the war effort. Its General Secretary wrote to the Defence Minister offering any assistance that might be required.[57]

Within days of the declaration of war precautionary measures were taken in deploying a complete brigade of infantry to act as mobile reserves in support of the Sydney coastal defences. The 25th Infantry Regiment was assigned responsibility for the city, Woolloomooloo, Miller's Point, Pyrmont and Ultimo.[58] Pyrmont was also the scene of an early act of patriotism when

---

55. *Catholic Press*, 13 August 1914.
56. *Catholic Press*, 13 August 1914.
57. *Catholic Press*, 27 August 1914.
58. *Sydney Morning Herald*, 6 August 1914.

John Bridge and Company offered their Pyrmont Wool Store for the indoor training of troops during winter months.[59]

One of the 'desirable results' of the conflict hoped for by all church leaders was an increase in church attendance. The first test for Pyrmont came with a mission in October preached by the familiar Missionaries of the Sacred Heart. There were reports of large congregations, evening services thronged, and 'practically every Catholic in the neighbourhood' approaching the sacraments of Confession and Holy Communion.[60]

In October 1915 the annual Communion Breakfast of the Hibernian-Australasian Catholic Benefit Society was held at the Town Hall following the 8 o'clock Mass at the Cathedral. Most of the speakers, including the Archbishop, stressed the loyalty of the Irish at home and abroad. Resuming his Home Rule theme, Archbishop Kelly declared his confidence that with the signing of peace, in the name of Irish heroes who were dying for the Empire, Home Rule would be automatically granted. Before the war Kelly had feared a violent Irish rising against England; he now saw the hope of a peaceful granting of Home Rule resulting from the violence of the Continental conflict. Sir Thomas Hughes, member of the Legislative Council, commented at the breakfast that Archbishop Kelly appeared to him to be a 'most active and successful recruiting officer'. Hughes reinforced pride in the Irish contribution to the war: 'Regarding the part the Irish were playing in the war, he could say from his own knowledge that 500 members of the Hibernian Society in New South Wales were at the war. That morning he was able to tell them that his two sons were now officers in the Dublin Fusiliers.'[61] One of those sons was killed in the following year.

One of the many addresses given at the Communion Breakfast was by Richard Meagher, Speaker of the Legislative Assembly and member for Phillip, and later Lord Mayor of Sydney. He remarked that he had recently attended a farewell for soldiers from his constituency in Pyrmont and Ultimo:

> They were saying good-bye to 85 fine types of young men who came from the neighbourhood of Harris street. 'Would you believe me,' said Mr Meagher, 'out of 85 men of different racial origin, 60 odd were of Irish parentage or Irish race.' The reason why he mentioned this circumstance was because no particular limelight had been focussed on the matter, and there were always people ready enough to go about doubting the loyalty of others. Moreover, no mention of it had been made in the daily

---

59. *Cobar Herald*, 7 August 1914.
60. *Catholic Press*, 29 October 1914.
61. *Freeman's Journal*, 21 October 1915.

press. However, it was as well that it should be known that members of the H.A.C.B. Society were prepared to do their little bit.[62]

A perusal of the names on the Pyrmont War Memorial ('those who died'—150; 'those who served'— 636) reveals many names of Irish origin and presumably of Catholic allegiance. A rough count of these comes nowhere near the 70% of Irish names claimed by Richard Meagher among the Pyrmont recruits in 1915. It was estimated that Catholics composed 19 per cent of the volunteers among the first contingent of troops in 1914, whereas they constituted 22 per cent of the Australian population.[63] Against Protestant accusations of Catholics not pulling their weight in volunteering, Melbourne's Archbishop Daniel Mannix commented wryly: 'Apparently not enough nuns are joining.'[64]

The war imposed new responsibilities on parish clergy. Father Hyland would have had the difficult duty, imposed on clergy by the Federal Government, of calling at the homes of any soldiers who were killed or injured in the various theatres of war and delivering the telegram bearing the tragic news. Beginning in May 1915, and throughout the year, the *Sydney Morning Herald* published lists of troop casualties under the heading 'Men of the Dardenelles'. As the months passed the number of deaths increased dramatically. In October and November there was a concerted recruitment effort. The large industrial sites in Pyrmont were visited by committees composed variously of repatriated wounded young soldier-heroes, politicians and senior military officers. Visits to the Colonial Sugar Refinery, the City Council's Electric Power-house and 'Goodlet and Smith', timber merchants, resulted in few volunteers. At the Powerhouse there was much cheering from the sixty workers for their nineteen-year-old mate, Private Saunders, a returned wounded soldier, but only one employee volunteered to join him.[65] Recruiting was a little more successful at the Sugar Refinery:

> Sergeant Cross, DCM, of the 'Gallant Thirteenth', related his experiences when at the front with his battalion, and said that Australia had every right and reason to be proud of the achievements of the boys on the other side, who are calling so insistently for assistance. One of the employees,

---

62. Freeman's Journal, 21 October 1915.
63. Patrick O'Farrell, *The Catholic Church and Community in Australia: a History* (Melbourne, 1977), 319.
64. James Griffin, 'Mannix, Daniel (1864–1963)', *Australian Dictionary of Biography*, National Centre of Biography, Australian National University, http://adb.anu.edu.au/biography/mannix-daniel-7478/text13033, published first in hardcopy 1986, accessed online 18 November 2015.
65. *Sydney Morning Herald*, 4 November 1915.

a fine stamp of a young fellow, held up a hand which was minus three fingers, and said that lie had made three attempts to enlist, but had been turned down each time. He was prepared to assist in any capacity. Sergeant Cross said that he had seen men on active service with one finger short, and advised the man to keep his maimed hand in his pocket when being tested. He gave in his name. Several other men, including his brother, also came forward, and were loudly cheered. Miss Smith, one of the employees, also addressed the men, advising them to get into khaki as soon as possible. 'Come on, men your duty,' she added. 'We have forty girls here, and we will guarantee to keep you in knitted socks.'[66]

In 1915 there was a new category added to the Archdiocesan questionnaire required to be completed by parish priests—'Special dangers to faith and morals in the district'. Father Hyland declined to respond to this question. In subsequent years his successors gave a range of answers: 1918—'mixed marriages, intemperance, negligent Catholics'; 1921—'seamen from Darling Harbour returning to ships at night'; 1932— 'mixed marriages, public schools'; 1938—'in Ultimo there is a good deal of Communism; gambling on the dogs; distribution of filthy reading matter'; 1941—'prone to gambling.'[67]

On 13 April 1916, just ten days before Easter Sunday, John Hyland was farewelled by his Pyrmont parishioners. At the gathering in the St Bede's school-room, he was thanked especially for his 'enthusiastic advocacy of the cause of the Catholic Federation' which had resulted in the establishment of 'such a flourishing branch' in Pyrmont and Ultimo.[68] In his new parish of Rockdale he would finally achieve stability, serving there as parish priest for 25 years. He died in July 1941 after a long illness. Norman Gilroy, who had automatically succeeded as archbishop after Michael Kelly's death in March 1940, presided at the Requiem Mass at St Joseph's, Rockdale. His Grace used his panegyric to draw lessons from the life of the deceased for the many priests gathered in the church. He described John Hyland as a 'straight man': 'and among men of this world there is no greater tribute they would pay to the honesty and integrity of a man than to say that of him—for it could not be said of many.' He would have had clerical gossip in mind when he highlighted the deceased's total lack of 'the defect of curiosity': 'His charity was remarkable. He was never heard to say a word that was derogatory to anybody.' He concluded by revealing details of Hyland's will: 'In his last will the first provision made was for a few Masses to be offered for the happy repose of his soul. The next was a bequest to the Archdiocese of Sydney

---

66. *Sydney Morning Herald*, 30 October 1915.
67. Pyrmont file, SAA.
68. *Freeman's Journal*, 20 April 1916.

for St Patrick's College, Manly.' Gilroy was much focused on the last will and testament of his clergy, expecting that the Archdiocese should be the major beneficiary, as he would again reveal in his gruff response in 1951 to the Brown Nurses regarding payment of a tombstone for Father Edward Gell. Perhaps Gilroy found in John Hyland a personality similar to his own: 'Father Hyland was a very shy man, continued his Grace. He was quiet and retiring. Because, perhaps, of these qualities, he went tranquilly through life, not making many friends, but never making an enemy. He was very just and efficient in the performance of his every duty.'[69]

---

69. *Catholic Freeman's Journal*, 24 July 1941.

Chapter 17
Impact of War

Succeeding John Hyland in April 1916, in time for Easter, was James Dalton. He had studied for the priesthood at St Kieran's College in Kilkenny, the cathedral city of the diocese of Ossory, where Patrick Moran had been bishop before his appointment to Sydney. The College was the first Catholic educational institution founded after the passing of the Relief Act of 1782, which allowed Catholics to establish schools, with the consent of the local Protestant bishop, for the first time since the Irish penal laws were introduced. The college's motto was 'Hiems Transiit', Latin for 'The Winter Has Passed', taken from the Song of Songs: 'My beloved speaks and says to me: Arise, my love, my fair one, and come away; for lo, the winter is past, the rain is over and gone.' The text was chosen to express relief at the relaxation of the penal laws which had kept Catholics as second class citizens in Ireland. The College was dedicated to Saint Kieran, known as 'Primogenitus Sanctorum Hiberniae', the first-born of the Irish saints and patron saint of the diocese of Ossory. St Kieran's College predated the national seminary at Maynooth by thirteen years and the Missionary College of All Hallows by sixty years. From this proud institution Cardinal Moran drew many recruits for his Archdiocese in the antipodes. Arriving in Sydney with James Dalton in October 1892 on the SS *Orizaba* were five other newly ordained Kilkenny priests.[1]

Soon after his arrival James was assigned to distant Cooma. After making the usual young curate's impact on the district, a popularity to which his horse contributed by winning the Hunter's Prize at the Cooma show in 1896, he was transferred to take charge of the nearby Bombala mission. His stay was surprisingly brief, and after just nine months he was sent as curate to Nowra. For ten years, from 1906 until his Pyrmont appointment, he was placed in various Sydney parishes.

At the time of the April 1916 hand-over at Pyrmont from John Hyland to James Dalton, the Australian 'birth of a nation' moment of the Gallipoli

---

1. *Freeman's Journal*, 22 October 1892.

landing was almost twelve months in the past, and the beginning of the birth pangs of the Irish republic were just days away. Ironically both events were devastating defeats which were turned into iconic 'creation stories'. On 25 April 1915, Australian and New Zealand troops were landed on a beach on the Gallipoli peninsula, and eight months later evacuated in defeat; on 24 April 1916, Easter Monday, 1200 Irish republicans rose in revolt in Dublin and surrendered five days later.

News of the rebellion in Ireland reached Australia on Thursday 27 April, while the rebels were still in occupation of the General Post Office and other Dublin locations. The *Sydney Morning Herald* headlined its report 'The Dublin Rioting'.[2] Two days previously the first anniversary of the Gallipoli landing had been celebrated throughout Australia and New Zealand. The *Herald* had opened its report: 'Australia's great heart is throbbing today as it has never throbbed before. For April 25—Anzac Day—is a day that will live in our hearts and in our history as long as Australia lasts.'[3] The 27 April edition of the weekly *Freeman's Journal* carried the headline: 'ANZAC DAY—THE BIRTH OF A NATION', but the only mention of Dublin was in a report on the state of health of the ailing Archbishop, William Walsh. Both Sydney's Catholic weekly newspapers would have to wait another week before being able to publish reports and comments on the 'rioting', by which time the execution of captured rebels by firing squad in Kilmainham gaol had already begun.

The reaction of all sectors of Australian society was one of condemnation of the Sinn Fein 'stab in the back', a betrayal of the Empire's war effort against Germany on behalf of small nations, especially Catholic Belgium. Archbishop Kelly proclaimed that 'the eruption in Dublin by the Sinn Feiners was a scandalous indecency'.[4] The *Freeman's Journal* concluded its article headed 'The Dublin Tragedy': 'With memories of Belgium's misery still fresh in their minds, the citizens of Dublin will doubtless congratulate themselves that this latest exhibition of German war tactics came speedily to an end'.[5] Even the Irish patriot, Coadjutor Archbishop Daniel Mannix in Melbourne, described it as 'truly deplorable', though he added that the rising was the 'natural, but regrettable sequence and response . . . to the campaign of armed resistance and civil war that the Carsonites had been allowed to preach and prepare for within the past few years'. He was among the first to signal the hasty executions as a future cause of a changed attitude to the rising.[6]

---

2. *Sydney Morning Herald*, 27 April 1916.
3. *Sydney Morning Herald*, 25 April 1916.
4. *Freeman's Journal*, 4 May 1916.
5. *Freeman's Journal*, 4 May 1916.
6. *Catholic Press*, 4 May 1916.

The British forces had retaliated against the Sinn Feiners with ferocity, arresting not just those directly involved in the Easter Rising, but anyone belonging to the movement. A total of 3,430 men and 79 women were rounded up and brought to Richmond Barracks in Dublin, where they were screened for trial, deportation or release. Nearly 2,000 were deported to England and interned; 160 prisoners were tried by courts martial. General John Maxwell, who had been appointed military commander of Ireland during the Rising, ordered that trials would take the form of 'Field General Court Martial', a stripped-down version of the standard court martial; proceedings were held behind closed doors and prisoners were not entitled to legal representation; most trials lasted about 20 minutes or less; 90 death sentences were handed down; 15 were carried out by firing squads over a two week period in the stone-breakers yard of Kilmainham gaol; the executed were buried uncoffined in quicklime.[7] The public was not to know when and whether the executions would cease. Advised of the darkening mood in Ireland, Prime Minister Asquith intervened on 10 May and ordered the cessation of executions.

The combination of the perceived vindictiveness of the executions, mass imprisonment, martial law, house raids and deportations soured the Irish and Irish-diaspora attitude to the British Government. The failure to implement the signed Home Rule Act of 1914 undermined the propaganda that the war against Germany was being fought for the freedom of small nations. In Ireland all these factors, together with the heavy Irish war casualties, which had begun at Gallipoli and continued on the Western Front, and the threat of conscription led away from the long-term support for the cautious policy of the Irish Parliamentary Party and towards Sinn Fein's doctrine of immediate independence as a republic through force of arms if necessary. Mannix artfully articulated this shift in a speech at the opening of a parish bazaar in July 1917:

> Nothing had ever been given in the way of redress until Ireland had used aggression and as much force as she could, moral or otherwise (Applause). Irishmen supported the Irish Parliamentary Party as long as they hoped against hope that their policy would result in redress. But Irish-Australia is tired of waiting, and, apparently, Ireland is tired of waiting, too (Loud applause). This accounts for the Sinn Fein victories all over the country (Applause). A few months ago, when hard words were being spoken, I ventured to predict that the time would inevitably come when the men who had suffered in Dublin, and the men who had been thrown into English prisons, would be taken to the heart of the people

---

7. Sean Enright, *Easter Rising 1916: the trials* (Sallins, Co. Kildare, 2014).

(Applause). The time has come already. Every election as it comes proves the truth of what I have said (Applause). Those who are more feeble and halting in their methods are thrown out of Parliament to make way for those who are in favour of a more strenuous and independent policy (Applause).[8]

The dramatic change of attitude in the Irish-Australian community was captured in the contrast between the reception received at the St Patrick's Day celebrations in 1916 and 1917 by Sydney's Lord Mayor, Richard Meagher, also speaker of the Legislative Assembly and member for the Pyrmont-Ultimo seat of Phillip. In 1916, a month before the Easter Rising in Dublin, he was cheered and applauded throughout his address. With his renowned eloquence, he traced the history of the movement towards Irish freedom. His speech culminated with the expression of great confidence that 'with the Act of the Imperial Parliament, Erin will again reflect her pristine brightness on the sun-kissed heights of her material, intellectual and spiritual glory. In her noontide radiance we shall behold her with her black robe of centuries of suffering cast aside, standing majestic and resplendent in her sheen of emerald green, as in the days of St Patrick'. Somewhat carried away by the cheering and applause he concluded:

> Countless bosoms in every clime on that proud day will heave with emotion, and fervently thank Providence that they have lived to see the day that their old folk, now passed away, ever dreamed of, ever longed for, and ever prayed for. God grant that before our next year's celebration the sea-divided Gael, with one triumphant and world-encircling 'Hosanna' will be able to greet grand old Erin, 'great, glorious, and free' (Great cheering).[9]

The 1917 celebration was held at the Agricultural Show Ground. Presiding was Archbishop Kelly accompanied by the Apostolic Delegate, Archbishop Bonaventura Cerretti. Special invited guests were Premier Holman and Lord Mayor Meagher. Kelly gave a long address which included remarks on Home Rule for Ireland. The politicians were called upon to give the vote of thanks to the Archbishop. But neither could make himself heard because of the hooting and howling from a section of the crowd. The attempts of the ecclesiastics, Irish and Italian, to quell the interruptions were in vain; even the Apostolic Delegate's thumping of the table with his cane failed to silence the dissenters.[10]

---

8. *Advocate*, 21 July 1917.
9. *Catholic Press*, 23 March 1916.
10. *Sunday Times*, 18 March 1917.

Both politicians were booed and jeered by the crowd because of their shared commitment to conscription, their adherence to the cautious Home Rule approach for Ireland and rejection of the Sinn Fein 'physical-force' campaign for independence. Holman and Meagher, together with Prime Minister William Morris Hughes, had been among the Labor politicians expelled from the Labor Party after the 1916 referendum because of their promotion of conscription contrary to party policy. Meagher, campaigning as a 'Labor Independent' would lose his seat of Phillip in the forthcoming state election; Holman would continue as Premier in coalition with the Nationals; Hughes, member for the Federal seat of West Sydney, which included Pyrmont-Ultimo, would abandon this working class electorate at the May 1917 Federal election and win the Victorian rural seat of Bendigo, under the banner of the break-away National Labor Party. West Sydney was easily retained by the Labor Party. During the 1916 campaign against conscription Hughes, 'Billy of Pyrmont', had been compared for his militarism to Kaiser Wilhelm, 'Billy of Potsdam', by the diminutive American peace-activist and 'mother of ten kids', Mrs Jennie Scott Griffiths, at a protest rally in Wollongong.[11]

The viciousness of the 1917 State election campaign, pitting old Labor colleagues against each other, was reflected in an accusation that Meagher had intervened with the Archbishop to have a popular local curate, an opponent of conscription, removed from his electorate of Phillip:

> Some of Mr R D Meagher's political opponents have not been playing the game. A story has been going the rounds in the Phillip electorate that the Lord Mayor used his influence to have a highly respected and popular curate removed to another district, because he opposed conscription and did not appreciate the Lord Mayor's political attitude. It was a silly suggestion in the first place; in the second, an insult to our revered Archbishop. Under the circumstances it might be well to publish the following correspondence without further comment:
>
> Town Hall, Sydney, 19-3-17
> Father J O' Gorman, Administrator, St Mary's Cathedral.
> Rev Sir, In view of the rumour persistently circulated in Phillip Electorate that I was instrumental in getting Dr Tuomey removed from St Benedict's, would you kindly ascertain from his Grace the Archbishop if directly or

---

11. *Illawarra Mercury*, 27 October 1916; T H Irving, 'Scott Griffiths, Jennie (1875–1951)', *Australian Dictionary of Biography*, National Centre of Biography, Australian National University, http://adb.anu.edu.au/biography/scott-griffiths-jennie-11641/text20793, published first in hardcopy 2002, accessed online 27 September 2015.

indirectly I have been identified in any such action regarding the rev gentleman named?
Yours truly, (Sgd) R D MEAGHER.

St Mary's Cathedral, Sydney, 19th March, 1917.
Right Hon R D Meagher, MLA, Lord Mayor of Sydney
My dear Lord Mayor, In reply to your question of even date, it will suffice to state:
1. No re-arrangement of mission would rightly be affected by political considerations.
2. No politician, to my knowledge, has sought directly or indirectly to influence ecclesiastical arrangements in this Archdiocese.

Your faithful servant in Christ, (Sgd) MICHAEL, Archbishop of Sydney.[12]

Patrick Tuomey, curate at St Benedict's, had been removed to rural Mittagong in December 1916, because of his clash with the Archbishop over his membership of the Irish National Association and support of the Easter Rebellion.[13] He was brought back briefly to Sydney by order of the magistrate's court in March 1919, charged with contravening the *War Precaution Regulations*. Unsuccessfully defended by barrister Edward McTiernan, a member of the Catholic Federation executive and future High Court justice, Tuomey was convicted of sedition for having encouraged disloyalty to the British Empire in a September 1918 speech at Paddington Town Hall critical of the oppressive English policy in Ireland. He was fined £30 and £6.12s costs. He was inclined to refuse the fine and go to gaol for two months. However, Archbishop Kelly intervened, the fine was paid and Tuomey was sent back south.[14]

Prime Minister Hughes had called the second conscription referendum for December 1917. The Australian community was deeply divided along class and religious lines, with trade unions, the Labor Party and a majority of Catholics opposed. The radicalisation of workers during the August-September General Strike consolidated opposition to conscription. Catholic bishops shifted from their neutral stand of 1916 and in 1917 tended to follow the lead of their Melbourne colleague Daniel Mannix, who had become Archbishop on the death of Thomas Carr in May 1917. Mannix was vigorously and controversially opposed to conscription in both referenda. He

---

12. *Freeman's Journal*, 22 March 1917.
13. Patrick O'Farrell, 'Archbishop Kelly and the Irish Question', *Journal of the Australasian Catholic Historical Society*, 4 (1974): 5.
14. *Evening News*, 20 March 1919; O'Farrell, *Archbishop Kelly and the Irish Question*, 6.

had also succeeded Carr as Catholic Chaplain-General. Prime Minister Billy Hughes found that 'his most implacable opponent on the conscription issue had become a Major-General in the Australian Army'.[15] The feisty Maurice O'Reilly, who, against the wishes of the Australian Vincentian authorities, had returned to Australia in 1915 as the new rector of St John's College at the University of Sydney, was a vocal supporter of his old Maynooth classmate. He became known as 'the Dr Mannix of New South Wales'.[16]

The belligerent Mannix had his belligerent critics. On the eve of the December 1917 referendum the Speaker of the Victorian Lower House called for his deportation:

> Sir Frank Madden said that Dr Mannix was an enemy of the country, and in his every action he betrayed his hostility to the British Empire. He was loyal only to the Sinn Fein, which had stirred up strife in Ireland, and sought to do the same out here. Some of its adherents in Ireland had been deservedly shot, and it was a pity that the authorities could not shoot a few in Australia, and thus avert future trouble . . . [T]he proper course for the Victorian Government to take would be to petition the Commonwealth authorities to deport Dr Mannix, and send him back to Ireland, where he could do no harm. He was not wanted in Australia, and he (Sir Frank Madden) would gladly pay his passage-money if only he could be induced to leave (Applause). It had been said, Sir Frank Madden added, that he was a Catholic. That was not true. He had been born a Catholic, but had left the church more than 50 years ago because he could not bear the domination of the priests.[17]

Such outbursts only served to strengthen Mannix's support in the Catholic community and led to the defeat of the referendum and to the defeat of Madden at the next Victorian State election. Conscription was rejected by an increased majority in December 1917.

During 1917 the Pyrmont-Ultimo branch of the Catholic Federation was still in operation and in January members had met under the presidency of Father Dalton to elect office bearers and delegates to the State Council. Those elected bore the names of prominent parishioners—'Messrs Chinchen and W Armstrong; vice presidents, Messrs M J Weslan and W Bradley; treasurer, Mr M O'Dwyer.' At the September meeting Norbert Chinchen advised that the branch now had a record membership. Father Dalton 'expressed his full

---

15. Tom Johnstone, *The Cross of Anzac: Australian Catholic Service Chaplains* (Toowoomba, 2003) 21.
16. J Wilkinson, 'Father Maurice O'Reilly, a Controversial Priest', *Journal of the Australian Catholic Historical Society*, 7(1983): 14.
17. *Argus*, 13 November 1917.

approval of the movement, and his hopes that all would become members', in order to 'secure their rights in regard to education . . . and strengthen the fight against materialism'. Also present at the meeting was curate Patrick McDonnell. The Federation played a controversial role later in the year by helping to mobilise the successful defeat of the second conscription referendum, a change from its neutral stance in 1916. Catholic opposition was partly based on the government's refusal to exempt seminarians and religious brothers from conscription: 'The omission to exempt Brothers and seminarists calls for action. Every ecclesiastical college in Australia, and every school taught by the Marist Brothers, the Christian Brothers, as well as those under the control of the Patrician and De La Salle Brothers, could be closed under the existing proposals.'[18] In the company of Archbishop Kelly at a chapel blessing in November the Federation president Patrick Cleary concluded his speech with a rallying cry to Catholic voters: 'Let us then, all Catholics worthy of the name, acting in unison, throw back this insulting conscription of God's anointed and keep Australia free.'[19] The Pyrmont priest-president of the local branch and his committee would have reinforced the message to the congregations of St Bede and St Francis Xavier in the weeks leading up to the 20 December referendum.

The wartime duty of informing families of war casualties continued to be a part of priestly ministry. On a sad day for an Ultimo family in December 1916, Father James Dalton would have made his way to the Doyle household at 342 Jones Street to inform the parents of the death in France of their twenty year old son Nicholas Joseph, and to console them as best he could. His death was noted in the *Freeman's Journal*:

> Mr and Mrs M J Doyle, of Jones street, Ultimo, on the 6th inst., received the sad intelligence of the death in France on the 5th October last of their second son, Private Nicholas, of the 3rd Battalion. The painful nature of the news was the more intensified as on the previous Sunday Mr and Mrs Doyle had received home their eldest son, Sergeant John Doyle, of the 55th Battalion, who had been wounded likewise in France. The bereaved parents are old and respected residents of the locality, and prominent Church workers in the parish of St Francis Xavier, Ultimo. Their good example has been followed by their children, who are as earnest and enthusiastic in their labours as their parents. Sergeant John Doyle is vice-president of the local conference of the Society of St Vincent de Paul. The parishioners of St Francis Xavier particularly and the residents of Ultimo and Pyrmont generally share in the grief of Mr and Mrs Doyle

---

18. *Catholic Press*, 13 December 1917.
19. *Catholic Press*, 22 November 1917.

and family, and deeply sympathise with them in the great loss they have sustained. The deceased son enlisted some eighteen months ago, and was but twenty years of age. RIP.[20]

At the time of his death Doyle was no longer a sergeant, having been demoted to private in September 1916 for absence from parade and using insolent language to an officer. Nick Doyle's personal effects were later returned to his father: three handkerchiefs, photos and a damaged soap box.[21]

The arrival of a curate at Pyrmont in January 1917 presented an opportunity for a holiday for the priest-in-charge, and in February James Dalton, accompanied by Father Roche of Petersham and Father Dunne of Wollongong, sailed to New Zealand. It proved to be a bit of a 'busman's holiday', as James found himself preaching 'a very earnest and practical sermon' in the Dunedin Cathedral.[22] The new curate was Patrick McDonnell, yet another All Hallows graduate newly arrived from Ireland. The division of duties between the two priests was exemplified on Easter Sunday 1917 with James Dalton presiding at the early Mass at Ultimo, during which he preached an 'eloquent sermon', and a 'large number approached the Holy Table'. The 10am Mass, a Missa Cantata, was sung by Patrick McDonnell. The choir extended its repertoire beyond the familiar Messe Solemnelle of Gounod to sing Luigi Bordese's Mass in G, though the *Gloria* was from Gounod's Fourth Mass.[23] Presumably the two Easter Masses at Pyrmont were similarly shared. McDonnell was obviously the more gifted musically; he would in later years be regularly called on to sing the Cathedral Masses.

The fiftieth anniversary of the establishment of Pyrmont as a separate mission and the opening of St Bede's occurred in September 1917. However, this golden jubilee seems to have passed without celebration.

In July 1918 Father Dalton offered advice to Archbishop Kelly concerning the value and the future of the Church properties at St Bede's—presbytery, church, school and cottages, with a total frontage of 160 feet. Excusing his boldness in proposing a suggestion to His Grace, he proceeded to explain that the Pyrmont properties were very valuable, and as the main entrance to Darling Island was close by, their value was enhanced ten-fold. He predicted that the property would be resumed within three years, and he advised His Grace to be very slow in signing any contract in the meantime. The

---

20. *Freeman's Journal*, 14 December 1916.
21. National Archives of Australia, B2455, DOYLE N J (http://recordsearch.naa.gov.au/SearchNRetrieve/Interface/ViewImage.aspx?B=3520987, accessed 16 December 2015)
22. *Freeman's Journal*, 1 March 1917.
23. *Freeman's Journal*, 19 April 1917.

prediction of the resumption of the Pyrmont Street church property would be a recurring theme throughout the century.

There was rejoicing in Sydney streets on 8 November 1918 when the morning newspapers prematurely reported that Germany had accepted the terms of an armistice:

> The storm of rejoicing, which broke over the city yesterday morning, showed us a Sydney capable of tremendous feeling. It also showed the grim spirit of restraint, determination to wait and see it through, under which the people have been living for four terrible years. Germany was finished, complete victory had been won, the war was over, the populace decided that the moment had come to be glad, and they simply let go and plunged into the joyous tide flowing strongly into the streets. The steam whistles on the railway engines and ferry boats spread the news abroad, discordantly but definitely. It got the thousands streaming into the city to work, by rail, tram and steamer, and it threw them off their accustomed balance, Anglo-Saxon reserve for once disappeared, and passengers everywhere formed themselves into groups, and cheered, and sang patriotic songs, and cheered again. There were tumultuous scenes on the ferry boats, where there is more freedom and less noise than on trains. Usually sober citizens jumped about, cheered, insisted on doing all sorts of wild things to show their delight.[24]

In October 1919 the Catholic Federation held its annual conference in the Cathedral Chapter Hall. On the agenda was the proposal to form a political party to contest the state elections in the following year. Delegates from the 331 branches, including Pyrmont, attended. The new strategy resulted from a change to proportional representation, a system which offered the possibility of gaining seats in the new multiple-seat electorates and thus holding the balance of power in the Legislative Assembly. The proposal was accepted by a majority of three to one.[25] All were agreed that the name of the new party should not include the word 'catholic', and names considered were 'Social Unity Party', 'Social Defence Party', 'People's Party'. Finally a unanimous vote resulted in adopting the name 'Democratic Party'. The editor of the *Freeman's Journal* expressed misgivings about the venture: 'The Democrats, if they appeal at all, must appeal largely to the present Catholic Labor vote. As it is from the Labor party Catholics have received most Parliamentary consideration, and as Catholics are really strong in the Labor Parliamentary party, is it a wise thing to risk weakening our influence there

---

24. *Sydney Morning Herald*, 9 November 1918.
25. *Catholic Press*, 9 October 1919.

whilst attempting to become a new influence elsewhere?'[26] The founder and president of the Federation, Patrick Scott Cleary, acknowledged the strong Catholic presence in the Labor Party, but emphasised the failure of the party to 'fight for fair treatment of our Catholic schools, hospitals and orphanages', a cause that Democratic Party members of Parliament would champion.[27] The Federation's gamble was that Catholics would vote for candidates espousing Catholic issues.

The decision was made to select candidates for the eight newly formed five-seat electorates of the Sydney city and suburban area. Cleary was endorsed as the candidate for the Sydney electorate, which had absorbed the former seat of Phillip and hence included the suburbs of Pyrmont and Ultimo. There were twenty candidates for Sydney, including five from the Labor Party, of whom four had been sitting members in the previous parliament. Also contesting the election as an independent was the ever hopeful Richard Meagher. The Democratic candidates were defeated in all electorates contested. Their gamble had failed; Catholic voting patterns did not change. In the electorate of Sydney four out of the five winning candidates came from the Labor Party and all were Catholics, one of them a Papal Knight of St Sylvester. Indeed Labor had a resounding victory over the previous government. Patrick Cleary received a disappointing 6.5% of the vote, not even representing the voting power of the members of the local Catholic Federation branches, let alone the total Catholic vote. Even the unsuccessful Meagher out-polled Cleary with 8.35%.[28]

In August 1920 the Federation flexed its muscles in calling a meeting in the Sydney Domain to protest the arrest on the high seas of Archbishop Daniel Mannix of Melbourne. Mannix was sailing from the United States to Ireland to visit his ninety year old mother, when his ship, within sight of the welcoming bonfires along the Irish southern coast, was intercepted at midnight by a British destroyer. He was arrested and removed from the SS *Baltic* to HMS *Wyvern*. Forbidden by the British government from landing at Cobh in County Cork, he was disembarked at Penzance in Cornwall. Styling himself the 'Pirate of Penzance', Mannix provided a perfect quote for the press and made the British government look foolish. In Sydney a 'tremendous crowd numbering tens of thousands' endorsed a resolution which concluded with a reference to Mannix's role in defeating the conscription referenda: 'We offer him our sympathy, encouragement and support, believing he will play as big a part in making Ireland free as he did in keeping Australia free from

---

26. *Freeman's Journal*, 16 October 1919.
27. *Catholic Press*, 26 February 1920.
28. A Green, *New South Wales Election Results 1856º2007* (http://www.parliament.nsw.gov.au/resources/nswelectionsanalysis/HomePage.htm [accessed 16 January 2015]).

military and Imperial tyranny.'[29] The Federation drew some encouragement from its ability to gather at short notice such a huge assembly of Sydney's Australian-Irish community, even though unable to enlist their support at the polls.

After Patrick McDonnell's departure from Pyrmont in February 1920, James Dalton was without a curate for the remaining two years of his appointment. During that time he would have called on the weekly assistance of supply priests for Sunday Masses at Ultimo or Pyrmont. The only indication of his absence from the parish in those two years was in July-August 1921 when the name of a Missionary of the Sacred Heart appeared in the baptismal register. Phillip O'Toole, a primary-school boy at the time, in old age recalled that Father Dalton 'always carried a walking stick (black with timber knots)'.[30]

St Bede's school was in the news in February 1920 because of a tragic accident which had occurred at the Pyrmont baths:

> A sad drowning fatality occurred at the Pyrmont Baths on Thursday afternoon last, when Mary Moynihan, aged 11 years, one of a party of school children from the local Good Samaritan Convent, who attended for their swimming lesson, by some unexplained means, unfortunately got out of her depth. When subsequently discovered in about eighteen feet of water her condition was such that all efforts to restore her to consciousness proved futile. The deceased was a daughter of Mr and Mrs Denis Moynihan, of Murray-street, Pyrmont, and much sympathy is felt for them in their sudden bereavement, especially when it considered this was the first visit of their daughter to the baths for a swimming lesson. The little girl's school mates from St Bede's Convent marched in the funeral procession from her parents' home to the mortuary station, during which, and later at the grave side, they sang hymns and recited the Rosary for the repose of her soul.[31]

Throughout 1920 and into 1921 several Pyrmont children took up their pens and wrote letters to 'Gumblossom', the editor of the children's page of the *Freeman's Journal*. From the letters it was clear that not all Pyrmont's Catholic children were attending St Bede's School. Five of the young writers were crossing Darling Harbour to attend the Marist Brothers primary school for boys at St Patrick's, Church Hill. The impressive Eucharistic Memorial School had been opened the previous year.[32] A three storied brick building

---

29. *Freeman's Journal*, 19 August 1920.
30. Phillip O'Toole to the author, 25 April 2006 (Archives of St Bede Pyrmont).
31. *Freeman's Journal*, 12 February 1920.
32. *Freeman's Journal*, 3 April 1919.

named in memory of the preservation of a consecrated host in a house at Church Hill during Sydney's priestless days, it would have proved a very attractive alternative to the old wooden school at Pyrmont. Also enticing would have been the prospect of being part of an all-boys school and being taught by an all-male staff. Some local families also chose to send their daughters to St Patrick's where the girls could pass from primary to high school on the same site, under the care of the Sisters of Mercy.

The Marist Brothers' boys were keen supporters of the *Freeman's Journal*, as reported by ten year old Verner Bodin of 148 Pyrmont Street: 'May the *Journal* spread far and wide; that is the wish of the St Patrick's boys.'[33] One precocious schoolboy, James Fitzgerald of 164 Pyrmont Street, sent 'Gumblossom' a lengthy essay on 'Progress of Catholicity in Australia'. Having read in a recent issue of the newspaper that there would be a prize for the best written letter, he was getting in early with a winning entry. His essay included a reference to the unusual name of his school:

> Men of all sects were compelled to attend the service of the Church of England. Refusal meant a flogging, and things became worse till the arrival of Father O'Flynn, the first priest with a commission from Rome. During these miserable and frightful times the Blessed Sacrament was miraculously preserved for two years in a small cottage at a place named the Rocks, where now stands the beautiful Church of St Patrick. In memory of this miracle a new St Patrick's Boys' School has been erected at a cost of £10,000. It is indeed a fitting monument to one of the most wonderful events that has happened in the history of the Catholic Church in Australia.

The influence of a parent, perhaps a member of the Catholic Federation, was evident in some of James' overwrought comments about the hierarchy. The names of the English Archbishops Polding and Vaughan were not mentioned. Of Cardinal Moran he wrote: 'Here at last was a person who could be a competent leader and thus lead them on to success and so achieve great works for the Church.' He had even higher praise for Melbourne's Archbishop:

> The Catholics of Australia owe much of their success at the present time to the indomitable spirit of the Most Rev Dr Mannix. It was he who voiced the opinion that this Sunny Land of Ours should not be crushed with the barbarous heel of conscription. One of the grandest and most impressive sights was to see those fourteen VC heroes, mounted on their

---

33. *Freeman's Journal*, 15 July 1920.

white chargers, acting as an escort to Dr Mannix through the streets of Melbourne on 17th March, 1920.[34]

Sydney's Archbishop Kelly was not mentioned in the essay. Gumblossom was rather reserved in her reply: 'Your letter is most instructive and most edifying. You have managed to crowd a great deal of information into your few pages of manuscript, and I must heartily congratulate you on the attention you have evidently given to the subject.'[35] There is no record of whether James of Pyrmont was favoured with the prize.

In May, ten year old Walter Greenall of 189 Pyrmont Street wrote a short letter to Gumblosson reporting on his attendance on Anzac Day at the Requiem Mass in St Mary's Cathedral for the souls of those who had fallen during the Great War. He explained that 'as a relative of mine had been killed there, I went to hear Mass at the Cathedral. The priest preached a sermon which was most interesting to grown-ups and children.'[36] Walter and his classmate Verner developed quite a taste for writing to Gumblossom and their many letters were published throughout 1921. Walter even ventured to imitate his Pyrmont Street neighbour James Fitzgerald, and submitted a lengthy letter on 'The New Trade Route to India.'[37] In the results for the 1924 Diocesan Examinations he was listed third in his class at the Marist school, Church Hill. In the same report the statistics for Pyrmont and Ultimo schools at the time of the 1924 inspections were given:

Pyrmont: enrolment 189; number present 176
Ultimo: enrolment 238; number present 201

Truancy had been and would continue to be a problem at both parish primary schools. As for Walter, in 1930 he was listed among the graduates in 'Fitting and Machining' at the Sydney Technical College.

Sydney's Catholic community mustered in huge numbers in August to welcome Daniel Mannix on his return to Australia. Despite strident demands from loyalist and Protestant groups for an Australian version of the British refusal of entry, or at least the imposition of an oath of loyalty prior to disembarkation, Mannix sailed into Brisbane and after days of triumphant welcome caught the train south to Sydney. In addition to the welcome and street parade organised by the Catholic Federation, he was controversially granted the freedom of the city by Sydney's Lord Mayor, William Lambert, one of Pyrmont's local aldermen. Perhaps Lambert's

---

34. *Freeman's Journal*, 5 August 1920.
35. *Freeman's Journal*, 5 August 1920.
36. *Freeman's Journal*, 19 May 1921.
37. *Freeman's Journal*, 7 July 1921.

gesture was not unrelated to his candidacy for Labor Party pre-selection for the September bi-election for the Federal seat of Western Sydney. The seat had been left vacant by the sudden death of Thomas Joseph Ryan, former premier of Queensland and focus of Labor's hopes for victory in the 1922 Federal election; Mannix had assisted at Ryan's Requiem on the day of his arrival in Brisbane. By hosting Mannix at the Town Hall Lambert would have emphasised his anti-conscription credentials and advanced his cause within the party. In his welcoming address Lambert lauded Mannix's leadership:

> We are under a debt of gratitude to his Grace, for his noble work . . . in connection with the effort made some years ago, when an attempt was made to place the people under the power of militarism (Applause). We respect and honor Dr Mannix for his democratic principles and for his outspoken and fearless advocacy on behalf of the working classes (Applause). In other respects he stands out as one of the most prominent of Irish patriots.[38]

There were three elements to the Town Hall welcome—the morning reception in the Mayoral Rooms with a large group of invited guests, followed by a public reception in the main hall, and an evening reception to which a disappointed overflow crowd of 'between 8,000 and 10,00' could not gain admittance. Mannix was in sparkling form at all three events. He returned the mayor's compliments with compliments of his own: 'It was fortunate for Sydney that it had as its first citizen such a man as the present Lord Mayor.' He concluded by claiming that 'behind closed doors he regarded Sydney as the capital city of the Commonwealth (laughter).' At the evening reception he delighted in having the title of 'digger' conferred on him by a returned soldier: 'The welcome from the Returned Soldiers and Sailors, where his enemies might be said to be found, was particularly gratifying. They saw on the platform a genuine Australian Digger, and his Grace was a proud man to have in Sydney soldiers and sailors gathered around him, and show their trust in him.'[39] The use of the adjectives 'genuine' and 'Australian' was an obvious challenge to Billy Hughes' proud claim of being 'the Little Digger'.

In December 1921, at the end of his Pyrmont appointment, James Dalton was given leave-of-absence to travel to Ireland for an extended holiday. He sailed on the *Ormonde* on 18 February 1922, having been farewelled by his parishioners—'about 500 assembled in the school hall, and at least 200 were unable to gain admission.'[40] He was also farewelled by his fellow swimmers at the Coogee Baths, a more salubrious spot than the Pyrmont pool, and

---

38. *Freeman's Journal*, 18 August 1921.
39. *Freeman's Journal*, 18 August 1921.
40. *Catholic Press*, 23 February 1922.

comfortably distant from his parishioners: 'Last Friday there was a happy little gathering at Jim McCauley's Coogee Baths, when Father Dalton who is off for a trip to the Old Country, was presented with a smoker's outfit and wallet by his friends of the "sun and no wind brigade". Mr J M Dunningham made the presentation, and he spoke of the popularity of the Reverend gentleman, and the esteem in which he is held by all.'[41] The Ireland that Dalton was sailing home to was about to enter into a devastating civil war over the peace treaty negotiated with the British, which granted dominion but not republican status, resulting in an Irish Free State without six of the Ulster counties.

On his return in February 1923 he was temporarily appointed as administrator of the Burwood-Enfield parish. He continued a 'locum tenens' role at Annandale in 1924, at Bondi in 1925 and at Naremburn in 1926. He finally achieved stability when he was appointed to Auburn as parish priest in December 1926. James Dalton died in September 1932 at the age of 67. The obituary notice in the *Freeman's Journal* recorded the names of his Kilkenny classmates, fellow passengers on the *Orizaba* in 1892, in order of ecclesiastical dignity:

> The present Bishop of Dunedin, the Most Rev Dr J Whyte, formerly of Sydney;
> Very Rev Father T Phelan, PP, Chancellor of the archdiocese and at present travelling companion of his Grace Archbishop Kelly, now on his way back from the Eucharistic Congress;
> the late Very Rev Father James Dunne of Wollongong;
> Rev Father M P Malone of Kiama,
> Rev Father M Hogan PP of Dulwich Hill.

James would have contentedly placed himself at the bottom of the list. Among the clergy at the Requiem Mass with a Pyrmont connection were the golden jubilarian Michael Macnamara and the newly ordained John O'Toole. The final word on James Dalton was that he was 'noted for the excellence of his well-reasoned and instructive sermons'.[42]

---

41. *Arrow*, 24 February 1922
42. *Freeman's Journal*, 8 September 1932.

Chapter 18
'Pyrmont Native' Ordained Priest

In February 1922 Michael O'Connell succeeded James Dalton at Pyrmont. O'Connell, born in 1883, was from Cloyne in County Cork and was educated at All Hallows. With three other newly ordained All Hallows graduates he arrived in Sydney by the mail steamer *Orient* at the end of October 1908. Within days the new arrivals had been dispersed as curates in Sydney and beyond. Michael O'Connell was assigned to assist in the parish of St Mary of the Suburbs at Erskineville, also called Macdonaldtown. In 1910 he was at Pymble where he remained until a transfer south to Moruya in 1913. In 1916 he received his first mission district when he was placed in charge of Helensburgh, a mining town in the Illawarra region. This appointment included chaplaincy at the Waterfall Sanitorium. A return to Erskineville was announced in February 1920 when he was asked to administer the parish in the absence overseas of the pastor. A similar appointment followed in 1921 when he administered Rockdale parish

O'Connell was installed at Pyrmont in time for the state election of March 1922. As parish priest he was ex-officio president of the local branch of the Catholic Federation. The Federation had selected only four Democratic Party candidates for the election. The seat of Sydney was not contested, so the Pyrmont president and branch members were not called on to campaign locally. The Democratic candidate for Eastern Suburbs, Doctor Cyril Fallon, was successful, but all hope of playing an influential role in favour of Catholic schools was dashed by the resounding victory of the Nationalists with the support of a highly successful campaign mounted by the rival Protestant Federation. The *Catholic Press* referred to the new government of Sir George Fuller as 'Premier Fuller and his Orange Ministry'.[1] Even in the electorate of Sydney, mainly working class, only three of the five elected members, all three Catholic, were from the Labor Party. The Catholic Federation was blamed for Labor's defeat, and in revenge it was dealt an insulting blow by

---

1. *Catholic Press*, 18 May 1922.

being listed by the Labor Party as a proscribed organisation along with the Loyal Orange Lodge and the Protestant Federation.

The last recorded meeting of the Pyrmont branch was held in September 1922: 'At the meeting held at Pyrmont on Sunday, 27th ult, the Rev Father M. O' Connell presided, and extended a welcome to the visiting delegate. Officers elected were Messrs M O'Dwyer and J Nicol, joint hon secretaries; Mr J Conlon, hon treasurer; Misses R Clarke and E Hallinan, delegates to the State Council. It was proposed to establish a sub-branch at Ultimo and then to combine the two sections.'[2] The Federation held its last annual conference in April 1923. The ever faithful Maurice O'Dwyer was one of Pyrmont's two delegates. Archbishop Kelly addressed the conference and expressed his pleasure at the presence of women among the delegates. The presence of women did not halt the steady decline in the Federation's numbers and influence. A year later the Federation's terminal condition was quietly indicated in an item in the *Freeman's Journal*: 'Through force of circumstances the Catholic Federation found itself unable to function this winter, and the necessity arose for an organisation to carry on the good work. The outcome has been the formation of a new body — the Catholic Evidence Guild — which will specialise in Catholic propaganda. His Grace the Archbishop is displaying great interest in the Guild, and it has the assurance of his active support and sympathy.'[3] The historian of the Catholic Federation, Jeff Kildea, headed his section on its demise, 'Not with a Bang . . .': 'There was no public announcement—no closing ceremony to mark the end of a once great Catholic organisation. The *Freeman's Journal*'s short statement was to be the Catholic Federation's epitaph—its poignancy magnified by the fact that the newspaper edited by P S Cleary, the founder and leading light of the Catholic Federation, appeared not to notice its passing.'[4] Doctor Fallon completed his term in the Legislative Assembly in April 1925, bringing to an end the brief existence of the Democratic Party. Fallon and another Federation stalwart, Peter Gallagher, stood as independents in that year's elections, but without success.

In April 1922 the Pyrmont War Memorial on the corner of Harris and Union streets was unveiled by the Governor of New South Wales, Sir Walter Davidson. The project had received approval from the works committee of the City Council. Gilbert Doyle was the sculptor, and the memorial was estimated to cost nearly £1000. The Sydney Morning Herald headlined its report of the opening, 'A FINE MONUMENT', and went on to declare

---

2. *Freeman's Journal*, 7 September 1922
3. *Freeman's Journal*, 29 May 1924.
4. J Kildea, *Tearing the Fabric: Sectarianism in Australia 1910 to 1925* (Sydney, 2000), 259.

it beautiful.[5] This was in contrast to the comments on the memorial in neighbouring Glebe which was inaugurated a few weeks later, on Anzac day 1922, by the Governor General, Lord Henry Forster. Before its unveiling the monument had been described by the architectural magazine *Building* as 'appalling': 'it appears as if it has been composed of discarded pieces found on the premises of a monumental mason.' In 1929 the same magazine added the scathing comment: 'Truly there are worse things than war when such horrible things as this can be perpetrated in times of peace'.[6]

At Pyrmont, a bronze angel of victory was placed on a plinth made, not of local sandstone, but of trachyte brought from the quarries at Bowral in the Southern Highlands of New South Wales. This tough, distinctively coloured igneous stone had begun appearing in the kerbs and gutters along Sydney's streets from the beginning of the century, and soon it had been adopted by builders and architects in its polished state for more monumental projects.[7] On the platform with the governor were local politicians, Federal member William Lambert and State member Alderman Michael Burke. The newspaper report described Pyrmont-Ultimo as 'probably one of the poorest districts of the metropolis, but what is lacking in material wealth is more than outweighed by the loyalty and patriotism of its people'. The monument was locally funded and 'there were few large contributions and the balance of the money—over £1000—was collected in small coins by the school children and by a house-to-house canvas'.[8]

Also present at the dedication were Rev Fr Michael O'Connell and the Rev Mr Edward Madgwick, acting rector of St Bartholomew's, who would go on to become the longest serving Anglican rector in Pyrmont, from his appointment in 1925 to his death in 1955. Both reverends spoke at the conclusion of the dedication ceremony. Reverend Madgwick would comment early in his ministry that the work in Pyrmont was 'tough', and that the heart of one of his predecessors, Maurice Gray, rector from 1902 to 1918, 'was broken as he saw the parish disfigured by the demolisher and families leaving by the hundred'.[9] His neighbours at St Bede's, a succession of 16 priests in residence during his incumbency of 30 years, would have readily concurred with the assessment of ministry at Pyrmont as 'tough' and 'heart-breaking'.

---

5. *Sydney Morning Herald*, 10 April 1922.
6. 'Unique Glebe WWI memorial gets timely facelift', *Sydney Morning Herald*, 7 February 2014.
7. R Irving & N Powell, *Sydney's Hard Rock Story: The Cultural Heritage of Trachyte* (Sydney, 2014).
8. *Sydney Morning Herald*, 10 April 1922.
9. *Sydney Diocesan Magazine*, 1 May 1930.

In neither St Bede nor St Francis Xavier churches was there any memorial related to the war, unlike at St Bartholomew's, where memorial gates were erected in 1927 and a plaque placed in the church:

> Although rain marred the outdoor activities in connection with the dedication of war memorials at St Bartholomew's Church, Pyrmont, on Saturday, the church was crowded for the indoor services. Dean Talbot dedicated the monument erected at the gates, the gates themselves, and the wall of the church. The sermon was preached by the Dean, and during the service Mr C E Guilford sang 'The Trumpeter'. The following inscription is engraved on the monument—'To the glory of God and to the appreciation of the men from this parish who served in the War, 1914-19.'[10]

Indeed the only reminder of the demolished Anglican church is that marble plaque now stuck on a retaining wall on the site where St Bartholomew's stood for 120 years.

Soon after his arrival at Pyrmont and Ultimo, Father O'Connell, at the urging of Archbishop Kelly, moved quickly to address an urgent need for new classroom facilities in both sections of the parish. At Pyrmont it was the 1880 dilapidated brick and timber school building that needed to be replaced. At Ultimo the problems of an unstable brick building, 'without any foundations', which served as both church and school, needed an urgent solution.

In a letter of June 1923 the pastor wrote to the Archbishop commenting on earlier discussions and arguing for a new proposal. Having spent eighteen months in the parish and realizing His Grace's anxiety for the welfare of the children of Pyrmont and Ultimo, he begged to make suggestions in reference to building new parochial schools.[11] The first approach had been to create one school in place of the two—a 'central school' mid-distance between St Bede's and Francis Xavier's. This involved purchasing land and building a new school. The project was to be funded by the sale of the Pyrmont property, including the church. The Ultimo church would serve both ends of the parish. Father O'Connell argued against the practicality of this plan, giving three reasons. Firstly, a site on Allen Street had been considered—a version of Father O'Callaghan's centralising plans of 1898— but it was not available for purchase: '[N]early all the property between Pyrmont and Ultimo has a nine and a half years lease to run, and is therefore not for sale.' Most of the property on the peninsula was held on a one hundred year lease dating from

---

10. *Sydney Morning Herald*, 4 April 1927.
11. O'Connell to Kelly, 8 June 1923 (Pyrmont Box, 1923 File, SAA).

the original development of the 1840s, after which leases would revert to the Macarthur family's Camden Estate. The 1940s became a focus of anxiety for residents who feared that, when the allotments were again available for purchase, the whole area would be totally given over to industry and houses demolished, and churches and schools would become redundant. In the meantime there was no property on which to build a 'central school'. Secondly, even if land were available, its cost, estimated at £7000, would exceed what the sale of the Pyrmont property could realise. Besides, it would be unwise to sell the church at the present time, when it could be expected that in ten years it would double in value. A final consideration was that access to a 'central school' would be difficult for the infants from Pyrmont who would have to cross 'two very heavy lines of traffic, Union Street and Bridge Road'. The dreaded Public School would be the only beneficiary.

This last consideration would be enough to open the Archbishop to O'Connell's alternative plan, which followed in the letter. It was to build a new school in each section of the parish at the present locations. He had to argue strongly for the retention of the Pyrmont school, whose numbers were lower than at Ultimo, stating that it could be expected that the current enrolment of 200 at Pyrmont would not decline over the next ten years, 'for most of the leases have that time to run, and even then resumptions could only be partial'. He made a case for the continuation of Pyrmont as a largely residential area based on the City Council's commitment 'to the erection of workmen's houses in the Pyrmont district'. He stated that the Council 'estimated they would settle 200 families in this area', and cited the example of the recent resumption of Church of England land on Way's Terrace for this purpose. He noted that if the school went, then the church too would go, but that 'the people have a pious and reverent affection for this church and do not want to lose it'.

Michael O'Connell had evidently done his homework, because he was able to present a detailed, costed plan for two new schools. At Pyrmont the three parish-owned cottages would be sold and demolished, the retrieved sandstone being used to build the new school on the site: 'In this way a great saving would be effected in not having to buy brick.' Attempting to cover all future contingencies, he proposed making the school-room 35 feet wide instead of the usual 30 feet, 'so that, in the event of the Pyrmont property being sold in years to come this building will command a price, being sufficiently wide for a big store, and strong enough to carry three stories [sic]'. The estimated total cost, including furnishings, was £1950. As for Ultimo, the present structure would have to be underpinned and extended so that a storey containing classrooms could be built on top of the ground floor space, which would then serve as a permanent church. With this new arrangement the weekly bother at Ultimo of transforming the week-day school into a weekend church, and vice versa, would be eliminated. The cost was estimated at £3800. The two buildings 'complete and fully equipped' were claimed to cost a manageable total of £5750. He concluded the letter, explaining that he had discussed the matter with the leading men of Pyrmont and Ultimo and that they had agreed this was the most useful and practical course to action. They were now awaiting the Archbishop's sanction. The nuns were also of the same opinion, and though they could not be relieved of the present inconvenience of having to walk daily from the Ultimo Convent to the Pyrmont School, they were quite agreeable to continuing the existing arrangement, realising the urgent necessity for new schools. He signed off offering the proposals for His Grace's consideration and earnestly hoping they would receive his approval.[12]

Eleven months later, in May 1924, the Archbishop came to Pyrmont to open the new school-hall, built not of stone, but brick. During the demolition and construction phase, classes had been held in the church, as recalled by Phillip O'Toole.[13] The Catholic organisations were lined up with the parish priest to welcome His Grace. The diocesan and local officials and members of the Australian Holy Catholic Guild, including the cross-bearer, were present in their regalia; the Hibernian-Australian Catholic Benefit Society was well represented. It was recorded that 'the guard of honour was strengthened by the presence of members of St Vincent de Paul Society, the little children of the Holy Angels Sodality, the Children of Mary'. Also prominent were the eight members of the St Bede church committee, 'the leading men', three of whom were members of the O'Toole family: Messrs M J Weslan (secretary), M O' Dwyer, J O'Toole, A O'Toole, A O'Toole, jun, J Leonard, M Daly and J Cavanagh. Among the clergy were former Pyrmont pastor Philip McIntyre and weekend assistant James Reynolds of the Sacred Heart Fathers. Politicians present were local alderman William Holdsworth and local member of the Legislative Assembly Michael Burke, both of whom had assured Father O'Connell regarding Pyrmont's future as a residential district. Prominent layman, Lieutenant Peter Gallagher LLB, president of the Catholic Returned Soldiers' Association and member of the Catholic Education Association, was present to lobby the politicians on Catholic demands for educational justice. Gallagher was the soldier who had so pleased Daniel Mannix at the Town Hall with his words of welcome in August 1921: 'His Grace is the elder brother of the soldiers, because he

---

12. O'Connell to Kelly, 8 June 1923 (Pyrmont Box, 1923 File, SAA).
13. Phillip O'Toole to the author, 25 April 2006 (Archives of St Bede Pyrmont).

fought for what we fought—the self-determination of small nations—the self-determination of Ireland.'[14]

In his words of welcome Father O'Connell recalled His Grace's desire for a new school at St Bede's and the parishioners' enthusiastic response:

> When I mentioned about 15 months ago to the people that your Grace desired the establishment of a new school in the parish . . . from that moment the people gave themselves whole-heartedly to the cause. The gathering here to-day is an indication of the generous spirit of devotion and loyalty to your Grace. I have to congratulate the people here on their earnestness, perseverance, and generosity, on the virile manner in which they took up the work of building this school. They have worked hard to achieve this object, and their efforts will be a source of pleasure to your Grace.[15]

Archbishop Kelly, using the much-favoured 'royal plural', referred to the new building in which they were gathered as 'a school which we have long desired'. As usual at school blessings he took the opportunity to state the Catholic case for government funding, highlighting a new injustice: 'The teachers of the public schools . . . wanting to perfect themselves for the work of teaching, go to the University, and they are admitted free. But if a Brother or a Sister of a teaching Order wishes to take the same course—and they have the same interest, perhaps greater, in their children—they must pay a heavy fee.' He concluded by congratulating the priest and people of St Bede's on their achievement. Peter Gallagher then stepped forward to initiate a subscription list. He took the opportunity to repeat the well-rehearsed argument about unjust taxation on Catholic parents: 'Half a million pounds was taken from the Catholic people of NSW each year for the purpose of contributing to the State system of education—free, compulsory and secular. In this parish, with 13000 [sic] or 1500 people, you are paying at least £1500 per year for the education of children who go to the public school. Such a state of affairs did not obtain in other countries.' The next month Gallagher would present the same argument, without success, to the Minister of Education at Parliament House.

The total cost of the Pyrmont project was £3802/2/7, double the estimate, and made up as follows: building, £2986/18/-; walls, fencing, etc., £218/5/-; demolishing cottages and cutting away stone for building and playground, £176/18/10; furniture, stage fittings and architect's fees, £438/1/9. The cottages were the three, numbers 33 to 37 Pyrmont Street, purchased by

---

14. *Freeman's Journal*, 15 August 1921.
15. *Freeman's Journal*, 15 May 1924.

Father O'Gorman for £850 in 1910. The income received to date against the debt was £650/10/- from the sale of stone and proceeds of a fete, and the respectable sum of £958/11/- collected at the opening ceremony, the subscription list being headed by a donation of an undisclosed sum from His Grace.[16]

At the conclusion of the ceremonies, Father O'Connell paid special tribute to Father James Reynolds, superior of the Sacred Heart monastery at Kensington, 'for the great assistance he had given him in the work of building the school'. Father Reynolds obviously did more than turn up at St Bede's for weekend 'supplies'. It was probably his friendship and company that was the source of greatest support for Michael O'Connell, whose vulnerabilities would emerge within a few years. Father Reynolds was described by his confreres as 'a servant of all, especially of the poor ... untiring in his visits to the sick, or to those in sorrow or affliction.'[17]

Ultimo's turn for celebrating the blessing of the reconstructed school-church came in December 1924. The Archbishop was again present, together with a group of Sacred Heart priests, regular assistants at St Francis Xavier, and Michael O'Connell's Rose Bay colleague, Richard Joseph O'Regan. The Federal Member of parliament and former Lord Mayor of Sydney, William Lambert, was present, as was the newly elected local Alderman John English. Both were Catholics and Labor Party members. The *Catholic Press* provided a full description of the completed project:

> The original church was one of the oldest in the city, and in very bad condition, being built of brick without any foundations. It had to be underpinned, and strengthened to support the classrooms over. It was 56 feet long, and has now been increased to 90 feet, in length, adding a very spacious sanctuary and sacristies. A simple but effective fibrous plaster ceiling, and new floors, plastering and seating and decorating has been carried out, the whole having a very fine effect. Three large classrooms and a stage have been erected above the church, capable of being divided by folding screens. The classrooms are exceptionally well lighted and ventilated, and have two wide and easy staircases leading on to a wide balcony, which is the whole length of the building.[18]

The parish priest was effusive in his praise of Archbishop Kelly: 'Rev Father O'Connell extended a hearty welcome to his Grace, remarking that it was the second time during the year that they had been honoured by a visit from

---

16. *Freeman's Journal*, 15 May 1924.
17. A Caruana, *Monastery on the Hill: A history of the Sacred Heart Monastery Kensington 1897–1997* (Kensington, 2002), 173.
18. *Catholic Press*, 11 December 1924.

the Archbishop, and both were concerned with schools. There was, perhaps, no period in the history of the Church in Australia when Catholic education had been advanced as it had been during the reign of the present Archbishop (applause).' Archbishop Kelly reciprocated; having spoken of the need of a school, his Grace referred to the parish's financial burden: 'We might say to God, "Rain down the means here". He has already rained down the means in Father O'Connell . . . Therefore, he would say, "Well done" to Father O'Connell, and he would say it in the name of Pyrmont and Ultimo, the Archdiocese of Sydney, and of Australia and the whole world.'[19] The *Catholic Press* journalist chimed in with more praise, at the same time referring to the slum reputation of the suburb in euphemistic terms: 'Ultimo and Pyrmont have now two schools in a congested district, much better than many in more nature-favoured localities, which are a credit to the Church, the parish, and Father O'Connell.'[20]

The cost of the Ultimo project was announced at the blessing:
Total cost £7688
Made up of:
Cost of upper-floor school rooms £5514
Cost of underpinning, extensions and renovation
of ground-floor church £1182
Sundries £ 992

As at Pyrmont, the cost again exceeded the estimate. The subscription list, opened by Alderman English, netted £970, not enough to cover sundries. The parish now had a combined debt of almost £11000, approximately double the original estimate. The Archbishop gave permission for a public appeal 'throughout the whole of Australasia'. Beginning on Christmas day 1924 and continuing throughout 1925, the two Sydney Catholic newspapers carried the Archbishop's letter authorising the appeal and encouraging a generous response.

Father O'Connell quickly formed a ladies committee drawn from parishes across Sydney to assist in the huge fund-raising task. He was also busy writing 'begging letters' to any likely benefactor whose name and address he get hold of. He introduced himself in the letter as the Pastor of a poor parish where a man's whole wealth is his weekly wage, and where the demon of want frequently entered many a Catholic home. He appealed directly to Catholics throughout Australia to come to the assistance of the parishioners and their parish priest, in order that the heavy burden undertaken by the

---

19. *Catholic Press*, 11 December 1924.
20. *Catholic Press*, 11 December 1924.

parish would not overwhelm them.[21] The true nature of the pastor's personal burden would only later become known to the Archbishop.

Early in December 1925 Michael O'Connell received news by cable from Ireland that his mother, Mrs Margaret O'Connell, had died on November 28. The news came as a great shock, because he had been planning to travel to Ireland to visit her in the near future. A few days after a Requiem Mass for his mother, clebarted at St Bede's, another cable brought the tragic news that his only married brother had died on 15 December. The shock of this double bereavement, combined with parish debt worries, seemed to lead to a breakdown in Michael O'Connell's physical and mental health, which found him struggling through the next two years. From December 1925 to November 1926 the baptismal register indicates an almost total dependence on the visiting Sacred Heart Fathers. O'Connell's name appears only on three occasions.

The final appeal of 1925 for funds to address the school debts was published on New Year's Eve. It concluded with acknowledgement of donations already received, including three guineas from Austin Walsh of Nowra, the great-uncle of Pyrmont's current parish priest, Dominican Father Anthony Walsh. The advertisements ceased in the New Year. The only indication of further fund-raising was in a letter to 'Gumblossom' from Ruth Cannon of Bowman Street. This school-girl's letter contained an indication that the parish was barely keeping up with interest payments:

> I go to St Bede's School, Pyrmont, where the Good Samaritan Sisters teach me. The school is quite new and up to date, but there is a very heavy debt still owing. We had a children's fete about six weeks ago, to help to pay the interest on the school, and a great many of the school children held back-yard bazaars. My two sisters (Madeline, Bonnie) and I organised a back-yard bazaar and raised £18, which made the total of the fete £120, and the Sisters were very pleased. Rev Father O'Connell, who is the parish priest, had quite a broad smile when we handed him the cheque. To help us, kind ladies and friends of the Sisters held a 'Chrysanthemum Ball' at the Wentworth Hotel, which brought our amount to over £200.[22]

Ruth, Madeline and Bonnie were sisters of Ernie Cannon, the benefactor of the John the Baptist sculpture placed in St Bede's church in 2013 and dedicated to the Cannon and O'Toole families. In 1951 Ernie married Joan Aldridge, a granddaughter of Tobias and Elizabeth O'Toole.

---

21. O'Connell to Mrs. Ryan, 29 October 1925 (Pyrmont Box, 1925 File, SAA)
22. *Freeman's Journal*, 5 August 1926.

The O'Toole family suffered the loss of a member of the second generation when Andrew, known as Dick, the youngest of the children of Tobias and Elizabeth, died in December 1926 at the age of 51. At various times he had been publican of local hotels—the *Green Tree*, the *Duke of Edinburgh* and the *Pacific*. Two former parish priests, Father McIntyre and Monsignor O'Gorman, joined Father O'Connell for the Requiem Mass. The *Freeman's Journal* paid tribute to the deceased:

> Mr O'Toole never did a bad turn to anyone and his innumerable gratuitous deeds and acts of self-sacrifice were performed in the most unassuming manner. His funeral last Saturday week provided one of Sydney's largest funerals. As the long, winding procession moved from St Bede's Church, Pyrmont, to the Mortuary Station, the pavements were lined with sorrowing mourners. A great crowd comprised of all classes and creeds gathered at the graveside to offer their last respects ... Deceased was 51 years of age and leaves a sorrowing family of wife, four sons and nine daughters.[23]

The three eldest daughters had joined the Sisters of the Good Samaritan.

The curate appointed in November 1926 was the newly ordained James Patrick Lynch from St Peter's College in Wexford. From the time of his arrival in the Pyrmont presbytery, he seemed to have taken over full responsibility from the troubled pastor. In May 1927 Michael O'Connell sailed from Sydney on the Royal Mail liner *Maloja*. It was only during his absence that the details of his troubles emerged, resulting in his being replaced in December, while still overseas, by Father William McDonald. In the meantime the inexperienced curate struggled on. He received high praise in June when the Archbishop visited St Bede's to preach yet another appeal for the completion of the Cathedral. This was a final archdiocesan appeal to complete St Mary's, in progress since 1865, in time for Sydney's hosting of the International Eucharistic Congress in 1928:

> Although burdened with a considerable debt of their own, the good people of the parish responded in a remarkably generous manner to the appeal of the Archbishop. The quota assigned was £220, and the amount contributed and promised reached the magnificent sum of £500. Speaking proportionately it can be said that Pyrmont's effort is a record, as it is the first parish which has more than doubled its quota. For this encouraging response credit is due to the priest in charge, Rev Father J Lynch, who was assiduous in visitation previous to the appeal ... The

---

23. *Freeman's Journal*, 23 December 1926.

gratitude of the Archbishop goes out to the subscribers, and he hopes that their goodwill and self-sacrifice will be an incentive to all to support him in his efforts to complete the Cathedral for the Eucharistic Congress.[24]

The details of the subscriptions were published in July. A most generous donation of £100 was recorded against the name of the absent Father O'Connell. The same amount was subscribed by Dick O'Toole's widow, now licensee of the *Duke of Edinburgh* Hotel in Harris Street. Father Lynch gave £25 from his modest curate's stipend. The familiar names of prominent parishioners were in evidence—O'Toole, O'Dwyer, Armstrong, Cannon.[25]

The new parish priest arrived in December 1927. He was William Henry McDonald, the first Australian-born pastor of Pyrmont since the brief incumbency of the Benedictine Daniel Maurus O'Connell in 1874. William McDonald was born in Brisbane in 1888. He studied at the Manly Seminary and was ordained for Sydney Archdiocese by Archbishop Kelly in 1915. His first appointment was to Lidcombe until 1917. From there he went to Enmore as assistant to the Venerable Archdeacon James Furlong, formerly pastor of Pyrmont. During the Archdeacon's final illness he was administrator of the parish. Following Furlong's death in November 1926 McDonald was sent to administer the Naremburn parish, and then to Ryde during the illness of Edward Gell, the former Pyrmont curate. From June 1927 he was in the Lismore diocese preaching an appeal for St Gabriel's Christian Brothers school for the deaf at Castle Hill. It was after this mission and a brief holiday in Queensland that he took up his Pyrmont appointment on 9 December 1927.

William McDonald was unique among Pyrmont priests in having left a hand-written summary of his administration.[26] He began his diary by explaining how he had come to be appointed to Pyrmont. Before his arrival the young curate Father Lynch had been 'locum tenens' in the absence of the parish priest in Europe. However, because Michael O'Connell had been relieved of his duties while on leave, McDonald had been appointed to the vacancy. From correspondence between Archbishop Kelly and Michael O'Connell upon his return in February 1928, it is evident that it was not just parish debts that were weighing on O'Connell, but, more heavily still, significant personal debts. Not only had he been relieved of his position at Pyrmont, but he had been suspended from all priestly ministry. His financial situation had come to light after his departure from Sydney and the Archbishop had moved quickly to terminate his appointment. He was

---

24. *Freeman's Journal*, 30 June 1927.
25. *Catholic Press*, 7 July 1927.
26. W McDonald, Diary 1927–1931, manuscript (McDonald file, SAA).

accused of very heavy betting on horse racing. On his return to Sydney, O'Connell desperately wanted to have his faculties restored so that he could save face and welcome and host his two brother priests, one from England and the other from the United States, who were planning to travel to Sydney for the 1928 International Eucharistic Congress and for a reunion with Michael. Faculties were not restored and the brothers' plans were cancelled.

Letters in October 1928 from Kelly to O'Connell, resident at Lewisham Hospital, referred to the burden of financial obligations brought upon the diocese, the parish of Pyrmont and O'Connell himself by maladministration and deceit unsuspected by the Archbishop. The letter of 12 October concluded that the idea of reinstatement as a priest was precluded by the negative attitude of fellow priests who might in other circumstances extend assistance to O'Connell. His Grace signed off with supplications to the Divine Mercy on behalf of his wayward priest.

A week later Kelly set out the conditions on which he hoped to restore the faculty of celebrating Mass to O'Connell:

1. Pending the repayment of £10,000 to the Australian Bank of Commerce and £8,000 to the Government Savings Bank, you will make provision to pay the annual interest.
2. That you will come to an agreement with your creditors concerning your private debts.
3. That you would observe total abstinence from intoxicating drinks.

These things are required to repair aggravated injustice and so remove an *obex* [barrier] to authorisation to a *celebret* [permission to celebrate Mass].[27]

In April 1929 Michael O'Connell was admitted to Callan Park Hospital for the Insane. One of his former Rockdale parishioners, on hearing that he had been committed to a state-run asylum, wrote an indignant letter to Archbishop Kelly stating that, with all due deference, he wished to state that many Catholic people were reasonably upset, because such a popular priest had been placed in a Public Institution to associate with the dregs of humanity.[28]

---

27. Kelly to O'Connell, 19 October 1928 (O'Connell file, SAA).
28. Jack Cronin to Kelly, 24 January 1931 (O'Connell file, SAA).

The *Catholic Directory* for 1931 and 1932 recorded O'Connell as being at Lewisham Hospital, where the sisters of the Little Company of Mary, who conducted the hospital, provided accommodation and care for alcoholic priests. After a failed placement as chaplain at the Westmead Boys' Home, he was in receipt of another harsh letter from the Archbishop in December 1935 stating that, in view of repeated relapses during recent years into scandalous intemperance, frequenting hotels, incurring debt by loans, non-payment of car fares and abuse of parochial trust at Pyrmont, the Archbishop must regard the report of the Brothers at Westmead and of the Parish Priest of Lewisham concerning recent relapses as leaving no option except the withdrawal of all Diocesan Faculties and immediate return to the Rest Home at Lake Macquarie.[29]

In 1934 the nuns had relocated their facility for troubled priests from the hospital at Lewisham to Morisset on Lake Macquarie, where a large homestead and estate, Kendall Grange, had been purchased. O'Connell's stay at St Joseph's Convalescent Home lasted until 1948, interrupted by two failed returns to parish ministry, at Strathfield in 1942 and Penshurst in 1944. His early years at St Joseph's would have coincided with the convalescence of his Pyrmont predecessor, the aged Philip McIntyre. In 1949 the St John of God Brothers purchased the Kendall Grange and established a residential training centre for 'sub-normal boys'. The Brothers also agreed to continue the work of the Sisters in caring for disturbed priests.

From 1950 to 1954 the 'Rev M O'Connell' was listed among the prize-winners in the *Sunday Herald*'s chess competitions. His locations, as indicated in these notices, were at Morisset, 1950-1951, Belmore [sic] Park, 1952, and Richmond, 1953-1954.[30] The Brothers had purchased a stately home and property, Belmont Park in Richmond, as announced in the *Catholic Weekly* under the heading: 'Catholic Hospital for Male Nervous Cases'.[31] The St John of God psychiatric hospital was blessed and opened by Cardinal Gilroy in September 1952.[32] It was at the Richmond hospital that Michael O'Connell died in July 1957. Brother Thaddeus wrote to inform Cardinal Gilroy that Father O'Connell was in good spirits up to the time of his death. However, on the Thursday night, after having his regular game of chess with one of his fellow patients, he retired at about 10pm. About eleven o'clock he was heard calling for help. Br Joseph went to see how he was and saw that he was in danger of death. The priest and doctor were called immediately and Michael

---

29. Kelly to O'Connell, 7 December 1935 (O'Connell file, SAA).
30. *Sunday Herald*, 19 March 1950; *Sydney Morning Herald*, 4 February 1951, 7 March 1951, 26 June 1951, 1 July 1951, 8 July 1952, *30 December 1953, 3 January 1954*.
31. *Catholic Weekly*, 3 January 1952.
32. *Catholic Weekly*, 25 September 1952.

O'Connell received the last Rites of the Church. He passed away peacefully at about five minutes to midnight. Br Thaddeus went on to emphasise that Father O'Connell would be very much missed by the Brothers and patients at Richmond; he was always ready to do all he could to help. The Brother movingly stated that Father O'Connell felt at home at Belmont Park, and that his conduct there was always most edifying at all times.[33]

The Cardinal expressed his appreciation of the kindness and consideration shown by the Brothers to Michael both at Morisset and Richmond.[34] The obituary published in the *Catholic Weekly*, referred to his years with the Saint John of God Brothers as 'chaplaincy'. His funeral took place at St Declan's, Penshurst, his last place of parish ministry.[35]

On arrival at St Bede's in December 1927, Father William McDonald's first impression was one of shock at the state of the clergy living conditions: 'I found the Presbytery was sadly in need of repair. Every dust blew in, every shower beat in the back of the house. Rats too had a happy hunting ground.' He quickly identified three sources of dust and grit so familiar to the locals— the chimney stacks of the Electric Power House in Pyrmont Street and the Colonial Sugar Refinery along John Street and the macadamised road surface in every street.

The new parish priest wasted no time in reporting to his parishioners on the financial situation of the parish. He published a complete list of the names of those who had contributed in 1927 and the amount that each had given. Heading the list was 'Mr And Mrs Joseph O'Toole and Family' with a contribution of £20.16s, which was three times the amount of the next highest contribution. A covering letter urged more people to join the list of contributors in the following year: 'Father Lynch and myself trust that the next list will be larger and more representative. Young man, young lady, do not leave all the contributions to mother; do your part as many others are doing.' Fr McDonald knew that it was the wife who held the purse-strings in the parish households.[36]

Plans for renovations of the presbytery were drawn up and tenders called for the demolition of the old detached kitchen and laundry and the building of extensions, including back veranda, kitchen and housekeeper's accommodation. The work was completed between June and October 1928

---

33. Br Thaddeus to Gilroy, 19 July 1957 (St John of God Brothers file, SAA).
34. Gilroy to Br Thaddeus, 25 July 1957 (St John of God Brothers file, SAA).
35. *Catholic Weekly*, 5 July 1957.
36. 'Parochial Collection' (Pyrmont Box, 1927 file, SAA)

and the renovated presbytery was ready to accommodate two priest-guests from Melbourne who were in Sydney for the Eucharistic Congress.

Under the diary heading 'March 1928: Epoch for Parish' was entered a jubilant announcement: 'His Grace Archbishop Kelly took over the major portion of the debt, leaving the parish to meet £7000. His Grace took over the debt as Archbishop of Sydney with the right of a rebate if or when the property is sold.' Pessimism about the survival of St Bede's was expressed in the following sentence: 'Eventually, all agree that the property will be sold on account of the area being purely for factories or stores (wool).'[37] McDonald's diary tracked the demolition of housing in Pyrmont and Ultimo and the emergence in their stead of huge wool-stores. The closest encroachment on St Bede's was the Shute-Bell wool-store, just two houses away to the south on Pyrmont Street. Earlier more extensive demolitions had removed housing from the northern end of the peninsula to accommodate the ever-expanding sugar refinery and from the eastern side of Pyrmont Street to make way for the power station.

Later in 1928 bazaars were held at Pyrmont and Ultimo. The Pyrmont event in May had the object of raising money to help pay off the debt still owing on the new schools. Monsignor O'Gorman, Cathedral administrator and former Pyrmont pastor, was invited to open the bazaar. Flattery was his way of loosening the purse strings:

> Monsignor O'Gorman, in declaring the bazaar open, said he had spent three of the happiest years of his life in Pyrmont, whence he took over the administratorship at St Mary's Cathedral. He left the district very reluctantly. The beautiful school that had been erected was a matter on which he would congratulate the people . . . Those in the hall could not put their money to better use than in patronage of the bazaar, which had for its object the liquidation of the debt on their school.[38]

In August the Ultimo bazaar was held to raise money for the presbytery renovations. Father McDonald added an element of friendly rivalry to encourage the Ultimo parishioners to contribute: 'The Pyrmont people had raised the interest due for the year, and he trusted that Ultimo would find the funds to pay for the kitchen.' Monsignor Moynagh from Rozelle declared the bazaar open and urged the people to support the project:

---

37. William McDonald, Diary 1927-1931, manuscript (McDonald file, SAA).
38. *Freeman's Journal*, 24 May 1928

Monsignor Moynagh who was received with applause, spoke very highly of the goodness of the people of the parish. In other parishes large sums are raised, but Pyrmont beats them all. Father McDonald is only asking for a new kitchen. He should ask for more, but this, he says, will make the presbytery comfortable. 'I cannot understand why this necessary work was not done years ago,' continued Monsignor Moynagh. 'Others were prepared to leave things as they were; but Father Mc Donald is asking for what should be done, and nothing more. The people do not wish the priest to have too much luxury, but expect and are prepared to give him at least the ordinary comforts of life; this has not been so up till now. I congratulate Father McDonald for doing this work, and am sure the people will respond generously, as I know you good people are generous. In fact, your pockets are often bigger than your hearts.'[39]

James Lynch, the curate, in proposing the vote of thanks to the Monsignor, remarked that 'a certain happy rivalry existed between Pyrmont and Ultimo parts of the parish, and he hoped when the results were published that Ultimo would at least equal Pyrmont in the amount raised'. Father McDonald's diary recorded the proceeds from the two bazaars: Pyrmont £377/16/5; Ultimo £306/18/3.

In November Archbishop Kelly blessed the presbytery renovations. In his address of welcome Father McDonald recalled that 'His Grace had told him long ago to make the house habitable', and he was pleased that, 'with the assistance of the people and the generous donations of many priests, he had been able to do this'. The Archbishop spoke of the need of a comfortable presbytery for the clergy. Referring to the locality as 'an industrial centre' he ventured to offer advice to the local union members:

> His Grace advised the men in the unions to exercise great care in electing their executive officials. They should not select men who had been failures, and who were merely talkers. Such were not fit to lead them. They certainly would not lead them to peace and progress. They wanted men who minded their own work and were of benefit to the country. Their duty was to secure the best men and place them at the head of their unions.[40]

Subscriptions on the day amounted to £107-15-0, which when added to the income from the bazaars covered the cost of the renovations.

---

39. *Catholic Press*, 16 August 1928.
40. *Freeman's Journal*, 22 November 1928.

It was noted that at the blessing, forming part of the guard of honour for His Grace, was a group of about 30 Goanese seamen from a liner in port. This was the first indication that the Pyrmont clergy had begun to participate in the ministry to seafarers, sponsored by the St Vincent de Paul Society. The ministry was based at the Stella Maris centre in Kent Street and the chaplain was a Marist priest from St Patrick's at Church Hill. Fathers McDonald and Lynch regularly visited ships berthed at Pyrmont, focusing on the Catholic Goanese crew. The Goans would have been particularly welcoming to a priest, who could boast of being pastor of a church dedicated to the Portuguese Jesuit missionary of Asia, Saint Francis Xavier, whose body was venerated in the Cathedral of Goa. At the end of his ministry at St Bede's, William McDonald was thanked for his assistance by the chaplain, Father Jeffcott, with the gift of a pipe and tobacco pouch, 'as a mark of appreciation for valuable services rendered in visiting seamen on ships and attending to their spiritual needs . . . The assistance afforded by Rev. Father Lynch to the untiring efforts of Father McDonald whilst in the Pyrmont parish was specially praised'.[41] This informal involvement in the seafarers' mission would be formalised with the combining of the chaplaincy with the role of Pyrmont parish priest in 1958.

In 1923 William McDonald had been appointed spiritual director of the Catholic Debating Societies Union. This was a role he continued throughout his priestly ministry. At Pyrmont, while he was busy with the Sydney-wide organisation, his curate James Lynch took charge of the local group. Debating between parish teams was a popular past-time among young Catholics during the 1920s and 30s.

McDonald's diary reported the removal of one of the causes of Pyrmont dirt and pollution—the macadamised street surfacing. The P&O Steamship Company whose ships berthed at Pyrmont asked the Municipal Council for better roads for access to and from the wharves. Father McDonald lent his weight to the proposal of woodblocking—he wrote to the city health officer complaining about air pollution on behalf of the children of the parish.[42] The replacement of the macadamised surface took place in Pyrmont and Union Streets and in Jones Bay Road. The other causes of pollution, the power station and sugar refinery, persisted and grew.

In August 1930 one of the most prominent parishioners of St Bede's, William Armstrong, died at his residence above the *Butcher's Arms* hotel, on the corner of Harris Street and Bridge Road. He had been a generous benefactor of Catholic charities and institutions in Sydney and beyond. For 35 years he had been the publican of the *Butcher's Arms*, 'which he

---

41. *Freeman's Journal*, 30 July 1928.
42. William McDonald, Diary 1927–1931, manuscript (McDonald file, SAA).

conducted with such consideration for his neighbour and such an obtrusive and abounding charity, that on his death he was accorded a more largely attended funeral than has ever before taken place in Pyrmont.[43] Father McDonald celebrated the Solemn Requiem Mass in the parish church, assisted by the curate James Lynch. Former parish priests, James Furlong and Philip McIntyre, returned to Pyrmont to honour the deceased. He was survived by his wife, six sons and four daughters, two of whom later joined the Little Company of Mary, known affectionately as the 'Blue Nuns'. William Armstrong's passing was noted in the sporting journal *Referee*, under the heading 'Raced a Few Horses'.[44]

The Armstrong sisters, Mary and Noreen, had each commenced a career—Mary in physiotherapy; Noreen as a secretary—and were often mentioned in the social columns of Sydney newspapers, before entering the convent in 1934 and 1942, at the ages of 22 and 25. Mary, Sister Rosalie, served as a nurse in various capacities in hospitals of the Order in Australia and New Zealand, dying at the age of 93 in 2006. Noreen, Sister Helen, served as nurse and administrator in all the Order's hospitals in Australia, predeceasing her older sister in 2000 at the age of 83. Both these 'Pyrmont girls', raised at the *Butcher's Arms*, are remembered with affection by members of the Little Company of Mary 'as women of spirit, deep commitment, piercing intelligence and who loved constructive debate'.[45]

In September 1930 James Lynch was transferred to Cronulla as curate. He was farewelled at a crowded function in St Bede's school rooms. Pyrmont's new curate, Father Patrick Treacy Boland, was present and was made welcome. But after just three weeks a smaller group of parishioners gathered to farewell him to his new placement at Drummoyne. His was the briefest clerical appointment in the history of St Bede's. In 1940 Boland joined the Australian Infantry Force as a chaplain, serving in the Mediterranean theatre and later in the Pacific. On his return to the Archdiocese at the end of the war, he was appointed as Parish Priest of Balmain, where he served for 27 years. In 1947 he was awarded the Order of the British Empire for his wartime service. He died in November 1998.

There was great celebration in the parish of St Bede in December 1930, as trumpeted in the *Catholic Times*: 'The first native of the district of Pyrmont to be ordained to the priesthood is a distinction enjoyed by Rev. Father J F O'Toole (son of Mr and Mrs Joe O'Toole), who was raised to that dignity in the Cathedral on the first of the month.'[46] Joseph and Mary Therese O'Toole

---

43. 'Obituary: MR WILLIAM ARMSTRONG', *Freeman's Journal*, 21 August 1930.
44. *Referee*, 20 August 1930.
45. Information communicated to author by email from LCM Provincialate, 2 April 2015.
46. *Catholic Press*, 18 December 1930.

had raised their family of nine children at 41 Point Street, in a house leased from the Macarthur foundation, the Camden Park Estate Limited. Joseph had begun his working life as a carrier with his own horses and carts and in 1916 he purchased three trucks and founded the Austral Sawdust Company, collecting sawdust from the seven timber mills at Pyrmont and selling it to butchers for their floors and to grocers for packaging. In 1930 the O'Toole clan, all children or grandchildren of Tobias and Elizabeth, was scattered in households throughout Pyrmont, in Harris, Cross, Scott, John, Little John, Harvey, McCredie, Point, Bowman, Bunn and Pyrmont streets and in Paternoster Row, Bulwara Road and Ways Terrace.[47] Over the next decades Pyrmont would lose all its O'Tooles as the families relocated to more salubrious Sydney suburbs.

The 1930 ordination class from St Patrick's National Seminary at Manly was twenty-four strong, with six seminarians ordained for Sydney, the rest being for other Australian dioceses. John Francis O'Toole's first Mass was celebrated at St Bede's on the morning of Tuesday 2 December, the day after the ordination ceremony in St Mary's Cathedral. Parish children made their First Holy Communion at the Mass, which was followed by a celebratory breakfast in the school-hall. The O'Toole tribe and parishioners gathered again in the evening as reported in the newspaper: 'It was a happy gathering, with Father McDonald presiding. In an address he said they had come together to honour the first priest of the parish, who, with his family, was loved by the people, as the ceremonies that morning had indicated.' Visiting clergy spoke in praise of the newly-ordained—a proud Father McIntyre who had baptised him, the two most recent curates, James Lynch and Treacy Boland and one of his fellow seminarians, Louis Tosi, who 'prayed that many young men of the Pyrmont parish would follow his example'.[48] That was a prayer which is yet to be answered as the sesquicentenary approaches. In the centenary booklet Father Victor Doyle claimed another Pyrmont vocation, Philip James Reeve of the 1926 ordination year, whose parents had 'a mixed foods business in Bunn St (since demolished)'.[49] However the family's stay in Pyrmont seems to have been very brief. The 'Secular Clergy Personal Information Form' completed by Father Reeve in 1937 indicated that he had attended a series of convent schools—Surry Hills, Pyrmont, Leichhardt, Glebe and Erskineville—and high school at Christian Brothers, Lewisham.[50] Pyrmont's claim on him as a local vocation could be challenged by several other parishes.

---

47. *City Assessment Book*, Pyrmont Ward 1930 (City of Sydney Archives: http://photosau.com.au/CosRates/scripts/home.asp, accessed January 21 2015)
48. *Catholic Press*, 18 December 1930.
49. Doyle, *Centenary*, 26.
50. Secular Clergy Personal Information Form 1937 (Reeve file, SAA)

The day after Father John O'Toole's first Mass at St Bede's it was Ultimo's turn to honour the newly ordained. The following Saturday he baptised a niece at St Bede's. In January he was entertained by the Pyrmont Debating Union and presented with 'a beautiful enlargement of the group photo taken of those present at his ordination breakfast'.[51] That photograph was presented to the parish many years later by the O'Toole family in memory of Father John, and it now hangs in a place of honour at the rear of the church, alongside a portrait of Archbishop John Bede Polding and a 1915 photograph of John's older brothers Tobias and Michael dressed as altar-boys.

Father O'Toole, now stationed at Belmore, made other return visits to St Bede's, both sad and happy. In February he presided at the Requiem Mass for his 23-year-old sister Kitty: 'The Relatives and Friends of Mr and Mrs JOSEPH O'TOOLE and FAMILY, of Point-street, Pyrmont, and of RICHARD LEWIN, are kindly invited to attend the Funeral of their beloved adopted DAUGHTER and SISTER, and his Friend, Catherine (Kitty); to leave St Bede's Church, Pyrmont, THIS TUESDAY, after Requiem Mass, commencing at 9 a.m., for Catholic Cemetery, Rookwood.'[52] The following month he baptised a nephew, and at the end of June joined parishioners in farewelling Father McDonald and welcoming the incoming pastor Daniel Hannan.[53] In October he returned to conduct the Requiem Mass of his father. The *Catholic Press* paid tribute to the deceased in an obituary:

> The recent death in St Vincent's Hospital of Mr Joseph O'Toole, took from the Pyrmont district an estimable parishioner who consistently coupled with devotion to his religious duties a generous activity on behalf of the parish and individuals in need. The Catholicity and charity of the deceased were only two of the aspects of a lovable type of man, whose personality endeared him to all his acquaintances. His upright character and kindness were nowhere more successful than in his own family, the members of which owe much to the good example of their father, and a loving mother who survives him. Mr O'Toole was an active member of the local conference of St Vincent de Paul Society, and, without notice, did a great amount of good.[54]

Fr John O'Toole's remarkable qualities were acknowledged in an unprecedentedly lengthy and glowing report of his farewell from Belmore parish. A neighbouring priest commented: 'Rarely a priest, said Father

---

51. *Catholic Press*, 22 January 1931.
52. *Sydney Morning Herald*, 24 February 1931.
53. *Catholic Press*, 9 July 1931.
54. *Catholic Press*, 15 October 1931.

Sheehy, got such a eulogy at the completion of his first charge after his ordination (Applause). It is, he said, more rarely still that a young priest deserves it.' His parish priest said that 'Father O'Toole was kindness itself, while his tact and courtesy brought peace and happiness everywhere'. The president of the local Vincent de Paul Society was a former Pyrmont parishioner and he reminisced about the O'Toole family: 'Mr A Meaney, president, spoke in a reminiscent vein when he recalled his early association, with Father O'Toole's family in the Ultimo and Pyrmont district, where they as stalwarts of the Church were ever to the fore in promoting everything that was best in the cause of religion, of education and charity. They, he said, carried out the best traditions of the Irish Catholics (Applause).'[55]

John's new appointment was to the Stanmore parish where, unsurprisingly, he made a big initial impact. However, after just seven months, following a series of unexplained fainting collapses, he was admitted to Lewisham Hospital suffering from a brain tumour. He was officially on sick leave from November 1935, being well enough briefly to act as chaplain at St Joseph's College at the commencement of the 1937 school year. After three years in and out of hospital, during which he underwent three operations and endured intense suffering, John O'Toole died on 19 August 1938, having just turned thirty. The Requiem was attended by 118 priests. Archbishop Norman Gilroy preached the panegyric during which he referred movingly to the O'Toole family: 'We shall likewise pray, continued his Grace, that God will comfort and console his beloved family. They had learned lessons from him that surely would influence their whole life, because they saw him day after day in his sufferings with never a word of complaint, and when they saw him so courageous they were inspired to bear their own cross with patience.'[56]

Father James Freeman, who had spoken at the Belmore farewell event and described himself as a 'college mate' of John O'Toole, both at St Mary's Cathedral College and St Patrick's College Manly, spoke movingly of his mate 'Johnny' in his weekly radio programme broadcast by radio station 2SM in August 1949. The theme of that programme was vocations to the priesthood. He spoke of a young man called Johnny, whom he 'remembered best for the graceful ease with which he could climb into a breaker on any beach and fly homewards with the foam all around him and the salt air on his face'. This was a reference to the O'Toole family custom of escaping Pyrmont and spending the long summer holidays at a beach house at Curl Curl on Sydney's northern beaches. Freeman commented that entering the seminary, Johnny 'said goodbye to the family that he loved most affectionately, took

---

55. *Catholic Freeman's Journal*, 11 April 1935.
56. *Catholic Freeman's Journal*, 25 August 1938.

one last look around the home that still meant so much to him and the first chapter of his life was closed'. The second chapter was concluded with his ordination at the early age of twenty-two. In his priestly ministry 'he learned from personal experience the triumphs and the disasters, the joys and heartbreaks, the wisdom and the foolishness that worked and played in the hearts of his fellow men'. But 'it so happened that the chapter which had scarcely opened was already destined to close':

> At last there came the day as it had to come when Johnny knew that the last chapter was closing too ... So on a bright sunny afternoon I sat beside his bed while he discussed plans that he himself could never fulfil ... Manly in everything he was never more a man than in those closing days. He suffered a lot without complaining. He still retained his sense of humour if only because he had increased his sanctity. The lustre had gone from his perfect physical frame but the brightness still lingered in his eyes ... So the athlete laid aside his games, the young man laid aside his earthly dream, the priest laid down his responsibilities, and calmly and quietly Johnny died ... It is a simple story of a young Australian who followed a vocation, followed it with loyalty and integrity as long as he was allowed and then laid down the charge when his Master called. It is simply the story of devotion and courage.[57]

James Darcy Freeman became Archbishop of Sydney in 1971 following the retirement of Cardinal Norman Thomas Gilroy. He received the cardinal's red hat in 1973. John O'Toole's last surviving sibling, Phillip Bede, who retained a great love of the family's parish church of St Bede, died, aged 94, in 2007, on the same August day of his brother John's death 69 years before.

Father McDonald continued alone in the Pyrmont presbytery after the departure of short-term curate Treacy Boland until his own transfer in June 1931 to Cronulla as parish priest, where he was welcomed by James Lynch who had been administering the parish since April. Archbishop Kelly's letter of appointment was very complimentary of William McDonald's ministry at St Bede and St Francis Xavier. In it he wrote that he regarded his term of office at Pyrmont as most fruitful from the spiritual point of view, especially for the visiting seamen.[58] In September 1933, he was appointed priest-in-charge of St Raphael's at South Hurstville. He often returned to St Bede's for funerals and celebrations, including the golden jubilee of the St Bede's Vincent de Paul Conference in 1939 and the conferring of a papal knighthood on Maurice O'Dwyer in 1954. William McDonald died in the

---

57. James Freeman, transcript of 2SM broadcast, 14 August 1949 (O'Toole file, SAA).
58. Kelly to McDonald, 4 June 1931 (McDonald file, SAA).

parish of South Hurstville, which he had served for 31 years, in November 1964, aged 75.

Chapter 19
Still a Mission District

William McDonald's successor was Daniel Hannan. This change marked a return to Irish rule in the Pyrmont mission district. Daniel was born in Listowel in County Kerry. He was a student at Collegium Omnium Sanctorum, as he chose to call All Hallows, and while there also attended the National University of Ireland, gaining a Bachelor of Arts degree in June 1913. He was ordained in 1917 and arrived in Sydney with two other Irish priests in October 1918, a month before the armistice ending the First World War. His first assignment was to Camperdown, a name that would have rankled with any Irishman with a sense of history. The defeat of the Dutch navy at Kamperduin by the British was one of the events preventing the French from landing troops in Ireland in support of the 1798 rebellion. Governor William Bligh, present at the battle as captain of HMS *Director*, imposed the anglicised Dutch name on his extensive landholdings just west of Sydney. The grant of land to the Catholic mission in the area was the only part of the former Bligh estate not designated for the campus of the University of Sydney.

In 1921 Hannan was at Wollongong and in 1924 he was back in Sydney at Kogarah. In February 1928 parishioners gathered to farewell him on a return trip to Ireland after nine years in Australia. Present was the secretary to the Apostolic Delegate, the Rev Dr N T Gilroy, who would become Archbishop of Sydney in 1940. In response to the speeches of appreciation and farewell Daniel Hannan made some observations about Australian Catholics: 'One thing he took particular notice of was the fact that the Australian Catholics never failed to honour their priests, and never let an opportunity go by without showing their appreciation of the Catholic faith . . . To the children attending the school he wished to say they were a credit to their teachers and the homes they came from. It was a pleasure to receive their daily greeting— Good morning, God bless you, Father!'[1]

1. *Freeman's Journal*, 1 March 1928.

On his return in January 1929 he was placed in charge of the district of Baulkham Hills, where he was a neighbour of Michael Macnamara, from whose parish at North Parramatta the Baulkam Hills parish of St Michael had been formed. It was from this semi-rural environment two years later that he was 'promoted to the charge of the large and important parish of Pyrmont-Ultimo'.[2] At the farewell, Father Macnamara 'spoke of the guest's unassuming manner, his diligent attention to duty, and his hard and successful work, qualities evidently noted and appreciated by his Grace, as shown by his promotion'. Macnamara, who in 1901 had not considered his own move from Kogarah to Pyrmont as a promotion, did not explain how the move of his neighbour to Pyrmont thirty years later was such. Father Hannan was especially thanked for his support of the deaf mute institute at Castle Hill conducted by the Christian Brothers and St Michael's Orphanage run by the Sisters of Mercy, interests he carried with him for the rest of his life. He handed over St Michael's to William McNally former curate at Pyrmont.

Daniel Hannan made his first appearance at Pyrmont at the farewell for his popular predecessor. His letter of appointment indicated that Pyrmont was still a mission district and had not joined the growing list of canonically formal parishes with irremovable parish priests. Archbishop Kelly's letter expressed every confidence that Hannan's ministry as Pastor of Pyrmont would be most beneficial both spiritually and temporally to the good people of the district.[3]

Within weeks of his arrival the Archbishop paid a Sunday visit to the parish and preached at the 9.30 Mass. He had a message for this industrial suburb hit hard by the onset of the Great Depression: 'Remember that the sufferings of this life were not worthy to be compared with the joys of the next that were in store for all those who loved and served God.' He later presided at a meeting of the church committee and encouraged them to work hard for the reduction of the parochial debt, quoting St Ignatius: 'Work as if everything depended on you, and pray as if everything depended on God.'[4] Work for most men in Pyrmont and Ultimo had always been casual and erratic and often hard to find. Unemployment rates were high even before the depression began to have its impact. But the situation worsened dramatically in the 1930s, even becoming desperate for many households. Even casual jobs on the waterfront, in the quarries and at the sugar refinery dried up, with the result that rents fell into arrears and evictions were threatened. The local conference of the Vincent de Paul Society under its president, Michael

---

2. *Catholic Press*, 9 July 1931.
3. Kelly to Hannan, 4 June 1931 (Hannan file, SAA).
4. *Catholic Press*, 2 July 1931.

Weslan, and secretary, Maurice O'Dwyer, was busy responding, where possible, to an increasing number of needy households. The local St Bede debating union kept up its range of sporting and social activities, helping parishioners put aside their worries for a few hours.

In February of the New Year, Father Hannan organised a harbour outing for the boys of St Gabriel's at Baulkam Hills. His continuation of Father McDonald's part-time ministry of visiting ships docked at Pyrmont put him in touch not only with Goan sailors, but also with ships' officers. With these he arranged for a tour of inspection for the boys of the liners in the harbour:

> Through the efforts and courtesy of Rev Father Hannan, of Pyrmont, an invitation came along to the boys to pay a visit of inspection on board the great liner of the P and O—the *Mooltan*. Several of the Christian Brothers accompanied the boys. The visitors were met at Pyrmont by their old friend, Father Hannan, and no time was lost in getting on board. One of the chief officers took the party in hand and in very painstaking fashion gave a most detailed and interesting explanation of the signalling, steering and many other apparatus which make the Mooltan and other big vessels veritable wonders . . . Nothing escaped the notice of these boys. The size of the funnels, the links of the anchor chains; each detail was of interest. They tested the comfort of the saloon chairs, etc., and seemed charmed. Their walk through the crew's quarters was quite a revelation. To see an altar with flowers and lights, made them forget they were on board ship.[5]

The visit concluded with a lavish afternoon tea which the boys devoured. The event was such a success that it was repeated in July with a visit to the navy cruiser HMAS *Canberra*, this time with the assistance of the official port chaplain, the Marist Father Aloysius Jeffcott.

In October 1934, a member of the prominent Pyrmont Catholic family, the Armstrongs, described as a 'hotelkeeper', won pre-selection as Labor Party candidate for the seat of Glebe in the upcoming State elections, defeating the sitting member, Tom Keegan, who had been a member of the Legislative Assembly since 1910. As noted by the historian of the Glebe Labor Party, Michael Hogan: 'There is some confusion about the identity of the Armstrong mentioned here. One report mentions J A Armstrong, another refers to W J Armstrong, while the future Senator and likely candidate was J I Armstrong.'[6] Family members confirm that it was John Ignatius Armstrong, and not his publican brother William, who had won the

---
5. *Catholic Press*, 10 March 1932.
6. Michael Hogan, *Local Labor. A history of the Labor Party in Glebe 1891–2003* (Sydney, 2004), 227 n 34.

controversial pre-selection.[7] The Party Executive declared the Armstrong election 'null and void following a protest challenging the continuity of the winner', and arranged another ballot. This second round, from which Armstrong withdrew, was not without incident:

> The Labor ballot for the selection of the candidate for the Glebe seat at the next State elections came to an abrupt finish on Saturday when a number of dissatisfied league members, who had been disfranchised, threw a bucket of water into the ballot box at the Pyrmont polling booth, drenching the ballot papers. 'We wanted to make sure that it was a clean ballot,' one of the disfranchised members said last night. 'We are confident now that it is the cleanest ballot the Labor party has ever held.'[8]

The Party Executive did not risk a third ballot and proceeded to endorse a new candidate who easily held the safe Labor seat.

In March 1935 Daniel Hannan was moved from Pyrmont and received the longed-for appointment as irremovable rector. Achbishop Kelly, in the letter of appointment, wished for Daniel success in his new posting at Watson's Bay as Rector Inamovibilis. The Archbishop recommended that Hannan pay special attention to pastoral visitation and the reduction of parochial debt, and he prayed that his new labours would be blessed by Providence with abundant fruits.[9] In 1960 he was granted the honour of being appointed a Papal Domestic Prelate, with the right to bear the title 'Monsignor'. In April 1962 he applied for and was granted the vacant parish of Clovelly. Ten years later, in April 1970, he resigned and returned to Ireland for retirement. He died at the age of 94 in July 1986 at his home town of Listowel, in the 'Kingdom of Kerry', as he was wont to call his home county. The *Catholic Weekly* obituary commented that 'he was still playing golf until three or four years ago'. It quoted a priest colleague: 'He was a very earnest, a very sensitive priest . . . a fine man, he had a very dry sense of humour.'[10]

Replacing Daniel Hannan at Pyrmont was Austin Bradstreet. Born in 1896 in the old gold-mining town of Hill End in the Bathurst Diocese, he was the son of the local public school teacher. Mr Bradstreet's various appointments led the family through a range of country towns, including Batlow, Hill End, Lake Cargelligo, Wilberforce and Dural. Austin entered the seminary at Manly and was ordained in 1919. His first appointment was to Maroubra, then, after two years, to St Benedict's, George Street West. In 1923 he was sent south to Moss Vale, then to Parramatta. There in 1924 he

---

7. Paul Armstrong, email to the author, 18 February 2015.
8. *Sydney Morning Herald*, 19 November 1934.
9. Kelly to Hannan, 7 March 1935 (Hannan file SAA).
10. *Catholic Weekly*, 23 July 1986.

had a motor cycle accident as reported in the local paper: 'An unfortunate accident happened to the Rev. Father Bradstreet, of St Patrick's Church, Parramatta, on Saturday morning last. It appears he was riding a motor cycle along Sydney-road, and when near Hampstead-road, Auburn, he collided with Tweedie's motor bus with such force as to sustain a fractured leg. He was removed in a motor lorry to St Joseph's Hospital, where he is reported to be doing well.'[11]

His recovery was slower than anticipated and he was not ready for re-appointment until November, when he was sent to Mascot. After an unusually lengthy stretch of seven years there as assistant, he was given charge of the Richmond district in June 1931. Austin brought to his mission a creative approach to fund-raising. He organised a 'popular girl competition' in which four parish girls would compete to raise the most money for the needs of the parish. At the social organised as a climax for the competition, the winner presented Fr Bradstreet with 'a handsome cigarette box well supplied with "soothers" in remembrance of his support for all the candidates'. The newspaper report gave him full marks: 'The Rev Father Bradstreet, who has charge of the parish of Richmond and Kurrajong, has, though only a comparatively short time in the district, won the goodwill and affection of his people, who have come to regard him as the ideal "Soggarth Aroon", and are working in a whole-hearted effort to assist him in the good works that he has undertaken.'[12]

In March 1935 he received a transfer from a district 'with such a charming combination of rustic life and rural scenes' to industrial Pyrmont. When Austin returned to Richmond for a farewell, he spoke of the contrast between the two parishes:

> An ovation greeted Father Bradstreet as he rose to speak. He thanked the people for their expressions of esteem, and rejoiced that the parish was holding its own. He went on to express his gratitude to his many loyal helpers, both in Richmond and Kurrajong, and regretted having to leave their beautiful district. He would surely revisit it. He found a marked contrast in his surroundings at Pyrmont, a congested area, where the people were poor. It was surprising the proportion of Catholics there. His area stretched from St Benedict's to the Harbour, taking in the wharves, warehouses and shipping. It was part of his duty to visit the boats, and that morning he had celebrated Mass at 5am on the *Moultan* [sic].

---

11. *The Cumberland Argus and Fruitgrowers Advocate*, 24 May 1924.
12. *Catholic Freeman's Journal*, 19 April 1934.

The local mayor was at the farewell and said how pleased he was to honour their guest, whom he had known as a boy 28 years ago, when the Bradstreet family lived in the schoolmaster's house at Dural.[13]

Austin would have barely had time to adjust to the smells of Pyrmont—the sour smell of milk from the dairies, the sweet smell of molasses from the Colonial Sugar Refinery, the stench of smoke and soot from the power stations—when his nostrils were assailed by the smell of the smoke and his eyes stung by tiny fragments of charred wool from the raging fire at the huge Goldsbrough Mort Woolstore. The *Sydney Morning Herald* reported after four days of burning:

> Last night a strong south-easterly breeze caused the flames to shoot up again, and they could be seen from all parts of the city. Up to a late hour it was not considered necessary to send reinforcements. Residents of the outer suburbs, as far as ten miles away from Pyrmont, have reported that they have been kept awake at night by the smell of the fire, and that tiny charred fragments of wool, which were apparently carried into the upper atmosphere with the smoke, are still descending.[14]

The wool-stores were highly inflammable because of the lanolin in the wool which soaked into the wooden floors. Fires were a regular occurrence in Pyrmont and Ultimo. The Goldsbrough Mort ruin smouldered for two weeks.

Austin Bradstreet brought to Pyrmont a variation of his successful fund-raising initiative—he organised a 'popular man competition'. The competitors came from three prominent parish families—Armstrong, Conlon and Cronin. John Ignatius Armstrong, whose brother William had succeeded their father as publican of the *Butchers Arms*, was the newly elected alderman for Phillip Ward, which he would represent until 1948. Each gentleman competitor had an organisational committee to assist, and they set to work over three months to raise money for the parish. The result was outstanding:

> Notwithstanding the great amount of unemployment in this industrial centre, the willingness manifested by supporters resulted in the splendid amount of £340 being collected during the three months. For a small parish this was a remarkable achievement, brought about by the holding of motor drives, euchre parties, dances, harbour excursions and house parties, the organisations of which showed the self sacrifice maintained

---

13. *Catholic Press*, 11 April 1935.
14. *Sydney Morning Herald*, 28 September 1935.

by the respective committees... Father Bradstreet must feel highly elated at the success of his first venture, and it is hoped that the same success attends the further ideas he is already forming for the future.[15]

One of Austin's young Ultimo parishioners wrote to the children's page of the *Catholic Press* in August 1936 giving a glimpse of parish life:

Dear Erica, This is my first letter to the 'Catholic Press'. My father gets it every week, and I like reading the Children's Page. I go to St Francis Xavier's School, Ultimo, and I am in fourth class. We have a new Sister teaching us. She came from Melbourne, and we all like her very much. We get prizes for mental arithmetic, dictation and cleanliness. We get so excited to see who is going to win. I often get one, and am pleased. Thirty children made their First Communion on Sunday, August 9. They looked heavenly, and we all went, too, in memory of our First Communion Day. The church was crowded, and Father Bradstreet gave a beautiful sermon. After Mass the children had a nice breakfast prepared for them in the school room by the Sisters. It had a lovely cake in the middle, with First Communion written in gold. Cheerio dear Erica. From your loving little friend, GLADYS O'KEEFE.[16]

In June 1937 there was a change in the governance of the Sydney archdiocese with the unexpected resignation of Michael Sheehan from his position as coadjutor archbishop with right of succession to Michael Kelly. Ecclesiastical speculation was that he had been informed by the Apostolic Delegate that the Holy See wanted an Australian to succeed to Sydney, and that his resignation was demanded. The previous month Justin Simonds had been consecrated and sent to Hobart as the first Australian-born archbishop. The attitude of Sheehan's fellow bishops to his resignation was made evident in a formal address prior to his departure: 'The news of your resignation, which came to us without warning through the daily Press, filled us all with sorrow and consternation.'[17] The 13 Irish-born among the 22 episcopal signatories would have been the ones feeling the 'sorrow and consternation'. The letter was reputed to have been written by Daniel Mannix who had travelled from Melbourne to be present at the farewell. He had successfully been resisting the pressure from Archbishop Giovanni Panico, the Apostolic Delegate, to accept an Australian coadjutor archbishop in Melbourne. The story was told in clerical circles that on one occasion in Melbourne, Panico was waxing enthusiastic about the day when Australia would have its first

---

15. *Catholic Press*, 17 October 1935.
16. *Catholic Press*, 17 August 1936.
17. *Catholic Press*, 1 July 1937.

native-born Archbishop. In reply Mannix, with biting wit, replied that he looked forward to the day when Australia would have its first native-born Apostolic Delegate. Sheehan uncharacteristically adopted Mannix's sharp wit when, at Auckland on his return journey to Europe, pressed about his future, he replied that 'he would act as Apostolic Delegate to the diocese of Germia'.[18] Germia was his titular See in Turkey. Mannix continued to taunt Panico. At the banquet following the consecration of Melbourne priest Matthew Beovich as archbishop of Adelaide in 1940, Mannix boasted about his archdiocese's 'big export trade in bishops', and expressed his confidence that he could also supply an Australian-born apostolic delegate when the next vacancy occurred.[19] After Panico had finally imposed Justin Simonds as coadjutor archbishop with right of succession in Melbourne in 1942, the 78 year old Mannix showed his disdain by refusing to consider resignation; he died at the age of 99 in 1963.

In Sydney, Sheehan was replaced one week after his departure by Norman Thomas Gilroy, the 41-year-old, Glebe-born, bishop of Port Augusta, the second most junior among Australia's bench of bishops. As a 19-year-old he had been present at the Gallipoli landing as a junior wireless officer on the transport *Hessen*, which was carrying 100 troops and 400 horses. Unlike Sheehan he could not recite the rosary in Gaelic, but his talents did include riding a camel, which he had learnt to do in the desert regions of South Australia.

The involvement of the Pyrmont priests with the seafarers' chaplaincy became a regular part of their ministry in the 1930s. The attendance of Father Bradstreet at the annual meetings of the Catholic Institute of Seamen was noted in each year of his stay at Pyrmont, and his assistance in the ministry was always acknowledged by the seafarers' chaplain, Father Aloysius Jeffcott. At the 1937 gathering the chaplain announced that a window dedicated to the memory of the Marist Father Peter Piquet, who had died in 1936, had been installed in the chapel: 'The cost of the window had been met by the contributions of the seamen, who realised all that Father Piquet had done for them.'[20] The chapel had been described in 1931 as a 'devotional little oratory' on the top storey of the Catholic Seamen's Mission and commanding 'a view of the lovely old harbor'.[21] The view across Darling Harbour to Pyrmont was obscured by the installation of stained-glass windows in 1937. The Piquet window depicted the Sacred Heart, with the text: 'Most Sacred Heart of Jesus have mercy on all seafarers'. There was a matching window depicting the Blessed Virgin Mary, with the inscription: 'Star of the Sea pray for

---

18. *Sydney Morning Herald*, 29 June 1937.
19. *Southern Cross*, 12 April 1940.
20. *Catholic Press*, 13 May 1937.
21. *Catholic Press*, 12 March 1931.

us'. Both windows were created in the Sydney studio of John Ashwin and Company, owned since 1920 by the company's chief designer, Polish born John Radecki. The windows were relocated to St Bede's when the Kent Street building was demolished in 1983. The Marian window had been donated to the Seamen's Institute by the St Raphael Conference of St Vincent de Paul at South Hurstville, at the urging of the priest-in-charge, William McDonald, formerly of Pyrmont.

At the 1938 annual meeting of the Institute, Rev Dr Eris O'Brien, recently returned from studies in Belgium, responded to the chaplain's report with an appeal for funds, in which he identified the growing menace of Adolf Hitler:

> As Catholics, you take your membership in the universal Apostolate of the Sea as the most ordinary of your duties, but the Hitlerian philosophy would contend that you were disloyal if you let your sympathy go out beyond your own country. The Catholic is trained to regard the world as his home and all the men as his brothers. When I read in your report that your Catholic institute received during the past year 15,000 Britishers, 2500 Germans, and hundreds of Italians, Norwegians, Goanese, Dutch, Americans, Swedes, French and Chinese—when I read these facts I can understand a little more clearly why Hitler fears that Catholics can never become the petty minded, parochial Germans that he wants them to become.[22]

Austin Bradstreet's term at Pyrmont came to an end in January 1939, when he was transferred to Chatswood as administrator during the absence overseas of the parish priest. His last duty at St Bede's was to preside at the end of year school concert and prize-giving. The event was honoured by the presence of the Mother Provincial of the Good Samaritans and Sisters from Rosebank College, Five Dock and St Scholastica's, Glebe. As well as Christmas carols and the usual repertoire of Irish melodies, the children performed an unusual little sketch, 'The Three Months and Napoleon's Farewell'. The item would have recounted the three month siege of Paris in 1814 which led to Napoleon's abdication, his farewell to his troops and the departure into exile on the island of Elba. The link between the departure into exile of Napoleon and the departure of Bradstreet from Pyrmont, was left to the imagination. The concert was concluded with 'a beautiful hymn to our Lady Help of Christians sung with great fervour by the school choir'. Father Bradstreet then gave out the prizes, some of which were sums of money for successful essays submitted to state-wide competitions.

---

22. *Catholic Press*, 12 May 1938.

Following his 'locum tenens' stint at Chatswood, Austin Bradstreet was assigned to Picton, where there were four Mass centres—Picton, Menangle, Bargo and Douglas Park. In 1943 he was made parish priest of the inner Sydney parish of Golden Grove. Editions of the *Catholic Directory* from 1958 to 1963 listed Bradstreet as 'chaplain' at the St John of God Hospital at Concord. He was listed as curate at Hurstville from 1964 to 1966. He died in May 1966 at the age of 70. The obituary in the *Catholic Weekly* gave a different account of his final years: '[I]n February, 1957, he was appointed in charge of Mortlake. Father Bradstreet took ill while at Mortlake and spent some years on relieving duties when illness permitted. In 1965 his health improved and he was appointed to Westmead Boys' Home where his love for children had a wonderful effect on the boys.'[23] His Requiem Mass was celebrated at the Hurstville parish church.

After Austin Bradstreet's transfer from Pyrmont, Coadjutor Archbishop Norman Gilroy summoned back to Sydney a priest who in 1937 had been sent south to be the first priest-in-charge at the new district of Port Kembla. Gilroy had assumed most administrative duties of the Archdiocese from the aging and ailing Michael Kelly. He wrote to the Rev M J Ryan BA, giving a positive spin to the unexpected and perhaps unwelcome move, saying that the change to a long established and well developed city district would afford him greater scope for his zeal and well known activity in parochial undertakings, and would also enable him to resume his care and direction of the various cultural movements with which he was previously so closely associated. Gilroy was confident that St Bede's would be a convenient centre and meeting place for the members the Gaelic language movement.[24] The extra-parochial interests of Michael Joseph Ryan were in the promotion of Gaelic language and culture, which had been interrupted, perhaps deliberately, by his assignment away from Sydney to Port Kembla.

Michael Ryan was born in 1893 at Kilmacduagh in the Gaeltacht, the Gaelic speaking area of County Galway. After graduating as a Bachelor of Arts from the National University of Ireland, he prepared for ordination at All Hallows College. He left Ireland for Australia in 1920, at the height of the Anglo-Irish war, arriving in Sydney in April. A *Catholic Press* article in 1934 explained the unusual circumstances of his coming to Australia:

> While a student of the National University of Ireland Father Ryan became actively identified with the Gaelic League and Irish Volunteer movements. His outstanding work in both won him the friendship of their leaders and the hatred of their foes. Constantly under enemy

---

23. *Catholic Weekly*, 26 May 1966.
24. Gilroy to Ryan, 26 January 1939 (M J Ryan file, SAA).

surveillance, frequently arrested, occasionally 'on the run', he was one of those marked down for execution in 1920. His early departure for Australia that year saved him from the cruel fate meted out later to some of his comrades and friends.[25]

He would later refer to his being in Sydney as a bitter exile. This attitude and the circumstances of his being sent from Ireland were in marked contrast to those of the annual contingent of Irish priests arriving in Australia. They had volunteered for the Australian mission early in their seminary formation. They looked forward to rapid promotion in contrast to the long wait for the move from curate to parish priest in Ireland, and they could look forward to a year's holiday back home after ten years of ministry in the antipodes. In many instances they already had family and townsmen in Australia, and there was also the prospect of sponsoring further family arrivals. Some even had a network of priest-relatives, as was the case with the long-serving parish priest of Annandale, the Venerable Archpriest Edward Rohan, who had a brother, two nephews, three cousins, and two distant cousins working as priests in Australia. Rohan also had a sister, Mother Mary Berchman, at nearby St Scholastica's Good Samaritan Training College, Glebe Point.[26] Most Irish priests in Australia, while asserting a deep love of the 'old country', regarded themselves as at home in the 'great southern land', and not as exiles. Michael Ryan would complain that his Irish colleagues' professed love of Ireland did not include any interest in Gaelic language and culture, stating that 'there was much indifference from the Irish clergy' in Sydney.[27]

Within weeks of his arrival in Australia, Ryan was recruited by the Irish National Association to give a lecture at St Patrick's on 'Modern Irish Literature'. He used the opportunity to express admiration of the rebellion of Easter 1916 and its 'martyrs', and the current Sinn Fein war with the British forces: 'Father Ryan began his lecture with a few sentences in Gaelic. Then he went on to tell how the Gaelic League, under Dr Douglas Hyde, arrested the decay of the national language, which Britain sought to destroy, and in reviving Gaelic succeeded in putting a new and invincible spirit into the Irish people ... Padraic Pearse, in Father Ryan's opinion, expressed in the highest manner the new spirit.'[28] Such sentiments so publicly expressed would not have pleased the cautious Archbishop Kelly.

In 1921 Ryan established a Sydney branch of the Gaelic League and became its president: 'The Gaels of Australia have now an opportunity of responding to this call of Eamon de Valera by joining the Sydney branch

---

25. *Catholic Press*, 18 January 1934.
26. *Catholic Weekly*, 1 October 1953.
27. *Freeman's Journal*, 9 December 1926.
28. *Catholic Press*, 26 August 1920.

of the Gaelic League, which has been recently established.'[29] By the end of the year members were sufficient in number and enthusiasm, but not in Gaelic, for Michael Ryan to advertise a performance in English translation of Pearse's one act play, 'The Singer', which he would direct. He promoted the event with passion:

> 'The Singer' is the story of Pearse's life and death, told with the vision of a prophet. It is not a mere piece of writing, more literature. It is more. It is flesh and blood—a dream come true—the confession of faith that brought him to martyrdom . . . It is not sufficient to know that Pearse died for Ireland. The living words that fell from his lips must be drunk into the soul in order to see by what process of reasoning he brought himself to die for Ireland.[30]

In 1922 Ryan further emulated Padraig Pearse in founding, as Pearse had done in Dublin in 1908, a school for the study of Gaelic dedicated to St Enda, as described in the *Catholic Press*: 'St Enda's Gaelic School, 614 George street, Sydney, conducted by the Gaelic League, is performing a notable work. The president of the school is the Rev Father M J Ryan, BA.'[31]

In November 1922 Sydney welcomed the coadjutor archbishop Michael Sheehan. The Irish National Association hosted a special welcome for the Gaelic speaker. Father Ryan, who presided at the event, took the opportunity to slight the Irish and Irish-Australian hierarchies, especially the local archbishop, Michael Kelly: 'He stated that this was the first time that an Archbishop had paid them the honor of a visit, and not only was Dr Sheehan the first Archbishop to visit them, but he was the first Irish Archbishop who could speak in the language of his own country. No doubt, he was the only member of the Irish Hierarchy in Australia who could do so.'[32]

In 1928 Ryan and Sheehan joined forces in organising an 'Irish National Session' during the International Eucharistic Congress held in Sydney. Ryan delivered a paper in Irish on 'The History of the Early Church in Sydney as a Source of Inspiration for Catholic Literature and Art in Australia', which

---

29. *Catholic Press*, 28 April 1921.
30. *Catholic Press*, 22 December 1921. Pearse was one of the 'martyrs' of the 1916 Easter Rising in Dublin.
31. *Catholic Press*, 11 March 1926. An historian of the 1916 Easter Rising has recently described Pearse's school as a 'kind of madrasa of revolutionary nationalism' (Roy Foster, *Vivid Faces; The Revolutionary Generation in Irleand1890–1923* [London: 2015], 42). Saint Enda is the patron saint of the Aran Islands; he was a fifth-century warrior-king in Ulster, who converted to Christianity and founded a monastery on Great Aran. He is revered as the 'Patriarch of Irish monasticism'.
32. *Catholic Press*, 22 December 1922.

concluded with a plea for 'collecting and promoting a knowledge of the early Catholic history of Australia'.[33] He was also responsible for preparing the musical programme and several tableaux, one of which depicted 'Irish prisoners deported to Sydney after the 1798 Insurrection beseeching God, the Blessed Virgin and the Irish Saints, in specially composed and selected poems, to send them Priests, Mass and Sacraments'. Archbishop Sheehan presided at the event held at the Saint Benedict Hall.[34]

On St Patrick's Day in 1933 Ryan gave an address following the recitation of the Rosary in Gaelic led by Archbishop Sheehan. The theme of the talk was the ministry of the earliest Irish priests in Australia—the three transported because of alleged involvement in the 1798 rebellion and Father Jeremiah O'Flynn. He waxed lyrical in describing O'Flynn as 'that fearless apostle with a Gaelic speech as swift as a mountain torrent, as soft as the coo of a dove on an April dawn, and as sweet as music flowing o'er chords of gold'.[35]

In January 1934 it was announced that Father Ryan was returning to Ireland to visit his family, 'some of whose members are in a critical state of health as a result of injuries received in the late Black and Tan War'.[36] At his farewell address to the Gaelic League, he referred to his exile:

> Though many changes have taken place in Ireland during my exile, I shall not be disappointed in it, for I realise that it is not in the power of any one generation of our nation to undo the conquest of many centuries. To every generation its own deed. The generation of Irishmen to which I have the honour to belong has done its deed, and done it nobly, bravely and honourably. It was one of the great privileges conceded to me by Almighty God to have a share in its performance—a privilege which has given me a memory to sweeten the bitterness of an exile endured even for the greatest of all causes.[37]

He nominated one of his anticipated joys on arriving in Ireland: 'To revisit the 'Gaeltacht' (Irish-speaking area), which stands firmly with its back to the Atlantic rollers and its face to the foe, its stubborn soul still undefiled by the corroding poison of Anglicisation, stoutly resisting the inroads of the Conquest.' For Ryan the final liberation of Ireland still awaited the restoration of the short-lived republic of 1919—the abolition of Dominion status and the breaking of all ties with the British monarchy. This would not formally happen until 1949.

---

33. *Freeman's Journal*, 30 August 1928.
34. *Southern Cross*, 7 September 1928.
35. *Catholic Press*, 30 March 1933.
36. *Southern Cross*, 26 January 1934.
37. *Freeman's Journal*, 8 February 1934.

He was back in Sydney in March 1935 in time to present the prize cup in the St Patrick's Day Irish dancing competition.[38] Beyond this date there are no newspaper reports of his involvement in matters of Irish culture and language. He was placed at Surry Hills and was acting as administrator in March 1937 when he faced court on an assault charge:

> At the Central Summons Court today an information against Father Michael Ryan, parish priest of St Peter's Church, Surry Hills, was dismissed. The case was one in which Joseph James Murphy, of Surry Hills, alleged assault against Father Ryan. Murphy said that on February 24th he called at St Peter's presbytery and saw Father Ryan, who took him by the arm so that he (Murphy) could not protect himself, carried him out to the street, and threw him to the road, where he struck the back of his head. They had had an altercation following a dispute of some months standing between himself and Father Ryan. In pleading not guilty, Father Ryan informed the magistrate he had not seen the man before in his life. In addition, on the day in question he was at Coogee from 11 o'clock until 5 p.m.[39]

In some newspaper reports the 74 year old Murphy admitted to having had 'some drink' on the day of the alleged assault.[40] In the light of subsequent revelations the magistrate would have done well to ask about Father Ryan's state of sobriety on the day. It is not recorded whether Ryan and Murphy exchanged words in Gaelic. Following the court appearance Ryan was swiftly relocated to Port Kembla where, in September 1938, he was suspended for a relapse into drunkenness. Norman Gilroy wrote to him communicating the decision of Archbishop Kelly that, in view of the relapse causing public distrust, the decision was made to reactivate the former withdrawal of Faculties. The Archbishop declared himself unable to ignore the scandal caused by Ryan. He was ordered to go and make a good retreat at Waratah.[41] A rather naive Redemptorist retreat master, with little experience of alcoholics, wrote to Kelly from the Waratah monastery after Ryan's brief stay, expressing confidence in handing the patient, cured of his spiritual ills, back to the Archbishop.[42] Ryan himself wrote declaring that he had taken a life pledge never to let strong drink pass his lips. He was restored to Port Kembla two weeks after his suspension.

Within two months of arriving at the Pyrmont presbytery in February 1939, complaints about his behaviour were being received at St Mary's

---

38. *Catholic Freeman's Journal*, 21 March 1935.
39. *The Sun*, 3 March 1937.
40. *Maitland Daily Mercury*, 4 March 1937.
41. Gilroy to Ryan, 21 September 1938 (Ryan file SAA).
42. D. Mitchell to Kelly, nd (Ryan file SAA).

Cathedral. Late in March, Nellie O'Dwyer of 12 Bunn Street, wife of parish stalwart Maurice and an O'Toole cousin, took courage and wrote a letter to Archbishop Gilroy. She specifically asked for Ryan to be removed and she expressed a longing for another good priest like Fr Hannan.[43] The next day, in commissioning Archpriest Martin of Enmore to visit Pyrmont and make a report, Gilroy listed the complaints:

a. drinking,
b. abusing people,
c. having a loaded gun,
d. that last Sunday week, March 12, the Masses of the parish were said by a Franciscan Father,
e. that a non-Catholic living next door to the presbytery complained about the language used by Father Ryan and brought the police to the presbytery.[44]

The Archpriest's report, based on interviews with the presbytery housekeeper, a neighbour and the accused himself, exonerated Ryan.[45] However, Gilroy chose to believe the influential O'Dwyers over a timid housekeeper and the practiced denials of the alcoholic priest. Ryan was required immediately to submit his resignation, which was dutifully received on 29 March, two months after receipt of his letter of appointment. The forced resignation avoided the need for formal consideration of the visitator's report.

During April further evidence of Ryan's drunkenness at Pyrmont emerged in a letter from the prominent Marist Father Leon Chaize, chaplain at the Mater Hospital, North Sydney, and former Provincial of the North Solomon Islands mission. He recounted an incident at the hospital on the night of 21 March. At about 10.30pm a telephone call was received at the Mater Hospital from the house-keeper of the Pyrmont presbytery. The woman asked for a bed for Father Ryan who was under the influence of drink. The nurse asked if he was quiet, and being answered in the affirmative, she decided to admit him.[46] Chaize proceeded to describe what happened after Ryan arrived at the Mater by taxi. Far from being quiet, he immediately began shouting in the corridors and refusing to enter his assigned room. The chaplain emerged, followed by a surgeon. The surgeon was assaulted, but the chaplain warmly embraced. The surgeon called the police who packed Ryan into a taxi and sent him back to the presbytery, where the long-suffering housekeeper would have had to look after him.

---

43. O'Dwyer to Gilroy, 24 March (Ryan file SAA).
44. Gilroy to Martin, 25 March 1939 (Ryan file SAA).
45. Martin to Gilroy, 28 March 1939 (Ryan file SAA).
46. Chaize to Kelly, 24 April 1939 (Ryan file SAA).

Michael Ryan's subsequent career was punctuated by repeated relapses. After a month's hospitalisation at St Vincent's the kind parish priest of Granville agreed to accept him as curate, but in December he contacted the Cathedral to report that Father Ryan was intoxicated for two days and had acted aggressively. The Parish Priest had his troublesome curate transported to the long-suffering nuns at the Mater Hospital.[47] From the Mater he was required to present himself at St Joseph's Convalescent Home at Morisset, where, except for a very brief appointment to Redfern, he remained until 1948 when the facility passed from the supervision of the Sisters of the Little Company of Mary to the Brothers of St John of God, newly arrived from Ireland.

The Brothers had agreed to continue St Joseph's Home in conjunction with their main work of caring for disabled boys. The memorandum of agreement between the Order of St John of God and the sponsoring body, the St Vincent de Paul Society, stated the aims of the Morisset establishment:

> #3. Nature of Undertaking: The Special Work beforementioned is for the spiritual welfare, physical care and training of mentally deficient and sub-normal boys from the age of approximately 6 years.
> #14. Care of Sick Priests: In addition to the work beforementioned the Society agrees to the Brothers caring for sick priests. The Society further agrees that the admission, care and discharge of sick priests are to be matters entirely subject to agreement between the Ecclesiastical Superiors of the Priests concerned and the brothers.[48]

The Brothers were trained in the various works undertaken by the Order, which included care of alcoholics, as at their Stillorgan Hospital outside Dublin, where four of Sydney's Irish clergy would be lodged during the 1950s, and where Pyrmont's Patrick O'Donnell would die in 1972. The Brother Prior, Killian Herbert, was cautiously critical of the work of the Sisters with the 'convalescing' priests:

> Owing to the fact that the Sisters could not have frequent access to the bedrooms and day-rooms of the Priests a grave lack of discipline has crept in. The Priests are frequently seen around the village of Morisset in an inebriated condition—due no doubt to the fact that they slip away through the bush, and, as the place is rather rambling in its structure they are not easily missed . . . Some of the priests have not been sober for weeks owing to the surreptitious way in which they are able to get

---

47. Memo, 30 December 1939 (Ryan file, SAA).
48. *Memorandum of Agreement*, 12 January 1948 (St John of God Brothers file, SAA).

the liquor brought in. Your Eminence will agree that the position is not a good one, for the danger of scandal in the locality is very great.

Brother Killian announced that he had requested that a Brother experienced in dealing with alcoholics be sent from Ireland. He proposed to make the priests' quarters a separate unit with the Brother residing with the them. The hope was that with this arrangement the Brother could check up on visitors to the priests and also prevent, to the best of his ability, their daily excursions to the village.[49]

Following a brief, failed chaplaincy trial at St Gabriel's School for the deaf at Castle Hill, Ryan was returned in February 1948 to Morisset, now under the new regime. Within a month Brother Killian wrote to Archbishop Gilroy informing him that Michael Ryan was showing definite signs of Chronic Alcoholic Insanity and it would be advisable to have him admitted to a mental Home without delay. It was no longer a question of drink but real mental instability or dementia. Brother Killian stated that his earlier suggestion that Father Ryan might be sent to the Stillorgan Institute in Dublin would no longer work, for he was too mentally deteriorated to make the journey to Ireland on his own. Also, it was observed that part of his delusion was about Ireland, and Ryan himself would refuse to return go back.[50]

Perhaps the Irish Brother-Prior's final comment hinted at the source of the instability of the radical Irish nationalist priest. Despite the dire warning, Michael Ryan was given another chance by the ever-hopeful Gilroy with the long-suffering Christian Brothers and boys at St Gabriel's in August 1949. Within months he had been returned to Morisset, declaring to Cardinal Gilroy that he would now spend his time preparing for death. He died on 26 November 1965. In the obituary notice the *Catholic Weekly* referred to his many years of residence at St Joseph's Convalescent Home as 'chaplaincy'.

Even in the emergency situation of having to supply a resident priest to Pyrmont in March 1939 following Ryan's removal, Norman Gilroy displayed his accustomed attention to the minor details of church finances. In appointing James Mullin as temporary 'acting administrator' he cautioned that, if possible, endeavour not to use any of the Easter dues.[51] After one month a more stable appointment was made when Cletus Heffernan was sent from Penrith to St Bede's. A follow-up letter from Gilroy's secretary again expressed a preoccupation with Easter dues. Gilroy's detailed instructions to the new priest-in-charge concerning the dues were that he was to give to the Rev M J Ryan, recent Pastor of the Parish, a 1/6th share of the total amount which would be received from the date of the letter for the 1939 Easter Dues,

---

49. Br Killian to Gilroy, 16 December 1947 (St John of God Brothers file, SAA).
50. Br Killian to Gilroy, 10 March 1948 (St John of God Brothers file, SAA).
51. Gilroy to Mullin, 29 March 1939 (Mullin file, SAA).

the other 5/6 share would be distributed between Heffernan and Mullin, the acting Administrator, in a proportion to be determined by Heffernan.[52]

James Mullin, Cletus Heffernan and James Massey, who would succeed Heffernan at Pyrmont in 1944, were members of the Manly ordination class of 1925. Despite the steady stream of ordinations from St Patrick's seminary in the early twentieth century, the Sydney Archdiocese was still heavily dependent on an annual influx of Irish-trained priests, and this situation would continue into the 1930s. In 1922 the Archdiocese had 26 students in theology classes in Irish seminaries—fourteen at All Hallows, four at St Kieran's, Kilkenny, three at St Patrick's, Thurles, two at both St John's, Waterford and St Patrick's, Carlow, and one at St Peter's, Wexford. In the same year there were only eighteen Sydney theology students at Manly, spread over six classes, providing a maximum of only three ordinations per year. During the 1920s 'the number of priests coming to Sydney annually from Ireland normally outstripped the number being ordained locally'.[53] In the parish of Pyrmont, despite the intermittent appointment of Manly-trained pastors, beginning with William McDonald in 1927, the partial dependence on Irish clergy would continue until 1987.

---

52. O'Donnell to Heffernan, 6 May 1939 (Heffernan file, SAA).
53. KJ Walsh, *Yesterday's Seminary. A history of St Patrick's Manly* (Sydney, 1998), 232.

Chapter 20
At War Again

James Mullin, the temporary administrator sent in place of the disgraced Michael Ryan, was not in residence at Pyrmont long enough to have conducted a baptism; his name is absent from the baptismal register. An old-boy of St Mary's Cathedral College, he had been guest of honour, together with James Freeman and John O'Toole, at the 1933 Old Boys Union Ball. Leaving Pyrmont after just five weeks he did brief periods of 'locum tenens' work for the rest of 1939 in six different parishes. In 1940 he received his first parish at Thirroul, followed by Sans Souci in 1947 and Auburn in 1956. He died in the following year at the age of 54. His seminary class-mate, Cletus Heffernan, who had succeeded him at Pyrmont, celebrated the Requiem Mass at the parish church of Auburn.[1]

At Father Heffernan's diamond jubilee of ordination the local Annandale parish historian found it necessary to enquire of him about his unusual Christian name. The family story was that his parents had chosen to name him Charles Joseph, but at the baptism the parish priest intervened and informed them that it was the feast day of Saint Cletus, pope and martyr, and proposed that the baby be given that name.[2] The story did not state whether the priest had been drinking. The Heffernans were third generation dairy farmers at Moruya on the New South Wales south coast. Born in 1899, Cletus was the eldest of four brothers and left school at the age of fourteen to begin work on the farm. After two years he left the homestead to travel to St Columba's Seminary at Springwood, where he completed his high-school and philosophy studies in preparation for transfer to the theological college at Manly.

Ordained in 1925 he spent a few months as curate in Belmore before being sent on loan to the newly created Wagga diocese. In January 1927 he

---

1. *Catholic Weekly*, 5 December 1957.
2. Judy Jones, 'Our Jubilarian', typescript of speech read at jubilee celebration in 1985 (Heffernan file, SAA).

was briefly back at Belmore, followed by a succession of appointments at Nowra, Enfield and Lewisham/Petersham. He was given his first appointment as pastor at Pyrmont in April 1939. The letter from Archbishop Gilroy's secretary, which followed his formal appointment and which began with the urgent matter of Easter dues, contained further instructions. On account of the special dangers to the people of the Pyrmont District from Communism and other evil influences, Archbishop Gilroy required Heffernan to give special and consistent attention to house to house pastoral visitation of his parishioners. He further required a written assurance that Cletus would carry out the Archbishop's directives in these matters.[3]

In August 1939 the Pyrmont Conference of the Saint Vincent de Paul Society celebrated its golden jubilee. Founded in 1889 with the encouragement of Father James Furlong, the conference had made a significant contribution to the welfare of parishioners and the general community of Pyrmont and Ultimo. There were two elements to the celebration—a Requiem Mass at St Bede's on Friday, 11 August, for deceased members and benefactors, and on the following Tuesday evening a festive gathering in the St Bede's school room. The Mass was celebrated by Cletus Heffernan and the guest preacher was Fr John Byrne of Enfield, who paid tribute to the record of good work of the local conference. Gathered at the Tuesday celebration were former Pyrmont priests William McDonald, Daniel Hannan and James Mullin. Also present was the port chaplain, Fr Aloysius Jeffcott, keen to show his appreciation of the growing involvement of the Pyrmont priests and parishioners in his ministry. Two hundred Vincentians from Sydney conferences had gathered, together with officials of the Society. William Coogan, the President of the Particular Council, a body responsible for the Society's special works, was present. He had accompanied Charles O'Neill to the inaugural Pyrmont meeting in 1889. Over those fifty years he had dedicated himself to the development of the widening range of special works, beginning with his cooperation with Frederick Shawelhood in the Surry Hills household for orphan boys which developed into the St Vincent's Boys Home, Westmead. His enthusiasm and energy also resulted in the emergence of the Catholic Seamen's Institute in Kent Street and the Matthew Talbot Hostel at Woolloomooloo. In his address at the festive meeting he recalled that it had been his privilege to establish 68 conferences of the Society and on each one of these he had always impressed the 'necessity of three things, namely, the love of charity, the love of humility, and the manifestation of respect and loyalty for the clergy'. In relation to the clergy 'it was quite safe to say that the society had succeeded because it had won

---

3. O'Donnell to Heffernan, 6 May 1939 (Heffernan file, SAA).

the esteem and the cooperation of the priests'.[4] At the funeral of William Joseph Coogan in December 1945, the preacher, Fr John Thompson, Rector of St John's College and spiritual director of the Superior Council of the Society, emphasised the deceased's relationship with the clergy: 'His faith was remarkable, too, in the great reverence he showed for Christ's priest. He saw in the priest not the frail mortal subject to failings, but the minister of God and the dispenser of the mysteries of Christ. I have known him accept adverse decisions of the priest with the humility of a child.'[5] At the Pyrmont jubilee gathering, after speeches by the clergy, closing prayers were recited, and 'the ladies of the parish served supper'.[6]

On 3 September 1939, Prime Minister Robert Menzies announced to the nation that Australia was at war with Germany. Within days a National Security Bill granting the Government wide-ranging powers in relation to the internment of enemy aliens and press and radio censorship was passed, despite the opposition of the Labor Party. Towards the end of October Menzies introduced three month compulsory military training for home service for all 21-year-old men. The decision resurrected the visceral opposition of 1916 and 1917 to the very word 'conscription', even though the decision did not as yet involve compulsory overseas service. The trade union movement went public with its opposition, seeing the move as preliminary to a Billy Hughes-type referendum. The *Catholic Press*, whose editor was Patrick Scott Cleary, founder of the Catholic Federation and the short-lived Democratic Party, commented: 'It will be time enough to fight against overseas conscription when and if it is proposed.'[7] In November former Premier Jack Lang addressed a crowded public meeting at St Bede's school at which he passionately proclaimed that the Labor Party would fight the Menzies plan: 'Four weeks ago the Menzies Government issued a regulation ordering those boys born in the year of the Armistice into Australia's first conscript army in the second world war ... We are not going to allow our sons to be slaughtered on a European battlefield in any useless war over European domination ... The Labor Party is going to fight against conscription.'[8] On the platform with Lang were Jack Beasley, local member in the House of Representatives, and John Armstrong, local alderman who had been elected to the Senate in 1938. Senator Armstrong made the concluding speech at the meeting: 'I feel a spark has been set alight tonight which will spread into a roaring conflagration, and will frighten the Federal Government away from

---

4. *Catholic Press*, 7 September 1939.
5. *Catholic Weekly*, 10 January 1946.
6. *Catholic Weekly*, 10 January 1946.
7. *Catholic Press*, 26 October 1939.
8. *Sydney Morning Herald*, 15 November 1939.

the conscription issue.[9] The secretary of the local Pyrmont-Denison branch of the Labor Party, Charles Hackett, had been instructed to postpone the meeting until after a speech regarding the war to be delivered by the Federal Party leader, John Curtin, in the following week. Hackett, known as the 'King of Ultimo'[10], ignored the instruction from headquarters. Lang, Beasley and Armstrong were censured by the executive of the party for pre-empting the leader's speech. Hackett was spared, but would be expelled from the party in 1959 for another infringement of party rules. In his much anticipated speech John Curtin, consistent with his strong stand against militarism during the First World War, enunciated the same opposition to conscription as Lang, but was less dismissive of Australia's involvement in the European war.[11]

Beasley and Armstrong were among the five members of Federal Parliament, who in 1940, together with nine state MLAs and six MLCs, joined a Lang breakaway party known as the Non-Communist Labor Party. The Pyrmont branch voted to join the breakaway party: 'The Pyrmont branch decided last night, by 68 votes to 1, to leave the official Labor Party and to join the Australian Labor Party (non Communist). When the dissenting member left, the branch carried a resolution congratulating Mr Beasley MP, Senator J Armstrong and Alderman E O'Dea of the City Council, "on their efforts to rehabilitate the Labor movement in New South Wales".[12]

In 1941 the new party was dissolved before it faced an election; its members, with the exception of Lang himself, were re-admitted to the Labor Party. This reconciliation allowed John Curtin to become Prime Minister at the head of a united party at the invitation of the Governor-General, following a vote of no confidence in the short-lived government of Arthur Fadden. When war against Japan was declared in December, Prime Minister Curtin reluctantly began moving towards implementing conscription to face the increased need for military personnel. After bitter debate within the party, he convinced his colleagues to accept a limited form of conscription for overseas service in February 1943, permitting conscripts to serve in Japanese-held territory south of the equator. Some Labor die-hards condemned Curtin as a traitor; others saw him as a pragmatist, forced to adjust his firmly held beliefs in response to the crisis. Jack Beasley facilitated Curtin's successful move to extend the area of compulsory military service. Lang was one of the die-hards maintaining in 1943 the same passionate opposition to any form of conscription proclaimed at St Bede's in 1939; he bitterly attacked Beasely for his abandonment of traditional Labor policy.[13]

---

9. *Newcastle Morning Herald and Miners' Advocate*, 15 November 1939.
10. MR Matthews, *Pyrmont and Ultimo. A history*, Sydney 1982, 97.
11. *Sydney Morning Herald*, 22 November 1939.
12. *Sydney Morning Herald*, 1 May 1940.
13. B Nairn, 'John Albert Beasley', *Australian Dictionary of Biography*, http://adb.

On 9 and 10 January 1940 the members of the Second Australian Infantry Force, an exclusively volunteer army, boarded four converted liners berthed at Pyrmont. The public was excluded from the wharves during embarkation to 'avoid the harrowing scenes which so often marked the departure of troops in the war of 1914-18':

> Strong police cordons guarded the road and rail approaches to the Pyrmont wharves. The only person successfully to break through the cordon was a six-year-old boy, who dodged behind a policeman and ran so fast that no one had the courage to pursue him. When at last he was caught, and it was learned that he only wanted to get a parting glimpse of his 'big brother', a sympathetic military policeman escorted him to the ship's side, where, scanning the crowded decks, he eventually espied brother Bill and piped him a last good-bye. On the hill behind the wharves relatives and friends kept a day-long vigil while the embarkation went on. Some of them, expecting the ships to sail at daybreak, assembled at 3 a.m. and stayed there, waving flags and handkerchiefs with pathetic patience, until the vessels pulled out from the wharves at mid-day and disappeared from view behind the buildings of the city.[14]

On the afternoon of 10 January the liners passed through the Heads and joined the waiting troopships from New Zealand and a naval escort of four warships. The convoy sailed to the Middle East.

On 26 February a public notice appeared in the *Sydney Morning Herald* declaring certain places in Sydney to be 'prohibited areas'. Included among these was the Pyrmont Power House. Attentive scutiny of the notice would have been needed by the priest and parishioners of St Bede to avoid infringement of the defined boundary, which ran along Pyrmont Street in front of the presbytery and church:

> Notice is hereby given that the places described in the schedule hereto have been declared PROHIBITED PLACES on the respective dates shown on the said schedule under and by virtue of Regulation 4 of the National Security (General) Regulations. Attention is directed to the part of this regulation which makes it unlawful to enter, approach, inspect, pass over or be in the neighbourhood of a prohibited place.
> The Schedule: PYRMONT POWER HOUSE.
> (a) Commencing at Intersection of Northern side of Marian Street with the eastern side of Pyrmont Street and bounded on the west by the eastern

---

anu.edu.au/biography/beasley-john-albert-jack-9461, accessed 9 February 2015.
14. *Sydney Morning Herald*, 13 February 1940.

side of Pyrmont Street, northerly to its intersection with the southern side of Jones Bay Road, thence on the north by the southern side of Jones Bay Road easterly to the western boundary of Darling Island Railway Yards thence . . . to the point of commencement.[15]

In March 1940 Archbishop Michael Kelly died at his palace at Manly, aged ninety, a priest for 67 years and a bishop for 39. Solemn mourning was initiated with the continuous ringing of the muffled Cathedral bells under the direction of the captain of the bell-ringers, Mr Robert McDonald, father of William McDonald, former pastor of Pyrmont:

> Throughout the week, from the time that his Grace's remains were first received on Sunday afternoon, at his Cathedral, muffled peals were being rung from the tower. There are few things more impressive than the muffling of the clamoring tongues of these bell-voices, which call, in normal times, so clamorously and loudly, to the worship of God. There can be no better expression of mourning—except it be the offering of the One Sacrifice at the Altar—than this soft-toned prayer for the soul of the departed . . . It is interesting to know, also, that the regular ringers of St Mary's were assisted at times, by Anglican ringers from Darling Point, and other places, while many noticed that the flag over the Anglican Church of St James' was lowered immediately it had been publicly announced that his Grace had passed onward. Such gestures are not without significance.[16]

Norman Thomas Gilroy, Coadjutor Archbishop with right of succession, automatically succeeded Michael Kelly in the See of Sydney, now no longer Irish. He was surrounded in his cathedral by visiting bishops and the clergy of Sydney at the Solemn Requiem Mass for his predecessor.

Soon after his appointment to Pyrmont, Father Heffernan had moved to establish the Holy Name Society in the parish. On a Sunday afternoon in May 1940 he led his recruits to a grand gathering of all branches of the HNS to St Mary's. An assembly reputed to be six thousand strong filled the Cathedral. The Society's diocesan spiritual director addressed the men and drew a timely parallel between volunteering for war service and defending the church through membership of the HNS: 'A country is at war and immediately men are implored to defend it with their lives. And they come forward voluntarily with the surrender of their lives. The citizens, no matter how law-abiding they may be, who will not help at such a time, are rightly

---

15. *Sydney Morning Herald*, 26 February 1940.
16. *Catholic Freeman's Journal*, 14 March 1940

regarded by all as useless citizens—selfish and therefore worthless citizens, and a danger to the common weal of their country.[17] The first annual retreat for the Pyrmont members was held at St Bede's the following month.[18]

The Holy Name Society had its Australia-wide debut in 1925. At a meeting of the Australasian hierarchy at Wagga, where bishops had gathered for the consecration of the cathedral, at the urging of the Dominican Archbishop of Adelaide, William Spence, 'their Lordships expressed the desire that the Holy Name Society would be established in every Diocese in Australia, and appointed the Rev Father Hogan OP, the National Director of the Society in Australasia'.[19] Another Irish Dominican, Vincent William McEvoy, was appointed Spiritual Director.[20] The Australasian bishops, in their statement of 1925, emphasised the Dominican role in the Society:

> The Holy Name Society is exclusively for men. It will be of assistance to priests who wish to establish the H.N.S. in their Church to note the following points: 1. Before the Society can be established in any Church or Parish the approbation of the Ordinary of the Diocese must be obtained in writing. 2. The Diploma authorising the establishment of the Society, in this Church or Parish must be obtained from the Father General of the Order of Preachers who alone has authority from the Holy See to issue this Diploma. Any branch of the H.N.S., established without this authorisation and Diploma is invalid, and the members of such a branch do not share in the privileges or Indulgences granted by the Holy See to the Holy Name Society.[21]

The bishops reminded parish priests of the indulgences attached to the daily invocation, 'Praised be the Holy Name of Jesus', and the wearing of the small, but unmistakeable lapel badge, designed in 1921 by Fr Vincent McEvoy, who succeeded Stanislaus Hogan as National Director in 1934. One of the rules for members was 'to remonstrate with those who blasphemed or used profane language in their presence'. This rule was accompanied by sensible advice: 'This must be governed by zeal, prudence and common sense.'[22] Rules for a junior Society for boys ranging in age from 12 to 16 years established practices which became widespread among Catholic men and boys: 'To

---

17. *Catholic Freeman's Journal*, 16 May 1940.
18. *Catholic Press*, 1 August 1940.
19. *Freeman's Journal*, 28 May 1928.
20. Peter J Naughton, *Australasian Dominicans*, (Melbourne, 2014), volume 3, 10.
21. Freeman's Journal, 28 May 1928.
22. John Dawes, 'The Inspiring Story of the Holy Name Society', *Catholic Weekly*, 9 April 1953.

salute the Blessed Sacrament by raising their hats or caps when passing a church; to honour and obey their parents and always to salute a priest.'

In establishing the HNS at Pyrmont, Father Heffernan brought to St Bede's and St Francis Xavier's a monthly pattern familiar to most Australian parishes—the all-male membership of the Society gathering together in a separate section of the parish church on the second Sunday of the month. On the first Sunday of each month the all-female membership of the Sacred Heart Society would occupy the same pews.

The war had an early minor impact on Pyrmont in October 1940 with the change of name of the Armstrong hotel from *The Butcher's Arms* to *The Dunkirk*, in honour of the heroic evacuation of allied troops that had taken place in May-June. In November a few days' notice of a more spectacular impact was given to Pyrmont readers of the *Sydney Morning Herald*: 'an explosive bomb and several incendiary bombs will be set off somewhere in Pyrmont on Sunday morning, as part of a realistic air-raid precautions exercise. For the purposes of the exercise, it will be assumed that hostile aircraft are bombing docks and houses in the district and that, while attempts are being made to save life and property, a steady shower of incendiary bombs continues.'[23] Further exciting details were provided in the Saturday edition of the paper:

> Rehearsal To-morrow. Planes and anti-aircraft guns will be used to give realism to the 'bombing' rehearsal at Pyrmont to-morrow from 10 am to noon. A siren will give the air-raid alarm at 10 am and planes of the RAAF will appear shortly afterwards. The anti-aircraft battery will fire from Harris Street. Incendiary and smoke bombs will be used to give emphasis to the attack and powder will be exploded to imitate high-explosive bombs. Bricks will be thrown across streets to represent falling buildings and indications will be given of areas where water and other essential services have been cut off.[24]

It all sounds like an average Saturday night in Pyrmont in 2016. Perhaps the number of worshippers and the collection at the late Mass at St Bede's were reduced, with locals keen to watch the spectacular happenings on their streets:

> Sydney's most realistic air raid exercise was held at Pyrmont yesterday, when Air Force planes, in waves, made a mock raid on a thickly-populated industrial area, for two hours. Plans for the raid included the

---

23. *Sydney Morning Herald*, 20 February 1940.
24. *Sydney Morning Herald*, 23 November 1940.

dropping of bombs on the Pyrmont power station, a school, a post-office and homes. Water and gas mains were presumed to have been burst, fires to have been started, electricity and telephone services interrupted, and many casualties caused. It was also assumed that gas and time bombs had been dropped in the streets. A.I.F. troops with two anti-aircraft guns and lighter arms were stationed at a big street intersection, their task being to try to drive off the 'raiders'. During parts of the exercise, when gas bombs were supposed to have been dropped, the A.R.P. squads and the soldiers wore gas masks. Smoke bombs were set off, and heaps of sand were blown up to represent the dropping of bombs . . . Some women's national emergency units helped to control the crowds.[25]

Ultimo's turn for a golden jubilee celebration came in August 1941 when the local branch of the Hibernian-Australasian Catholic Benefit Society welcomed visitors from twenty other branches to celebrate fifty years of service to the local community. The HACBS was established in the 19th century to provide insurance against unemployment and hospital and funeral expenses for Catholic workers. In doing so it joined a growing list of friendly societies providing the same range of benefits for other sections of society, such as the Freemasons, the various groups of Oddfellows and the Orange Lodges. In 1891 Ultimo became the thirteenth branch of the HACBS in Sydney. The speeches at the jubilee celebrations recalled the glories of the local branch in providing so many high officials to the Society, especially the first National President, John McElhone. But regrets were also expressed— 'that the urge of industrial expansion was elbowing many of the grand old families out of the district'. Brother Maurice O'Dwyer, in proposing the toast to the 'Hierarchy and Clergy', 'assured the parish priest that the Hibernians were always anxious and willing to cooperate with him in parochial work', and that 'they were pleased to welcome Father Heffernan, who had gained the affection of the Ultimo people'. Cletus Heffernan replied that 'his experiences in Ultimo were of a happy nature; and the disposition of the people was excellent. He realised that on his appointment he had to follow in the footsteps of a long line of distinguished priests, but the assistance given by the parishioners was most helpful. He gratefully welcomed the preferred cooperation of the Hibernians, whose history in the district he had listened to with great interest'.[26]

In the month following the Ultimo celebration Cletus Heffernan was appointed to Penrith. In 1948 he applied successfully for appointment to Annandale, where he was parish priest until his retirement in 1983, when he

---

25. *Sydney Morning Herald*, 25 November 1940.
26. *Catholic Freeman's Journal*, 14 August 1941.

was formally named 'pastor emeritus', continuing to reside at the presbytery with his successor. He died in July 1993.

At Pyrmont in September 1941 James Massey succeeded his Manly classmate. The district to which he was now assigned had continued to experience social hardship throughout the years of the Great Depression. The demolition of housing to make way for wool stores and industrial plants, which William McDonald had predicted in 1927 would lead to the abandonment of St Bede's church and school, had led to increased overcrowding. One resident observed in 1937: 'In Pyrmont people cannot afford to go out of the district. I know some houses where they have had to put beds in the back yard in a small shed.'[27] There was no overcrowding at the Pyrmont Street presbytery, because there had not been a curate assigned to the parish since 1930. The staffing of two churches each weekend continued to depend on the assistance of 'supplies' from members of religious congregations.

The Secord World War had brought some relief from the depression and unemployment with the prospect for enlisting in the armed forces. There was also an increase in local employment in Pyrmont—for men on the wharves with the increase in shipping, and for women in the local textile and garment industry, supplying the needs of the troops. At Pyrmont there were constant reminders that Australia was at war—the transporting of troops from and into Darling Harbour; the disembarking and transporting of Italian prisoners of war to rural camps; the increase in the shipping of materiel and supplies. With the arrival of the American forces into Sydney, the pace of life in the district became hectic and sometimes a little tense. Indeed, as reported in 1992 to authors Shirley Fitzgerald and Hilary Golder by Otto Kruger of Ways Terrace, 'there was a moment when one section of the Pyrmont Peninsula's population did directly go to war—not with the enemy, but with the American allies':

> When the United States troops began arriving, the local children were glad to catch the chocolates and 'Lucky Strikes' which the men threw onto the wharves in a typical display of Yankee largesse. However, when they built a shed on Wharf 25 which blocked access to the swimming pool, relationships quickly deteriorated. But as one resident recalls it, Pyrmont was good billy-cart country, so their owners converted the carts into makeshift tanks, and led the attack down the hill and into the gates. It was the United States army against the children. Eventually an access plan was negotiated, without a shot being fired.[28]

---

27. S Fitzgerald & H Golder, *Pyrmont and Ultimo Under Siege* (Sydney, 1994), 109.
28. Fitzgerald & Golder, Pyrmont and Ultimo Under Siege, 109.

American servicemen were the targets of other local attacks. In November 1943 the publican of the Terminus Hotel was sentenced to one month's imprisonment with hard labour by a special Federal tribunal for having sold a bottle of Australian whisky to a member of the U.S. Military Police for £2/10/- when the fixed price for it was 12/9p.[29]

The first Pyrmont casualty among the AIF volunteers was recorded on a list published in May 1941.[30] The question of the clergy's role in informing families of war casualties was not defined by government and military authorities as during the First World War. A decision of the War Cabinet in January 1941 delegated local postmasters to fulfil this duty:

> A variation in the method of notifying fatal casualties to the next-of-kin in the fighting services has been approved by the War Cabinet. As far as practicable, the Postmaster-General will see that where casualty telegrams to next-of-kin are reporting deaths, the message will be personally conveyed by the postmaster himself, or some person to whom he has delegated authority. This will make it possible for the news of death to be broken by a clergyman, or by some close friend of the family concerned.[31]

Many mayors approached the clergy to assume the responsibility in their localities, as happened in the Penrith district where James Massey's brother Bernard was curate:

> In reply to inquiries by St Mary's Council of the local clergymen as to whether they would co-operate with the local postmaster in the notification of fatal war casualties to next-of-kin, favourable replies were received in each case at the meeting of Council on Tuesday evening. Rev. H Broadley (C of E), Rev AJ Cutler (Methodist), and Rev AJ Barrett (Presbyterian) stated that they would be willing to act in this way, and Father Hollands wrote that he and Father Massey would be available for notification of next-of-kin. The Mayor said that this was very satisfactory.[32]

On Passion Sunday, 26 March 1944, a Pastoral Letter from Archbishop Gilroy was read at Sunday Masses in all Sydney parishes. The letter deplored the Allies' bombing of the city of Rome. It began by quoting the words of Pope Pius XII addressed to the people of Rome, in which the pope expressed

---

29. *Sydney Morning Herald*, 27 November 1943.
30. *Sydney Morning Herald*, 7 May 1941.
31. *Picton Post*, 19 February 1941.
32. *Nepean Times*, 17 July 1941.

his shock that such attacks could be taking place: 'How can we believe that anyone could ever dare to desecrate this dear city, which belongs to all peoples, and upon which the Christian of the civilised world is now gazing with anxiety?' The Archbishop's letter concluded:

> To-day is Passion Sunday. Each successive day now brings before us a more intense realisation of Our Divine Saviour's sufferings, culminating in His crucifixion on Good Friday. That appalling tragedy, however, was shortly followed by the glorious Resurrection. So may our union in spirit with our Divine Redeemer in His Passion merit to obtain from the Heavenly Father release from the agony being suffered by His Vicar on earth, our Holy Father.[33]

In November 1944 the alarming results of a housing survey in some of Sydney's worst slum areas, Surry Hills and Pyrmont, were published:

> City Council officers who surveyed slum pockets in Surry Hills and Pyrmont found that only 13 out of every 100 houses either conformed or could be made to conform at reasonable cost to minimum standards of health and comfort. Of the houses inspected 37 per cent were damp and had leaking roofs and eight per cent, were vermin-infected. Of a group of 222 dwellings sanitary plumbing was defective in 183. Of 635 houses 291 had no kitchen sinks. Of all the houses surveyed 93 per cent were substandard, and only 6.34 per cent could be made standard at reasonable cost. The areas surveyed were selected because they are substantially residential, the street systems are bad and the houses are worse than in adjoining areas.[34]

Father McDonald, now residing in Hurstville, would have been reminded by these findings of the state of the Pyrmont presbytery as he found it in 1927.

There was great rejoicing in the city with the announcements of the end of the war in Europe in May 1945, and and in the Pacific in August. In September the first of the liberated prisoners returned from Europe and were driven in buses labelled 'Returned Prisoners of War' over the Glebe Island Bridge, through Pyrmont and across Pyrmont Bridge into the city, where crowds gathered to cheer them.[35]

In June 1946 James Massey applied to the Cardinal for permission to accept a quotation for £110-10-00 to replace the slate on the church roof. A less demanding financial burden on the parish had been his request in 1944

---

33. *Catholic Weekly*, 30 March 1944.
34. *Sydney Morning Herald*, 2 November 1944.
35. *Sydney Morning Herald*, 7 September 1945.

for permission to raise the Sisters' annual subsidy from £30 to £43. In October 1946 he was ready for greener pastures and he applied unsuccessfully for a move to the more salubrious parish of Ashbury. In February of the following year he managed to gain appointment to Sans Souci at Botany Bay. Three months later he died from coronary occlusion in Lewisham hospital at the age of 47. His brother Bernard presided at the Solemn Requiem Mass; his ordination class-mates filled the other liturgical roles—Cletus Heffernan as deacon, John McCooe as subdeacon and Dominic Furlong as master of ceremonies. The *Catholic Weekly* obituary noted that 'Father Massey had a particularly attractive voice, both for singing and in speech, combined with a prepossessing physique, prominent characteristics of his father'.[36]

Succeeding James Massey at Pyrmont in February 1947 was Richard Funcheon. He had arrived in Sydney from Ireland in November 1932 in a group of five newly ordained priests. Four of them were graduates of All Hallows, but Richard had studied at St Kieran's College, Kilkenny, in the diocese of Ossory. He was a beneficiary of a bequest for 'the foreign missions' received by Moran when bishop of Ossory and applied by him to supporting students for the Australian mission.[37] His first appointment was to Sacred Heart, Darlinghurst, where he dedicated most of his four years in residence to the chaplaincy of St Vincent's Hospital. Brief appointments to St Mary's and to Holy Cross, Woollahra, followed in 1939 and 1940. He returned to the cathedral staff in 1941 where he had special responsibility for St Columbkille's Church at Woolloomooloo, then a tough dockside district, which would have helped prepare him for his future mission at Pyrmont. He became a renowned preacher at the Cathedral, often quoted in the *Sydney Morning Herald*. In September 1941 the *SMH* quoted from sermons preached the previous day on the theme 'Duty of Church and State' at a range of Sydney churches—St Stephen's Presbyterian in the city, the Methodist churches at Newtown and Chatswood, the Congregational church at Bexley and St Mary's Cathedral. In his sermon Richard touched on the traditional just war theory: 'There were a number of misguided people who called themselves pacifists said Father Funcheon. They had no right to arrogate to themselves that title. The word simply implied peace-maker and that was what all right minded people must be. A nation engaged in a just war might employ all the usual means to destroy the enemy's power and gain victory.'[38] The just war was dramatically expanded three months later, on 8 December, with Prime Minister John Curtin's radio announcement: 'Men and women of Australia, we are at war with Japan.'[39]

---

36. *Catholic Weekly*, 15 May 1947.
37. KJ Walsh, *Yesterday's Seminary*, 231.
38. *Sydney Morning Herald*, 8 September 1941.
39. John Curtin Prime Ministerial Library (http://john.curtin.edu.au/diary/

'Dick' Funcheon had an unusually limited number of appointments during his fifteen years as a curate. Unusual also was the fact that over those years his ministry was exclusively within the Sydney metropolitan area. Within six months of arriving at Pyrmont he applied for extended leave in Ireland during 1948. In granting permission Cardinal Gilroy referred to 'the gravity of your request', and specified 'the condition that you guarantee D.V. ['deo volente', 'God willing'] to be available for duty in the Archdiocese on the 1st of February, 1949'.[40] On 18 January 1949 a telegram arrived in Sydney for 'Cardinal Milroy' from Richard Funcheon: 'Regret sudden appendicitis operation prevents return by Orion as arranged.'[41] This news threw into disarray the administrative arrangements that had been made for Pyrmont parish, where Father Thomas Keogh was packing to move to his next assignment at Belmore. James Byrne, the senior curate at neighbouring at St James, Forest Lodge, took up residence at St Bede's as 'locum tenens'.

Dick Funcheon was back in harness at St Bede's in September 1949. The steam ship *Ormonde* had delivered him to the Pyrmont wharves, within walking distance of his front door. The *Ormonde* had served as a troop ship in both world wars and was now serving as a migrant ship. Funcheon had obtained the job of chaplain to the Catholics among the migrants, as he had informed Cardinal Gilroy in July.[42] After the war the Pyrmont wharves, particularly the legendary 'Wharf 13', had resumed their role as the main Sydney terminal for passenger ships, now carrying the influx of British migrants and 'displaced persons', 'DPs', from continental Europe.

In 1944 Prime Minister John Curtin had committed the government to an expanded immigration programme once the war had ended. The experience of labour shortages, not least in Pyrmont, indicated the need for such a programme. There was an urgent need to address infrastructure shortcomings—housing, schools, hospitals, transport systems, electricity and water supply. The pre-war programmes of child migration were no longer adequate. In 1946 the Australian and British Governments signed an agreement to provide free passage to Australia for British ex-servicemen and their families. Then in 1947 the Government signed an agreement with the International Refugee Organisation to bring 12,000 displaced persons each year from refugee camps in Europe. This resulted in the Displaced Persons' Resettlement Scheme. During the war many people were taken from their occupied homelands in eastern and central Europe to work in German industry. Others had fled their homes ahead of advancing armies.

---

primeminister/fulltext/fulltext%20prime%20minister_1941_4.html; accessed 9 February 2015).
40. Gilroy to Funcheon, 8 August 1947 (Funcheon file, SAA).
41. Telegram, 18 January 1949 (Funcheon file, SAA).
42. Funcheon to Gilroy, 28 July 1949 (Funcheon file, SAA).

After the war they were unable or unwilling to return to their homelands and thousands found themselves stranded in refugee camps. For a country whose immigration policies had always given almost exclusive priority to people of Anglo-Celtic heritage, it was a significant political shift, which in turn resulted in cultural transformation of Australian society.

For most of the new arrivals at Pyrmont wharves, the local suburb was merely a place of transit. On disembarkation they were escorted to trains and taken to camps in the Sydney region and beyond. By 1951 over 460,000 migrants and refugees had arrived in Australia:

> Of the 460,560 migrants who have come here since October, 1945, 230,000 are British, 4,989 American, and 225,571 European. The great mass of the Europeans are displaced persons, rendered homeless, and in many cases stateless, by the Second World War. Latest available figures on nationalities are to June, 1950, when there were 190,000 DPs in Australia. Poles headed the list with 55,330 followed by Italians (not essentially DPs) 19,472, Latvians 16,379, Ukrainians 15,750, Yugoslavs 14,573, Lithuanians 9,293. The remainder is made of small groups from places like Estonia and Greece.[43]

The Australian bishops were conscious of the significant number of Catholics among the DPs, especially Poles, Ukrainians, Lithuanians, Dutch, Maltese and Italians, and by 1951 they had taken steps to cater for their needs with the establishment of a National Migration Committee, with agencies in each capital city. The first step was to recruit ethnic chaplains, some of whom were themselves displaced persons. Secular priests and Jesuits, Capuchins, Franciscans, Vincentians were among the 50 chaplains brought to Australia. By 1953 the number of migrant chaplains had grown to 100. In a July edition of Sydney's *Catholic Weekly* there was published 'A Page of Information for Our Catholic New Australians'. It provided the times of Masses for different language groups in Sydney churches and at the camps, variously called 'holding centres' and 'immigration centre'.[44] A Mass in Dutch was celebrated each Sunday at the Seamen's Mission in Kent Street. The largest of the camps was at Scheyville in the Windsor region. Here in 1954 a church was built and dedicated to St Vincent de Paul. It had been funded by the regional conference of the St Vincent de Paul Society. Attached to the church was basic accommodation for a full-time chaplain, a priest of the Archdiocese. A future pastor of St Bede's, Victor Doyle, would serve as chaplain at Scheyville from 1956 to 1963, when he was appointed to Pyrmont.

---

43. *Sunday Mail*, 25 February 1951.
44. *Catholic Weekly*, 26 July 1951.

Not only were priests disembarking at the Pyrmont wharves, but they were also embarking, for the Australian bishops had taken the initiative of calling for volunteers for missionary work in post-war Japan. Cardinal Gilroy and Bishop McCabe of Port Augusta, who visited Japan on behalf of the Australian Hierarchy in 1946, had 'observed both the chaotic conditions and the opportunities to spread the Faith'.[45] The volunteer priests would be on loan to Japanese bishops for five years and were to be supported by the Society for the Propagation of the Faith in Australia. In 1947 and 1948 the first two groups of priests left for various dioceses in Japan—a total of six from Sydney, two from Port Augusta and one from Perth. One of the first volunteers was Father Eamonn Dundon who would be appointed to Pyrmont parish in 1961. Sailing with the first group of priests in October 1947 were six Good Samaritan sisters who had responded to a direct request of Bishop McCabe. The Mother General had written to Cardinal Gilroy in March 1947: 'In view of the findings of your Eminence during your visit to Japan regarding the favourable position of the country for the reception of Christianity, we humbly offer ourselves for the evangelising of these pagan souls, if God so wills. Although our home needs are pressing and our numbers few, we feel that any sacrifice made will be amply rewarded by Him Who loves the Japanese as well as ourselves.'[46] They sailed from Sydney on the *Changte*, a 4,324 ton *steamship* built in Hong Kong in 1925. After a rough passage on the small ship, the missionaries arrived in Japan five weeks later, and the priests moved to Osaka and the nuns to Nagasaki.

Back in Pyrmont, despite the huge numbers of people passing through, the attraction of the district as a suitable residential location, a place to settle, continued to decline, as summarised by historians Shirley Fitzgerald and Hilary Golder:

> Soon after World War II Sydney was becoming a city of rapid suburban sprawl. A pent-up housing demand translated into miles of freestanding cottages built at ever increasing distances from the city centre, and accessed by a burgeoning population of privately owned motor cars. The process of preference for suburban living had already had a long history going back at least to the turn of the century, but never before had it been such a widespread possibility as it became after World War II. The lifestyle was extolled and promoted by means of legislative and financial incentives, and consequently places like Pyrmont and Ultimo had never

---

45. *Catholic Weekly*, 5 March 1953.
46. Mother Oliviero to Cardinal Gilroy, 4 March 1947, in Marilyn Kelleher, *Annals of the Sisters of the Good Samaritan*, Sydney 2010, volume 2, 149.

been held in such low esteem. The population aged, as a generation of young adults fled.[47]

The population decline was exacerbated by the continuing encroachment of industry and warehouses.

Early in 1952 a sister of Richard Funcheon wrote to Cardinal Gilroy. She was Sister Kieran of the Holy Family Sisters at Pietermaritzburg in South Africa. She nervously asked whether His Eminence would consider allowing her brother, whom she had not seen for twenty years, to 'carry his bags' on the Cardinal's planned visit to the Marian Congress being held at Durban later in the year. She begged him not to tell Dick that she was making this request. She concluded by stating 'how eager I am to pull his ears as he never writes to me', and pledging to offer 'Novenas to St Jude for the success of my appeal'.[48] His Eminence replied, regretting that his plans to travel to South Africa had been cancelled, and stating that her brother was one of the best priests of the Archdiocese of Sydney.[49] He did not, however, offer to facilitate the reunion of brother and sister.

In 1944 Richard's younger brother Patrick, having been ordained in Ireland in 1940 and delayed by the War from sailing to Australia, had arrived in Sydney on his way to the diocese of Lismore, where he held appointments at Lismore, Kyogle, Bowraville and Kempsey. In July 1952 Richard received a letter from Patrick's bishop containing the devastating news that his brother Patrick had left Lismore diocese and that there was no news of his whereabouts. Bishop Farrelly went on to explain that Patrick had departed Kempsey in the company of a young married woman. He concluded the letter expressing his astonishment at the turn of events as 'Father Pat' had seemed to be very happy and very interested in the work of the Pilgrimage of the statue of Our Lady of Fatima. The bishop shared with Richard the hope that perhaps Our Lady would bring Pat back.[50] This news was deeply troubling for Richard and eventually led to his announcement to Cardinal Gilroy in 1954 that he was considering joining a religious order. He explained that he had been thinking of this move since early days on the mission, but that the attraction was more assertive and persistent since the sad news of his brother's defection. He expressed his attraction to the Redemptorists. His hope was that such a change would lead to personal sanctification and would be instrumental in securing much needed graces of repentance,

---

47. Fitzgerald & Golder, *Pyrmont and Ultimo*, 111.
48. Sister Kieran Funcheon to Cardinal Gilroy, 10 February 1952 (Funcheon file, SAA).
49. Cardinal Gilroy to Sister Kieran Funcheon, 23 February 1952 (Funcheon file, SAA).
50. Farrelly to Funcheon, 17 July 1952 (Funcheon file, SAA).

conversion and rehabilitation for a lapsed brother.[51] The Cardinal invited him to come to the Cathedral Presbytery and discuss the matter.[52] Dick continued as a diocesan priest. His brother was formally laicised in 1975 and died in Melbourne in 1978.

From Pyrmont Richard had gone north in September 1952 to Gosford where he ministered for six years. His next appointment was south to Sutherland as parish priest. In 1972 he applied for and was appointed to the smaller parish of Ashbury. In 1987 one of his parishioners wrote anonymously to the Archbishop complaining that Father Funcheon was quite deaf, and questioned whether he should be hearing confessions.[53] Many Catholics would regard a deaf confessor as a distinct advantage, as attested by Frank McCourt in his book *Angela's Ashes*, in which he related his and his mates' preference for the confessional box of a deaf Dominican.

Richard Funcheon died in 1989 at the age of 80. At the Requiem Mass Bishop David Cremin reminisced fondly about his Kilkenny colleague. He recalled his reputation as a fine preacher, with 'a rich and pleasant voice', and 'a beautiful command of the English language'. He described him as 'a most private person', 'a real contemplative', and cited the example of his walks every afternoon with his dog, Red, in the national park during his term at Sutherland. He did not state whether it was shyness or Canon Law that led 'Dick' to place Red in the front seat and the lady-catechists in the back, when driving to the state school for religious instruction. Bishop Cremin referred to the Funcheon siblings, Patrick, who had died in 1978, Elizabeth in Ireland, and Peggie, Sister Kieran, still in South Africa.[54]

---

51. Funcheon to Gilroy, no date (Funcheon file, SAA).
52. Gilroy to Funcheon, 27 March 1954 (Funcheon file, SAA).
53. 'Concerned parishioner' to Cardinal Clancy, 30 Semptember 1987 (Funcheon file, SAA).
54. *Catholic Weekly*, 27 September 1989.

Chapter 21
Parish Decline & Port Chaplaincy

Succeeding Richard Funcheon at Pyrmont and Ultimo in October 1952 was Sidney Robert Thorne. Born in Wollongong in 1908, he belonged to a well-known local family. His father was a tobacconist and 'master billiard player of semi-professional status'. Sidney learnt to play the game from his earliest years.[1] He went to the local convent school and then to the public high school. He trained as a primary school teacher, completing the two year course at Sydney Teachers College, newly located on the campus of the University of Sydney. After a short period of school teaching he decided to study for the priesthood. He was ordained in November 1936, together with two cousins, the brothers Gregory and John Madden. Sidney was hailed as Wollongong's first local-born priest, and given a grand reception after the celebration of his first Mass at St Francis Xavier Church.

After four years as curate in a range of Sydney parishes—Bondi, Camperdown, Haberfield, Lane Cove—Thorne was sent on a one-year loan to Hobart Archdiocese in 1940. On his return he resumed ministry as an assistant at Balmain and then at Forest Lodge. In 1942 he volunteered as a chaplain in the Royal Australian Air Force, and was based variously at Richmond, Darwin and Townsville. He was in Darwin when the town was the target of a Japanese air raid in May 1943; his dramatic report of the event was published in the *Illawarra Mercury* under the headline, 'PADRE IN AIR RAID':

> Ft-Lt Sidney K Thorne; RAAF, Catholic Chaplain, was caught in the Jap air raid on Darwin on Monday, but was unharmed . . . The padre's story was: 'Military, police had warned me that a raid was due, but I had to try to get to the air station in case there were casualties. A bomb fell a few yards behind my car and the blast sent the car zigzagging all over the

---

1. Sidney Thorne obituary, *Catholic Weekly*, 18 February 1987.

road. This probably saved my life, because a Jap plane just then came down strafing. Bits started to fly out of the bonnet of the car and shrapnel and bullets were whipping down, so I swerved the car off the road and jumped clear. I dived into a trench, but was able to come out a bit later and watch the Spitfires chase the Japs off. At an earlier Mass those Spitfire boys had been urging me to hurry the service through, because they were expecting the Japs.'[2]

In December 1944 Cardinal Gilroy received a letter from Bishop Hugo Ryan of Townsville relaying complaints from local Catholics that Fr Thorne was taking a little too much drink, and urging that he be recalled.[3] The administrator of the Townsville Cathedral, Peter Vandeleur, followed up with a letter seeking to moderate his bishop's alarmist focus on a drink problem, but agreeing that a transfer would be good for Thorne for general health reasons. He explained that when Father Thorne came down from Darwin he was a little on the nervy side and that he had not fully regained his equilibrium. Vandeleur considered, therefore, that a transfer from Townsville or a withdrawal from the Air Force would be helpful to him.[4] Gilroy initially wrote to the Chaplain General, Archbishop Daniel Mannix in Melbourne, urging that immediate action be taken in removing Thorne from Townsville and possibly from the RAAF.[5] However, following Vandeleur's clarification and further investigation, he wrote to Rev John Pierce, acting staff chaplain at the Air Board in Melbourne, that there did not seem to be sufficient reason to take the drastic step of asking for his withdrawal from the RAAF.[6] Thorne continued as chaplain, but was moved from Townsville. A story from his Air Force days was recounted at his funeral in February 1987 by Bishop David Cremin: 'He was, on another occasion, the hero of the Air Force when he took on and roundly thrashed a billiards or pool "hustler" who happened to be an American officer and who, it seems, had left most of the Australian officers minus their shirts.'[7]

In April 1946 Flight Lieutenant Thorne was discharged from the RAAF after bouts of sickness and hospitalisation at Yaralla Military Hospital in Concord. He became available for assignment again in the Sydney Archdiocese and was sent to Brighton-le-Sands as assistant. Two years later he was at Bankstown. His first assignment in charge of a parish was to rural Burragorang, of which Bishop Cremin would comment in his eulogy:

---

2. *Illawarra Mercury*, 25 June 1942.
3. Ryan to Gilroy, 7 December 1944 (Thorne file SAA).
4. Vandeleur to Gilroy, 7 December 1944 (Thorne file SAA).
5. Gilroy to Mannix, 9 December 1944 (Thorne file SAA).
6. Gilroy to Pierce, 3 January 1945 (Thorne file SAA).
7. *Catholic Weekly*, 18 February 1987.

'Now Burragorang had a certain "Siberia" element in it and priests tend to say "what hath he done?" to deserve such a sentence.'[8] From 'Siberia' he was assigned to Pyrmont in October 1952 as priest-in-charge, 'parochus amovibilis' or removable pastor.

Within weeks of his arrival at St Bede's he wrote to the Archbishop requesting approval of a summer change to the Sunday Mass schedule—at Pyrmont from 7am to 6.30am, and at Ultimo from 9.30am to 8.30am—citing the desire of parishioners to get away to the beaches as early as possible: 'One can easily understand the desire of the people to spend a day away from these localities whenever possible.'[9]

The new pastor would have soon learnt of the high regard in which the President of the local conference of the St Vincent de Paul Society, Maurice O'Dwyer, was held. Father Thorne decided to honour Maurice's 55 years in the parish and 54 years as member of the Society. He wrote to Cardinal Gilroy recommending a papal award. He supported the request with high praise of Maurice: 'his long life of constant virtue, generous assistance in all parish undertakings, heroic relief of the misery of the poor, visitation of the sick in hospitals and institutions, helpful co-operation with the priest for the good of the people, and ever present example of the Christian virtue of charity.'[10] The Cardinal forwarded the request to the Vatican via the Apostolic Delegate. In January 1954, Gilroy informed Thorne that an award had been granted, concluding with his customary focus on the matter of payment due:

> Herewith is the honour that you requested for Mr Maurice O'Dwyer, which the Holy Father has graciously granted. Will you please convey my cordial congratulations to the recipient with the expression of my hope that he will be long spared to enjoy the honour.
> Begging God's blessing on yourself and the parish.
> PS The Tax for the concession of the honour is £7, which amount I would ask you kindly to remit to His Excellency, the Apostolic Delegate, directly.[11]

In February the *Catholic Weekly* announced that Maurice O'Dwyer had been awarded the 'Cross of Leo' by His Holiness Pope Pius XII. The 'Pro Ecclesia et Pontifice' ('For Church and Pope') medal was established by Leo XIII in 1888 to commemorate his golden jubilee of priesthood, and was originally bestowed on those men and women who had aided and promoted the jubilee and by other means assisted in making the jubilee and the associated Vatican

---

8. *Catholic Weekly*, 18 February 1987.
9. Thorne to Gilroy, November 1952 (Pyrmont file, SAA)
10. *Catholic Weekly*, 4 February 1954.
11. Gilroy to Thorne, 20 January 1954 (Pyrmont file, SAA)

Exposition successful. It was later broadened for distinguished service to the church by lay people and clergy. It is the highest award that can be granted to the laity by the Pope. The medal, hanging from a ribbon of papal colours, is in the form of a cross and carries the profile of Pope Leo on the front and the words 'Pro Ecclesia et Pontifice' on the reverse.

The *Catholic Weekly* summarised Maurice's career:

> Mr O'Dwyer, who is 74 years of age, lives with his wife, Mrs Ellen O'Dwyer, in Bunn-street, Pyrmont, and came to the parish after spending his youth at Dunmore and Albion Park on the South Coast and a further six years at Leichhardt. He has been a member of St Bede's Conference of the Society of St Vincent de Paul for 54 years, being secretary for 35 years and president for the past 10 years. A member of the Hibernian Australasian Catholic Benefit Society he has also belonged to the Holy Name Society since its inauguration in Pyrmont parish. Mr O'Dwyer has taken an active part helping the Special Works of the Society of St Vincent de Paul and has been a constant Sunday visitor to the sick in Sydney Hospital for the past 10 years.[12]

A week later it was announced that the presentation would take place at St Bede's school-hall 'during a *musicale* arranged by Radio 2SM in honor of Mr O'Dwyer'. It was also announced that the presentation would be made, not by His Eminence or either of the auxiliary bishops, but by a minor prelate, Monsignor Bond of Concord. The Right Reverend Monsignor would have added a touch of colour with the purple of his quasi-episcopal garb.[13] Admission to the 'musicale' was free and 'the pastor of Pyrmont (the Rev. Father S. Thorne) particularly invites former parishioners of Pyrmont and Ultimo'. Maurice was well known to generations of parishioners not only for his prominence in church matters, but also because he was the local milkman. Phillip O'Toole, a cousin of Mrs Nellie O'Dwyer, wrote down his reminiscences of the 1920s, when he was a schoolboy at St Bede's, and he recalled fondly that Maurice was the man who delivered fresh milk daily to the O'Toole family home in Point Street, pouring it into a billy-can kept at the front door.[14] Already in 1915 tribute had been paid to Pyrmont's milkman:

> The medical profession is forever impressing on their clients the absolute necessity of drinking none but pure milk, and this means doing business with none but registered milk vendors. In the district of Pyrmont people are to be congratulated on having such an exceptionally conscientious

---

12. *Catholic Weekly*, 4 February 1954.
13. *Catholic Weekly*, 11 February 1954.
14. Phillip O'Toole, 'Some Memories' (manuscript 2003 [Pyrmont Archives]).

milk vendor as M. O'Dwyer, of 12 Bunn street. Those who have had even the experience of a rather short trial are ever anxious to give testimonials of the pure quality of the milk and of the satisfactory way in which M. O'Dwyer meets all customers.[15]

The gathering for the conferral of the papal award was very well attended: 'At the function former residents of Pyrmont and Ultimo mixed with members of the present community and renewed old friendships with them and Mr and Mrs O'Dwyer. Practically all the suburbs of Sydney were represented, and many relatives of Mr O'Dwyer travelled from Bathurst, Berry, Kiama, Shellharbour, Dunmore and Wollongong.' Former parish priests turned up to add their congratulations—William McDonald of South Hurstville, Richard Funcheon from Gosford and Thomas Keogh from Riverstone. Also present was Father Edward Drohn, the Sacred Heart priest, who had been intermittently commuting on weekends to Pyrmont from Kensington and Randwick since 1923.[16] Telegrams were received from former Pyrmont clergy—Austin Bradstreet of Golden Grove and James Lynch of North Leichhardt. Local politicians were in attendance—Dan Minogue MHR and Dan Clyne MLA—as well as Senator John Armstrong and his brother Dr Edward Armstrong. Present too was the Reverend Edward Madgwick, who, as long-serving rector of St Bartholomew's Anglican church, had known Maurice longer than any of the Catholic clergy present.[17]

In making the presentation Monsignor Bond praised Maurice's achievements:

> He said that even when he was Administrator at the Cathedral, the virtues and the work of corporal mercy of Mr O'Dwyer were well known. Mr O'Dwyer had practised, throughout a lifetime, and to an eminent degree, all the virtues instilled into members of the Society of St Vincent de Paul, and had stored up riches for himself in the life to come. However, he had well earned the notice of the Universal Church and had been rewarded while still in this life.

He paid due honour to Maurice's wife Nellie: 'He said Mrs Maurice O'Dwyer certainly shared in the honor that had come to her husband, because of her homely virtues, and the self-effacing and courageous assistance and encouragement she had given him throughout the years.' Nellie and Maurice had also shared duty at the organ keyboard at St Bede's over many years. The

---

15. *Catholic Press*, 4 March 1915.
16. Father Edward Drohn received the author's father into the Catholic Church at Randwick in 1944.
17. *Catholic Weekly*, 25 February 1954.

honoured and humbled Maurice O'Dwyer responded, sharing his award with his wife and fellow parishioners:

> In reply Mr O'Dwyer said that he did not think himself worthy of the honour given him, but was most grateful to the Holy Father for bestowing such distinction upon Pyrmont and Ultimo. He thanked His Eminence Cardinal Gilroy for recommending the decoration and the Apostolic Delegate, His Excellency Archbishop Carboni, for granting him a personal audience at the Apostolic Delegation. Mr O'Dwyer also thanked Monsignor Bond and Father Thorne and all associated with the function and expressed gratitude to his wife and all those who had assisted him in his work for the Church.[18]

Towards the end of the school year in 1954 the Mother General of the Good Samaritan Sisters, Mother Oliverio, wrote to Father Thorne concerning the future of St Bede's school. Citing staffing difficulties and the decline in the number of pupils, she proposed that the school be closed. In November the parish priest wrote to the Director of Catholic Education, Monsignor John Slowey, whose brother was the publican of the Pyrmont Arms Hotel, outlining the school situation. He revealed that the Mother General had first raised the question of closure in 1952, but that he had resisted the suggestion. Thorne tried to find a group of nuns to replace the Good Samaritans in both schools of the parish.

In September 1953 he wrote to the Mother General of the Sisters of St Joseph of Cluny in Melbourne.[19] The Cluny Sisters were a French Order founded in 1807. In 1848 they established communities in the French and British colonies in the Pacific. In 1903 when the French Government passed Laicisation Laws which enforced the closing of the novitiate in New Caledonia, the nuns came to Australia, eventually locating their work in Melbourne. Fr Thorne explained that the Order had been recommended to him by Sydney's auxiliary bishop, Patrick Lyons, former Vicar General of the Melbourne Archdiocese. He stated that the Good Samaritans had been 'unable to provide suitable staff' for the schools: 'I have spoken several times with the Mother General, and whilst she appreciates the necessity of virile sisters for the difficult work here, she can do nothing about it.' He went on to describe the parish, the schools and the convent. He was quite open about the challenging situation to which he was inviting a group of at least six Sisters: 'You see that this is not an invitation to a wealthy concern. It is an invitation to a parish situated next to the Cathedral parish, and one

---

18. *Catholic Weekly*, 25 February 1954.
19. Thorne to Mother General, 23 September 1953 (Pyrmont Box, SAA).

which may eventually disappear altogether; it is an invitation to the special work of the poor in a parish in which the majority of the 1200 Catholics are indifferent to religion.' He referred to the recent arrival in Sydney of another French Order, the Daughters of Charity, who had begun work in the 'slum section' of the Cathedral parish, and expressed the hope that the Sisters of St Joseph of Cluny would have a similar impact in Pyrmont: 'This parish is crying out for Sisters to come here and do the same. The people are very friendly, and will quickly take the Sisters to their hearts. I can assure you that, if you can take on this parish, the Cardinal, the auxiliary bishop, the priests, the people and indeed the whole diocese will be deeply grateful to you.'[20] The Sisters were unable to accept Father Thorne's invitation.

Having failed to entice a new group of nuns to take over both schools, as a last resort he attempted to find a lay teacher to replace the Good Samaritans at St Bede's, so that the school could stay open for the twenty children enrolled for 1955. He confidently informed Monsignor Slowey: 'You may notify the Superior General of the Good Samaritans that the Order will no longer be expected to provide Sisters for the St Bede's School, Pyrmont.'[21] However, in January he reluctantly accepted the inevitable and wrote to Mother Oliverio: 'If approached by the Education Office, I would give the necessary permission for the closing of the Pyrmont School.'[22] St Bede's did not open for the 1955 scholastic year, and the children were offered places at St Francis Xavier School in Ultimo, where the Good Samaritans would continue teaching until 1973. The Pyrmont School building was henceforth listed as 'Church Hall', which drew the attention of the Town Clerk regarding liability of the parish for payment of rates. Father Thorne replied to the Council: 'This property may again be used as a school in the future. The Church-hall is not registered as a public hall, nor is it hired out to anyone for a profit.'[23]

During 1954 the parish priest had repeatedly complained to the local member of the Legislative Assembly, Daniel Clyne, in his eleventh term as representative for the electorate of King, about the noise and nuisance of construction work in the vicinity of the church and school. Fr Thorne's first focus was on a compression engine located close to the school. He asked for its removal because of the impossibility of the Sisters to conduct classes due to the noise. The compression engine was just one of many nuisances adding to the disruption of the school: 'The children enrolled are very young; the noise, added to intermittent blasting in the railway cutting and noise from the power houses and coal-trucks, has a most deleterious effect upon the

---

20. Thorne to Mother General, 23 September 1953 (Pyrmont Box, SAA).
21. Thorne to Slowey, 27 November 1954 (Pyrmont Box, SAA).
22. Thorne to M. Oliviero, 19 January 1955 (Pyrmont Box SAA)
23. Thorne to Town Clerk, 20 March 1955 (Pyrmont Box, SAA).

children's health.' Invoking a widespread anxiety among residents about the future of the district, he pleaded: 'Until this area is declared industrial and the people are moved away, consideration should be shown to these poor children as much as to those in better circumstances.'[24]

In January 1955 the parish made a claim against the Minister of Transport for damage to the church windows caused by blasting in the nearby railway cutting. A department investigation concluded that there was only a very remote possibility that the damage had been caused by the excavation work and a token offer of £60 was made. The local Member of Parliament, on behalf of Father Thorne, rejected the findings and the offer. The final outcome, accepted by the parish, was that no liability was acknowledged by the Minister and the 'ex gratia' offer was raised to £100.[25]

Advice about the damaged windows was sought from Stephen Moor of Ars Sacra Studio, who submitted the following recommendations: 'Those windows would need a complete re-leading which would be too expensive a matter owing to the cheap quality of the glass used. Therefore, my suggestion is to make new lead lights and, instead of diamonds, squares (which are constructionally much stronger) and not in lead but in metal which is much more durable and is slightly lower in price, too.'[26] No repair of the windows was undertaken. However, many years later Stephen Moor would have an indirect impact on the damaged windows he had inspected in 1955. Born in Hungary in 1915, he arrived in Australia in 1950 as a war refugee. Before the War he had been teaching stained glass at the Budapest Academy. After assembly-line work in Sydney, Moor learnt English and gained employment as a stained glass artist, establishing his own practice, *Ars Sacra*, at Burwood: 'He became a dominant figure in the stained glass scene in Sydney, bringing his distinctive European/Germanic style to bear on a craft largely mired in the 19th century ... He reinvigorated the liturgical and residential stained glass of the time.'[27] Several of the current generation of stained glass practitioners received their training under Moor, including Paddy Robinson and Jeffrey Hamilton, both of whom contributed in the 2000s to the replacement of the original, temporary and damaged diamond leadlights at St Bede's with stained glass.

In May 1955 Father Thorne had the privilege of announcing that the parish was finally debt-free. In August the O'Dwyers joined the exodus from the district and retired to a more salubrious suburb. Sidney Thorne was

---

24. Thorne to Clyne, 2 February 1954 (Pyrmont Box, SAA).
25. Correspondence 1955 (Pyrmont Box, SAA).).
26. Moor to Thorne, 26 March 1954 (Pyrmont Box, SAA).
27. http://www.artrecord.com/index.cfm/artist/11384-moor-stephen/ (accessed 24 March 2015).

not far behind in moving out; in January 1956 he was sent, not to a leafier destination, but to Erskineville, another inner-city working-class district.

In 1958 he was invited by Cardinal Gilroy to be chaplain to the Genesian Theatre Company. The Company had been formed as an offshoot of the Catholic Youth Organisation in 1944, and named after Genesius, a comedian and actor who worked in a series of plays that mocked Christianity. The legend stated that one day, while performing in a work that made fun of baptism, he had a conversion experience on stage. He announced his new faith, and refused to renounce it, and was martyred by the Emperor Diocletian in the year 303 A.D. He became the patron saint of actors. The Sydney Genesians' first play, opening on January 1945, was *The Comedian* by Henri Ghèon, a drama about St Genesius. Between 1945 and 1954 the Company's productions were performed at a variety of venues—the Australian Hall (later Rivoli Theatre), the Sydney Radio Theatre, the Conservatorium, Manresa Hall in North Sydney, and the Capitol Theatre. In 1954 the Company moved to the former St John's church-school in Kent Street. The building, opened in 1868, had ceased to function as church and school in 1932, and had its first incarnation as a theatre, becoming the home of the Sydney Repertory Company. From 1938 to 1953 it served as the first Matthew Talbot Hostel, and then underwent a makeover: 'The former Matt Talbot Hostel in Kent Street, shortly to become Australia's first permanent Catholic theatre, is at present undergoing a complete "face-lift". The Genesians, Sydney's Catholic drama group, are enthusiastically converting it into an up-to-date "Little Theatre".'[28] In the 1970s the players rehearsed their productions and prepared their stage props in the old school of St Bede at Pyrmont.

After thirteen years at Erskineville, Sidney Thorne raised with Cardinal Gilroy his desire for a new appointment, writing that His Eminence would appreciate the hardships he had faced over the past twenty years in Burragorang, Pyrmont and Erskineville. He expressed his confidence that the Cardinal would sympathise with his desire to experience normal living conditions for a few years.[29] In May 1969 he formally applied for and was granted the parish of Flemington. Sidney Thorne continued as Genesian chaplain until his retirement from the Flemington parish in 1971. He had never failed to send an invitation to the Archbishop at the commencement of each theatre season. To mark his thirteen years as chaplain he was granted a farewell Testimonial Dinner by the Genesians in February 1971. He retired to the specially created facility for priests, the Saint John Vianney Villa, within the grounds of the Little Sisters of the Poor at Randwick, where he died in January 1987. The *Catholic Weekly* headlined the announcement of

---

28. *Catholic Weekly*, 30 July 1953.
29. Thorne to Gilroy, 25 September 1968 (Thorne file, SAA).

his death: 'Theatre priest takes his final bow'.[30] Bishop Cremin shared a final story with the congregation at the Requiem Mass at St Mary's Cathedral: 'One evening last November, he was awakened in his sick bed to find a figure in white hovering over him. He was assured that it was not the Angel Gabriel but none other than His Holiness Pope John Paul II, who came to bless him and kiss him with affection.'[31]

Succeeding Father Thorne at Pyrmont in February 1956 was Ashley Jones. Born at Hobart in 1913 his family relocated to Sydney where he attended high school at the Marist Brothers College, Darlinghurst. He was among the first priests to be ordained in the Cerretti Chapel at Manly College in 1937. His unusually lengthy first appointment was to Parramatta where he was curate until 1942. From 1943 to 1946 he was on loan to the diocese of Goulburn, serving as curate firstly at the Goulburn Cathedral and then at Cooma and finally at St Bede's, Braidwood. On his return to Sydney he was appointed as assistant at Malabar parish, and then in 1951 at Lidcombe. In 1953 he became administrator of Mount Carmel parish at Waterloo. It was from there that he came to Pyrmont as administrator.

In January 1958 the Pyrmont parish became the location of an experiment in a new approach to parish missions. The classic model, often experienced at St Bede's, had been the arrival in a parish of two priests belonging to a religious order to conduct a week, from Sunday to Sunday, of intensive preaching and home visitation. The emphasis would be on increased availability of Mass and confession, and on the theme of conversion. The Redemptorists, the only order in Australia to have avoided the bishops' usual requirement of conducting parishes or schools as a condition of entry into the diocese, had been discussing among themselves a new approach to parish missions, especially for so-called 'industrial areas in our big cities'. In January 1958 the superior of their Sydney monastery at Pennant Hills, Austin Brennan, wrote to Cardinal Gilroy outlining the proposal. He expressed his community's assessment of the inadequacy of ordinary missions in bringing back to the Church the large numbers, 'even the big majority of baptised Catholics' in industrial suburbs, who have 'fallen away almost completely from the practice of their faith'.[32] The problem was that such lapsed Catholics did not attend the parish church based missions, and the proposed solution was 'to take the message of the mission to them in their own homes and in a convenient place near where they live'. To make this possible, more missioners would be needed and the mission period would have to be significantly extended. The Redemptorists had received the permission of their Father General in Rome to proceed with the experiment and the Provincial had approved the

---

30. *Catholic Weekly*, 11 February 1987.
31. *Catholic Weekly*, 18 February 1987.
32. Brennan to Gilroy, 20 January 1958 (Pyrmont Box, SAA).

details of a proposal involving a commitment of four or five priests for a period of six weeks. Father Brennan was able to inform the Cardinal that the Redemptorists had located a parish priest willing to welcome the new style of mission into his parish. The priest was Ashley Jones and his parish in the inner Sydney industrial area of Pyrmont-Ultimo. There would be no charge on the parish. Cardinal Gilroy granted permission and bestowed his blessing on the venture.

At the end of 1958 a report on the experiment was prepared with the heading: '*Outside the City*—the Story of the First Industrial Parish Mission.'[33] The solemn opening of the mission took place in Wentworth Park, which was technically outside the western border of the parish. There were about 300 in attendance. Father Jones addressed the assembly in carefully crafted words and dramatic tones, probably written by the Redemptorists:

> I turn my eyes to the City in the outskirts of which you live; I lift my voice and speak to you the people of Pyrmont and Ultimo. You have come out of the City this afternoon to sit down here and listen to God's voice speaking to you through these priests, just as the woman in St John's Gospel came out of the ancient city of Sichar in Samaria and listened to the Son of God. I call for the conversion of the people of this Parish to God and to a Christian life. I plead on behalf of Christ, I plead with you, every one of you, to accept this great Mission as a special grace from God, as the Samaritan woman accepted Christ, gave up sin and spent the rest of her life calling others to come and know and follow Christ. I ask you in heaven's name to do this now, that you may be worthy of forgiveness and Heaven too.[34]

His words had a decidedly old-fashioned Redemptorist mission ring to them. If there were any lingering doubts about the theme of the six weeks to follow they were quickly dispelled when Father Brennan spoke or bellowed, as was the Redemptorist style: 'Enter ye in at the narrow gate: for wide is the gate and broad is the way that leadeth to destruction and many there are who go thereat. How narrow is the gate, and straight is the way that leadeth to life and few there are that find it.'[35]

Over the next six weeks the four mission priests visited local households, 'by day and by night, hampered by rain and blistering heat'. They were given the use of a large truck by one of the parishioners, to which they attached a tall crucifix, and from Monday night to Friday night they preached for a

---

33. 'Outside the City'—the Story of the First Industrial Parish Mission', no date (Pyrmont Box, SAA).
34. 'Outside the City' (Pyrmont Box, SAA).
35. Matt 7:13–14.

fortnight in the streets of Pyrmont and Ultimo: 'This most important part of the Mission amazed the local inhabitants. They threw up their windows to listen; they gathered in groups round the truck and as the word of God fell upon their ears and entered their minds and hearts there could be seen in the eyes of many admiration for these priestly men who were doing so much for the salvation of souls, particularly the souls of the Pyrmont parish.' During the next fortnight the focus was on the two churches of the parish— St Bede Pyrmont and St Francis Xavier Ultimo—with morning Masses, instructions, evening sermons and Benediction. On the final Sunday night there was another outdoor gathering, beginning with a procession led by the truck carrying the crucifix followed by parishioners, missioners, parish priest and altar boys, along Bulwara Road to the Ultimo church.

Before giving an assessment of the mission the report focused on some of the observed challenges of the industrial district, especially the perilous situation of the children:

> Spiritually speaking at least, the lot of many of the children in this parish is a sad and tragic one. Almost half the Catholic children of this parish are attending a Public School, which means that during their impressive years, they are deprived of the cultured influence of the best of Catholic womanhood—our Nuns. The homes of many children in this area are unhappy, made so by drink mainly, in some cases immorality, and by the pagan lives of their parents who have no interest in God or religion whatsoever.

Included in the report was an expression of thanks to the girls of the Theresian Club 'whose work for the Mission Fathers was devoted and invaluable. It was a further extension of the magnificent Apostolate performed by them in this parish, so silently and unostentatiously for 19 years.' The Theresians began as a group of Sydney girls formed into a 'club' in 1918 by a Sister of Charity at St Vincent's Hospital. Their two aims were personal sanctification and responding to the spiritual needs of poor children in the congested areas of the city. During the 1920s, the activities of the young single women focused on the religious education of Catholic children attending state schools, not by entering the schools, but by visiting homes and bringing children to the parish Sunday Mass, followed by catechism classes. Theresian Clubs were established in Sydney parishes; they totalled 27 in 1939, one of which was in the Pyrmont-Ultimo parish. By then the members were conducting classes in the public schools.[36]

---

36. Ann Maree Whenman, *In Good Faith: a historical study of the provision of religious education for Catholic children in Catholic schools in New South Wales*, thesis submitted in School of Religious Education, Australian Catholic University,

The assessment of the Mission was posed in terms of the question 'Was there a harvest?' The frank answer was 'Yes, with reservations'. The reservations were dealt with first: 'Sad, as it is to have to say, but the largest proportion of the parish's lapsed Catholics (about 800 approximately) did not attend the Mission at all. There was no hostility, there were a few refusals, but for the most part, it was a question of indifference.' Leaving the final harvest assessment to God's reaping, the report concluded by enumerating 'a few tangible results' of the Mission: approximately 30 Catholics returned to their religious duties; 60 children, who had not been attending Sunday Mass, began regularly receiving the Sacraments; four men and one woman, all alcoholics, abandoned drink and returned to religious practice; two elderly women received the sacraments of confession and communion after fifty years absence; one woman received her First Communion at the age of 75.[37] It is not known whether the Redemptorist mission experiment was ever repeated.

Ashley Jones was absent on extended leave during the second half of 1961. When he became available again for ministry in 1962 he was assigned to West Pymble. In 1986 he opted to join the new diocese of Broken Bay which had been created out of the northern section of Sydney Archdiocese. He continued as parish priest of West Pymble until retirement in 1997. He died in 1999.

Replacing Father Jones at Pyrmont as administrator during his leave of absence was Eamonn Dundon. Eamonn was born in County Carlow in 1918. He was one of the last of the priests of St Patrick's College, Carlow, to come to Australia. The long and distinguished line of Carlow graduates began with John Joseph Therry in 1821 and included the founder of Saint Bede's at Pyrmont, Timothy McCarthy.[38] Ordained in 1940 for the Archdiocese of Sydney, Eamonn was prevented from travelling to Australia because of the War. With the permission of Archbishop Gilroy, he sought a placement in the English Diocese of Lancaster, where he worked as a curate in the parish of St Annes-on-Sea from September 1944 to February 1946. On arrival in Sydney in May 1946 he was assigned as assistant to Flemington parish. In 1947 he volunteered for the post-war mission in Japan. For the next six years he was stationed with his fellow Irishman Father Tom Fennell in the diocese of Osaka. Japan was in a devastated condition. Food was so scarce that the Australian priests and nuns heading there in 1947 were required to take

---

Sydney, 2011, 99–107.
37. 'Outside the City'—the Story of the First Industrial Parish Mission', no date (Pyrmont file, SAA).
38. Janice Garaty, 'The Carlow connection: the contribution of Irish seminarians to 19th century Australia', *Journal of the Australian Catholic Historical Society*, 35 (2014): 10–21.

several tons of food on board with them as a condition of being allowed entry.[39] On his return to Sydney in July 1953 he was placed at St Mary's Cathedral. No sooner was he back than he was volunteering for another overseas assignment, this time to Singapore.

Back in Australia in April 1958 he was briefly at Strathfield and then Elizabeth Bay, before Cardinal Gilroy called on him in December to take on the double role of National Director of the Apostleship of the Sea and Port Chaplain in Sydney. The Marist Fathers of St Patrick's, Church Hill, had conducted this ministry over many years, based for the national role in Harrington Street, and for the local role at the Seamen's Club in Kent Street, both within the Marist city parish. However, in December 1958 the then Marist chaplain, Denis Donovan, resigned 'following tension with his support agency, the St Vincent de Paul Society'.[40]

Eamonn moved into the Redfern presbytery, but then relocated to a vacancy in the more conveniently located parish of Balmain. When, in July 1961, an administrator was needed at Pyrmont, an even more convenient location for the seafarers' ministry, Cardinal Gilroy assigned him to St Bede's. The letter of appointment carried the usual Gilroy emphasis on matters financial: 'During the period that you will be in charge, you will please assume the responsibility of celebrating the 'Missa pro Popolo'. For this you will recompense yourself at the rate of one pound (£1) for each Mass . . . At the conclusion of your period of administration kindly forward to me a statement of Accounts, together with a cheque for any surplus Pastoral revenue, made payable to the Surplus Revenue Fund.'[41] With this appointment began the formal Pyrmont parish connection with the Apostleship of the Sea. There had been an informal connection beginning with Father McDonald's volunteer ship visits in 1930, and this had been continued, with more or less enthusiasm, by some of his successors.

In 1960 Dundon had presented his first report as National Director. The ministry in local ports around Australia had developed the pattern of being located at Stella Maris Clubs, from where a chaplain and volunteers would conduct ship visits and at which seafarers could gather for rest and recreation while in port. In the report he strongly advocated that Port Chaplaincy in major centres should be a full-time position: 'It is essential, I would say, to have a full-time Chaplain before a proper Club can be formed or run in any port. The Chaplain is an essential part of any club; without him it means nothing.'[42] This was a theme that would resurface in Sydney twenty years

---

39. *Catholic Weekly*, 5 February 1986,
40. P McMurrick, *The Harmonious Influence of Religion: St Patrick's Church Hill, 1840 ro the Present* (Sydney:2011), 80.
41. Gilroy to Dundon, 8 December 1961 (Dundon file, SAA)
42. *Apostleship of the Sea: 1960 Annual Report* (Apostleship of the Sea file, SAA).

later. The significance of the ministry was indicated in the report where he indicated a total attendance of 23,000 sailors at the Sydney Club during 1960. However, he expressed disappointment with this statistic because 'the number represents a very small proportion of sailors who come to the city'. Here he raised the question of the provision of a liquor licence for the Club, a subject that would continue to be controversial over many years. Another source of tension was the status of the Seafarers' ministry as a 'special work' of the St Vincent de Paul Society. The chief work was the visiting of ships, which he compared to the house to house visitation, then so normal in a parish. Part of the ship visit routine was to make available suitable reading matter for the sailors. On this matter he offered some advice 'Each bundle of literature should be approximately 50% secular and 50% Catholic. Not all secular magazines are put on board, only those that would be found in a respectable Catholic home.' He concluded his report with a paragraph on the menace of Communism, which Cardinal Gilroy had identified as a particular danger on the Pyrmont peninsula when appointing Cletus Heffernan 1939: 'There is no doubt that the biggest single factor acting against the sailor practicing his religion is Communism. The members of the Communist Party are as active as ever on board the Australian ships. Every battle that their union wins is claimed as a victory for Communism. They hide behind every good that is obtained for the sailor. Capitalism and Church are identified.' Despite the challenges Father Dundon was glad to be able to claim 'some definite progress during 1960'.[43]

The Cardinal was pleased with the way the double role of Port Chaplain and National Director was being performed, writing to Eamonn in August 1961: 'Congratulations upon what you have achieved in Sydney and what you endeavour to achieve elsewhere. I hope you will receive here and elsewhere the assistance you need to fulfil this most important apostolate.'[44] Gilroy, ever attentive to minor matters, raised an issue with Dundon in June 1962: 'A whisper reached me that there have been occasions when non-Catholic Ministers have used a Mass kit. Would it not be an advantage to have a prominent notice on the Kits "Reserved exclusively for Roman Catholic Clergy" or some such inscription?'[45] Dundon replied at considerable length, stating that he was aware of the problem and that he had taken the initiative of having all Catholic chalices inscribed 'Apostolatus Maris'. However, he noted that 'recently the opposite happened': 'One of our priests used the Church of England chalice for saying Mass over a period of weeks.' He concluded in a 'P.S.' that the problem was that the shipping companies supplied kits for

---

43. Apostleship of the Sea: 1960 Annual Report (Apostleship of the Sea file, SAA).
44. Gilroy to Dundon, 10 August 1961 (Dundon file, SAA)
45. Gilroy to Dundon, 15 June 1962 (Dundon file, SAA)

Low Church services only, and that it was the High Church Anglicans 'who cause the trouble' in seeking out the Catholic kits replete with vestments and vessels more suited to their style.[46]

After spending 1962 at Pyrmont, assisted in both parochial and extra-parochial duties by a curate, Frank Higgins, Eamonn was summoned by the Cardinal to be administrator of St Mary's Cathedral—on a salary of £35 per month. He retained the national element of the seafarers' ministry, being designated 'Merchant Navy Chaplain' in the *Catholic Directory*, while his successor as parish priest of Pyrmont, Victor Doyle, took on the local aspects of the ministry with the title 'Port of Sydney Chaplain'.[47]

Eamonn Dundon's ministry at St Mary's came to an abrupt end when he suffered a severe heart attack in 1967. Following convalescence he was assigned to the small parish of Northbridge. On Cardinal Gilroy's recommendation he had been appointed in 1966 an honorary Chaplain to Pope Paul VI with the tile of 'Monsignor'. He continued at Northbridge for 18 years, dying in 1986 at the age of 67. At his Requiem Mass Bishop Geoffrey Robinson, who had shared the Northbridge presbytery with him for twelve years, recalled his love of boats, quite a development for a native of a landlocked Irish county:

> One Saturday he was working on his boat, but was due to say the evening Mass. At five to six I came out of the confessional to see what was happening and found him just arriving home. He put his cassock over the clothes he was wearing. Because it was cold and wet, over that he put the wind jacket he had been wearing, with an Irish flag on one breast and an Australian flag on the other. The top of his head was covered with marine varnish. Thus attired, he proceeded to the church.[48]

---

46. Dundon to Gilroy, 25 June 1962 (Dundon file, SAA)
47. *Catholic Directory*, volumes 1963–64, 1964–65, 1965–66.
48. *Catholic Weekly*, 5 February 1986.

Chapter 22
Centenary Celebrated

Victor Doyle, aged forty-four when he arrived at Pyrmont in May 1963, was a priest of unusually wide pastoral experience. In addition to the usual series of appointments as parish curate following ordination in 1945—at Erskineville, Concord, Liverpool—he had also served as an army chaplain at Holsworthy camp from 1951 to 1954 and as migrant chaplain based at the Scheyville Immigration Centre in the Windsor district from 1956 to 1963. On being informed of the appointment to Pyrmont he wrote to Cardinal Gilroy: 'I feel sure that my five years as an Army Chaplain, and my six and a half years here as a Migrant Chaplain will be of some assistance in enabling me to carry out my new duties.'[1]

Welcoming him to the presbytery was the curate, Frank Higgins, who had been appointed to St Bede's at the same time as Eamonn Dundon. Ordained in 1955, Higgins served as assistant priest at Enmore and Kogarah before coming to Pyrmont where, as well as being parish curate, he was also Assistant Port Chaplain. He continued in this double role until 1966, after which he served as curate at Richmond and Waitara. Succeeding Higgins in parish and seafarer ministry at Pyrmont was Ronald Hickman. Born of English migrant parents in 1924, he was baptised in the Anglican Church at Leeton. In 1934 the whole family was received into the Catholic Church at St Joseph's, Rozelle. He attended the local Catholic schools under the Good Samaritan Sisters and Christian Brothers. In 1942 at the age of 18 he enlisted in the army, becoming a member of the 2/17th Battalion, serving in New Guinea and Borneo. Back in Australia he resumed work at the Sydney County Council. Following a parish mission at Punchbowl in 1947 he was determined to follow a call to the priesthood. He completed his Leaving Certificate through attending night school at St Patrick's, Church Hill. In 1948 he began ecclesiastical studies at St Columba's, Springwood. He was part of the Manly ordination class in 1954. Before coming to Pyrmont he

---

1. Doyle to Gilroy, 12 April 1963 (Doyle file, SAA).

was curate at Tempe, Auburn, Cabramatta and Lidcombe. After finishing at Pyrmont in 1972, his career took him to a dizzying range of Sydney parishes, mostly in his preferred role as curate, but also in charge at Blacktown, Revesby and Sadleir-Miller. His last placement was chaplain at Cardinal Gilroy Retirement Village in 2003. He died in February 2010 aged 85. At his Requiem Mass Bishop Geoffrey Robinson explained Ronald's aversion to being in charge: 'He loved being a priest but he hated administration, all that practical part of being a parish priest that they never taught you about in the seminary, and which takes up much of a parish priest's time. . . . If you check it out you will find that he was a parish priest for only 15 of the 50 years that he worked as a priest. But then Ron was not an administrator. He was affectionately and always a people person.'[2]

As for Eamonn Dundon, so for Victor Doyle, it was the Port Chaplaincy ministry that constituted his major commitment. The population of Pyrmont-Ultimo was continuing to decline and parish ministry was far from being a full-time job, especially with a second priest in the presbytery. Already the number of Sunday Masses in the parish had been halved, from four to two, 7am at St Bede's and 9am at St Francis Xavier.

Within a few months of commencing at St Bede's, Father Doyle received high praise from the President of the NSW Central Council of the St Vincent de Paul Society, who in a letter to Cardinal Gilroy concluded that 'complete harmony prevails' between the National Director and the Port Chaplain and the Seafarers' Committee. The main content of the letter was a focus on the lack of harmony, indeed incompatibility, between the 'Rule of the Society' and that of the 'Apostolatus Maris'.[3] Conflicts invariably involved questions of jurisdiction and finance. The Society was responsible for financing the Clubs and providing Chaplains with stipends, and it was expected that the ministry would be governed by the Society's rule and spirit. Its highest governing body, the Superior Council of Australia, early in August, had published eight resolutions to be communicated to the Australian bishops. On the question of the Clubs, the Council set out conditions which must be adhered to for their management to be compatible with the Rule of the Society:

1. The managing body of the Club must consist of members of the Society duly appointed by the appropriate council.
2. The financial affairs of the Club must be under the direct control of the Society.
3. Members of the Society must be involved in the work.[4]

---

2. *Catholic Weekly*, 21 March 2010.
3. LJ Keegan to Cardinal Gilroy, 13 August 1963 (Apostleship of the Sea file, SAA).
4. 'Text of Resolutions relating to Stella Maris Clubs', Plenary meeting of the Superior Council of the St Vincent de Paul Society, held in Sydney, 3rd & 4th

The tensions identified were never satisfactorily resolved and in 1982 the Vincent de Paul Society would arrive at the conclusion that, with improved conditions and pay for seamen, the work of the Apostleship of the Sea was not compatible with the Society's mission to the poor. In Sydney this involved the handing over of the Kent Street premises and responsibility for the funding of the Stella Maris Club to the Archdiocese.

The parish school at Ultimo received a gift in 1965 which, it was hoped, would go some way to solving the generations-old problem of truancy in the district—a two hundredweight bronze bell, which would be rung to summon the local children at the beginning of the school day. The hundred-year-old bell had been cast in the United States and installed at the old Belmore Market in George Street, and was later taken across the road to the new site at Haymarket. It became redundant with the installation of an electric bell system at the market and sat gathering dust in storage. Through the influence of the local Ultimo alderman, Sid Fegan, the City Council donated the bell to St Francis Xavier School. An old-boy of the school, Sid Malone, led a team of five in installing the bell; Sister Edith Edwards, Superior of the Good Samaritan Convent, had the honour of being the first to ring it.[5]

Victor Doyle had identified a bright spot on the rather gloomy horizon of the parish. He was the right man for recognising the upcoming centenary of the blessing of St Bede's Church. The first requirement had been to get the date correct. His predecessors since 1944 had been recording the year of opening as 1856 in the intermittent reports for the Archdiocesan Chancery, despite 'Anno Domini 1867' being clearly engraved on the facade of the church. Doyle got the date right in 1965 when he crossed out 1856 and wrote 1867 in his report. There had been no recognition of the fiftieth or seventy-fifth anniversaries, and he was determined that 1967 would not pass without a celebration. He formed a fifteen member Centenary Committee with himself as chairman and his curate, Ron Hickman, as vice-chair. Cardinal Gilroy was in January invited to preside at the Centennial Mass to be celebrated on Sunday 24 September. The invitation was 'provisionally' accepted. In July the Cardinal informed the Committee that he had unfortunately been called to Rome and was due to sail from Sydney on the *Galileo* in August 1967. He delegated his auxiliary bishop, James Carroll, to represent him at the celebration and provided a foreword for the centennial booklet.[6] Before sailing, Gilroy granted permission for the centenary Mass to be concelebrated. Concelebration was one of the liturgical fruits of the recent Vatican Council. However, the Cardinal found himself unable to give

---

August, 1963 ((Apostleship of the Sea file, SAA).
5. *Sydney Morning Herald*, 15 May 1965; *Catholic Weekly*, 17 August 1965.
6. See Appendix 1 below.

permission for 'bination', the celebration by a priest of a second Mass on the same day: 'My Faculties do not seem to include the granting of permission to binate simply to be one of the Concelebrants.' Another request from the Parish Priest was referred to the auxiliary bishop: 'You may arrange with Archbishop Carroll for the consecration of the St Bede's Church, Pyrmont.'[7] The consecration did not take place in conjunction with the centenary celebration.[8]

The next dignitary to be invited was John Ignatius Armstrong, Lord Mayor of Sydney and former Senator, who had been born in Pyrmont in 1908, the son the publican of the *Butcher's Arms*. He had been baptised at St Bede's and had attended the parish primary school before proceeding to the Marist Brothers' High School in Darlinghurst. The Right Honourable Mayor was more effusive in his response than His Eminence, accepting the invitation 'with much pleasure', and offering to honour the occasion by wearing the mayoral robes and gold chain of office.[9] The local Federal Member, Dan Minogue, was sent a rather last-minute invitation on 12 September; he also was delighted to accept.

A full week of celebration was planned beginning with the Sunday evening Mass, the first to be concelebrated at St Bede's, in the presence of Archbishop Carroll, the Lord Mayor and past and present parishioners. This would be followed by a 'Grand Concert' in the parish hall, the former parish school building. On the Tuesday evening Bishop Muldoon would confirm children of the parish. On the Wednesday a luncheon for past priests of the parish was planned. The following evening a Requiem Mass was to be celebrated for all deceased members of the parish. The week would conclude with a Cabaret Dance on the Saturday evening.

Father Doyle had prepared a thirty page illustrated booklet on the story of St Bede's, past and present. It was published by the Lyons printery around the corner in Harris Street. The Lyons family had been the official printers for the parish for two generations, and would continue in the role for a third, preparing Annual Reports of the Stella Maris Club and parish bulletins until 2002 when the business closed. The family were generous benefactors of St Bede's; they would fund the Marian grotto in the church grounds during the incumbency of Father James Fowler, 1987 to 1991.

Newspaper announcements of the planned centenary celebration emphasised the changed environment of St Bede's over the hundred years of its existence: 'Built of sandstone hewn on the site, St Bede's once had an unimpeded view of the harbour, but now takes its place with wool stores

---

7. Gilroy to Doyle, 3 August 1967 (Centenary File, Pyrmont Box, SAA).
8. The present Parish Priest is hoping to include the formal consecration of the church as part of the Sesquicentennial celebrations.
9. Armstrong to Doyle, 23 March 1967 (Centenary File, Pyrmont Box, SAA).

and the Pyrmont wharves opposite.'[10] 'At the time the church stood above a grassy slope which stretched down to the sand at the water's edge . . . Today the chimneys of big industry belch forth smoke and soot at the rate of 28 tons per square mile each month.'[11]

Concelebrating with the Parish Priest for the centennial Mass were former Pyrmont clergy, Monsignor Eamonn Dundon from St Mary's Cathedral and Fathers Ashley Jones from West Pymble, Cletus Heffernan from Annandale and Frank Higgins from Richmond. Other visiting clergy gathered with the congregation. Archbishop Carroll and Monsignor Duffy, the Archdiocesan historian, flanked the sanctuary, and the robed Lord Mayor was in a place of honour outside the altar rails. James Carroll chose to deliver himself of a long address on the much overworked question of State aid for Catholic education. With minimal reference to St Bede's, he rehearsed the long and often bitter and now tedious debate, quoting at length from Archbishop Vaughan. The Archbishop's speech occupied five columns of the *Catholic Weekly*. It was left to Monsignor Duffy briefly to pay due honour to the one hundred years of Pyrmont parish.[12] The Grand Concert that followed the Mass consisted of choirs from the parish school at Ultimo and from St Mary's Cathedral College, 'McEwan's School of Irish Dancing', a singing clergyman, Father John O'Neill, 'MacNamara's Band', a female soloist, 'The Roster Sisters' and a performance of an operetta, 'Cinderella', by the children of St Francis Xavier School. The Lord Mayor wrote to Father Doyle during the following week, commenting generously on the celebration: 'Congratulations on the Centenary. It was wonderfully done and everyone enjoyed it. I was thrilled to be there.'[13]

As St Bede's celebrated its centenary, St Bartholomew's Anglican Church, seventeen years older, stood abandoned on the heights of Pyrmont. In 1963 it had faced closure, with a Sunday congregation reduced to between six and a dozen. There was a plan for the church to be pulled down and moved stone by stone to a new site at Balgowlah. The few parishioners at the time were determined not to lose their historical church perched on the highest point of Pyrmont, and they appealed to the archdeacon, who gave a reprieve and said that if they wanted the church it would stay.[14] The parish had lost its resident rector in 1955 following the end of Edward Madgwick's thirty year incumbency, and was combined with the parishes of Rozelle and Balmain. The district was later annexed to St Barnabas at Broadway. According to the Reverend Barnett, during the brief period he was in charge the congregation

---

10. *Sydney Morning Herald*, 23 September 1967.
11. *Catholic Weekly*, 14 September 1967.
12. *Catholic Weekly*, 28 September 1967.
13. Armstrong to Doyle, 26 September 1967.
14. *The Sun*, 17 October 1969.

consisted of his wife and the catechist.[15] By 1967 services were suspended. An article in the *Sydney Sun* of October 1969 was headed 'End Near for the Sailors' Church'. The article was full of inaccuracies, including the designation of St Bartholomew's as 'the sailors' Church ... full of memories and half-forgotten prayers of a thousand seamen'.[16] The Anglican seafarers' mission had always been located across Darling Harbour in the Rocks area. Nor was the description of the church as 140 years old accurate; the foundation stone of St Bartholomew's was laid in 1849 and opened in 1850.[17] In 1836 Edward Macarthur had proposed a subdivision of the Pyrmont estate, and he set aside an acre of land, at the location of the old windmill on the hill overlooking Darling Harbour, for the erection of an Anglican church, rectory and school, and the creation of a burial ground. Part of the land had been resumed by the City Council in 1916 for the eventual building of the Ways Terrace flats. With the compensation money the parish built a new rectory and parish hall; the school, like most Anglican parish schools, had been relinquished following Henry Parkes' Public Instruction Act of 1880. An article in the journal of the Church of England Historical Society in 1964 described the contemporary state of the church and parish:

> Today there are about fifty Anglican families amongst the two hundred in the district. The roof of Church is in a bad state. One wonders what is to become of this Church. Surely such a parish is a challenge to the whole Church. It seems that lengthy ministries, whatever their cause, are detrimental to the life of a parish, and hard on the clergy concerned. As a church we seem to be lacking in a brotherly spirit. The wealthier parishes could help a place such as this more directly than at present. It seems bad policy to haul down the flag of our Church, as we seem to be doing in these inner areas. We should keep our properties as far as possible, and see that they are used for the purposes for which they were given. If we lose them, we may not be able to secure others. Conditions in these districts could easily change in these days of multi-storied buildings, and we would find it difficult to buy similar lands in the future.[18]

In May 1970 the *Sydney Morning Herald* published a photograph captioned 'St Bartholomew's—wrecking under way'. The forlorn image showed that slate tiles had been ripped off the roof, the windows smashed; a bulldozer, surrounded by rubble, was at work at the side of the church. The

---

15. *Sydney Morning Herald*, May 1970.
16. *The Sun*, 17 October 1969.
17. *Sydney Morning Herald*, 25 August 1849.
18. E Middleton, 'St Bartholomew's, Pyrmont', *Church of England Historical Society Journal*, 7(1964): 239.

accompanying article, headed 'No one to save St Bartholomew's', detailed the process of demolition:

> The roof has gone, its furnishings have been ripped out, the floors burnt away to expose the foundations. An old baptismal font still stands at one end of the church, and the stained-glass window behind the altar area is intact. The rest is a mass of charred and broken wood. The rectory has almost totally disappeared and the bedraggled remains of crepe-paper streamers still hang forlornly in the church hall. The cedar pews have been sold for $60 to other churches. The stone, of such poor quality the parish authorities could not even give it away, has been left to the demolishers.[19]

The journalist explained that the Church of England still owned the land and had leased it to developers. The Reverend Barnett did not agree that the Anglican Church should keep its properties 'as far as possible, and see that they are used for the purposes for which they were given'. His comment to the journalist reporting the demolition was: 'We cannot keep useless monuments, simply for the sake of nostalgia.'[20] The 24,000 square-foot site would remain abandoned for thirty years. Multi-storied apartment buildings now stand on the former Anglican property. The only record of St Bartholomew's 120 years on the site is a marble plaque inscribed to the memory of the fallen soldiers, but which does not name the parish church:

\+

TO THE GLORY OF GOD

AND

IN APPRECIATION OF THE MEN

OF THIS PARISH WHO SERVED IN

1914   THE GREAT WAR   1918

The church's fine, single manual organ had been created locally by William Davidson in about 1870 and originally installed in St John's, Ashfield. It had been relocated to Saint Bartholomew's in 1882. In 1970, prior to the demolition of the church, the organ was retrieved and restored for installation in St Luke's at Northmead.[21] Efforts by the Pyrmont Anglican community to revive a parish in recent years, even to the extent of recruiting a resident minister as 'curate in charge' in 2007, came to naught, due largely to the

---

19. *Sydney Morning Herald*, May 1970.
20. *Sydney Morning Herald*, May 1970.
21. Graeme D Rushworth, *Historic Organs of New South Wales: The Instruments, Their Makers and Players, 1791–1940* (Sydney, 1988), 99.

lack of church property, a situation about which the wise Mr Middleton had warned in 1964, and which was acknowledged by the bishop for South Sydney, Robert Forsyth, in 2008: 'With hindsight you wonder whether this has taught us a lesson about trying to grow churches in extremely expensive areas where you don't own buildings.'[22]

The year following the church demolition, the State Government of Robin Askin produced the 1971 City of Sydney Plan, whose accompanying map of Pyrmont-Glebe showed only one tiny portion of the peninsula designated as 'residential'. This was the 1923 Ways Terrace Flats; the rest was designated 'industrial', including, of course, St Bede's Church. Shown in the plan were two major expressways through Pyrmont and Ultimo. Demolition of local housing was again on the agenda. The City Council countered with its 1971 Strategic Plan in which the bulk of the peninsula was designated residential, leaving the waterfront and rail network, the Sugar Refinery and Power Station as industrial. All the areas then occupied by the many giant wool-stores were to be converted to residential use. However, the State Plan was law, and the only power still in the hands of the Council was the right to limit the height of any proposed development. The Council imposed a holding operation 'by placing a 1:1 floor space ratio prescription over the area.'[23] Not able to prevent the handing over of the peninsula to wholesale industrial and commercial development, because of the gazetted State Plan, the Council used its limited power to make such development economically unviable by effectively limiting any new building to one or two storeys. This seemed to provide the suburb with a reprieve from relentless demolition. However, nothing could prevent demolition of housing for freeways and parking lots.

In May 1971 Vic Doyle was interviewed by journalist Alan Gill for an article about the peninsula entitled, 'Decline and fall of a bit of old Sydney':

> The sole surviving church with an active congregation is the Roman Catholic St Bede's, Pyrmont. The parish priest is Father Victor Doyle. Officially his church is in an area designated for light industry ... Father Doyle ... treats property men the way that St George tackled the dragon. On the day he was interviewed for this article he had just had a visit from a developer. The priest told him: 'I'm NEVER going to sell my church.' Answered the developer: 'That's why I want it.' Father Doyle told the

---

22. Joseph Smith, 'Our 'worthwhile' ministry risk', *Sydney Anglicans*, 28 February 2008 (http://sydneyanglicans.net/news/pyrmont_church_story [accessed 19 March 2015]).
23. Michael R Matthews, *Pyrmont and Ultimo. A history* (Sydney 1982), 104.

Herald: 'In Pyrmont-Ultimo we have a devoted community, possibly unique in Australia. At all costs it must be kept.'[24]

After nine years at Pyrmont Vic Doyle was looking for a change of scene. In May 1972 he applied for appointment as parish priest of Harbord, one of Sydney's northern beach suburbs, and the traditional holiday destination of Pyrmont's O'Toole family. The vacancy at Harbord had occurred when the well-known priest, Roger Pryke, for many years chaplain at the University of Sydney, wrote to his parishioners in April 1972: 'With much and with deep feeling I want to tell you of a decision I have made after several years of difficulty, doubts and indecision. Though I realise it will cause some people surprise, even pain, I have decided painfully at this stage of my life and work, to retire from Ministry and to live the rest of my life as a private person and citizen rather than as a public official of the church.'[25]

In his application Vic Doyle reminded the newly appointed Archbishop James Freeman that he had been Port Chaplain for over nine years; he was seeking 'a more settled parish where I could be more actively engaged in the pastoral field': 'I have thoroughly enjoyed every Parish that I have been in, especially Pyrmont, but as my years here have been exceeded by no one since 1899, I feel that I have done reasonably well here.' The reference was to Philip McIntyre, whose ten years at Pyrmont, 1899-1909, constituted the longest appointment among Doyle's many predecessors at St Bede's. Father Doyle seemed to be suggesting that ten years service on the Pyrmont peninsula was the most that could be expected of any priest. He even submitted to the Archbishop a list of the names of six priests whom he considered suitable to succeed him as port chaplain. Included on the list was 'Ron Hickman who has been here for six years and is thoroughly conversant with every aspect of the Port'.[26] Vic Doyle was not successful in his application for Harbord parish and he continued at St Bede's for another two years. His total of eleven years made him the longest serving parish priest in the 150 years of Pyrmont parish. It is doubtful whether any other parish in Sydney has recorded so short a 'longest term'.

His failure to achieve a transfer in 1972 meant that he faced another episcopal visitation of Pyrmont in 1973. The auxiliary Bishop, Thomas Muldoon, conducted the bi-annual review of the parish in June of that year. The 31 page document is a sad record of the declining state of the parish in the early years of its second century, as concluded by Bishop Muldoon in his

---

24. *Sydney Morning Herald*, 8 May 1971.
25. Letter of Pryke to Harbord parishioners, 16 April 1972, in Francis Ravel Harvey, *The Roger Pryke Story: Traveller to Freedom*, (Sydney: Freshwater Press, 2011), 343.
26. Doyle to Freeman, 1 May 1972 (Doyle File, SAA).

summary: 'Sad to see the old place going down. However, we must hang on to it and give the adequate pastoral care.'

The 'Report of Episcopal Visitation' was prefaced by the canonically enumerated purposes of diocesan visitations:
1. To preserve sound and orthodox doctrine.
2. To foster good morals.
3. To correct evil customs.
4. To promote peace, innocence, piety and discipline among clergy and laity.
5. As far as circumstances permit to regulate everything for the best interests of Religion.

The document to be completed was divided into four sections: Persons; Places and Things; The Sacraments; Parochial Administration. The very last question elicited a pessimistic answer:

> What notable changes have taken place in the Parish since the last Visitation (e.g. increase or decrease of population; new buildings or properties; factors effecting development, such as new housing, migrant influx, etc; parochial debt.)?
> Decrease in population; many houses being demolished for Expressway and Parking Lots.[27]

This was the same observation that had been made in Father McDonald's diary entry of 1928, except that in that year the houses were making way for factory and warehouse expansion. The evidence of the population decrease was given in the comparison of parishioner numbers in the 1970 and 1973 visitation documents:

	1970	1973
Parishioners	974	612
Catholic families	229	180
Catholic children of school age	186	132

These figures represented a decrease of parishioners by a third in three years, and a decrease in families and school age children by a quarter. Over the same period the parish school enrolment suffered a decrease of fifty per cent, from 117 to 55. The percentage of parish children at the parish school declined from 63% to 42%.[28] These were the statistics that gave rise to Bishop Muldoon's lament about 'the old place going down'.

---

27. 'Report of Episcopal Visitation', Pyrmont 1973, 29 (Pyrmont Box, SAA).
28. 'Report of Episcopal Visitation', Pyrmont 1973, 2 (Pyrmont Box, SAA).

The detailed, probing questions relating to worship and sacraments yielded succinct answers: 'What is the average length of the instruction at the early Mass?'—10 minutes; 'What time is usually given to the Sermon at the late Mass?'—10 minutes. This was an improvement over the 20 minute sermons at the late Mass in 1947 by the eminent preacher Dick Funcheon. The episcopal preoccupation with marriage found expression in a range of questions:

> Is a special Instruction given at least once a year on the evils of Mixed Marriages?—Yes
> How many purely Catholic Marriages took place since last Visitation?—12
> How many mixed marriages occurred since last Visitation?—13
> How many Catholics were civilly married (a) before a heretical minster; (b) by a civil Registrar?—(a) nil; (b) nil
> How many 'ne temere' cases in the Parish now?—50

'Ne temere' cases were marriages involving a Catholic partner that had not been performed by a Catholic priest. Such marriages were regarded as invalid and parish priests, through their visits to parish households, were required to keep a record of such cases and persevere in trying to have them regularised. The irksome task was often delegated to the curate, as historian John Challis recalled in his reminisces about his first parish appointment as a curate in the Archdiocese of Perth: 'One of the first tasks Fr Kieran gave me was to go and visit the "Ne Tem cases", as they were called in clerical parlance—people who were married outside the church and therefore "living in sin". I said to Fr Kieran: "What shall I say to them?" and he said: "Tell them they have to live as brother and sister".'[29]

Adding to the perception of 'the old place going down' was Fr Doyle's response to the question concerning lay organisations in the parish. Of the eighteen groups named in the document only four were in existence at Pyrmont-Ultimo in 1973. Associations which had had a proud history at St Bede's and at St Francis Xavier's were no longer functioning—the Hibernians, the AHC Guild, the Children of Mary, Holy Name Society, Catholic Youth Organisation. The Theresians, who had received high praise from Vic Doyle in the centenary booklet in 1967 for their work with State School children, were no longer functioning six years later. Even the groups still in existence were reduced to very low membership: Christian Doctrine (catechetics)—assistant priest and one laywoman; Sacred Heart Sodality

---

29. John Challis, 'Recollections of a Perth Movement Chaplain', *Journal of the Australian Catholic Historical Society*, 35 (2014): 75. See Brigid Moore, 'Sectarianism in NSW: the *Ne Temere* Legislation 1924-1925', *Journal of the Australian Catholic Historical Society*, 9(1987): 3–15.

for women—6 members; St Vincent de Paul Society—3 members[30]; Altar Society—4 members. A group not mentioned on the form was the Rosary Confraternity which, when established in the parish in 1952 by Dominican Thomas Fitzgerald, had enrolled 138 members. Groups that had the custom of gathering in the parish church on a particular Sunday of the month, such as the Sacred Heart Sodality and the Holy Name Society, had been somewhat undermined by the liturgical changes brought about at the Second Vatican Council, which met from 1962 to 1965.

Bishop Muldoon, despite his sadness at the parish statistics, was adamant that the parish should not be suppressed as happened just three years earlier to the Anglican parish, when St Bartholomew's church had been demolished: 'We must hang on to it and give it adequate pastoral care. The people look to the priest, who is just about the only stable and secure thing in their lives.' And he made a practical proposal and a final plea: 'One extra man working part-time at Broadway would be a great help—and adequate. It is greatly desired that the Sisters stay in the area.'[31] Father Brian Charlton was sent as curate the next year, but the Good Samaritan Sisters had already left the Ultimo convent and were commuting from the St Benedict's convent. St Francis Xavier school would close at the end of the year, just six months after the visitation. The *Catholic Weekly* announced the closure, citing the reduced enrolment of 35 pupils: 'One of Sydney's oldest and most historic parish schools will close on Thursday, December 13.'[32] The evening before the closure a Mass of Thanksgiving was celebrated at St Francis Xavier's Church, Ultimo, for 'the many graces received . . . as a result of the self-sacrifice of the Sisters of the Good Samaritan'. Ten priests who had participated in the ministry at Ultimo returned to take part, including Monsignor Dundon who reminded the congregation that the church-school was the first to be dedicated to St Francis Xavier in the Archdiocese.[33] The 1851 Church at Berrima was first dedicated to St Scholastica and only in the late 1890s, after the naming of the Ultimo church, was the dedication changed to that of the great Jesuit missionary and co-patron of the Church in Australia.

Father Vic Doyle was finally released from Pyrmont in July 1974 with his appointment to Mount Carmel parish at Waterloo, another challenging inner-city parish, far from his preferred beachside suburbs. In October he wrote from Waterloo to his successor at Pyrmont, Brian Charlton, thanking him for organising a farewell, and for the gift of a 'reclining chair for my

---

30. One of the three Pyrmont Conference members was a young city-based lawyer, Michael Whittemore, who had joined in 1966. Fifty years later he is still an active Vincentian.
31. 'Report of Episcopal Visitation', Pyrmont 1973, 31.
32. *Catholic Weekly*, 6 December 1973.
33. *Catholic Weekly*, 10 January 1974.

declining years, and your generous cheque': 'I enjoyed my years in Pyrmont and Ultimo, and I will always remember with deep gratitude the generosity of the People of the Parish. I pray that God will prosper your work among them and that He will bless you and them always.'[34] Father Vic Doyle spent 26 years as parish priest of Waterloo, retiring in 1990. On Australia Day 2004 he was awarded the Order of Australia medal. The citation read: 'For service to the community, particularly through the social welfare programs of the Catholic Church.'[35] He died in October that year aged 83.

Brian Charlton had been ordained in 1955 in the same group of Manly graduates as Frank Higgins. In the chaplain's report for 1974 he wrote glowingly of the work of Vic Doyle in the seafarers' apostolate: 'His energy, enthusiasm and zeal for the Church's work for Seafarers moved at a pace that has been impossible to duplicate. . . . Without help the Port Chaplain would be most ineffectual. I take this opportunity of recording my gratitude to Father Doyle for introducing me into this work.'[36] Father Charlton's ministry in Pyrmont and at Kent Street came to an abrupt end when he abandoned the presbytery in October 1975, leaving a brief note for the Archbishop informing him of his resignation from the priesthood, and where the keys for the Seafarers Club could be found.[37]

In November 1975 an interim appointment was needed to secure church services in the parish after Brian Charlton's sudden withdrawal. A young priest, Luke Rawlings, from the Dominican Priory in Wahroonga, took up residence at St Bede's for three months. Luke's total lack of experience in parish matters was displayed in his cry for help placed in the Parish Bulletin below the weekly entry 'Silver Circle Winners for this week': 'The Silver Circle is a complete mystery to me—even after a fine explanation from Fr Ingham, I shall have to get someone to come down and explain it to me. Hopefully everything will be cleared up next week.'[38]

In December 1975 Cardinal Freeman received a letter of complaint from a parishioner of St Benedict's accusing the priest at Pyrmont of allowing a political rally to be held in St Bede's Church. Proof was supplied in an enclosed publication, a copy of the election edition of 'The Pyrmont and Ultimo Gazette' which had announced: 'ALP Rally 7.30pm, Thursday, December 4, Pyrmont: election rally at St Bede's, Catholic Church, Pyrmont Street. Come and hear Les McMahon the ALP endorsed candidate.'[39] Luke

---

34. Doyle to Charlton, 31 October 1974 (Doyle File, SAA).
35. *Catholic Weekly*, 1 February 2004.
36. Brian Charlton, 'Port Chaplain's Report', *Stella Maris Club Annual Report*, July 1974.
37. Charlton to Freeman, 5 October 1975 (Charlton File, SAA).
38. *Pyrmont Parish Newsletter*, 9 November 1975 (Pyrmont Box, SAA).
39. *Pyrmont and Ultimo Gazette*, November 1975.

Rawlings, in granting permission for the event, was delightfully free of detailed knowledge of Canon Law. The complainant did not seem to receive a reply from the Cardinal. Les McMahon, a parishioner of neighbouring St James, Forest Lodge, was successful in holding the electorate of Sydney for Labor in the 1975 landslide swing against the party. In his maiden speech in the House of Representatives McMahon paid homage to a Pyrmont identity, Elizabeth Healey, a foundation member of the local party branch, for her influence on his political career, which took him from city alderman to MHR: 'I feel it would be remiss if I did not pay tribute to Mrs Elizabeth Healey who is 97 years of age and has been a member of the Australian Labor Party for over 75 years. Despite being confined to a wheelchair she still works actively for the ALP as she has done most of her life. I thank this great old lady for her dedication to the ALP and her assistance to me.'[40] It is not recorded whether Elizabeth attended the rally at St Bede's in December 1975. She died in 1977 at the age of 99. She is remembered in the 'Elizabeth Healy Reserve', opposite the *Quarryman's* Hotel.

A formal appointment to Pyrmont-Ultimo took place in January 1976 with the arrival of Father John Ford, who was taking charge of a parish for the first time.

---

40. *House of Representatives Hansard*, 4 March 1976.

Chapter 23
Continued Population Decline

John Ford was ordained in 1958, and he experienced the usual wide range of appointments as a young curate—Eastwood, Annandale, Penrith, Liverpool, Baulkham Hills, Kogarah, StMary's Cathedral. The Liverpool appointment, however, turned into an army chaplaincy. His role as chaplain was threefold: at the married quarters in Anzac Village, Moorebank, at the Corrective Establishment , Holsworthy, and to the engineers unit, which had a chapel where Mass was celebrated each week. John Ford has spoken of this period:

> It was of course during the Vietnam War and lots of the soldiers were over there, and their families were always in fear of them not coming back as some of them didn't. It was one of the hardest things I ever had to do—tell the wife that her soldier husband would not be returning alive. There were also a number of full time chaplains, Gerry Cudmore, a Melbourne priest ordained the same year as me, 1958, now deceased, being the first to go to Vietnam. They were all fine priests who worked under great difficulty. I was very fortunate that I was not called on to make that journey.[1]

He was based for three years, from 1971 to 1973, at St Patrick's College, Manly, as Director of Students and Bursar. In 1974, during four months sabbatical leave in the United States, he worked in a Minneapolis parish: 'I did not do official study leave but learnt a lot from there. It was a big parish with four priests and a deacon and one church on top of the other. Interesting to note that there is only one priest there now. It was a great time, just after Vatican II, and I still correspond with friends I made.'[2] On return to Australia he acted as curate at Malabar, where he was also chaplain to the hospital at Little Bay, until his appointment to the Pyrmont-Ultimo parish

---

1. Email from John Ford to the author, 4 March 2015.
2. Email from John Ford to the author, 4 March 2015.

and the seafarers' chaplaincy. It was a widely experienced and energetic priest who introduced himself to his parishioners in the parish bulletin of Sunday 25 January 1976: 'My Dear People, I would like to express to you all my sincere joy in coming to Pyrmont. It is a Parish of great traditions. I hope that, together, we might come to love the Lord in a more fervent and more fruitful way and that the love that the Lord shares with us, we might share more with others. Please feel free to visit me at any time.'[3]

One of his first duties in the parish was to preside at the funeral of Charlie Hackett at St Francis Xavier church in Ultimo in February. Until his final years, Hackett, the 'King of Ultimo', had a well-deserved reputation of being a 'fix-it man' when it came to finding jobs for locals, especially on the payroll of the City Council. This focus led to a practical suggestion about eliminating the word 'lane' from the Ultimo map: 'In 1950 Charlie told the aldermen that kids from Kirk Lane were going for jobs and getting knocked back because they lived in a lane. He wanted it changed to a street, and as with most things he wanted, he was successful. On the same day the aldermen honoured Charlie by renaming Bulwara Lane, Hackett Street.'[4] He was also a patron of local aspiring aldermen and State and Federal politicians. He had been a member of the NSW Legislative Council for twenty years from 1943 and was Secretary of the Pyrmont-Denison branch of the Labor Party for forty years, until his expulsion from the Party in 1959 for crossing the floor in Parliament to vote against the Labor Government Bill to abolish the Upper House:

> On the 14 December 1959, at 70 years of age, Charlie attended his last Labor Party Branch meeting. 'It was like a funeral', he later said. He took along the Branch's record books and formally tendered his resignation as Secretary . . . Charlie was politically dead, but not buried. He still had 6 years of his 12 year term to serve . . . In 1965 he could only muster one vote in the election for new MLCs—'I didn't even bother going in to vote for myself' . . . Right to the end, Charlie would attend City Council meetings, sit in the public gallery, chomp on his oversized cigar and ruminate on how those who grew up in his shadow were looking after the interests of Pyrmont and Ultimo. In 1971 he told Alan Gill on the Herald that the only way he would leave Ultimo would be 'when he was carried out feet first'. This was how he did leave his home at 70 Macarthur Street.[5]

---

3. *Pyrmont Parish Newsletter*, 25 January 1976 (Pyrmont Box, SAA).
4. Michael Matthews, *Pyrmont & Ultimo. A History* (Sydney, 1982), 97.
5. Matthews, *Pyrmont & Ultimo*, 97.

In 1976 a new system of funding the agencies of the Sydney Archdiocese was introduced. Father Ford was a foundation member of the new Charitable Works Fund Committee that was tasked with setting assessments for each parish's contribution to the central fund. The annual amount expected from Pyrmont was $500, to be collected on three designated Sundays throughout the year. The congregation was gently encouraged to be 'extra generous' to these special collections. By the time of the third collection only $187 had been contributed, and the parish priest's appeal was a little more pressing: 'I do ask you to be as generous as you are able to be.'[6] A sigh of relief could be detected in the Bulletin of the following week: 'I wish to express very sincere thanks to those who made contributions to the Appeal last Sunday. The sum of $146 was collected and for a parish as small as ours this is excellent. May you be blessed in your generosity.' There was a shortfall of $165. The Pyrmont parish assessment forty years later is $54,900.

Also new were aspects of the liturgical life of parishes flowing from decisions made at the Second Vatican Council. During February 1976 it was announced in the Parish Bulletin that from the first Sunday of March it would be permissible to receive Holy Communion in the hand. During Lent of that year, John Ford, like all parish priests in Sydney, was required to introduce his parishioners to a new 'Rite of Penance' which would come into effect in Advent.

With the continuing decline in the local population the principal work of the resident priest of Pyrmont became his ministry as Sydney Port Chaplain, into which Father Ford entered with enthusiasm and energy, taking on the running of the Stella Maris Club and its events, as well as maintaining a busy schedule of ships' visits. The Chaplain's report of 1978 gave an insight into the scope of this ministry:

> There was a Korean fishing vessel that came into Sydney early in June. Repairs were needed to the engine. One of the crew, unable to speak any English, had been seriously hurt when hurled against a winch and was taken to Sydney Hospital. With the help of Raphael Byun, a Korean Seaman on the *Diamond Star*, we were able to visit him, help the nursing sisters understand him and arrange for some of the Korean ministry to visit him when the ship had to leave. Others of the crew visited the Club almost daily. This crew had left their homes in Korea in September 1976 and will only return next year—a period of thirty months living in confined quarters—their only homes away from home being places like this. These are the ones for whom this Club and this work exists.[7]

---

6. *Pyrmont-Ultimo Parish Bulletin*, 10 October 1976 (Pyrmont Box, SAA).
7. John Ford, 'Port Chaplain's Report', *Stella Maris Club Annual Report*, July 1978.

Back in the parish there was drama later in 1978. In the early hours of Monday 27 November the parish priest was awakened by the smell of smoke. He discovered a raging fire in the church and immediately called the fire brigade. The parish bulletin for the following Sunday informed the Pyrmont congregation, now gathered with their fellow parishioners at the Ultimo church, about the damaged state of St Bede's:

> The fire was deliberately set, the back sacristy having been broken into and the front door left open. Thanks to the prompt action by the fire brigade there was no damage to the roof or the external walls of the church. If anyone saw what appeared to be suspicious action at that time you might let Father know. The church is now in the process of being restored and it will be some considerable time until this is complete. The damage is estimated in the vicinity of possibly $50,000, which will be covered by insurance.[8]

The *Catholic Weekly* later provided more details and information:

> A fire which extensively damaged the interior of one of Sydney's most historic inner city churches recently was deliberately lit, the parish priest revealed. The fire took place in the small church of St Bede, in Pyrmont Street, Pyrmont, early last Monday morning. It completely destroyed the gallery, confessionals and storeroom at the back of the church, and the heat and smoke damaged the altar and sanctuary fittings so badly that they will have to be removed.... Father Ford said that those who had left the door to the church slightly ajar, thus allowing the wind to spread the fire rapidly through the interior.[9]

The article ended on an optimistic note provided by the parish priest: 'Father Ford said that when the 111-year-old church was eventually restored he hoped that there would be a "Back to Pyrmont" Mass and a celebration that would be attended by many present and past parishioners.'[10]

The fire led to the renovation of the church and its adaptation to the reformed liturgy of the Vatican Council. The fire-damaged ornate wooden altar was removed from the sanctuary and replaced with a free standing stone altar, brought forward to the edge of the sanctuary. A new carved stone tabernacle was created and placed at the right-hand side of the sanctuary, a position made available by the removal of damaged plaster statues. The smoke damaged original blue-painted plaster was removed from the walls

---

8. *Parish Bulletin*, 3 December 1978 (Pyrmont Box, SAA).
9. *Catholic Weekly*, 17 December 1978.
10. *Catholic Weekly*, 17 December 1978.

and the honey-coloured sandstone was revealed. The confessional box was removed and not replaced; the large, framed paintings of the Stations of the Cross were replaced with small ceramic representations; a new gallery with stair case was installed. The work was overseen by Father John Ford and carried out by volunteer builders and craftsmen and their apprentices. The result was the uncluttering of the interior of a traditional 19th century Roman Catholic Church and the creation of a simple and beautiful space for community prayer and worship. In the words of ancient theology it could be said that the lighting of the fire, for which three local teenagers were charged and convicted, was a 'felix culpa', a fortunate mishap.

The population of the peninsula had peaked at the turn of the century to an estimated 30,000 and after steady decline reached its nadir in the late eighties at approximately 1500. The Catholic congregations in Pyrmont and Ultimo experienced a proportionately dramatic decline. When, in July 2009, Father John Ford celebrated the late morning Mass at St Bede's, which was attended by the usual congregation of approximately 100 parishioners, he informed them that when he had celebrated his last Sunday Mass before leaving Pyrmont in 1991, there were seven people in the congregation, and two of them were nuns! This was not quite the low experienced at St Bartholomew's in 1966—with the rector, his wife and the catechist in attendance. The Parish of Pyrmont-Ultimo had retained its resident priest through the 1960s into the 1990s because of the convenient location of the presbytery for conducting the Port of Sydney chaplaincy. This meant that its two churches remained open despite the declining population.

The larger of the parish's two small Sunday congregations gathered at St Francis Xavier Church in Ultimo and Father Ford was anxious to provide pastoral care for that southern section of the parish. Sister John (Mary Constable), who had been the last principal of the infant school in 1973, continued the Good Samaritan presence by conducting catechism classes in the local State School, leading the Rosary in the church and visiting the sick. She kept an office in the small room at the rear of the old convent, which had served as a music room during the life of the school. The rest of the convent was being used by the Vincent de Paul Society for Vietnamese refugee accommodation. A Josephite sister, Teresa Noon, was in 1977 looking for a change after forty years of school teaching, and seeking pastoral work in a poor area of Sydney. Based at the Arncliffe convent, she visited all the fringe parishes of the city, in the hope of finding a location where she could be of assistance. At Ultimo she met Sister John and Father Ford, who convinced her of the great needs of the area. Sister Teresa was given permission by her superiors to dedicate her time to developing a pastoral ministry in the parish. For two years she commuted each day by train and bus from Arncliffe to Ultimo. She began her ministry by visiting families named on a list provided by Sister John. When in 1980 another Josephite sister expressed interest in participating in this ministry, Father Ford arranged accommodation for them by having half of the old school on the top floor of the church-school building converted into an improvised convent. Each day found the traditionally habited nuns walking along the streets of Ultimo and Pyrmont, visiting the many needy households.

John Ford became active in a local group established to oppose the ongoing demolition of housing on the peninsula. He made common cause with the founders of Sydney's Green Ban movement, Jack Mundey and Joe Owens, leaders of the New South Wales Builders Labourers Federation and both members of the Communist Party of Australia. Late in 1980 Father Ford's activism resulted in threatened repercussions for his seafarers' ministry, as recounted by Michael Matthews, who had been elected Sydney's first independent alderman, for Phillip Ward, that September:

> CSR [Colonial Sugar Refinery] announced that they were going to demolish the Smooges Terrace in Jones Street for a level carpark. There was considerable local opposition to this and I wrote a feature letter to *SMH* decrying council's support of the proposal. The lord mayor, Doug Sutherland, then wrote a reply defending CSR and saying that council had no power over demolition. I wrote another letter and then John Ford wrote to *SMH* saying that 'he has followed this debate and is familiar with the issues, and believes that Alderman Matthews has the more supportable position', or words to that effect, or perhaps stronger words. All of this would have been in October or November 1980. The very next week, by coincidence, all the annual community grants came before council for renewal or commencement. The Stella Maris Club's grant [$1,000] was taken away by the Labor majority. Fr Ford's letter was not of course mentioned as being the reason, but I was told by the left side of the Labor caucus that this was the reason. The decision was circulated in the community and in Town Hall circles. About two meetings later the ALP could see the political fall-out beginning and reversed their decision.[11]

The so-called Smooges or Smoodgers Cottages, on the eastern side of Jones Street, between Bowman and Harvey, were a row of houses, larger than usual in Pyrmont. They were owned by CSR and rented out to the more senior managerial staff. The name carried the implication that the occupiers had done more than just a good day's work to merit such superior accommodation.

---

11. Michael Matthews, email communication to author, 8 March 2015.

Living in less elegant company-housing in John Street, around the corner from Smoodgers, was Mrs Ethel Carmichael, who became known as the 'Queen of Pyrmont'. Born in Pyrmont in 1886, she had strong CSR connections—her father in law, her husband, one son and a granddaughter all worked for CSR. Ethel herself, after a career as a tailoress, became a cleaner at the CSR research laboratory for 14 years, retiring in 1958. In 1986 the *Sydney Morning Herald*'s religious affairs reporter, Allan Gill, wrote an article to honour her hundredth birthday under the headline: QUEEN OF ULTIMO CELEBRATES A 'QUIET' CENTURY.

> No smoking, no drinking, plenty of exercise and a 'quiet life' is the recipe offered by Mrs Ethel Carmichael, 'Queen of Pyrmont-Ultimo', who is 100 years old today. Quiet? Perhaps. But not uneventful. Mrs Carmichael, who must be the fittest centenarian in Australia, was for 70 years an active member of Sydney Flying Squadron 18-Footer Sailing Club, and continued to attend meetings until last year . . . Easily the best known person in Pyrmont-Ultimo, Mrs Carmichael accepts her regal status with aplomb, and says she knows 'absolutely everybody' on the peninsula . . . She has lived on the peninsula all her life. When she was a girl Pyrmont boasted shipyards, a tin smelter, the famous Pyrmont Baths—she was a member of Pyrmont Ladies' Amateur Swimming Club—and 25 hotels. At 16 she went to work for a city tailor, hand stitching waistcoats. In 1906, when she was 20, she married Robert Carmichael at St Bartholomew's Anglican Church, Pyrmont, now demolished . . . Mrs Carmichael has outlived her husband, who died 44 years ago, and both her sons. As compensation she has 58 grandchildren, great-grandchildren and great-great-grandchildren. I asked her if she would like to live to see the Bicentenary. 'Not really,' she said. 'They're spoiling Sydney like they spoilt Ultimo.'[12]

Ethel Carmichael did not live to celebrate Australia's Bicentenary; she died in August 1987. She had been baptised and married at the local Anglican church, but St Bartholomew's was no longer standing to receive and farewell her body. Instead she was received at St Bede's, down the hill, and a Requiem Mass was celebrated by Father Jim Fowler. Sisters Teresa and Margaret, who used to lead the Rosary in Ethel's John Street home, and cared for her in her last years, said of her: 'She was like a little cock-sparrow, but she had a wonderful alertness of mind. Her life had given her great wisdom and

---

12. *Sydney Morning Herald*, 3 September 1986.

a sense of real values. She was not swept away by affluence, like so many people are today. We will treasure her spirit. No-one will ever replace her.'[13]

In 1981 John Ford had applied for and received appointment as parish priest of Avalon, on Sydney's Northern Beaches, the preferred destination of many ex-Pyrmonites. There followed appointments at Stanmore and North Leichhardt, from where he retired in 1999. His retirement has been very active, especially in the early years with involvement in the parish of St Vincent's at Redfern, assisting the legendary pastor, Ted Kennedy.[14]

Succeeding John Ford at Pyrmont 1981 was Brian James Hume Tierney. A convert from Anglicanism, he was ordained in 1964 and began his priestly ministry as a curate at Harris Park in western Sydney, followed by appointments to Strathfield, Ryde and Penrith. Prior to seminary studies, he had graduated in 1958 as Bachelor of Science with a Diploma in Education at the University of Sydney. During his undergraduate years he was a member of the University Regiment, rising to the rank of a Staff Sergeant. His training and interest in education led him in 1974 to establish at Parramatta the Cardinal Newman Catechist Centre, of which he remained the owner and director until 2000. His military background resulted in a rather combative approach to what he perceived as the failures of Catholic education. His resourcing and promotion of traditional catechetical methods and content became his life's work. In an article in 2010 recounting the saga of his campaign, writing in the third person and referring to himself as 'Fr T', he stated: 'The link with Newman was clear: the upholding of Tradition and orthodoxy in Christian Doctrine. It became Fr T's life's work. From then on he became a controversial figure, even a clerical pariah, and harassed by educrats, bureaucrats and some bishops.'[15] In 1980, the year before his appointment to Pyrmont, Cardinal Freeman, after four years of persistent requests from Tierney, granted a year free of pastoral commitments to complete his controversial book *Catholic Family Catechism*.

It was in August 1981 that James Tierney was appointed to Pyrmont as administrator and Port of Sydney chaplain. In addition he brought with him his role of director of the Newman Centre. He introduced himself in *Wavelength*, the Stella Maris Club newsletter, by describing his first visit to one of the ships in Sydney Harbour: 'It was certainly an eye-opener for one who had never been on a ship in his life. It also gave me an inkling of the life and work on board—a hint of what is involved in being a seafarer. It will certainly make it easier for me to get down to the work of systematically

---

13. *Sydney Morning Herald*, 25 August 1987.
14. On Kennedy's ministry see Edmund Campion, *Ted Kennedy, Priest of Redfern* (Melbourne, 2009).
15. 'Vera Doctrina', *Cardinal Newman Faith Resources*, March 2010.

visiting the ships in Port Jackson and Port Botany.'[16] The transfer of commercial shipping from Sydney Harbour to Botany Bay was already underway, with the opening of Port Botany in 1979.

Tierney indicated that his work in the parish would be more demanding than it had been for his immediate predecessors, hinting that this could have an impact on his Club attendance and ship visits:

> Almost daily in the news is the forthcoming expansion of Pyrmont and Ultimo, with 4000 home units to be built over the next few years. Already some are nearing completion. Coupled with this change in the area is the tremendous re-routing of the traffic in the area and the controversy over the future of the old Pyrmont Bridge, which at the present is the last hope for a quick walking route to the heart of the city (and to the Club in Kent Street) from Pyrmont.[17]

In April 1982 he submitted to Cardinal Freeman a report on the Stella Maris Club and Pyrmont parish. The document opened with the announcement that he had brought a significant change to the seafarers' ministry: 'Formerly the chaplain ran the club. By personal temperament, by prudence in a new and unusual ministry, and by Vatican II's teaching on the place of the laity in Church organisations, I felt disinclined "to take charge" in the Club itself.'[18] This change 'brought to a head those problems that have increasingly beset the Club over recent year'. Tierney identified the problems as sharp decline in volunteers for the apostolate—'moving away, getting married, sick, or even frustrated by internal disagreements with each other'. The impact on the functioning of the Club was the abandonment of the regular dances in 1980, the inability to staff the coffee bar and to process the important service of providing telephone facilities for the visiting sailors. And there were few helpers to simply welcome and chat with them. Topping all these personnel problems was the financial crisis of the Club. Tierney informed Freeman that the Vincent de Paul Society had initiated an investigation, and that initial findings were inclining the Society to withdraw from the Apostolate of the Sea: 'They think that the SVdeP money should not be spent on any seafarers who are not materially poor.' One immediate result of the investigation was the termination of 'the illegal sale of canned beer', which made the Kent Street facility the only dry Club in Australia, except for Sydney's Anglican seafarers' facility, the Flying Angel. Tierney speculated that the closure of 142 Kent Street would necessitate the temporary use of the Parish Hall at

---

16. *Wavelength*, August 1981.
17. *Wavelength*, August 1981.
18. Brian Tierney, 'Port Chaplain's Report on Stella Maris Club and Pyrmont Parish', 30 April 1982 (Pyrmont Box, SAA).

Pyrmont for Club purposes. He also suggested grander proposals, based on the possible transfer of the city building to the archdiocese, and on the appointment of a chaplain with qualifications he did not possess: 'If the Chaplain was the sort of priest capable of organising big building projects, he would redevelop the site at 192 Kent Street, or else sell it and build a wholly new club on the site of the Pyrmont Parish Hall and its yard.'

The Report next addressed the state of the 'financial and management problems' of the parish. The first point was the insurer's push to increase significantly the premiums, a move that had been actively advocated since the 1978 fire. Tierney noted that such an increase would absorb almost the total annual income of $3000 from the weekly collection. He then detailed the 'dire need of maintenance' on all parish buildings—church, presbytery and hall at Pyrmont, and church and two houses at Ultimo. He identified the fretting stone-work of St Bede's, a problem which only began to be addressed thirty years later in 2013 with the letting of tenders for major restoration and conservation work, and the commencement of the project in 2015. The final item in this section of the report was headed: 'None of the tenants pay sufficient rent'. Details were provided:

- Trading Partners in St Bede's Hall pay $60 weekly ($260 monthly), but the parish pays for their electricity.
- Two sister of St Joseph live on one stipend paid by their Order and occupy what was an upstairs classroom and stage [Ultimo]; the Parish pays all outgoings including the phone; they work in the Parish.
- The Marillac Centre occupies the remaining two classrooms upstairs at St Francis Xavier's; they sort old clothing for the Daughters of Charity; rent is $10 weekly, and the Parish pays all outgoings.
- St Vincent de Paul restored and continues to maintain St Anne's [former convent in Bulwara Road], and pays most of the outgoings and rent of $30 weekly.
- The Barrows family, migrants, in the Parish Cottage, pay $30 weekly and most of the outgoings.

The final section of the Report was headed: 'The Priest'. Herein was found a final plea for help from a priest to his bishop. Tierney, with his well-known commitment to his catechetical crusade, found his present situation untenable. He argued the case for his unsuitability for the appointment he had been given. Of the parish ministry he stated: 'While the population has so far increased only a little, as people move into new home units, the priest's time on Parish affairs is incommensurate with the 40 people who attend the two Sunday morning Masses. Further, a priest is needed who is good with tenants, rents, maintenance and building.' He advocated the need for a full-time Port Chaplain, taking up Dundon's proposal of twenty years earlier, and of the incompatibility of the parish and seafarer ministry. He proposed a solution for both ministries: 'In view of the situation at the Stella Maris Club, it seems that the priest is needed as a full-time chaplain, preferably living at the club itself; in this case, the Parish of Pyrmont and Ultimo might be added to neighbouring parishes.' There then followed an alternative suggestion: 'If the Stella Maris Club has to forsake its present site and move to Pyrmont, the priest could live as now in the present Presbytery; St Bede's Church would become the Seafarers' chapel, and a Mass centre for local residents, with the Ultimo Church and its properties and problems, and the bulk of home units, added to a neighbouring parish.'[19] Neither of these proposals involved the continuing presence in Pyrmont of Father James Tierney.

Cardinal Freeman's delayed response in June was to ask Father Tierney to call a meeting of his predecessors in the double ministry to discuss the situation and to present recommendations. The St Vincent de Paul Society had by then resolved to withdraw from the Apostleship of the Sea. Within days the four priests—Dundon, Doyle, Ford and Tierney—gathered at St Bede's presbytery. The next day Jim Tierney sent to the Cardinal a letter containing a summation of the unanimous recommendations of the group, accompanied by detailed comments on each item.[20] The six recommendations, 'based on a combined experience going back over nearly 23 years', were submitted for the Archbishop's consideration:

1. There needs to be a full-time Catholic Port Chaplain to build up the Seafaring Apostolate.
2. The ownership of the present Stella Maris building and land needs to be handed over by the St Vincent de Paul Society to the Archdiocese of Sydney.
3. The Port Chaplain should live in the flat on the fifth level of the Club's premises and not at Pyrmont presbytery.
4. The Club should be financially viable even without the St Vincent de Paul funding from 30th September, as long as the Archdiocese provides the salary, keep and travel allowance for the Port Chaplain.
5. There needs to be a properly constituted Apostleship of the sea for the Club members who serve the seafarers.
6. The Parish of Pyrmont and Ultimo should be given to a priest who might otherwise be choosing retirement, or to a priest assigned to a Special Work, e.g. the Immigration Chaplain.

---

19. Brian Tierney, 'Port Chaplain's Report on Stella Maris Club and Pyrmont Parish', 30 April 1982 (Pyrmont Box, SAA).
20. Tierney to Freeman, 19 June 1982 (Seafarers Box, SAA).

A final point was contrary to Tierney's earlier suggestion that Pyrmont-Ultimo should, in part or whole, be absorbed into another parish: 'All the priests were again assertive of the advisability and the practicality of keeping the Parish of Pyrmont and Ultimo—the population is growing again, and there are certain categories of priests suited to its situation.'

In July auxiliary bishop John Heaps was sent to Pyrmont to communicate verbally the decision of the Archdiocesan Council of Bishops. The points were summarised by Tierney in a letter to Cardinal Freeman a week later.[21] The Port Chaplaincy was to remain the responsibility of the parish priest of Pyrmont who would continue to reside in the presbytery. It was suggested that Father Tierney apply for a vacant parish or offer himself as an administrator or curate.

In Cardinal Freeman wrote to the State President of the Vincent de Paul Society asking for a twelve month delay in the handing over of the Stella Maris Apostolate to the Archdiocese.[22] One of the reasons given was the need to appoint a new chaplain; Father Tierney had resigned. For the joint ministry at Pyrmont Cardinal Freeman turned to a relatively recent arrival in the archdiocese, an Irish priest, not from All Hallows or another of the Irish seminaries, but from a monastery in rural Victoria. Kevin Cox, born in Ireland of an Irish father and Australian mother, had joined the Cistercian community in Roscrea, County Offaly, after graduating from school, and became Brother Dominic. He arrived in Australia with a group of monks in 1954 to establish a Trappist monastery at Tarrawarra in Victoria. The following year he was ordained by Archbishop Mannix at St Patrick's Cathedral, Melbourne. In 1974 he took leave of absence from the monastery and was received into the Sydney Archdiocese where he was appointed assistant priest at Kogarah and then from 1975 to 1982 at Caringbah. In the *Catholic Directory* of 1981-82 the letters OCSO, designating membership of the Cistercian Order, were still attached to his name. The following year, dispensed from his monastic vows he became a priest of the Sydney Archdiocese and dropped the religious name Dominic, reverting to his baptismal name Kevin.

He succeeded James Tierney at Pyrmont in October 1982, at the very end of Cardinal Freeman's term as Archbishop, and served until 1986. Despite the demands of the Port Chaplaincy, which continued to be the main work of the Pyrmont incumbent, he set himself to undertake major repair and renovation projects in the parish. The presbytery underwent a significant makeover with the generous assistance of his Sydney-based family members. Nor was the church neglected. After the closure of the Kent Street Stella

---

21. Tierney to Freeman, 14 July 1982 (Seafarers Box, SAA).
22. Freeman to Blackstock, 30 September 1982 (Seafarers Box, SAA).

Maris Club, he negotiated the transfer of the two stained glass windows, depicting the Sacred Heart and Madonna with child, from the Club's chapel to St Bede's, where they were fitted into two of the eight nave windows; the rectangular windows needed to be lengthened and fitted into the arched spaces. This was the first stained-glass placed in the church windows since the installation of temporary glass in the new building in 1867. He also completed the work begun by John Ford, by removing the last of the plaster from the walls of the sanctuary.

In 1983, again with funding from his family, Kevin Cox commissioned a pipe organ for the church. The organ builder, Geoffrey Kendall, described the instrument as having been 'developed over the last ten years' and involving 'four significant innovations not previously used in pipe organ construction'. It was installed and blessed in November. The programme produced for the event further described the new organ as having 'a life span of 250 years, with refurbishing every fifty years'. The faulty instrument was dismantled in 2010 and replaced by a 1963 Moller pipe organ imported from the United States.

Kevin Cox concluded his ministry at Pyrmont in 1986. Appointments to Auburn, Woollahra and Enmore followed. He was withdrawn from active ministry in 1996 and died in 2008. He had been succeeded at St Bede's by James Fowler. Born in Petersham in 1923, Jim had entered the seminary as a young man in 1950, being supported financially by the Repatriation Department, because his father had died on active service in Palestine during the Second World War. However, he left Springwood after two years, and after some years as a clerk in the Department of Justice, he began studying for the Solicitors Admissions Board examinations, being admitted as a solicitor in 1967. He later completed a postgraduate degree in criminology. His career in the law was crowned by appointment as a stipendiary magistrate in 1968. His attraction to the priesthood had never left him, and after his mother's death he resumed theological studies at St Paul's Seminary for 'late vocations' at Kensington. Ordained in 1981, he was appointed as curate in a range of Sydney parishes—Concord, Winston Hills, Blacktown, Lalor Park and Cronulla—before becoming administrator at Pyrmont. Jim's ministry became somewhat limited among Ultimo locals when it became known that he had been a magistrate. More than one dying gentleman refused to receive the ministrations of a priest who had sat on the wrong side of the bench.

In May 1982 Sister Teresa Noon had been joined by Sister Margaret Gooley at Ultimo. After her initial shock at the run-down condition of the suburb, especially the housing and footpaths, walking along which required very attentive foot placement, Margaret resolved that the only way she could survive in this environment would be to glide through the suburb with a smile on her face. Teresa and Margaret continued their ministry together in Ultimo and Pyrmont for thirty years. In 1989 the sisters moved from their improvised accommodation which was accessed by an unsafe, rickety external stair case, to the house next door. The house had been purchased by the parish in 1924 in order to prevent the building of a factory next to the church-school and had been rented out until the sisters moved in. It became St Joseph's House, a place of welcome and hospitality in Ultimo for the next 22 years.

With the final closure of the Kent Street Stella Maris Club in 1987, an interim ecumenical arrangement had been made with the Anglican 'Flying Angel Club' at Millers Point: 'Present Port Chaplain, Fr Jim Fowler has been welcomed by the Anglican chaplain, Rev Owen Dykes and his crew. The future seems to indicate that something of the nature of a small "home" type mission needs to be established by the Apostleship of the Sea, Sydney. Steps are being taken to do something in this regard. In the meantime, Fr Jim visits the ships in combination with the Flying Angel Club.'[23] In 1990 Jim Fowler made some basic changes to the presbytery to create a modest Stella Maris centre—the small room under the house was equipped with two telephone booths for seafarers' calls to home; the courtyard at the rear of the house was made suitable for fair-weather gatherings. The church was declared to be the Seafarers Chapel, and the arrangement was blessed on 29 April 1990, by Cardinal Edward Clancy, who had been appointed Archbishop of Sydney in succession to James Freeman in February 1983:

> Compared with the former premises of the Stella Maris . . . the new Centre is in the words of Cardinal Clancy, 'modest'. Yet in some ways the complex is beyond compare. St Bede's church . . . has a simple, warm charm which is indescribable. Two stained glass windows taken from the now demolished chapel of the old Stella Maris adorn each of the transepts [sic] . . . The plans are not to cater for large numbers of seafarers but merely provide a homely base for catholic seafarers requiring the Mass centre and the basic services of telephone and mail communications with home . . . Stella Maris Sydney could well become a model to be emulated by many port parishes throughout Australia.[24]

Jim Fowler had grander plans in mind for significant extensions on top of the housekeepers flat at the rear of the presbytery. He commissioned an architect to prepare specifications for an expanded Stella Maris centre and submitted them to Cardinal Clancy, but these did not receive approval,

---

23. *Beacon: Australian Apostleship of the Sea Newsletter*, Melbourne, July 1988.
24. *Beacon: Australian Apostleship of the Sea Newsletter*, Melbourne, May 1990.

and the seafarers' facility remained confined to the small room below the presbytery.

On the parochial front Father Fowler, in 1990, was faced with significant maintenance problems at the Ultimo end of his parish. Despite the fact that St Francis Xavier's church drew a congregation twice the size of that at St Bede's, his solution was to propose to the Archdiocesan authorities the closure of the church and the sale of the property. Predictably this proposal was a source of great distress to the local community. His rather naive suggestion was that the Ultimo people could attend Mass at Pyrmont. He announced that a free bus service would be available each Sunday morning to transport parishioners to St Bede's for the 8am Mass, where there were plenty of empty pews to accommodate them. Angry parishioners approached the local member of the Legislative Assembly, Sandra Nori, for assistance in organising resistance to the proposed closure of their church. A petition was quickly organised and gathered two hundred signatures. Nori wrote a covering letter and submitted the signed petition to Cardinal Clancy:

> Your Eminence, I am enclosing a petition from the residents of Pyrmont and Ultimo, who have approached me over the proposed closure of their local parish church, St Francis, in Bulwara Road, Ultimo. The residents and parishioners feel that this church has both historical and sentimental significance and that it would be a great blow to them and the character of the area to lose it . . . I therefore request that you consider the petition before you with the aim of halting, if not stopping completely, the sale of this historic and important building.[25]

The petition emphasised the passionate attachment of the people to their church: 'There is much sadness at the loss of this church. There are many memorial plaques and tributes to past parishioners inside the church that will be lost forever.' It concluded: 'Your parishioners, therefore, humbly pray that your Eminence will ensure that the Church of St Francis will remain available.'[26]

Father Fowler's plans had already received archdiocesan approval; the last Mass was celebrated in the church on 5 May 1991. It was attended by previous pastors—Fathers Doyle, Ford, Hickman and Cox—and a large congregation of past and present parishioners, lamenting the closure of the church. Sadly, just ten weeks before, the centenary of the original St Francis Xavier's church, built by Father James Furlong, and blessed by Cardinal Moran on Sunday, 22 February 1891, had passed without celebration or

---

25. Nori to Clancy, 5 June 1991 (Pyrmont Box SAA).
26. Petition to Cardinal Clancy, 5 June 1991 (Pyrmont Box SAA).

comment. Father Fowler's Sunday bus from Ultimo to Pyrmont was soon cancelled because of lack of passengers. Ultimo locals still wanting to attend Mass turned their backs on St Bede's and its parish priest and headed south to St Benedict's or east to one of the city churches. The Ultimo church and the former convent were sold to the City Council and adapted for use as a child-care centre. The parish retained ownership of the small house occupied by the Josephite Sisters.

The parish priest and the archdiocesan authorities were woefully short-sighted in 1991 in urging and approving the sale of church property on the peninsula. In 1989 Elizabeth Farrelly, future City Alderman-Councillor and professor of architecture at the University of Sydney, had published a feature article in which she reviewed the past and raised questions about the future of the district:

> The issues are many and complex. Pyrmont is no tabula rasa. Much of the infrastructure—the streets, the services, the topography, even an existing rail line—that will form the peninsula's new urban skeleton is already in existence. That is part of the problem—and part of the solution.
>
> In early days after settlement, Pyrmont was largely farmland [sic], but the mid-century expansion of coastal shipping established Sydney as a regional, mercantile centre, bringing to Pyrmont not only dockyards, woolstores and grainstores, but industry; foundries, flour mills, factories (including, by 1876, the Colonial Sugar Refinery, which still occupies something over 12 hectares of the peninsula's north-western tip), and in 1853 a quarry, which provided high-grade sandstone for many of Sydney's finest buildings and left Pyrmont with its dramatically shaped land-form, while the opening of the Glebe Island bridge locked Pyrmont into Sydney's increasingly complex transport net.
>
> Most of those who worked in Pyrmont not only shopped, socialised, worshipped and educated their offspring locally, but lived in the peninsula's expanding clusters of two-storeyed, terrace housing along Miller Street and the Harris Street 'ridge'. By the end of the century Pyrmont had the highest population density in the colony.
>
> Since then, however, the story has been one of decline; population shrinkage at a continuing average of 5 per cent per year, closed schools, churches and pubs. By the 1970s Pyrmont was classifiable as a stagnant, inner suburb—and so it remains, with a residential population now around 1,000.
>
> In recent years, of course, things have changed again. Darling Harbour, while so far only marginally successful in commercial terms, has swung the CBD's centre of gravity sideways and south, bringing Pyrmont within the mental range of your average city developer. Development

proposals—for hotels, office blocks, tourist attractions, retail centres and luxury residential developments—proliferate. At the same time and, in part, for the same reasons (harbour views, proximity to the city, etc) house prices on Pyrmont have been doubling and tripling. Suddenly, Pyrmont is under pressure: developers want zoning and height restrictions lifted, residents want their 'rights' (security, views, amenities, parking) guaranteed; and everyone looks expectantly to the planners to arbitrate. As indeed they must. What is likely to come of it all?[27]

That final question was one which Church authorities did not seem to pause to consider when they moved to close and sell the Ultimo church. Something of the determination and vision of Vic Doyle twenty years previously, in a time of dramatic population decline—'I'm NEVER going to sell my church'—should have prevailed in a period of population growth.

A few months after the closure of St Francis Xavier's, the Cardinal sent a letter to be read at the only Sunday Mass now celebrated in the parish— 8am at St Bede's. It announced a new plan for the parishes of Pyrmont, Forest Lodge and Annandale. All three would be administered by a priest resident at St James, Forest Lodge. The shortage of priests and the 'sharp decrease in resident population in these areas' were cited as the reasons for the 'rationalization of city-fringe parishes'.[28] For the first time since 1880 the parish was not served by a resident pastor.

Following the controversial closure of the church, the presence in Ultimo of Sisters Teresa and Margaret became even more significant. They became the darlings not just of the local Catholics, but of the wider community. The patrons of the Lord Wolseley Hotel, a few paces along Bulwara Road from St Joseph's House, held raffles throughout the year with the aim of raising money for the Sisters. In the week before Christmas it became a custom to welcome them to the crowded pub. A milk crate was placed in front of the bar, and the publican would step up and give a rousing speech in praise of the work of Teresa and Margaret, and hand over the substantial proceeds of the year's fund-raising. It was then Sister Teresa's turn to mount the crate and express thanks, and give a summary of their work during the year. Finally, Sister Margaret climbed up and gave a Christmas blessing. As the Holy Water was being splashed the drinkers protectively covered their schooners.

From the first of January 1992 Pyrmont, together with Annandale, came under the administration and pastoral care of the Parish Priest of Forest Lodge, Alexander Johnson. Jim Fowler continued in residence at the presbytery as Port Chaplain until March 1993 when he was appointed as

---

27. *Sydney Morning Herald*, 21 July 1989.
28. Cardinal Clancy to Parishioners of Pyrmont, 23 July 1991 (Pyrmont Box, SAA).

Parish Priest of Darlinghurst. The work of the Apostleship of the Sea was then taken over by a Josephite Sister, Mary Leahy, as 'pastoral assistant', while Jim retained the title of Port Chaplain until his retirement in 1996. Mary Leahy was then named Director of the Apostleship of the Sea in Sydney. Even though the work of ship visits and care of seafarers had been largely relocated from Sydney Harbour to Botany Bay, the Pyrmont connection with the ministry continued with Sister Mary's office located under the presbytery.

In 2006 Jim Fowler returned to St Bede's to celebrate Mass on the occasion of his silver jubilee of ordination. Concelebrating was the then Parish priest, Colin Fowler, not a relative, who welcomed Jim, noting that 'every Father Fowler in Australia has gathered for this celebration'. Jim, who had been living in retirement at Rockdale for seven years, died in February 2013 after a long illness. He was 74. While his Requiem Mass was being celebrated at Brighton-le-Sands, the bell of St Bede's at Pyrmont was being re-erected on a new wooden frame. When secured in place, the bell was tolled in memory of the deceased former pastor. It continues to be rung to announce the commencement of Sunday Masses and to celebrate baptisms and weddings, and it is tolled for the dead.

Chapter 24
Revival of Peninsula and Parish

Lex Johnson was born in Sydney in 1940 and he attended the Jesuit schools of St Aloysius Milson's Point and St Ignatius Riverview. He entered the Springwood Seminary in 1959 and after theological studies at St Patrick's, Manly, he was ordained in 1965. His appointments over the next twenty years took him to Sydney parishes of widely ranging socio-economic status—Pennant Hills, Elizabeth Bay, Waitara, Lane Cove and Mount Druitt—first as curate and then as parish priest. In 1984, the year of the first visit of Pope John Paul II to Australia, he was promoted to the key position of administrator of St Mary's Cathedral. In 1986 he was raised to the dignity of a Monsignor. In 1990, after six years at St Mary's, he was appointed to the parish of St James at Forest Lodge in the suburb of Glebe. He was sent with a mandate from Cardinal Clancy to devise new approaches to inner city parishes in a situation of shrinking congregations and declining clergy numbers. Consolidation of the many parishes on the western edge of the city was his advice to the Archbishop. The result was that in January 1992 he was asked to accept the administration of the neighbouring parishes of Pyrmont to the east and Annandale to the west, in addition to his responsibility for St James parish. All three parishes were to remain canonically distinct. For most of his incumbency he was not assisted by a resident curate at St James. However, there were priests in residence at St Bede's and St Brendan's during his term of office. Julian Porteous resided at Annandale as official curate to all three parishes, thus making him the only 'Pyrmont priest' to become a bishop—firstly as auxiliary in Sydney in 2003, and then as archbishop of Hobart in 2013. At St Bede's, Jim Fowler continued as Port Chaplain in residence until early 1993, when Peter Fitzgerald, whose main commitment was ministry to the deaf, moved into the presbytery. The Cardinal's letter announcing the Fitzgerald appointment, stated that he had been instructed to make arrangements with Lex 'to be of such assistance as is possible and consistent with his ministry to the hearing impaired'.[1]

Lex Johnson was the first monsignor in charge at St Bede's since John Lynch in 1878. Lynch had also administered the Pyrmont district 'from a distance', from his residence in Glebe. Forest Lodge, a more prosperous and prestigious parish than Pyrmont-Ultimo, has had quite a number of monsignori as parish priests since its inception in 1877.

Lex moved quickly to schedule a Thursday morning Mass at St Joseph's House in Ultimo, in an attempt to provide in a small way for a community that had so recently and controversially lost its church. Over the next twenty years the Josephite Sisters built their ministry around this small weekly gathering for the celebration of the Eucharist.

In September 1991 CSR had announced that it would close its sugar refinery in the following year. The eventual development of residential buildings on this vast site, covering the northern shoreline of the peninsula, branded 'Jackson's Landing' by the developers, would significantly accelerate the population increase. Also adding to the growth were plans for the conversion of some of the huge historic bond-stores in Ultimo and Pyrmont into apartments.

By 1995 Monsignor Johnson was taking note of this potential growth in his Pyrmont parish. In January he wrote to Cardinal Clancy:

> A drive around the Pyrmont-Ultimo peninsula reveals many large apartment buildings being built. Within a few years there will be a population of some 16,000, with another 16,000 coming to work here. Most of the workers will be at the new casino, which as you know, is over the road from St Bede's church . . . St Bede's is the only church of any denomination on the peninsula and will need the normal parish infrastructure fairly soon. At the moment with only 400 Catholics, pastoral care is at a minimum, as the annual returns indicate. Peter Fitzgerald helps as much as he can on weekends in the three parishes, and he has some excellent insights into the local area. In February I hope to set up the beginnings of a pastoral plan together with the people, Peter and the Sisters at Ultimo.[2]

He concluded that 'with the Pyrmont-Ultimo end coming more on line it will require more of my time, and less spent here at St James and St Brendan's'. Consequently he proposed that he be released from the administration of Annandale, and that the resident priest there, Julian Porteous, be appointed

---

1. Clancy to Johnson, 18 March 1993 (Johnson File, SAA).
2. Johnson to Clancy, 13 January 1995 (Johnson File, SAA).

parish priest. The Cardinal's reply came two months later; the status quo was to be maintained.[3]

A year later, in March 1996, Lex Johnson submitted his resignation as administrator of Annandale, citing the following reasons:

1. I cannot cope with 3 parishes, with 3 different communities, even though there is much lay involvement.
2. I detect a deterioration in my health situation with a general tiredness.
3. Pyrmont is about to explode numerically. The casino is really irrelevant for pastoral care, but gets all the publicity. The population is about to move in, and I have done little down there other than just keeping the place ticking over.[4]

This time the Cardinal concurred and two weeks later Porteous was appointed parish priest at Annandale. Lex's responsibilities were now reduced to a more manageable combination of two parishes.

In 1997, at the end of his six-year appointment, Lex Johnson applied for reappointment as parish priest Forest Lodge and Pyrmont. He focused on the changing situation at Pyrmont as his reason for wanting to continue:

> The Pyrmont is at a most interesting stage of development, with more people coming to Mass (this means about 40), and more and more people coming to live on the peninsula ... I am working with a number of parishioners to see what pastoral response might be appropriate. St Bede's is the only operational church in Pyrmont-Ultimo of any denomination, and we are in a marvellous position to make some impact on the new community.[5]

The uniqueness of St Bede's as the only functioning church in Pyrmont, led to its use by other Christian denominations. In 1996 a small number of local Protestants of various denominations, calling themselves the Mustard Seed Group, approached Lex Johnson requesting access to St Bede's on Sundays for an informal service. Robin Davies, who would become the minister of the Uniting Church in Ultimo, has told the story:

> The Casino had just been completed dwarfing St Bede's. I spoke to Lex and he said that he had been to a meeting with his colleagues where they were discussing what to do about the declining churches and the fact that

---

3. Clancy to Johnson, 21 April 1995 (Johnson File, SAA).
4. Johnson to Clancy, 8 March 1996 (Johnson File, SAA).
5. Johnson to Clancy, 7 & 10 October 1997 (Johnson File, SAA).

they were under-utilised. He saw the opportunity of sharing the church as a positive initiative for a local church . . . we could use it as we wished but not have communion. We would meet at 9.30am, turning the pews around so that we were facing each other. It never grew beyond about 8-10 because within a year the Ultimo Church became available and we moved into that property.[6]

The church in Ultimo, built in 1883 for the Presbyterian community, is on the corner of Bulwara Road and Quarry Street, adjacent to the Lord Wolseley Hotel and along the road from St Francis Xavier. With the union of a group of Protestant churches in 1977 it became a place of worship for the new Uniting Church and served Sydney's Dutch community. In 1997 the church became available for the Mustard Seed group to gather and develop a congregation with Robin Davies as minister.

Some years later, in 2002, a local Anglican group, the Peninsula Community Church, gathered at St Bede's on Sunday evenings over a period of several months. At Easter 2002 Cardinal Pell received a letter from the same complainant who, in 1975, had protested the holding of an ALP rally in St Bede's church. She again enclosed a local pamphlet, this one announcing the holding of an Anglican Easter Sunday service at 'the Sandstone Church' in Pyrmont Street. The Cardinal's private secretary replied, explaining that diocesan policy and the policy of the universal church make provision for ecumenical cooperation.[7] Stuart Robinson was the minister of the Peninsula Community Church at the time. He was consecrated and installed as the 10th Bishop of the Anglican Diocese of Canberra and Goulburn in January 2009 at St Saviour's Cathedral, Goulburn. In February 2008 the Anglican Archdiocese of Sydney announced that 'Pyrmont Anglican Church, known as Peninsula Community Church (PCC) to its parish, held its final service on December 30 after an exciting five years of experimental ministry'.[8] Local Anglicans were advised that they were now part of the parish of St Philip at Church Hill, across Darling Harbour from Pyrmont, the oldest parish in Australia.

1992 saw the final resolution of a local dispute thanks largely to the intervention of a nun with strong family connections in Pyrmont. She was Josephite Sister Christine, born Maria Watkinson, the granddaughter of a famous Pyrmont identity, James Watkinson, known affectionately as 'Watto' or 'Wokko'. He had grown up in Pyrmont Street, just along from St

---

6. Rev Robin Davies, email to the author, 16 March 2015.
7. Michael Casey to 'Complainant', 22 April 2002 (Pyrmont Box, SAA)
8. Joseph Smith, 'Our "worthwhile" ministry risk', *Sydney Anglicans*, 28 February 2008 (http://sydneyanglicans.net/news/pyrmont_church_story; accessed 19 March 2015).

Bede's church and then lived in Bowman Street for the whole of his married life. He taught hundreds of children to swim in the baths at the bottom of Point Street and was a driving force in the emergence of Pyrmont as a dominant water polo and swimming club in Sydney. He competed against legendary Olympic swimmer Andrew 'Boy' Charlton, at both the Pyrmont and Woolloomooloo baths. He also had hero status for his celebrated water rescues at the northern beaches and in Darling Harbour. In 1926 the Sydney sporting journal, *The Arrow*, carried an article headlined 'WATTO ON THE JOB: Congratulations to James Watkinson, one of Pyrmont's champion polo players. He is spending a holiday at Narrabeen, and last Sunday fished out a young fellow named Blacki who was in difficulties. Blacki got into trouble about 200 to 300 yards out from the beach, and after others had missed him, "Watto" got a grip and brought him ashore.'[9] He was perhaps the best known identity in Pyrmont and certainly one of the most respected and well-liked, a pillar of the local community. He successfully fought against the CSR's attempt to demolition of the Pyrmont Baths in 1929. The baths were finally removed in 1946 causing lasting community bitterness.

Following his death in 1954 the Council named in his honour a reserve on the eastern side of the Ways Terrace flats, where the 'flags of Pyrmont', the residents' washing, flapped in the prevailing north-easterly breeze. Jim Watkinson's widow, still living in their old terrace in Bowman Street, kept the memorial plaque polished. However, the park had not been formally gazetted, and in 1986 the State Government sold the reserve to a private developer to build 'Jones Bay apartments' and the plaque disappeared. Sister Christine Watkinson, then at Lalor Park, heard by chance about what had happened to her grandfather's memorial. She appealed to Independent alderman Frank Sartor, who tracked down the plaque through the developers and presented a residents' petition to Council calling for the restoration of the reserve. Finally in 1992 this was achieved, and now the James Watkinson Reserve overlooks the modern apartments which nearly caused it to be wiped off the map. Sister Christine commented at the time: 'It's part of our family heritage—and part of Pyrmont's heritage, too.'[10] She was a renowned music teacher in Josephite schools from Bombala to Nelson Bay, specialising in teaching the violin and she served as President of the New South Wales Music Teachers' Association. Her preferred water recreation was not the water polo of her grandfather 'Watto', but fishing: 'She

---

9. *Arrow*, 15 January 1926.
10. See *Sydney Morning Herald*, 26 October 1990 and City of Sydney Website, http://www.cityofsydney.nsw.gov.au/learn/sydneys-history/people-and-places/park-histories/james-watkinson-reserve, accessed 10 March 2015.

never lost the excitement of feeling a bite, or of encouraging and helping novice "fisherladies" bait their hooks.'[11] She died in 1993.

Responsibility for the development of the Peninsula was shared between government and private enterprise. The State Government in 1992 had formed the City West Development Corporation to manage the planning and construction of infrastructure and the marketing and sale of surplus government land in the area, which constituted about 30 per cent of the total to be developed. By 1997 extensive subsidised flats had been built at the Pyrmont point and in Ultimo, focused on providing affordable housing for local people, and the Lend Lease development of the CSR site was well underway. The number of new apartments on the peninsula already numbered 2000, and still the Corporation had twenty major sites available for development, including Darling Island. On the non-residential side of development, the new Sydney Casino had been completed on the site of the former power station and was looming over St Bede's to a height rivalling that of the demolished chimneys.

In November 1998 Father Johnson reluctantly agreed to a request from Cardinal Clancy that he take on the responsibility of another Sydney parish: 'I have considered your suggestion of moving to a bigger parish and after much thought, I agree that it would be worthwhile.'[12] He had barely begun the parish revival that was getting underway in Pyrmont. In January 1999 he moved to the parish of Earlwood with responsibility also for Clempton Park, land-locked dormitory suburbs in the south of Sydney. Three years later a new Archbishop, George Pell, asked him to move to Mascot. Lex Johnson died suddenly of a heart attack in April 2002, at the age of 61. Large congregations gathered for the Vigil Mass at the Earlwood parish church, presided over by Auxiliary Bishop Peter Ingham and at the Requiem Mass at St Mary's Cathedral, celebrated by a seminary classmate and life-time friend, Patrick Power, Auxiliary Bishop of Canberra-Goulburn. The obituary in the *Catholic Weekly* began by quoting the words of a parishioner and friend: 'Lex genuinely cared about people. His faith was deeply personal and I never doubted his love of God. I do not doubt God has brought home one of the great Aussie rough diamonds of the Catholic Church: opinionated, militant and sometimes obnoxious, but always deeply faithful to the Truth and his life within the Church.'[13]

The successor at Forest Lodge and Pyrmont/Ultimo in January 1999 was a 72-year-old priest, the oldest incumbent at St Bede's in its history to

---

11. Obituary, Archives of the Sisters of St Joseph.
12. Johnson to Clancy, 30 November (Johnson File, SAA).
13. *Catholic Weekly*, 28 April 2002.

that date. Lester Cashen had written to Cardinal Clancy in December 1998 offering himself as pastor for a small parish:

> In the reshuffle of pastors of parishes to be considered on Dec 17th may I be considered for appointment as pastor to a small parish if one were to become available? I do not wish to be considered for the parish of Surry Hills, as I have no wish to be faced with a demanding maintenance programme, nor does the prospect of sharing the presbytery with a religious order appeal to me. It may possibly happen that another inner city parish may become vacant. In that case I would be happy to be appointed as administrator until such time as the parish were to be advertised, in which case I would apply to be appointed pastor.[14]

The Cardinal seemed to have considered that the parishes of St Bede and St James together were the equivalent of one small parish and he appointed Father Cashen as parish priest. In fact the letter of appointment referred to 'the Parish of Forest Lodge/Pyrmont'. This was canonically incorrect, because neither parish had been suppressed to create a new single entity, as a future parish priest would have to establish in canon and civil law in response to a legal challenge from commercial tenants of Glebe parish properties. Also ignored by His Eminence was Cashen's request to avoid 'a demanding maintenance programme'. The collection of buildings in both parishes had major maintenance problems. A future pastor would be informed by the archdiocesan property manager in 2004 that 'the maintenance problem in these parishes is a train-wreck waiting to happen'.

Les Cashen may have been close to the official retirement age of 75 for Catholic clergy, but he brought a great deal of experience to his new posting. After graduating from Sydney High School he began studies in pharmacy at the University of Sydney, gaining his degree in 1946. In the following year he founded the National Association of Pharmaceutical Students. After a few years working at his profession he chose a new direction, courageously joining a bunch of school-leavers at St Columba's Springwood. After theological studies at St Patrick's Manly, he was ordained by Cardinal Gilroy in 1958. A series of appointments as curate took him across Sydney—Central Bankstown, Dundas-Carlingford and Balmain. Then, in 1967, less than ten years ordained, he boldly applied for the position of parish priest at Forest Lodge. He was appointed assistant there instead. Granville and Croydon followed. In 1959 he was appointed as vice-rector of St John's College at his Alma Mater, the University of Sydney. From 1973 to 1978 he was director of the Catholic Enquiry Centre. In 1980 he was elected by the

---

14. Cashen to Clancy, 3 December 1998 (Cashen File, SAA)

Fellows of St John's as College Rector. He continued in that role until January 1992. At his retirement as Rector he was awarded the honorary degree of Master of Philosophy in recognition of his contribution to the life of the University and College. On his return from a period of leave in Europe, where he attended a renewal course in theology at the University of Leuven in Belgium, he served as administrator at Caringbah and then at Balmain, after which he applied for and was appointed parish priest of Lane Cove. From 1987 to 1992 he had also served as member and then chairman of the Board of Directors the *Catholic Weekly*, the Archdiocesan newspaper that had replaced the *Freeman's Journal* and *Catholic Press* in 1942. He was well known and respected among Australian clergy as a founding activist in the National Council of Priests.

The growth in Cashen's new area of responsibility as parish priest of Glebe and Pyrmont was located in the eastern section, in the parish of Pyrmont-Ultimo. In November 1999 the real-estate section of the *Sydney Morning Herald* presented an update on development on the peninsula:

> Nowhere has the scale and speed of urban renewal and gentrification happened more dramatically than at Pyrmont. Where a power station and incinerator once fouled the city air and wharfies spilled out of pubs of the 'public lavatory' school of design, million-dollar apartments are sprouting and hectares of new open space are blooming with Gymea lilies. Baby boomers whose parents wouldn't be seen dead in old Pyrmont are now migrating there from the North Shore.... Government planning for Pyrmont's rebirth began 10 years ago when its population was down to 3,000. Billions of dollars later, that population is about 12,000 and will grow to 20,000. There's no doubting the appeal of living at Pyrmont. It offers a more human scale of inner-city living than the sunlight-challenged canyons across the other side of Pyrmont Bridge. It's on the very doorstep of Darling Harbour—with its restaurants, shops, museums and entertainment venues—and is remarkably blessed with buses, ferries, a light rail system (to be extended soon) and the monorail.[15]

Despite the continued momentum of development and population growth, the new parish priest did not seem to inherit the enthusiasm of his predecessor for devising pastoral strategies for forming a community at St Bede's. During Father Cashen's incumbency the one Sunday Mass continued to be celebrated at 8am, not a time to attract a population of young city workers. Any Pyrmont residents wanting to attend a later Sunday Mass had plenty of options in every direction—east to St Patrick's and the Cathedral;

---

15. *Sydney Morning Herald*, 6 November 1999.

south to St Peter Julian in George Street and St Benedict's at Broadway; north to St Augustine's at Balmain; west to St James at Glebe. The parish priest's attention was focused on his parish of St James, where there was a demanding range of challenges—pastoral, administrative, financial, property and building maintenance and a parish school. While challenges were not absent from the Pyrmont parish, especially pastoral and maintenance, the presence of a resident priest at St Bede's allowed the effortless continuation of a minimum ministry of Mass and sacraments. Peter Fitzgerald continued at Pyrmont until his transfer to the parish of Hoxton Park-Hinchinbrook in January 2000, when he was replaced in the presbytery by Michael Walsh, a Vincentian priest, whose full-time work was as prison chaplain at Long Bay and Silverwater Gaols. Both priests were deservedly much appreciated by the small local congregation.

Les Cashen had wider interests than just his two parishes, which briefly became three with Annandale again added from October 1999 to May 2000. He maintained an active involvement with the National Council of Priests and kept a critical eye on the hierarchy of the Australian Church. Tension on multiple fronts, parochial, diocesan and national, took its toll on the ageing parish priest. Lester Cashen died in April 2003 at the St John Vianney Villa where he had been recuperating from a recent illness. He had reached the age of 77. On the Australia Day before his death he had been awarded the Medal of Australia in the General Division 'for service to the Catholic Church, particularly in the area of education and in the administration of St John's College at the University of Sydney'. A former Chairman of the College Council commented that he was 'a man of commanding presence, he was good at handling people and had a wry sense of humour'.[16] The Sydney University Pharmacy Alumni Association established the 'Les Cashen Pharmacy Travel Scholarship' in his memory.

Following Father Cashen's death, Michael Walsh, whose residence in the Pyrmont presbytery was by invitation of the late parish priest, wrote to Archbishop Pell asking for the continuation of this arrangement: 'Pyrmont is very suitable for my ministry as full time Chaplain to Corrective Services. I am able to travel to Long Bay complex via the Eastern Distributor and to Silverwater complex via the Anzac Bridge. Also, I am very pleased that I am so close to the courts in the city. I often attend there to offer support and to pray with the prisoners, especially with those who have no families/ friends'.[17] He also explained his ministry at St Bede's and the importance of this contact to him personally: 'I have appreciated this opportunity to join

---

16. *Catholic Weekly*, 20 April 2003.
17. Walsh to Cardinal Pell, 1 May 2003 (quoted with the permission of Michael Walsh).

with "mainstream" Catholics in Sunday worship and to join in other aspects of normal parish life. This has been very valuable to me, as the prisoners are a special culture with very different needs and cultures.' His residence and ministry at St Bede's was much appreciated by the parishioners, as conveyed to him by Les Cashen in a letter of April 2002, in which he stated that the Parish Pastoral Council of Forest Lodge and Pyrmont had recently expressed its deep appreciation of the high level of Michael's pastoral work in St Bede's parish. The parish priest further expressed his satisfaction with the way in which Michael was supervising the maintenance of both the church and the presbytery.[18] The Cardinal replied to Michael expressing appreciation of his ministry in prisons and at Pyrmont, and assuring him that he would recommend to a new Administrator that the present housing arrangements be continued.[19] Within a few months George Pell chose to fill the vacancy at Glebe and Pyrmont by inviting the Dominican Order to establish a community of friars at the St James presbytery and to nominate one of them as parish priest of Forest Lodge and Pyrmont.

In October 2003 Robert Mutlow, a senior priest of the Dominican Order, was formally appointed as parish priest of St James and St Bede. A clause in the agreement between the Archdiocese and the Dominicans stated that the Community of friars would reside at Glebe, and that the Archdiocese would find a 'suitable tenant' for the Pyrmont presbytery. Moves were immediately made to terminate Father Michael Walsh's occupancy of the presbytery and to make it available to a part-time lay member of the Archbishop's personal staff. The parishioners of Pyrmont, deprived of their own resident pastor since 1992, now witnessed perhaps the lowest point in the history of the parish—the removal of any priestly presence at a time when the district was rapidly increasing in population. Both Lex Johnson and Les Cashen, as non-resident pastors, had been determined in ensuring that there was a priest residing at St Bede's from 1992 to 2003. With the new arrangements the parishioners also suffered another loss in being deprived of access to the meeting and gathering space in the presbytery. This was not an auspicious start for the pastoral renewal needed among the expanding population, nor for Dominican ministry at St Bede's. The 8am Sunday Mass continued as the only occasion when the church was opened for prayer and worship. As one parishioner expressed it in a letter to the newly elevated Cardinal Pell, it seemed that St Bede's had become simply a Mass Centre. He concluded with a plea to the Cardinal not to let St Bede's slide into oblivion.[20] The coming of the Dominican friars seemed set to reflect the style of the remote ministry

---

18. Cashen to Walsh, 28 April 2002 (Pyrmont Box, Correspondence 2002, SAA).
19. Pell to Walsh, 13 May 2003 (Pyrmont Box, Correspondence 2003, SAA).
20. Brian Ell to Cardinal Pell, 1 February 2004 (Pyrmont Box, Correspondence 2004, SAA).

of the Benedictines in Pyrmont from 1870 to 1875, when the monks resided in community at St Benedict's and rode along Harris Street to St Bede's to conduct liturgies and then trotted back home. The friars, resident at St James Priory, drove from Glebe to St Bede's for Sunday Mass and weddings, baptisms and funerals, and then drove back home.

Robert Mutlow's fragile state of health led to his replacement at the end of 2004 by another Dominican, the author of this sesquicentennial history. At his first meeting with the Parish Council, the new parish priest made the observation that Pyrmont seemed to him like 'sleep-in territory', and suggested that a second, later Sunday morning Mass ought to be scheduled. It was decided that 11am would fit in best with the Mass schedule in place at St James. However, it was discovered that there was a wedding booked at that time on a Sunday later in the year. This awkwardness led to a search for an alternative location for Mass on the Sunday of the clash. The neighbouring Casino, to which the parish priest had been called following a death, was approached and the generous offer of a conference room was made to accommodate the 11am Mass. This was a fortuitous arrangement, because in 2006 there would be need to relocate Sunday Masses from the church for seven weekends, while the termite-riddled floor was being replaced. The Archbishop was informed that services were to be held at 'a nearby conference centre'. The congregations, which had grown significantly by then, did not lose a single member during this 'Babylonian Exile'; in fact, the numbers increased.

An update of the growth of the local population had been given in 2004, in a publication of the Sydney Harbour Foreshore Authority: 'Historical reckonings have the resident workforce peaking at 19,000 in 1901, a population that declined to about 1,590 in 1981. The 1986 Census recorded 2,631 people living in the two postcodes. With urban renewal, this number increased to 12,708 residents by 2001. Recent estimates have about 13,300 people living in the precinct, with the likely population rising to 17,000 by 2011.'[21]

A sure sign of an emerging community spirit at St Bede's was the enthusiastic response to a call for local parishioners to resume responsibility for the work of the Vincent de Paul Society in the district. For a long period, the many needy households of Pyrmont, Ultimo and Glebe had been dependent on visits by the members of the Pymble Parish Conference of the Society, who drove down from the upper North Shore each Saturday morning. Many parishioners of both Glebe and Pyrmont came forward and

---

21. Sydney Harbour Foreshore Authority, *Pyrmont + Ultimo: decade of renewal*, (Sydney, 2004), 13.

formed a strong local conference, which was soon able to take on the major portion of the visits to local households, averaging 800 per year.

Another sign of the growing sense of community was the response to the proposal of regular working-bees in and around the church. The volunteers formed themselves into a very active maintenance committee, with Ron Gattone and Laurie Zammit in the lead. In 2005 the parish regained access to the presbytery and in 2008 the committee initiated major renovations to maximise community access to the building, while retaining a residential component. The walls within the 1930s extension at the rear of the house—containing kitchen and housekeepers rooms—were demolished, creating one large room, with folding doors opening onto the courtyard. The parish now had a welcoming space for community events, especially regular gatherings after Sunday Masses. The church was made available for wider community access, becoming the rehearsal location for the Jackson's Landing Choir and the Gregorian Schola, as well as for regular concerts.

The old school building had been leased to commercial tenants since 1982, and with the lease set to expire in March 2009, the Finance Committee and Parish Council early in 2008 began to seek and assess expressions of interest to ensure continuity of tenancy. An application for a group to conduct a child care centre in the premises, seen as a use in continuity with the original purpose of the building, was submitted to the Archbishop in October. It was rejected in February 2009 on the grounds that the principals, not being 'practicing Catholics'—one being Anglican, the other Buddhist—failed a recently devised 'Catholicity clause'. After this setback, the property was eventually leased to restauranteurs without an imposition of 'Catholicity' conditions on their suitability to conduct their business of providing Taiwanese cuisine.

The restored flow of rental income allowed the community to begin to replace the temporary plain leadlight glass of 1867 with stained-glass. Apart from the two windows relocated to St Bede's from the Seamen's Chapel in 1983, the hope of the pioneers for a complete set of stained glass windows for the church had awaited fulfilment for almost 150 years. The installation of the porch window and its dedication by the parish community of 2009 to the parishioners of 1867 began the process towards fulfilling the pioneers' dreams. The theme chosen for the window comes from the time of Bede the Venerable (672-735). The dominant image of Christ in that Romanesque period, represented in manuscript illumination and stone, was the *Maiestas Domini*—the beardless Lord seated in majesty, his right hand raised in blessing, his left hand holding the book of the Gospels and surrounded by four winged figures, symbols of the evangelists. The cover of the book is inscribed with the word PAX. Being the motto of the Benedictine Order, the word Pax/Peace creates a link with the Benedictine Archbishop Bede

Polding who consecrated the church and with the Benedictine Sisters of the Good Samaritan who conducted the parish schools.

The symbols of the four evangelists are the man, the ox, the lion and the eagle: Matthew, Luke, Mark and John. Each identifies one evangelist, and the four together represent the Gospel as a whole. In addition, the four symbols represent the key moments of Christ's life celebrated in the liturgical year: they recall in turn the birth, sacrifice, resurrection and ascension of Jesus. The symbols are derived from the opening chapter of the book of the prophet Ezekiel. There the prophet had a vision of four winged living creatures in the middle of a glowing fire fanned by a stormy north wind. The figures appear again in chapter four of St John's Book of Revelation. The description of their mysterious appearance and their dynamic movement made such an impact that the first Christian generations saw in their appearance a foreshadowing of the Gospel of Jesus presented by the four evangelists. The human figure signifies Matthew, who begins his Gospel with the human descent of Jesus, his genealogy. The lion represents the evangelist Mark, whose Gospel begins with John the Baptist in the wilderness, the domain of the lion. Luke's account of the infancy of Jesus places the child in the Temple, the place of animal sacrifice. Hence the ox became the symbol of Luke. In the prologue of his Gospel, John intently gazes on the eternal Word, the light who scatters the darkness of the world. This recalls the eagle that in legend soars while looking directly at the sun. In this way tradition has assigned each evangelist his own distinct symbol.[22] These winged creatures surround the figure of Christ and carry his gospel message into the world. As the congregation leaves the church each Sunday the image in the porch window is a reminder of the Lord's blessing of peace which has been received and of the shared task of spreading the Gospel message, the Good News of salvation; as the words of dismissal at the end of Mass proclaim: 'Go in peace to love and serve the Lord.' The window was created by Jeffrey Hamilton of Hamilton Design Glass, Surry Hills.

Music for liturgy and concerts was greatly enhanced by the installation of a replacement pipe organ in the church gallery. The saga of the project was related by the organ builders Darrell Pitchford and Dean Yates in the journal of the Organ Music Society of Sydney:

> A pipe organ had been installed in the church in 1981 [sic]. The console was playable from the back of the church and the main body of the organ was situated in the gallery at the rear of the church. The organ

---

22. See St Jerome, *Commentary on Ezekiel*, 1.7 (Latin text in Migne, *Patrologia Latina*, volume 25, col 22).

was built using an accumulation of different ranks of pipes from various redundant instruments . . .

In 2007, Father Colin Fowler, parish priest for both St James, Forest Lodge and St Bede's, Pyrmont, asked us to repair a 'few faults' occurring on the St Bede's organ. We were reluctant to maintain the organ on a permanent basis. However, because of our association with the Whitehouse organ in St James' Church, Forest Lodge, we agreed to keep St Bede's pipe organ functional, with the understanding that the parish members consider a long term solution to their existing pipe organ. St Bede's committee considered a few options:
1. rebuild their existing organ;
2. purchase a new pipe organ;
3. purchase a second-hand redundant pipe organ;
4. replace their existing pipe organ with an electronic instrument.

Options one, two and four were dismissed for various reasons, cost being a main consideration. The church committee asked us to search for a redundant pipe organ in Australia or overseas. A suitable organ would need to meet the following criteria:
(a) it must be less than 8 feet or 2.4 metres in height;
(b) it must be able to fit within an allocated area of the gallery;
(c) it must be able to lead a congregation of 120 people;
(d) it must be tuned to equal temperament at A440 pitch as many other instruments including violin, flute and guitar are included in the musical liturgy at St Bede's . . .

The Organ Clearing House in America had a few interesting small pipe organs for sale and one in particular looked promising. The Moller Artiste, built in 1963, Opus 9816 would certainly fit in the gallery and the specification, having four extended ranks would give the versatility required in a parish organ . . .

The shipping container travelled through China, New Zealand and Tasmania and was delivered to St Bede's on 13 May 2010 . . . Whilst installing the organ, it was quite evident that the quality of the workmanship was first class. It was important to the church that the organ should look like a pipe organ. We constructed a 'dummy front' using eleven pipes from the previous organ. These pipes are painted gold. Removal of the old organ left a 2.6 metre hole in the handrail of the gallery. Together with a parish member, Mr Ron Gattone, it was decided to construct a Juliet or Minstrel balcony to fill the area. The completed structure gives more space for the various musicians and aesthetically it complements a very attractive, historic church . . .

Mr Peter Kneeshaw [St Mary's Cathedral organist] played the opening recital at a dedication service on Sunday 24 October 2010. A full congregation was well entertained by Peter's recital, demonstrating the versatility of a small parish organ.[23]

During the dismantling of the old organ and the installation of the new, St Bede's was given use of a portable pipe organ thanks to the generosity of St John the Baptist parish in Woy Woy.

In 2011 the parish community resumed the project of completing the installation of stained-glass. Paddy Robinson of Finglinna Studios at Sofala was commissioned to give contemporary expression to an ancient Christian theme—the cross as the source of life. This theme, depicted in stone and manuscript, was widespread in the time of the Venerable Bede. The cross was to be represented in the two lancet windows in the sanctuary, and from the cross a vine would curl and waters flow, spreading through the windows of the nave, enfolding the gathered congregation. The two windows from the seafarers' chapel were skilfully brought into the overall scheme, by incorporating the water theme at the base of each of them, and by repeating the colours and shapes of the rich foliage background of the figures of Jesus and Mary. The whole stained-glass project was completed by the repair and restoration of these windows.

Represented in the lower portion of the sanctuary windows are two deer drinking from the water flowing from the cross, a beautiful symbol of human longing drawn from Psalm 42:

Like the deer that yearns for running streams,
so my soul is yearning for you, my God.
My soul is thirsting for God, the God of my life;
when can I enter and see the face of God?

The sanctuary window is dedicated to all the priests and nuns who ministered at St Bede's from 1867. The window was funded jointly by the parish and the Dominican community of St James. Past and present parishioners sponsored the six nave windows in memory of their families. At the base of each is a plaque bearing a biblical text expressing the vine or water theme and carrying a dedicatory text.

In 2013 the parish commissioned a sculpture of St John the Baptist to be placed on the wall behind the baptismal font. This was an attempt to correct the neglect of the iconography of John the Baptist in the Western Latin

---

23. Darrell Pitchford, 'St Bede's Catholic Church, Pyrmont—Möller', *Sydney Organ Journal*, 42/1 (Summer 2010/11): 23, 31–32, 62–63.

tradition. In the Orthodox or Eastern tradition the Baptist is always found in conjunction with icons of Christ and Mary. The sculptor, Jane Dawson, was commissioned to apply her renowned work with copper to create a full length figure to be placed adjacent to the Jesus and Mary windows.[24] The sculpture was donated by former parishioner Ernie Cannon, who had grown up at his parents' general-store on the corner of Harris and Bowman streets and had married one of his O'Toole neighbours. In August 2013, in the presence of the artist and her family, members of the Cannon and O'Toole families participated in the dedication of the sculpture.

As early as 2011 the Pyrmont parish community had begun to prepare for the 2017 sesquicentenary by commissioning conservation reports on the sandstone of the church, with the assistance of a City Council grant. The main problem to be addressed was the deterioration of some of the blocks through damp, aggravated by the repointing of the joints with concrete that had taken place many years before. There had also been some impact-damage to some of the blocks. A final report was accepted by the Parish Council and Finance Committee in 2013. A preliminary project involving new drainage on the northern side of the church was undertaken at the beginning of 2014. The stonework project was commenced in February 2015.

Some of the details from the 'Stonework Conservation and Repairs Specification' document, prepared by Jasper Swann, give glimpses of the skills that were used in the building of the church in 1867, and others that were unknown to the quarrymen and stonemasons of that period. The major difference is the source of the replacement blocks of sandstone. These are sourced, not from Pyrmont, but from quarries in the Gosford region. However, the specifications emphasised that the quality should match that of the best that Pyrmont had to offer: 'The sandstone for new works, indents and the like, shall be a good quality oxidising yellowblock sandstone.'[25] The document further specified that 'replacement stones are to match original profiles and original surface finishes; all finishes shall match the existing original finishes, including hand-tooled finishes where necessary to match existing'. Those original, hand-tooled finishes reflected a wide variety of styles used by the team of stonemasons at work on St Bede's from February to August 1867. Each distinctive style stands like a personal signature of the many pioneer parishioners at work on fashioning their new parish church.

Reference to the restrained use of modern products and tools is found in relation to the desalination of external and internal surfaces: 'The sandstone shall be desalinated, where scheduled, using a poultice... Prior to application

---

24. *Sculpture Society Bulletin*, September–October 2013, 9.
25. Jasper Swann, 'Stonework Conservation and Repairs Specification', October 2013 (St Bede, Pyrmont, Archives).

of the poultice, all loose and friable stone shall be removed from the surface using a stiff bristle nylon brush. Flaking, delaminating or exfoliating stone shall be dressed back with a light chisel using pneumatic or hand tools prior to application of the poultice.'

Preliminary to the major task of repointing every joint over the whole external surface of the building, it was necessary to rake out the thick and damaging concrete that had been so roughly applied in the 1950s. Again, caution about the tools to be used was specific: 'Existing mortar shall be raked out using hand-tools or Fein tools only. No other power tools of any kind shall be used at any time.' The use and application of a traditional recipe for the replacement mortar is a work of major restoration, of which the stonemasons of 1867 would have approved: 'Pointing mortar shall consist of: 1 part off white cement; 1 part slaked lime; 6 parts clean sharp sand. The repointing mortar shall be placed cleanly and under compression into the joint without smearing the stonework either side of the joint. No voids shall be left in the joint behind the pointing mortar.'

The final aspect of the stonework conservation is the removal from the stone of 150-years accumulation of algal and other biological deposits, as well as the grime of Pyrmont's industrialised era, principally from the smoke and soot from the neighbouring power station chimneys. However, an emphatic specification was: 'Do not attempt to produce a new stone appearance.' The governing document expressed a very respectful and gentle approach to the cleaning of the 'very neat elegant structure':

> Where currently soiled with algal and other biological deposits, the sandstone shall be cleaned using clean fresh water and a stiff bristle nylon scrubbing brush. Bronze brushes may be used to remove stubborn soiling or staining. No steel brushes are to be used. Do not use severely worn brushes. Clean the existing stonework to remove harmful or unsightly deposits of foreign material and salts from the building fabric, without damage to the stonework, and leave the stonework surface clean. Provide an even final appearance, without overlaps between bays which may cause streaks of over-cleaning.[26]

The work of restoration has been completed under the new parish priest, Anthony Walsh, and the parish committees. The present generation of parishioners has contributed significantly to the preservation of St Bede's for future worshippers.

---

26. Swann, 'Stonework Conservation and Repairs Specification', October 2013 (St Bede, Pyrmont, Archives).

Chapter 25
Patron Saint

At the laying of the foundation stone in February 1867 it was announced that the new church at Pyrmont would be placed under the patronage of the Venerable Bede (673-735). Saint Bede was the eighth century English monk whose name was given to John Polding when he received the Benedictine habit in 1810 at the age of sixteen. There is no documentation relating to the choice of the name for Pyrmont's church. However, it may be supposed that the decision was made deliberately to honour the Archbishop. Such decisions would normally have been made by the bishop himself in consultation with the local priest-in-charge. In the absence of Polding in Europe, to where he had sailed in November 1865, it would have been the Vicar-General, Austin Sheehy, in consultation with Timothy McCarthy, the pastor of the mission district, who chose the Venerable Bede as patron saint. Both priests were very fond of and very dedicated to the Archbishop—Sheehy was a member of the Sydney Benedictine community and had been recently successfully proposed by Polding to be his assistant bishop; McCarthy was a particular favourite of the Archbishop and entrusted with a succession of important missions. The name of Bede was also a strong link with the mother church of the district dedicated to St Benedict (480-543), the fifth century author of the monastic rule which gave rise to a multitude of monasteries of monks and nuns throughout Europe, including the seventh century foundations at the mouth of the river Wear in remote north-eastern England, to which Bede belonged.

In 1867 there were already three churches in New South Wales dedicated to Saint Bede. The Catholic Church at Appin, south of Sydney, had been begun by Father John Joseph Therry in 1837, the year in which he was reinstated on the list of official chaplains. His intention was that the new church would be dedicated to Mary under the title of 'Immaculate Conception'. However, after Therry was transferred to Hobart in 1838, the project came directly under the oversight of Polding, who adjusted the building plans and in 1842, in conjunction with the new pastor, Father Bede Sumner, changed the dedication to Saint Bede, the personal patron of both these English monks. The church was officially dedicated in October 1843.[1]

Much further south at Braidwood, the centre of a gold-mining district, the foundation stone for a church was laid by Archbishop Polding in 1853, during one of the pastoral tours of his favourite southern districts. However, a church did not emerge on that site, and in 1858 the local priest-in-charge, Edward O'Brien, made a new beginning at a more salubrious location. On this site was built the Church of St Bede. 'Mr Monro' was named as the church 'designer', the same William Munro, who was the architect of the Pyrmont church.[2] However, Munro's involvement with the project was short-lived; he was replaced by William Kemp, an architect with better connections in the distant district.[3] In January 1861 the church was solemnly blessed by Archdeacon John McEncroe.[4] There is no record of the decision to dedicate the church to the Venerable Bede; the choice could have been that of the Archbishop in 1853 out of personal devotion to the saint, or of Father O'Brien in 1858 out of devotion to the Archbishop. In 1862 a huge bell, cast in England, arrived at Braidwood for the new church. It was inscribed with the name of the patron—'Bedae venerabilis nomen'. The translation of the full inscription, addressed to the bell, read:

> Bronze cast in holy service, vibrant will re-echo your voice,
> Awaking day from veil of darkness, proclaiming abroad the dawn of light.
> The name of venerable Bede you bear, engraved to make it known.
> May this recall to exiled hearts the blessed love of distant home.[5]

Dean Edward O'Brien, as he became, continued his church-building career in rural parishes until 1887, when he made the unusual decision for a diocesan priest to join a religious order, entering the Jesuit Novitiate at the age of 70 and dying at North Sydney in 1900.

At Morpeth in the Hunter River valley, north of Sydney, Archbishop Polding laid the foundation stone for a temporary church and school-house

---

1. TJ Whitty, 'The Origins of the Church of St Bede, Appin, and the History of the Appin Catholic School', *Journal of the Australian Catholic Historical Society*, 7(1982): 23–33; Marie Holmes, *St Bede's Church Appin*, Minto, Campbelltown and Airds Historical Society, 1987.
2. *Freeman's Journal*, 30 October 1858.
3. Robert Parkinson, *The House of Prayer: St Bede's Catholic Church, Braidwood, NSW*, (Braidwood, 2003), 5–7.
4. *Freeman's Journal*, 26 January 1861.
5. Translation by Sr M Peter Damian McKinlay SGS, in Parkinson, *The House of Prayer*, 21.

in November 1861. He had sailed by steamer from Sydney, accompanied by Austin Sheehy. Gathered with them at the ceremony were priests who would have a Pyrmont connection in future years—the Benedictine Dean Maurus O'Connell of East Maitland, Dean John Lynch of West Maitland and Father Eugene Luckie of Raymond Terrace. Perhaps it was not surprising that, with the Archbishop and two high-ranking Benedictines present, the patron chosen for the new church was the Venerable Bede. Newspaper reports noted that 'Mr William Munro, of the Glebe Road, is the architect'.[6]

In 1875 a fifth church in the Sydney Archdiocese was dedicated to Saint Bede, at Cobargo on the far south coast of New South Wales, as reported in the *Freeman's Journal*:

> This handsome little church, recently opened by Archbishop Vaughan, forms a valuable addition to the rising township of Cobargo. The church stands on a beautiful site on the bill overlooking Bredbatoura, the land on which it has been erected being the gift of W. D. Tarlinton, Esq. The building is thirty-eight feet long by eighteen broad, and is of weatherboard, lined throughout with pine. The internal fittings are of cedar, and are really very beautiful; the communion railing and altar being after a design by Mr Barlow, of Moruya; the latter especially is a most elegant and elaborate piece of workmanship. It speaks well for the liberality of Catholic residents in this locality, that this church has been erected almost free of debt.[7]

Two of the five churches dedicated to the Venerable Bede underwent subsequent changes in dedication. When a new church was built at Morpeth in 1898 it was given the name 'Immaculate Conception' by its Irish parish priest, Patrick Corcoran, who was the first resident priest and who served from 1875 to 1929. This name change was the reverse of that at Appin in 1842. There were no longer any Benedictines, bishop or priests, in the Diocese of Maitland to advocate retention of the dedication to Saint Bede. The Morpeth parish school, however, which inherited the original church building, kept Bede as its patron, as did the very active local branch of the Holy Catholic Guild. At Cobargo a new brick church was built and dedicated under the title of 'Our Lady of Good Counsel'.

The 'Sisters of the Good Samaritan of the Order of St Benedict' expressed their fondness for their co-founder, John Bede Polding and his patron and also honoured the new Archbishop, Roger Bede Vaughan, who shared that patron, when they dedicated a new convent and high school at Newtown to

---

6. *Freeman's Journal*, 20 November 1861.
7. *Freeman's Journal*, 8 May 1875.

Saint Bede in 1883. St Bede's Convent was opened by Archbishop Vaughan on 7 January shortly before his departure for his 'ad limina' visit to Rome. Roger Bede did not reach Rome, dying a few days after his arrival in England in August 1883. 'Bede' would next appear in the name of a Sydney Archbishop in 1983 with the appointment of Edward Bede Clancy (1923-2014). The first bishop of Parramatta diocese, separated from the Sydney archdiocese in 1986, was Bede Heather. The name of Bede had disappeared from Newtown with the closing of the high school in 1961.

Bede was a particularly popular name among the members of the English Benedictine Congregation, to which Polding and the early Sydney monks belonged. The EBC was created from among the exiled English and Welsh monks in the early seventeenth century. They formed communities at various locations on the Continent, from which individual monks would enter England clandestinely for missionary work. Whole communities began to return to England after the French Revolution, and with the lifting of restrictions on Roman Catholic organisations in Great Britain. Polding's plans for his Vicariate were that he would establish a branch of the Anglo-Benedictines in the Antipodes. On the evening of his day of consecration as a bishop in London, he wrote to the President of the Congregation, Dr Augustine Birdsall, advocating this missionary plan: 'Let me be considered only as a Deputy of our Congregation, extending the wing of its care over a land far distant and very wicked . . . I do hope that . . . in a few years the Benedictine Province of N S Wales shall be deemed no inconsiderable or uninteresting part of our Holy Institute.'[8] On the eve of his sailing he wrote to Cardinal Fransoni, Prefect of Propaganda Fide, with great pride in the missionary tradition of the Benedictines: 'As it has been found from experience that the Benedictine spirituality has virtually from its beginning produced missionaries well adapted for the conversion of pagan peoples . . . I plead with the Holy See to be permitted to establish my vicariate, if it seems reasonable, the same Rule of life as is now in England, with the same provisions.'[9]

John Bede Polding clung to his Benedictine dream from 1834 until his death in 1877. In 1845 he reiterated the ideal in a letter to a lay benefactor in England: 'We shall, in our institute, come as near as to the form of the Benedictine Institute as it existed before the Reformation in England as we can, blending as it did in perfect harmony the Episcopal authority with the Apostolical, and producing missionaries who more zealously fulfilled their duty from the habitual renunciations of all things, the consequence of their monastic profession.'[10] The dream was not shared by all, not even fellow

---

8. Polding to Birdsall, 29 June 1834 (Polding Letters I.32).
9. Polding to Fransoni, 26 March 1835 (Polding Letters I.53).
10. Polding to William Leigh, 7 January 1845 (Brian Condon, *Letters and Documents in 19th Century Australian Catholic History*, http://www.library.unisa.edu.au/

Benedictines. In 1838 it was already perceived by Ullathorne as a daydream and by Vaughan in 1877 as a nightmare.

The 'Obit book of the English Benedictines, 1600-1912', compiled by Dom Norbert Birt, listed fourteen monks with the name Bede.[11] This was the highest occurrence of any religious name among the 350 Benedictines whose deaths occurred in the nineteenth century. One of these Bedes was an uncle of Polding and another a cousin. The cousin, Edward Bede Slater, had exercised ecclesiastical jurisdiction over New Holland from 1819 to 1832 as Vicar Apostolic on Mauritius, without ever sailing to the eastern extremity of his Vicariate.

John Bede Polding found much in common with his patron saint. Both were orphaned in childhood and placed under the guardianship of a monk. Bede at the age of seven became the ward of Abbot Benedict Biscop, founder of the twin monasteries of Saint Peter and Saint Paul at Wearmouth and Jarrow, where Bede would spend the rest of his life. Polding at the age of eight was placed under the care of his maternal uncle, Dom John Bede Brewer, and in 1810, at the age of 16, he joined the Benedictine community in Shropshire that had relocated to England from Douai in 1795, following the French Revolution.

Even in the great contrast between the sedentary Bede, who rarely left his monastery, and the itinerant Polding, who was always on the move, there was a deep affinity. The mission of the two monks was identical, namely, the communication of the Gospel message, and the formation of Christian communities in union with the successors of St Peter, the Bishops of Rome. Both were teachers in their own time and place. In worlds apart in time, 1200 years, and place, 11000 miles, Bede achieved this by his prayer and writing, Polding by his prayer and preaching journeys. Similar also was an attractive gentleness of character. In 1844 William Duncan in his *Weekly Register* published a biography of Polding which was reprinted in the *Sydney Morning Herald*, and which concluded: 'Of the personal character of Dr Polding there is but one opinion in the colony: those who are most opposed to his religion being among the readiest to bear testimony to the many amiable qualities which adorn its local head, but which qualities those only who know him intimately can appreciate in the fullest degree.'[12] Australian Catholics did not hesitate to name their first Archbishop 'the Venerable Bede of the Australian Church', as articulated by an episcopal colleague, Christopher Reynolds of

---

condon/CatholicLetters/18410412.htm)

11. Henry Norbert Birt, *Obit Book of the English Benedictines from 1600 to 1912*, (Edinburgh, 1913).
12. *Weekly Register*, 30 March 1844; *Sydney Morning Herald*, 1 April 1844.

Adelaide, at the Requiem Mass for Australia's deceased prelates during the 1885 Plenary Council at St Mary's Cathedral.[13]

A thematic thread running through Bede's *Ecclesiastical History of the English People*, written in 731, was the strong bond between the English Church and the Church of Rome. Benedict Biscop had made six journeys to Rome to study monastic practices, to collect Roman liturgical and theological manuscripts, and to recruit experts to instruct the English in all fields of Roman practice, in music and in skills such as building in stone and the glazing of windows. His dedication of his twin monasteries to Peter and Paul was an emphatic statement of his links with Rome and its apostles, and a repetition of Saint Augustine's naming of his monastery at Canterbury one hundred years before. Bede emphasised in his history the adoption of the Roman calculation of Easter by the Celtic church under the influence of the Roman missionaries, Augustine and Paulinus. Bede's account of the Synod of Whitby in 664, where the decision in favour of the Roman tradition was made, presents the outcome as the triumph of universal practice over provincial custom.[14]

Polding would have found in the writings of St Bede the basis of his own role as a monk-bishop, especially in the biographies of the exemplary monk-bishops such as Aidan and Cuthbert. Bede's letter of 734 to Egbert, bishop of York, set out the high ideal of the episcopal office, to which Polding was committed:

> I therefore exhort your Holiness, my beloved Bishop in Christ, to conform both by holy life and by holy teaching, the sacred dignity which God, the Author of dignities and Giver of spiritual gifts, hath bestowed upon you. For neither of these is complete without the other: if the bishop whose life is pure, omits the duty of preaching, or the good teacher neglects to practise what is right. But he who faithfully does both, is that servant who shall with joy await the coming of the Lord, hoping soon to hear 'Well done, good and faithful servant.'[15]

---

13. *Freeman's Journal*, 5 December 1885.
14. John Moorhead, 'Bede on the Papacy', *Journal of Ecclesiastical History*, 60 (2009): 217–232.
15. 'An Epistle from Bede to Bishop Egbert', in J.A. Giles (ed./transl.), The Complete Works of Venerable Bede, in the original Latin, collated with the Manuscripts, and various printed editions, and accompanied by a new English translation of the Historical Works, and a Life of the Author, London, Whittaker and Company, 1843, volume II, 138-155.

Bede scholar Simon Coates' conclusion to his article on 'Bede and the spiritual authority of the monk-bishop' could stand as the ideal lived by John Bede Polding:

> Though a monk, Bede carefully enunciated a view of episcopal authority which was marked by a long-established literary tradition that had related asceticism to a world beyond the monastery. The mainspring of his intellectual activity was pastoral. As ascetics and pastors monk-bishops did not live double lives. Their ability to move inward to embrace a life of contemplation and meditation was linked to their ability to move outward to embrace the wider needs of the world. The practice of ascetic virtue was related to the preaching of the Gospel. Bede recognised that it was in the figure of the monk-bishop that these two activities could be most effectively realised.[16]

The Monastic Library at St Mary's Cathedral, later relocated to Lyndhurst College and then to St John's College, was well stocked with the works of Bede. The earliest holding was a volume with the title, *Tomvs tertius collectaneorum Venerabilis Bedae presbyteri in Epistolas D. Pauli Apostoli,* published in Paris in 1521. It was the third of a three volume set of Bede's New Testament commentaries. The complete works of Bede were found in the eight volumes of the 1612 Cologne edition.[17] The description of Saint Bede in the title is worthy of translation: 'The Venerable Bede, the Anglo-Saxon Priest, the most learned man of his time'. The St Mary's library also contained six of the eight volumes of the Reverend JA Giles' 1843 edition of Bede's Complete Works.[18] John Allen Giles (1808–1884) was an Anglican priest and scholar, an expert in Anglo-Saxon language and history. Between 1837 and 1843 the prolific Giles published the *Patres Ecclesiæ Anglicanæ* ('Fathers of the English Church') a series of thirty-four volumes, culminating with the Bede volumes. Sydney's Benedictine library contained more of Giles' translations of Bede's works in a series published by Henry George Bohn in one of his

---

16. Simon J Coates, 'The bishop as pastor and solitary: Bede and the spiritual authority of the monk-bishop', *Journal of Ecclesiastical History*, 47(1996), 618-619.
17. *Venerabilis Bedae Presbyteri Anglo-Saxonis viri sua aetate doctissimi opera, quotquot reperiri potuerunt omnia. Hac ultima impressione ornatius in lucem edita,* Coloniae Agrippinae sumptibus Anton. Hierati et Ioan. Gymnici, Anno 1612
18. *The Complete Works of Venerable Bede, in the original Latin, collated with the Manuscripts, and various printed editions,* and *accompanied by a new English translation of the Historical Works, and a Life of the Author,* published in London by Whittaker and Company.

many *Bohn's Libraries* collections: in 1845 *The biographical writings and letters of Venerable Bede* and in1847 *The Ecclesiastical history of the English People*. The volumes of Bede produced by Giles and Bohn reflected and promoted a growing interest in the saint during the 1840s in connection with the Oxford Movement. This interest was already strongly present in Polding's Sydney monastery, and was greatly increased with the purchase of the new editions in translation.

The St Mary's monastic library had its origins in the large collection of books brought to Sydney by William Bernard Ullathorne in 1832. It was supplemented by the books of subsequent Benedictine missionaries and by Polding's purchases during his five voyages to Europe. In 1852 the growing collection was moved from St Mary's to the Lyndhurst Monastery and College in The Glebe. In 1877, following Archbishop Vaughan's dissolution of the monastery and closure of the college, the library was relocated to St John's College within the University of Sydney, where Vaughan maintained his residence. The books became a substantial part of his personal library and its acquisition may have been a motivation in his precipitate, mid-academic year closure of Lyndhurst. The Benedictine Collection, as it became known, was transferred to St Patrick's College at Manly in 1889, and now constitutes a special section of the Veech Library at the Catholic Institute of Sydney at Strathfield. Early catalogue cards contain information about the provenance of the books through 'ex libris' entries. The only Bede volume with such a detail is the 1845 publication, *The biographical writings and letters of Venerable Bede*, which bears the name of Dom Placid Quirk followed by that of WA Duncan. It was Duncan who, commissioned by Archbishop Vaughan, had collected the scurrilous rumours about Dom Placid and his fellow Sydney monks, which contributed to the closure of the monastery and removal of the library.

The feast day of Saint Bede was traditionally celebrated on 27 May, on which date his name appeared in the Roman Martyrology. Even in the civil calendar published in the *Sydney Gazette*, in which were listed birthdays of members of the royal family and historical figures, anniversaries of major civil events and ecclesiastical feasts, the name of the Venerable Bede was always listed on that date, sometimes sharing the day with 'Dante born 1265' or 'Expedition against Holland, 1799'.[19] The Catholic clergy needed more than the *Gazette*'s calendar to guide them through the liturgical year; they needed the approved liturgical calendar so they could confidently celebrate the right feasts on the correct days of the year. The arrival of the annual official directory from England was often frustratingly uncertain, as flippantly indicated by Bishop Polding writing to his monk-agent and

---

19. *Sydney Gazette*, 1829, 1831.

cousin, Dom Paulinus Heptonstall: 'And what is Mr Scott about, to leave us so long without Directories? Half the Saints of the foregone months, for aught I know, may have entered suits at law against us for deprivation of due honour and service.'[20] When the *Freeman's Journal* began publication in 1850 it printed a liturgical calendar at the beginning of each month. In 1850, when 27 May occurred on the Monday after Trinity Sunday, the feast of St Bede was relocated to a traditional alternative date, 29 October, a date associated with the translation of his body to Durham. The English Benedictine, Alban Butler, explained the variations in dates in his 1864 edition of 'The Lives of the Fathers, Martyrs and Other Principal Saints':

> His feast was kept in England in some places on the 26th of May, with a commemoration only in the office of St Austin; in others it was deferred to the 27th, on which it occurs in the Roman Martyrology. In the constitution of John Alcock, bishop of Ely, for the festivals of his diocese, printed in 1498 by Pynson, Bede's feast is ordered to be kept with an office on the 13th of March, the day of his death being taken up by the office of St Austin. Certain congregations of the Benedictine order have long kept his office on the 29th of October, perhaps on account of some translation. On the same day it is celebrated at present in England.[21]

In November 1899, in response to an 1859 petition from the English bishops, the celebration of the feast of the Venerable Bede was extended to the universal church by Pope Leo XIII. The day named in the Decree for the observance of the Saint's Feast was 27 May. In the same document Bede was declared to be a Doctor of the Church. Even before the formal petition of 1859 Polding had been actively lobbying for this outcome on behalf of his patron saint during the great gathering of bishops in Rome, in December 1854, for the solemn declaration of the doctrine of the Immaculate Conception. He wrote optimistically to Dame Scholastica Gregson, the Lady Abbess of Stanbrook Abbey: 'We have been making a great attempt to have the Feast of my Patron, Venerable Bede, made a double for the Universal Church, as it is now for England; and also this great saint declared a Doctor of the Church. The Pope has given his consent; upwards of 250 B[isho]ps and Prelates signed the Supplication.'[22]

---

20. Polding to Heptonstall, 1 May 1836 (Letters I.58).
21. A Butler, *The Lives or the Fathers, Martyrs and Other Principal Saints*, London 1864, volume V (http://www.ewtn.com/library/MARY/STBEDE.htm; accessed 9 February 2015).
22. Polding to Abbess of Stanbrook, 15 January 1855 (Polding Letters II.221).

There were some years when the feast was transferred to a ferial day in June, as happened in 1866 when Archbishop John Bede Polding was visiting Prior Roger Bede Vaughan's community near Hereford

> The Most Rev Dr Polding OSB, Archbishop of Sydney, visited the Cathedral Priory of St Michael, near Hereford, on Saturday last, June 16th, and remained there for a few days. His Grace, who is looking well and vigorous in spite of the weight of his years and labours, attended the offices of the Church, in the Cathedral, on Sunday. On the following day, which chanced to be the very day on which the English Benedictines kept the transferred feast of Venerable Bede (whose name the Archbishop assumed on receiving the religious habit), after conventual Mass, celebrated by himself, he received the following address . . . : 'May it please your Grace: We the Cathedral Prior and community of St Michael's desire to take advantage of your visit and of this day, the festival of your patron, the Venerable Bede, to assure you how deeply gratified and highly honoured we are by your presence among us . . . As a Bishop and Primate in the Church of God, we must honour you. As another pastor in the line of pastors that have come from the Benedictine cloister, we must feel proud of you. As the English founder and venerable ruler of a sister Church that is bound to us by a thousand ties and sympathies, we must feel enthusiasm for you . . . We wish you with the utmost respect, all the happiness that is suggested to our hearts to pray for, by your presence among us, by your connection with us, by your high position, and by the festival of your patron saint . . .'[23]

Back in Sydney the feast was celebrated on 15 June 1866, as noted at the conclusion of a letter from Austin Sheehy to the absent archbishop: 'Today we keep the feast of St Bede. I celebrated Mass for Your Grace at the Good Shepherd, and in addition to prayers I think all the Communions were offered for you. Wishing Your Grace a happy feast and begging your blessing, I remain Your obed[ient] Child, S J A Sheehy.'[24]

The feast of Saint Bede is now celebrated universally on 25 May. On that day, in the Office of Readings in the Roman Breviary, the following charming text, 'Letter on the Death of Bede [735]', is read:

> On Tuesday before the feast of the Ascension, Bede's breathing became labored and a slight swelling appeared in his legs. Nevertheless, he gave us instruction all day long and dictated cheerfully the whole time. It

---

23. *The Tablet*, 23 June 1866.
24. Sheehy to Polding, 15 June 1866 (Polding Letters III. 148).

seemed to us, however, that he knew very well that his end was near, and so he spent the whole night giving thanks to God. At daybreak on Wednesday he told us to finish the writing we had begun. We worked until nine o'clock, when we went in procession with the relics as the custom of the day required. But one of our community, a boy named Wilbert, stayed with him and said to him, 'Dear master, there is still one more chapter to finish in that book you were dictating. Do you think it would be too hard for you to answer any more questions?' Bede replied: 'Not at all; it will be easy. Take up your pen and ink, and write quickly,' and he did so. At three o'clock, Bede said to me, 'I have a few treasures in my private chest, some pepper, napkins, and a little incense. Run quickly and bring the priests of our monastery, and I will distribute among them these little presents that God has given me.' When the priests arrived he spoke to them and asked each one to offer Masses and prayers for him regularly. They gladly promised to do so. The priests were sad, however, and they all wept, especially because Bede had said that he thought they would not see his face much longer in this world. Yet they rejoiced when he said, 'If it so please my Maker, it is time for me to return to him who created me and formed me out of nothing when I did not exist. I have lived a long time, and the righteous Judge has taken good care of me during my whole life. The time has come for my departure, and I long to die and be with Christ. My soul yearns to see Christ, my King, in all his glory.' He said many other things which profited us greatly, and so he passed the day joyfully till evening. When evening came, young Wilbert said to Bede, 'Dear master, there is still one sentence that we have not written down.' Bede said, 'Quick, write it down.' In a little while, Wilbert said, 'There; now it is written down.' Bede said, 'Good. You have spoken the truth; it is finished. Hold my head in your hands, for I really enjoy sitting opposite the holy place where I used to pray; I can call upon my Father as I sit there.' And so Bede, as he lay upon the floor of his cell, sang, 'Glory be to the Father, and to the Son and to the Holy Spirit.' And when he had named the Holy Spirit, he breathed his last breath. We believe most firmly that Bede has now entered into the joy of the heaven he longed for, since his labors here on earth were always dedicated to the glory of God.[25]

The feast, on whatever day designated, was always celebrated with exuberance at Polding's Cathedral Church and monastery of St Mary. For example, in 1849 the monk chronicler made the following entry in the

---

25. 'Letter on the Death of Bede', in *Bede: The Ecclesiastical History of the English People*, edited by Judith McClure & Roger Collins (Oxford, 2008), 300–303.

Benedictine Journal: '[Monday] Oct 29th. Feast of St Bede, Patron of His Grace the Archbishop. The bells were rung from 3½ to 4½ AM. Matins was said ¼ before 5, then prime was said—after which Meditation followed. His Grace celebrated the conventual Mass at ¼ to 7. An extraordinary communion was permitted to the brethren.'[26] The celebrations of St Bede's Day at the monastery were not restricted to the liturgy. The ranking of the feast as a 'Double' indicated that it was a day of rest, no work or study, and this was reflected in the continuation of the *Journal* entry for 29 October 1849: 'About 10am. The F[ather] Subprior accompanied the Religious, Novices and Postulants to Wooloomooloo [sic] Bay . . . They embarked on two other boats, and after some smart, but rather moist, sailing arrived at Garden Island . . . Various little parties set out in quest of sport—some to procure specimens for the museum . . . and others to procure the treasures the sea-beaten rocks afforded, a few oysters—and the wild goats were hunted by the young ones in the party.'[27] The former Benedictine John Henry Curtis (Brother Anselm) in his 1902 memoir on the Archbishop recalled St Bede's day at St Mary's monstery: 'Whenever the junior ecclesiastics went, according to the custom in religious houses, to wish him 'a happy feast' on St Bede's day, he would let them know how much he loved his patron saint. I daresay many of them, in the boyish way, thought more of the holiday that followed the greeting. But many caught the infection of the good prelate's love.'[28] During the life of the Sydney monastery, at the Cathedral and then at Lyndhurst, four young recruits were given the name Bede: Bede Bowler in 1849, Bede McNamara in 1856; Bede Field in 1863; Bede Brady circa 1873. Only one of the four died as a Benedictine—Bede Brady in 1876 at the age of 18.[29] The giving of the name Bede was not restricted to the monks. The Good Samaritan Sisters honoured their founder, John Bede Polding, by making sure that there was always at least one of the sisters who bore his monastic name. The first was Sister Bede Kelleher who entered the convent in 1864 and died in 1915; the last was Sister John Bede Lambert who died in 1994, after 80 years as a nun. Within those 130 years, Sister John Bede Harrington also upheld the tradition, from 1920 to 1979. The custom among the Sisters of imposing a religious name at the reception of the habit faded away in recent years. The name was also being given by parents to their sons throughout New South Wales in honour of the first bishop and his successor. It is no surprise that the St Bede's Baptismal Register at Pyrmont contains a sprinkling of the name 'Bede', usually as a second Christian name. It was not unusual for Catholic parents to choose the name of the parish patron

---

26. *Benedictine Journal*, 29 October 1849.
27. *Benedictine Journal*, 29 October 1849.
28. JHB Curtis, 'John Bede Polding', *Austral Light*, Oct. 1902, 699.
29. T Kavenagh, 'Poldings Monks', *Tjurunga*, 8(1974), Appendix 1, i-xviii.

saint for their child, and sometimes the parish priest imposed the name of his favourite saint in place of the parents' choice. The historian, Bede Nairn, author of the Polding entry in the *Australian Dictionary of Biography*, used to retell the family story that at his baptism at Mudgee in 1917 the Irish parish priest refused to pronounce the name proposed by the parents, 'Lloyd George', the name of the British Prime Minister who favoured the partition of Ireland. The priest imposed instead the name 'Bede'.[30]

There was a remarkably high instance of the occurrence of the unusual name throughout Sydney and rural New South Wales from the 1850s into the twentieth century. The choice of the name reflected the affection in which John Bede Polding and Roger Bede Vaughan were held by the Catholic community. An online search of the NSW Registry of Births for the years 1870 to 1911 revealed a total of 360 occurrences of 'Bede': 153 as a first name, 33 as 'John Bede', 20 as 'Roger Bede'.[31] In other instances the name 'Bede' was registered as the initial 'B' and did not emerge from the online search. Such, for example, was the case for the Dalley family. William Dalley (1831-1888) was given the name Bede by Polding at his confirmation in 1843. A pupil at St Mary's Seminary, he formed a life-long friendship with the Archbishop. The 21-year-old Dalley, a budding public speaker and student of the law, chose the Venerable Bede as the subject of a lecture given at a meeting of the newly founded Catholic Association in 1853.[32] The name would become part of the Dalley family tradition, even with the fading of the Catholic connection in the younger generations. William's brother Richard also bore the name and William Bede shared it with his sons, William Bede, John Bede and Charles Bede. William Bede junior, in defiance of gender, even gave the name to his daughter, Yolande Bede Dalley.

There is a Sydney street which bears the name of the saint—in the area now called South Strathfield, where in 1854 the entrepreneurial Father Joseph Therry drew up plans for 'St Anne's Village'. At the centre of the village stood the church of St Anne, completed in 1864; it is identical in style to St Bede's at Pyrmont. The streets radiating out from the central village square were named by Therry in honour of the archbishop, two of Sydney's Benedictine monks, a fellow pioneer priest and himself: John, Bede, Gregory, Anselm, McEncroe and Therry Streets.

The Venerable Bede was depicted in a window in St Mary's Cathedral, taking his place among New Testament figures and doctors of the Church. The window was dedicated in memory of Cardinal John Henry Newman and installed in 1902. The image of the central Christ figure is in the eighth

---

30. 'Obituary', *Sydney Morning Herald*, 15 May 2006.
31. NSW Registry of Births, Deaths and Marriages: http://www.bdm.nsw.gov.au/ (accessed 14 September 2014).
32. *Benedictine Journal*, 27 January 1853.

century style of 'Maiestas Domini', as also found in the new porch window at St Bede's, Pyrmont:

> In the centre, seated on a rainbow, and surrounded by the sun in its golden splendour, is a figure of the Divine Lord, the fountain and source of life and light to man. He is clothed in brilliant white garments. spangled with stars, and holds up in one hand a burning lamp, the other hand resting on the book of the Holy Gospels, as the treasury wherein is contained the record of His earthly life and teaching. An aureole of winged seraphs and light clouds surround this part of the composition, together with a scroll held by angels bearing the text in Latin: 'The Lord is my light and my salvation' (Ps. Xxvi.1). On either side, as far as space would permit, are placed various figures of Apostles, doctors of the Church, Greek and Latin saints, who by their lives and writings have illustrated, expounded, and defended the Christian faith, and many of whose characteristics were reflected in the life and work of the illustrious Cardinal commemorated. These consist of St John the Baptist, St John the Evangelist, Holy Simeon, St Paul, the Apostle of the Gentiles, St Ambrose, St Augustine, St John Chrysostom, St Athanasius, St Basil, and Venerable Bede.[33]

A much earlier Sydney appearance of Bede in glass is found, not in a church, but in the Great Hall of the University of Sydney. Installed in 1859, the windows in the northern wall are 'filled with large and beautifully executed figures, in stained glass, representing, in a splendid historical series, the worthies of England, Scotland and Ireland, beginning at the Venerable Bede . . .'[34]

Saint Bede is no longer honoured in the parish of Pyrmont by the baptismal names given to the parish children—the last entry of the name Bede in the baptismal register was in November 1937: 'Norman Bede', possibly honouring the new Coadjutor Archbishop, Norman Gilroy, as well as Sydney's first Archbishop. The parish's venerable patron is now remembered in an inscription placed beneath the porch window of the Christ figure, dedicated to the 'Pioneers of this Parish' in 2009. The words are taken from Bede's commentary on the Book of the Apocalypse, the young monk's first venture into biblical exegesis, as inscribed over his tomb in Durham Cathedral:

---

33. *Sydney Mail and New South Wales Advertiser,* 14 June 1902.
34 *Sydney Morning Herald,* 13 July 1859.

Christus
est stella
matutina qui nocte
saeculi transacta
lucem vitae
sanctis promittit
et pandit aeternam

Christ is the morning star
who when the night
of this world is past
brings to his saints
the promise of
the light of life
and opens everlasting day."[35]

Australia's own 'Venerable Bede', John Bede Polding, is remembered in a portrait of the young bishop over the sacristy fireplace, and in an image of the aged archbishop in the church nave.

---

35. Faith Wallis (translator), *Bede: Commentary on Revelation* (Liverpool: Liverpool University Press, 2013).

Bibliography

Matthew Allen, 'Sectarianism, respectability and cultural history: the St Patrick's Total Abstinence Society and Irish Catholic temperance in mid-nineteenth century Sydney', *Journal of Religious History*, 35(2011), 374-92.
Brian Andrews, 'St Francis Xavier's Church, Berrima, New South Wales', Pugin Foundation (http://www.puginfoundation.org/assets/Berrima_Essay.pdf)
John Arnold & John Hay (eds), *The Bibliography of Australian literature to 2000*, St Lucia 2000.
P Ayres, *Prince of the Church. Patrick Francis Moran, 1830-1911*, Sydney 2007
Carol J Baxter (ed), *1805-06 Musters of New South Wales and Norfolk Island*, Sydney 1989
Benedictine Monks of Buckfast Abbey, 'The Laying of the Foundation-Stone of a Church', *Homiletic & Pastoral Review*, January 1927.
Delia Birchley, *John McEncroe, Colonial Democrat*, Sydney 1986.
Henry Norbert Birt, *Benedictine pioneers in Australia*, **2 vols,** London 1911.
Henry Norbert Birt, *Obit Book of the English Benedictines from 1600 to 1912*, Edinburgh 1913.
D Bowen, *Paul Cardinal Cullen and the Shaping of Modern Irish Catholicism*, Dublin 1983
Francis Bertie Boyce, *Fourscore Years and Seven. The memoirs of Archdeacon Boyce, for over sixty years a clergyman of the Church of England in New South Wales*, Sydney 1934
Brian Byron, 'The Stability Necessary for a Parish Priest', *Australasian Catholic Record*, 73(1996), 304-322
H Campbell, 'Dean Lynch: laying the foundations for Maitland Diocese', *Journal of the Australian Catholic Historical Society*, 3 (1971) 46-71.
Malcolm Campbell, 'John Redmond and the Irish National League in Australia and New Zealand, 1883', *History* 86 (2002), 348-362.
Edmund Campion, *Rockchoppers. Growing up Catholic in Australia*, Ringwood, 1982.
Edmund Campion, *Ted Kennedy, Priest of Redfern*, Melbourne 2009
A Caruana, *Monastery on the Hill: a history of the Sacred Heart Monastery Kensington 1897-1997*, Kensington 2002
Kelvin Cavanagh, *St Benedict's School, Broadway: a history of a Catholic school*, Sydney 2014.
John Challis, 'Recollections of a Perth Movement Chaplain', *Journal of the Australian*

Catholic Historical Society, 35 (2014), 75-86.
C M H Clark, *A History of Australia*, Melbourne 1968
A M Clarke, *Life of Reverend Mother Mary of St Euphrasia Pelletier, First Superior General of the Congregation of Our Lady of Charity of the Good Shepherd of Angers*, London 1895
Simon J Coates, "The bishop as pastor and solitary: Bede and the spiritual authority of the monk-bishop", *Journal of Ecclesiastical History*, 47(1996), 601-619.
Paul Collins, *A very contrary Irishman: the life and journeys of Jeremiah O'Flynn*, Northcote, Victoria, 2014.
M. Xavier Compton et al (eds), *The Letters of John Bede Polding OSB*, 3 vols, Sydney 1994.
M. Xavier Compton et al (eds), *Adjutor Deus. Documents and resource material relating to the episcopacy of Archbishop John Bede Polding OSB*, 2 vols, Sydney 2000
Brian Condon: *Letters and Documents in 19th Century Australian Catholic History*, http://www.library.unisa.edu.au/condon/CatholicLetters/18410412.htm
P Crittenden, *Changing Orders. Scenes of clerical and academic life*, Blackheath 2008
A E Cunningham, *The Price of a Wife? The priest and the divorce trial*, Sydney 2013
JM Curran, 'Julian Tenyson Woods', *Centennial Magazine*, 2(1889-1890).
JHB Curtis, 'John Bede Polding', *Austral Light*, October 1902.
Mella Cusack, 'Kevin Izod O'Doherty and the Roman Catholic Bishops of Hobart and Brisbane', *Journal of the Australian Catholic Historical Society*, 22(2001), 59-70.
RA Daly, *One Hundred Years on Grose's Farm: the story of the College of St John the Evangelist, within the University of Sydney*, typed manuscript, 1977.
John de Luca, 'Disharmony among bishops: On the binding nature of a papal *motu proprio* on music', *Journal of the Australian Catholic Historical Society*, 35(2014), 28-37.
Everard Digby (ed), *Australian men of mark* (2 vols), Sydney 1888.
Christopher Dowd, *Rome in Australia: The Papacy and Conflict in the Australian Catholic Missions* (2 vols), Leiden, 2008.
Victor J Doyle, *St. Bede's Church Pyrmont. Centenary 1867-1967*, Sydney 1967.
Barrie Dyster, *Servant & Master: building and running the grand houses of Sydney 1788-1850*, Kensington 1989
Sean Enright, *Easter Rising 1916: the trials*, Sallins, Co. Kildare, 2014.
W Fanning, 'Secret Societies', *Catholic Encyclopedia*, New York, 1912, vol 14.
J J Farrell, *A Great Storm Arose: the saga of the resignation of Bishop Timothy O'Mahony*, unpublished manuscript based on a thesis 'The O'Mahony Case' submitted for Degree of Master of Letters at the University of New England, 1991.
Shirley Fitzgerald, *Lord Wolseley Hotel: a social history of a very small pub*, Sydney 2016.
Shirley Fitzgerald and Hilary Golder, *Pyrmont and Ultimo Under Siege*, Sydney 1994.
J Fletcher & M Hogan, *St James' Parish, Forest Lodge. 125 years: 1877-2002*, Forest Lodge 2002
Roy Foster, *Vivid Faces. The revolutionary generation in Ireland 1890-1923*, London 2015.
Janice Garaty, 'The Carlow connection: the contribution of Irish seminarians to 19th

century Australia", *Journal of the Australian Catholic Historical Society*, 35 (2014), 10-21.
Patrick M Geoghegan, "The Catholics and the Union", *Transactions of the Royal Historical Society*, 30(2000), 243-258.
JA Giles (ed), *The Complete Works of Venerable Bede, in the original Latin, collated with the Manuscripts, and various printed editions, and accompanied by a new English translation of the Historical Works, and a Life of the Author*, London 1843
Damian Gleeson, *Irish Dusk Colonial Dawn: the Dooly, Hickey, O'Brien, O'Neill (Neale), O'Toole (Toole) and Ryan Septs*, manuscript, 1999.
Damian Gleeson, "Marriages performed at St Bede's Catholic Church, Pyrmont, 1868-69", manuscript, Sydney 2000.
DJ Gleeson, "Tobias (O')Toole in History", manuscript, Sydney 2011.
L Grant, *Salt of the Earth: a Bathurst Necrology*, Bathurst 2005
A Green, *New South Wales Election Results 1856-2007* (http://www.parliament.nsw.gov.au/resources/nswelectionsanalysis/HomePage.htm
Francis Ravel Harvey, *The Roger Pryke Story: traveller to freedom*, Sydney 2011
Elizabeth Hellwig (ed), *An Account of a Journey from Kingstown, Ireland, to Maitland, Australia, in 1867 during the Age of Sail*, Strathfield 2001
Michael Hogan, *The Sectarian Strand. Religion in Australian history*, Ringwood 1987.
Michael Hogan, *Local Labor. A history of the Labor Party in Glebe 1891-2003*, Sydney 2004,
Marie Holmes, *St Bede's Church Appin*, Minto, 1987.
Mark Edward Horn, *William Munro: a report*, B Arch Thesis, Department of Architecture, University of NSW, 1973
R Irving & N Powell, *Sydney's Hard Rock Story: the Cultural Heritage of Trachyte*, Sydney 2014.
Ruth Marchant James, *Fields of Gold: a history of the Dominican Sisters in Western Australia*, Doubleview, WA, 1999
Patrick Kavanagh, *A Popular History of the Insurrection of 1798*, Dublin 1870.
T Kavenagh, 'Polding's Monks', *Tjurunga*, 8(1974), Appendix 1, i-xviii.
T Kavenagh, 'Vaughan and the monks of Sydney', *Tjurunga* 25 (1983), 183-206
T Kavenagh, "Romanticism and Recrimination: the Boy Postulants at St. Mary's, Sydney", *Tjurunga* 46 (1994), 21-42.
Vivienne Keely, *Dixon of Botany Bay: the convict priest from Wexford*, Sydney 2003.
Marilyn Kelleher, "Sister Scholastica Gibbons Co-Founder of the Sisters of the Good Samaritan", *Journal of the Australian Catholic Historical Society*, 20/1999, 17-30.
MA Kelleher, *Compassionate Samaritans. The experiences of active Benedictine women in New South Wales from 1857 to 1877*, PhD thesis submitted to Department of Studies of Religion, University of Sydney, 2000.
Marilyn Kelleher, *The Annals of the Sisters of the Good Samaritan of the Order of Saint Benedict, 1938-1959*. Sydney, 2010
Joan Kerr, *Our Great Victorian Architect, Edmund Thomas Blacket, (1817–1883)*, Sydney 1983.
J Kildea, *Tearing the Fabric: sectarianism in Australia 1910 to 1925*, Sydney 2000
J Kildea, 'Troubled times: an overview of the history of the Catholic Federation of New South Wales', *Journal of the Australian Catholic Historical Society*, 23 (2002), 9-22.

Henry J Koren, *The Spiritans. A History of the Congregation of the Holy Ghost*, Pittsburgh 1958.
TJ Linane & F A Mecham (eds), *The Men of '38 and other pioneering priests by 'John O'Brien'*, Kilmore 1975.
TJ Linane, *From Abel to Zundolovich. Biographies of priests on the Australian scene up to 1900* (vol. 2, Byrne to Dixon), Armadale 1979.
Kevin Livingston, *The Emergence of the Australian Catholic Priesthood*, Sydney 1977.
M Macnamara, 'The Catholic Church in NSW and the Census', *Australasion Catholic Record*, 8(1902), 292-315.
Brian Maher, *Planting the Celtic Cross: foundations of the Catholic Archdiocese of Canberra and Goulburn*, Canberra 1997.
MR Matthews, *Pyrmont and Ultimo. A history*, Sydney 1982
Henry Mayer, *The Press in Australia*, Melbourne 1968
Judith McClure & Roger Collins (eds), *Bede: The Ecclesiastical History of the English People*, Oxford 2008.
John F McMahon, *Randwick Catholic Church Centenary*, Kensington 1985
P McMurrich, *The Harmonious Influence of Religion: St Patrick's Church Hill, 1840 to the present*, Sydney 2011
F Mecham & A Brown, 'Eveleigh House', *Footprints* 9(1973), 9-10.
E Middleton, 'St Bartholomew's, Pyrmont', *Church of England Historical Society Journal*, 7(1964).
John Molony, *The Roman Mould of the Australian Church,* Melbourne 1969.
Brigid Moore, 'Sectarianism in NSW: the *Ne Temere* Legislation 1924-1925', *Journal of the Australian Catholic Historical Society*, 9(1987), 3-15.
John Moorhead, 'Bede on the Papacy', *Journal of Ecclesiastical History*, 60 (2009), 217-232.
Patrick Moran, *History of the Catholic Church in Australasia*, Sydney, 1895-96.
Patrick O'Farrell, "Archbishop Kelly and the Irish Question", *Journal of the Australasian Catholic Historical Society*, 4(1974), 1-19.
Patrick O'Farrell, *The Catholic Church and Community in Australia: a history*, Melbourne 1977.
Robert Parkinson, *The House of Prayer: St Bede's Catholic Church, Braidwood, NSW*, Braidwood 2003.
Darrell Pitchford, 'St. Bede's Catholic Church, Pyrmont – Möller', *Sydney Organ Journal*, 42/1 (Summer 2010/11), 23, 31-32, 62-63.
Margaret Press, *Julian Tenison Woods: 'Father Founder'*, 2nd edition, North Blackburn 1994.
Graeme D Rushworth, *Historic organs of New South Wales: the instruments, their makers and players, 1791-1940*, Sydney 1988.
Sister de Sales Smith, *The Annals of the Institute of the Sisters of the Good Samaritan from 1857 to1938*, Sydney 1939.
Joseph Smith, 'Our "worthwhile" ministry risk', *Sydney Anglicans*, 28 February 2008 (http://sydneyanglicans.net/news/pyrmont_church_story)
Keith Vincent Smith, *Eora Clans: A History of Indigenous Social Organisation in Coastal Sydney, 1770–1890*, MA thesis, Macquarie University, Sydney 2004.
Samuel Hanbury Smith, *Medicinal Mineral Waters, Natural and Artificial: their efficacy in the treatment of chronic diseases*, Hamilton, Ohio, 1855.
Max Solling, *Sydney's Aldermen* (http://www.sydneyaldermen.com.au).

WT Southerwood, *The Convict's Friend: Bishop R W Willson*, Hobart 1989.
Sydney Harbour Foreshore Authority, *Pyrmont + Ultimo: decade of renewal*, Sydney 2004.
Jasper Swann, 'Stonework Conservation and Repairs Specification', October 2013, St. Bede, Pyrmont, Archives.
S Utick, *Captain Charles, Engineer of Charity: the remarkable life of Charles Gordon O'Neill*, Sydney 2008.
Roger Bede Vaughan, 'Report on the Australian Benedictines' (October 27 1877) in T. Kavenagh, 'Vaughan and the monks of Sydney', *Tjurunga* 25 (1983), 183-206.
Faith Wallis (trans), *Bede: Commentary on Revelation*, Liverpool 2013.
KJ Walsh, *Yesterday's Seminary. A history of St Patrick's Manly*, Sydney 1998,
Anne Wark, *Armour of light: the stained glass windows of St James' Church, Forest Lodge, those to whom they are dedicated and their families*, Forest Lodge 2010.
Ian Waters, *Australian Conciliar Legislation prior to the 1917 Code of Canon Law: a comparative study with similar conciliar legislation in Great Britain, Ireland, and North America*, dissertation submitted to the Faculty of canon Law, Saint Paul University, Ottawa, in partial fulfilment of the requirement for the degree of Doctor of canon Law, 1990.
Ian Waters, "Stability of parish priests: the Australian History", *Australasian Catholic Record*, 74 (1997), 307-314.
Ann Maree Whenman, *In Good Faith: a historical study of the provision of religious education for Catholic children in Catholic schools in New South Wales*, thesis submitted in School of Religious Education, Australian Catholic University, Sydney 2011.
Charles White, *John Vane, bushranger: Being a true narrative of his career faithfully depicted*, Sydney 1908.
TJ Whitty, 'The origins of the Church of St Bede, Appin and the history of the Appin Catholic School', *Journal of the Australian Catholic Historical Society*, 7(1982), 23-33.
J Wilkinson, "Father Maurice O'Reilly, a controversial priest", *Journal of the Australian Catholic Historical Society*, 7 (1983), 3-23.
PJ Wilkinson, 'Daniel Vincent Maurus O'Connell OSB: first Australian-born priest', *The Swag*, February 2013
Patrick Woulfe, *Irish names and surnames*, Dublin, 1922.
Roger Wynne, 'The unfortunate business of '98', *Australasian Catholic Record*, 42(1965), 202-208
Roger Wynne, 'The coming of Cardinal Moran', *Australasian Catholic Record*, 47 (1970), 202-208
Roger Wynne, "Dean Flanagan's last years", *Australasian Catholic Record*, 48(1971), 171-172.
Roger Wynne, 'From Portland Bay to Moreton Bay', *Australasian Catholic Record*, 53(1976), 275-284
'Zero', *The Secret History of the Coningham Case*, Sydney 1901.

Appendix 1

ST. BEDE'S CHURCH
Pyrmont

CENTENARY
1867–1967

Centenary of the Solemn Blessing and Opening of St. Bede's Church, Pyrmont

1867—1967

Foundation Stone Laid, 6th February, 1867
Solemn Blessing and Opening, 1st September, 1867

CENTENARY COMMITTEE:

Rev. V. J. Doyle (Chairman)
Rev. R. Hickman (Vice-Chairman)
Mr. Ken Lewis (Secretary)

Messrs. Ted Cruickshank, John O'Regan, Frank Harbrow, Fred Schembri, Hugh Molin.

Mesdames Shirley Cruickshank, Joan O'Regan, Annie Reedie, Shelah Wormleaton, Joan Garner, Alice Barker, Joan Dattilino, Joan Griffiths, Nellie Campise, and Miss Monica Fay.

His Eminence N. T. Cardinal Gilroy, Archbishop of Sydney, with the T/V "Galileo" on which he sailed to Rome on 11th August, 1967.

Appendix 1

St. Mary's Cathedral
Sydney... 2000.

FOREWORD.

In our young Country a Centenary is an event that dips back into the early history of Australia.

For that reason, it is worthy of commemoration.

One hundred years ago Pyrmont was a well established suburb of Sydney.

St. Bede's, which on the the 7th of September will be 100 years old, was the Parish Church of a flourishing and devoted Catholic population.

The solid structure of the building is an indication of the belief of the pioneers that however Sydney developed St. Bede's would always be needed as a centre of Catholic devotion.

In this they were right. It is interesting to note that St. Bede's was built only two years after the original St. Mary's Cathedral was destroyed by fire. This is an indication of the courage and the generosity of the parishioners of Pyrmont.

Their interest went out beyond their own parish. While they erected and paid for their own Parish Church, they were among the more generous contributors towards the construction of the new St. Mary's Cathedral.

Let us learn from our pioneer Catholics to be courageous in our undertakings for God and His Holy Church.

May God bless abundantly today's Priests, Religious and Parishioners of St. Bede's.

N. Cardinal Gilroy
ARCHBISHOP OF SYDNEY.

29th July 1967.

Solemn Blessing and Opening of St. Bede's Church, Pyrmont

1st September, 1867

On Sunday, September 1, 1867, Archbishop Polding, O.S.B., first Archbishop of Sydney, came to the harbourside suburb of Pyrmont to bless the handsome stone Church which still stands proudly as a monument to the faith, generosity and fortitude of our forefathers.

The pioneer settlers had built the Church stone by stone, giving voluntarily of their labour.

The site selected for St. Bede's was on the original grant of 55 acres made over to Thomas Jones on March 14, 1795, for a shilling a year rental, to be known as "Jones' Farm", on the western side of Cockle Bay. Portion of this land passed later to Edward Macarthur, who in turn sold it to Thomas Ware Smart, who sold it to Archbishop Polding on December 11, 1865, for the sum of £330 (with co-signatures: Rev. Timothy McCarthy, John Henry Wiles and Patrick O'Toole (cf. Registrar-Gen. No. 256, Book 97; Vol. 6614, Folio 200).

Some of the stones for St. Bede's were quarried on the spot, and some from the Saunders' Quarry nearby, famous for its Pyrmont Sandstone.

The Church, worthy of the specially selected site, stands back from the waterfront.

On that historic day in 1867, its stone facade, lifting the two artistically fashioned stone Crosses high above its surroundings, stood well above a grassy slope which stretched down to the sand at the water's edge. Port Jackson fig trees here and there provided shade on the warm Spring day selected for the Blessing. The crowd which had assembled before 11 a.m. to welcome their Archbishop, waited calmly in the sunshine. Then excitement grew as the Archbishop's carriage was seen to approach, followed by many visitors from Sydney and neighbouring Parishes.

Only seven months before, the Vicar General had blessed the Foundation Stone of this Church. Now another stone like one of the many hewn from the nearby quarry was inscribed carefully for the benefit of later generations. Many are the stories told by the children and grandchildren of the Catholic men who quarried these stones and then actually climbed the growing walls to fit each particular stone into its rightful place in the Sacred Edifice.

Small wonder then, that the people of Pyrmont rejoiced as they followed their Archbishop as he made a circuit of the building, blessing the very walls that they had made. Archbishop Polding in a few words, then explained that "the walls were sprinkled with Holy Water to remind us of the Blood of Christ by which we have been redeemed". The prayer was added: "That Thou wouldst deign to cleanse and to bless this Church and altar in Thine honour and in the name of Thy Saint Bede." After the Litany of the Saints was recited, Psalms 119, 120, 121 were sung.

The interior of the Church being blessed, the assembled people were admitted and the first High Mass was sung in the Church of St. Bede. The Archbishop presiding in the Sanctuary, the Mass was sung by Father M. J. Dwyer, Father Crone acting as Deacon, and Father Luckie as Sub-Deacon. Father Colletti was Master of Ceremonies. Also present in the Sanctuary were Fathers McCarthy, Keating, Bersanti and Athy. Amongst the laity, names noted (in Freeman's Journal, September 7, 1867) were W. B. Dalley, Esq., W. Cummins, M.L.A., Alderman Caraher, Messrs. Mullins, Hurley, Moore, Bubie, Curran, O'Neill, Clune, McCarthy, etc.

The Choir (from St. Benedict's) was very highly praised.

After the Gospel, Father Bersanti ascended the altar steps, and preached a most eloquent sermon. He took the following words for his text:—

"I have chosen and have sanctified this place that my name may be there for ever, and my eyes and my heart may remain there perpetually" (2nd Book of Paralipomenon, c. vii). He said the people of Israel, the chosen of God from the beginning of the world until the reign of Solomon, were persecuted and wandered about, having no fixed place of abode. They had no material temples, but the temple of nature, under the vast canopy of heaven was the place where they first offered up sacrifices which consisted of the best and fattest of their flocks. Enoch was the first to supplicate and call upon God in public places. Noah built an altar to God, to offer up a clean holocaust on the very spot where he stepped forth from the Ark; Abraham also in the solitude of the wilderness offered up a sacrifice to the most High; Jacob, rising early one morning, took the stone upon which his head had been reclining, poured oil upon it and called it a temple of God; Melchisedech the high priest offered up bread and wine; Moses constructed in the desert the tabernacle of the covenant which was a portable structure, and was carried about when the camp of the Jews was moved. David, who ruled over the kingdom of Israel, was the first who felt the necessity of temples, but having engaged in so many wars and shed so much blood, he was deprived of the privilege of building a suitable temple to God. This glory was reserved for his son Solomon, styled the wisest of men. His kingdom being at peace with the whole world, he sent messengers to all the neighbouring kings to obtain presents and material to build a temple suitable to the Most High. Solomon erected the temple and when it was solemnly opened the Lord gave a visible mark of his presence, for while the Levites were singing canticles to the Lord, a cloud representing the majesty of the Almighty filled the temple, a fire from heaven consumed the sacrifice, and the Lord said: "I have chosen, and have sanctified this place, that my name may be there for ever, and my eyes and my heart may remain there perpetually." The solemn and consoling ideas concerning the temples of Solomon and the ceremonies with which it was blessed furnished the subject of his (the preacher's) discourse, which would be about the blessing and dedication of a church to the service of the Almighty. The triumphs of Solomon were a figure of the benefits which would here befall us, for the Lord was ready to shower his mercies, if his people will only show their love for him by erecting temples to his holy name. In directing Solomon in the steps he should follow He had in view the course which the true Christian Church should take to emulate him in their fervour in performing the public and solid act of religion.

Not very long ago the present spot upon which the Church stood was rough even when the foundation stone was laid, and if a stranger had passed and had not known the influence which the Catholic Church exercises over her children he could never have believed that so great a change could have taken place. The spot had now become the royal palace of the Most High, which He has filled with His majesty, where the unbloody sacrifice of the cross shall be offered up, and where hymns and canticles shall be sung. He will reside there like a father amongst His children and he will ever be ready to pity and assist them. If threatened to be struck by an angry God, they can seek shelter in that place, and if He send misery and pestilence and His face be sought in that place He will forgive their sins, for His eyes shall always be open to see them, and His heart to show compassion for He has said: "I have chosen, and have sanctified this place, that my name may be there for ever, and my eyes and my heart may remain there perpetually." The present ceremony was not merely an outward form of religion, it was also a majestic and solemn act of religion paid to the Almighty Creator of the Universe. The very ground and stones with which the church is built all belong to man, and his donations and contributions to the Almighty were offerings made to Him in virtue of his supreme domination over all things.

It is in the Church that man is regenerated to a new life and hope, in the church he is strengthened in his faith by confirmation and his soul nourished with the sacred food which leads to life everlasting, and in the church he is allowed the privilege of being present at the adorable sacrifice of the Mass.

In blessing a church, men, therefore, acknowledge God as the author of all things, and they are reminded that they were precious stones chosen to build up the heavenly Jerusalem. They were also reminded that they were a spiritual building of which Christ is the cornerstone, and where the head is, there also should the members be; they were reminded of the difference between the tabernacle of old and the church of the present time whenever they were present at the sacred mysteries. There were, therefore, many consoling ideas in connection with the ceremony of blessing a church, because it was an act of glory to God and was a tribute of honour and veneration to Him. ("Freeman's Journal", September 8, 1867. Page 15.)

Erected to the Honour of God

"In the Faith of Jesus Christ, and to the honour of the Most High God, this Foundation Stone of the Church of St. Bede, was laid by the Very Rev. S. F. A. Sheey, V.G., on the 6th day of February, in the year of salvation, 1867, the Rev. T. McCarthy, missionary presbyter of the District, and many other priests assisting, a very large concourse of the faithful being also in attendance; Pope Pius IX, happily reigning; the most illustrious and Most Rev. John Bede being Archbishop of Sydney; Victoria, Queen of Britain and its Dependencies; the Honourable Sir John Young, Governor of the Colony."

(A translation of the Latin inscription written on vellum and placed under the Foundation Stone.)

100 Years Ago ...

When St. Bede's was opened 100 years ago the following appeared in the "Freeman's Journal" of 7th September, 1867, together with the write-up of the Blessing and Opening:—

Thunderbolt, the bushranger, was chased by the police — "Every time they came within firing distance letting fly with a will" — he got away. (Page 7).

Randwick Races: Spring Meeting last Saturday — only one favourite won. Main race was the Australian Derby Stakes, won by Fireworks (6-4); The Italian (6-1) second. (Page 7).

Rev. W. F. Payne delivered a sermon in St. Joseph's Cathedral, Buffalo, complaining about ladies' "Short skirts and short hair". (Pages 12-13).

"Coals and every description of Fuel and Produce delivered with despatch." — Worburton & Sons, Pyrmont. (Page 14).

"Tweed Suits to measure, well shrunk," were selling for £2.10.0. (Page 14).

Potatoes were 3/- a hundredweight. Eggs were 4d. a dozen. Butter was 9d. a pound. (Page 16).

Omnibus fares between Glebe Point and Wynyard Square were reduced to half original price. Buses were better patronised as a result. (Page 7).

Cooke, Zoyara & Wilson's Circus was in Sydney. (Entrance Elizabeth St., opposite Hyde Park). "The tumbling and athletic feats marvellous to behold." (Page 7).

They were still digging the Suez Canal. "The Maritime Canal is now about twelve feet deep, but is intended to hold twenty-six feet of water when finished." (Page 11).

And Holloway's Ointment was being advertised as a cure for all ailments of New Settlers. (Page 16).

St. Charles' Church and School (Waverley) held a Raffle:—
1st Prize: A Thoroughbred Bay Filly with Saddle and Bridle.
2nd Prize: A Fine Grey Filly (no saddle or bridle).
3rd Prize: A Gold Watch.
4th Prize: A Silver Watch. (Page 16).
Tickets 2/6 each

Some of the ships to arrive here in September 100 years ago included:— Susannah Cuthbert from Grafton; Wonga Wonga from Melbourne; Kembla from Moruya and the Clyde; Lady Bowen from Brisbane.

One hundred years later some of the September arrivals are:— City of Adelaide from New York; Oriana from Southampton; Ventoux from Dunkirk; Wanliu from Japan; Port Brisbane from London; Monterey from San Francisco.

Blessing of the Foundation Stone of St. Bede's Church

6th February, 1867

Now in September, 1967, St. Bede's Church, Pyrmont, looks out over the same harbour, and the same bays and headlands as it did in 1867, when the foreshores were untouched, but the changes of waterfront and skyline are phenomenal; their history is manifest in the growth and development of New South Wales from 1867 to 1967.

The vast growth of Sydney since the turn of the century is responsible for the great volume of traffic which roars past St. Bede's, up and down to the wharves and back to the city. This is in strong contrast to the gentle lap of the water on sandy shores of a century past when the Ceremony of the Blessing of the Foundation Stone was performed by the Vicar-General of the Archdiocese, Very Reverend S. A. Sheehy, V.G.

Extract from "Freeman's Journal," February 9, 1867, page 2:—

"On Wednesday morning the foundation stone of a new Catholic Church in Pyrmont, was laid by the Very Rev. the Vicar-General, in presence of several clergy and a numerous body of the laity . . . Until the gallery is built there will be accommodation for 400 seats. The church will be called Saint Bede's, after the learned English saint of the same name, and will be under his special patronage.

"By eleven o'clock, the time fixed for the ceremony, a very large number of people had assembled from all parts of Sydney, and the whole of the resident Catholics were present and having ranged themselves around the spot occupied by the foundation, the clergy approached in procession . . . The stone having been blessed and the appointed prayers having been said and ceremonies performed, the stone was placed in its proper position. Under the stone a bottle containing some coins of the realm, copies of the Freeman's Journal, Sydney Morning Herald, and Empire, and the inscription (see page 7) written on vellum.

"When the ceremony was concluded the Rev. T. Keating delivered a most appropriate discourse, taking for his text the following words of Saint Matthew: 'And the mustard seed became a mighty tree, so that the birds of the air came and dwelt in the branches thereof'."

NOTES FROM THE PAST

£136.2.10 was collected at the laying of the Foundation Stone of St. Bede's School in 1880. The total amount raised in conjunction with the laying of the foundation stone amounted to £189.0.4.

* * *

Pyrmont: On 29th August, 1880, first Holy Communion at 7.30 a.m. Mass was followed by the Confirmation of 40 boys and 56 girls at 11 a.m.

Father Garavel records that "On the same day (29th August, 1880), the foundation stone of the addition to the school was laid by His Grace Archbishop Roger Bede Vaughan, O.S.B., at 3.30 p.m. in the presence of a crowded assembly." (Parish archives.)

* * *

At the conclusion of the first Mass ever said in St. Bede's on 1st September, 1867, Father McCarthy announced that the church and land had cost £1,100, and that every shilling had been paid on the building. More than half the purchase money of the land had yet to be paid, plus altar furnishings and seats, but these, he hoped, would soon be paid for. (Freeman's Journal, 7th September, 1867.)

* * *

Fr. Eugene Luckie, the first priest in charge of Pyrmont, was Secretary of the Catholic Association, a body formed for the support of Catholic schools. The Freeman's Journal of 13th November, 1867, gives his speech for the preservation of Catholic schools. He was later transferred to Woollahra and Fr. J. A. Byrne was made Parish Priest when St. Bede's Parish was established as such in 1870.

* * *

Attendances at St. Bede's School:
          In 1867 there were   86 children
             1868   ,,   ,, 116 children
             1869   ,,   ,, 102 children
             1881   ,,   ,, 250 children
             1886   ,,   ,, 220 children
             1891   ,,   ,, 244 children.

* * *

There were 1,000 Catholics in the Parish of Pyrmont in 1881. Today there are 1,156.

* * *

Mgr. John Lynch, P.P., Pyrmont (1877) was preaching at St. Benedict's, Broadway, when a messenger, Andy Macaulay, brought word of Archbishop Polding's death.

* * *

On 8th June, 1867, the Pyrmont Concert was held. These concerts were a great source of revenue for the parish.

Appendix 1 495

The Lord Mayor, Alderman John Armstrong

Sydney's Lord Mayor Native of Pyrmont

The fourth youngest of ten children, John Ignatius Armstrong was born on 6th July, 1908, at Pyrmont of the late William and Ellen Armstrong (nee Hannan). At that time his parents were living at the Dunkirk Hotel, 205 Harris Street, Pyrmont, where an elder brother, William, now resides.

The Baptismal Register kept at Pyrmont shows that in entry No. 585 of 26th July, 1908, John Armstrong was baptized by Rev. Fr. P. McIntyre, his sponsors being James Crowe and Annie Hannan. There were six brothers and four sisters in the Armstrong family as follows:—

Doctor Eddie (dec'd), Kathleen (dec'd), William, James, Patrick (dec'd), Doctor Thomas, John (Lord Mayor), Mary (Sister Mary Rosalie of Calvary Hospital, Wagga), Eileen (recently dec'd), and Noreen (Sister Mary Helen of Mount St. Margaret's, Ryde).

Alderman Armstrong was educated at St. Bede's, Pyrmont, and the Marist Brothers' School, Darlinghurst.

In October, 1945, he married Miss Joan Curran, and they have been blessed with a family of one son and four daughters.

Alderman Armstrong became an Alderman of Sydney Municipal Council in 1934 at the age of 25, for Phillip Ward. He was elected to the Senate in 1938 at the age of 29 years, and remained a Senator until 1962. From 1951 to 1956 he was Deputy Opposition Leader in the Senate, and was Minister for Supply and Development from 1946 to 1949. He was Chairman of the Sydney County Council from 1963 to 1965.

In December, 1965, he was elected by the citizenry as Lord Mayor of Sydney. He will be in attendance for the Mass and Concert for the Centenary celebrations on 24th September.

Rev. T. McCarthy, P.P.

A Tribute...

During its 100 years, St. Bede's has enjoyed the fruits of a sound and apostolic foundation laid by its early Pastors.

It was only two days prior to the Blessing and Opening of the Church that Archbishop Polding had created it a separate Parochial District, and had appointed Father Luckie as the first resident priest. Since then succeeding Priests have laboured long and zealously. The present Parish Priest is Rev. Father Doyle and his assistant is Rev. Father Hickman. But the name of Rev. Father McCarthy is carved deep into the Foundation Stone, since it was he who laboured untiringly in the supervision of the building, while at the same time devotedly carrying out his duties as assistant priest of St. Benedict's, to which the Pyrmont district was then attached.

Fire at Catholic School, Pyrmont.

A hall, later destroyed by fire, in Harris Street near Union Street, was used as the first church in Pyrmont. It was next to the present post office which was then a butcher's shop. (Maurice O'Dwyer and Sister Elizabeth.)

The Freeman's Journal of 22nd June, 1867 (page 10) under the heading of "Town News" tells us that "The school building was wilfully, maliciously and unlawfully set on fire by Alexander Downie and that Edward John Buckman was accessory thereto."

* * *

On 13th January, 1897, Church Committe moved that a Gallery be erected at St. Bede's at a cost of £50. Tenders were to be called for this work.

* * *

Those present at the inaugural meeting of the Church Committee held on 17th August, 1896:—
Father Ed. O'Callaghan (chairman), Messrs. Costigan, English, Bergin, Leonard, Crowe, Healy, Toohey, Connelly, Cassidy and Doyle.

Parish Dates

St. Bede's Foundation Stone laid 6th February, 1867.
St. Bede's Blessed and Opened 1st Sept., 1867.
St. Bede's School Foundation Stone 29th Sept., 1880.
New St. Bede's School Blessed and Opened 9th May, 1924.
St. Bede's Presbytery Blessed 29th July, 1880.
St. Francis Xavier's Church/School Foundation Stone, 22nd February, 1891.
St. Francis Xavier's Church/School Blessed 4th October, 1891.
New St. Francis Xavier's Church/School Opened and Blessed 5th December, 1924.

Appendix 1 497

A Coincidence

On 13th January, 1897, Mr. Doyle at St. Bede's Church Committee Meeting, moved that the shed roof be raised 5 ft. Exactly 69 years later on 13th January, 1966, Father Doyle (no relation) lowered the roof 5 ft. for the two remodelled garages!

* * *

Father W. H. McDonald in 1928 had the front of the Presbytery altered. He glassed-in the verandah and effected a double entrance to the steps, plus other improvements to the Presbytery. These were blessed by Archbishop Kelly in November, 1928.

* * *

"As you know, most of the old buildings of Sydney were built of Pyrmont sandstone, and my father used to tell us about the times when he and other boys used to walk from Ultimo to St. Bede's along a very rough road cut through the sandstone, to serve at Benediction at night. It was so dark and lonely that they used to sing all the way. They knew that if they dared stop, their courage would fail, and they would run home again. However, they felt well rewarded when a kind old French priest (Father Garavel) would greet them with: 'I will give you a cheque on Heaven'. This saying was passed on to us down through the years." (Extract from letter of Mrs. Thom, nee Mary Maher, to Father Doyle on 13th August, 1967.)

First Marriage — First Baptisms

The first recorded marriage at Pyrmont was on 29th August, 1874, between James Marsh and Mary O'Neill.

* * *

Mrs. J. Power, of 92 O'Connor St., Haberfield, says that her mother, Elizabeth O'Toole and Tobias O'Toole (twins) were the first baptized in St. Bede's.

[No baptismal records from 1867 to 1874. Maurice O'Dwyer states that these were burned.]

First Baptismal Register: First baptism — William Follers, baptized 30th July, 1874 by Fr. W. McCormack.

Second Baptismal Register: First baptism — Esther Charlotte Johnson, baptized 29th June, 1876 by Mgr. T. Lynch.

Third Baptismal Register: First baptism — John Bede O'Toole, baptized 23rd September, 1910 by Fr. A. J. Goodman, M.S.C.

Fourth (latest) Baptismal Register: First baptism — Kerry May Lillian Therese Allport, baptized on 10th April, 1960, by Fr. Ashley Jones.

CATHOLIC CHURCH, PYRMONT

On to-morrow morning, St. Bede's Church, Pyrmont, will be solemnly Blessed and Opened by His Grace the Archbishop. The Service will commence at 11 o'clock.

(Advertisement from "Freeman's Journal", August 31, 1867.)

Father V. J. Doyle inspecting the Foundation Stone of the original St. Bede's School, Pyrmont

The 1880 St. Bede's School

On the 28th June, 1880, the land for St. Bede's School at Pyrmont, adjoining the Church, was purchased by Archbishop Roger Bede Vaughan.

From the Freeman's Journal of 4th September, 1880, we have the following account:—

BLESSING OF FOUNDATION STONE

"His Grace the Archbishop of Sydney (Archbishop Roger Bede Vaughan) laid the corner stone of the new school attached to St. Bede's Church, Pyrmont, in the presence of a large assemblage, on Sunday afternoon . . .

"The esteemed pastor of the district, the Rev. Père Garavel, commenced the proceedings by requesting His Grace to lay the corner stone of the new building."

The following is an extract from the Archbishop's famous sermon:—

[To fully appreciate His Grace's words it is well to know that Henry Parkes had just introduced in 1879 his Bill to repeal the Public School Act of 1866. The main import of the Bill, which came into force on 1st May, 1880, was that from the 31st December, 1882, all financial assistance to Catholic and Denominational Schools was to end. — Editor.]

" . . . Accept your cross manfully, and throw your energies into building, when necessary, your own schools, and into supporting them when built. If we let the colony see that we are thoroughly in earnest, and if we prove, by our acts, that we believe what we say, justice will be done us all the sooner. Do not allow your action and generosity to be paralyzed by the delusion that you will get any help from any except yourselves. Take for granted that State aid has gone, and gone for you do not know how long. And take one thing more for granted — that the more zealously and earnestly you rely on yourselves now, so much the sooner will the majority come to your relief. I say, then, let us build as many schools as we can, and pay for the Catholic training of our children in them, and stand on our own feet, and be brave, and cheerful, and manly under difficulties (great cheers). The Catholic body is fairly well off. There is money enough amongst us to do all we really want; and if we are true to each other, and true to ourselves, the Catholic Church in this colony will flourish . . .

"And I would say to you, fathers of the children — husbands of their mothers — teach the children to love you, and to fear you, too. Let them, from earliest days, look on you with reverence, as the very model of a Christian man. Teach them to be truthful — to prefer to suffer anything than to tell a lie. To be honest — to keep their fingers off what does not belong to them. Teach them to be brave, not to fear the dark, and to suffer pain without crying — to suffer it courageously and with self-control. The gentleness of the mother, and the strength of the father will stamp the golden coin on either side; and a Christian will be minted in your happy homes who will pass current, as bearing the image of Christ and of Caesar, too. You will be formers and fashioners of good sterling Christians and of loyal citizens; brave, true and honest. At all events, you will thus give your children the best possible preparation for school, and bring a blessing on your homes, and on the country of your adoption (cheers). I must say I have great faith in the good nature of my fellow man, and cannot help being persuaded that, if we are earnest and self-denying, and true to the principles of our faith for a few years, the sympathy of the public will of itself grow towards us; and that, being convinced of our sincerity and our straight-forwardness, they will provide some scheme by means of which we shall get equal help with others — though we do bring up Catholics as Catholics — for the secular portion of the children's education. Meanwhile, let us throw all our energies into the great, the most holy work, of providing schools and funds for the thorough Catholic training and education of Catholic children . . ." (Cheers and applause.)

Pupils of St. Bede's School. Father John O'Toole is on the left bottom row; John Armstrong, the future Lord Mayor of Sydney, is fourth from left.

In St. Bede's School yard after Father John O'Toole

Pyrmont Memories

Pyrmont's first native priest, Father John O'Toole, son of Joseph and Teresa O'Toole, was ordained on 1st December, 1930; he celebrated his first Holy Mass in the church of his baptism, i.e. St. Bede's, and his second Mass in St. Francis Xavier's, Ultimo. On both days there was a First Communion of the children. After eight years of zealous performance of priestly duties, Father O'Toole was suddenly called to his Eternal Home. He had "fulfilled a long life in a short space of time."

※　※　※

Memories of old Pyrmont go back to the stories of boys and girls rowing across Cockle Bay to the only school available, that in Kent Street, City.

※　※　※

Captain Matthew Byrnes ran the ferry from the foot of John Street, Pyrmont, to Erskine Street, City. He donated the cedar pulpit made by Lockley Brothers for St. Bede's. Later this was cut up to make the Sacred Heart Altar. Captain Byrnes was the father of Sister Mary Matthew of the Good Samaritan Order.

※　※　※

Organists still remembered at St. Bede's and St. Francis Xavier's: Mrs. Maurice O'Dwyer (Nellie O'Toole), Mrs. Mary Thompson (Mary Cannon), Mrs S. Gray (Shirley Josephs), and Miss Gladys Scanlon.

※　※　※

"Another memory of Pyrmont . . . Parish Picnics . . . usually to Fig Tree Avenue. Great days." (Mrs. Thom.)

's first Mass on 2nd December, 1930

St. Bede's Picnic, Saturday, September 11, 1880 (Freeman's Journal)
"The annual picnic in connection with St. Bede's Christian Doctrine Confraternity took place at Chowder Bay on Tuesday last and was successful in every respect. There were nearly eight hundred visitors, including the Very Rev. Dr. Quirk, Rev. J. J. Pollard, Rev. D. McCarthy and Rev. Father Kavanagh. The children enjoyed themselves thoroughly, and their comfort and pleasure were well looked after by the good pastor of St. Bede's (Père Garavel) and the teachers.

From the Freeman's Journal of 9th February, 1867, we read of a tea-party and musical soirée held in the Masonic Hall to celebrate the laying of St. Bede's foundation stone. "The floor of the large hall was crowded as well as the gallery . . . there could not have been less than 1500 persons present and Father McCarthy can congratulate himself on having got up the largest tea-party ever held in Sydney."

A much respected and well-remembered family name in the parish is that of the O'Toole family, who, along with others, helped build up the traditional spirit of the parish.

St. Bede's Church is full of memories. In it the pioneers were married; to its font they brought their children for baptism; and in obedience to the sound of the little bell they came in their numbers each Sunday to assist at Holy Mass.

"I am very sorry that I will not be able to come to the Celebrations . . . I would enjoy every minute of them, bubbling over with pride that I once belonged there. Pyrmont has a spirit of its own — and I still love its people and the dear old spot." (Sister M. Elizabeth O'Toole, 14th Sept., 1967.)

St. Francis Xavier's, Ultimo
Laying of Foundation Stone

St. Francis Xavier's Church and School at the other end of Pyrmont parish, also have an interesting history.

The land was bought on 29th December, 1890, by His Eminence Cardinal Moran, then Archbishop of Sydney. Originally it was part of a Crown grant of 35 acres made to John Harris, 1st January, 1806 (Reg. Gen. Vol. 6697, Folio 128), (Fol. 887, Book 1410).

"Father Furlong decided for a beginning to put up a building which would do duty both as a Church and School. The new Church would thus accommodate some 300 people. It was mentioned that the cost of the building would be £1,904, with an additional expenditure of £700 for fittings and furniture.

"Cardinal Moran introduced to the assembled parishioners of Pyrmont-Ultimo, the Bishop of Grafton, Dr. Doyle, who stated that 'he need hardly offer them his assurance that it was a very great pleasure on the eve of leaving their shores to visit the other side of the world, to have the privilege of assisting at a ceremony of so interesting and so important a character. The event they were celebrating — and every ceremony of the kind was an event in the history of the church in Australia — was to him a fresh proof, if indeed any were required, of the devotion of the Catholic people of the colony to the cause of religion and religious education. Every laying of a foundation stone of a Catholic school was an argument that they did more work than talk. They had taken up this work of religious education in a spirit of thorough earnestness, and while asking only fair play and no favour, they were determined that their schools should be in every way equal, if not superior, to any secular schools in existence in this colony or any of the other colonies. He congratulated His Eminence on this the latest addition to the long list of schools and churches it had been his happiness to establish in the Diocese of Sydney, and he congratulated not less heartedly Father Furlong and the good people of Pyrmont on the earnestness and generosity of which this school-church was the form and expression . . .'

"His Eminence, after announcing the amount collected, took advantage of the occasion to congratulate Father Furlong on the initiation of this most necessary work. He desired to congratule the pastor and his devoted people on their choice of St. Francis Xavier as the patron of the new school-church. This was the first sacred edifice in Australia bearing the name of St. Francis Xavier of which the foundation stone had been laid since the special feast in honour of the illustrious saint which was celebrated by the church in India with so much solemn pomp and religious ceremonial."

We are indebted to the Freeman's Journal (page 17, Saturday, February 28, 1891) for the account of the laying of the foundation stone of the School Church at Ultimo.

Opening and Blessing — 4th October, 1891

St. Francis Xavier's was blessed and opened by His Lordship Bishop Higgins, Auxiliary to His Eminence Cardinal Moran on 4th October, 1891. The first Mass was celebrated by Father P. M. Ryan.

During the Mass appropriate music was rendered by the choir with Miss Toohey at the organ and Mr. M. J. Maher as leader. At the Offertory Mr. Maher sang Himmel's O Salutaris. In appealing to the congregation after a brief address from Bishop Higgins, Father Furlong explained that the building, with the cost of the ground, had involved the parish to the amount of £1,960, towards which £758.13.4 had been subscribed since the work was undertaken. The response on Sunday amounted to £115. Bishop Higgins offered his warmest congratulations to the Catholics of Ultimo on the practical spirit of faith manifested in the erection of this very necessary building, and complimented Father Furlong on the success of his well-directed efforts for the improvement of the parish. The opening of the school-church was marked by two special sermons of a particularly interesting and impressive kind. The Very Rev. John Ryan, S.J. (Rector of St. Ignatius' College), was the morning preacher, and the Very Rev. C. Morrogh, S.J., President of St. Aloysius' College, preached in the evening. At the morning ceremony the members of the new local branch of the Hibernian Society joined by a number of the St. Benedict's branch, attended in regalia and took part in the procession.

(Page 16, Freeman's Journal, 10th October, 1891)

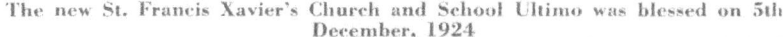

The new St. Francis Xavier's Church and School Ultimo was blessed on 5th December, 1924

New Church and School at Ultimo 1924

On 8th June, 1923, Fr. Michael O'Connell, in a letter to His Grace Archbishop Kelly, proposed building a school at both the Pyrmont and Ultimo ends of the parish as against only the one in the centre of the parish as had been canvassed. He thought that a Central School would mean the selling of the church property at Pyrmont. He says: "If the School in Pyrmont were to go, the Church also would have to go, and the people have a pious and reverent affection for this Church and do not want to lose it."

In 1924 both schools were built. The one at Pyrmont served the district for 30 years until closed in 1954.

However, additions to the school accommodation at Ultimo were made, when a large sum of money was expended once again. The total amounted to £7,688.0.0, a very large sum for those days, and was raised by the self-denial and the generosity of the people of Ultimo and Pyrmont. From 1924, the Ultimo school attained its present proportions, with its well-lighted and well-ventilated classrooms.

On 5th December, 1924, Archbishop Kelly said:

"May God multiply our private schools — I am not saying Catholic schools — because parents wishing to save their children will be imbued with Christianity from the beginning, and their children will be made practical Christians, thus living as Christ would have them live. Therefore, I would urge them to build these private schools. We pray to God for patience. Multiply the schools, and the churches will be filled; we would have social peace and equity. Therefore, he (Archbishop Kelly) would say "Well done" to Father O'Connel, and he would say it in the name of Pyrmont and Ultimo, the Archdiocese of Sydney, and of Australia and the whole world."

(Cf. "The Catholic Press," 11th December, 1924. Page 29)

FIRST IN AUSTRALIA

At the laying of the Foundation Stone of St. Francis Xavier's on 22/2/1891 His Eminence Cardinal Moran said: "This is the first sacred edifice in Australia bearing the name of St. Francis Xavier of which the foundation stone has been laid since the special feast in honour of the illustrious Saint." (Freeman's Journal, 28th February, 1891. Page 17.)

Advertisement on Page II of the Freeman's Journal dated 21st February, 1891:—

"*His Eminence Cardinal Moran will lay the Foundation Stone of St. Francis Xavier's School-Church, Crown Road, Ultimo, on Sunday, 22nd February, at 3.30 p.m.*"

Sisters of The Good Samaritan at St. Francis Xavier's on 13th August, 1967

Sisters of the Good Samaritan

At the request of the Archbishop in 1880, the Sisters of the Good Samaritan came daily from their Convent in Pitt Street, Sydney (where the Central Railway Station now stands) to teach the boys and girls of Pyrmont. This Religious Congregation was as yet in its infancy. Founded by Archbishop Polding in 1857, it was the first Institute of religious women to be actually founded and established in Australia. Its numbers in 1880 were still less than one hundred, but in response to the great need of the time, the Sisters travelled each day to many of the schools in the growing areas of Sydney. In 1900, the Sisters took up residence in the house (since demolished) adjoining St. Bede's School, Pyrmont, but after a few years, in the time of Fr. John O'Gorman, moved to Bulwara Road, Ultimo, where they still reside. The happy association between the Sisters of the Good Samaritan and the people of the parish of Pyrmont-Ultimo has continued right through the years, to the present day.

Indeed, many of the pupils of the Sisters generously gave themselves to God in this same Congregation, while others felt called to serve in other Religious Institutes.

Church Furnishings at St. Bede's

The Monstrance at St. Bede's was given in honour of the Blessed Sacrament as a gift from Maurice and Nellie O'Dwyer on 18th July, 1924.

* * *

The Credence Table was donated by Mrs. C. O'Toole in memory of her deceased husband, Thomas.

* * *

The Communion Plate was given by Mrs. Gerathy in memory of her late husband, Patrick Clifford Gerathy, on 16th April, 1930.

* * *

The Tabernacle at St. Bede's is inscribed "In memory of John, Alice and James Slyney".

* * *

The picture of Our Lady of Perpetual Succour was given by Mrs. Slyney.

* * *

Our Lady's statue at St. Bede's was donated by Mrs. Ellen Minogue in memory of her husband, Patrick.

* * *

The Sacred Heart statue was given by Mrs. Russell in memory of her husband.

* * *

The statue of St. Vincent de Paul was given by Mrs. Lydia O'Toole in memory of her husband, Dick.

* * *

St. Patrick's statue was the gift of Patrick O'Donnell. His sister gave the statue of St. Joseph.

* * *

The Conlon Brothers, Bill and Ernie, gave the Stations of the Cross.

* * *

The picture of the Sacred Heart was given by Mrs. W. Daly.

* * *

Mrs. M. O'Dwyer gave the statue of the Little Flower.

* * *

The large crucifix at the back of the church was donated by Joseph O'Toole.

Forty hours adoration at St. Francis Xavier's about 1944 before repainting of church. Walls of blue with a surround of gold grapes and motifs.

Blessing and Opening of New St. Bede's School

St. Bede's School Hall
Pyrmont

The new St. Bede's School was blessed and opened by His Grace Archbishop Michael Kelly on Sunday, 9th May, 1924, in the presence of a vast number of people.

Father O'Connell welcomed the Archbishop and went on to praise the people of Pyrmont: "I have to congratulate the people here on their earnestness, perseverence, and generosity, on the virile manner in which they took up the work of building this school." (Freeman's Journal, 15th May, 1924.)

He also mentioned that the architect was Mr. W. J. Gilroy and the builder Mr. W. J. Malcolm, and the school enrolment was 220 children. Soon, he hoped that the new school at Ultimo would be completed. Total cost of the building, plus demolishing cottages and cutting away stone for the building and playground, was £3,802.2.7. (This school was in use till 1954.)

* * *

Programme of Events for St. Bede's Centenary, 1967

Sunday, 24th September:—
    Concelebrated Mass at St. Bede's, 6 p.m., Archbishop J. Carroll presiding.
    Lord Mayor J. Armstrong in attendance.
    Supper to follow.
    Concert in St. Bede's Hall.

Tuesday, 26th September:—
    9.30 a.m. Children's Mass and Parish Visitation by His Lordship Bishop Muldoon.
    7.30 p.m. Confirmation.

Wednesday, 27th September:—
    Clergy Dinner, 1 p.m.
    Year of Faith Mass, 7.30 p.m.

Thursday, 28th September:—
    Requiem Mass for all deceased Parishioners of St. Bede's, 7.30 p.m.

Friday, 29th September:—
    School Picnic — harbour cruise.

Saturday, 30th September:—
    Cabaret Dance and Social, St. Bede's Hall, 8 p.m.

CHURCH FURNISHINGS, ULTIMO:—

The Chalice at Ultimo is inscribed 1891.

* * *

Missal Stand is dedicated to the memory of Charlotte Bannon, who died 21st December, 1928.

* * *

The Sanctuary Lamp was given in memory of William Bradley by his brothers and sisters. William Bradley died 1st June, 1922.

* * *

One set of Brass Vases bears the inscription: "In memory of Eric, 26th May, 1939."

* * *

The statue of St. Francis Xavier was presented in loving memory of Catherine and William John Benn, R.I.P.

* * *

The Communion Plate at St. Francis Xavier's is inscribed 12th June, 1931, and the Monstrance, 1891.

* * *

The large Mass Bell was given: "In Loving Memory of William Benn. Killed in France, Feast of Corpus Christi, 1917."

* * *

The Holy Water font was given in memory of Nicholas Joseph Doyle, killed in action in France, 5th November, 1916. His sister is Mrs. Annie Reedie, of 314 Jones Street, Ultimo, and his brother is Greg Doyle, of Point Street, Pyrmont.

* * *

The pulpit in St. Francis Xavier's, Ultimo, came from Fr. Dominic Furlong, of Lakemba, when he built the new church there in 1963. The seats and Vestment Press at St. Bede's, Pyrmont, also came from Lakemba. When Fr. Dominic Furlong (R.I.P.) was transferred to Bondi he gave the seats from that church to St. Francis Xavier's, Ultimo.

* * *

Mr. H. Wordell (son of the Architect of St. Mary's Cathedral) was the Architect for the original St. Francis Xavier's, Ultimo, in 1891.

HISTORY REPEATING ITSELF

His Lordship Bishop Doyle, of Grafton, spoke at the laying of the Foundation Stone of St. Francis Xavier's, Ultimo, on 22nd February, 1891.

Bishop Higgins, Auxiliary to Cardinal Moran, blessed and opened St. Francis Xavier's on 4th October, 1891.

Father Doyle and Father Higgins were later to be associated together at St. Francis Xavier's for several years!

Fete time — the Jacaranda Stall, St. Bede's School

His Eminence, N.T. Cardinal Gilroy, had accepted an invitation to come to the Centenary Mass as early as January, 1967. However, he left for Rome on the T/V "Galileo" on 11th August to attend the Episcopal Synod and will not be able to be present. He will be ably represented by His Grace, Archbishop James Carroll, D.D., D.C.L., Auxiliary to His Eminence.

The new set of white gothic vestments to be worn by the main celebrant at the Centenary Mass has been donated in memory of Christina Magee.

In preparation for the Centenary a Mission was given by the Redemptorist Fathers in St. Bede's from 13th to 20th August. The church was packed each evening.

The Centenary Mass will be concelebrated by five priests of Pyrmont: Rev. Father C. J. Heffernan (Annandale), Rev. Ashley Jones (West Pymble), Very Rev. Mgr. Eamonn Dundon (Administrator St. Mary's Cathedral), Rev. F. Higgins, representing all past Curates (Richmond), and Rev. V. J. Doyle, the present Pastor.

Pyrmont Presbytery

The 1880 Presbytery in Bunn Street

On 25th August, 1879, Fr. Garavel recorded that the Presbytery was a house in Bowman Street, Pyrmont, rented at £5 per month.

On 27th January, 1880, Fr. Garavel moved from Bowman Street to Bunn Street to a house rented at £6 per calendar month.

On 29th July, 1880, the house next to the church was bought from Mrs. Brennan as a Presbytery and mortgaged for the sum of £625. The Presbytery was blessed and opened in 1880 (Parish Archives).

Religious from Pyrmont

Over the years Pyrmont has given generously of the flower of its parishioners to the religious life. The list as far as I have been able to ascertain is as follows:—

SISTERS OF THE GOOD SAMARITAN
Sr. M. Anthony (Foley), Sr. M. Blandina (Alice Burns)
Sr. M. Virgillus (Scott), Sr. Bridget Mary (Mary O'Toole)
Sr. M. Matthew (Annie Byrnes)
Sr. M. Alphonsus Liguori (Maggie Boylon)
Mother Mary Elizabeth (Christine O'Toole), Coffs Harbour.
Sr. M. Lidwina (Katie O'Toole), Rozelle
Sr. M. Celestine (Ester Magee), Nowra
Sr. M. Bernard (Doreen Riley), Coorparoo, Qld.

SISTERS OF ST. JOSEPH
Sr. M. Pius (Mary Lane), Riverwood
Sr. M. Christine (Maria Watkins), Riverwood

LITTLE COMPANY OF MARY
Sr. M. Rosalie (Mary Armstrong), Calvary Hospital, Wagga
Sr. M. Helen (Noreen Armstrong), Mt. St. Margaret's, Ryde

SISTERS OF THE SACRED HEART
Sr. M. Adelaide (Betty Whalquist), Kilburn, S.A.

PRIESTS
Father John Francis O'Toole, son of Mr. and Mrs. Joseph O'Toole.
Father Phil Reeves, late P.P. of Ryde, once lived at Pyrmont. His parents had a mixed goods business in Bunn St. (since demolished).
Father Tom Crowley, D.D., of West Tamworth. Mr. and Mrs. F. Crowley now live at 200 Harris St., Pyrmont.
Very Rev. Mgr. John Slowey has a brother, Denis, the proprietor of the Pyrmont Arms Hotel.

MORE RECENT EVENTS

On 14th February, 1953, St. Bede's Hall was used as a Polling Booth for the General Elections.

The Confraternity of the Holy Rosary was established officially on 18th June, 1952, in the time of Fr. R. Funcheon.

In 1950 there was a flourishing C.Y.O. in Pyrmont. A regular Club Paper was produced under the title of "The Cloud".

On the 25th May, 1955, Father S. Thorne wrote to His Eminence Cardinal Gilroy informing him that the Parish was now free of debt. In his reply, the Cardinal said that "this has been possible only through the vigilance and energy of the Pastor and the generosity of the parishioners. To both Pastor and people I offer the expression of my sincere thanks and cordial congratulations."

Paul Garner was the first person in the parish to act as a Lay Reader (Easter, 1967).

St. Francis Xavier's School football team, coached by John O'Regan, won the final of the District Convent Schools Competition by beating St. Benedict's (our Mother Parish) by 36 to 0 on 27th August, 1967, for the Joe Coffey Trophy.

The girls from St. Francis Xavier's School won the South Sydney Convent School Basketball Competition for 1967 by defeating Botany 11 to 7 in the final.

Very Rev. Monsignor Eamonn Dundon, now Administrator of St. Mary's Cathedral, was formerly Pastor of Pyrmont and Port Chaplain of Sydney. These two portfolios are still combined in the present Pastor. Hence the picture of Cardinal Gilroy on page 2 against a shipping background.

For many New Australians who arrive here by ship at No. 13 wharf, Pyrmont, St. Bede's is the first church in which they worship God in their new country.

To show the Ecumenical spirit pervading the parish in 1967, it is worthy of note to record that the Fisherman's Club, with headquarters at the Terminus Hotel, gave $60 towards the costs of the Centenary celebrations. A Children's Fancy Dress Ball raised $110.

An appeal for old gold was made in 1930 for a chalice. Father W. McDonald's father "did the work". Again in 1961, in the time of Father Ashley Jones, another appeal was made for old gold for the beautiful chalice which St. Bede's now possesses. It is inscribed as follows: "Donated by Parishioners of St. Bede's, Pyrmont, April, 1930 and 1961."

Presbytery and Church 13th August, 1967

Our Patron: Saint Bede

Venerable Bede, whose feast day is May 27, was consecrated to God at the age of seven. Later he became a monk at Jarrow. To the toils of teaching he added long hours of private prayer, and the study of every branch of science and literature then known. He was familiar with Latin, Greek and Hebrew. He put together all that the world then knew of history, chronology, physics, music, philosophy, poetry, arithmetic and medicine. In his Ecclesiastical History he has left us beautiful lives of Anglo-Saxon Saints and the holy Fathers, while his commentaries on the Holy Scriptures are still in use by the Church. He had little aid from others, and during his later years suffered from constant illness; yet he worked and prayed up to his last hour.

The Saint was employed in translating the Gospel of St. John from the Greek up to the hour of his death, which took place on Ascension Day, 735 A.D.

The Priests of Pyrmont

From the Baptismal Records kept at St. Bede's we have the names of the 51 priests who have served the parish over the past 100 years. The list does not include the names of priests who performed baptisms, but who were obviously visitors:—

Name	First Entry	Last Entry
Timothy McCarthy (1867)	No record	
Eugene Luckie (1867)	No record	
J. A. Byrne (1870)	No record	
W. McCormack	30/ 8 /1874	3/ 9 /1875
I. T. Lynch	14/11/1875	27/ 5 /1878
J. A. Quirk	23/ 6 /1878	13/ 7 /1879
G. M. Garavel	30/ 8 /1879	9/ 3 /1884
Joseph M. Peuyer	5/ 2 /1882	2/ 4 /1882
M. McKernan	14/ 2 /1884	24/ 2 /1884
E. Walsh	23/ 3 /1884	31/ 3 /1889
R. O'Regan	3/ 2 /1889	28/ 4 /1889
Jas. Furlong	7/ 4 /1889	2/12/1893
Thomas Ryan	20/ 4 /1890	11/10/1891
Edmund Creagh	8/11/1891	5/ 7 /1892
Patrick O'Shea	23/10/1892	30/ 4 /1893
Daniel O'Reilly	14/ 5 /1893	26/ 8 /1900
P. M. Ryan	4/ 2 /1894	19/ 7 /1896
Ed. O'Callaghan	2/ 8 /1896	21/ 1 /1899
Phillip McIntyre	19/ 2 /1899	23/ 6 /1909
P. Power	9/12/1900	10/ 2 /1901
W. MacNamara	3/ 3 /1901	2/ 3 /1902
Peter Donnelly	14/12/1902	16/ 7 /1905
Edward Gell	20/ 8 /1905	26/ 4 /1906
Joseph Bowers	11/11/1906	16/ 1 /1908
R. Woulfe	8/ 3 /1908	8/ 5 /1909
John O'Gorman	27/ 6 /1909	17/11/1912
Matthew Smith	31/10/1909	26/ 6 /1910
A. G. Clarke	12/10/1910	20/ 1 /1911
J. P. Hyland	23/ 2 /1911	19/ 3 /1916
J. M. Curran	11/ 8 /1912	10/11/1912
William P. McNally	15/12/1912	26/10/1913
Thomas O'Farrell	16/11/1913	1/ 3 /1914
J. Dalton	3/ 4 /1916	18/ 2 /1922
P. McDonnell	18/ 1 /1917	25/ 1 /1920
Michael O'Connell	19/ 2 /1922	18/ 3 /1927
M.S.C.'s	29/ 7 /1923	6/11/1927
J. P. Lynch	21/11/1926	16/ 8 /1930
W. H. McDonald	18/12/1927	8/ 6 /1931
P. T. Boland	No entry	
Daniel Hannan	14/ 6 /1931	10/ 3 /1935
A. J. Bradstreet	17/ 3 /1935	18/12/1938
C. J. Heffernan	9/ 5 /1939	7/ 9 /1941

Name	First Entry	Last Entry
J. J. Massey	2/11/1941	26/1/1947
R. Funcheon	2/2/1947	23/9/1952
Thomas Keogh	7/3/1948	30/1/1949
James Byrne	17/2/1949	7/8/1949
S. Thorne	5/10/1952	21/1/1956
Ashley J. Jones	5/2/1956	23/12/1961
F. P. Higgins	12/1/1962	9/1/1966
Eamonn P. Dundon	18/2/1962	1/5/1963
Victor J. Doyle	17/5/1963	To present date
R. Hickman	5/2/1966	To present date

Old Bell Rings a New Tune

A bell which used to proclaim the opening and closing of the Sydney Markets will be heard again soon after years of disuse.

The 2 cwt. bell, cast in bronze, has been collecting dust in storage since the Markets installed an electric buzzer.

Sydney City Council has presented it to St. Francis Xavier's School in Bulwara Road, Ultimo.

It will be handed over today on behalf of the Council by the vice-chairman of the finance committee, Alderman S. Fegan.

Yesterday a team of five workmen hoisted the bell on to a school balcony.

Its chimes will ring for the start and finish of the school day when the May holidays are over.

It is believed that the bell was originally installed at the Belmore markets, on the site of the Hotel Sydney and the Tivoli Theatre.

Later it was removed to the present site of the Markets.

The leader of the team which put the bell in position is Mr. S. Malone, of Blackwood Avenue, Clovelly, whose father placed a bell in a tower at the school 45 years ago.

(This extract from the Sydney Morning Herald of 15th May, 1965, is full of meaning for the present-day pupils of St. Francis Xavier's, Ultimo.)

A Committee met several times during 1967 at St. Bede's Presbytery to arrange fitting celebrations in connection with the Centenary.

* * *

The first Concelebrated Mass in St. Bede's Church will be the Centenary Mass on 24th September.

* * *

Mrs. Margaret Ryan (nee Murphy), aged 84 years, now living at 30 Flinders Street, Darlinghurst, is a cousin of Father T. McCarthy, who built St. Bede's.

* * *

Dick Whalquist opens and closes St. Bede's Church each day.

Maurice O'Dwyer

Maurice O'Dwyer was born at Shellharbour 87 years ago last October. He was the fourth youngest of sixteen children of the late Thomas and Mary O'Dwyer. He came to Pyrmont in 1899 and remained here for 57 years. He is the oldest living member of the St. Vincent de Paul Society in N.S.W. and the only one left who knew Charles O'Neill who founded the Society in New South Wales at St. Patrick's, Church Hill.

"As a tangible acknowledgement of, and reward for his long life of constant virtue and generous assistance in all parish undertakings, heroic relief of the poor, visitation of the sick in hospital and institutions, helpful co-operation with the priest for the good of the people and the ever-present example of the christian virtue of charity," His Holiness Pope Piux XII conferred on Maurice O'Dwyer the signal honour of the Cross Pro Ecclesia et Pontifice of St. Leo.

* * *

Sacred Heart Sodality

The Sacred Heart Sodality consists of about 20 ladies. Throughout the years they and other such members have been a source of inspiration to the rest of the parish. They have helped keep the Faith alive and strong by their living example.

* * *

Altar Boys

Altar boys and their value can easily be overlooked. In Pyrmont today's altar boys are carrying on the noble traditions of days gone by. A word of thanks to them goes a long way — a picnic makes up for everything!

Society of St. Vincent de Paul, Pyrmont

The Conference of St. Bede's, Pyrmont, was established on Sunday, 17th August, 1889. This fact is recorded by the late Brother Charles O'Neill, the founder of the St. Vincent de Paul Society in Australia, in his personal manual. The Conference was the sixteenth formed by the Society.

The earliest available records of the Conference are contained in a Minute Book covering a period from 15th October, 1899 to the latter end of 1903. This book is retained in the archives of the Society at Ozanam House and a perusal of the minutes clearly indicates the vast amount of charitable work performed by members of the Conference during those years. An outstanding member of the Conference who gave devoted service to the Society's work was the late Brother Michael J. Weslan, who took over as President in 1900 and continued in this position for over 40 years. Another member of note is Brother Maurice O'Dwyer who, after joining the Conference in 1899, served the Society for 57 years in Pyrmont, first as Secretary, then Treasurer and President for 12 years. On leaving the parish, he transferred to Belmore Conference where he is still an active member. The Conference, although now numbering four, is still carrying on the charitable works of the Society which commenced in the parish 78 years ago. At present the President is John Dunn. Two past Presidents of note were Kevin Gagen and Ken Lewis.

The Theresians

The parish owes a debt of gratitude to the Theresians who instruct the State School children in their religion. They can be seen any Sunday gathering these children from the various homes in the district and bringing them to Mass; afterwards taking them for instructions in their religion; preparing them for first Holy Communion and Confirmation. Names we remember well: Joan Humphries and Meg Rochford.

Children of Mary

The Children of Mary number about 40 at present. Betty Salvia and Helen Slowey have been instrumental in encouraging these young girls to edify the parishioners by their attendance at Mass, Benediction and processions, thus adding dignity and reverence to the sacred ceremonies. They are a source of great admiration in the parish.

ACKNOWLEDGMENTS

I am grateful to Very Rev. Mgr. C. Duffy, D.D., D.Ph., P.C., Archivist of the Archdiocese of Sydney, for research done in St. Mary's Cathedral Archives; The "Catholic Weekly" for access to archives; the Registrar-General's Department for access to land grant titles; Mother M. Peter and Mother M. Imelda of St. Scolastica's, Glebe Point, for typing the script and valuable help in compiling this booklet; Misses Kay Ashbourn, Pat McDonnell, Betty Church and Annette Dinham for typing from the original sources.

Without their generous assistance and enthusiasm this Centenary Booklet could not have been written.

VICTOR J. DOYLE,

Pyrmont. 1/9/1967

Appendix 2
Priests of Pyrmont

PASTOR	ADMINISTRATOR	ASSISTANT [Locum Tenens]	TERM
Eugene Luckie			1867-1869
James Austin Byrne OSB			1869-1873
Daniel Maurus O'Connell OSB			1874
John Thomas Lynch			1875-1878
John Norbert Quirk OSB			1878-1879
Joseph-Marie Garavel			1879-1884
Edmund Walsh			1884-1889
		Richard O'Regan	1889
James Furlong			1889-1893
		Richard O'Regan	1889
		Thomas Ryan	1890-1891
		Edmund Creagh	1891-1892
		Patrick O'Shea	1892-1893
		Daniel O'Reilly	1893-1900
Patrick Matthias Ryan			1894-1896
		Daniel O'Reilly	1893-1900
Edward O'Callaghan			1896-1899
Philip McIntyre			1899-1909
		Peter Power	1900
	Michael Macnamara		1900
		Michael Macnamara	1901
		Peter Donnelly	1902

PASTOR	ADMINISTRATOR	ASSISTANT [Locum Tenens]	TERM
		Edward Gell	1905
		Joseph Bowers	1906-1907
		Richard Woulfe	1908
John O'Gorman			1909-1912
		MSC Priests [Sundays]	1909-1910
		Alfred Clarke	1910-1911
	John Hyland		1911
		John Milne Curran	1912
		William McNally	1912-1913
John Hyland			1913-1916
		Thomas O'Farrell	1913-1914
James Dalton			1916-1922
		Patrick McDonnell	1917-1920
Michael O'Connell			1922-1927
		MSC Priests [Sundays]	1923-1926
		James Lynch	1926-1930
William McDonald			1927-1931
		Patrick Treacy Boland	1930
Daniel Hannan			1931-1935
Austin Bradstreet			1935-1938
Michael Ryan			1939
	James Mullin		1939
Cletus Heffernan			1939-1941
James Massey			1941-1947
Richard Funcheon			1947-1952
	Thomas Keogh		1948-1949
	James Byrne		1949
Sidney Thorne			1952-1956
Ashley Jones			1956-1961
	Eamonn Dundon		1961

PASTOR	ADMINISTRATOR	ASSISTANT [Locum Tenens]	TERM
Eamonn Dundon			1962-1963
		Francis Higgins	1962-1966
Victor Doyle			1963-1974
		Ronald Hickman	1966-1972
		Brian Charlton	1974
Brian Charlton			1975
		[Luke Rawlings OP]	1975
John Ford			1976-1981
James Tierney			1981-1982
Kevin Cox			1983-1987
James Fowler			1987-1991
Alexander Johnson			1992-1999
		Julian Porteous	1992-1995
		[Peter Fitzgerald]	1995-1999
Lester Cashen			1999-2003
		[Michael Walsh CM]	2000-2003
Robert Mutlow OP			2003-2004
Colin Fowler OP			2004-2013
Anthony Walsh OP			2014-

Name Index

A

Adamson, Mother Magdalen, nun, 181, 183.
Allworth, William, clergyman, 104.
Armstrong, John Ignatius, politician and mayor, 361, 364, 380, 399, 414, 415.
Armstrong, Mary (Sister Rosalie), nun, 353.
Armstrong, Noreen (Sister Helen), nun, 353.
Armstrong, William, publican, 295, 352, 353, 361, 364.
Ashwin, John, stained-glass artist, 367.
Askin, Robin, politician, 418.
Athy, Myles Edmund, monk, 80, 123, 224.

B

Balfe, John Donnellan, publisher, 234.
Barker, Frederick, bishop, 56, 58, 59, 170.
Barnabo, Alessandro, cardinal, 50, 62, 78, 79, 115, 180.
Barry, William, bishop, 221.
Barsanti, Octavio, priest, 80, 172.
Barton, Edmund, politician, 271, 272.
Battaillon, Pierre-Marie, bishop, 14.
Beasley, John Albert (Jack), politician, 379, 380, 381.
Beovich, Matthew, archbishop, 366.
Bermingham, Patrick, priest, 69, 70.
Birdsall, Augustine, monk, 463.
Birt, Norbert, monk and historian, 55, 464, 475.
Biscop, Benedict, monk and abbot, 464, 465.
Blacket, Edmund, architect, 14, 64, 66, 477.
Blaxcell, Garnham, 5.
Bligh, William, Governor, 6, 359.
Bodenham, Thomas, auctioneer, 9.
Bodin, Verner, pupil, 331.
Bohn, Henry George, publisher, 466, 467.
Boland, Patrick Treacy, priest and Army chaplain, 353, 354, 357, 515.
Bourke, Richard, Governor, 19, 59, 103.
Boyce, Francis Bertie, clergyman, 174, 175, 517.
Bow, John, bushranger, 42.
Bowers, Joseph, priest, 285, 286, 287, 288, 289, 290, 515.
Bowler, Bede, monk, 471.
Bowman, James, surgeon, 10, 23.
Bradstreet, Austin, priest, 224, 307, 362, 363, 364, 365, 366, 367, 368, 399, 515.
Bradley, Pat, boxer, 261.
Brennan, Austin, priest, 404, 405.
Brewer, John Bede, monk, 464.
Broughton, William, bishop, 9, 10, 64.

Buchan, Edward, apprentice, 74, 75, 76.
Buchan, James, clergyman, 212.
Bunbury, Joseph, priest, 229, 230, 231, 242, 243, 244 245, 250.
Bunn, George, ship's captain, 7.
Bunn, George Harris, 7.
Burke, Mickey, bushranger, 34.
Burke, Michael, alderman and politician, 337, 340.
Burke, Thomas, 206.
Butler, Alban, monk and historian, 468.
Butler, Edward, politician, 296.
Butler, Thomas, publisher, 242.
Byrne, James Austin, monk, 120–129, 132, 166, 392, 483.
Byrnes, Catherine (Sister Matthew), nun, 185, 190, 193, 195.
Byrnes, Mary Maria, teacher, 193.
Byrnes, Matthew, captain and shipowner, 152, 167, 169, 172, 185, 186, 187, 188, 189, 190, 191, 192, 193, 210, 218.

C

Callachor, Bernard, monk, 81, 216, 217, 224.
Cannon, Ernie, benefactor, 346, 458.
Cannon, Ruth, pupil, 344.
Capel, Thomas John, priest, 200.
Cardorna, Raffaele,General, 162.
Carmichael, Ethel ('Queen of Pyrmont -Ultimo'), 431.
Carr, Sister Elizabeth, nun, 196.
Carr, Thomas, archbishop, 309, 324, 325.
Carroll, Sister Hyacinth, nun, 227.
Carroll, James, archbishop, 241, 413, 414, 415.
Carrington, Charles Robert, governor, 212, 213.
Cashen, Lester, priest, 449, 450, 451, 452, 516.
Cavendish, Lord Frederick, Irish Chief Secretary, 206.

Cerretti, Bonaventura, Cardinal, 322.
Chaize, Leon, priest, 373.
Challis, John, author, 421, 475.
Charlton, Brian, priest, 422, 423, 447, 516.
Chinchen, Norbert, Pyrmont parishioner, 257, 325.
Chisholm, Caroline, philanthropist, 114.
Cheeke, Alfred, judge, 76.
Clancy, Edward Bede, Cardinal, 394, 438, 439, 441, 443, 444, 445, 448, 449, 463.
Cleary, Patrick Scott, journalist, 309, 310, 311, 313, 326, 329, 336, 379.
Clyne, Daniel, politician, 399, 401, 402.
Coates, Simon, historian, 466, 476.
Colletti, Angelo, priest, 80, 81, 201.
Collingridge, Charles, priest, 249, 284.
Coogan, William, philanthropist, 221, 250, 378, 379.
Coonan, Patrick, priest, 215.
Constable, Mary (Sister John), nun, 429.
Corcoran, James, priest, 9.
Corcoran, Patrick, priest, 462.
Cordner, William, musician, 78.
Corish, Michael Mellitus, monk, 24, 25, 26, 27, 28, 49, 54, 113.
Coveny, Christopher, teacher, 270.
Cowper, Charles, politician, 62, 63.
Cox, Kevin, priest, 436, 437, 439, 516.
Creagh, Edmund, priest, 226, 227, 228, 514.
Creed, William, publican, 74, 75.
Crick, William Patrick (Paddy), politician, 267, 268, 272.
Croke, Thomas, Archbishop, 199, 200.
Crookall, John, priest, 146.
Cullen, Paul, Cardinal, 47, 72, 113, 141, 147, 228, 229, 475.
Curr, Bonaventure, monk, 81.
Curran, John Milne, priest and geologist, 271, 287, 302, 303, 304, 476, 515.

Curtin, John, politician, 380, 389, 390.
Curtis, Henry Anselm, monk, 24, 25, 26, 33, 128, 133, 471.
Curtis, James, undertaker, 90.

D

Daley, Patsy, bushranger, 34.
Dalley, William Bede, lawyer and politician, 36, 76, 80, 110, 184, 212, 248, 472.
Dalton, James, priest, 319, 325, 326, 327, 328, 330, 333, 334, 335, 515.
Darboy, Georges, Archbishop, 162.
Darby, James, apprentice, 163.
Davidson, Walter, governor, 336.
Davidson, William, organ builder, 417.
Davies, Robin, clergywoman, 445, 446.
Davis, Charles, bishop, 69, 150.
Davitt, Michael, politician, 240, 241.
Dawson, Jane, sculptor, 457.
de Valera, Eamon, politician, 369.
Denison, William, Governor, 66.
Dillon, George, priest, 29, 70, 201, 202.
Dillon, John, politician, 188, 189.
Dixon, James, priest, 4, 9, 228, 477, 478.
Dolman, William, publisher, 105, 129.
Donnelly, Peter, priest, 279, 281, 514.
Donova, Sister Clement, nun, 182.
Donovan, Denis, priest, 408.
Dowling, Christopher Vincent, priest, 9, 105, 234.
Downie, Alexander, wheelwright and landlord, 74, 75, 76, 82.
Doyle, Gilbert, sculptor, 336.
Doyle, Jeremiah Joseph, bishop, 217.
Doyle, John, soldier and parishioner, 326
Doyle, Nicholas Joseph, soldier and parishioner, 327.
Doyle, Victor, priest and Army Chaplain, 50, 128, 247, 291, 299, 354, 391, 410–415, 418, 419, 421, 422, 423, 435, 439, 441, 476. 516.

Drohn, Edward, priest, 399.
Duncan, Mary (Sister Clare), nun, 118.
Duncan, William Augustine, publisher, 87, 118, 127, 128, 132, 134, 139, 464, 467.
Dundon, Eamonn, priest, 392, 407, 408, 409, 410, 411, 412, 415, 422, 435, 515.
Dunn, Johnnie, bushranger, 34.
Dunne, James, priest, 327, 334.
Dwyer, Michael, emancipist, 110, 253, 258.
Dwyer, John Michael, monk, 62, 80, 110, 123, 125, 129, 132, 133, 135, 172,
Dykes, Owen, clergyman, 438.

E

Edmunds, Walter, judge, 47.
Edwards, Sister Edith, nun, 413.
Egan, Sister Catherine, nun, 181, 182, 183.
Ellard, William ('Tim Fogarty'), journalist, 256.
English, John, alderman, 342.
Epalle, Jean-Baptiste, bishop, 21.

F

Fadden, Arthur, politician, 380.
Fallon, Cyril, doctor and politician, 313, 335, 336.
Farrelly, Elizabeth, alderman and professor of architecture, 440.
Farrelly, Patrick Joseph, bishop, 393.
Fegan, Sidney (Sid), alderman, 413.
Fennell, Thomas, priest, 407.
Finlay, John, parish secretary, 63.
Fitzgerald, Edward, Lord, 258.
Fitzgerald, James, pupil, 331, 332.
Fitzgerald, Paul, monk, 183.
Fitzgerald, Peter, priest, 443, 444, 451, 516.
Fitzgerald, Shirley, historian, 14, 16, 249, 386, 392, 476.
Fitzgerald, Thomas, priest, 253, 422.

Fitzroy, George Augustus, Governor, 103.
Flanagan, Michael, priest, 172, 173, 479.
Foley, John, bushranger, 35, 37.
Foley, Michael, priest, 138, 151.
Ford, John, priest, 424, 425, 427, 429, 430, 432, 437, 516.
Forrest, John, priest, 124, 125, 130, 160, 162, 172.
Forster, Lord Henry, Governor-General, 337.
Forsyth, Robert, bishop, 418.
Fowler, Colin, priest, 442, 456, 516.
Fowler James, priest, 414, 431, 437, 438, 439, 440, 441, 442 443, 516.
Fransoni, Giacomo Filippo, Cardinal, 25, 463.
Freehill, Francis Bede, lawyer, 209, 210, 241.
Freeman, James Darcy, Cardinal, 295, 356, 357, 377, 419, 423, 432, 433, 435, 436, 438.
Fuller, George, politician, 335.
Funcheon, Sister Kieran, nun, 393, 394.
Funcheon, Patrick, priest, 393, 394.
Funcheon, Richard, priest, 389, 390, 391, 393, 394, 395, 399, 421, 515.
Furber, Sister Mary Barbara, nun, 185.
Furlong, Dominic, priest, 389.
Furlong, James, priest, 215, 217, 219, 221, 223, 224, 225, 230, 232, 234, 270, 288, 346, 353, 378, 389, 439, 514.

G

Gallagher, John, bishop, 231.
Gallagher, Peter, lawyer and soldier, 336, 340, 341.
Garavel, Joseph-Marie, priest, vii, 50, 54, 113, 115, 116, 125, 151, 155–167, 169, 172–177, 188, 201, 263, 514.
Gardiner, Frank, bushranger, 34, 42.
Gattone, Renato (Ron), Pyrmont parishioner, 454, 456.
Gell, Edward, priest, 281, 283, 284, 285, 293, 294, 307, 318, 346, 515.
Ghèon, Henri, author, 403.
Gibbons, Scholastica, nun, 78, 177, 179, 181, 477.
Gilbert, John, bushranger, 34, 36.
Giles, John Allen, clergyman and scholar, 465, 466, 467, 477.
Gill, Alan, journalist, 418, 426, 431.
Gilroy, Norman Thomas, Cardinal, 278, 284, 285, 289, 317, 318, 348, 349, 356, 357, 359, 368, 372, 375, 378, 382, 387, 390, 391, 392, 393, 394, 396, 397, 400, 404, 403, 404, 405, 407–414, 449, 473.
Gladstone, William, politician, 206, 209, 210.
Golder, Hilary, historian, 14, 16, 386, 392, 393, 476.
Gorman, Ellen, 94.
Gorman, Patrick, shipwright, 116.
Gorman, William, convict, 3.
Goold, James Alipius, bishop, 22, 59, 88, 204.
Gooley, Sister Margaret, nun, 437.
Gounod, Charles, composer, 252, 264, 327.
Gray, Maurice, clergyman, 338.
Greenall, Walter, pupil, 332.
Greenway, Francis, architect, 7.
Gregory, Henry, monk, 18, 30, 32, 34, 78, 105, 106, 113, 120, 128, 132, 472.
Gregson, Dame Scholastica, abbess, 468.
Griffiths, Jennie Scott, peace-activist, 323.
Groberty, Annie Mary, pupil-teacher, 90.
Groberty, Catherine, schoolmistress, 82, 86, 88, 89, 91, 94.
Groberty, Edwin, convict and musician, 88, 89, 90.
Grose, Francis, acting Governor, 2, 14, 66, 106, 476.

H

Hackett, Charles, politician, 380, 426.
Halfpenny, James and Stephen, convicts, 3.
Hall, Ben, bushranger, 34, 36.
Hamilton, Jeffrey, stained-glass artist, 402, 455.
Hanly, James, priest, 146.
Hannan, Daniel, priest, 307, 355, 359, 360, 361, 362, 373, 378, 515.
Harold, James, priest, 4.
Harris, John, Corps Surgeon, 2, 6, 7, 8, 10, 14.
Hartigan, Patrick (John O'Brien), priest and poet, 138, 139, 151, 286.
Hayes, James Bernard, priest, 145, 146.
Healey, Elizabeth, 424.
Heaps, John, bishop, 436.
Heather, Bede, bishop, 463.
Heptonstall, Paulinus, monk, 468.
Herbert, Brother Killian, 374.
Heffernan, Cletus, priest, 116, 375, 375, 376, 377, 378, 385, 389, 409, 415, 515.
Heydon, Louis Francis, politician, 282.
Hickman, Ronald, soldier and priest, 411, 413, 419, 439, 516.
Higgins, Francis, priest, 410, 411, 415, 423, 516.
Higgins, Joseph, bishop, 190, 194, 218, 259, 266.
Highfield, Sister Mary Elizabeth, nun, 197.
Hogan, Michael, historian, 361, 477.
Hogan, Stanislaus, priest, 383.
Holdsworth, William, alderman, 340.
Holman, William, politician, 311, 312, 313, 322, 323.
Howard, Sister Ligouri, nun, 182, 183.
Huggard, William, pupil, 246.
Hughes, John, merchant and pastoralist, 296.
Hughes, William Morris, politician, 323, 324, 325, 333, 379.
Hunt, John Ignatius ('The Flaneur'), journalist, 136.
Hurley, John, alderman, 29, 80.
Hyde, Douglas, professor, 369.
Hyland, John, priest, 298, 301, 303–309, 316–319, 515.
Hynes, Bridget, pupil, 275.

I

Ingham, Peter, bishop, 423, 448.

J

Jeffcott, Aloysius, priest, 361, 366, 378.
John Paul II, Pope, 404, 443.
Johnson, Alexander, priest, 441, 443, 444, 445, 448, 452, 516.
Joly, Claude Marie, priest, 167.
Jones, Ashley, priest, 404, 405, 407, 415, 515.

K

Kavanagh, Patrick, priest and author, 207, 477.
Keating, Thomas, priest, 71, 80.
Kelleher, Sister Bede, nun, 182, 183, 185, 471.
Kelleher, Sister Marilyn, nun, vii, 39, 78, 392, 477.
Kelly, James, convict, 3.
Kelly, Michael, archbishop, 206, 221, 228, 230, 232, 274, 275, 288, 293, 294, 304, 310, 317, 324, 334, 340, 342, 346, 347, 348, 360, 365, 368, 369, 370, 372, 382.
Kelly, William, priest, 124.
Kemp, William, architect, 461.
Kendall, Geoffrey, organ builder, 437.
Kenny, Edward, pupil, 97.
Kenny, John, priest and historian, 149.
Kenny, John ('Zero'), priest, 268, 278.
Keogh, Thomas, priest, 390, 399, 515.
Kildea, Jeff, lawyer and historian, 207, 311, 336, 477.
King, Philip Gidley, Governor, 1, 4, 6.

L

La Perouse, Jean François de Galaup, comte de, explorer, 162.
Lambert, Sister John Bede, nun, 471.
Lambert, William, mayor and politician, 332, 333, 337, 442.
Lang, Catherine, pupil-teacher, 94, 97.
Lang, John Dunmore, clergyman, 12, 28, 106, 114, 144, 163.
Lang, John Thomas (Jack), politician, 379, 380.
Lanigan, William, bishop, 77, 99, 100, 146, 147, 202, 266.
Le Rennetel, Pierre François, priest, 220, 241.
Leahy, Sister Mary, nun, 442.
Leahy, Thomas, publican, 249.
Leo XIII, Pope, 167, 397, 468.
Lowry, Fred, bushranger, 35.
Luckie, Eugene John, priest, 30, 77, 80, 85, 86, 92, 93, 99–112, 116–121, 123, 149, 154, 166, 168, 202, 225, 234, 462, 514.
Lynch, James, priest, 345, 346, 349, 351, 352, 353, 354, 357, 359, 515.
Lynch, John Thomas, priest, 18, 30, 32, 37, 43, 113, 115, 116, 132, 138–155, 166, 169, 174, 224, 305, 446, 148, 150, 152, 154, 155, 167, 175, 225, 306, 444, 462, 514.
Lyons, Patrick, bishop, 400.

M

Massey, James, priest, 376, 386, 387, 388, 389, 515.
Macarthur, John, pastoralist and politician, 2, 6, 7, 8, 9.
Macarthur, Elizabeth, grazier, 2, 45.
Macarthur, Edward, soldier, 10, 12, 23, 117, 416.
Macarthur, Hannibal, pastoralist and politician, 65.
Macarthur, James, landowner and politician, 2, 7.
Macarthur, Mary, 2.
Macarthur, William, landowner, 2.
MacCarthy, Charles, doctor, 253, 255, 257, 258, 259.
Macnamara, Michael, priest, 51, 153, 265, 268, 269–279, 293, 294, 302, 304, 307, 310, 312, 334, 360, 415, 478, 514.
Macquarie, Lachlan, Governor, 4, 213.
Mackinson, Thomas, clergyman, 24.
Madden, Frank, politician, 325.
Madgwick, Edward, clergyman, 337, 399, 415.
Maher, Sister Laurentia, nun, 182, 185.
Mahoney, Edmund, priest, 138, 119.
Manning, Henry Edward, Cardinal, 235, 244.
Mannix, Daniel, archbishop, 316, 320, 321, 324, 325, 329, 331, 332, 333, 340, 365, 366, 396, 436.
Matthews, Michael, alderman and author, 380, 418, 426, 430, 478.
Maunsell, Daniel, policeman, 251.
Maunsell, Nellie, singer, 251, 301.
Martin, James, politician, 62.
Mathew, Theobald, priest, apostle of total abstinence, 139, 140.
Mazzinghi, Joseph, composer, 88.
McDonald, William, priest, 305, 346, 349–355, 357, 358, 359, 361, 367, 376, 378, 382, 386, 388, 399, 408, 420, 515.
McDonnell, Patrick, priest, 326, 327, 330, 515.
McElhinney, Thomas, merchant, 75.
McElhone, John, Pyrmont parishioner, 385.
McEncroe, John, priest, 9, 56, 66, 70, 71, 72, 84, 85, 103, 130, 154, 158, 178, 271, 461, 472, 475.
McEvoy, Vincent William, priest, 88, 383.
McGirr, James, priest, 127.
McGrath, Edward, priest, 172, 283.
McGuirk, Tom, pupil, 273.
McIntyre, Philip, priest, 51, 142, 143, 144, 175, 262–266, 268, 270, 273, 274, 276, 279, 280,

282–286, 289, 290–295, 298 305, 340, 345, 348, 354, 419, 514.
McKillop, Mother Mary, nun and foundress, 177, 277, 278.
McMahon, James Leslie (Les), politician. 423, 424.
McNally, William, priest, 306, 307, 308, 309, 360, 515.
McNeill, John, politician, 282.
McTiernan, Edward, lawyer, politician and judge, 324.
Meagher, Richard (Dick), politician and mayor, 312, 315, 316, 322, 323, 324, 329.
Menzies, Robert, politician, 379.
Minogue, Daniel, politician, 399, 414.
Monnier, Joseph, priest, 121, 122.
Moor, Stephen, stained-glass artist, 402.
Moore, Thomas, poet and songwriter, 285.
Moran, Patrick Francis, Cardinal, 23, 116, 141, 154, 179, 183, 187, 190, 197, 199, 200, 203, 204, 205, 206, 211, 212, 213, 215, 218, 220, 221, 222, 225, 228, 230, 235, 240, 241, 244, 245, 249, 254, 255, 256, 257, 258, 259, 263, 264, 265, 267, 268, 269, 271, 274, 275, 276, 277, 289, 280, 282, 286, 287, 291, 296, 301. 303, 309, 319, 331, 374, 389, 439, 475, 478, 479.
Moynagh, John Patrick, priest, 350, 351.
Moynihan, Mary, pupil, 330.
Muldoon, Thomas, bishop, 414, 419, 420, 422.
Mullin, James, priest, 375, 376, 377, 378, 515.
Mullooly, Joseph, priest, 117.
Mundey, Jack, union activist, 430.
Munro, William, architect, 64–69, 83, 84, 461, 462. 477.
Muraire, Zépherin Felicien, priest, 167.
Murphy, Bernard, priest, 32, 33.
Murphy, Daniel, bishop, 30.
Murphy, Francis, bishop, 22, 139, 140.
Murphy, Joseph James, litigant, 372.

Murphy, Mother Oliverio, nun, 400, 401.
Murray, Anna Maria (Bunn), 7.
Murray, James, bishop, 154, 184, 199, 200, 234, 235, 266.
Murray, Terence, Army Captain, 7.
Murray, Terence Aubrey, politician, 57.
Mutlow, Robert, priest, 452, 453, 516.

N

Nairn, Bede, historian, 268, 296, 380, 472.
Nathan, Isaac, composer and choirmaster, 87, 88.
Newman, John Henry, cardinal, 59, 432, 472.
Noon, Sister Teresa, nun, 429, 437.
Nori, Sandra, politician, 439.

O

O'Brien, Edward, priest, 461.
O'Brien, Eris, archbishop, 233, 367.
O'Brien, James, priest, 244, 302.
O'Callaghan, Edward, priest, 244, 245, 246, 247, 248, 250, 252, 253, 254, 258, 259, 260, 261, 262, 269, 338, 514.
O'Connell, Daniel, Irish liberator, 11, 47, 48, 109. 129.
O'Connell, Daniel Maurus, monk, 128, 133, 138, 462, 479.
O'Connell, Dean, priest, 62, 130, 131, 132, 149.
O'Connell, Michael, priest, 335, 337, 338, 339, 340–349, 462, 484.
O'Connor, Daniel, politician, 166, 218.
O'Connor, Eileen, visionary and foundress, 283, 284.
O'Connor, Richard, politician, 271.
O'Doherty, Kevin Izod, politician, 208, 210.
O'Doherty, Mary Anne ('Eva of the Nation'), poet, 208.
O'Donovan, Sister Clement, nun, 182.

O'Dwyer, Maurice, Pyrmont parishioner and milkman, 128, 295, 298, 325, 336, 361, 387, 397, 398, 399, 400.
O'Dwyer, Nellie, parishioner, 373, 400.
O'Farrell, Henry James, would-be assassin, 92, 110.
O'Farrell, Patrick Francis, priest, 127, 128.
O'Farrell, Thomas, priest, 308, 313, 515.
O'Flaherty, Sister Alexius, nun, 183.
O'Flaherty, John, priest, 224.
O'Gorman, James Hugh, priest, 298.
O'Gorman, John, priest, 196, 197, 269, 276, 290, 291, 297-306, 310, 327, 342, 345, 350, 515.
O'Haran, Denis, priest, 215, 230, 253, 259, 265, 266, 267, 268-281, 291, 297, 298, 305.
O'Keefe, Gladys, pupil, 365.
O'Mahony, Timothy, bishop, 138, 147, 148, 149, 150, 151, 476.
O'Meally, John, bushranger, 34.
O'Neill, Charles Gordon, engineer and philanthropist, 219, 220, 221, 226, 238, 299, 380, 479.
O'Neill, George, priest and biographer, 277, 278.
O'Neil, John, priest, 415.
O'Neil, Peter, priest, 4.
O'Regan, Richard, priest, 175, 213, 215, 216, 225, 226, 342, 514.
O'Reilly, Daniel, priest, 62, 192, 193, 223, 225, 232, 236, 244, 245, 251, 260, 269, 514.
O'Reilly, Maurice, priest, 310, 311, 312, 313, 325, 481.
O'Shea, Patrick, priest, 228, 239, 231, 514.
O'Sullivan, Edward, politician, 210, 230.
O'Toole, Andrew, publican, 49, 196, 197, 347.
O'Toole, Catherine Mary (Sister Mary Lidwina), nun, 196.
O'Toole, Christina Ann (Sister Mary Elizabeth), nun, 196, 197.
O'Toole, Elizabeth (Sister Brigid Mary), nun, 183, 184, 185, 195, 197, 346.
O'Toole, Hannah (Sister Elizabeth), nun, 48.
O'Toole, Hugh, 46, 47.
O'Toole, Michael, 29, 49, 51.
O'Toole, John Francis, priest, 196, 294, 334, 355, 356, 357, 358, 377.
O'Toole, Joseph, carrier, 351, 355.
O'Toole, Patrick, stonemason, 29, 40, 41, 44, 45, 47, 48, 50, 61, 63, 64, 75, 107, 186.
O'Toole, Phillip, union officer, 197, 330, 340, 398.
Owens, Joe, union activist, 430.
Oxford, Edward, would-be assassin, 110.

P

Palmer, J H, clergyman, 35, 104.
Panico, Giovanni, archbishop, 365, 366.
Parkes, Henry, politician, 108, 111, 168, 170, 171, 241.
Parnell, Charles Stewart, politician, 206, 208, 209, 210, 241.
Paterson, Robert Smith, clergyman, 92, 106, 107.
Patterson, James Laird, bishop, 200.
Pearse, Padraic, lawyer, teacher, poet and rebel, 369, 370.
Pegum, Stephen, teacher, 94, 95, 96, 97.
Pell, George, Cardinal, 446, 448, 451, 452.
Phelan, Andrew, priest, 144, 145, 224.
Phillip, Arthur, Governor, 2.
Pilgrim, James, playwright, 257.
Piquet, Peter, priest, 269, 298, 366.
Pitchford, Darrell, organ builder, 455, 457, 478.
Pius IX, Pope, 70, 79, 117, 154, 161.
Pius X, Pope, 252, 261, 301.

Pius XII, Pope, 387, 397.
Plunkett, John Hubert, Attorney
    General, 19, 140.
Polding, John Bede, monk and
    bishop, 9, 10, 18, 19, 20, 21, 22,
    24, 25, 26, 30, 32, 33, 34, 37, 38,
    50, 53, 56, 57, 59, 60, 61, 62, 64,
    65, 66, 69, 71, 77, 78, 79, 80, 85,
    99, 100, 101, 103, 110, 113, 115,
    120, 122, 126, 127, 128, 129, 130,
    132 133, 134, 1411, 142, 144,
    145, 146, 147, 150, 151, 154, 158,
    162, 170, 178, 180, 181, 201,
    203, 204, 225, 263, 271, 274, 331,
    355, 454, 460–474, 476, 477.
Pollard, John, priest, 150, 168, 172.
Pompallier, Jean-Baptiste,
    bishop, 156, 157, 158.
Porteous, Julian, priest,
    443, 444, 445, 516.
Power, Patrick, bishop, 448.
Power, Peter, priest, 269,
    270, 271, 298, 483.
Pryke, Roger, priest, 419, 477.
Pugin, Augustus, architect,
    20, 59, 64, 65, 66, 475.
Pugin, Edward, architect, 226.

Q

Quinn, James, bishop, 47,
    78, 141, 147, 204,
Quinn, Matthew, bishop,
    270, 281, 302.
Quirk, John Norbert, monk, 115, 116,
    133–138, 154, 156, 166, 172, 514.

R

Radecki, John, stained-
    glass artist, 367.
Raphael, Joseph, alderman, 56.
Rawlings, Luke, priest, 423, 424, 516.
Redmond, John, politician,
    206, 207, 259.
Redmond, William, politician, 206.
Reeve, Philip James, priest, 354.

Reid, Reginald, doctor, 164, 165, 166.
Reynolds, Christopher,
    archbishop, 464.
Reynolds, James, priest, 340, 342.
Richardson, Sarah, widow, 165, 166.
Riddell, Campbell Drummond,
    public servant, 103.
Rigney, John, priest, 139, 140, 153, 154.
Robertson, John, politician,
    62, 63, 95.
Robinson, Geoffrey, bishop, 410, 412.
Robinson, Stuart, bishop, 446.
Robinson, Mother Mary
    Gabriel, nun, 196.
Robinson, Paddy, stained-
    glass artist, 402, 457.
Rohan, Edward, priest, 369.
Rohan, Mother Mary
    Berchman, nun, 369.
Rowe, Mother Mary De
    Sales, nun, 196.
Rusden, George, educationalist
    and civil servant, 102.
Russell, Jimmy, boxer, 261.
Ryan, Hugo, bishop, 396.
Ryan, Martin, pupil, 286.
Ryan, Matthew Patrick, 97.
Ryan, Michael Harrington,
    priest, 101, 102, 225, 234,
    235, 369, 371, 372, 374.
Ryan, Patrick Matthias, priest, 190,
    192, 243, 244, 245, 253, 259, 514.
Ryan, Thomas, priest, 225, 227, 514.
Ryan, Thomas Joseph, politician, 332.

S

Sartor, Frank, politician
    and mayor, 447.
Saunders, Charles, quarry owner, 15.
Saunders, Robert, quarry
    owner, 15, 130.
Shawelhood, Frederick, teacher,
    soldier and musician, 242,
    248, 249, 250, 251, 252,
    259, 260, 264, 378.
Sheedy, James, convict, 3.

Sheehy, Samuel Austin, monk, 59, 60, 62, 63, 64, 69, 70, 78, 79, 94, 125, 128, 133, 144, 145, 146, 199, 201, 266, 283, 356, 460, 462.
Sheridan, John Felix, monk, 199, 122, 123, 124, 175, 201.
Simeoni, Giovanni, Cardinal, 38, 39.
Simonds, Justin, archbishop, 233, 288, 307, 365, 366.
Slater, Edward Bede, monk and bishop, 119, 464.
Slowey, John, priest, 400, 401.
Smart, Thomas Ware, auctioneer and politician, 10, 11, 61.
Smith, Sister de Sales, nun, 177, 181, 184, 196.
Smith, William Saumarez, archbishop, 267.
Spence, Robert William, archbishop, 309, 383.
Stephen, Alfred, judge, 36.
Swann, Jasper, heritage and masonry consultant, 458 459, 479.

T

Tawhiao, Maori King, 173.
Telfer, Archibald, stonemason and builder, 40, 41, 42, 43, 45, 64.
Therry, Roger, lawyer and judge, 19, 65, 69.
Thorne, Sidney, priest and Air Force chaplain, 395, 402, 403, 515.
Tierney, James, priest, 432, 433, 434, 435, 436, 516.
Toohey, James, brewer and politician, 209, 210.
Toole, Bridget, 45, 48.
Toole, Elizabeth, licensee, 128, 195.
Toole, Ellen, 48.
Toole, Hannah, dairywoman, 48.
Toole, James, dairyman, 29.
Toole, Michael, labourer, 29.
Toole, Thomas, labourer, 48.
Toole, Tobias, quarryman and publican, 48.
Torregiani, Eleazar, bishop, 39.
Tuomey, Patrick, priest, 323, 324.

U

Ullathorne, William Bernard, priest, 9, 19, 101, 138, 178, 464, 467.

V

Vandeleur, Peter, priest, 396.
Vane, Johnny, bushranger, 34, 35, 36, 37, 42, 479.
Vaughan, Herbert, Cardinal, 174.
Vaughan, Jerome, monk, 199.
Vaughan, Roger Bede, monk and Archbishop, 15, 38, 80, 119, 127, 129, 131, 132, 133, 134, 136, 148, 149, 150, 153, 154, 168, 169, 170, 173, 174, 187, 188, 199, 200, 202, 234, 235, 242, 262, 263, 265, 286, 331, 415, 462, 463, 464, 467, 469, 472.
Vaughan, Theresa, schoolmistress, 82.
Veech, Thomas, priest, 23.
Vonwiller, Oscar Ulrich, professor of physics, 307.

W

Walsh, Andrew, priest, 204.
Walsh, Anthony, priest, vii, 344, 459, 516.
Walsh, Austin, businessman, 344.
Walsh, Edmund, priest, 70, 115, 116, 175, 190, 201, 202, 203, 207, 213, 214, 215, 514.
Walsh, Louis, pupil, 289, 290.
Walsh, Michael, priest, 451, 516.
Walsh, William, Archbishop, 200, 320.
Wardell, Herbert, architect, 217.
Wardell, William Wilkinson, architect, 15, 59, 60, 66, 67
Wardrop, Joseph, blacksmith, 82.
Watkinson, James ('Watto'), swimming coach, 447, 448.
Watkinson, Maria (Sister Christine), nun, 446.

Weslan, Michael, Pyrmont
    parishioner, 251, 340, 361.
Wiles, John Henry, teacher, 61.
Wilkins, William, educationalist
    and civil servant, 63, 64,
    85, 130, 197, 217.
Wilkinson, Leslie, professor
    of architecture, 46.
Wilson, John Henry, architect, 67.
Wiseman, Nicholas,
    Cardinal, 234, 252.
Wolseley, Garnet Joseph,
    General, 249, 250.
Woods, John, mayor, 56.
Woods, Julian Tenison, priest
    and scientist, 270, 276,
    277, 279, 302, 303, 476.
Woulfe, Richard, priest, 289,
    290, 297, 479, 515.

Y

Yates, Dean, organ builder, 456.
Young, John, Governor,
    56, 57, 58, 59, 70.

Z

Zammit, Laurie, Pyrmont
    parishioner, 454.

Place Index

A

Adelaide, 22, 146, 215, 227, 302, 309, 366, 383, 465.
Adelong, 250.
Albion Park, 263, 270, 285, 398.
Anatolia, 10.
Angers, 178, 180, 478.
Antwerp, 156.
Apia, 14.
Appin, 202, 230, 235, 263, 460, 461, 462, 479.
Arabia, 117.
Araluen, 131, 202, 226, 246, 275, 278, 293, 310, 312.
Ardagh, 47, 119.
Armagh, 101, 105, 113, 279.
Armidale, 30, 31, 32, 34, 39, 102, 133, 138, 139, 141, 145, 146, 147, 149, 150, 151, 155, 166, 201, 225.
Arncliffe, 429.
Ashbury, 389, 394.
Ashfield, 417.
Athol Gardens, 173.
Auburn, 270, 290, 293, 300, 334, 363, 377, 412, 437.
Auckland, 156, 157, 158, 173, 199, 223, 300, 366.
Australia, *passim*
Avalon, 432.

B

Baerami Creek, 91.
Balgowlah, 415.
Ballinhassig, 30.
Balmain, 12, 16, 22, 23, 25, 29, 48, 70, 82, 89, 90, 177, 181, 183, 186, 188, 190, 192, 193, 248, 285, 306, 307, 353, 395, 408, 415, 449, 450, 451.
Balmoral Gardens, 73.
Balthenglass, 188.
Baltimore, 43.
Ballyheeda, 39.
Bankstown, 396, 449.
Bargo, 368.
Bathurst, 4, 13, 26, 32, 35, 36, 37, 38, 55, 57, 127, 142, 143, 237, 248, 260, 265, 270, 271, 276, 281, 282, 302, 303, 304, 310, 312, 362, 399, 479.
Batlow, 362.
Baulkam Hills, 307, 360, 361.
Bay of Islands, 158, 159.
Bega, 279, 281, 306.
Belfast, 254, 256, 259.
Belgium, 215, 233, 320, 367, 450.
Belley, 156.
Belmore, 348, 355, 356, 377, 378, 390, 413.
Berrima, 64, 65, 146, 422, 477.
Berry, 399.
Bethsaida, 69, 283.
Bexley, 273, 389.
Birmingham, 20, 101, 178.
Blacktown, 412, 437.
Blackwattle Bay, Cove, Creek, Swamp, 1, 7, 23.
Blue Mountains, 26, 104, 120, 194, 287.

Bombala, 319, 447.
Bookham, 250.
Botany, 26, 27, 160, 209, 210.
Botany Bay, 4, 23, 33, 78, 103, 162, 209, 389, 433, 442, 479.
Bourke, 270.
Bowraville, 393.
Braidwood, 7, 181, 185, 202, 228, 263, 275, 278, 290, 291, 292, 293, 404, 461, 480.
Branxton, 139.
Brighton-le-Sands, 396, 442.
Brisbane, 38, 47, 78, 102, 141, 142, 147, 204, 208, 300, 332, 333, 346, 478.
Brisbane Water, 90, 131.
Broadway, 61, 198, 415, 422, 451, 478.
Broken Bay, 5, 407.
Bungendore, 270, 281.
Bungonia, 99, 105, 201.
Burragorang, 94, 96, 226, 307, 396, 397, 403.
Burrangong, 32.
Burrowa, 60, 99.
Burwood, 289, 334, 402.

C

Cabramatta, 412.
Cairo, 249.
Callan Park, 41, 347.
Camden, 45, 96, 97, 215, 228, 230, 235, 306, 339, 354.
Camperdown, 26, 89, 160, 235, 359.
Canada, 72, 101, 148.
Canterbury, 22, 108, 120, 175, 465.
Carcoar, 28, 30, 32, 33, 34, 35.
Caringbah, 436, 450.
Carlingford, 449.
Carlow, 30, 225, 376, 407, 478.
Castle Hill, 4, 226, 346, 360, 375.
Castlereagh, 126, 226.
Centennial Park, 267, 304.
Ceylon, 117, 147, 300.
Charters Towers, 183, 194.
Chatswood, 288, 367, 368, 389.
Chippendale, 91, 183.

Chowder Bay, 130, 151, 172, 175, 187, 188, 189, 240.
Church Hill, 20, 23, 117, 220, 248, 269, 331, 332, 352, 408, 411.
Circular Quay, 152, 172, 219, 220, 222, 238.
Clare, 247, 297.
Clontarf, 47, 92, 108, 109, 111.
Clovelly, 362.
Cloyne, 335.
Cobargo, 51, 275, 279, 462.
Cockatoo Island, 20.
Cockle Bay, 1, 2, 5, 6, 7, 8.
Coffs Harbour, 195.
Colombo, 300.
Concord, 18, 48, 140, 141, 215, 279, 368, 396, 398, 411, 437.
Cooba Creek, 250.
Cook's River, 26, 90, 135.
Coogee, 164, 283, 284, 285, 333, 334, 372.
Cooma, 226, 319, 404.
Cootamundra, 311, 312.
Cork, 30, 39, 182, 193, 329, 335.
Cronulla, 353, 357, 437.
Crow's Nest, 437.
Crystal Creek, 194.
Cue, 227.
Cumberland County, 45.

D

Dardenelles, 316.
Darling Harbour, 5, 9, 10, 11, 12, 13, 15, 16, 23, 52, 70, 74, 77, 78, 83, 122, 124, 186, 191, 219, 221, 222, 237, 238, 317, 330, 366, 386, 416, 440, 446, 447, 450.
Darling Point, 282, 296, 382.
Darlinghurst, 25, 37, 41, 42, 55, 76,125, 110, 121, 127, 150, 169, 201, 268, 281, 296, 297, 305, 389, 404, 414, 442.
Darwin, 395, 396.
Denison Ward, 45, 47.
Dinalong, 250.
Douglas Park, 368.

Douai, 464.
Drumcondra, 101, 119.
Drummoyne, 353.
Dubbo, 183, 282, 302.
Dublin, 44, 101, 119, 129, 138, 140, 141, 144, 185, 189, 191, 192, 200, 201, 206, 207, 208, 215, 226, 234, 243, 245, 249, 254, 256, 257, 258, 260, 261, 300, 302, 305, 313, 315, 320, 321, 322, 370, 374, 375.
Dulwich Hill, 334.
Dumbarton, 219.
Dun Laoghaire, 185.
Dunedin, 327, 334.
Dunmore, 398, 399.
Dunn's Plain, 35.
Dural, 362, 364.
Durham, 468.

E

Eastwood, 425.
Edgecliff, 112.
Edinburgh, 143.
Egypt, 117, 249, 283.
Elizabeth Bay, 10, 11, 296, 297, 408, 443.
Elizabeth Farm, 2, 6.
England, 2, 4, 7, 20, 22, 30, 31, 34, 35, 41, 47, 55, 57, 59, 60, 64, 66, 68, 72, 91, 101, 102, 104, 112, 113, 119, 124, 136, 138, 141, 145, 147, 150, 151, 174, 202, 208, 220, 226, 245, 262, 275, 281, 300, 302, 315, 321, 331, 339, 347, 409, 416, 417, 460, 461, 463, 464, 467, 468, 473.
Enmore, 225, 232, 346, 373, 411, 437.
Erskineville, 244, 245, 246, 248, 260, 335, 354, 403, 411.

F

Farm Cove, 54.
Fiji, 204.
Fish River, 35.
Five Dock, 181, 183, 185, 250, 367.
Forbes, 32.

Forest Lodge, vii, 67, 81, 168, 181, 183, 198, 215, 216, 217, 224, 225, 230, 390, 395, 424, 441, 443, 444, 445, 448, 449, 452, 456.
Fort Augustus, 199.
France, 108, 117, 124, 156, 161, 167, 178, 283, 309, 326.

G

Galle, 147.
Gallipoli, 283, 319, 320, 321, 366.
Galway, 368.
Geelong, 145, 161.
Geraldton, 227, 228.
Germany, 10, 117, 302, 309, 320, 321, 328, 379.
Germia, 366.
Glasgow, 41, 217, 219, 226, 249.
Glebe, viii, 23, 24, 30, 37, 61, 65, 67, 81, 115, 149, 150, 151, 166, 184, 186, 195, 308, 337, 354, 361, 362, 366, 367, 369, 388, 418, 440, 443, 444, 449, 450, 451, 452, 453, 462, 467, 479.
Glen Innes, 91, 146
Goa, 352, 361, 367.
Goat Island, 20.
Gordon, 271.
Gosford, 225, 226, 228, 270, 394, 399, 458.
Goulburn, 34, 38, 60, 77, 99, 100, 105, 142, 146, 170, 201, 202, 228, 229, 231, 233, 248, 266, 270, 281, 291, 292, 404, 446, 448, 480.
Granville, 214, 374, 449.
Great Britain, 11, 22, 89, 114, 205, 210, 369, 463, 481.
Greenough, 227, 228.
Gundagai, 250.
Gunning, 60.

H

Haberfield, 395.
Hampshire, 234.
Harbord, 419.

Hartley, 37.
Hawkesbury, 4, 126, 271.
Haymarket, 122, 159, 183, 235, 288, 413.
Helensburgh, 335.
Helidon, 330.
Hereford, 469.
Hiero-Caesarea, 10.
Hilton, 142.
Hinchinbrook, 451.
Hobart, 20, 30, 47, 146, 208, 221, 233, 365, 395, 404, 443, 460, 478.
Holland, 302, 467.
Holy Land, 117.
Hot Springs, 173.
Hoxton Park, 451.
Hungary, 402.
Hurstville, 236, 273, 368, 388, 399.
Hyde Park, 52, 54, 110.
Hyderabad, 30, 183.

I

Illawarra, 18, 70, 103, 104, 130, 140, 241, 242, 263, 275, 323, 335, 395, 396.
India, 7, 30, 117, 161, 183, 302, 332.
Inverell, 149.
Ipswich, 30, 101, 102, 104, 141, 225.
Ireland, 4, 11, 19, 22, 30, 31, 32, 38, 39, 44, 47, 48, 51, 58, 72, 73, 89, 90, 91, 101, 206, 207, 102, 107, 109, 110, 113, 114, 117, 118, 130, 133, 138, 140, 144, 149, 151, 152, 184, 187, 188, 201, 205, 208, 209, 210, 213, 215, 225, 226, 230, 232, 233, 243, 248, 250, 253, 254, 256, 258, 259, 260, 265, 268, 269, 270, 273, 276, 285, 288, 289, 290, 296, 300, 301, 306, 308, 313, 314, 319, 320, 321, 324, 325, 327, 329, 333, 334, 341, 344, 359, 362, 368, 369, 370, 371, 374, 376, 389, 390, 393, 394, 436, 472, 473.
Isabel Island, 21.
Italy, 18, 117, 161, 162.

J

Jarrow, 464.
Jersey, 300.
Johnston Bay, 1, 23, 70, 77.
Jones Bay, 352, 382, 447.
Junee, 250.

K

Kamperduin, 359.
Kempsey, 139, 393.
Kensington, 298, 342, 399, 437.
Kerry, 359, 362.
Khartoum, 249.
Kiama, 78, 275, 334, 399.
Kilkenny, 215, 296, 306, 319, 334, 376, 389, 394.
Kilmacduagh, 368.
Kilmainham, 320, 321.
Kimberley, 203.
Kincumber, 90, 91, 293.
Korea, 427.
Kyogle, 393.
King's Plains, 32.
Kingstown, 185.
Kogarah, 235, 268, 269, 271, 273, 359, 360, 411, 425, 436.

L

Lake Cargelligo, 362.
Lake Macquarie, 294, 348.
Lalor Park, 437, 447.
Lambing Flat, 34.
Lancaster, 407.
Lane Cove, 395, 443, 450.
Lawson, 194.
Leeds, 300.
Leichhardt, 160, 175, 176, 235, 241, 264, 285, 354, 398, 399, 432.
Lewisham, 226, 281, 287, 347, 348, 354, 356, 378, 389.
Lidcombe, 293, 346, 404, 412.
Limerick, 90, 91, 225, 270.
Lismore, viii, 244, 245, 346, 393.
Listowel, 359, 362.

Lithgow, 282, 283.
Liverpool, 31, 64, 118, 168, 411, 425.
Lochinvar, 95, 139.
London, 4, 8, 9, 13, 72, 87, 101, 192, 210, 234, 236, 245, 248, 254, 300, 463.
Long Bay, 451.
Lourdes, 228.
Louvain, 215, 233, 288.
Lyndhurst, 14, 23, 24, 25, 46, 65, 71, 81, 120, 122, 123, 127, 128, 132, 133, 134, 135, 137, 150, 184, 286, 466, 467, 471.

M

Macarthur Estate, 2, 5, 7.
Maitland, 18, 30, 32, 38, 41, 43, 68, 89, 95, 96, 130, 132, 138, 139, 140, 141, 142, 143, 144, 145, 146, 151, 152, 154, 155, 184, 189, 194, 199, 200, 211, 224, 234, 235, 248, 266, 372, 462, 477.
Manchester, 41, 43, 73.
Manly, 169, 181, 183, 184, 185, 187, 188, 194, 204, 233, 255, 286, 287, 289, 290, 304, 306, 318, 346, 354, 356, 357, 362, 376, 377, 382, 386, 404, 411, 423, 425, 443, 449, 467, 481.
Maroubra, 362.
Marrickville, 183, 246, 248, 298.
Mauritius, 119, 464.
Maynooth, 30, 101, 138, 200, 296, 319, 325.
McDonald Town, 244, 245, 271, 335.
Melbourne, viii, 2, 18, 22, 33, 34, 47, 55, 59, 66, 73, 88, 91, 103, 110, 112, 113, 114, 124, 128, 146, 153, 161, 180, 194, 204, 212, 233, 242, 248, 252, 260, 274, 275, 288, 297, 309, 316, 320, 324, 329, 331, 332, 350, 365, 366, 383, 394, 396, 400, 425, 432, 436, 438, 477.
Menangle, 182, 368.
Merrygoen, 183.
Metz, 161.

Michelago, 226, 297.
Middle Harbour, 73, 92, 108.
Millchester, 194.
Miller's Forest, 105.
Miller's Point, 222, 314.
Millwall, 236, 245.
Milton, 226, 281.
Minneapolis, 425.
Mittagong, 307, 324.
Moreton Bay, 30, 101, 102, 141, 481.
Morisset, 348, 349, 374, 375.
Morpeth, 66, 68, 78, 95, 96, 461, 462.
Mortlake, 368.
Moruya, 181, 183, 279, 335, 377, 462.
Mosman, 246, 308.
Mount Druitt, 443.
Mudgee, 35, 66, 472.
Mulgoa, 226.
Murrumburrah, 228.
Muswellbrook, 91, 139, 140.

N

Naremburn, 334, 346.
New Caledonia, 161, 300, 400.
New England, 30, 31, 35, 91, 145, 147, 151.
New Hebrides, 300.
New Holland, 10, 18, 30, 119, 138, 464.
New South Wales, 1, 2, 4, 18, 19, 32, 33, 38, 41, 58, 60, 67, 73, 87, 96, 101, 102, 104, 110, 111, 124, 135, 154, 174, 186, 187, 194, 200, 201, 212, 219, 234, 239, 243, 248, 249, 253, 263, 266, 270, 272, 275, 282, 287, 289, 290, 299, 303, 304, 310, 311, 315, 325, 337, 377, 380, 406, 417, 430, 447, 460, 462, 471, 472, 472, 477.
New Zealand, 54, 73, 80, 101, 156, 157, 158, 159, 164, 173, 175, 204, 207, 223, 243, 250, 300, 323, 320, 327, 353, 381.
Newcastle, 30, 94, 96, 105, 114, 115, 147, 186, 202, 234, 380.
Newtown, 26, 128, 131, 135, 136, 160,

161, 173, 181, 183, 224, 225, 232, 246, 389, 462, 463.
Norfolk Island, 3, 4, 102, 225, 234, 477.
North Parramatta, 275, 276, 278, 230.
North Sydney, 294, 373, 403, 419, 432, 461.
Northbridge, 410.
Northcote, 194.
Northmead, 417.
Nowra, 185, 307, 319, 344, 378.
Numba, 66.

O

Omaha, 281.
Orange, 281.
Osaka, 392, 407.
Ossory, 199, 200, 240, 296, 319, 389.

P

Paddington, 112, 304, 324.
Palestine, 56, 437.
Pambula, 103, 223, 281.
Paris, 69, 156, 162, 208, 234, 258.
Parkes, 127.
Parramatta, 1, 4, 6, 9, 18, 25, 29, 33, 65, 89, 153, 172, 179,184, 185, 225, 226, 248, 263, 275, 276, 278, 279, 305, 360, 362, 363, 404, 432, 463.
Pennant Hills, 404, 443.
Penola, 276.
Penrith, 224, 226, 375, 385, 387, 425, 432.
Penshurst, 348, 349.
Perth, 392, 421.
Petersham, 23, 25, 50, 90, 94, 104, 154, 175, 176, 245, 263, 270.
Picton, 289, 297, 368, 387.
Pietermaritzburg, 393.
Pirrama, 2.
Pittwater, 271.
Ponsonby, 300.
Pont-de-Beauvoisin, 156, 161.
Port Augusta, 366, 392.
Port Hacking, 55.
Port Kembla, 368, 372.

Port Macquarie, 139, 245.
Port Phillip, 102.
Port Pirie, 194.
Port Stephens, 105.
Portsmouth, 300.
Potsdam, 323.
Prussia, 124, 125, 161, 162.
Punchbowl, 411.
Pymble, 306.
Pyrmont, *passim*

Q

Queanbeyan, 181, 183, 202, 210, 270, 301, 306.
Queensland, 30.

R

Randwick, 41, 162, 163, 164, 166, 283, 399, 403.
Raymond Terrace, 66, 99, 104, 105, 462.
Redfern, 26, 175, 226, 238, 374, 418, 432, 477.
Richmond, 36, 37, 125, 126, 183, 307, 348, 349, 363, 395, 411, 415.
Riverstone, 399.
Riverview, 155, 306, 443.
Rockdale, 273, 317, 335, 347, 442.
Rockhampton, 194, 259, 266.
Rome, 4, 10, 18, 25, 35, 37, 38, 56, 62, 65, 69, 70, 78, 79, 80,102, 113, 117, 133, 134, 141, 142, 146, 147, 148, 161, 162, 170, 174, 180, 187, 200, 215, 230, 245, 260, 265, 266, 279, 281, 300, 305, 306, 308, 331, 404, 413, 463, 404, 413, 463, 464, 465, 468, 478.
Rookwood, 215, 292, 293, 355.
Rooty Hill, 226.
Roscrea, 436.
Rose Bay, 342.
Rosebank, 183, 185, 367.
Rozelle, 23, 181, 183, 285, 306, 312, 350, 411, 415.
Rozelle Bay, 23.

Place Index

Rydalmere, 226, 235.
Ryde, 66, 167, 283, 284, 293, 346, 432.

S

Salford, 173, 174, 199.
Sans Souci, 377, 389.
Sardinia, 156.
Savoy, 156, 158, 161.
Scheyville, 391, 411.
Scotland, 64, 101, 142, 199, 226, 473.
Shellharbour, 399.
Shropshire, 464.
Silverwater, 451.
Singleton, 32, 66, 96, 139, 140.
Solomon Islands, 21, 373.
Smithtown, 226.
Sofala, 104, 106, 457.
Solomontown, 195.
South Africa, 101, 203, 252, 253, 264, 393, 394.
South Australia, 51, 366.
South Hurstville, 357, 358, 367, 399.
South Yarra, 194.
Southampton, 146, 161.
Springwood, 233, 287, 377, 411, 437, 443, 449.
St Albans, 279.
St George, 271.
St Leonard's, 66.
Stanmore, 356, 432.
Strasbourg, 161.
Strathfield, 184, 275, 348, 408, 432, 467, 472.
Subiaco, 25, 65, 184, 226, 235.
Sudan, 248, 249, 250, 288.
Surry Hills, 8, 172, 181, 223, 230, 232, 250, 269, 279, 287, 304, 306, 354, 372, 378, 388, 449, 455.
Sutherland, 273, 394, 430.
Switzerland, 86, 302.
Sydney, *passim*

T

Tasmania, 129, 132, 208, 234, 456.
Tauranga, 173.

Tempe, 183, 246, 412.
Tenterfield, 30, 146, 147.
The Rocks, 8, 9, 20, 176, 220, 269, 331, 416.
Tipperary, 183, 201, 226, 254, 302.
Toronto, 148.
Townsville, 395, 396.
Transvaal, 203.
Tuam, 215.
Tumut, 250.
Turkey, 366.
Turnham Green, 234.

U

Ultimo, *passim*.
United States, 44, 101, 117, 200, 254, 268, 281, 290, 304, 329, 347, 386, 413, 425, 437.

V

Van Dieman's Land, 9, 102, 129, 234.
Victoria, 180, 323, 325, 436.
Vietnam, 219, 425, 429.

W

Wagga Wagga, 270.
Wahroonga, 423.
Waitematta, 278.
Waikato, 157, 173.
Waitangi, 159.
Waitara, 411, 443.
Waratah, 372.
Ware, 234.
Waterford, 201, 376.
Waterloo, 26, 27, 66, 226, 262, 288, 306, 307, 404.
Watson's Bay, 362.
Waverley, 66, 82, 106, 118, 151, 157, 158, 162, 163, 164, 166, 190, 192, 247, 251, 257, 258.
Wearmouth, 464.
Webb's Creek, 279.
Weddin Mountain, 34.
Wellington, 32, 219, 281.

West Indies, 101.
West Pymble, 306, 407, 415.
Western Australia, 227.
Westmead, 250, 300, 348, 368, 378.
Westmeath, 234.
Westminster, 19, 174, 199, 200, 206, 234, 235, 240, 244, 245.
Wexford, 48, 215, 233, 345, 376, 479.
Wicklow, 44, 48, 188.
Wilberforce, 362.
Windsor, 125, 131, 181, 226, 270, 307, 391, 411.
Winston Hills, 437.
Wiseman's Ferry, 279.
Woden, 7.
Wollongong, 103, 104, 172, 181, 183, 195, 248, 263, 307, 323, 327, 334, 359, 395, 399.
Woolloomooloo, 8, 20, 22, 222, 239, 296, 314, 378, 389, 447.
Woy Woy, 457.
Wyalong, 228.

Y

Yarralumla, 7.
Yass, 60, 142, 146.
York, 300, 465.
Young, 34, 99,